IM~~PORTA~~NT.

SO-AKF-686

REGISTRATION CODE

HERE IS YOUR REGISTRATION CODE TO ACCESS
YOUR PREMIUM McGRAW-HILL ONLINE RESOURCES.

For key premium online resources you need THIS CODE to gain access. Once the code is entered, you will be able to use the Web resources for the length of your course.

If your course is using **WebCT** or **Blackboard**, you'll be able to use this code to access the McGraw-Hill content within your instructor's online course.

Access is provided if you have purchased a new book. If the registration code is missing from this book, the registration screen on our Website, and within your WebCT or Blackboard course, will tell you how to obtain your new code.

Registering for McGraw-Hill Online Resources

TO gain access to your McGraw-Hill web resources simply follow the steps below:

sandstones-95160522

1. USE YOUR WEB BROWSER TO GO TO: **www.mhhe.com/lucas8**

2. CLICK ON **FIRST TIME USER**.

3. ENTER THE REGISTRATION CODE* PRINTED ON THE TEAR-OFF BOOKMARK ON THE RIGHT.

4. AFTER YOU HAVE ENTERED YOUR REGISTRATION CODE, CLICK **REGISTER**.

5. FOLLOW THE INSTRUCTIONS TO SET-UP YOUR PERSONAL UserID AND PASSWORD.

6. WRITE YOUR UserID AND PASSWORD DOWN FOR FUTURE REFERENCE.
   KEEP IT IN A SAFE PLACE.

TO GAIN ACCESS to the McGraw-Hill content in your instructor's **WebCT** or **Blackboard** course simply log in to the course with the UserID and Password provided by your instructor. Enter the registration code exactly as it appears in the box to the right when prompted by the system. You will only need to use the code the first time you click on McGraw-Hill content.

Thank you, and welcome to your McGraw-Hill online Resources!

Mc Graw Hill **Higher Education**

*YOUR REGISTRATION CODE CAN BE USED ONLY ONCE TO ESTABLISH ACCESS. IT IS NOT TRANSFERABLE.

0-07-288661-7 T/A LUCAS: THE ART OF PUBLIC SPEAKING, 8E

THIS WEBSITE INFORMATION CARD WILL BE INCLUDED IN ALL STUDENT TEXTBOOKS. THE PASSWORD ON IT PROVIDES ACCESS TO THE PREMIUM CONTENT AVAILABLE ON "POWERWEB: PUBLIC SPEAKING". STUDENT CENTER MATERIALS ON THE WEBSITE OTHERWISE REQUIRE NO PASSWORD. YOU SHOULD STILL CONTACT YOUR LOCAL SALES REP FOR THE SEPARATE USER NAME AND PASSWORD TO ACCESS THE INSTRUCTOR MATERIALS INCLUDED ON THIS WEBSITE.

THE ART *of* PUBLIC SPEAKING

Eighth Edition

STEPHEN E. LUCAS

University of Wisconsin–Madison

Boston   Burr Ridge, IL   Dubuque, IA   Madison, WI   New York   San Francisco   St. Louis
Bangkok   Bogotá   Caracas   Kuala Lumpur   Lisbon   London   Madrid   Mexico City
Milan   Montreal   New Delhi   Santiago   Seoul   Singapore   Sydney   Taipei   Toronto

The McGraw·Hill Companies

 Higher Education

THE ART OF PUBLIC SPEAKING
Published by McGraw-Hill, a business unit of The McGraw-Hill Companies, Inc., 1221 Avenue of the Americas, New York, NY, 10020. Copyright © 2004, 2001, 1998, 1995, 1992, 1989, 1986, 1983, by Stephen E. Lucas. All rights reserved. No part of this publication may be reproduced or distributed in any form or by any means, or stored in a database or retrieval system, without the prior written consent of The McGraw-Hill Companies, Inc., including, but not limited to, in any network or other electronic storage or transmission, or broadcast for distance learning.
Some ancillaries, including electronic and print components, may not be available to customers outside the United States.

This book is printed on acid-free paper.

1 2 3 4 5 6 7 8 9 0 QPD/QPD 0 9 8 7 6 5 4 3

ISBN   0-07-256296-X (student edition)
ISBN   0-07-256406-7 (annotated instructor's edition)

Publisher: *Phillip A. Butcher*
Senior sponsoring editor: *Nanette Kauffman Giles*
Director of development and media technology: *Rhona Robbin*
Editorial coordinator: *Josh Hawkins*
Senior marketing managers: *Sally Constable and Daniel M. Loch*
Producer, Media technology: *Jessica Bodie Richards*
Lead project manager: *Susan Trentacosti*
Manager, New book production: *Sandra Hahn*
Design manager: *Laurie J. Entringer*
Lead supplement producer: *Marc Mattson*
Freelance supplement editor: *Kassi Radomski*
Associate photo research coordinator: *Natalia C. Peschiera*
Photo researcher: *Barbara Salz*
Cover and interior design: *Laurie J. Entringer*
Cover illustration: *Riccardo Vecchio*
Typeface: *10/12 Melior*
Compositor: *The GTS Companies*/York, PA Campus
Printer: *Quebecor World Dubuque Inc.*

Library of Congress Control Number: 2003104880

www.mhhe.com

The Art of Public Speaking   Eighth Edition

Bringing Public Speaking to Life

The publication of this Eighth Edition marks 20 years of Stephen Lucas' *The Art of Public Speaking*. Why has the Lucas text been the leader in public speaking for a generation of students, teachers, and professionals? The answer is simple. *The Art of Public Speaking* brings public speaking to life with its clear, jargon-free writing style and vivid examples.

The *Art of Public Speaking* offers an outstanding supplements package, an integrated presentation of every major aspect of speech preparation and presentation, and sensitivity to the diverse needs of today's students and instructors. Lucas teaches public speaking skills in the text, student CD-ROM, and Online Learning Center website through creative activities, vivid examples, annotated speech samples, and a foundation of classical and contemporary rhetoric.

In keeping with this tradition of leadership, the Eighth Edition features many new sections and updates, including the following: an exciting new PowerPoint appendix; a new section on the tradition of public speaking; newly revised materials to aid in assessing, citing, and utilizing Internet resources for research; new sections on inclusive language, the importance of persuasion, and ethics and persuasion; and new and updated sample speeches and examples throughout the book.

Bridging the Printed Page

Enhanced Student CD-ROM and Online Learning Center Website

Bridging the gap between the printed page and the spoken word has always been the biggest challenge for a public speaking textbook. Not any more. The Lucas Student CD-ROM (two disk set) and Online Learning Center website bring public speaking to life. As students read the book, specially marked icons in the margins guide them to corresponding features on the CD-ROM and website. A dynamic approach to learning, the CD-ROM and Online Learning Center are fully integrated with *The Art of Public Speaking*.

CD Icons

CD icons in the margins guide students to corresponding features on the CD.

Video Clips

Video excerpts and full speeches by students and public figures illustrate the principles of public speaking.

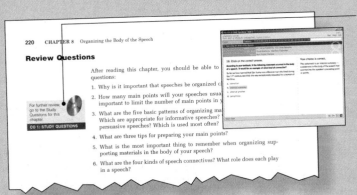

Study Questions

Self-study quizzes for each chapter of the book reinforce key principles and concepts.

Other Features of the Student CD

Speech preparation checklists, Speech Outliner, outline exercises, key-term flashcards, bibliography formats, a glossary, a notepad, and a link to the Lucas website.

and the Spoken Word

You are a management trainee in a large corporation. Altogether, there are seven trainees in the program. One of you will get the lower-management job that has just opened. There is to be a large staff meeting at which each of the trainees will discuss the project he or she has been developing. One by one your colleagues make their presentations. They have no experience in public speaking and are intimidated by the higher-ranking managers present. Their speeches are stumbling and awkward. You, however, call upon all the skills you learned in your public speaking course. You deliver an informative talk that is clear, well reasoned, and articulate. You get the job.

You are married and have three children. One of your children has a learning disability. You hear that your local school board has decided, for budget reasons, to eliminate the special teacher who has been helping your child. At an open meeting of the school board, you stand up and deliver a thoughtful, compelling speech on the necessity for keeping the special teacher. The school board changes its mind.

You are the assistant manager in a branch office of a national company. Your immediate superior, the branch manager, is about to retire, and there will be a retirement dinner. All the executives from the home office will attend. As his close working associate, you are asked to give a farewell toast at the party. You prepare and deliver a speech that is both witty and touching—a perfect tribute to your retiring superior. After the speech, everyone applauds enthusiastically, and a few people have tears in their eyes. The following week you are named branch manager.

Fantasies? Not really. Any of these situations could occur in daily life. In a survey of 480 companies and public organizations, communication skills—including public speaking—were ranked first among the personal qualities of college graduates sought by employers.[2] The importance of this skill holds true across the board—for accountants and architects, teachers and technicians, scientists and stockbrokers. Even in highly specialized fields such as civil and mechanical engineering, employers consistently rank the ability to communicate above technical knowledge when deciding whom to hire and whom to promote.

Nor has the growth of the Internet and other new technologies diminished the need for public speaking. As one communication consultant states, "There are more avenues to reach people than ever before, but none of them substitute for face-to-face communication." To be successful, according to civic leader Midge Costanza, you must have "the ability to stand on your feet, either on a one-to-one basis or before a group, and make a presentation that is convincing and believable."[3]

The same is true in community life. Public speaking is a vital means of civic engagement. It is a way to express your ideas and to have an impact on issues that matter in a democratic society. Look back for a moment at the second of our three hypothetical situations, the one in which you persuade the school board to keep the special teacher who has been helping your child. Why did the school board change its mind? Not simply because the facts were on your side (though they may have been) or because you knew more about education than the school board (which you probably do not). The school board changed its mind because of your *speech*—in which you presented a compelling case for keeping the special teacher.

The point is that public speaking is a form of empowerment. It can—and often does—make a difference in things people care about very much. The key phrase here is "make a difference." This is what most of us want

To read the words of famous speakers, log on to the Top 100 American Speeches of the 20th Century at www.mhhe.com/lucastop100

ONLINE LEARNING CENTER

speech class, have them make a list of their career goals. Then lead a class discussion on how public speaking can help them achieve those goals.

Online Learning Center Icons
Online Learning Center icons in the margins direct students to corresponding features of the text's website.

Top 100 American Speeches of the 20th Century
A unique site that gives students access to the complete text, historical background, and audio of major speeches of the 20th century.

Key Terms

ethics (34)
ethical decisions (35)
name-calling (39)
Bill of Rights (40)
plagiarism (42)

global plagiarism (43)
patchwork plagiarism (43)
incremental plagiarism (45)
paraphrase (45)

Review these terms by doing the Chapter 2 crossword puzzle at www.mhhe.com/lucas8

ONLINE LEARNING CENTER

Review Questions

After reading this chapter, you should be able to answer the following questions:

1. What is ethics? Why is a strong sense of ethical responsibility important for public speakers?

2. What are the five guidelines for ethical speechmaking discussed in this chapter?

3. What is the difference between global plagiarism and patchwork plagiarism? What are the best ways to avoid these two kinds of plagiarism?

4. What is incremental plagiarism? How can you steer clear of it when dealing with quotations and paraphrases?

5. What are the three basic guidelines for ethical listening discussed in this chapter?

The Art of Public Speaking
Eighth Edition
Stephen E. Lucas

Crossword Puzzles
Key-term crossword puzzles help students test their mastery of key concepts.

Other Features of the Online Learning Center
Internet exercises, learning objectives, practice quizzes, key-term flashcards, PowerPoint tutorials, speech evaluation forms, worksheets, PowerWeb resources.

Introducing New Features That

Figure A.4
Sample PowerPoint Slide

you wish to communicate. There are also many kinds of images available to you, ranging from video to still images such as photographs, clip art, and graphs. Let's look at each individually.

Text

Most PowerPoint slides contain some kind of text. The text might be no more than a title indicating the subject of the slide, or it might include several lines in the body of the slide. Text can be used by itself, and it can be used in conjunction with photographs, clip art, or other images. For the most part, any text appropriate for a traditional visual aid can be included on a PowerPoint slide.

For example, Figure A.4 shows a slide from the speech on the Great Wall of China. The speaker used this slide in conjunction with his explanation of the first stage of building the Great Wall, during the Qin dynasty. In addition to an image of Qin Shi Huang, the emperor who started construction of the Wall, the slide contains a title plus text identifying Qin Shi Huang and the dates of the Qin dynasty. The slide also includes copyright information for the drawing of Qin Shi Huang.

Photographs

One of the benefits of PowerPoint is the ease with which it allows you to spice up a speech with photographs. If you're speaking on a topic drawn from your personal experience, you can use PowerPoint to display your own photographs. For other topics, you can download photographs from the Web. Here are some of the best online sources for photographs on topics of current and historical interest:

■ *Google Image Search* (www.google.com/imghp?hl=en&ie=UTF-8&oe=UTF-8&q=). The Web's most comprehensive image resource. Allows you to search for photographs on virtually any topic across thousands of websites.

New Appendix on Using PowerPoint
"Using PowerPoint" (which follows Chapter 13, "Using Visual Aids,") gives students the tools they need to create and efficiently use PowerPoint presentations to accompany their speeches. A sample speech on the student CD-ROM shows the effective use of PowerPoint. The Online Learning Center features PowerPoint tutorials with technical instructions on how to create PowerPoint slides.

The Tradition of Public Speaking

Related Reading
For an insightful view of rhetorical practices and principles around the globe, see George A. Kennedy, *Comparative Rhetoric: An Historical and Cross-Cultural Introduction* (New York: Oxford University Press, 1998). For more detail, consult Thomas O. Sloane (ed.), *Encyclopedia of Rhetoric* (New York: Oxford University Press, 2001).

Given the importance of public speaking, it's not surprising that it has been taught and studied around the globe for thousands of years. Almost all cultures have an equivalent of the English word "orator" to designate someone with special skills in public speaking. The oldest known handbook on effective speech was written on papyrus in Egypt some 4,500 years ago. Eloquence was highly prized in ancient India, Africa, and China, as well as among the Aztecs and other pre-European cultures of North and South America.[4]

In classical Greece and Rome, public speaking played a central role in education and civic life. It was also studied extensively. Aristotle's *Rhetoric*, composed during the third century B.C., is still considered the most important work on its subject, and many of its principles are followed by speakers (and writers) today. The great Roman leader Cicero used his speeches to defend liberty and wrote several works about oratory in general.

Over the centuries, many other notable thinkers have dealt with issues of rhetoric, speech, and language—including the Roman educator Quintilian, the Christian preacher St. Augustine, the medieval writer Christine de Pizan, the British philosopher Francis Bacon, and the American critic Kenneth Burke.[5] In recent years, communication researchers have provided an increasingly scientific basis for understanding the methods and strategies of effective speech.[6]

New section on "The Tradition of Public Speaking"
This section in Chapter 1, "Speaking in Public," helps students appreciate the long-standing importance of rhetoric and public speaking in global culture and the role of public speaking as a mode of civic engagement.

Keep Your Course Current

Citing Internet Sources

Careful listeners are skeptical. They keep an ear out both for the speaker's information and for the sources of that information. Whether your research is based primarily on the Internet or on print works such as books, newspapers and magazines, you need to identify the sources of the facts, figures, and testimony you cite in your speeches.

One step in identifying your sources is to include them in your speech bibliography. As you prepare your bibliography, don't forget to mention the Internet sources, as well as the print sources, that you used in preparing the speech. When citing Internet sources, include the same information you provide for print works—author, title, date of publication, and the like. You should also include the URL for each Internet document, plus the date on which you accessed the document.

On CD 1, you will find a complete set of sample bibliography citations for various kinds of Internet sources formatted according to American Psychological Association (APA) and Modern Language Association (MLA) guidelines. Check these formats and follow the one your instructor specifies for your class.

In addition to including Internet sources in your speech bibliography, you need to cite them in the speech itself so listeners will know what those sources are. It would take far too much time if you recited orally the full citation as written in your bibliography. On the other hand, you should not simply say, "As I found on the Web," or "As the Internet states."

If you are citing the testimony of a specific person, you should identify her or him and the website on which you found the testimony. If you are citing an organization rather than an individual, you need to provide the name of the organization. Here, for example, are two Internet citations from student speeches. The first is from an informative speech about sign language:

> Some people think that sign language is a primitive substitute for spoken language, but in fact sign language is just as rich and expressive as spoken language. For example, Karen Nakamura states in the online *Deaf Resources Library* that American Sign Language "should not be considered in any way to be a broken, mimed, or gestural form of English." According to Nakamura, ASL is a complex, full, and natural language in its own right, with "its own beautiful grammar."

The second is from a persuasive speech urging the audience to become blood donors:

> According to the American Red Cross Web pages, where I obtained an enormous amount of information, in the United States alone someone undergoes a blood transfusion once every three seconds, which amounts to 3,000 gallons of blood every hour, day and night.

In both cases, the speaker makes clear exactly where she obtained her information. You should do the same when citing Internet sources in your speeches.

Go to the Bibliography Formats for a complete set of sample APA and MLA citations.

CD 1: BIBLIOGRAPHY FORMATS

View these excerpts from Leah Pogorski, "Sign Language," and Jennifer Conard, "The Ultimate Gift."

CD 1: VIDEO 6.1

Updated Coverage of Internet Research
Chapter 6, "Gathering Materials," offers an updated discussion to keep pace with changes in information technology, both in the library and on the Internet. There is expanded coverage of evaluating Internet sources and a new section on citing Internet documents in a speech.

Ethics and Persuasion

As we saw in Chapter 2, questions of ethics come into play whenever a speaker addresses an audience. No matter what the speaking situation, you need to make sure your goals are ethically sound and that you use ethical methods to communicate your ideas. Meeting these obligations can be especially challenging when you speak to persuade. Would you be willing to shade the truth "just a bit" if it would guarantee a successful speech? How about juggling statistics, doctoring quotations, passing off opinions as facts, or pandering to prejudice and stereotypes?

Unfortunately, there is no shortage of speakers—and other persuaders—who are willing to take ethical shortcuts to achieve their objectives. Yet, as Martin Luther King stated years ago, it is not possible to bring about a truly beneficial result by using unethical methods. Maintaining the bond of trust with listeners is also vital to a speaker's credibility. As in other kinds of public speaking, the ideal of effective persuasion is the good person speaking well.

When you work on your persuasive speech, keep in mind the guidelines for ethical speaking discussed in Chapter 2 and do your best to follow them every step of the way. Make sure your goals are ethically sound and that you can defend them if they are questioned or challenged. Study the topic thoroughly so you won't mislead your audience through shoddy research or muddled thinking. Learn about all sides of an issue, seek out competing viewpoints, and get your facts right.

Related Reading
For a more detailed look at this subject, see Richard L. Johannesen, "Perspectives on Ethics in Persuasion," in Charles U. Larson, *Persuasion: Reception and Responsibility*, 9th ed. (Belmont, CA:

New Material on Persuasion
Chapter 15, "Speaking to Persuade," includes new sections on the importance of persuasion and on ethics and persuasion and has been updated throughout.

Reflecting the Rich Diversity

Public speaking is a vital mode of communication in most cultures around the world. Here Philippine President Gloria Macapagal Arroyo addresses a mass meeting in Manila.

Public Speaking in a Multicultural World
Chapter 1, "Speaking in Public," includes a discussion that places public speaking in the context of today's global multiculturalism.

As this scenario illustrates, public speakers can ill afford to overlook their listeners' cultural values and customs. This is true whether you are speaking at home or abroad, in Atlanta or Rio de Janeiro, in a college classroom or at a meeting of community volunteers. Because of the increasing diversity of modern life, many—perhaps most—of the audiences you address will include people of different cultural backgrounds.

As you read the rest of this book, you will learn the methods of effective public speaking. Almost all those methods will be helpful to you in speaking to culturally diverse audiences. Here we need to stress the i[...] of avoiding the ethnocentrism that often blocks communication [...] speakers and listeners of different cultural, racial, and ethnic bac[...]

Related Reading
Roger Axtell, *Gestures: The Do's and Taboos of Body Language Around the World*, rev. ed. (New York: Wiley, 1998). This entertaining book by a veteran international communicator provides a wealth of examples that can be used

Avoiding Ethnocentrism

Ethnocentrism is the belief that our own group or culture—whate[...] be—is superior to all other groups or cultures. Because of ethnoce[...] identify with our group or culture and see its values, beliefs, and [...] "right" or "natural"—in comparison to the values, beliefs, and custo[...] groups or cultures, which we tend to think of as "wrong" or "un[...]

Teaching Tip
Mary Fisher's "A Whisper of AIDS" is one of the most eloquent public addresses of recent years. Have students analyze how Fisher uses the resources of language discussed in this chapter to sharpen her message and bring it home to listeners. The text of Fisher's speech is printed in the appendix of sample speeches that follows Chapter 18, and a video of it is available on *Speaking of Diversity: A Videotape Supplement to The Art of Public Speaking*. For full discussion of the speech, see the *Instructor's Manual*, pp. 335–339.

honoring the crew of the space shuttle *Columbia*. The first two topics call for straightforward description and explanation. The latter two call for special language skills to evoke emotion, admiration, and appreciation.

Appropriateness to the Speaker

No matter what the occasion, audience, or topic, language should also be appropriate to the speaker. Imagine the effect if Dick Cheney tried to adopt the religious imagery and rhythmical cadence of Jesse Jackson. The results would be comical. Every public speaker develops his or her own language style.

"Terrific," you may be thinking. "I have my own style too. I feel more comfortable using abstract words, slang, and technical jargon. That's just me. It's *my* way of speaking." But to say that language should be appropriate to the speaker does not justify ignoring the other needs for appropriateness. There is a difference between one's everyday style and one's *developed* style as a public speaker. Accomplished speakers have developed their speaking styles over many years of trial, error, and practice. They have *worked* at using language effectively.

You can do the same if you become language-conscious. One way to develop this consciousness is to read and listen to the speeches of effective speakers, whether they are current public figures such as Colin Powell and Hillary Clinton or historical figures such as Barbara Jordan and Martin Luther King. Study their techniques for achieving accuracy, clarity, and vividness, and try to adapt those techniques to your own speeches. But do not try to "become" someone else when you speak. Learn from other speakers, blend what you learn into your own language style, and seek to become the best possible you.

Inclusive Approach to Public Speaking
Attention to diversity is evident throughout the book. There is a new section on inclusive language in Chapter 11, "Using Language," as well as numerous discussions, sample speeches, and examples that reflect the diversity of life in the modern world and that encourage an inclusive approach to the art of public speaking.

A Note on Inclusive Language

"When a soldier goes to war, he should have the best possible equipment."

"Improving education has always been a high priority for Negro leaders."

"Any discrimination against crippled people is completely unacceptable."

Forty years ago, most people in the United States who heard these statements in a speech would not have given them a second thought. Today the same statements would raise more than a few eyebrows—and perhaps tempers—in almost any audience. Here's why:

Soldiers in the U.S. military include women as well as men. To say, "When a soldier goes to war, he should have the best possible equipment," ignores the existence of female soldiers. It can also be interpreted as meaning that only male soldiers should go to war with the finest possible equipment—hardly a comforting thought to female soldiers or their loved ones!

The word "Negro" has fallen out of common usage and has changed in meaning. While this term was considered acceptable through the 1960s and was used by civil rights leaders such as Martin Luther King, it is now considered offensive. Today the preferred terms are "black" and "African American."

# of Today's World

Racial, Ethnic, and Cultural Background

Class Activity
For a class activity that encourages students to explore the role of ethnic and gender differences in communication, see Ken Hawkinson, "Two Exercises on Diversity and Gender," in *Selections from the Speech Communication Teacher, 1991–1994,* pp. 24–25, which accompanies *The Art of Public Speaking.*

As we saw in Chapter 1, the United States has long been a multicultural society. Populated originally by Native Americans and then by immigrants from all over the world, it is today a multiracial, multiethnic country of unmatched diversity. Although there are exceptions, the majority of Americans support this diversity and see it as a positive development in today's globalized world. Attitudes about race and ethnicity are quite different from what they were even a few decades ago.

Understanding those attitudes is crucial for public speakers whether they are addressing a mixed-race audience or one with little apparent racial diversity. Consider, for example, the case of U.S. Senator Trent Lott:

First elected to Congress in 1972 from the state of Mississippi, Trent Lott rose steadily through the ranks of the Republican Party from one leadership post to another. By the end of 2002, he was poised to become Senate majority leader, one of the most powerful positions in all of American politics.

Then Lott made the following statement during an informal speech at the 100th-birthday party of South Carolina Senator Strom Thurmond: "I want to say this about my state: When Strom Thurmond ran for president, we voted for him. We're proud of it. And if the rest of the country had followed our lead, we wouldn't have had all these problems over all these years, either."

Lott's listeners were shocked, and a number gasped. When Thurmond campaigned for president in 1948, he did so on a platform of . . . words appeared to indicate that he still supported tha . . .

Good speakers use a lively voice to help bring their ideas to life. They also use gestures, eye contact, and facial expressions to create a strong bond with members of the audience.

At this stage of your speaking career, you have many more important things to concentrate on than how to gesture. Gesturing tends to work itself out as you acquire experience and confidence. In the meantime, make sure your hands do not upstage your ideas. Avoid flailing them about, wringing them together, cracking your knuckles, or toying with your rings. Once you have eliminated these distractions, forget about your hands. Think about communicating with your listeners, and your gestures will probably take care of themselves—just as they do in conversation.

Eye Contact

The eyeball itself expresses no emotion. Yet by manipulating the eyeball and the areas of the face around it—especially the upper eyelids and the eyebrows—we are able to convey an intricate array of nonverbal messages. So revealing are these messages that we think of the eyes as "the windows of the soul." We look to them to help gauge the truthfulness, intelligence, attitudes, and feelings of a speaker.

Like many aspects of communication, eye contact is influenced by cultural background. When engaged in conversation, Arabs, Latin Americans, and Southern Europeans tend to look directly at the person with whom they are talking. People from Asian countries and parts of Africa tend to engage in less eye contact. In Kenya a discussion between a woman and her son-in-law may well be conducted with each person turning her or his back to the other![12]

eye contact
Direct visual contact with the eyes of another person.

Retaining Signature Features

You may be surprised to learn that one of your first assignments is to give a speech. You say to yourself, "What am I going to do? I have barely started this course, yet I'm supposed to stand up in front of the whole class and give a speech! I've only read a few pages in the textbook, and I don't know much about public speaking. Where do I begin?"

If these are your thoughts, you aren't alone. Most beginning speech students have a similar reaction. Fortunately, giving your first speech sounds a lot harder than it is. The purpose of this appendix is to help you get started on preparing and delivering your speech.

Preparing Your Speech

Usually a brief, simple presentation, the first assignment is often called an ice-breaker speech because it is designed to "break the ice" by getting students up in front of the class as soon as possible. This is an important step because much of the anxiety associated with public speaking comes from a lack of experience giving speeches. Once you have broken the ice by giving a speech, you will feel less anxious and will have taken the first step on the road to developing sound public speaking habits that lead to confidence.

Speech Apprehension
To give students confidence in their speaking abilities, Chapter 1, "Speaking in Public," provides practical tips for understanding and coping with stage fright. The appendix, "Giving Your First Speech," now appears at the end of Part I and includes two new sample speeches.

THE INTERNET Connection

Looking for a quotation to use in the introduction or conclusion of your speech? Visit Yahoo! (http://dir.yahoo.com/Reference/Quotations/) for a comprehensive roster of links to collected quotations on the Web.

Are you interested in reading introductions and conclusions from important speeches in U.S. history? You can find them at Douglass: Archives of American Public Address (http://douglassarchives.org/).

You can link to these websites at www.mhhe.com/lucas8.
ONLINE LEARNING CENTER

Consider, for example, the story one student, an education major, told to open his speech about the ways American teachers are adapting to the cultural diversity of today's school-age population:

The Internet Connection
This valuable feature that appears in most chapters provides extra help on using the Web effectively and responsibly.

Guidelines for Ethical Speaking

Make Sure Your Goals Are Ethically Sound

Not long ago, I spoke with a former student—we'll call her Melissa—who had turned down a job in the public relations department of the American Tobacco Institute. Why? Not because of the salary (which was generous) or the work schedule (which was ideal). Melissa declined the job because it would have required her to lobby on behalf of the cigarette industry. Knowing that cigarettes are the number one health hazard in the United States, Melissa did not believe she could ethically promote a product that she saw as responsible for thousands of deaths and illnesses each year.

Discussion Prompt
Students can easily agree that a speaker's goals should be ethically sound, yet some may be inclined to select speech topics such as "How to Make a Fake I.D." or "How to Make Long-Distance Phone Calls without Paying for Them." Discuss whether certain topics are unethical in a public speaking classroom and why.

Given Melissa's view of the dangers of cigarette smoking, there can be no doubt that she made an ethically informed decision to turn down the job with the American Tobacco Institute. On the other side of the coin, someone with a different view of cigarette smoking could make an ethically informed decision to *take* the job. The point of this example is not to judge the rightness or wrongness of Melissa's decision (or of cigarette smoking), but to illustrate how ethical considerations can affect a speaker's choice of goals.

Your first responsibility as a speaker is to ask whether your goals are ethically sound. During World War II, Hitler stirred the German people to condone war, invasion, and genocide. More recently, we have seen politicians who betray the public trust for personal gain, business leaders who defraud investors of millions of dollars, preachers who lead lavish lifestyles at the expense of their religious duties. There can be no doubt that these are not worthy goals.

Strong Coverage of Ethics
Chapter 2, "Ethics and Public Speaking," presents guidelines for ethical speaking, discusses the problem of plagiarism and how to avoid it, and provides guidelines for ethical listening. A new section on plagiarism on the Internet has been added to this chapter.

That Work in the Classroom

Written for Students

Rich with examples, *The Art of Public Speaking* has engaged student interest since its first edition. Reflecting current topics, cultural diversity, and a wide range of speaking challenges, each example in the book clearly illustrates a concept. The author's highly praised writing style enlivens the reading for traditional and nontraditional students alike.

Chapter Focus
This chapter begins by showing how public speaking empowers people to make a difference in their lives. After looking at the long tradition of public speaking, it then explores similarities and differences between public speaking and everyday conversation, techniques students can use to combat stage fright, the basic elements of the speech.

Wilma Subra had no intention of becoming a public speaker. After graduating from college with degrees in chemistry and microbiology, she went to work at Gulf South Research Institute in New Iberia, Louisiana. As part of her job, she conducted field research on environmental toxins—often in minority communities located near large industrial polluters. She found that many families were being exposed to high, sometimes deadly, levels of chemicals and other toxins, but she was not allowed to make her information public.

Frustrated by these restrictions, Subra left her job in 1981, created her own company, and has devoted the past two decades to helping people fight back against giant industrial polluters. She works with families and community groups to conduct environmental tests, interpret test results, and organize for change. Because of her efforts, dozens of toxic sites across the country have been cleaned up, and one chemical industry spokesperson calls her "a top gun for the environmental movement."

How has Wilma Subra achieved all this? Partly through her scientific training, partly through her commitment to environmental justice. But just as important is her ability to communicate with people through public speaking. "Public speaking," she says, "is the primary vehicle I use for reaching people. When you have an important message, it's the best way to engage people and get them involved."

Thorough Coverage of the Basics

Through each edition, instructors and students have praised *The Art of Public Speaking* for its clear, straightforward approach that gives students the tools they need to prepare and present speeches. Weaving theory and practice, the text skillfully guides students through the challenging but essential basics of topic selection, outlining, delivery, audience analysis, research, persuasion, and visual aids.

Sample Speeches with Commentary

The following speeches were presented by students in beginning speech classes at the University of Wisconsin. The first is a speech of self-introduction; the second is a speech introducing a classmate. As you read the speeches, notice how clearly they are organized and how creatively they are developed.

View Bekah Diehl "The Rare Phobia," and Mike Davis II "Steady and True."
CD 2: FULL SPEECH

The Rare Phobia

Commentary	Speech
	Bekah Diehl
Beginning with a series of statements about different kinds of phobias helps the speaker gain attention and arouses curiosity about where the speech will go next. The specific details make the introduction much more effective than if the speaker had simply said, "Lots of people suffer from phobias."	Everyone in the world today suffers from some kind of fear. However, about 4 to 5 percent experience a more severe form of fear known as phobias. Some of the most common phobias are claustrophobia, agoraphobia, which is the fear of public spaces, and arachnophobia, the fear of spiders. Then there are the more uncommon phobias—such as peladophobia, the fear of bald people, or geniophobia, the fear of chins. There is even a name for the fear of Friday the 13th—paraskevidekatriaphobia.
The speaker completes her introduction by revealing her particular phobia—the fear of baseballs. As you can see from CD 1: Video A1.5, she presents her ideas with strong eye contact and excellent vocal variety.	According to the latest count, there was a total of 530 named phobias. However, my particular phobia is so rare that it doesn't even have a name. It is simply called the fear of baseballs. That's right, you heard me, the fear of baseballs. I know it sounds stupid, but it's true. I am terrified of baseballs. Even holding one in my hand sends shivers down my spine.

Learning Aids

The learning aids include margin glossary, chapter outlines, speech outlines, sample speeches, chapter summaries, key-terms lists with page references, review questions, and critical thinking exercises.

Key Terms

Review these terms by doing the Chapter 9 crossword puzzle at www.mhhe.com/lucas8.
ONLINE LEARNING CENTER

rhetorical question (229)
credibility (233)
goodwill (233)

preview statement (235)
crescendo ending (238)
dissolve ending (238)

Review Questions

For further review, go to the Study Questions for this chapter.
CD 1: STUDY QUESTIONS

After reading this chapter, you should be able to answer the following questions:

1. What are four objectives of a speech introduction?
2. What are seven methods you can use in the introduction to get the attention and interest of your audience?
3. Why is it important to establish your credibility at the beginning of your speech?
4. What is a preview statement? Why should you nearly always include a preview statement in the introduction of your speech?
5. What are five tips for preparing your introduction?
6. What are the major functions of a speech conclusion?
7. What are two ways you can signal the end of your speech?
8. What are four ways to reinforce the central idea when concluding your speech?
9. What are four tips for preparing your conclusion?

Exercises for Critical Thinking

Cross-Reference
For discussion of the Exercises for Critical Thinking, see the Instructor's Manual, pp. 207–209, for additional

1. Here are six speech topics. Explain how you might relate each to your classmates in the introduction of a speech.

Social Security   laughter
illiteracy   steroids

Setting New Standards on CD

This unique, fully integrated resource brings *The Art of Public Speaking* to life. As your students read about public speaking in the text, they can watch videos of student and professional speakers in action, use outlining software, benefit from outline exercises and speech preparation checklists, and test their knowledge of the principles and concepts presented in the book.

Videos

Video Clips

Full Speeches

Study Aids

Study Questions

Outline Exercises

Tools

Speech Outliner

The CD also includes bibliography formats, key terms, key-term flashcards, a notepad, and a link to the book's website.

Speech Preparation Checklists

Setting New Standards Online

The Lucas Online Learning Center connects you to a host of resources, including the new *Public Speaking PowerWeb* and the Top 100 American Speeches site.

Top 100 American Speeches of the 20th Century

Internet Connection

Crossword Puzzles

Public Speaking PowerWeb

Worksheets

Key-Term Flashcards

The Online Learning Center also includes learning objectives, chapter outlines and overviews, practice quizzes, speech evaluation forms, PowerPoint tutorials, and a glossary.

The Integrated Teaching
and Learning System

The Lucas integrated teaching and learning system continues to drive the unprecedented popularity of this text. Stephen Lucas writes his own *Annotated Instructor's Edition, Instructor's Manual*, and *Test Bank*. These materials, as well as the Student CD and the Online Learning Center with *PowerWeb* that accompany this text, are crossed-referenced to provide an exemplary integrated system. Two new supplementary booklets accompany this edition.

- *From Oratory to Public Speaking*, written by Stephen Lucas, presents a synoptic view of major developments in the practice and teaching of public speaking in the 20th century, and it illuminates the role of public speaking as a powerful historical force.

- *Teaching Public Speaking Online with The Art of Public Speaking*, written by Jennifer Cochrane of Indiana University–Purdue University at Indianapolis, is a practical guide to creating and implementing public speaking courses online.

Offers a Rich Array of Resources for Students and Instructors

Print

- **Instructor's Manual** 0-07-256410-5
- **Annotated Instructor's Edition** 0-07-256406-7 with Topic Finder Booklet 0-07-292348-2 and Student CD-ROM Guidebook 0-07-256415-6
- **Test Bank** 0-07-256411-3
- **Overhead Transparencies** 0-07-256412-1
- **Teaching Public Speaking Online with The Art of Public Speaking** 0-07-256418-0
- **Student Workbook** 0-07-256407-5
- **The McGraw-Hill Guide to Electronic Research and Documentation** 0-07-290306-6
- **Selections from the Communication Teacher,** Volumes I (0-07-038988-8); II (0-07-039030-4); III (0-07-039076-2); IV (0-07-238396-8); and V (0-07-256409-1)
- **From Oratory to Public Speaking by Stephen E. Lucas** 0-07-256417-2 [reprinted from the Encyclopedia of Rhetoric (Oxford University Press, 2001)].
- **Handbook for Teachers of Non-Native Speakers of English** 0-07-039032-0
- **The Heritage of Rhetorical Theory** 0-07-027133-X

Media

- **Online Learning Center** at www.mhhe.com/lucas8 including PowerWeb: Public Speaking
- **WebCT, Blackboard, and eCollege Cartridges**
- **Instructor's Resource CD-ROM** (with Instructor's Manual, Computerized Test Bank and Power Point Slides) 0-07-256413-X
- **Student CD-ROM Version 3.0** 0-07-256415-6
- **VHS Video: Commencement Speeches at Wellesley College** 0-07-038991-8
- **VHS Video: Great Speeches,** Volumes I (ISBN 0-07-540823-6); 2 (0-69-711399-X); 3 (0-07-255161-5); 4 (0-07-255162-3); 5 (0-07-540824-4); 6 (0-07-020028-9); 7 (0-07-255163-1); 8 (0-69-720101-5); 9 (0-07-255164-X); 10 (0-69-723232-8); 11 (0-07-255165-8); 12 (0-07-039073-8); 14 (0-07-238491-3); 15 (0-07-249598-7); 16 (0-07-256419-9); 17 (0-07-288185-2)
- **VHS Video: Be Prepared to Speak** (Toastmasters) 0-07-540825-2
- **VHS Video: Speaking Effectively to 1 or 1000** 0-07-039051-7
- **VHS Video: Student Speeches for Analysis and Discussion,** Volumes 4 (0-07-912170-5); 5 (0-07-027492-4); 6 (0-07-238490-5); 7 (0-07-256408-3)
- **VHS Video: Contemporary Women Speakers** 0-07-027581-5
- **VHS Video: History of American Public Address** 0-07-289576-4
- **Video Disk: Great Moments from Great Speeches** 0-07-020921-9

As a full service publisher of quality educational products, McGraw-Hill does much more than just sell textbooks to your students. We create and publish an extensive array of print, video, and digital supplements to support instruction on your campus. Orders of new (versus used) textbooks help us defray the cost of publishing supplements, which is substantial. Please consult your local McGraw-Hill representative to learn about the availability of the supplements that accompany this text.

THE ART *of* PUBLIC SPEAKING

Eighth Edition

STEPHEN E. LUCAS

University of Wisconsin–Madison

Mc
Graw
Hill

Boston   Burr Ridge, IL   Dubuque, IA   Madison, WI   New York   San Francisco   St. Louis
Bangkok   Bogotá   Caracas   Kuala Lumpur   Lisbon   London   Madrid   Mexico City
Milan   Montreal   New Delhi   Santiago   Seoul   Singapore   Sydney   Taipei   Toronto

The McGraw·Hill Companies

Higher Education

THE ART OF PUBLIC SPEAKING
Published by McGraw-Hill, a business unit of The McGraw-Hill Companies, Inc., 1221 Avenue of the Americas, New York, NY, 10020. Copyright © 2004, 2001, 1998, 1995, 1992, 1989, 1986, 1983, by Stephen E. Lucas. All rights reserved. No part of this publication may be reproduced or distributed in any form or by any means, or stored in a database or retrieval system, without the prior written consent of The McGraw-Hill Companies, Inc., including, but not limited to, in any network or other electronic storage or transmission, or broadcast for distance learning.
Some ancillaries, including electronic and print components, may not be available to customers outside the United States.

This book is printed on acid-free paper.

1 2 3 4 5 6 7 8 9 0 QPD/QPD 0 9 8 7 6 5 4 3

ISBN   0-07-256296-X (student edition)
ISBN   0-07-256406-7 (annotated instructor's edition)

Publisher: *Phillip A. Butcher*
Senior sponsoring editor: *Nanette Kauffman Giles*
Director of development and media technology: *Rhona Robbin*
Editorial coordinator: *Josh Hawkins*
Senior marketing managers: *Sally Constable and Daniel M. Loch*
Producer, Media technology: *Jessica Bodie Richards*
Lead project manager: *Susan Trentacosti*
Manager, New book production: *Sandra Hahn*
Design manager: *Laurie J. Entringer*
Lead supplement producer: *Marc Mattson*
Freelance supplement editor: *Kassi Radomski*
Associate photo research coordinator: *Natalia C. Peschiera*
Photo researcher: *Barbara Salz*
Cover and interior design: *Laurie J. Entringer*
Cover illustration: *Riccardo Vecchio*
Typeface: *10/12 Melior*
Compositor: *The GTS Companies*/York, PA Campus
Printer: *Quebecor World Dubuque Inc.*

Library of Congress Control Number: 2003104880

www.mhhe.com

About the Author

Stephen E. Lucas is Professor of Communication Arts and Evjue-Bascom Professor in the Humanities at the University of Wisconsin–Madison, where he has taught since 1972. He received his bachelor's degree from the University of California, Santa Barbara, and his master's and doctorate degrees from Penn State University.

Professor Lucas has been recognized for his work as both a scholar and a teacher. His first book, *Portents of Rebellion: Rhetoric and Revolution in Philadelphia, 1765–1776,* received the Golden Anniversary Award of the National Communication Association in 1977 and was nominated for a Pulitzer Prize. His major articles include "The Schism in Rhetorical Scholarship" (1981), "The Renaissance of American Public Address: Text and Context in Rhetorical Criticism" (1988), "The Stylistic Artistry of the Declaration of Independence" (1990), and "The Rhetorical Ancestry of the Declaration of Independence" (1998), for which he received the Golden Anniversary Monograph Award of the National Communication Association. His most recent book is *The Quotable George Washington* (1999).

Professor Lucas has received a number of teaching awards, including the Chancellor's Award for Excellence in Teaching at the University of Wisconsin and the National Communication Association's Donald Ecroyd Award for Outstanding Teaching in Higher Education. His lecture course on "The Rhetoric of Campaigns and Revolutions" is among the most popular on campus and has twice been selected for statewide broadcast in its entirety by Wisconsin Public Radio. Professor Lucas is featured in the Educational Video Group's program on the history of American public address, and he has appeared on the History Channel's documentary on the Declaration of Independence.

Professor Lucas has directed the introductory public speaking course at the University of Wisconsin–Madison since 1973. Over the years he has been responsible for numerous teaching innovations and has supervised the training of hundreds of graduate assistants. He has also participated in public speaking workshops and colloquia at schools throughout the United States. In 2002 he served as a judge at China's national collegiate English-language public speaking competition sponsored by Ericsson and *21st Century,* and he has lectured at several Chinese universities, including Beijing University, Sichuan University, and the University of International Business and Economics, where he holds an honorary professorship.

Stephen Lucas and his wife, Patty, live in Madison, Wisconsin, and have two sons, Jeff and Ryan. His interests include travel, sports, art, and photography.

Contents in Brief

Contents

PART I   Speaking and Listening

2 Ethics and Public Speaking — 32

3 Listening — 54

Part II   Speech Preparation: Getting Started

4   Selecting a Topic and Purpose — 84

5   Analyzing the Audience — 106

6   Gathering Materials — 134

7 Supporting Your Ideas — 172

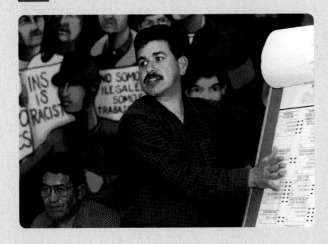

PART III Speech Preparation: Organizing and Outlining

8 Organizing the Body of the Speech — 200

9 Beginning and Ending the Speech — 222

10 Outlining the Speech — 246

Part IV   Presenting the Speech

13   Using Visual Aids   320

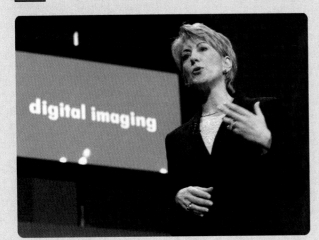

Appendix Using PowerPoint 343

Part V   Varieties of Public Speaking

14 Speaking to Inform ────────────────────────────── 364

17 Speaking on Special Occasions —————————— 462

18 Speaking in Small Groups —————————— 478

Preface

If it is true, as Walter Pater said, that "a book, like a person, has its fortunes," then fortune has indeed smiled upon *The Art of Public Speaking*. As the book enters its eighth edition, I am deeply appreciative of the students and teachers who have made it the leading work on its subject at colleges and universities across the United States.

In preparing this edition, I have retained what readers have identified as the main strengths of previous editions. The book continues to be informed by classical and contemporary theories of rhetoric but does not present theory for its own sake. Keeping a steady eye on the practical skills of public speaking, it offers full coverage of all major aspects of speech preparation and presentation.

Throughout *The Art of Public Speaking* I have followed David Hume's advice that one "who would teach eloquence must do it chiefly by examples." Whenever possible, I have tried to *show* the principles of public speaking in action in addition to describing them. Thus you will find in the book a large number of narratives and extracts from speeches—set off from the text in a contrasting typeface. There are also many speech outlines and sample speeches. All these are provided so students can *see* how to formulate specific purpose statements, how to analyze and adapt to audiences, how to organize ideas and construct outlines, how to assess evidence and reasoning, how to use language effectively, and so forth.

Because the immediate task facing students is to present speeches in the classroom, I have relied heavily on examples that relate directly to students' classroom needs and experiences. The speech classroom, however, is a training ground where students develop skills that will serve them throughout life. Therefore, I have also included a large number of illustrations drawn from the kinds of speaking experiences students will face after they graduate—in their careers and in their communities.

Also as in previous editions, I have been guided by the belief that a book intended for students who want to speak more effectively should never lose sight of the fact that the most important part of speaking is thinking. The ability to think critically is vital to a world in which personality and image too often substitute for thought and substance. While helping students become capable, responsible speakers, *The Art of Public Speaking* also aims at helping them become capable, responsible thinkers.

Features of the Eighth Edition

Given the extremely favorable response of teachers and students to the changes made in the 7th edition, I have kept the basic philosophy and approach of the book intact. At the same time, I have made a number of improvements in response to changes in world events, to advances in technology, and to the evolving needs of students and instructors. The improvements cover a broad range of subjects and are discussed below.

PowerPoint

As the use of PowerPoint has become more ubiquitous in every venue for public speaking, the need for students to understand how to use it has grown apace. Many schools now provide students the opportunity to employ Power-Point in the classroom, and employers increasingly assume that students who have taken a public speaking class have had some exposure to PowerPoint.

Unfortunately, PowerPoint is not always used well, a fact that has led many professors to lament the banality of a "typical" PowerPoint presentation, in which the content of a speech is reduced to a set of bulleted lists that a speaker reads off the screen to a bored audience sitting in a darkened room. Discontent with this kind of discourse has been captured perfectly in Peter Norvig's parody of what the Gettysburg Address might have looked like if Abraham Lincoln had presented it with PowerPoint ("The Gettysburg PowerPoint Presentation" at www.norvig.com/Gettysburg/).

When used properly, however, PowerPoint is a rich resource that allows a speaker to integrate text, photographs, charts, graphs, sound, and even video into a speech. Accordingly, following Chapter 13, I have added a new appendix that explains how PowerPoint can be used to enhance a speech without either dominating it or enfeebling its content. This appendix explains the pluses and minuses of PowerPoint, how to plan where to employ PowerPoint in a speech, how to use the resources of PowerPoint most effectively, and how to work PowerPoint into the delivery of a speech smoothly and expertly. It also provides guidance for students with regard to the use of copyrighted materials on PowerPoint slides.

Because PowerPoint is a visual medium, the appendix includes a five-minute informative speech on the Great Wall of China that illustrates the use of PowerPoint. This speech is available on both the Student CD-ROM and the speech videotape that accompanies the book, and it is reprinted in full—with commentary—at the end of the PowerPoint appendix.

Finally, for students who need more guidance on the technical details of PowerPoint than can be covered in the appendix, the Online Learning Center website for *The Art of Public Speaking* includes step-by-step tutorials for PowerPoint 2000 and PowerPoint 2002. The tutorials can be accessed at www.mhhe.com/lucaspowerpoint.

Taken together, the PowerPoint appendix, the CD-ROM, and the online tutorials provide the most comprehensive set of teaching materials for PowerPoint available with any speech textbook. I have worked hard to make sure they provide the kind of guidance students need to use PowerPoint effectively and responsibly—in the classroom and beyond.

The Tradition of Public Speaking

Today, more than ever, students need to understand that public speaking is a subject of rich lineage that has been vital in cultures around the globe for several millennia. Much more than a manner of winning friends and influencing people, it is a vital mode of civic engagement through which people express their ideas and influence their society. I have rewritten the opening pages of Chapter 1 to make this point more explicitly than in previous editions—partly through the addition of a new section titled "The Tradition of Public Speaking" and partly through the reworking of existing material. This new emphasis seeks to provide a sharper intellectual foundation for the book and for the public speaking course in general.

Plagiarism and the Internet

When it comes to plagiarism, no subject causes more confusion—or more temptation—than the Internet. Because it is so easy to copy information from the Web, many students do not understand the lines between plagiarism and the legitimate use of Internet materials. Nor do they understand the need to cite sources when using such materials.

To address these concerns, I have added a new section to Chapter 2 titled "Plagiarism and the Internet." In addition to explaining how to avoid inadvertent plagiarism when working with the Internet, this section addresses the problem of websites that sell complete speeches and papers. Here, as elsewhere in the book, I emphasize the importance of firm ethical standards in every aspect of public speaking.

Audience-Centeredness

As the world has become more complex, so have the challenges of audience analysis and adaptation. The revised version of Chapter 5 reflects that fact in several ways. First, it grounds the process of audience analysis and adaptation in the concept of identification. As with several other changes in the book, this change makes explicit a theoretical orientation that had been implicit in previous editions. Second, Chapter 5 contains a new section on sexual orientation as a factor in demographic audience analysis.

Third, I have reworked the sections on religion and racial, ethnic, and cultural background to make sure both are as current as possible. Finally, I have added a caution against stereotyping at the beginning of the section on demographic audience analysis. Looking at demographic factors can provide important clues about an audience, but those clues need to be used prudently, responsibly, and in combination with situational audience analysis.

The importance of audience-centeredness to effective speechmaking has been a point of emphasis from the very first edition of *The Art of Public Speaking*. So, too, has the fact that the speech class is a vital forum for engagement on ideas and issues of consequence. Rather than dismissing the classroom as an artificial speaking situation, it needs to be treated as a real situation in which students can—and do—affect the knowledge, values, beliefs, and opinions of their classmates. This edition continues that emphasis. By doing so, I hope it will contribute to the reinvigoration of participatory democracy on campus and off.

Internet Research

Students and instructors alike have responded favorably to the section in Chapter 6 titled "Searching the Internet" ever since I added it in the 6th edition. Readers of this edition will continue to find coverage of search engines, metasearch engines, and virtual libraries—as well as a compendium of specialized research sources—but each of these subjects has been thoroughly updated to keep pace with technological changes and the emergence of new websites.

I have also expanded the existing section on "Evaluating Internet Documents" and have added a new section on "Citing Internet Documents." Too often, students either forget to cite Internet materials in their speeches or cite them in passing by saying something like, "As I found on the Web," or "As the Internet states." In addition to explaining the need for precise, accurate citation of Web sources, I provide two examples of such citation from classroom speeches. These excerpts are included on the CD-ROM, so readers can see how Internet citations can be woven into the delivery of a speech.

Inclusive Language

The Art of Public Speaking has long been a leader in emphasizing the need for inclusive language as a matter of ethics, accuracy, and audience-centeredness in speechmaking. In the past editions, that emphasis ran subtly throughout the text and was discussed at length in "A Note on Nonsexist Language" in Chapter 11. In addition to continuing to underscore the need for inclusiveness throughout the book, I have replaced the discussion of nonsexist language in Chapter 11 with a new section titled "A Note on Inclusive Language."

This section includes material on nonsexist language, but it has been broadened to reflect the fact that as society has become more diverse, language has evolved to reflect that diversity. Regardless of the situation, audiences today expect speakers to be respectful of the different groups that make up American society. The new section on inclusive language helps explain how speakers can achieve that goal.

Persuasion and Ethics

In addition to Chapter 2, which focuses exclusively on the ethics of public speaking, a concern with ethics runs through *The Art of Public Speaking* like a theme in a symphony. In keeping with that approach, I have added a new section early in Chapter 15 on ethics and persuasion. This section reminds students of their ethical responsibilities as speakers and helps ensure that they keep those responsibilities in mind as they work on their persuasive speeches. As in previous editions, there is also a discussion of the ethics of emotional appeal in Chapter 16.

There are two other changes in Chapter 15 that warrant mention. First, I have added a section on "The Importance of Persuasion" at the start of the chapter. This section grounds the subject of persuasive speaking more firmly within the general subject of persuasion than had been the case in previous editions. Second, I have expanded the discussion of the potential range of persuasive responses in the section on "The Challenge of Persuasive Speaking." A new figure illustrating the degrees of persuasion will also help students grasp this important subject.

Diversity

As society has changed since the first edition of *The Art of Public Speaking* in 1983, so has the book. In each edition, I have sought to relate the principles of effective speechmaking to students of diverse backgrounds, values, and aspirations. This new edition continues my efforts to make sure the book is respectful of and applicable to all its readers.

Rather than treating diversity as a subject to be highlighted in boxes for marketing purposes or to be tossed into a chapter or two for its own sake, I have woven the subject into the fabric of the book from beginning to end. This is evident from the section on public speaking in a multicultural world in Chapter 1 to the treatment of audience analysis in Chapter 5 to the material on inclusive language in Chapter 11 to the speech by Nelson Mandela accepting the Congressional Gold Medal in Chapter 17.

In addition, there are scores of stories, speech excerpts, outlines, examples, photographs, and other materials that reflect the diversity of contemporary life and its implications for speechmaking. This new edition also reflects the increasingly global context in which much public speaking takes place—including excerpts from student speeches delivered in China's 2001 and 2002 collegiate English-language speech competition. In a variety of ways, large and small, I have sought to instill respect for people of diverse cultures, backgrounds, and orientations and to encourage an inclusive approach to the art of public speaking.

Student CD-ROM

Bridging the gap between the printed page and the spoken word has always been the greatest challenge facing a public speaking textbook. The innovative student CD that accompanied the 7th edition brought the art of public speaking to life, and it has been fully revised and updated for this new edition. Specially marked icons in the margins of the book direct readers to the appropriate resources on the CD. Those resources have been carefully designed to help students master the skills, concepts, and principles discussed in the text. Let me say a word about each.

Speech Videos

Continuing one of the most popular features of the 7th-edition CD, the updated version contains 58 video clips that demonstrate the principles of public speaking in action—including more than a dozen brand new clips. Fully integrated with the text, each clip has been chosen to illustrate a specific aspect of speechmaking. Running in length from 20 seconds to a minute and a half, the clips are distributed evenly throughout the book. Three-fourths are from student presentations. The remainder are from public figures and include such models of rhetorical excellence as Winston Churchill, Martin Luther King, Ronald Reagan, Mary Fisher, Jesse Jackson, and Elizabeth Dole.

In response to requests from users of the 7th edition, a second CD presents 11 full student speeches for analysis and discussion. Included are ice breaker speeches, informative speeches, persuasive speeches, and commemorative speeches. Together, the excerpts and full speeches provide students with approximately two hours of video.

Interactive Study Questions

To reinforce key principles and ideas, the CD contains a comprehensive set of study questions for each chapter. These questions are fully interactive, use a variety of formats, and systematically cover all the major concepts discussed in the book. Entirely different from items in the *Test Bank,* the questions have been written both to quiz students and to help them learn. After students enter their answer for each question, they receive not just an indication of whether the answer is right or wrong, but *feedback* that explains the correct answer.

Speech Outliner

In addition to video clips and study questions, the CD includes a speech outliner that guides students systematically through the process of organizing and outlining their speeches. As students use the outliner, they move step by step through each element of the speech from title through bibliography. Tutorial screens explain the organizational methods involved in composing each part of the speech, and the outliner automatically formats the speech in accordance with proper outlining principles. It also allows students to save, revise, and print their work, as well as export it to their own word processors.

Outline Exercises

New to this edition, five interactive outlining exercises give students additional help in developing their skills of speech organization. These exercises present scrambled outlines that students can rearrange in the correct order by using standard drag-and-drop procedures. As in other parts of the CD, the aim of these exercises is to put the resources provided by computer technology to the best possible pedagogical use.

Bibliography Formats

The CD also presents a comprehensive set of sample citations for both the Modern Language Association (MLA) and American Psychological Association (APA) formats. Covering more than 30 types of source material—from books, essays, and newspaper articles to government publications, personal interviews, television programs, and Internet documents—these sample citations have been fully updated for the new edition and are especially valuable to students as they prepare their speech bibliographies.

Speech Preparation Checklists

A dozen checklists help students keep on track as they prepare their speeches. Included are checklists for ethical public speaking, for framing the specific purpose and central idea, for phrasing and organizing main points, for creating the preparation outline, for composing introductions and conclusions, for using supporting materials, and for preparing and presenting visual aids.

Glossary of Key Terms

Throughout the book, key terms are defined in the margin as they appear in the text. Those key terms are reproduced on the CD, where they can be accessed either by chapter or via a master glossary arranged in alphabetical order. Whether students are reviewing for exams or working with the study questions on the CD, they can instantly check the meaning of any key term at the click of a mouse.

Key-Term Flashcards

A set of electronic flashcards for each chapter provides another resource for studying key terms. In addition to being fully interactive, the flashcards include an audio option for students who are aural learners. Developed especially for this edition of *The Art of Public Speaking,* the flashcards provide another example of how students can profit from advancements in instructional technology.

Notepad

New to this edition, the Notepad feature allows students to take notes as they are using the CD and to save those notes as a .txt file on their computer's hard drive.

Online Learning Center with PowerWeb

Accessible at www.mhhe.com/lucas8, the Online Learning Center provides a wealth of resources that supplement *The Art of Public Speaking.* Among those resources is the Top 100 American Speeches of the 20th Century. Based on a nationwide survey of 137 communication scholars I conducted at the end of 1999 with Professor Martin Medhurst, the top 100 speeches were rated on two criteria: rhetorical artistry and historical impact.

The Online Learning Center includes at least one link to a website with a transcript of each speech. Many of the links also furnish historical background about the speech and/or links to additional sites with information about the speaker, speech or occasion. Whenever possible, a link has been provided to a site that contains a full or partial audio presentation of the speech.

My aim in developing the Top 100 website was to provide a readily accessible way for students to learn more about the rich history of public speaking. One way to incorporate the site into class is to have each student give an informative presentation about one of the Top 100 speeches. Students often find this a fascinating assignment that broadens their horizons beyond the boundaries of their classroom.

The Online Learning center also includes practice quizzes, worksheets, speech evaluation forms, and key-term crossword puzzles, as well as overviews, outlines, and learning objectives for each chapter of the book. In addition, it is integrated with McGraw-Hill's Public Speaking PowerWeb, which keeps students up to date and helps them find topics for their presentations by reprinting recent speeches of public interest, plus news and journal articles related to current issues and to public speaking in general. The PowerWeb also provides weekly updates, links to *New York Times* articles, and a powerful search capability.

As with the CD, icons in the margins of the book guide readers to specific elements of the Online Learning Center.

Other Improvements

Beyond the changes described above, I have made a number of other improvements in this edition, including:

■ A sharper focus in Chapter 3 on active listening. In addition, the chapter now contains a Listening Self-Evaluation Form that students can use to gauge their own listening skills.

■ Moving the appendix on "Giving Your First Speech" from the end of the book to the end of Part I (following Chapter 3) so as to give it more visibility early in the term. The appendix also contains two new sample classroom introductory speeches, both of which are available for viewing on the Student CD.

■ Updating the section of Chapter 6 on library research to reflect current developments in information technology and the ongoing evolution of electronic databases.

■ Updating the treatment of nonverbal communication in Chapter 12. The chapter now contains sections on "The Speaker's Voice" and "The Speaker's Body" to provide parallel treatment of these two aspects of speech delivery. A definition of nonverbal communication at the start of the chapter makes clear that nonverbal communication covers both vocalics and physical action. This approach is more consistent with current scholarship than was the previous edition and should make for an easy transition when students go from the public speaking course to the nonverbal communication course.

■ Three new sample speeches in Chapter 17. The first two are companion pieces—Bill Clinton presenting the Congressional Medal of Honor to Nelson Mandela, and Mandela accepting the Medal. An excerpt from Mandela's speech is included on the CD-ROM. The chapter also has a new student commemorative speech on the Massachusetts 54th, the African-American regiment from the U.S. Civil War featured in the movie *Glory*. A full video of this speech is available on the Student CD.

■ Thorough reworking of examples throughout the book to keep the material clear, interesting, and relevant to today's readers.

Besides these revisions, I have tried in every chapter to make sure the endnote references reflect current theory and research. My aim has been to maintain the readability of the text while using the endnotes to help students understand that the principles of effective speechmaking have been confirmed by substantial contemporary scholarship as well as by centuries of practical experience.

Integrated Teaching and Learning System

The Art of Public Speaking has an exceptional set of print, video, and electronic resources for students and teachers alike. Some of these resources are found in the book itself; others are supplemental to it. Taken together, they provide a fully integrated teaching and learning system. In addition to the On-line Learning Center and the Student CD, both of which were described earlier, the integrated teaching and learning system includes the following elements.

Sample Speeches

Chapters 7, 14, 15, and 16 contain full sample speeches with commentary, as do the appendixes on "Giving Your First Speech" and "Using Power-Point." Chapter 10 has complete preparation and speaking outlines, both with commentary, and Chapter 17 has four full sample speeches. The end-of-book appendix consists of seven additional speeches for discussion and analysis, all of which are also available on video.

Critical Thinking Exercises

A set of Exercises for Critical Thinking accompanies each chapter, and the *Instructor's Manual* provides dozens of additional exercises that can be used as homework assignments or as the basis for classroom activities and discussion. In keeping with the experiential nature of speechmaking, these exercises require that students *work with* (rather than simply memorize) the principles presented in the book.

Student Workbook

Containing exercises, checklists, worksheets, evaluation forms, and other materials, the workbook gives students additional assistance with all the major elements of effective speechmaking. Instructors teaching online classes have found it highly valuable, but it has become a staple in many traditional classes as well.

Annotated Instructor's Edition

The *Annotated Instructor's Edition* provides a wealth of teaching aids for each chapter in the book. These aids include instructional strategies, class activities, discussion questions, speech assignments, and related readings. The *Annotated Instructor's Edition* is also cross-referenced with the *Instructor's Manual* and the other supplements that accompany *The Art of Public Speaking*.

Instructor's Manual

Running to more than 500 pages, the *Instructor's Manual* provides a comprehensive guide to teaching from *The Art of Public Speaking*. The manual contains outlines for each chapter of the book; discusses the end-of-chapter exercises; furnishes supplementary exercises, speeches, and classroom activities; offers suggested course outlines and speaking assignments; and provides over two dozen additional speeches for discussion and analysis.

Test Bank

The *Test Bank* furnishes more than 1,900 examination questions based on *The Art of Public Speaking*. As a special feature, it also offers preconstructed quizzes for each chapter in the book, as well as three complete final examinations. In addition to a print version, an electronic version is available for computerized test construction.

Selections from the *Communication Teacher*

This edition marks the fifth volume of selections from the *Communication Teacher* (formerly the *Speech Communication Teacher*) that I have compiled to accompany *The Art of Public Speaking.* Like its predecessors, the new collection covers a host of topics related to the teaching of public speaking, including audience analysis, critical thinking, diversity and multiculturalism, ethics, organization and outlining, speech anxiety, persuasion, testing and evaluation, and general instructional methods. All five volumes are available with this edition of the book. Taken together, they reprint almost 350 brief articles that offer a wealth of practical ideas for classroom use.

Videos

There are several videotapes of student presentations that accompany *The Art of Public Speaking,* including a new tape that offers 17 speeches, eight of which are new to this edition. Instructors who adopt *The Art of Public Speaking* can also select from 20 "Great Speeches" videotapes that accompany the book. Among the selections on these are Martin Luther King's "I Have a Dream," Barbara Bush's 1990 commencement speech at Wellesley College, and Mary Fisher's "A Whisper of AIDS"—all of which are reprinted in the book.

Two other videos—*Be Prepared to Speak* and *Speaking Effectively to 1 or 1,000*—introduce students to the public speaking process and provide helpful advice on dealing with stage fright. Both tapes are entertaining as well as informative, and either can be shown early in the course to help prepare students for their ice breaker speeches.

Overhead Transparencies

The 8th edition of *The Art of Public Speaking* comes with a binder of more than 120 full-color overhead transparencies. Created to be of maximum value for lecture presentations and classroom discussions, they include a wide range of graphics, illustrations, and exercises from the textbook, as well as additional exercises and classroom activities from the *Instructor's Manual.*

PowerPoint Slides with Video Clips

There is also a collection of more than 400 slides for instructors who use PowerPoint in their lectures and discussions. Instructors can use these slides just as they are, or they can modify the slides to fit the special needs of individual classes. As a new feature, 40 of the slides include video speech clips as well as text. The PowerPoint slides can be found on the Instructor's Resource CD-ROM described on the next page.

Teaching Public Speaking Online

This new supplement provides a wealth of practical guidance for instructors who are adapting *The Art of Public Speaking* for use in an online environment. Written by Professor Jennifer Cochrane of Indiana University–Purdue University at Indianapolis, it draws upon her experience with online instruction to explore how one can teach an intellectually rich, practically rewarding public speaking course via the Web.

Instructor's Resource CD-ROM

For the convenience of instructors, the *Instructor's Manual, Test Bank, Teaching Public Speaking, Teaching Public Speaking Online, Selections from the Communication Teacher, Handbook for Teachers of Non-Native Speakers of English,* and PowerPoint slides are all available on a single CD. Like the other computerized resources that accompany *The Art of Public Speaking,* this CD is available in both Mac and Windows versions.

From Oratory to Public Speaking

Reprinted from my essay on "Public Speaking" in the *Encyclopedia of Rhetoric* (Oxford University Press), this pamphlet is a new supplement to the 8th edition of *The Art of Public Speaking.* It presents a synoptic view of major developments in the practice and teaching of public speaking during the 20th century, and it illuminates the role of public speaking as a powerful historical force.

Teaching Public Speaking

Written primarily for beginning instructors, *Teaching Public Speaking* reprints my essay of the same title from *Teaching Communication: Theory, Research, and Methods* (Lawrence Erlbaum Associates). This essay presents an overview of the pedagogical philosophy behind *The Art of Public Speaking* and discusses a number of practical classroom issues.

Handbook for Teachers of Non-Native Speakers of English

Developed for instructors who have ESL students in their public speaking classes, this 60-page handbook focuses on the central issues that should be considered when working with students from different linguistic and cultural backgrounds.

Online Resources

Instructors and students alike can take advantage of several outstanding online resources in conjunction with this edition, including the Online Learning Center with PowerWeb, which we discussed on page xxv. In addition, instructors using *The Art of Public Speaking* have full access to McGraw-Hill's PageOut, which allows teachers to create personal course websites by using a template provided by McGraw-Hill.

Special features of PageOut include an interactive course syllabus, an online gradebook, online testing, and capability for posting personal files and discussions. All online content for *The Art of Public Speaking* is supported by Web CT, Blackboard, and eCollege.com. For more details, check with a McGraw-Hill representative or visit www.mhhe.com.pageout.

Acknowledgments

"'Tis the good reader," said Ralph Waldo Emerson, "that makes the good book." I have been fortunate to have very good readers indeed, and I would like to thank the reviewers and focus group participants whose names appear on page xxxii for their many helpful comments and suggestions.

In addition, I would like to express my gratitude to the students at the University of Wisconsin whose speeches provided the material for so many of the examples in the text; to Mary Rossa, Ted Schroeder, and Melissa Magreta, who assisted with the research for this edition; to Jim Ferris, who once again provided a valuable sounding board on numerous issues; and to members of the Communication Arts 100 teaching staff at the University of Wisconsin, who helped me by collecting sample speeches and by identifying rough spots in the 7th edition.

I wish to extend a special thanks to Amy Slagell, who did a marvelous job generating new questions for the *Test Bank* and steering the final version into production; to Jennifer Cochrane, who produced a wonderful supplement on using *The Art of Public Speaking* in an online course; and to Sue Vander Hook, who, as in previous editions, did an exceptional job formatting the *Instructor's Manual, Test Bank,* and *Student Workbook.* She has once again made it possible to offer the finest set of supplements available with any public speaking textbook.

I am also indebted to Carl Burgchardt, who provided permission for me to incorporate parts of his pamphlet *How to Give Your First Speech,* originally written to accompany the 5th edition of *The Art of Public Speaking,* into the appendix on "Giving Your First Speech"; to Randy Fitzgerald, Director of Public Relations at the University of Richmond, and Paul Porterfield, Director of the Media Resource Center at the same school, for their time and effort in helping me secure the videotape of Sajjid Zahir Chinoy's "Questions of Culture"; and to Nie Lisheng, Editor-in-Chief of *21st Century,* for permission to include on the Student CD video excerpts from speeches presented at China's 21st Century Ericsson Cup National English Speaking Competition.

I am especially beholden to my colleague Susan Zaeske, whose assistance and counsel have been indispensable. In addition to preparing the initial draft of the PowerPoint appendix and the online PowerPoint tutorials, she worked with me in revising the entire book and the *Instructor's Manual.* As always, I have profited from her insight and enterprise, and the book is demonstrably better as a result of her contributions.

I also owe thanks to many people at McGraw-Hill. Nanette Kauffman Giles provided overall editorial direction and a powerful sense of energy that helped keep the book on track even through her wedding and the inevitable vicissitudes of any large-scale project. Rhona Robbin proved again why she is regarded as a masterful editor by authors who have had the privilege of working with her. She is truly a gem. So, too, is Jessica Bodie Richards, who coordinated the book's ever-growing technology program, including the splendid revision of the Student CD, which she undertook with a blend of dedication, grace, and patience that made working with her an unqualified joy.

Sally Constable was another key member of the book team. She spearheaded a superlative marketing campaign and provided helpful advice on numerous other matters. Susan Trentacosti proved once again the value of a top-flight project manager. I have no idea how she coordinated everything so as to get the book through production on schedule, but I am deeply thankful. Laurie Entringer made sure the book continued its tradition of having a striking cover and an appealing, user-friendly interior design.

As in the 7th edition, I was fortunate to have Barbara Salz as the book's photo researcher. Notwithstanding the changes roiling her industry, Barbara again produced a superb photo program. It was also a pleasure to work with Kassi Radomski, who managed the supplements, and Marc Mattson, who superintended production of them. I would be remiss if I did not also thank Phil Butcher, Thalia Dorwick, Steve Debow, and Ed Stanford—all of whom lent steadfast support to the book and its commitment to excellence.

It is amazing to me that the publication of this edition marks the 20th anniversary of *The Art of Public Speaking*. My younger son, Ryan, was born the year before I began work on the first edition. He is now a grown man and I am still working on the book—a fact of which he often reminds me. My older son, Jeff, can remember a time before the book became a part of our family routine, but it has overlapped with a major part of his life as well. Like Ryan, he always seemed to understand when it was time for another edition, and he made allowances for my preoccupation at those times. Nobody, however, has been more supportive or more understanding than my wife, Patty. There might be an *Art of Public Speaking* without her, but there would be no one with whom to share it.

Stephen E. Lucas

Madison, Wisconsin

Reviewers and Focus Group Participants

Kari A. Manuel
State University of West Georgia

David D. Allison
Liberty University

Rick Armstrong
Wichita State University

Krista Appelquist
Moraine Valley Community College

Christa Arnold
University of Florida

Elizabeth Bernat
State University of New York College at Plattsburgh

Judy Castle
Southwest Virginia Community College

Jennifer Cochrane
Indiana University–Purdue University, Indianapolis

William Cue
Longview Community College

Linda Davis
Northeast State Technical Community College

Tom Diamond
Montana State University

Michael Dillon
Duquesne University

D. Michael Ehret
Columbus State Community College

Jerry K. Frye
Stephen F. Austin University

Gayle Garner
Cleveland State Community College

Marcia Goldberg
Ursinus College

Dayle Hardy-Short
Northern Arizona University

Kim Higgs
University of North Dakota

Lisa Hogan
Pennsylvania State University

William Hysell
Mohawk Valley Community College

Brenda Jolley
Stillman College

Debra S. Jones
Chattanooga State Technical College

Carl Kell
Western Kentucky University

David Kosloski
Clark College

Patricia Scileppi Krivanek
Riverside Community College

Katheryn C. Maguire
Colorado State University

Sujanet Mason
Luzerne County Community College

Lee Mazmanian
University of San Francisco

Patrick Mills
Palomar College

Maurice Odine
Tennessee State University

James Prohs
Black Hawk College

Jeff Przybylo
Harper College

James Putz
University of Wisconsin–LaCrosse

Rebecca Roberts
University of Wyoming

Douglas Rosentrater
Bucks County Community College

Mary Sandoz
Vanderbilt University

Lynae Sanford
Lamar University

Kristi Schaller
University of Hawaii at Manoa

Jennifer Scharf
Marshall University

Amy R. Slagell
Iowa State University

David Sprague
Liberty University

James J. Spurrier
Vincennes University

Linda Loomis Steck
Benjamin Franklin International School, Barcelona, Spain

Elena C. Strauman
Auburn University

Elliott Street
Meridian Community College

Katherine B. Taylor
University of Louisville

Michael Tew
Eastern Michigan University

Donna Thomsen
Johnson & Wales University

Shaun R. Treat
Louisiana State University

Paul Trent
Mercy College

F. Kim Wilcox
Penn Valley Community College

THE ART *of*
PUBLIC SPEAKING

Chapter One

SPEAKING IN PUBLIC

Chapter Focus
This chapter begins by showing how public speaking empowers people to make a difference in their lives. After looking at the long tradition of public speaking, it then explores similarities and differences between public speaking and everyday conversation, techniques students can use to combat stage fright, the basic elements of the speech communication process, and the role of public speaking in a multicultural world. For a full outline of the chapter, see the *Instructor's Manual*, pp. 60–65.

W ilma Subra had no intention of becoming a public speaker. After graduating from college with degrees in chemistry and microbiology, she went to work at Gulf South Research Institute in New Iberia, Louisiana. As part of her job, she conducted field research on environmental toxins—often in minority communities located near large industrial polluters. She found that many families were being exposed to high, sometimes deadly, levels of chemicals and other toxins, but she was not allowed to make her information public.

Frustrated by these restrictions, Subra left her job in 1981, created her own company, and has devoted the past two decades to helping people fight back against giant industrial polluters. She works with families and community groups to conduct environmental tests, interpret test results, and organize for change. Because of her efforts, dozens of toxic sites across the country have been cleaned up, and one chemical industry spokesperson calls her "a top gun for the environmental movement."

How has Wilma Subra achieved all this? Partly through her scientific training, partly through her commitment to environmental justice. But just as important is her ability to communicate with people through public speaking. "Public speaking," she says, "is the primary vehicle I use for reaching people. When you have an important message, it's the best way to engage people and get them involved."

If you had asked Subra before 1981, "Do you see yourself as a major public speaker?" she would have laughed at the idea. Yet today she gives more than 100 presentations a year, not including radio, television, and newspaper interviews. Along the way she has lectured at Harvard, testified before Congress, and addressed audiences in 40 states, as well as in Mexico, Canada, and Japan. "When I was in college," she says, "I never dreamed I'd need public speaking, but now I use it almost every day."

The Power of Public Speaking

Throughout history people have used public speaking as a vital means of communication. What the Greek leader Pericles said more than 2,500 years ago is still true today: "One who forms a judgment on any point but cannot explain" it clearly "might as well never have thought at all on the subject."[1] Public speaking, as its name implies, is a way of making your ideas public—of sharing them with other people and of influencing other people.

During modern times many women and men around the globe have spread their ideas and influence through public speaking. In the United States, the list includes Franklin Roosevelt, Billy Graham, Cesar Chavez, Barbara Jordan, Ronald Reagan, Martin Luther King, Jesse Jackson, and Elizabeth Dole. In other countries, we see the power of public speaking employed by such people as former British Prime Minister Margaret Thatcher, South African leader Nelson Mandela, Guatemalan human rights activist Rigoberta Menchu, and Burmese democracy champion Aung San Suu Kyi.

As you read these names, you may think to yourself, "That's fine. Good for them. But what does that have to do with me? I don't plan to be a president or a preacher or a crusader for any cause." Nevertheless, the need for public speaking will almost certainly touch you sometime in your life—maybe tomorrow, maybe not for five years. Can you imagine yourself in any of these situations?

View John F. Kennedy, Martin Luther King, Barbara Jordan, Ronald Reagan, and other speakers in action.

CD 1: VIDEO 1.1

You are a management trainee in a large corporation. Altogether, there are seven trainees in the program. One of you will get the lower-management job that has just opened. There is to be a large staff meeting at which each of the trainees will discuss the project he or she has been developing. One by one your colleagues make their presentations. They have no experience in public speaking and are intimidated by the higher-ranking managers present. Their speeches are stumbling and awkward. You, however, call upon all the skills you learned in your public speaking course. You deliver an informative talk that is clear, well reasoned, and articulate. You get the job.

You are married and have three children. One of your children has a learning disability. You hear that your local school board has decided, for budget reasons, to eliminate the special teacher who has been helping your child. At an open meeting of the school board, you stand up and deliver a thoughtful, compelling speech on the necessity for keeping the special teacher. The school board changes its mind.

You are the assistant manager in a branch office of a national company. Your immediate superior, the branch manager, is about to retire, and there will be a retirement dinner. All the executives from the home office will attend. As his close working associate, you are asked to give a farewell toast at the party. You prepare and deliver a speech that is both witty and touching—a perfect tribute to your boss. After the speech, everyone applauds enthusiastically, and a few people have tears in their eyes. The following week you are named branch manager.

Fantasies? Not really. Any of these situations could occur. In a recent survey of 480 companies and public organizations, communication skills—including public speaking—were ranked first among the personal qualities of college graduates sought by employers.[2] The importance of such skills is true across the board—for accountants and architects, teachers and technicians, scientists and stockbrokers. Even in highly specialized fields such as civil and mechanical engineering, employers consistently rank the ability to communicate above technical knowledge when deciding whom to hire and whom to promote.

Nor has the growth of the Internet and other new technologies reduced the need for public speaking. As one communication consultant states, "There are more avenues to reach people than ever before, but there's no substitute for face-to-face communication." To be successful, says business leader Midge Costanza, you must have "the ability to stand on your feet, either on a one-to-one basis or before a group, and make a presentation that is convincing and believable."[3]

The same is true in community life. Public speaking is a vital means of civic engagement. It is a way to express your ideas and to have an impact on issues that matter in a democratic society. Look back for a moment at the second of our three hypothetical situations, the one in which you persuade the school board to keep the special teacher who has been helping your child. Why did the school board change its mind? Not simply because the facts were on your side (though they may have been) or because you knew more about education than the school board (which you probably do not). The school board changed its mind because of your *speech*—in which you presented a compelling case for keeping the special teacher.

The point is that public speaking is a form of empowerment. It can—and often does—make a difference in things people care about very much. The key phrase here is "make a difference." This is what most of us want to do in life—to make a difference, to change the world in some small way. Public speaking offers you an opportunity to make a difference in something you care about very much.

The Tradition of Public Speaking

Given the importance of public speaking, it's not surprising that it has been taught and studied around the globe for thousands of years. Almost all cultures have an equivalent of the English word "orator" to designate someone with special skills in public speaking. The oldest known handbook on effective speech was written on papyrus in Egypt some 4,500 years ago. Eloquence was highly prized in ancient India, Africa, and China, as well as among the Aztecs and other pre-European cultures of North and South America.[4]

In classical Greece and Rome, public speaking played a central role in education and civic life. It was also studied extensively. Aristotle's *Rhetoric,* composed during the third century B.C.E., is still considered the most important work on its subject, and many of its principles are followed by speakers (and writers) today. The great Roman leader Cicero used his speeches to defend liberty and wrote several works about oratory in general.

Over the centuries, many other notable thinkers have dealt with issues of rhetoric, speech, and language—including the Roman educator Quintilian, the Christian preacher St. Augustine, the medieval writer Christine de Pizan, the British philosopher Francis Bacon, and the American critic Kenneth Burke.[5] In recent years, communication researchers have provided an increasingly scientific basis for understanding the methods and strategies of effective speech.[6]

Your immediate objective is to apply those methods and strategies in your classroom speeches. What you learn in your class, however, will be applicable long after you leave college. As you read this book, keep in mind that the principles of public speaking are derived from a long tradition and have been confirmed by a substantial body of research.[7] The more you know about those principles, the more effective you will be in your own speeches—and the more effective you will be in listening to the speeches of other people.

Related Reading
For an insightful view of rhetorical practices and principles around the globe, see George A. Kennedy, *Comparative Rhetoric: An Historical and Cross-Cultural Introduction* (New York: Oxford University Press, 1998). For more detail, consult Thomas O. Sloane (ed.), *Encyclopedia of Rhetoric* (New York: Oxford University Press, 2001).

Similarities Between Public Speaking and Conversation

How much time do you spend each day talking to other people? The average adult spends about 30 percent of her or his waking hours in conversation. As you will see, there are many similarities between daily conversation and public speaking.

Children learn the art of conversation by trial and error. A toddler says "Cookie!" to persuade her father to give her a snack. A five-year-old tells a little story to entertain Grandma and gain admiration. If neither of these things works—the cookie isn't forthcoming, Grandma is not amused— well, back to the drawing board. Next time the child will try it a slightly different way.

By the time you read this book, you will have spent much of your life perfecting the art of conversation. You may not realize it, but you already employ a wide range of skills when talking to people. These skills include the following:

1. *Organizing your thoughts logically.* Suppose you were giving someone directions to get to your house. You wouldn't do it this way:

> When you turn off the highway, you'll see a big diner on the left. But before that, stay on the highway to Exit 67. Usually a couple of the neighbors' dogs are in the street, so go slow after you turn at the blinking light. Coming from your house you get on the highway through Maple Street. If you pass the taco stand, you've gone too far. The house is blue.

Instead, you would take your listener systematically, step by step, from his or her house to your house. You would organize your message.

2. *Tailoring your message to your audience.* You are a geology major. Two people ask you how pearls are formed. One is your roommate; the other is your nine-year-old niece. You answer as follows:

> *To your roommate:* "When any irritant, say a grain of sand, gets inside the oyster's shell, the oyster automatically secretes a substance called nacre, which is principally calcium carbonate and is the same material that lines the oyster's shell. The nacre accumulates in layers around the irritant core to form the pearl."

> *To your niece:* "Imagine you're an oyster on the ocean floor. A grain of sand gets inside your shell and makes you uncomfortable. So you decide to cover it up. You cover it with a material called mother-of-pearl. The covering builds up around the grain of sand to make a pearl."

Teaching Tip
On the first or second day of class, have students fill out and return the Student Introduction Questionnaire on p. 68 of the *Instructor's Manual.* This will give you a good picture of the public speaking experiences of the students in your class. It will also allow you to see what specific goals individual students have for improving their speaking. At the end of the term, you can return the questionnaires to students so they can assess how successful they have been in meeting their goals.

Many skills used in conversation also apply in public speaking. As you learn to speak more effectively, you may also learn to communicate more effectively in other situations.

3. *Telling a story for maximum impact.* Suppose you are telling a friend about a funny incident at last week's football game. You don't begin with the punch line ("Keisha fell out of the stands right onto the field. Here's how it started. . . . "). Instead, you carefully build up your story, adjusting your words and tone of voice to get the best effect.

4. *Adapting to listener feedback.* Whenever you talk with someone, you are aware of that person's verbal, facial, and physical reactions. For example:

You are explaining an interesting point that came up in biology class. Your listener begins to look confused, puts up a hand as though to stop you, and says "Huh?" You go back and explain more clearly.

A friend has asked you to listen while she practices a speech. At the end you tell her, "There's just one part I really don't like—that quotation from the attorney general." Your friend looks very hurt and says, "That was my favorite part!" So you say, "But if you just worked the quotation in a little differently, it would be wonderful."

Each day, in casual conversation, you do all these things many times without thinking about them. You already possess these communication skills. And these are among the most important skills you will need for public speaking.

To illustrate, let's return briefly to one of the hypothetical situations at the beginning of this chapter. When addressing the school board about the need for a special teacher:

- You *organize* your ideas to present them in the most persuasive manner. You steadily build up a compelling case about how the teacher benefits the school.

- You *tailor your message* to your audience. This is no time to launch an impassioned defense of special education in the United States. You must show how the issue is important to the people in that very room—to their children and to the school.

- You tell your story for *maximum impact.* Perhaps you relate an anecdote to demonstrate how much your child has improved. You also have statistics to show how many other children have been helped.

- You *adapt to listener feedback.* When you mention the cost of the special teacher, you notice sour looks on the faces of the school board members. So you patiently explain how small that cost is in relation to the overall school budget.

In many ways, then, public speaking requires the same skills used in ordinary conversation. Most people who communicate well in daily talk can learn to communicate just as well in public speaking. By the same token, training in public speaking can make you a more adept communicator in a variety of situations, such as conversations, classroom discussions, business meetings, and interviews.

Teaching Tip
Telling a story for maximum impact is a strategy that most successful comedians have mastered. Bring in a short video of one or two comedians and have students comment on how each comic builds up the story and adjusts his or her timing to get the best effect.

Class Activity
On the first day of class, have students introduce themselves, name their hometowns, identify their intended major and career goals, and provide one unusual fact about themselves (traveled abroad, worked in a television newsroom, lived through a hurricane, etc.). Afterward, point out that everyone in the class has just made an impromptu speech, even though they probably did not think of it that way. Note, too, that they have made many such speeches in their lives. In addition to reinforcing the similarities between public speaking and daily conversation, this activity allows students to learn about each other and sets a positive tone for the rest of the class.

Differences Between Public Speaking and Conversation

Despite their similarities, public speaking and everyday conversation are not identical. Imagine that you are telling a story to a friend. Then imagine yourself telling the story to a group of seven or eight friends. Now imagine telling the same story to 20 or 30 people. As the size of your audience grows, the manner in which you present the story will change. You will find yourself adapting to three major differences between conversation and public speaking:

1. *Public speaking is more highly structured.* It usually imposes strict time limitations on the speaker. In most cases, the situation does not allow listeners to interrupt with questions or commentary. The speaker must accomplish her or his purpose in the speech itself. In preparing the speech, the speaker must anticipate questions that might arise in the minds of listeners and answer them. Consequently, public speaking demands much more detailed planning and preparation than ordinary conversation.

2. *Public speaking requires more formal language.* Slang, jargon, and bad grammar have little place in public speeches. As angry as she is about industrial pollution, when Wilma Subra speaks to a congressional committee, she doesn't say, "We've damn well got to stop the greedy creeps who pollute whole communities just to make a few more bucks." Despite the growing informality of all aspects of American life, listeners usually react negatively to speakers who do not elevate and polish their language when addressing an audience. A speech should be "special."

3. *Public speaking requires a different method of delivery.* When conversing informally, most people talk quietly, interject stock phrases such as "like" and "you know," adopt a casual posture, and use what are called vocalized pauses ("uh," "er," "um"). Effective public speakers, however, adjust their voices to be heard clearly throughout the audience. They assume a more erect posture. They avoid distracting mannerisms and verbal habits.

With study and practice, you will be able to master these differences and expand your conversational skills into speechmaking. Your speech class will provide the opportunity for this study and practice.

Class Activity
For an interesting assignment that reinforces the applicability of a public speaking course to many aspects of daily life, see Jodi R. Cohen, "The Relevance of a Course in Public Speaking," in *Selections from the Speech Communication Teacher, 1986–1991,* pp. 2–3, which accompanies *The Art of Public Speaking.*

Developing Confidence: Your Speech Class

One of the major concerns of students in any speech class is stage fright. We may as well face the issue squarely. Many people who converse easily in all kinds of everyday situations become frightened at the idea of standing up before a group to make a speech.

If you are worried about stage fright, you may feel better knowing that you are not alone. A survey conducted in 1973 asked more than 2,500 Americans to list their greatest fears. To the surprise of the researchers, the largest number of people—41 percent—listed speaking before a group among their greatest fears.[8] Amazing as it may seem, many Americans appear to consider public speaking a fate worse than death.

stage fright
Anxiety over the prospect of giving a speech in front of an audience.

In a more recent study, researchers concentrated on social situations and, again, asked their subjects to list their greatest fears. Here is how they responded:[9]

Greatest Fear	Percent Naming
A party with strangers	74
Giving a speech	70
Asked personal questions in public	65
Meeting a date's parents	59
First day on a new job	59
Victim of a practical joke	56
Talking with someone in authority	53
Job interview	46
Formal dinner party	44
Blind date	42

Again, speechmaking ranks near the top in provoking anxiety.

Nervousness Is Normal

Actually, most people tend to be anxious before doing something important in public. Actors are nervous before a play, politicians are nervous before a campaign speech, athletes are nervous before a big game. The ones who succeed have learned to use their nervousness to their advantage. Listen to tennis star Serena Williams, speaking after her 2002 Wimbledon title match against her sister Venus. Asked by a reporter if she was nervous playing in the Wimbledon final, Williams responded, "Oh, yes—especially in the second set when I had a chance to close out the match." Putting her butterflies to good use, Serena did indeed close out the match, defeating Venus in straight sets to claim her first Wimbledon championship.

Much the same thing happens in speechmaking. Surveys show that 76 percent of experienced speakers have stage fright before taking the floor.[10] But their nervousness is a healthy sign that they are getting "psyched up" for a good effort. Novelist and lecturer I. A. R. Wylie explains, "Now after many years of practice I am, I suppose, really a 'practiced speaker.' But I rarely rise to my feet without a throat constricted with terror and a furiously thumping heart. When, for some reason, I *am* cool and self-assured, the speech is always a failure."[11]

In other words, it is perfectly normal—even desirable—to be nervous at the start of a speech. Your body is responding as it would to any stressful situation—by producing extra *adrenaline.* This sudden shot of adrenaline is what makes your heart race, your hands shake, your knees knock, and your skin perspire. Every public speaker experiences all these reactions to some extent. The question is: How can you control your nervousness and make it work for you rather than against you?

Discussion Prompt
Ask students to discuss specific reasons they fear speaking in public. For example, are they afraid of being boring? Of shaking or blushing? Of forgetting what they plan to say? Research has shown that it can be reassuring to learn that others in class share similar fears.

Discussion Prompt
Have students relate their experience in sports, music, or theater and discuss the stage fright they felt in those activities. What strategies did students use to control their nervousness and make it work for them? Point out that many of the same strategies can be used in public speaking.

adrenaline
A hormone released into the bloodstream in response to physical or mental stress.

Dealing with Nervousness

Rather than trying to eliminate every trace of stage fright, you should aim at transforming it from a negative force into what one expert calls *positive nervousness*—"a zesty, enthusiastic, lively feeling with a slight edge to it. . . . It's still nervousness, but it feels different. You're no longer victimized by it; instead, you're vitalized by it. You're in control of it."[12] Here are six time-tested ways you can turn your nervousness from a negative force into a positive one.

positive nervousness
Controlled nervousness that helps energize a speaker for her or his presentation.

Acquire Speaking Experience

You have already taken the first step. You are enrolled in a public speaking course, where you will learn about speechmaking and gain speaking experience. Think back to your first day at kindergarten, your first date, your first day at a new job. You were probably nervous in each situation because you were facing something new and unknown. Once you became accustomed to the situation, it was no longer threatening. So it is with public speaking. For most students, the biggest part of stage fright is fear of the unknown. The more you learn about public speaking and the more speeches you give, the less threatening speechmaking will become.

Your speech class will provide knowledge and experience to help you speak with confidence. Of course, the road to confidence will sometimes be bumpy. Learning to give a speech is not much different from learning any other skill—it proceeds by trial and error. The purpose of your speech class is to shorten the process, to minimize the errors, to give you a nonthreatening arena—a sort of laboratory—in which to undertake the "trial."

Your teacher recognizes that you are a novice and is trained to give the kind of guidance you need to get started. In your fellow students you have a highly sympathetic audience who will provide valuable feedback to help you improve your speaking skills. As the class goes on, your fears about public speaking will gradually recede until they are replaced by only a healthy nervousness before you rise to speak.[13]

Teaching Tip
Dealing sensitively and sympathetically with stage fright is especially crucial at the beginning of a public speaking course. No matter what their age, gender, ethnic background, year in school, major, or grade point average, most students enter the course highly apprehensive about the prospect of presenting a formal speech. One of your most important tasks is to create a supportive classroom atmosphere in which students feel free to discuss their anxiety and to take the risks necessary to overcome it. It is crucial, as the class progresses, that you provide feedback to students about their speeches in a kind, optimistic tone that is realistic about their strengths and weaknesses while also providing hope and encouragement for their future speeches.

Prepare, Prepare, Prepare

Another key to gaining confidence is to pick speech topics you truly care about—and then to prepare your speeches so thoroughly that you cannot help but be successful. Here's how one student combined enthusiasm for her topic with thorough preparation to score a triumph in speech class:

Tia Betances was concerned about taking a speech class. Not having any experience as a public speaker, she got butterflies in her stomach just thinking about talking in front of an audience. But when the time came for Tia's first speech, she was determined to make it a success.

Tia chose the Special Olympics as the topic for her speech. Her younger brother suffered from Down's syndrome, and for the past five years Tia had worked as a volunteer at the local Special Olympics competition. The purpose of her speech was to explain the origins, events, and philosophy of the Special Olympics.

As Tia spoke, it became clear that she cared deeply about her subject and genuinely wanted her audience to care about it too. Because she was intent on communicating with her audience, she forgot to be nervous. She established eye contact with her listeners and spoke clearly, fluently, and dynamically. Soon the entire class was engrossed in her speech.

Afterward, Tia conceded that she had surprised even herself. "I could hardly believe it," she said. "Once I got through the introduction, I didn't think about being nervous—I just concentrated on what I wanted to say. It was even sort of fun."

How much time should you devote to preparing your speeches? A standard rule of thumb is that each minute of speaking time requires one to two hours of preparation time—perhaps more, depending on the amount of research needed for the speech. This may seem like a lot of time, but the rewards are well worth it. Like an actor who rehearses a role until it is just right, you will find that your confidence as a speaker increases when you work on a speech until it is just right. One professional speech consultant estimates that proper preparation can reduce stage fright by up to 75 percent.[14]

If you follow the techniques suggested by your teacher and in the rest of this book, you will stand up for every speech fully prepared. Imagine that the day for your first speech has arrived. You have studied your audience and selected a topic you know will interest them. You have researched the speech thoroughly and practiced it several times until it feels absolutely comfortable. You have even tried it out before two or three trusted friends. How can you help but be confident of success?

Think Positively

Confidence is mostly the well-known power of positive thinking. If you think you can do it, you usually can. On the other hand, if you predict disaster and doom, that is almost always what you will get. This is especially true when it comes to public speaking. Speakers who think negatively about themselves and the speech experience are much more likely to be overcome by stage fright than are speakers who think positively. Here are some ways you can transform negative thoughts into positive ones as you work on your speeches:

Cross-Reference
Many instructors assign an ungraded ice breaker speech in the first week or two of the term to help increase students' comfort with the class. The appendix following Chapter 3, "Giving Your First Speech" (pp. 73–83), is designed to help students get ready for this speech.

Negative Thought	**Positive Thought**
I wish I didn't have to give this speech.	This speech is a chance for me to share my ideas and gain experience as a speaker.
I'm not a great public speaker.	No one's perfect, but I'm getting better with each speech I give.
I'm always nervous when I give a speech.	Everyone's nervous. If other people can handle it, I can too.
No one will be interested in what I have to say.	I have a good topic and I'm fully prepared. Of course they'll be interested.

Many psychologists believe that the ratio of positive to negative thoughts in regard to stressful activities such as speechmaking should be at least five to one. That is, for each negative thought, you should counter with a minimum of five positive ones. Doing so will not make your nerves go away completely, but it will help keep them under control so you can concentrate on communicating your ideas rather than on brooding about your fears and anxieties.

Use the Power of Visualization

Visualization is closely related to positive thinking. It is a technique used by many people—athletes, musicians, actors, speakers, and others—to enhance their performance in stressful situations. How does it work? Listen to Olympic long-distance runner Vicki Huber:

> Right before a big race, I'll picture myself running, and I will try and put all of the other competitors in the race into my mind. Then I will try and imagine every possible situation I might find myself in . . . behind someone, being boxed in, pushed, shoved or cajoled, different positions on the track, laps to go, and, of course, the final stretch. And I always picture myself winning the race, no matter what happens during the event.[15]

Of course, Huber does not win every race she runs, but research has shown that the kind of mental imaging she describes can significantly increase athletic performance. Research has also shown that the same technique is of great benefit in helping speakers control their stage fright.[16]

The key to visualization is creating a vivid mental blueprint in which you see yourself succeeding in your speech. Picture yourself in your classroom rising to speak. See yourself at the lectern, poised and self-assured, making eye contact with your audience and delivering your introduction in a firm, clear voice. Feel your confidence growing as your listeners get more and more caught up in what you are saying. Imagine your sense of achievement as you conclude the speech knowing you have done your very best.

As you create these images in your mind's eye, be realistic but keep focused on the positive aspects of your speech. Don't allow negative images to eclipse the positive ones. Acknowledge your nervousness, but picture yourself overcoming it to give a vibrant, articulate presentation. If there is one part of the speech that always seems to give you trouble, visualize yourself getting through it without any hitches. And be specific. The more lucid your mental pictures, the more successful you are likely to be.[17]

As with your physical rehearsal of the speech, this kind of mental rehearsal of the speech should be repeated several times in the days before you speak. It doesn't guarantee that every speech will turn out exactly the way you envision it—and it certainly is no substitute for thorough preparation. But used in conjunction with the other methods of combating stage fright, it is a proven way to help control your nerves and to craft a successful presentation.

Know That Most Nervousness Is Not Visible

In addition to being anxious about giving a speech, many novice speakers are worried about appearing nervous to the audience. It's hard to speak with poise and assurance if you think you look tense and insecure. One of the most valuable lessons you will learn as your speech class proceeds is that only a fraction of the turmoil you are feeling inside is visible on the outside.

visualization
Mental imaging in which a speaker vividly pictures himself or herself giving a successful presentation.

Related Reading
Steven Ungerleider, *Mental Training for Peak Performance* (Emmaus, PA: Rodale Press, 1996). Although Ungerleider focuses on the use of visualization in Olympic-level athletics, most of the methods he discusses are applicable to public speaking.

The need for public speaking arises in many situations. Here world-champion cyclist Lance Armstrong addresses doctors and fellow cancer survivors in Annapolis, Maryland.

Teaching Tip

It is very comforting for students to learn that the butterflies they feel inside are usually not visible to listeners. One of the best ways to reinforce this point is to ask students, after their ice breaker speeches, if they were nervous while speaking. Almost all will respond that they were extremely nervous. Then ask other members of the class if the speaker looked nervous. In most cases, the class will state that the speaker looked just fine. This will allow you to stress the fact that even speakers who feel they are "dying" on the inside usually remain fairly calm and collected on the outside.

"Your nervous system may be giving you a thousand shocks," says one experienced speaker, "but the viewer can see only a few of them."[18]

Even though your palms are sweating and your heart is pounding, your listeners probably won't realize how tense you are—especially if you do your best to act cool and confident on the outside. Most of the time when students confess after a speech, "I was so nervous I thought I was going to die," their classmates are surprised. To them the speaker looked calm and assured.

Knowing this should make it easier for you to face your listeners with confidence. As one student stated after watching a videotape of her first classroom speech, "I was amazed at how calm I looked. I assumed everyone would be able to see how scared I was, but now that I know they can't, I won't be nearly so nervous in the future. It really helps to know that you look in control even though you may not feel that way."

Don't Expect Perfection

It may also help you to know that there is no such thing as a perfect speech. At some point in every presentation, every speaker says or does something— no matter how minor—that does not come across exactly as he or she had planned. Fortunately, as with one's nerves, such moments are usually not evident to the audience. Why? Because the audience does not know what the speaker *plans* to say. It hears only what the speaker *does* say. If you momentarily lose your place, reverse the order of a couple statements, or forget to pause at a certain spot, no one need be the wiser. When such moments occur, don't worry about them. Just proceed as if nothing happened.

Even if you do make an obvious mistake during a speech, that is no catastrophe. If you have ever listened to Martin Luther King's famous "I Have a Dream" speech, you may recall that he stumbles over his words twice during the speech. Most likely, however, you don't remember. Why? Because you were focusing on King's message rather than on the fine points of his delivery.

One of the biggest reasons people are concerned about making a mistake in a speech is that they view speechmaking as a kind of performance rather than as an act of communication. They feel the audience is judging them against a scale of absolute perfection in which every misstated word or awkward gesture will count against them. But speech audiences are not like judges in a violin recital or an ice-skating contest. They are not looking for a virtuoso performance, but for a well-thought-out address that communicates the speaker's ideas clearly and directly. Sometimes an error or two can actually enhance a speaker's appeal by making her or him seem more human.[19]

As you work on your speeches, make sure you prepare thoroughly and do all you can to get your message across to your listeners. But don't panic about being perfect or about what will happen if you make a mistake. Once you free your mind of these burdens, you will find it much easier to approach your speeches with confidence and even with enthusiasm.[20]

Besides stressing the six points just discussed, your teacher will probably give you several tips for dealing with nervousness in your first speeches. They may include:

- Be at your best physically and mentally. It's not a good idea to stay up until 4:00 A.M. partying with friends or cramming for an exam the night before your speech. A good night's sleep will serve you better.

- As you are waiting to speak, quietly tighten and relax your leg muscles, or squeeze your hands together and then release them. Such actions help reduce tension by providing an outlet for your extra adrenaline.

- Take a couple slow, deep breaths before you start to speak. Most people, when they are tense, take short, shallow breaths, which only reinforces their anxiety. Deep breathing breaks this cycle of tension and helps calm your nerves.

- Work especially hard on your introduction. Research has shown that a speaker's anxiety level begins to drop significantly after the first 30 seconds of a presentation.[21] Once you get through the introduction, you should find smoother sailing the rest of the way.

- Make eye contact with members of your audience. Remember that they are individual people, not a blur of faces. And they are your friends.

- Concentrate on communicating with your audience rather than on worrying about your stage fright. If you get caught up in your speech, your audience will too.

- Use visual aids. They create interest, draw attention away from you, and make you feel less self-conscious.[22]

Cross-Reference
Refer students to Chapter 12 for a five-step method of speech rehearsal they can use for their class presentations.

Related Reading
Karen Kangas Dwyer, *Conquer Your Speechfright* (Fort Worth, TX: Harcourt Brace, 1998). Firmly grounded in the research on speech anxiety, this book provides practical, step-by-step strategies, exercises, and activities to overcome the fear of public speaking.

If you are like most students, you will find your speech class to be a very positive experience. As one student wrote on her course evaluation form at the end of the class:

> I was really dreading this class. The idea of giving all those speeches scared me half to death. But I'm glad now that I stuck with it. It's a small class, and I got to know a lot of the students. Besides that, this is one class in which I got to express *my* ideas, instead of spending the whole time listening to the teacher talk. I even came to enjoy giving the speeches. I could tell at times that the audience was really with me, and that's a great feeling.

Discussion Prompt
Ask whether students have other methods of combating stage fright to add to those presented in this chapter.

Over the years thousands of students have developed confidence in their speechmaking abilities. As your confidence grows, you will be better able to stand before other people and tell them what you think and feel and know—and to make them think and feel and know those same things. The best part about confidence is that it nurtures itself. After you score your first triumph, you will be that much more confident the next time. And as you become a more confident public speaker, you will likely become more confident in other areas of your life as well.

Public Speaking and Critical Thinking

> That guy at the party last night really demolished me when we got into a discussion. I know my information is right, and I'm sure there was something wrong with his argument, but I can't put my finger on it.

> I need a computer, and every advertisement says its brand is state-of-the-art. But which is really the best buy for me?

> I've worked hard on my term paper, but I'm not satisfied. It just doesn't seem to hang together, and I can't figure out what's wrong.

> Political speeches are so one-sided. The candidates talk and talk, and they make everything sound rosy, but I still don't know whom to vote for.

critical thinking
Focused, organized thinking about such things as the logical relationships among ideas, the soundness of evidence, and the differences between fact and opinion.

Do any of these situations sound familiar? Have you ever found yourself in similar situations? If so, you may find help in your speech class. Besides building confidence, a course in public speaking can develop your skills as a critical thinker. Those skills can make the difference between the articulate debater and the pushover, the careful consumer and the easy mark, the A student and the C student, the thoughtful voter and the coin tosser.

What is critical thinking? To some extent, it's a matter of logic—of being able to spot weaknesses in other people's arguments and to avoid them in your own. It also involves related skills such as distinguishing fact from opinion, judging the credibility of statements, and assessing the soundness of evidence.

In the broadest sense, critical thinking is focused, organized thinking—the ability to see clearly the relationships among ideas. It has often been said that there are few new ideas in the world, only reorganized ideas. The greatest thinkers, scientists, and inventors have often taken information that was readily available and put it together differently to produce new insights. That, too, is critical thinking.[23]

If you are wondering what this has to do with your public speaking class, the answer is quite a lot. As the class proceeds, for example, you will probably spend a good deal of time organizing your speeches. While this may seem like a purely mechanical exercise, it is closely interwoven with critical thinking. If the structure of your speech is disjointed and confused, odds are that your thinking is also disjointed and confused. If, on the other hand, the structure is clear and cohesive, there is a good chance your thinking is too. Organizing a speech is not just a matter of arranging the ideas you already have. Rather, it is an important part of shaping the ideas themselves.

Teaching Tip
Students often think the word "critical" means "harsh" or "negative." Stress that thinking critically means not accepting ideas or claims at face value and consciously acknowledging the reasons for one's decisions.

What is true of organization is true of many aspects of public speaking. The skills you learn in your speech class can help you become a more effective thinker in a number of ways. As you work on expressing your ideas in clear, accurate language, you will enhance your ability to think clearly and accurately. As you study the role of evidence and reasoning in speechmaking, you will see how they can be used in other forms of communication as well. As you learn to listen critically to speeches in class, you will be better able to assess the ideas of speakers (and writers) in a variety of situations.[24]

To return to the four examples at the beginning of this section:

That guy at the party last night—would sharpened critical thinking have helped you pounce on the flaws in his argument?

Buying a computer—are advertisements a reliable source of information, or should you try to find out more about prices and the features you need?

The term paper—would better organization and a clear outline help pull it together?

The politicians—once you filter out the fluff, are they drawing valid conclusions from sound evidence?

Related Reading
See Sherry Diestler, *Becoming a Critical Thinker: A User Friendly Manual,* 3rd ed. (Upper Saddle River, NJ: Prentice Hall, 2001), for concepts, strategies, and exercises that can help students improve their critical thinking skills.

If you take full advantage of your speech class, you will be able to enhance your skills as a critical thinker in many circumstances. This is one reason public speaking has been regarded as a vital part of education since the days of ancient Greece.[25]

The Speech Communication Process

As you begin your first speeches, you may find it helpful to understand what goes on when one person talks to another. Regardless of the kind of speech communication involved, there are seven elements—speaker, message, channel, listener, feedback, interference, and situation. Here we shall focus on how these elements interact when a public speaker addresses an audience.

Speaker

Speech communication begins with a speaker. If you pick up the telephone and call a friend, you are acting as a speaker. (Of course, you will also act as a listener when your friend is talking.) In public speaking, you will usually present your entire speech without interruption.

Your success as a speaker depends on *you*—on your personal credibility, your knowledge of the subject, your preparation of the speech, your manner of speaking, your sensitivity to the audience and the occasion. But successful speaking is more than a matter of technical skill. It also requires enthusiasm. You can't expect people to be interested in what you say unless you are interested yourself. If you are truly excited about your subject, your audience is almost sure to get excited along with you. You can learn all the techniques of effective speechmaking, but before they can be of much use, you must first have something to say—something that sparks your own enthusiasm.

speaker
The person who is presenting an oral message to a listener.

Message

The message is whatever a speaker communicates to someone else. If you are calling a friend, you might say, "I'll be a little late picking you up tonight." That is the message. But it may not be the only message. Perhaps there is a certain tone in your voice that suggests reluctance, hesitation. The underlying message might be "I really don't want to go to that party. You talked me into it, but I'm going to put it off as long as I can."

message
Whatever a speaker communicates to someone else.

Your goal in public speaking is to have your *intended* message be the message that is *actually* communicated. Achieving this depends both on what you say (the verbal message) and on how you say it (the nonverbal message).

Getting the verbal message just right requires work. You must narrow your topic down to something you can discuss adequately in the time allowed for the speech. You must do research and choose supporting details to make your ideas clear and convincing. You must organize your ideas so listeners can follow them without getting lost. And you must express your message in words that are accurate, clear, vivid, and appropriate.

Discussion Prompt
Have students ever been in a situation where a speaker's verbal and nonverbal messages seemed contradictory? What aspects of the speaker's behavior led students to this conclusion?

Besides the message you send with words, you send a message with your tone of voice, appearance, gestures, facial expression, and eye contact. Imagine that one of your classmates gets up to speak about student loans. Throughout her speech she slumps behind the lectern, takes long pauses to remember what she wants to say, stares at the ceiling, and fumbles with her visual aids. Her intended message is "We must make more money available for student loans." But the message she actually communicates is "I haven't prepared very well for this speech." One of your jobs as a speaker is to make sure your nonverbal message does not distract from your verbal message.

Channel

The channel is the means by which a message is communicated. When you pick up the phone to call a friend, the telephone is the channel. Public speakers may use one or more of several channels, each of which will affect the message received by the audience.

channel
The means by which a message is communicated.

Consider a speech to Congress by the President of the United States. The speech is carried to the nation by the channels of radio and television. For the radio audience the message is conveyed entirely by the President's voice.

They can hear him, but they can't see him. For the television audience the message is conveyed by both the President's voice and the televised image of the President and his surroundings. The people in Congress have a more direct channel. They not only hear the President's voice as amplified through a microphone, but they see him and the setting firsthand.

In a public speaking class your channel is the most direct of all. Your classmates will see you and hear you without any electronic intervention.

Listener

The listener is the person who receives the communicated message. Without a listener, there is no communication. When you talk to a friend on the phone, you have one listener. In public speaking you will have many listeners.

Everything a speaker says is filtered through a listener's *frame of reference*—the total of his or her knowledge, experience, goals, values, and attitudes. Because a speaker and a listener are different people, they can never have exactly the same frame of reference. And because a listener's frame of reference can never be exactly the same as a speaker's, the meaning of a message will never be exactly the same to a listener as to a speaker.

You can easily test the impact of different frames of reference. Ask each of your classmates to describe a chair. If you have 20 classmates, you'll probably get 20 different descriptions. One student might picture a large, overstuffed easy chair, another an elegant straight-backed chair, yet another an office chair, a fourth a rocking chair, and so on. Even if two or more envision the same general type—say, a rocking chair—their mental images of the chair could still be different. One might be thinking of an early American rocker, another of a modern Scandinavian rocker—the possibilities are

listener
The person who receives the speaker's message.

frame of reference
The sum of a person's knowledge, experience, goals, values, and attitudes. No two people can have exactly the same frame of reference.

The powers of critical thinking you develop when researching and organizing your speeches can be applied in many forms of communication, including presenting ideas in your other classes.

unlimited. And "chair" is a fairly simple concept. What about "patriotism" or "freedom"?

Because people have different frames of reference, a public speaker must take great care to adapt the message to the particular audience being addressed. To be an effective speaker, you must be *audience-centered.* You must do everything in your speech with your audience in mind. You cannot assume that listeners will be interested in what you have to say. You must understand their point of view as you prepare the speech, and you must work to get them involved. You will quickly lose your listeners' attention if your presentation is either too basic or too sophisticated. You will also lose your audience if you do not relate to *their* experience, interests, knowledge, and values. When you make a speech that causes listeners to say "That is important to *me,*" you will almost always be successful.

Feedback

When the President addresses the nation on television, he is engaged in one-way communication. You can talk back to the television set, but the President won't hear you. Most situations, however, involve *two-way* communication. Your listeners don't simply absorb your message like human sponges. They send back messages of their own. These messages are called feedback.

For example, when you phone your friend to say you will be late, you may hear, "Oh, no you don't! I don't care *what* your problem is; you get here on time!" That is feedback.

This kind of verbal give-and-take is unusual in public speaking. Still, there is always plenty of feedback to let you know how your message is being received. Do your listeners lean forward in their seats, as if paying close attention? Do they applaud in approval? Do they laugh at your jokes? Do they have quizzical looks on their faces? Do they shuffle their feet and gaze at the clock? The message sent by these reactions could be "I am fascinated," "I am bored," "I agree with you," "I don't agree with you," or any number of others. As a speaker, you need to be alert to these reactions and adjust your message accordingly.

Like any kind of communication, feedback is affected by one's frame of reference. How would you feel if, immediately after your speech, all your classmates started to rap their knuckles on the desks? Would you run out of the room in despair? Not if you were in a European university. In many parts of Europe, students rap their knuckles on their desks to show admiration for a classroom lecture. You must understand the feedback to be able to deal with it.

There are still two more elements we must consider to understand fully what happens in speech communication.

Interference

Interference is anything that impedes the communication of a message. When you talk on the telephone, sometimes there is static, or wires get crossed so that two different conversations are going on at once. That is a kind of interference.

Cross-Reference

Chapter 5 contains a full discussion of the importance of taking an audience-centered approach to public speaking.

feedback

The messages, usually nonverbal, sent from a listener to a speaker.

Teaching Tip

Stress to students the importance of providing positive feedback during their classmates' speeches. As explained in Chapter 2, listening attentively and courteously is an important ethical responsibility.

In public speaking there are two kinds of interference. One, like the static or crossed wires in a phone conversation, is *external* to the audience. Many classrooms are subject to this kind of interference—from traffic outside the building, the clatter of a radiator, students conversing in the hall, a room that is stifling hot or freezing cold. Any of these can distract your listeners from what you are saying.

A second kind of interference is *internal* and comes from within your audience rather than from the outside. Perhaps one of your listeners has a bad mosquito bite or a patch of poison ivy. She may be so distracted by the itch that she doesn't pay attention to your speech. Another listener could be worrying about a test coming up in the next class period. Yet another could be brooding about an argument he had with his girlfriend.

As a speaker, you must try to hold your listeners' attention despite these various kinds of interference. In the chapters that follow you will find many ways to do this.

Situation

The situation is the time and place in which speech communication occurs. Conversation always takes place in a certain situation. Sometimes the situation helps—as when you propose marriage over an intimate candlelight dinner. Other times it may hurt—as when you try to speak words of love in competition with a blaring stereo. When you have to talk with someone about a touchy issue, you usually wait until the situation is just right.

Public speakers must also be alert to the situation. Certain occasions—funerals, church services, graduation ceremonies—require certain kinds of speeches. Physical setting is also important. It makes a great deal of difference whether a speech is presented indoors or out, in a small classroom or in a gymnasium, to a densely packed crowd or to a handful of scattered souls. When you adjust to the situation of a public speech, you are only doing on a larger scale what you do every day in conversation.

Now let us look at a complete model of the speech communication process, as shown in Figure 1.1.[26]

interference
Anything that impedes the communication of a message. Interference can be external or internal to listeners.

situation
The time and place in which speech communication occurs.

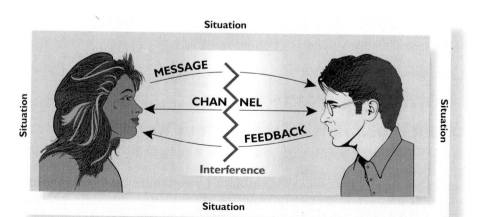

Figure 1.1

Overhead Transparency
For ease of classroom discussion, this model of the speech communication process is available in the binder of full-color overhead transparencies that accompanies *The Art of Public Speaking*.

The Speech Communication Process: Example with Commentary

The following example shows how the various components of the speech communication process interact:

Class Activity
The first Exercise for Critical Thinking at the end of this chapter provides an effective vehicle for class discussion about the basic elements of the speech communication process. By stressing the strategic aspects of everyday conversation, this exercise also points to the similarities between conversation and public speaking.

Situation	It was 9:30 on a rainy Tuesday night. A series of routine reports had taken much longer than expected, and the meeting of the neighborhood association was running late.
Speaker	Angela Morales was worried. As the founder of Pathways, a nonprofit organization devoted to operating group homes for developmentally disabled adults, she was the last speaker on the agenda. As Angela rose to address the association, she knew she faced a difficult task. She wanted to explain the purpose of Pathways and to get support for locating a group home for developmentally disabled adults in the neighborhood.
Channel Interference	Angela stepped to the microphone and began speaking. She could see members of the audience looking at their watches. They were worried about getting home on such a rainy night; some had even started putting on their coats and getting out their umbrellas.
Adapting to Interference	"Good evening," Angela began, "and thank you for staying a little longer. I promise I'll take no more than five minutes. Would anyone care to time me?" She was relieved to see several people chuckle as they checked their watches and settled back into their seats.
Message	Now that she had the attention of her audience, Angela quickly sketched the origins of Pathways and the needs of developmentally disabled adults. She ended by stating that she hoped to be able to address the association in more detail at a later meeting. She was delighted to see heads nodding at that suggestion, and was even more encouraged when one woman asked for Pathways' phone number. Several people jotted it down.
Feedback	True to her word, Angela finished in five minutes. "Time's up," she laughed. "Thanks for listening, and don't forget your umbrellas!" Afterward, the association's president complimented Angela on dealing so well with a tough situation. "Next time, we'll make sure you're first on the agenda," the president said. "I know people are looking forward to hearing what you have to say."

Related Reading
For other models of the speech communication process, see Stephen W. Littlejohn, *Theories of Human Communication*, 6th ed. (Belmont, CA: Wadsworth, 2002); Em Griffin, *A First Look at Communication Theory*, 5th ed. (New York: McGraw-Hill, 2003).

Public Speaking in a Multicultural World

Cultural Diversity in the Modern World

The United States has always been a diverse society. In 1673, more than three centuries ago, a visitor to what is now New York City was astonished to find that 18 languages were spoken among the city's 8,000 inhabitants.[27] By the middle of the nineteenth century, so many people from so many lands had come to the United States that novelist Herman Melville exclaimed, "You cannot spill a drop of American blood without spilling the blood of the whole world."[28]

One can only imagine what Melville would say today! The United States has become the most diverse society on the face of the earth. For more than a century, most immigrants to the U.S. were Europeans—Irish, Germans, English, Scandinavians, Greeks, Poles, Italians, and others. Together with African Americans, they made America the "melting pot" of the world.[29] Today another great wave of immigration—mostly from Asia and Latin America—is transforming the United States into what one writer has called "the first universal nation," a multicultural society of unmatched diversity.[30]

The diversity of life in the United States can be seen in cities and towns, schools and businesses, community groups and houses of worship all across the land. Consider the following:

- There are 215 nations in the world, and every one of them has someone living in the United States.

- New York City has over 170 distinct ethnic communities.

- Houston has two radio stations that broadcast in Chinese and a daily newspaper that prints in Chinese.

- Nearly 61 percent of the people in Miami were born outside the United States.

- More than 32 million people in the U.S. speak a language other than English at home.

- Asian Americans make up 45 percent of first-year students at the University of California, Berkeley.

These kinds of changes are not limited to the United States. We are living in an age of international multiculturalism. The Internet allows for instant communication almost everywhere around the world. CNN is broadcast in more than 200 countries. International air travel has made national boundaries almost meaningless. All nations are becoming part of a vast global village. For example:

- There are 60,000 transnational corporations around the world, and they account for more than a quarter of the world's economic output.

- Restaurants in coastal towns of Queensland, Australia, print their menus in both Japanese and English.

- McDonald's sells more hamburgers and french fries abroad than it does in the United States; Gillette makes 70 percent of its sales through exports.

- In Geneva, Switzerland, there are so many people from around the world that nearly 60 percent of the school population is non-Swiss.

- France has more Muslims than practicing Catholics; radio CHIN in Toronto, Canada, broadcasts in 32 languages.

- Four of every five new jobs in the U.S. are generated as a direct result of international trade.

Discussion Prompt
Over the years various metaphors have been used to describe the mix of cultures in the United States. They include the notion of the U.S. as a melting pot, as a river or stream, as a garden salad, and as a quilt or tapestry. Lead a class discussion on the strengths and weaknesses of each metaphor. For a full explanation of this activity, see the *Instructor's Manual*, pp. 69–70.

Speech Assignment
For speech assignments designed to increase students' awareness of cultural diversity, see the *Instructor's Manual*, pp. 71–72. Also consult the entries under "Diversity and Multiculturalism" in the five volumes of *Selections from the Speech Communication Teacher* that accompany *The Art of Public Speaking*.

Cultural Diversity and Public Speaking

"That's all very interesting," you may be saying to yourself, "but what does it have to do with my speeches?" The answer is that diversity and multiculturalism are such basic facts of life that they can play a role in almost any speech you give. Consider the following situations: A business manager briefing employees of a multinational corporation. A lawyer presenting her closing argument to an ethnically mixed jury. A minister sermonizing to a culturally diverse congregation. An international student explaining the customs of his land to students at a U.S. university. A teacher addressing parents at a multiethnic urban school. These are only a few of the countless speaking situations affected by the cultural diversity of modern life.

As experts in intercultural communication have long known, speechmaking becomes more complex as cultural diversity increases. Part of the complexity stems from the differences in language from culture to culture. As we will see in Chapter 11, language and thought are closely linked. So, too, are language and culture. Nothing separates one culture from another more than language. Not only do words change from language to language, but so do ways of thinking and of seeing the world. Language and culture are so closely bound that "we communicate the way we do because we are raised in a particular culture and learn its language, rules, and norms."[31]

The meanings attached to gestures, facial expressions, and other nonverbal signals also vary from culture to culture. Even the gestures for such basic messages as "yes" and "no," "hello" and "goodbye" are culturally based. In the United States people nod their heads up and down to signal "yes" and shake them back and forth to signal "no." In Thailand the same actions have exactly the opposite meaning! To take another example, the North American "goodbye" wave is interpreted in many parts of Europe and South America as the motion for "no," while the Italian and Greek gesture for "goodbye" is the same as the U.S. signal for "come here."[32]

Many stories have been told about the fate of public speakers who fail to take into account cultural differences between themselves and their audiences. Consider the following scenario:[33]

The sales manager of a U.S. electronics firm is in Brazil to negotiate a large purchase of computers by a South American corporation. After three days of negotiations, the sales manager holds a gala reception for all the major executives to build goodwill between the companies.

As is the custom on such occasions, time is set aside during the reception for an exchange of toasts. When it is the sales manager's turn to speak, he praises the Brazilian firm for its many achievements and talks eloquently of his respect for its president and other executives. The words are perfect, and the sales manager can see his audience smiling in approval.

And then—disaster. As the sales manager closes his speech, he raises his hand and flashes the classic U.S. "OK" sign to signal his pleasure at the progress of the negotiations. Instantly the festive mood is replaced with stony silence; smiles turn to icy stares. The sales manager has given his Brazilian audience a gesture with roughly the same meaning as an extended middle finger in the United States.

The next day the Brazilian firm announces it will buy its computers from another company.

Discussion Prompt

If you have international students in your class, ask them to discuss the role of public speaking in their home cultures. What are the major similarities and differences between speeches in the United States and those in the international students' native countries?

Discussion Prompt

Have students think of a situation in which they sought to understand the message of, or to convey a message to, someone from a different culture. What barriers did students encounter in their attempts at communication? What steps did they take to overcome those barriers? What did they learn from their experience about the process of communicating across cultures?

Public speaking is a vital mode of communication in most cultures around the world. Here Philippine President Gloria Macapagal Arroyo addresses a mass meeting in Manila.

As this scenario illustrates, public speakers can ill afford to overlook their listeners' cultural values and customs. This is true whether you are speaking at home or abroad, in Atlanta or Rio de Janeiro, in a college classroom or at a meeting of community volunteers. Because of the increasing diversity of modern life, many—perhaps most—of the audiences you address will include people of different cultural backgrounds.

As you read the rest of this book, you will learn the methods of effective public speaking. Almost all those methods will be helpful to you in speaking to culturally diverse audiences. Here we need to stress the importance of avoiding the ethnocentrism that often blocks communication between speakers and listeners of different cultural, racial, and ethnic backgrounds.

Related Reading

Roger Axtell, *Gestures: The Do's and Taboos of Body Language Around the World*, rev. ed. (New York: Wiley, 1998). This entertaining book by a veteran international communicator provides a wealth of examples that can be used for class discussion.

Avoiding Ethnocentrism

Ethnocentrism is the belief that our own group or culture—whatever it may be—is superior to all other groups or cultures. Because of ethnocentrism, we identify with our group or culture and see its values, beliefs, and customs as "right" or "natural"—in comparison to the values, beliefs, and customs of other groups or cultures, which we tend to think of as "wrong" or "unnatural."[34]

Ethnocentrism is part of every culture. If you were born and raised in the United States, you may find it strange that most people in India regard the cow as a sacred animal and forgo using it as a source of food. On the other hand, if you were born and raised in India, you might well be shocked at the use of cows in the United States for food, clothing, and other consumer goods. If you are Christian, you most likely think of Sunday as the "normal" day of worship. But if you are Jewish, you probably regard Saturday as the "correct" Sabbath. And if you are Muslim, you doubtless see both Saturday and Sunday as unusual times for worship. For you, Friday is the "right" day.

ethnocentrism
The belief that one's own group or culture is superior to all other groups or cultures.

THE
INTERNET
Connection

As we shall see throughout this book, there are many resources on the World Wide Web for public speakers. One of those resources is an extensive collection of speeches from U.S. history, which you can access at Douglass: Archives of American Public Address (http://douglassarchives.org/).

Thousands of people in the United States earn their living as professional public speakers. You can learn about their activities at the National Speakers Association website (www.nsaspeaker.org/).

Ethnocentrism can play a positive role in creating group pride and loyalty. But it can also be a destructive force—especially when it leads to prejudice and hostility toward different racial, ethnic, or cultural groups. To be an effective public speaker in a multicultural world, you need to keep in mind that all people have their special beliefs and customs.

Avoiding ethnocentrism does not mean you must agree with the values and practices of all groups and cultures. At times you might try to convince people of different cultures to change their traditional ways of doing things—as speakers from the United Nations seek to persuade farmers in Africa to adopt more productive methods of agriculture, as Muslim parents in the United States urge public school officials to accommodate Muslim customs for children who adhere to Islam, or as delegates from the U.S. and Japan attempt to influence the other country's trade policies.

If such speakers are to be successful, however, they must show respect for the cultures of the people they address. They cannot assume that their cultural assumptions and practices will be shared—or even understood— by all members of their audience. They need to adapt their message to the cultural values and expectations of their listeners.

When you work on your speeches, keep in mind the growing diversity of life in the modern world and be alert to how cultural factors might affect the way listeners respond to your speeches. As we shall see in Chapter 5, for classroom speeches you can use audience-analysis questionnaires to learn about the backgrounds and opinions of your classmates in regard to specific speech topics. For speeches outside the classroom, the person who invites you to speak can usually provide information about the audience.

Once you know about any cultural factors that might affect the audience's response to your speech, you can work on adapting the speech to make it as effective and appropriate as possible. As you prepare the speech, try to put yourself in the place of your listeners and to hear your message through their ears. If there is a language difference between you and your audience, avoid any words or phrases that might cause misunderstanding. When researching the speech, keep an eye out for examples, comparisons, and other supporting materials that will relate to a wide range of listeners. Also, consider using visual aids in your speech. As we shall see in Chapter 13, they can be especially helpful in bridging a gap in language or cultural background.

When delivering your speech, be alert to feedback that might indicate the audience is having trouble grasping your ideas. If you see puzzled expressions on the faces of your listeners, restate your point to make sure it is understood. With some audiences, you can encourage feedback by asking, "Am I making myself clear?" or "Did I explain this point fully enough?"

If you pose such questions, however, be aware that listeners from different cultures may respond quite differently. Most Arabs, North Americans, and Europeans will give you fairly direct feedback if you ask for it. Listeners from Asian and Caribbean countries, on the other hand, may not respond, out of concern that doing so will show disrespect for the speaker. (See Chapter 5 for a full discussion of audience analysis and adaptation.)[35]

Finally, we should note the importance of avoiding ethnocentrism when listening to speeches. As we shall see in Chapters 2 and 3, speech audiences have a responsibility to listen courteously and attentively. When you listen to a speaker from a different cultural background, be on guard against the temptation to judge that speaker on the basis of his or her appearance or manner of delivery. Too often we form opinions about people by the way they look or speak rather than by listening closely to what they *say*. No matter what the cultural background of the speaker, you should listen to her or him as attentively as you would want your audience to listen to you.

Related Reading

For an instructive guide to creating speeches for international audiences, see Patricia L. Kurtz, *The Global Speaker: An English Speaker's Guide to Making Presentations Around the World* (New York: AMACOM, 1995).

Summary

Public speaking has been a vital means of personal empowerment and civic engagement throughout history. The need for effective public speaking will almost certainly touch you sometime in your life. When it does, you want to be ready. But even if you never give another speech in your life, you still have much to gain from studying public speaking. Your speech class will give you training in researching topics, organizing your ideas, and presenting yourself skillfully. This training is invaluable for every type of communication.

There are many similarities between public speaking and daily conversation. In conversation, almost without thinking about it, you employ a wide range of skills. You organize your ideas logically. You tailor your message to your audience. You tell a story for maximum impact. You adapt to feedback from your listener. These are among the most important skills you will need for public speaking.

Public speaking is also different from conversation. First, public speaking is more highly structured than conversation. It usually imposes strict time limitations on the speaker, and it requires more detailed preparation than does ordinary conversation. Second, public speaking requires more formal language. Listeners react negatively to speeches loaded with slang, jargon, and bad grammar. Third, public speaking demands a different method of delivery. Effective speakers adjust their voices to the larger audience and work at avoiding distracting physical mannerisms and verbal habits.

One of the major concerns of students in any speech class is stage fright. Actually, most successful speakers are nervous before making a speech. Your speech class will give you an opportunity to gain confidence and make your nervousness work for you rather than against you. You will take a big step toward overcoming stage fright if you think positively, prepare thoroughly, visualize yourself giving a successful speech, keep in mind that most nervousness is not visible to the audience, and think of your speech as communication rather than as a performance in which you must do everything perfectly. Like other students over the years, you too can develop confidence in your speechmaking abilities.

Besides building your confidence, a course in public speaking can help develop your skills as a critical thinker. Critical thinking is the ability to perceive relationships among ideas. It can help you spot weaknesses in other people's reasoning and avoid them in your own. Critical thinking can make a difference in many areas of your life, from your schoolwork to your activities as a consumer to your responsibilities as a citizen.

The speech communication process as a whole includes seven elements—speaker, message, channel, listener, feedback, interference, and situation. The speaker is the person who initiates a speech transaction. Whatever the speaker communicates is the message, which is sent by means of a particular channel. The listener receives the communicated message and provides feedback to the speaker. Interference is anything that impedes the communication of a message, and the situation is the time and place in which speech communication occurs. The interaction of these seven elements is what determines the outcome in any instance of speech communication.

Because of the growing diversity of modern life, many—perhaps most—of the audiences you address will include people of different cultural, racial, and ethnic backgrounds. When you work on your speeches, be alert to how such factors might affect the responses of your listeners and take steps to adapt your message accordingly. Above all, avoid the ethnocentric belief that your own culture or group—whatever it may be—is superior to every other culture or group. Also keep in mind the importance of avoiding ethnocentrism when listening to speeches. Accord every speaker the same courtesy and attentiveness you would want from your listeners.

Key Terms

Review these terms by doing the Chapter 1 crossword puzzle at www.mhhe.com/lucas8.

ONLINE LEARNING CENTER

stage fright (9)
adrenaline (10)
positive nervousness (11)
visualization (13)
critical thinking (16)
speaker (18)
message (18)

channel (18)
listener (19)
frame of reference (19)
feedback (20)
interference (21)
situation (21)
ethnocentrism (25)

Review Questions

After reading this chapter, you should be able to answer the following questions:

1. In what ways is public speaking likely to make a difference in your life?

2. How is public speaking similar to everyday conversation?

3. How is public speaking different from everyday conversation?

4. Why is it normal—even desirable—to be nervous at the start of a speech?

5. How can you control your nervousness and make it work for you in your speeches?

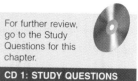

For further review, go to the Study Questions for this chapter.

CD 1: STUDY QUESTIONS

6. What are the seven elements of the speech communication process? How do they interact to determine the success or failure of a speech?

7. What is ethnocentrism? Why do public speakers need to avoid ethnocentrism when addressing audiences with diverse cultural, racial, or ethnic backgrounds?

Exercises for Critical Thinking

1. Think back on an important conversation you had recently in which you wanted to achieve a particular result. (*Examples:* Asking your employer to change your work schedule; explaining to a friend how to change the oil and filter in a car; attempting to talk your spouse or partner into buying the computer you like rather than the one he or she prefers.) Work up a brief analysis of the conversation.

   In your analysis, explain the following: (1) your purpose in the conversation and the message strategy you chose to achieve your purpose; (2) the communication channels used during the conversation and how they affected the outcome; (3) the interference—internal or external—you encountered during the conversation; (4) the steps you took to adjust to feedback; (5) the strategic changes you would make in preparing for and carrying out the conversation if you had it to do over again.

Cross-Reference
For discussion of the Exercises for Critical Thinking, see the *Instructor's Manual*, pp. 65–66. For additional exercises, check the *Instructor's Manual*, pp. 67–72, as well as the five volumes of *Selections from the Speech Communication Teacher* that accompany *The Art of Public Speaking*.

2. Divide a sheet of paper into two columns. Label one column "Characteristics of an Effective Public Speaker." Label the other column "Characteristics of an Ineffective Public Speaker." In the columns, list and briefly explain what you believe to be the five most important characteristics of effective and ineffective speakers. Be prepared to discuss your ideas in class.

3. On the basis of the lists you developed for Exercise 2, candidly evaluate your own strengths and weaknesses as a speaker. Identify the three primary aspects of speechmaking you most want to improve.

Applying the POWER of PUBLIC SPEAKING

It has been three years since you finished college. After gaining experience as an administrative assistant at a major publishing company, you have just been promoted to marketing manager for a children's book series. Though you have occasionally given brief reports to other members of your work team, you are now facing your first speech to a large audience. At your company's annual sales meeting, you will address the sales force about the company's new books and how to sell them to wholesalers and retail bookstores.

Cross-Reference
For discussion of this Applying the Power of Public Speaking scenario, see the *Instructor's Manual*, pp. 66–67.

You're pleased to have this opportunity and you know it shows the company's faith in your abilities. Yet the closer you get to the day of the speech, the harder it is to control the butterflies in your stomach. There will be 150 people in your audience, including all the senior editors and regional managers, in addition to the sales force. All eyes will be on you. It's important that you come across as confident and well informed, but you're afraid your stage fright will send the opposite message. What strategies will you use to control your nerves and make them work for you?

Notes

[1]Pericles, quoted in Richard Whately, *Elements of Rhetoric,* 7th ed. (London: John W. Parker, 1846), p. 10.

[2]*The Wall Street Journal,* December 29, 1998, p. A1.

[3]Stephanie Armour, "Failure to Communicate Costly for Companies," *USA Today,* April 30, 1998, p. 1B; Midge Costanza, quoted in Sharon Nelson, "Address for Success," *Nation's Business* (February 1991), pp. 43–44.

[4]George A. Kennedy, *Comparative Rhetoric: An Historical and Cross-Cultural Introduction* (New York: Oxford University Press, 1998).

[5]For an excellent selection of works from the figures discussed in this and the previous paragraph, see Patricia Bizzell and Bruce Herzberg (eds.), *The Rhetorical Tradition: Readings from Classical Times to the Present,* 2nd ed. (New York: Bedford/St. Martin, 2001). For a comprehensive overview, see Craig R. Smith, *Rhetoric and Human Consciousness,* 2nd ed. (Prospect Heights, IL: Waveland, 2003).

[6]See, for example, James Price Dillard and Michael Pfau (eds.), *The Persuasion Handbook: Developments in Theory and Practice* (Thousand Oaks, CA: Sage, 2002).

[7]For an overview of that tradition, see David Cohen, "Oratory," and Stephen E. Lucas, "Public Speaking," in Thomas O. Sloane (ed.), *Encyclopedia of Rhetoric* (New York: Oxford University Press, 2001), pp. 538–547, 640–647.

[8]"What Are Americans Afraid Of?" *The Bruskin Report,* 53 (July 1973).

[9]Daniel Goleman, "Social Anxiety: New Focus Leads to Insights and Therapy," *New York Times,* December 18, 1984, "How Americans Communicate," a 1999 study commissioned by the National Communication Association, found that only 24 percent of Americans are "very comfortable" giving a speech or other formal presentation. The study can be accessed at www.natcom.org/research/Roper/how_americans_communicate.htm.

[10]Jeffrey C. Hahner, Martin A. Sokoloff, and Sandra L. Salisch, *Speaking Clearly: Improving Voice and Diction,* 6th ed. (New York: McGraw-Hill, 2002), p. 12.

[11]Quoted in Bert E. Bradley, *Fundamentals of Speech Communication: The Credibility of Ideas,* 6th ed. (Dubuque, IA: W. C. Brown, 1991), p. 36.

[12]Elayne Synder, *Speak for Yourself—With Confidence* (New York: New American Library, 1983), p. 113.

[13]A number of studies have shown that taking a public speaking course is effective in reducing stage fright. See, for example, Rebecca B. Rubin, Alan M. Rubin, and Felicia F. Jordan, "Effects of Instruction on Communication Apprehension and Communication Competence," *Communication Education,* 46 (1997), pp. 104–114.

[14]Lilly Walters, *Secrets of Successful Speakers* (New York: McGraw-Hill, 1993), pp. 32–36.

[15]Quoted in Steven Ungerleider, *Mental Training for Peak Performance* (Emmaus, PA: Rodale Press, 1996), p. 9.

[16]Joe Ayres, Tim Hopf, and Debbie M. Ayres, "Visualization and Performance Visualization: Applications, Evidence, and Speculation," in John A. Daly, James C. McCroskey, Joe Ayres, Tim Hopf, and Debbie M. Ayres (eds.), *Avoiding Communication: Shyness, Reticence, and Communication Apprehension,* 2nd ed. (Cresskill, NJ: Hampton Press, 1997), pp. 401–422.

[17]See Marie Dalloway, *Visualization: The Master Skill in Mental Training* (Phoenix, AZ: Optimal Performance Institute, 1992).

[18]Dick Cavett, quoted in Steve Allen, *How to Make a Speech* (New York: McGraw-Hill, 1986), p. 10.

[19]For more detail on the ideas in this paragraph, see Michael T. Motley, *Overcoming Your Fear of Public Speaking: A Proven Method* (Boston: Houghton Mifflin, 1998).

[20]For additional research on the benefits of viewing public speaking as an act of communication rather than a rule-governed performance, see Amy M. Bippus and John A. Daly, "What Do People Think Causes Stage Fright? Naive Attributions About the Reasons for Public Speaking Anxiety," *Communication Education,* 48 (1999), pp. 62–72.

[21]Michael T. Motley, "Taking the Terror Out of Talk," *Psychology Today* (January 1988), p. 47.

[22]For fuller discussion of these and other approaches to controlling stage fright, see Karen Kangas Dwyer, *Conquer Your Speechfright* (Fort Worth, TX: Harcourt Brace, 1998); Janet E. Esposito, *In the Spotlight: Overcome Your Fear of Public Speaking and Performing* (Southington, CT: Strong Books, 2000).

[23]For more detail on the dimensions of critical thinking, see M. Neil Browne and Stuart M. Keeley, *Asking the Right Questions: A Guide to Critical Thinking,* 6th ed. (Englewood Cliffs, NJ: Prentice Hall, 2001).

[24]For the transference of critical thinking skills from public speaking to other activities, see Mike Allen, Sandra Berkowitz, Steve Hunt, and Allen Louden, "A Meta-Analysis of the Impact of Forensics and Communication Education on Critical Thinking," *Communication Education,* 48 (1999), pp. 18–30. Also see Virginia O'Keefe, *Developing Critical Thinking; The Speaking/Listening Connection* (Portsmouth, NH: Boynton/Cook, 2000).

[25]See Bruce A. Kimball, *Orators and Philosophers: A History of the Idea of Liberal Education* (New York: College Board, 1995).

[26]For other models of the speech communication process, see Stephen W. Littlejohn, *Theories of Human Communication,* 7th ed. (Belmont, CA: Wadsworth, 2002); Em Griffin, *A First Look at Communication Theory,* 5th ed. (New York: McGraw-Hill, 2003).

[27]John Elson, "The Great Migration," *Time* (Fall 1993), p. 30.

[28]Quoted in Ronald Takaki, *A Different Mirror: A History of Multicultural America* (Boston: Little, Brown, 1993), p. 427.

[29]See Michael Barone, *The New Americans: How the Melting Pot Can Work Again* (New York: Regnery, 2001).

[30]Ben J. Wattenberg, *The First Universal Nation: Leading Indicators and Ideas About the Surge of America in the 1990s* (New York: Free Press, 1991).

[31]William B. Gudykunst and Young Yun Kim, *Communicating with Strangers: An Approach to Intercultural Communication,* 4th ed. (New York: McGraw-Hill, 2003), p. 4. For more detail, see Fred E. Jandt, *Intercultural Communication: An Introduction,* 3rd ed. (Thousand Oaks, CA: Sage, 2001).

[32]Carley H. Dodd, *Dynamics of Interpersonal Communication,* 5th ed. (New York: McGraw-Hill, 1998), pp. 133–153; Dale Marco, "Doing Business Overseas: It's a Whole New Ballgame," *USA Today,* September 1998, pp. 20–22.

[33]Adapted from Roger E. Axtell (ed.), *Do's and Taboos around the World,* 3rd ed. (New York: John Wiley and Sons, 1993), p. 41.

[34]Myron W. Lustig and Jolene Koester, *Intercultural Competence: Interpersonal Communication Across Cultures,* 4th ed. (Boston: Allyn and Bacon, 2003), pp. 148–150.

[35]For a comprehensive review of scholarship on multiculturalism and communication, see William B. Gudykunst and Bella Moody (eds.), *Handbook of International and Intercultural Communication,* 2nd ed. (Thousand Oaks, CA: Sage, 2002).

Chapter Two

ETHICS AND PUBLIC SPEAKING

Chapter Focus
Questions of ethics arise
whenever a speaker ad-
dresses an audience. This
chapter explains the importance of ethics and explores
the ethical responsibilities of
speakers and listeners. It also
includes a section on plagiarism and how to avoid it.
For a full outline of the
chapter, see the *Instructor's
Manual*, pp. 88–91.

K athryn Luedtke, a manager in the state Department of Development and Natural Resources, was in charge of planning a multipurpose center for business and educational retreats on a little-used stretch of riverfront in the northwest tip of the state. There was just one catch. The year before, a local environmental group had raised funds to create a small wildlife park on one cor- ner of the site. Although final plans for the center had not been drawn, Kathryn knew the park would have to be closed to make way for an access road.

Shortly before the plans were finished, Kathryn was asked to speak at a meeting of the local group. Recognizing the positive economic impact the center would have on their community, the group's members were willing to support it as long as it did not disrupt the wildlife park. Reasoning to herself that the group was small and located far from the state's media centers, Kathryn assured them the park would be protected. The group voted to endorse the proposal.

Two days after final plans for the center were presented to the legislature, a re- porter who had been contacted by the local group called Kathryn to ask how she could sacrifice the park after promising to do the opposite. Kathryn tried to talk her way out of it, but she had no defense. The legislature withdrew funding for the center, a na- tional environmental group put Kathryn on their annual "Liars List," and she was fired from her position with the Department of Development and Natural Resources.

This is not a happy story, but it shows why speechmaking needs to be guided by a strong sense of integrity. Kathryn Luedtke was persuasive when speak- ing to the local enviornmental group, but she was unethical in not telling the truth about the impact of her project on the wildlife park. As a result, the project was abandoned, Kathryn lost her job, and her reputation was left in tatters.

You might be saying to yourself, "Yes, that's very unfortunate. But lots of people lie and cheat, and many of them don't get caught." And you would be correct—many people don't get caught. But that doesn't make their be- havior right. In public speaking, as in other areas of life, there are standards for ethical conduct.

The goal of public speaking is to gain a desired response from listeners— but not at any cost. Speechmaking is a form of power and therefore carries with it heavy ethical responsibilities. As the Roman rhetorician Quintilian stated 2,000 years ago, the ideal of commendable speechmaking is the good person speaking well. In this chapter, we explore that ideal by look- ing at the importance of ethics in public speaking, the ethical obligations of speakers and listeners, and the practical problem of plagiarism and how to avoid it.

The Importance of Ethics

ethics
The branch of philosophy
that deals with issues of
right and wrong in human
affairs.

Ethics is the branch of philosophy that deals with issues of right and wrong in human affairs. Questions of ethics arise whenever we ask whether a course of action is moral or immoral, fair or unfair, just or unjust, honest or dishonest.[1]

We face such questions daily in almost every part of our lives. The par- ent must decide how to deal with a child who has been sent home from school for unruly behavior. The researcher must decide whether to shade her data "just a bit" in order to gain credit for an important scientific break-through. The shopper must decide what to do with the $5 extra change mistakenly given by the clerk at the grocery store. The student must decide whether to say anything about a friend he has seen cheating on a final exam.

Questions of ethics also come into play whenever a public speaker faces an audience. In an ideal world, as the Greek philosopher Plato noted, all public speakers would be truthful and devoted to the good of society. Yet history tells us that the power of speech is often abused—sometimes with disastrous results. Adolf Hitler was unquestionably a persuasive speaker. His oratory galvanized the German people into following one ideal and one leader. But his aims were horrifying and his tactics despicable. He remains to this day the ultimate example of why the power of the spoken word needs to be guided by a strong sense of ethical integrity.

As a public speaker, you will face ethical issues at every stage of the speechmaking process—from the initial decision to speak through the final presentation of the message. This is true whether you are speaking in the classroom or the courtroom, whether you are participating in a business meeting or a religious service, whether you are addressing an audience of two people or 2,000 people. And the answers will not always be easy. Consider the following example:

> Felicia Robinson is running for school board in a large eastern city. Her opponent is conducting what Felicia regards as a highly unethical campaign. In addition to twisting the facts about school taxes, the opponent is pandering to racial prejudice by raising resentment against African Americans and newly arrived immigrants.
>
> Five days before the election, Felicia, who is slightly behind in the polls, learns that the district attorney is preparing to indict her opponent for shady business practices. But the indictment will not be formally issued until after the election. Nor can it be taken as evidence that her opponent is guilty—like all citizens, he has the right to be presumed innocent until proven otherwise.
>
> Still, news of the indictment could be enough to throw the election Felicia's way, and her advisers urge her to make it an issue in her remaining campaign speeches. Should Felicia follow their advice?

There are creditable arguments to be made on both sides of the ethical dilemma faced by Felicia Robinson. She has tried to run an honest campaign, and she is troubled by the possibility of unfairly attacking her opponent—despite the fact that he has shown no such scruples himself. Yet she knows that the impending indictment may be her last chance to win the election, and she is convinced that a victory for her opponent will spell disaster for the city's school system. Torn between her commitment to fair play, her desire to be elected, and her concern for the good of the community, she faces the age-old ethical dilemma of whether the ends justify the means.

"So," you may be saying to yourself, "what is the answer to Felicia Robinson's dilemma?" But in complex cases such as hers there are no cut-and-dried answers. As Richard Johannesen, a leader in the study of communication ethics, states, "We should formulate meaningful ethical guidelines, not inflexible rules."[2] Your ethical decisions will be guided by your values, your conscience, your sense of right and wrong.

Class Activity
Divide the class into groups, each of which is to function as a consultant to Felicia Robinson on the question of whether she should or should not make the impending indictment of her opponent an issue in her remaining campaign speeches. Assign each group the task of formulating a recommendation to Robinson and a rationale in support of that recommendation. Have one person from each group present the group's recommendation and rationale to the class. Follow up with a general class discussion on the issues raised in the groups' deliberations.

ethical decisions
Sound ethical decisions involve weighing a potential course of action against a set of ethical standards or guidelines.

But this does not mean such decisions are simply a matter of personal whim or fancy. Sound ethical decisions involve weighing a potential course of action against a set of ethical standards or guidelines. Just as there are guidelines for ethical behavior in other areas of life, so are there guidelines for ethical conduct in public speaking. These guidelines will not automatically solve every ethical quandary you face as a speaker, but knowing them will provide a reliable compass to help you find your way.

Guidelines for Ethical Speaking

Make Sure Your Goals Are Ethically Sound

Not long ago, I spoke with a former student—we'll call her Melissa—who had turned down a job in the public relations department of the American Tobacco Institute. Why? Not because of the salary (which was generous) or the work schedule (which was ideal). Melissa declined the job because it would have required her to lobby on behalf of the cigarette industry. Knowing that cigarettes are the number one health hazard in the United States, Melissa did not believe she could ethically promote a product that she saw as responsible for thousands of deaths and illnesses each year.

Discussion Prompt
Students can easily agree that a speaker's goals should be ethically sound, yet some may be inclined to select speech topics such as "How to Make a Fake I.D." or "How to Make Long-Distance Phone Calls without Paying for Them." Discuss whether certain topics are unethical in a public speaking classroom and why.

Given Melissa's view of the dangers of cigarette smoking, there can be no doubt that she made an ethically informed decision to turn down the job with the American Tobacco Institute. On the other side of the coin, someone with a different view of cigarette smoking could make an ethically informed decision to *take* the job. The point of this example is not to judge the rightness or wrongness of Melissa's decision (or of cigarette smoking), but to illustrate how ethical considerations can affect a speaker's choice of goals.

Your first responsibility as a speaker is to ask whether your goals are ethically sound. During World War II, Hitler stirred the German people to condone war, invasion, and genocide. More recently, we have seen politicians who betray the public trust for personal gain, business leaders who defraud investors of millions of dollars, preachers who lead lavish lifestyles at the expense of their religious duties. There can be no doubt that these are not worthy goals.

But think back for a moment to the examples of speechmaking given in Chapter 1. What do the speakers hope to accomplish? Report on a business project. Improve the quality of education. Pay tribute to a fellow worker. Protect communities against industrial pollution. Support the Special Olympics. Few people would question that these goals are ethically sound.

As with other ethical issues, there can be gray areas when it comes to assessing a speaker's goals—areas in which reasonable people with well-defined standards of right and wrong can legitimately disagree. But this is not a reason to avoid asking ethical questions. If you are to be a responsible public speaker, you cannot escape assessing the ethical soundness of your goals.

Questions of ethics arise whenever a speaker faces an audience. Former South African president Nelson Mandela is highly regarded for his ethically sound goals and powerful persuasive appeal.

Be Fully Prepared for Each Speech

"A speech," as Jenkin Lloyd Jones states, "is a solemn responsibility." You have an obligation—to yourself and to your listeners—to prepare fully every time you stand in front of an audience. The obligation to yourself is obvious: The better you prepare, the better your speech will be. But the obligation to your listeners is no less important. Think of it this way: The person who makes a bad 30-minute speech to an audience of 200 people wastes only a half hour of her or his own time. But that same speaker wastes 100 hours of the audience's time—more than four full days. This, Jones exclaimed, "should be a hanging offense!"

At this stage of your speaking career, of course, you will probably not be facing many audiences of 200 people. And you will probably not be giving many speeches in which the audience has come for the sole purpose of listening to you. But neither the size nor the composition of your audience changes your ethical responsibility to be fully prepared. Your speech classmates are as worthy of your best effort as if you were addressing a jury or a business meeting, a union conference or a church congregation, the local Rotary club or even the United States Senate.

Being prepared for a speech involves everything from analyzing your audience to creating visual aids, organizing your ideas to rehearsing your delivery. Most crucial from an ethical standpoint, though, is being fully informed about your subject. Why is this so important? Consider the following story:

Several years ago Manuel Higuera, a student at a large California university, gave a classroom speech demonstrating how to use the Heimlich maneuver to dislodge a piece of food trapped in a person's windpipe. Manuel had learned the maneuver from his mother, a Red Cross worker, but he did not rely on that knowledge alone in

Speech Assignment
One way to give ethics a prominent place in the class is to have students give a speech in which they discuss an example of an ethical or unethical speech act. For one approach, see W. Bradford Mello, "Ethics Speech Assignment," in *Selections from the Speech Communication Teacher, 1996–1999,* pp. 48–49, which accompanies *The Art of Public Speaking.*

preparing his speech. He read several magazine articles about the Heimlich maneuver, and he picked up a pamphlet from the local fire department explaining how to perform the maneuver.

In addition to his research, Manuel gave a lot of thought to organizing and delivering his speech. He even got a friend to serve as a volunteer on whom he could demonstrate the steps of the Heimlich maneuver for his classmates. By the day of his speech, Manuel was thoroughly prepared—and he gave an excellent presentation.

No more than a week later, one of Manuel's classmates, Alison Bartlett, was eating dinner in her apartment when her roommate began choking on a piece of food. Remembering Manuel's speech, Alison went into action with the Heimlich maneuver. First she got her roommate to stand up. Then she put her arms around her roommate's waist, made a fist with one hand, pressed it into her roommate's abdomen, and exerted several quick upward thrusts until the food popped out. Alison saved her roommate's life, thanks to Manuel's speech.

This is an especially dramatic case, but it demonstrates how your speeches can have a genuine impact on your listeners' lives. As a speaker, you have an ethical responsibility to consider that impact and to make sure you prepare fully so as not to communicate erroneous information or misleading advice. Imagine what might have happened if Manuel had not done such a thorough job researching his speech. He might have given his classmates faulty instructions about the Heimlich maneuver—instructions that might have had tragic results.

No matter what the topic, no matter who the audience, you need to explore your speech topic as thoroughly as possible. Investigate the whole story; learn about all sides of an issue; seek out competing viewpoints; get the facts right. Not only will you give a better speech, you will also fulfill one of your major ethical obligations.

Be Honest in What You Say

Nothing is more important to ethical speechmaking than honesty. Public speaking rests on the unspoken assumption that "words can be trusted and people will be truthful."[3] Without this assumption, there is no basis for communication, no reason for one person to believe anything that another person says. Once the bond of trust between a speaker and listener is broken, it can never be fully restored.

Does this mean *every* speaker must *always* tell "the truth, the whole truth, and nothing but the truth"? We can all think of situations in which this is impossible (because we do not know the whole truth) or inadvisable (because it would be tactless or imprudent). Consider a presidential press secretary who denies the existence of secret diplomatic negotiations because she does not know they are taking place. Or a parent who tells his two-year-old daughter that her screeching violin solo is "beautiful." Or a speaker who tells a falsehood in circumstances when disclosing the truth might touch off mob violence. Few people would find these actions unethical.[4]

In contrast, think back to the case of Kathryn Luedtke at the start of this chapter. Kathryn knew the center she was developing would require closing the local wildlife park. Yet she told the environmental group that the center could be built without harming the park. The group accepted her word and voted to support the center. There is no way to excuse Kathryn's conduct. She told a flat-out lie without regard for its consequences on the audience.

Teaching Tip
It is very important to stress that the speech classroom is not an artificial speaking situation. Each person in the class is a real person with real ideas, attitudes, and feelings. For fuller discussion of this point, see Chapter 5, pp. 112–113.

Teaching Tip
If your class meets during an election year, ethical issues are bound to arise in relation to the candidates' campaign rhetoric. Such issues might include the use of negative campaigning, the distortion of evidence in campaign speeches, and the tendency of candidates to say different things to different groups of voters. Set aside time during the term to deal with such issues—especially when they achieve prominence in press coverage of the campaign.

Such blatant contempt for the truth is one kind of dishonesty in public speaking. But there are more subtle forms of dishonesty that are just as unethical. They include juggling statistics, quoting out of context, misrepresenting the sources of facts and figures, painting tentative findings as firm conclusions, portraying a few details as the whole story, citing unusual cases as typical examples, and substituting innuendo and half-truths for evidence and proof. All of these violate the speaker's duty to be accurate and fair in presenting information.

While on the subject of honesty in speechmaking, we should also note that ethically responsible speakers do not present other people's words as their own. They do not plagiarize their speeches. This subject is so important that we devote a separate section to it later in this chapter.

Avoid Name-Calling and Other Forms of Abusive Language

"Sticks and stones can break my bones, but words can never hurt me." This popular children's chant could not be more wrong. Words may not literally break people's bones, but they are powerful weapons that can leave psychological scars as surely as sticks and stones can leave physical scars. As one writer explains, "Our identities, who and what we are, how others see us, are greatly affected by the names we are called and the words with which we are labeled."[5] This is why almost all communication ethicists warn public speakers to avoid name-calling and other forms of abusive language.

Name-Calling and Personal Dignity

Name-calling is the use of language to defame, demean, or degrade individuals or groups. When applied to various groups in America, it includes such epithets as "fag," "kike," "nigger," "wop," "jap," "chink," and "spic." Such terms have been used to debase people because of their sexual orientation, religious beliefs, or ethnic background. These words dehumanize the groups they are directed against. They imply that the groups are inferior and do not deserve to be treated with the same dignity and respect as other members of society.

In Chapter 11 we will look at ways you can avoid biased language in your speeches. For now, the point to remember is that, contrary to what some people claim, avoiding racist, sexist, and other kinds of abusive language is not simply a matter of political correctness. Such language is ethically suspect because it devalues the people in question and stereotypes them in ways that assume the innate superiority of one group over another.

Such language is also a destructive social force. When used repeatedly and systematically over time, it helps reinforce attitudes that encourage prejudice, hate crimes, and civil rights violations.[6] This is true whether the group is being maligned for its gender, religion, ideology, ethnic background, sexual orientation, or physical or mental disability. The issue is not one of politics, but of respecting the dignity of the diverse groups in contemporary society.

Name-Calling and Free Speech

Name-calling and abusive language also pose ethical problems in public speaking when they are used to silence opposing voices. A democratic society depends upon the free and open expression of ideas. In the United

---

Teaching Tip
Because some students may seek to dismiss questions related to name-calling and personal dignity as nothing more than political correctness, it is important to stress that the issues raised in this section of the book are ethical rather than political. It is also vital to present the issues in such a way that students do not believe instructors are forcing their political beliefs on the class.

name-calling
The use of language to defame, demean, or degrade individuals or groups.

Related Reading
Alexander Tsesis, *Destructive Messages: How Hate Speech Paves the Way for Harmful Social Movements* (New York: New York University Press, 2002) provides an insightful look at the negative long-range consequences of name-calling and other forms of abusive language.

States, all citizens have the right to join in the never-ending dialogue of democracy. As a public speaker, you have an ethical obligation to help preserve that right by avoiding tactics such as name-calling that automatically impugn the accuracy or respectability of public statements made by groups or individuals who voice opinions different from yours.

This obligation is the same regardless of whether you are black or white, Christian or Muslim, male or female, gay or straight, liberal or conservative. A pro-environmentalist office seeker who castigated everyone opposed to her ideas as an "enemy of wildlife" would be on as thin ice ethically as a politician who labeled all his adversaries "tax-and-spend liberals" when he knew full well that the charge was untrue. No matter what your stand on particular issues, you have an ethical responsibility to avoid name-calling and other tactics that harm the free and open expression of ideas.

Like other ethical questions in public speaking, name-calling raises some thorny issues. Although name-calling can be hazardous to free speech, it is still protected under the free-speech clause of the Bill of Rights. This is why the American Civil Liberties Union, a major defender of constitutional rights, has opposed broadly worded codes against abusive speech on college campuses. Such codes usually prohibit threatening or insulting speech against racial or religious minorities, women, gays and lesbians, and people with physical disabilities. To date, these codes have not survived legal challenges, and a number of schools are now developing more narrowly focused regulations that they hope will stand up in court.[7]

But whatever the legal outcome may be, it will not alter the ethical responsibility of public speakers—on or off campus—to avoid name-calling and other kinds of abusive language. Legality and ethics, though related, are not identical. There is nothing illegal about falsifying statistics in a speech, but there is no doubt that it is unethical. The same is true of name-calling. It may not be illegal to cast racial, sexual, or religious slurs at people in a speech, but it is still unethical. Not only does it demean the dignity of the groups or individuals being attacked, but it undermines the right of all groups in the U.S. to be fairly heard.

Put Ethical Principles into Practice

We are all familiar with people who say one thing and do another. It is easy to pay lip service to the importance of ethics. It is much harder to act ethically. Yet that is just what the responsible public speaker must do. As one popular book on ethics states, "Being ethical means behaving ethically *all the time*—not only when it's convenient."[8]

As you work on your speeches, you will ask yourself such questions as, "Is my choice of topic suitable for the audience?" "Are my supporting materials clear and convincing?" "How can I phrase my ideas to give them more punch?" These are *strategic* questions. As you answer them, you will try to make your speech as informative, as persuasive, or as entertaining as possible.

But you will also face moments of *ethical* decision—similar, perhaps, to those faced by Kathryn Luedtke, Felicia Robinson, and the other speakers in this chapter. When those moments arrive, don't simply brush them aside

---

Bill of Rights
The first 10 amendments to the United States Constitution.

Related Reading
For an excellent discussion of the issues raised here, see Thomas L. Tedford, and Dale A. Herbeck, *Freedom of Speech in the United States*, 4th ed. (State College, PA: Strata Publishing, 2001), pp. 174–180, which is reprinted in the *Instructor's Manual*, pp. 97–104.

and go on your way. Take your ethical responsibilities as seriously as your strategic objectives. Keep in mind the guidelines for ethical speechmaking we have discussed and do your best to follow them through thick and thin. Make sure you can answer yes to all the questions on the Checklist for Ethical Public Speaking (Figure 2.1).

Figure 2.1

CHECKLIST FOR ETHICAL PUBLIC SPEAKING

1. Have I examined my goals to make sure they are ethically sound?

    a. Can I defend my goals on ethical grounds if they are questioned or challenged?
    b. Would I want other people to know my true motives in presenting this speech?

2. Have I fulfilled my ethical obligation to prepare fully for the speech?

    a. Have I done a thorough job of studying and researching the topic?
    b. Have I prepared diligently so as not to communicate erroneous or misleading information to my listeners?

3. Is the speech free of plagiarism?

    a. Can I vouch that the speech represents my own work, my own thinking, my own language?
    b. Do I cite the sources of all quotations and paraphrases?

4. Am I honest in what I say in the speech?

    a. Is the speech free of any false or deliberately deceptive statements?
    b. Does the speech present statistics, testimony, and other kinds of evidence fairly and accurately?
    c. Does the speech contain valid reasoning?
    d. If the speech includes visual aids, do they present facts honestly and reliably?

5. Do I use the power of language ethically?

    a. Do I avoid name-calling and other forms of abusive language?
    b. Does my language show respect for the right of free speech and expression?

6. All in all, have I made a conscious effort to put ethical principles into practice in preparing my speech?

To help foster responsible communication, the National Communication Association has developed a Credo for Ethical Communication. You can access it at www.natcom.org/policies/External/EthicalComm.htm.

You can learn a great deal about free-speech issues on the Internet. One source is the American Civil Liberties Union Free Speech website at www.aclu.org/FreeSpeech/FreeSpeechmain.cfm. Another is the Freedom Forum's First Amendment site at www.freedomforum.org/first/.

You can link to these websites at www.mhhe.com/lucas8.

ONLINE LEARNING CENTER

Plagiarism

plagiarism
Presenting another person's language or ideas as one's own.

"Plagiarism" comes from *plagiarius,* the Latin word for kidnapper. To plagiarize means to present another person's language or ideas as your own—to give the impression you have written or thought something yourself when you have actually taken it from someone else.[9] We often think of plagiarism as an ethical issue in the classroom, but it can have repercussions in other situations:

As a senior member of the Senate Foreign Relations Committee, Joseph Biden of Delaware is a major voice in public discussions about terrorism and foreign policy. With his expertise, high public profile, and dynamic speaking skills, he would seem to be a contender for the Democratic Party's presidential nomination. Yet every time his name crops up, so too does the fact that he is haunted by a history of plagiarism.

In 1987 Biden was emerging as a candidate for the nomination when it was reported that his eloquent conclusion to a speech at the Iowa State Fair was lifted, almost word for word, from an address by British political leader Neil Kinnock. Biden claimed the similarity between his speech and Kinnock's was purely accidental, but it was soon discovered that in an earlier speech he had pirated, almost verbatim, the words of Robert Kennedy. Even more damage was done a few days later when Biden admitted he had been found guilty of plagiarism while a law student at Syracuse University.

Although Biden tried to pass the whole matter off as "much ado about nothing," his standing in the polls plummeted and his campaign for president was ruined. Even though more than 15 years have passed since Biden admitted to plagiarizing, doubts about his credibility linger today and continue to pose obstacles to his political aspirations.

As this story shows, plagiarism is a serious matter. If you are caught plagiarizing a speech in class, the punishment can range from a failing grade to expulsion from school. If you are caught plagiarizing outside the classroom, you stand to forfeit your good name, to damage your career, or, if you are sued, to lose a large amount of money. It is worth your while, then, to make sure you know what plagiarism is and how to avoid it.[10]

Teaching Tip
Make sure students are aware of your school's policies regarding plagiarism and the penalties you will impose on students found guilty of plagiarism in their speeches. Often the Dean of Students or the Office for Academic Affairs will have a formal statement about plagiarism and a specific set of procedures to be followed in dealing with cases of plagiarism and other forms of academic dishonesty.

Global Plagiarism

Global plagiarism is stealing your speech entirely from another source and passing it off as your own. The most blatant—and unforgivable—kind of plagiarism, it is grossly unethical.

When global plagiarism takes place in a college classroom, it is sometimes the result of deliberate dishonesty. More often it happens because a student puts off the assignment until the last minute. Then, in an act of desperation, the student downloads a speech from the Internet or gets one written by a friend during a previous term, and delivers it as his or her own. Or the student dashes to the library, finds a suitable magazine article or encyclopedia entry, copies it more or less verbatim, and turns that in as the assigned speech.

The best way to avoid this, of course, is not to leave your speech until the last minute. Most teachers explain speech assignments far enough in advance that you should have no trouble getting an early start. By starting early, you will give yourself plenty of time to prepare a first-rate speech— a speech of your own.

If, for some reason, you fail to get your speech ready on time, do not succumb to the lure of plagiarism. Whatever penalty you suffer from being late will pale in comparison with the consequences if you are caught plagiarizing.

global plagiarism
Stealing a speech entirely from a single source and passing it off as one's own.

Patchwork Plagiarism

Unlike global plagiarism, in which a speaker pirates an entire speech from a single source, patchwork plagiarism occurs when a speaker pilfers from two or three sources. Here's an example:

Kevin Moss chose "The Paintings of Georgia O'Keeffe" as the topic for his informative speech. In his research, Kevin found three especially helpful sources. The first was a pamphlet about O'Keeffe published by the local art center, which was showing an exhibit of her work. The second was an entry in the online *Encyclopaedia Britannica.* The third was an article from the O'Keeffe Museum website. Working from these sources, Kevin put together a speech dealing with O'Keeffe's early life, the major features of her paintings, and her contributions to modern art.

Unfortunately, instead of using his research materials creatively to generate a speech in his own words, Kevin lifted long passages from the pamphlet, the encyclopedia entry, and the Internet article and patched them together with a few transitions. When he was finished, he had a speech that sounded wonderful—but it was not truly *his* speech since it was composed almost entirely of other people's words.

As it turned out, Kevin's teacher had been to the same art show and thought parts of his speech sounded familiar. After checking her copy of the art center's pamphlet, her suspicions were confirmed. Fearful that Kevin might have filched from more than the pamphlet, she went online and checked websites with information about O'Keeffe. In a few minutes she found both the museum article and the encyclopedia entry. Kevin was caught red-handed.

patchwork plagiarism
Stealing ideas or language from two or three sources and passing them off as one's own.

Related Reading
Robert A. Harris, *The Plagiarism Handbook: Strategies for Preventing, Detecting, and Dealing with Plagiarism* (Los Angeles: Pyrczak Publishing, 2001). For a quick reference, check Harris' website, "Anti-Plagiarism Strategies for Research Papers," at www.virtualsalt.com/antiplag.htm.

This story illustrates an important point about plagiarism. Kevin did not take his speech from a single source. He even did a little research. But copying word for word from a few sources is no less plagiarism than is copying from a single source. When you give a speech, it is just like putting your name on a paper in your English class. You declare that the speech is your

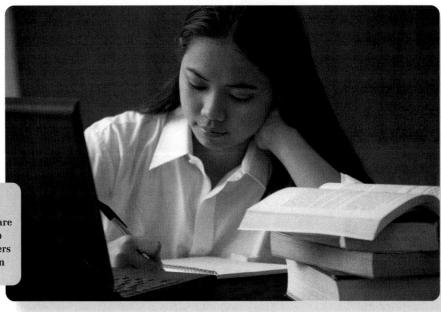

Speakers who begin work on their speeches early and consult a wide range of sources are less likely to fall into the trap of plagiarism than are speakers who procrastinate and rely on a limited number of sources.

Teaching Tip
Students may believe that "doing enough research" means reading a couple magazine articles or visiting a couple websites. Make clear your standards for the amount of research you expect students to put in for their speeches. Many instructors find it helpful to require a specific number of research sources for each speech.

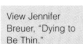

View Jennifer Breuer, "Dying to Be Thin."

CD 2: FULL SPEECH

work—that it is the product of your thinking, your beliefs, your language. Kevin's speech did not contain any of these. Instead it was cut and pasted wholly from other people's ideas, other people's words.

"But," you may be thinking, "not many students are experts on their speech topics. Why should they be expected to come up with new ideas that even the experts haven't thought of?" The answer is they aren't. The key is not whether you have something absolutely original to say, but whether you do enough research and thinking to come up with your own slant on the topic.

How can you do this? There is no formula, but perhaps an example will help. In "Speeches for Analysis and Discussion," the appendix following Chapter 18, you will find a speech on anorexia titled "Dying to Be Thin." The speaker, Jennifer Breuer, a biochemistry major, is hardly an expert on eating disorders. The inspiration for her speech came from a high-school friend who had died of anorexia nervosa. Because of that experience, Jennifer cared deeply about the topic and wanted to inform her audience about it.

As Jennifer did her research, she learned a number of important facts about anorexia—many more than she could ever include in a six-minute speech. Noticing that much of what she found dealt with the causes, effects, and treatment of anorexia, she decided to focus her speech on those three areas. From all the materials she gathered in her research, she selected for her speech those that best illustrated her ideas. Because those ideas were truly hers, she had no trouble expressing them in her words. By the time she was done, she had blended the raw materials amassed during her research into a speech that was distinctively her own.

As with global plagiarism, one key to averting patchwork plagiarism is to start working on your speech as soon as you possibly can. The longer you work on it, the more apt you are to come up with your own approach. It is also vital to consult a large number of sources in your research. If you have only two or three sources to turn to for inspiration, you are far more likely to fall into the trap of patchwork plagiarism than if you consult a wide range of research materials.

Incremental Plagiarism

In global plagiarism and patchwork plagiarism the entire speech is cribbed more or less verbatim from a single source or a few sources. But plagiarism can exist even when the speech as a whole is not pirated. This is called incremental plagiarism. It occurs when the speaker fails to give credit for particular parts—increments—of the speech that are borrowed from other people. The most important of these increments are quotations and paraphrases.

Quotations

Whenever you quote someone directly, you must attribute the words to that person. Suppose you are giving a speech on Malcolm X, the famous African-American leader of the 1960s. While doing your research, you run across the following passage from Bruce Perry's acclaimed biography, *Malcolm: The Life of the Man Who Changed Black America:*

> Malcolm X fathered no legislation. He engineered no stunning Supreme Court victories or political campaigns. He scored no major electoral triumphs. Yet because of the way he articulated his followers' grievances and anger, the impact he had upon the body politic was enormous.[11]

This is a fine quotation that summarizes the nature and importance of Malcolm's impact on American politics. It would make a strong addition to your speech—as long as you acknowledge Perry as the author. The way to avoid plagiarism in this instance is to introduce Perry's statement by saying something like:

> In *Malcolm: The Life of the Man Who Changed Black America,* historian Bruce Perry says the following about Malcolm's impact on American politics. . . .

Or,

> According to historian Bruce Perry in his book *Malcolm: The Life of the Man Who Changed Black America,* . . .

Now you have clearly identified Perry and given him credit for his words rather than presenting them as your own.

Paraphrases

When you paraphrase an author, you restate or summarize her or his ideas in your own words. Suppose, once again, that your topic is Malcolm X. But this time you decide to paraphrase the statement from Bruce Perry's biography rather than quoting it. You might say:

> Malcolm X was not a politician. He did not pass any laws, or win any Supreme Court victories, or get elected to any office. But he stated the grievances and anger of his followers so powerfully that the whole nation took notice.

incremental plagiarism
Failing to give credit for particular parts of a speech that are borrowed from other people.

Class Activity
Lead a class discussion in which students develop a code of ethical speaking for their classroom. The final product of the discussion will be a list entitled "Ethical Speaking for Our Speech Class." For full discussion of this activity, see the *Instructor's Manual,* p. 94.

paraphrase
To restate or summarize an author's ideas in one's own words.

Even though you do not quote Perry directly, you still appropriate the structure of his ideas and a fair amount of his language. Thus you still need to give him credit—just as if you were repeating his words verbatim.

It is especially important in this case to acknowledge Perry because you are borrowing his opinion—his judgment—about Malcolm X. If you simply recount basic facts about Malcolm's life—he was born in Omaha, Nebraska, converted to the Nation of Islam while in prison, traveled to Mecca toward the end of his life, was assassinated in February 1965—you do not have to report the source of your information. These facts are well known and can be found in any standard reference work on Malcolm X.

On the other hand, there is still considerable debate about Malcolm's views of other African-American leaders, the circumstances surrounding his death, and what he might have done had he lived. If you were to cite Perry's views on any of these matters—regardless of whether you quoted or paraphrased—you would need to acknowledge him as your source. If you did not, you could very well be charged with plagiarism.

As more than one speaker (and writer) has discovered, it is possible to commit incremental plagiarism quite by accident. This is less offensive than deliberate plagiarism, but it is plagiarism nonetheless. There are two ways to guard against incremental plagiarism. The first is to be careful when taking research notes to distinguish among direct quotations, paraphrased material, and your own comments. (See Chapter 6 for a full discussion of research methods.) The second way to avoid incremental plagiarism is to err on the side of caution. In other words, when in doubt, cite your source. This way, you cannot go wrong.

Plagiarism and the Internet

When it comes to plagiarism, no subject poses more confusion—or more temptation—than the Internet. Because it's so easy to copy information from the Web, many people are not aware of the need to cite sources when they use Internet materials in their speeches. Just as you need to give credit to the authors of print books and articles, you also need to give credit to the authors of documents found online. If you don't cite Internet sources, you are just as guilty of plagiarism as if you take information from print sources without proper citation.

One way to avoid patchwork plagiarism or incremental plagiarism when working with the Internet is to take careful research notes. Make sure you keep a record of the following: (1) the title of the Internet document, (2) the author or organization responsible for the document, (3) the date on which the document was last updated, (4) the address of the website, and (5) the date on which you accessed the site. You will need all this information for your speech bibliography.

You will also need to identify your Internet sources when you present the speech. It's not enough to say, "As I found on the Web" or "According to the Internet." You need to specify the author and website—just as you would identify the author and publication for a print source. In Chapter 6,

Class Activity
Students often benefit from working with the distinctions between paraphrase and direct quotation. Bring to class several short newspaper or magazine articles. Divide the class into small groups. Give each group one article and have the group summarize the article in a single paragraph. Also have each group identify one or two quotations from the article that could be used in a speech.

Teaching Tip
There are a number of websites that provide information and resources for combating the plague of Internet plagiarism. Two of the most helpful are "The Virtual Professor: Dealing with Plagiarism in Online Courses" (www.ibritt.com/resources/vp_plagiarism.htm) and "Anti-Plagiarism Resources" (www3.la.psu.edu/hrsweb/fac-news/apr.htm).

we'll look more closely at how to cite Internet documents (see page 157). For now, keep in mind that providing such citations is another of your ethical responsibilities as a public speaker.

Another problem with regard to the Internet is the large number of websites that sell entire speeches or papers. In addition to being highly unethical, using material from one of these sites is extremely risky. The same technology that makes it easy to plagiarize from the Web makes it easy for teachers to locate material that has been plagiarized and the exact source from which it has been taken. Some schools even subscribe to Internet services that specialize in identifying papers, speeches, and other kinds of academic work that are plagiarized from the Web.

You should also know that almost all the speeches (and papers) offered for sale on the Web are of very low quality. If you are ever tempted to purchase one of these items, keep in mind there is a good chance you will waste your money and get caught in the process. Here, as in other aspects of life, honesty is the best policy.

Teaching Tip
Some instructors have found that the most effective way to prevent plagiarism is to ask students to sign an honor pledge indicating that they understand the different kinds of plagiarism and promising that they will not engage in plagiarism in their speeches.

Guidelines for Ethical Listening

So far in this chapter we have focused on the ethical duties of public speakers. But speechmaking is not a one-way street. Listeners also have ethical obligations. They are (1) to listen courteously and attentively; (2) to avoid prejudging the speaker; and (3) to maintain the free and open expression of ideas. Let us look at each.

Be Courteous and Attentive

Imagine that you are giving your first classroom speech. You have put a great deal of time into writing the speech, and you have practiced your delivery until it is just right. You have not had much experience giving speeches, but you are confident you can do well—especially once you get over the initial rush of stage fright.

You have worked hard on your introduction, and your speech gets off to a fine start. You are pleased to see that most of your classmates are paying close attention. But you also notice that some are not. One appears to be doing homework for another class. Another keeps sneaking glances at the school newspaper. Two or three are gazing out the window, and one is leaning back in his chair with his eyes shut!

You try to block them out of your mind—especially since the rest of the class seems interested in what you are saying—but the longer you speak, the more concerned you become. "What am I doing wrong?" you wonder to yourself. "How can I get these people to pay attention?" The more you think about your inconsiderate and inattentive listeners, the more your confidence and concentration waver.

When you momentarily lose your place halfway through the speech, you start to panic. Your nerves, which you have held in check so far, take the upper hand. Your major thought now becomes, "How can I get this over as fast as possible?" Flustered and distracted, you rush through the rest of your speech and sit down.

Class Activity
The third Exercise for Critical Thinking at the end of this chapter provides an excellent activity for generating discussion about the kinds of ethical decisions students face in speech class. For full discussion of the exercise, see the *Instructor's Manual,* pp. 92–93.

Teaching Tip
One way to discourage
listeners from engaging in
discourteous or inattentive
behavior during classroom
speeches is to have students
fill out evaluation forms on
their peers' speeches. Sample forms can be found in
the *Instructor's Manual*,
pp. 49–55.

How would you feel if this happened to you? Angry? Frustrated? Discouraged? Certainly you would not regard your speech as a positive experience. Nor would you be brimming with confidence as you worked on your next speech. Perhaps you would be soured on speechmaking altogether.

Just as public speakers have an ethical obligation to prepare fully for each speech, so listeners have a responsibility to be courteous and attentive during the speech. This responsibility—which is a matter of civility in any circumstance—is especially important in speech class. You and your class-mates are in a learning situation in which you need to support one another. Professional speakers are trained to deal with inconsiderate or unrespon-sive audiences, but novices need encouraging, sympathetic listeners to help maintain their morale and confidence.[12]

When you listen to speeches in class, give your fellow students the same courtesy and attention you want from them. Come to class prepared to lis-ten to—and to learn from—your classmates' speeches. As you listen, be con-scious of the feedback you are sending the speaker. Sit up in your chair rather than slouching; maintain eye contact with the speaker; show support and encouragement in your facial expressions. Keep in mind the power you have as a listener over the speaker's confidence and composure, and exer-cise that power with a strong sense of ethical responsibility.

Avoid Prejudging the Speaker

We have all heard that you can't judge a book by its cover. The same is true of speeches. You can't judge a speech by the name, race, lifestyle, appear-ance, or reputation of the speaker.

Related Reading
For fuller treatment of many
of the issues discussed in this
chapter, see Richard L.
Johannesen, *Ethics in Human
Communication*, 5th ed.
(Prospect Heights, IL:
Waveland Press, 2002).

As we shall see in Chapter 3, jumping to conclusions about a speaker's ideas before hearing the speech is one of the major barriers to effective lis-tening. But it also has ethical implications. If a speaker has fulfilled her or his responsibility to prepare fully and conscientiously, the audience has an obligation to listen to that speaker before deciding whether to accept or re-ject what she or he is saying. As the National Communication Association states in its Credo for Ethical Communication, listeners should "strive to understand and respect" speakers "before evaluating and responding to their messages."[13]

This does not mean you must agree with every speaker you hear. You do not want to be a "rubber-stamp" listener any more than you want to be a closed-minded one. Your aim is to listen carefully to the speaker's ideas, to assess the evidence and reasoning offered in support of those ideas, and to reach an intelligent judgment about the speech. In Chapter 3, we will dis-cuss specific steps you can take to improve your listening skills. For now it is enough to know that if you prejudge a speaker—either positively or negatively—you will fail in one of your ethical responsibilities as a listener.

Maintain the Free and Open Expression of Ideas

As we saw earlier in this chapter, a democratic society depends on the free and open expression of ideas. The right of free expression is so important that it is protected by the First Amendment to the U.S. Constitution, which declares, in part, that "Congress shall make no law . . . abridging the freedom

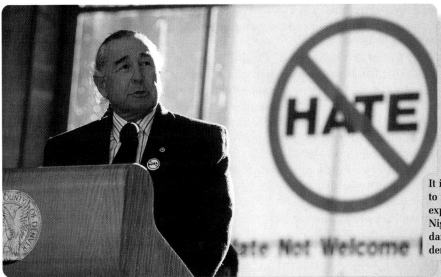

It is vital for a democratic society to maintain the free and open expression of ideas. Here Ben Nighthorse Campbell explains the dangers that hate speech poses to democratic ideals.

of speech." Without the right of individual citizens to speak their minds on public issues, free government cannot survive. Just as public speakers need to avoid name-calling and other tactics that can undermine free speech, so listeners have an obligation to maintain the right of speakers to be heard.

As with other ethical issues, the extent of this obligation is open to debate. Disputes over the meaning and scope of the First Amendment arise almost daily in connection with issues such as terrorism, pornography, and hate speech. The question underlying such disputes is whether *all* speakers have a right to be heard.

There are some kinds of speech that are not protected under the First Amendment—including defamatory falsehoods that destroy a person's reputation, threats against the life of the President, and inciting an audience to illegal action in circumstances where the audience is likely to carry out the action. Otherwise, the Supreme Court has held—and most experts in communication ethics have agreed—that public speakers have an almost unlimited right of free expression.

In contrast to this view, it has been argued that some ideas are so dangerous, so misguided, or so offensive that society has a duty to suppress them. But who is to determine which ideas are too dangerous, misguided, or offensive to be uttered? Who is to decide which speakers are to be heard and which are to be silenced? As Edward Kennedy explains in his acclaimed speech "Truth and Tolerance in America," once we succumb to the temptation of censoring ideas with which we disagree, "we step onto a slippery slope where everyone's freedom is at risk."[14]

No matter how well intentioned they may be, efforts to "protect" society by restricting free speech usually end up repressing minority viewpoints and unpopular opinions. In U.S. history such efforts were used to keep women off the public platform until the 1840s, to stop abolitionist orators from exposing the evils of slavery before the Civil War, to muzzle labor

Class Activity

Lead a class discussion in which students develop a code of ethical listening for their classroom. The final product of the discussion will be a list entitled "Ethical Listening for Our Speech Class." For full discussion of this activity, see the *Instructor's Manual,* pp. 94–95.

View Edward Kennedy's warning against censorship in his "Truth and Tolerance in America."

CD 1: VIDEO 2.1

organizers during the 1890s, and to impede civil rights leaders in the 1960s. Imagine what American society might be like if these speakers had been silenced!

It is important to keep in mind that ensuring a person's freedom to express her or his ideas does not imply agreement with those ideas. You can disagree entirely with the message but still support the speaker's right to express it. As Colin Powell stated in a highly publicized presentation at Howard University in 1994, "freedom of speech means permitting the widest range of views to be presented, however controversial those views may be. The First Amendment right of free speech is intended to protect the controversial and even the outrageous word and not just comforting platitudes too mundane to need protection."[15] In the long run, there is no better way to maintain liberty and protect human dignity than to protect the free and open expression of ideas.

View these words from Colin Powell's speech at Howard University.

CD 1: VIDEO 2.2

Summary

Because public speaking is a form of power, it carries with it heavy ethical responsibilities. Today, as for the past 2,000 years, the good person speaking well remains the ideal of commendable speechmaking.

There are five basic guidelines for ethical public speaking. The first is to make sure your goals are ethically sound—that they are consistent with the welfare of society and your audience. The second is to be fully prepared for each speech. Every audience you address—in class and out—deserves your best effort. You do not want to waste their time or mislead them through shoddy research or muddled thinking. The third guideline is to be honest in what you say. Responsible speakers do not distort the truth for personal gain. They are accurate and fair in their message and in their methods.

The fourth guideline for ethical speaking is to avoid name-calling and other forms of abusive language. Name-calling is the use of language to defame or degrade other individuals or groups. It is ethically suspect because it demeans the dignity of the people being attacked and because it can undermine the right of all groups in American society to be fairly heard. The final guideline is to put ethical principles into practice—to follow them through thick and thin, not just when it is convenient.

Of all the ethical lapses a public speaker can commit, few are more serious than plagiarism. Global plagiarism is lifting a speech entirely from a single source and passing it off as your own. Patchwork plagiarism involves stitching a speech together by copying more or less verbatim from a few sources. Whenever you give a speech, you must be sure it represents your work, your thinking, your language. You must also take care to avoid incremental plagiarism, which occurs when a speaker fails to give credit for specific quotations and paraphrases that are borrowed from other people.

In addition to your ethical responsibilities as a speaker, you have ethical obligations as a listener. The first is to listen courteously and attentively. The second is to avoid prejudging the speaker. The third is to support the free and open expression of ideas. In all these ways, your speech class will offer a good testing ground for questions of ethical responsibility.

Key Terms

ethics (34)

ethical decisions (35)

name-calling (39)

Bill of Rights (40)

plagiarism (42)

global plagiarism (43)

patchwork plagiarism (43)

incremental plagiarism (45)

paraphrase (45)

Review these terms by doing the Chapter 2 crossword puzzle at www.mhhe.com/lucas8.

ONLINE LEARNING CENTER

Review Questions

After reading this chapter, you should be able to answer the following questions:

1. What is ethics? Why is a strong sense of ethical responsibility vital for public speakers?

2. What are the five guidelines for ethical speechmaking discussed in this chapter?

3. What is the difference between global plagiarism and patchwork plagiarism? What are the best ways to avoid these two kinds of plagiarism?

4. What is incremental plagiarism? How can you steer clear of it when dealing with quotations and paraphrases?

5. What are the three basic guidelines for ethical listening discussed in this chapter?

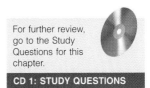

For further review, go to the Study Questions for this chapter.

CD 1: STUDY QUESTIONS

Exercises for Critical Thinking

1. Look back at the story of Felicia Robinson on page 35. Evaluate her dilemma in light of the guidelines for ethical speechmaking presented in this chapter. Explain what you believe would be the most ethical course of action in her case.

2. The issue of insulting and abusive speech—especially slurs directed against people on the basis of race, religion, gender, or sexual orientation—is extremely controversial. Do you believe society should punish such speech with criminal penalties? To what degree are colleges and universities justified in trying to discipline students who engage in such speech? Do you feel it is proper to place any boundaries on free expression in order to prohibit insulting and abusive speech? Why or why not? Be prepared to explain your ideas in class.

3. All the following situations could arise in your speech class. Identify the ethical issues in each and explain what, as a responsible speaker or listener, your course of action would be.

   a. You are speaking on the topic of prison reform. In your research, you run across two public opinion polls. One of them, an independent survey by the Gallup Organization, shows that a majority of people in your state oppose your

Cross-Reference

For discussion of the Exercises for Critical Thinking, see the *Instructor's Manual,* pp. 91–93. For additional exercises, check the *Instructor's Manual,* pp. 94–104, as well as the five volumes of *Selections from the Speech Communication Teacher* that accompany *The Art of Public Speaking.*

position. The other poll, suspect in its methods and conducted by a partisan organization, says a majority of people in your state support your position. Which poll do you cite in your speech? If you cite the second poll, do you point out its shortcomings?

b. When listening to an informative speech by one of your classmates, you realize that much of it is plagiarized from a magazine article you read a couple weeks earlier. What do you do? Do you say something when your instructor asks for comments about the speech? Do you mention your concern to the instructor after class? Do you talk with the speaker? Do you remain silent?

c. While researching your persuasive speech, you find a quotation from an article by a highly respected expert that will nail down one of your most important points. But as you read the rest of the article, you realize the author does not in fact support the policy you are advocating. Should you still include the quotation in your speech?

Applying the POWER of PUBLIC SPEAKING

Having graduated with a degree in public administration and hoping to pursue a career in politics, you have been fortunate to receive a staff position with one of the leading senators in your state legislature. Since your arrival two months ago, you have answered phones, ordered lunch, made copies, stapled mailings, and stuffed envelopes. Finally you have been asked to look over a speech the senator will deliver at your alma mater. Surely, you think, this will be the first of many important assignments once your value is recognized.

Cross-Reference
For discussion of this Applying the Power of Public Speaking scenario, see the *Instructor's Manual*, pp. 93–94.

After reading the speech, however, your enthusiasm is dampened. You agree wholeheartedly with its support of a bill to fund scholarships for low-income students, but you're dismayed by its attack on opponents of the bill as "elitist bigots who would deny a college education to those who need it most." You haven't been asked to comment on the ethics of the speech and you certainly don't want to jeopardize your position on the senator's staff. At the same time, you think his use of name-calling may actually arouse sympathy for the opposition. The senator would like your comments in two hours. What will you tell him?

Notes

1. Steven Luper, *A Guide to Ethics* (New York: McGraw-Hill, 2002), p. 15.
2. Richard L. Johannesen, *Ethics in Human Communication,* 5th ed. (Prospect Heights, IL: Waveland Press, 2002), p. 15.
3. Johannesen, *Ethics in Human Communication,* p. 14.
4. See, for example, Vincent Ryan Ruggiero, *Thinking Critically About Ethical Issues,* 5th ed. (New York: McGraw-Hill, 2001).
5. Haig A. Bosmajian, *The Language of Oppression* (Washington, DC: Public Affairs Press, 1974), p. 5.
6. The negative effects of name-calling and other forms of abusive language are discussed especially well by Alexander Tsesis, *Destructive Messages: How Hate Speech Paves the Way for Harmful Social Movements* (New York: New York University Press, 2002).
7. Thomas L. Tedford and Dale A. Herbeck, *Freedom of Speech in the United States,* 4th ed. (State College, PA: Strata Publishing, 2001), pp. 174–180.

[8]Kenneth Blanchard and Norman Vincent Peale, *The Power of Ethical Management* (New York: Ballantine Books, 1988), p. 64.

[9]Joseph Gibaldi, *MLA Handbook for Writers of Research Papers,* 5th ed. (New York: Modern Language Association of America, 1999), p. 30.

[10]For a fascinating look at the history of plagiarism in a variety of contexts, see Thomas Mallon, *Stolen Words: Forays into the Origins and Ravages of Plagiarism,* updated ed. (New York: Harvest Books, 2001).

[11]Bruce Perry, *Malcolm: The Life of the Man Who Changed Black America* (Tarrytown, NY: Station Hill, 1991), p. 380.

[12]For research on the impact of audience members on a speaker's self-confidence, see Peter D. MacIntyre, Kimly A. Thivierge, and J. Renee MacDonald, "The Effect of Audience Interest, Responsiveness, and Evaluation on Public Speaking Anxiety and Related Variables," *Communication Research Reports,* 14 (1997), pp. 157–168.

[13]The credo is available at www.natcom.org/policies/External/EthicalComm.htm.

[14]Edward M. Kennedy, "Truth and Tolerance in America," October 3, 1983, in Lloyd Rohler and Roger Cook (eds.), *Great Speeches for Criticism and Analysis,* 4th ed. (Greenwood, IN: Alistair Press, 2001), pp. 323–324.

[15]Colin Powell, Commencement Address at Howard University, May 14, 1994, in Rohler and Cook, *Great Speeches,* p. 344.

Chapter Three

LISTENING

I t was a hot afternoon in May. The professor of ancient history was lecturing on the fall of the Roman Empire. She began: "Yesterday we discussed the political and social conditions that weakened the empire from within. Today we will talk about the invasions that attacked the empire from the outside—the Visigoths from the northwest, the Ostrogoths from the northeast, the Vandals from the south, the Huns from the west, and Homer Simpson from the southeast."

Nobody batted an eye. Nobody looked up. The classroom was quiet, except for the scratch of pens as the students took notes—presumably recording Homer Simpson as an invader of the Roman Empire.

hearing
The vibration of sound waves on the eardrums and the firing of electrochemical impulses in the brain.

listening
Paying close attention to, and making sense of, what we hear.

This story illustrates what one research study after another has revealed—most people are shockingly poor listeners. We fake paying attention. We can look right at someone, appear interested in what that person says, even nod our head or smile at the appropriate moments—all without really listening.

Not listening doesn't mean we don't hear. *Hearing* is a physiological process, involving the vibration of sound waves on our eardrums and the firing of electrochemical impulses from the inner ear to the central auditory system of the brain. But *listening* involves paying close attention to, and making sense of, what we hear. Even when we think we are listening carefully, we usually grasp only 50 percent of what we hear. After 24 hours we can remember only 10 percent of the original message.[1] It's little wonder that listening has been called a lost art.[2]

Listening Is Important

Chapter Focus
Students often say that one of the unexpected benefits of their speech class is that it improves their listening skills. This chapter begins by explaining the importance of listening and the relationship between listening and critical thinking. Then it explores four major causes of poor listening and offers strategies for becoming a more effective listener. For a full outline of the chapter, see the *Instructor's Manual*, pp. 108–111.

Although most people listen poorly, there are exceptions. Top-flight business executives, successful politicians, brilliant teachers—nearly all are excellent listeners. So much of what they do depends on absorbing information that is given verbally—and absorbing it quickly and accurately. If you had an interview with the president of a major corporation, you might be shocked (and flattered) to see how closely that person listened to your words. One business executive admitted, "Frankly, I had never thought of listening as an important subject by itself. But now that I am aware of it, I think that perhaps 80 percent of my work depends upon my listening to someone, or upon someone listening to me."[3]

In our communication-oriented age, listening is more important than ever. This is why, in most companies, effective listeners hold higher positions and are promoted more often than people who are ineffective listeners.[4] When business managers are asked to rank-order the communication skills most crucial to their jobs, they usually rank listening number one.[5] Listening is so important that in one survey of America's Fortune 500 companies, almost 60 percent of the respondents said they provide some kind of listening training for their employees.[6]

Even if you don't plan to be a corporate executive, the art of listening can be helpful in almost every part of your life. This is not surprising when you realize that people spend more time listening than doing any other communicative activity—more than reading, more than writing, more even than speaking.

Think for a moment about your own life as a college student. Close to 90 percent of class time in U.S. colleges and universities is spent listening to discussions and lectures. A number of studies have shown a strong correlation between listening and academic success. Students with the highest grades are usually those with the strongest listening skills. The reverse is also true—students with the lowest grades are usually those with the weakest listening skills.[7]

There is plenty of reason, then, to take listening seriously. Employers and employees, parents and children, wives and husbands, doctors and patients, students and teachers—all depend on the apparently simple skill of listening. Regardless of your profession or walk of life, you never escape the need for a well-trained ear.

Listening is also important to you as a speaker. It is probably the way you get most of your ideas and information—from television, radio, conversation, and lectures. If you do not listen well, you will not understand what you hear and may pass along your misunderstanding to others.

Besides, in class—as in life—you will listen to many more speeches than you give. It is only fair to pay close attention to your classmates' speeches; after all, you want them to listen carefully to *your* speeches. An excellent way to improve your own speeches is to listen attentively to the speeches of other people. One student, reflecting on her speech class, said, "As I listened to the speeches, I discovered things that seemed to work—things I could try. I also learned what didn't work—what to avoid. That helped a lot in my own speeches." Over and over, teachers find that the best speakers are usually the best listeners.

A side benefit of your speech class is that it offers an ideal opportunity to work on the art of listening. During the 95 percent of the time when you are not speaking, you have nothing else to do but listen and learn. You can sit there like a stone—or you can use the time profitably to master a skill that will serve you in a thousand ways.

Discussion Prompt
Can students think of speakers to whom they nearly always pay attention? Why are some speakers "easier to listen to" than others?

Listening and Critical Thinking

One of the ways listening can serve you is by enhancing your skills as a critical thinker. We can identify four kinds of listening:[8]

- *Appreciative listening*—listening for pleasure or enjoyment, as when we listen to music, to a comedy routine, or to an entertaining speech.

- *Empathic listening*—listening to provide emotional support for the speaker, as when a psychiatrist listens to a patient or when we lend a sympathetic ear to a friend in distress.

- *Comprehensive listening*—listening to understand the message of a speaker, as when we attend a classroom lecture or listen to directions for finding a friend's house.

- *Critical listening*—listening to evaluate a message for purposes of accepting or rejecting it, as when we listen to the sales pitch of a used-car dealer, the campaign speech of a political candidate, or the closing arguments of an attorney in a jury trial.

appreciative listening
Listening for pleasure or enjoyment.

empathic listening
Listening to provide emotional support for a speaker.

comprehensive listening
Listening to understand the message of a speaker.

critical listening
Listening to evaluate a
message for purposes of
accepting or rejecting it.

Although all four kinds of listening are important, this chapter deals primarily with the last two—comprehensive listening and critical listening. They are the kinds of listening you will use most often when listening to speeches in class, when taking lecture notes in other courses, when communicating at work, and when responding to the barrage of commercials, political messages, and other persuasive appeals you face every day in our fast-paced society. They are also the kinds of listening that are most closely tied to critical thinking.

As we saw in Chapter 1, critical thinking involves a number of skills. Some of those skills—summarizing information, recalling facts, distinguishing main points from minor points—are central to comprehensive listening. Other skills of critical thinking—separating fact from opinion, spotting weaknesses in reasoning, judging the soundness of evidence—are especially important in critical listening. When you engage in comprehensive listening or critical listening, you must use your mind as well as your ears. When your mind is not actively involved, you may be hearing, but you are not *listening*.[9] In fact, listening and critical thinking are so closely allied that training in listening is also training in how to think.[10]

At the end of this chapter, we'll discuss steps you can take to improve your skills in comprehensive and critical listening. If you follow these steps, you may also become a better critical thinker at the same time.

Four Causes of Poor Listening

Not Concentrating

The brain is incredibly efficient. Although we talk at a rate of 120 to 150 words a minute, the brain can process 400 to 800 words a minute.[11] This would seem to make listening very easy, but actually it has the opposite effect. Because we can take in a speaker's words and still have plenty of spare "brain time," we are tempted to interrupt our listening by thinking about other things. And thinking about other things is just what we do. Here's what happens:

spare "brain time"
The difference between
the rate at which most
people talk (120 to 150
words a minute) and the
rate at which the brain
can process language
(400 to 800 words
a minute).

> Rico Salazar is the youngest member of the public relations team for a giant oil company. He is pleased to be included in the biweekly staff meetings. After two dozen or so meetings, however, he is beginning to find them tedious.
>
> This time the vice president is droning on about executive speechwriting—an area in which Rico is not directly concerned. The vice president says, "When the draft of a speech hits the president's desk . . ."
>
> "Desk," thinks Rico. "That's my big problem. It's humiliating to have a metal desk when everyone else has wood. There must be some way to convince my boss that I need a new wooden desk." In his imagination, Rico sees himself behind a handsome walnut desk. He is conducting an interview, and his visitor is so impressed . . .
>
> Sternly, Rico pulls his attention back to the meeting. The vice president has moved on to a public relations problem in Latin America. Rico listens carefully for a while, until he hears the words "especially in the Caribbean."

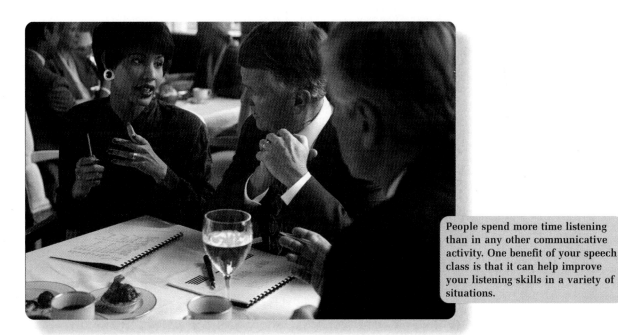

People spend more time listening than in any other communicative activity. One benefit of your speech class is that it can help improve your listening skills in a variety of situations.

"Oh, if only I could get away for a winter vacation this year," he thinks. He is lost in a reverie featuring white beaches, tropical drinks, exotic dances, scuba diving, sailboats, himself tanned and windblown . . .

". . . will definitely affect salary increases this year" brings him back to the meeting with a jolt. What did the vice president say about salary increases? Oh, well, he can ask someone else after the meeting. But now the vice president is talking about budgets. All those dreary figures and percentages . . . And Rico is off again.

His date last night, Celine, really seemed to like him and yet . . . Was it something he did that made her say goodnight at the door and go inside alone? Could she have been *that* tired? The last time she invited him in for coffee. Of course, she really did have a rough day. Anybody can understand that. But still . . .

". . . an area Rico has taken a special interest in. Maybe we should hear from him." Uh, oh! *What* area does the vice president mean? Everyone is looking at Rico, as he tries frantically to recall the last words said at the meeting.

It's not that Rico *meant* to lose track of the discussion. But there comes a point at which it's so easy to give in to physical and mental distractions—to let your thoughts wander rather than to concentrate on what is being said. After all, concentrating is hard work. Louis Nizer, the famous trial lawyer, says, "So complete is this concentration that at the end of a court day in which I have only listened, I find myself wringing wet despite a calm and casual manner."[12]

Later in this chapter, we will look at some things you can do to concentrate better on what you hear.

Listening Too Hard

Until now we have been talking about not paying close attention to what we hear. But sometimes we listen *too* hard. We turn into human sponges, soaking up a speaker's every word as if every word were equally important.

Class Activity
Have students keep a personal journal of their listening activities for a full day. The journal should include brief descriptions of all the listening situations each student experiences during that day. It should also include the student's analysis of how well she or he listened in each situation and of why she or he did (or did not) listen effectively in each situation. For full discussion of this activity, see the *Instructor's Manual*, p. 116.

We try to remember all the names, all the dates, all the places. In the process we often miss the speaker's point by submerging it in a morass of details. What is worse, we may end up confusing the facts as well.

Shortly after graduating from college, Erik Nakamura landed an excellent job at a graphics design firm. Knowing that he had never been good at budgeting his money, he was determined to improve and to begin thinking about his long-range economic future. When his employer circulated an e-mail announcing a financial planning workshop, Erik signed up right away.

The first session was about retirement planning. Simone Fisher, who was conducting the workshop, explained that 7 of 10 Americans between the ages of 22 and 35 do not have either a monthly budget or a regular savings plan. Erik wrote down every number Simone mentioned.

"If you want to have a retirement income equal to 75 percent of your current salary," Simone continued, "you will need to invest at least 6 percent of your present earnings, and beyond that you need to figure in future inflation rates. We have set aside time this afternoon to meet with you personally to calculate your individual savings needs. In the meantime, I want to stress that the most important thing is to start saving now."

Erik wrote furiously to record all the statistics Simone cited. When she opened the floor for questions, Erik raised his hand and said, "I have two questions. When is the best time to start saving for retirement? And how am I supposed to figure out my savings target if I don't know what inflation rates will be in the future?"

This is a typical example of losing the speaker's point by concentrating on details. Erik had fixed his mind on remembering all the statistics in Simone's presentation—period. In doing so, he blocked out the main message— that it is best to start saving now and that he would get help developing an individual plan.

Rather than trying to remember everything a speaker says, efficient listeners usually concentrate on main ideas and evidence. We'll discuss these things more thoroughly later in the chapter.

Jumping to Conclusions

Renee Anello, a recent college graduate, took a job as an editorial assistant in the research department of a regional magazine. Shortly after Renee arrived, the editor in charge of the research department left the magazine for another job. For the next two months, Renee struggled to handle the work of the research department by herself. She often felt in over her head, but she knew this was a good opportunity to learn, and she hated to give up her new responsibilities.

One day Seiji Tomasu, the editor in chief of the magazine, comes into Renee's office to talk. The following conversation takes place:

Seiji: You've done a great job these last two months, Renee. But you know we really need a new editor. So we've decided to make some changes.

Renee: I'm not surprised. I know I've made my share of mistakes.

Seiji: Everyone makes mistakes when they're starting out. And you've been carrying a lot of responsibility. Too much. That's why . . .

Renee: That's okay. I'm grateful to have had a chance to try my hand at this. I know I'm inexperienced, and this is an important department.

Discussion Prompt

The problem of poor listening is nothing new. In his play *King Henry the Fourth, Part II*, Shakespeare referred to "the disease of not listening." Lead a class discussion in which students identify causes of poor listening that are not discussed in the textbook. After the causes are identified, ask students what steps can be taken to overcome each cause.

Class Activity

Lead a class discussion in which students develop a code of listening behavior for your classroom. The final product of this discussion will be a list entitled "Listening Behavior for Our Speech Class." For further discussion of this activity, see the *Instructor's Manual*, p. 114.

Seiji: Yes, it is. And it's not an easy job. We really need an editor and an assistant to handle all the work. That's why I wanted to tell you . . .

Renee: You're right, of course. I hope you've found somebody good to be the new editor.

Seiji: I think so. But, Renee, I don't think you understand . . .

Renee: No, I understand. I knew all along that I was just filling in.

Seiji: Renee, you're not listening.

Renee: Yes, I am. You're trying to be nice, but you're here to tell me that you've hired a new editor and I'll be going back to my old job.

Seiji: No, that's not it at all. I think you've done a fine job under difficult circumstances. You've proved yourself, and I intend to make *you* the editor. But I think you'll need an assistant to help you.

Why is there so much confusion here? Clearly, Renee is unsure about her future at the magazine. Although she has worked hard, she knows she has made some mistakes that a more experienced person might have avoided. So when Seiji starts to talk about making some changes, Renee jumps to a conclusion and assumes the worst. The misunderstanding could have been avoided if, when Seiji had said, "We've decided to make some changes," Renee had asked, "What changes?"—and then *listened.*

This is one form of jumping to conclusions—putting words into a speaker's mouth. It is one reason why we sometimes communicate so poorly with people we are closest to. Because we are so sure we know what they mean, we don't listen to what they actually say. Sometimes we don't even hear them out.

Another way of jumping to conclusions is prematurely rejecting a speaker's ideas as boring or misguided. We may decide early on that a speaker has nothing valuable to say. Suppose you are passionately committed to animal rights and a speaker's announced topic is "The Importance of Animals to Scientific Research." You may decide in advance not to listen to anything the speaker has to say. That would be a mistake. You might pick up useful information that could either strengthen or modify your thinking. In another situation, you might jump to the conclusion that a speech will be boring. Let's say the announced topic is "Looking Toward Jupiter: Science and the Cosmos." It sounds dull. So you tune out—and miss a fascinating discussion of possible extraterrestrial life-forms.

Nearly every speech has something to offer you—whether it be information, point of view, or technique. You are cheating yourself if you prejudge and choose not to listen.

Focusing on Delivery and Personal Appearance

Even though Tim and Suzanne had been born in Nebraska, they had lived in Brooklyn for 15 years and had come to love it. But when Suzanne's company offered her a promotion and a new position in the Omaha office, they decided to move.

Soon after they arrived in Omaha, Suzanne saw a notice in the local paper about an Audubon Society lecture on the annual Sandhill Crane migration. She asked Tim if he'd like to attend, and they decided to go the following weekend. "This may come

Discussion Prompt
We are all guilty of jumping to conclusions at one time or another. Ask students to discuss the people with whom they are most likely to jump to conclusions— parents, friends, teachers, roommates, spouses, etc. What impact can jumping to conclusions have on one's ability to listen ethically to public speakers?

as a surprise," Tim said when they arrived at the lecture, "but I'm really looking forward to this. I remember watching the crane migration with my grandfather when I was a kid. It's an amazing spectacle."

The speaker, a professor at a nearby college, began by discussing the geography of the migration and pointing out the stretch of wetlands on the Platte River where half a million cranes stop every year. He explained how cranes have followed the same route from Mexico to Alaska for more than 9 million years, and he showed dramatic color slides of the birds that had most of the audience spellbound.

"That was great," exclaimed Suzanne when they got back to the car. "I definitely want to see the migration next spring." But Tim was scowling. "What's wrong?" Suzanne asked.

"I know you're going to think this is stupid," Tim began, "but once I realized the speaker had a Brooklyn accent, I didn't hear a word he said."

"But you love Brooklyn," Suzanne protested. "That professor is a great speaker, and he gave a terrific presentation."

"I know, I know," Tim admitted. "I guess I just wanted him to sound like my grandfather."

Cross-Reference
Be sure to remind students of the criteria for ethical listening discussed in Chapter 2.

This story illustrates a very common problem. We tend to judge people by the way they look or speak and therefore don't listen to what they *say*. Some people become so distracted by a speaker's accent, personal appearance, or vocal mannerisms that they lose sight of the message. As in Tim's case, this can happen even when a listener is interested in the topic and looking forward to the presentation. Focusing on a speaker's delivery or personal appearance is one of the major sources of interference in the speech communication process, and it is something we always need to guard against.

How to Become a Better Listener

Take Listening Seriously

The first step toward becoming a better listener is to accord listening the seriousness it deserves. Good listeners are not born that way. They have *worked* at learning how to listen effectively. Good listening does not go hand in hand with intelligence, education, or social standing. Like any other skill, it comes from practice and self-discipline. Check your current skills as a listener by completing the Listening Self-Evaluation form on page 63 (Figure 3.1).[13] Once you have identified your shortcomings as a listener, make a serious effort to overcome them.

Be an Active Listener

Teaching Tip
The "Listening Self-Evaluation" form is reprinted on p. 113 of the *Instructor's Manual*. Make copies of the form and distribute it in class. Have students fill out the form and return it to you. In cases where you find significant differences between a student's positive self-evaluation and your observation of the student's negative listening behavior in class, set up a conference in which you discuss the differences with the student.

So many aspects of modern life encourage us to listen passively. We listen to a CD while studying or listen to the television while moving about from room to room. Parents listen to their children while fixing dinner; students listen to a lecture while doing the crossword puzzle; television reporters listen to a politician's speech while walking around the auditorium looking for their next interview.

This type of passive listening is a habit—but so is active listening. Active listeners give their undivided attention to the speaker in a genuine effort to understand his or her point of view. In conversation, they do not interrupt

Figure 3.1

LISTENING SELF-EVALUATION

How often do you indulge in the following 10 bad listening habits? Check yourself carefully in each one.

HABIT	FREQUENCY					SCORE
	Almost Always	Usually	Some-times	Seldom	Almost never	
1. Giving in to mental distractions			✓			4
2. Giving in to physical distractions		✓				8
3. Trying to recall everything a speaker says		✓				
4. Rejecting a topic as uninteresting before hearing the speaker				✓		4
5. Faking paying attention					✓	2
6. Jumping to conclusions about a speaker's meaning				✓		6
7. Deciding a speaker is wrong before hearing everything she or he has to say			✓			6
8. Judging a speaker on personal appearance				✓	✓	10
9. Not paying attention to a speaker's evidence				✓		2
10. Focusing on delivery rather than on what the speaker says				✓		

TOTAL _____

How to score:

For every "almost always" checked, give yourself a score of   2
For every "usually" checked, give yourself a score of   4
For every "sometimes" checked, give yourself a score of   6
For every "seldom" checked, give yourself a score of   8
For every "almost never" checked, give yourself a score of   10

Total score interpretation:

Below 70	You need lots of training in listening.
From 71–90	You listen well.
Above 90	You listen exceptionally well.

the speaker or finish his or her sentences. When listening to a speech, they do not allow themselves to be distracted by internal or external interference, and they do not prejudge the speaker. They take listening seriously and do the best they can to stay focused on the speaker and his or her message.

Of course, there are some situations in which active listening is not necessary—when you are joking around with friends or talking casually with a stranger while waiting in line. But there are many more situations in which active listening is imperative. If you develop the habit of being an active listener, you will reap the rewards in your schoolwork, in your personal and family relations, and in your career.[14]

There are a number of steps you can take to improve your skills of active listening. They include resisting distractions, not allowing yourself to be diverted by a speaker's appearance or delivery, suspending judgment until you have heard the speaker out, focusing your listening, and developing note-taking skills. We'll discuss each of these in turn.

active listening
Giving undivided attention to a speaker in a genuine effort to understand the speaker's point of view.

Resist Distractions

In an ideal world, we could eliminate all physical and mental distractions. In the real world, however, this is not possible. Because we think so much faster than a speaker can talk, it's easy to let our attention wander while we listen. Sometimes it's very easy—when the room is too hot, when construction machinery is operating right outside the window, when the speaker is tedious. But our attention can stray even in the best of circumstances—if for no other reason than a failure to stay alert and make ourselves concentrate.

Whenever you find this happening, make a conscious effort to pull your mind back to what the speaker is saying. Then force it to stay there. One way to do this is to think a little ahead of the speaker—try to anticipate what will come next. This is not the same as jumping to conclusions. When you jump to conclusions, you put words into the speaker's mouth and don't actually listen to what is said. In this case you *will* listen—and measure what the speaker says against what you had anticipated.

Another way to keep your mind on a speech is to review mentally what the speaker has already said and make sure you understand it. Yet another is to listen between the lines and assess what a speaker implies verbally or says nonverbally with body language. Suppose a politician is running for reelection. During a campaign speech to her constituents she makes this statement: "Just last week I had lunch with the President, and he assured me that he has a special concern for the people of our state." The careful listener would hear this implied message: "If you vote for me, there's a good chance more tax money will flow into the state."

To take another example, suppose a speaker is introducing someone to an audience. The speaker says, "It gives me great pleasure to present to you my very dear friend, Nadine Zussman." But the speaker doesn't shake hands with Nadine. He doesn't even look at her—just turns his back and leaves the podium. Is Nadine really his "very dear friend"? Certainly not.

Attentive listeners can pick up all kinds of clues to a speaker's real message. At first you may find it difficult to listen so intently. If you work at it, however, your concentration is bound to improve.

Class Activity
For an excellent activity that helps students learn to listen respectfully and carefully, see Richard Bruce Hyde, "Council: Using a Talking Stick to Teach Listening," in *Selections from the Speech Communication Teacher, 1991–1994,* pp. 41–42, which accompanies *The Art of Public Speaking.*

Effective listeners take their task seriously. If you approach listening as an active process, you will significantly sharpen your powers of concentration and comprehension.

Don't Be Diverted by Appearance or Delivery

If you had attended Abraham Lincoln's momentous Cooper Union speech of 1860, this is what you would have seen:

> The long, ungainly figure upon which hung clothes that, while new for this trip, were evidently the work of an unskilled tailor; the large feet and clumsy hands, of which, at the outset, at least, the orator seemed to be unduly conscious; the long, gaunt head, capped by a shock of hair that seemed not to have been thoroughly brushed out, made a picture which did not fit in with New York's conception of a finished statesman.[15]

But although he seemed awkward and uncultivated, Lincoln had a powerful message about the moral evils of slavery. Fortunately, the audience at Cooper Union did not let his appearance stand in the way of his words.

Similarly, you must be willing to set aside preconceived judgments based on a person's looks or manner of speech. Gandhi was a very unimpressive-looking man who often spoke dressed in a simple white cotton cloth. Helen Keller, deaf and blind from earliest childhood, always had trouble articulating words distinctly. Renowned physicist Stephen Hawking is severely disabled and can speak only with the aid of a voice synthesizer. Yet imagine if no one had listened to them. Even though it may tax your tolerance, patience, and concentration, don't let negative feelings about a speaker's appearance or delivery keep you from listening to the message.

On the other hand, try not to be misled if the speaker has an unusually attractive appearance. It's all too easy to assume that because someone is good-looking and has a polished delivery, he or she is speaking eloquently.

Discussion Prompt
Often the physical environment of a listening situation can affect one's ability to concentrate. Ask students if they believe they concentrate better when they sit toward the front of the classroom. As the term progresses, you may want to have different students sit in the front of the classroom to see what impact it has on their listening.

Some of the most unscrupulous speakers in history have been handsome people with hypnotic delivery skills. Again, be sure you respond to the message, not to the package it comes in.

Suspend Judgment

Unless we listen only to people who think exactly as we do, we are going to hear things with which we disagree. When this happens, our natural inclination is to argue mentally with the speaker or to dismiss everything she or he says. But neither response is fair—to the speaker or to ourselves. In both cases we blot out any chance of learning or being persuaded.

Does this mean you must agree with everything you hear? Not at all. It means you should hear people out *before* reaching a final judgment. Try to understand their point of view. Listen to their ideas, examine their evidence, assess their reasoning. *Then* make up your mind. The aim of active listening is to set aside "one's own prejudices, frames of reference and desires so as to experience as far as possible the speaker's world from the inside."[16] If you're sure of your beliefs, you need not fear listening to opposing views. If you're not sure, you have every reason to listen carefully. It has been said more than once that a closed mind is an empty mind.

Focus Your Listening

As we have seen, skilled listeners do not try to absorb a speaker's every word. Rather, they focus on specific things in a speech. Here are three suggestions to help you focus your listening.

Listen for Main Points

Most speeches contain from two to four main points. Here, for example, are the main points of a recent speech on women's health issues delivered by AARP President Tess Canja:[17]

1. Women are living longer, healthier lives today than ever before.

2. There is still a shortage of research that takes gender differences into account when considering medical diagnosis, prevention, and treatment.

3. Public policy needs to be adjusted to account for the growing majority of women among America's elderly population.

4. Women should take charge of their own personal health through awareness, prevention, and public activity.

These four main points are the heart of Canja's message. As with any speech, they are the most important things to listen for.

Unless a speaker is terribly scatterbrained, you should be able to detect her or his main points with little difficulty. Often a speaker will give some idea at the outset of the main points to be discussed in the speech. For example, at the end of her introduction, Canja said, "Today I'm going to focus on four key areas." Noticing this, a sharp listener would have been prepared for a speech with four main points. Canja also gave a preview statement identifying each of the points before she started the body of her speech.

Related Reading

Diana Bonet, *The Business of Listening: A Practical Guide to Effective Listening*, 3rd ed. (Menlo Park, CA: Crisp Publications, 2001) contains numerous checklists, activities, and exercises that can help students sharpen their listening skills.

Class Activity

Show your class a selection from one of the videotapes of student speeches that accompanies *The Art of Public Speaking*. Have students take notes in which they demarcate where the introduction of the speech ends, list the main points and subpoints in the body, and identify where the conclusion begins. Check the results in a class discussion and give pointers for listening and taking notes more effectively.

Just as there are organizations devoted to public speaking, so there is a major group devoted to the study of listening. It's called the International Listening Association, and you can visit its website at www.listen.org.

Do you wish you could listen to the words of historical figures such as Amelia Earhart, Winston Churchill, Mohandas Gandhi, and Malcolm X? You can by logging on to The History Channel: Great Speeches (www.historychannel.com/speeches/index.html).

You can link to these websites at www.mhhe.com/lucas8.

ONLINE LEARNING CENTER

As the speech progressed, she enumerated each point to help her audience keep track of them. After this, only the most inattentive of listeners could have been in the dark about Canja's main points.

Listen for Evidence

Identifying a speaker's main points, however, is not enough. You must also listen for supporting evidence. By themselves, Canja's main points are only assertions. You may be inclined to believe them just because they come from the president of a major national organization. Yet a careful listener will be concerned about evidence no matter who is speaking. Had you been listening to Canja's speech, you would have heard her support her claims about the special health needs facing women with a mass of verifiable evidence. Here is an excerpt:

> Eighty percent of people with osteoporosis are women. Women who smoke are 20 to 70 percent more likely to develop lung cancer than men who smoke the same amount. Women are more likely to suffer from autoimmune diseases—including rheumatoid arthritis, lupus, and multiple sclerosis. Nearly 26.4 million of the 42.7 million Americans with arthritis are women. By the age of 65, 80 percent of women report some problem with arthritis. . . .
>
> Heart disease kills more women than all kinds of cancer combined. Women are more likely to suffer a second heart attack within one year of their first heart attack. More women die from heart disease than men.

There are four basic questions to ask about a speaker's evidence:

Is it *accurate*?

Is it taken from *objective* sources?

Is it *relevant* to the speaker's claims?

Is it *sufficient* to support the speaker's point?

In Canja's case, the answer to each question is yes. Her figures about the incidence of osteoporosis, lung cancer, autoimmune conditions, arthritis, and heart disease among women are well established in the public record and can be verified by independent sources. The figures are clearly relevant

Class Activity
Students may feel overwhelmed by the sheer number of items to listen to and evaluate during a classroom speech. To ease the task of listening early in the course, divide the class into groups and have each group assess a single element of a speech. Assign one group to evaluate the introduction, a second to assess the organization of main points, a third to appraise the use of evidence, a fourth to judge delivery, etc. Have each group report its conclusions to the class.

to Canja's claim that women need to take special health issues into account as they age, and they are sufficient to support that claim. If Canja's evidence were inaccurate, biased, irrelevant, or insufficient, you should be wary of accepting her claim.

We shall discuss these—and other—tests of evidence in detail in Chapters 7 and 16. For now, it's enough to know that you should be on guard against unfounded assertions and sweeping generalizations. Keep an eye out for the speaker's evidence and for its accuracy, objectivity, relevance, and sufficiency.

Listen for Technique

Class Activity

For at least one round of speeches, have students prepare evaluations of their classmates' speeches using the evaluation form on p. 51 of the *Instructor's Manual*. This form is designed to gauge students' listening competence by requiring them to state the speaker's specific purpose, main points, pattern of organization, and types of supporting materials. If you use this form for each round of speeches, it can be of great help in sharpening your students' listening skills by the end of the course.

We said earlier that you should not let a speaker's delivery distract you from the message, and this is true. However, if you want to become an effective speaker, you should study the methods other people use to speak effectively. When you listen to speeches—in class and out—focus above all on the content of a speaker's message; but also pay attention to the techniques the speaker uses to get the message across.

Analyze the introduction: What methods does the speaker use to gain attention, to relate to the audience, to establish credibility and goodwill? Assess the organization of the speech: Is it clear and easy to follow? Can you pick out the speaker's main points? Can you follow when the speaker moves from one point to another?

Study the speaker's language: Is it accurate, clear, vivid, appropriate? Does the speaker adapt well to the audience and occasion? Finally, diagnose the speaker's delivery: Is it fluent, dynamic, convincing? Does it strengthen or weaken the impact of the speaker's ideas? How well does the speaker use eye contact, gestures, and visual aids?

As you listen, focus on the speaker's strengths and weaknesses. If the speaker is not effective, try to determine why. If he or she is effective, try to pick out techniques you can use in your own speeches. If you listen in this way, you will be surprised how much you can learn about successful speaking.

Develop Note-Taking Skills

Speech students are often amazed at how easily their teacher can pick out a speaker's main points, evidence, and techniques. Of course, the teacher knows what to listen for and has had plenty of practice. But the next time you get an opportunity, watch your teacher during a speech. Chances are she or he will be listening with pen and paper. When note taking is done properly, it is a surefire way to improve your concentration and keep track of a speaker's ideas.

Discussion Prompt

Almost 700 years ago the Italian poet Dante wrote in his classic work *The Divine Comedy*, "He listens well who takes notes." Ask students to explain, on the basis of their experience, why note taking is such an important aid to good listening.

The key words here are *when done properly*. Unfortunately, many people don't take notes effectively. Some try to write down everything a speaker says. They view note taking as a race, pitting their handwriting agility against the speaker's rate of speech. As the speaker starts to talk, the note taker starts to write. But soon the speaker is winning the race. In a desperate effort to keep up, the note taker slips into a scribbled writing style with incomplete sentences and abbreviated words. Even this is not enough. The speaker pulls so far ahead that the note taker can never catch up. Finally, the note taker concedes defeat and spends the rest of the speech grumbling in frustration.[18]

Research confirms that listening carefully and taking effective notes are vital skills for success in college. They will also benefit you in countless situations throughout life.

Some people go to the opposite extreme. They arrive armed with pen, notebook, and the best of intentions. They know they can't write down everything, so they settle comfortably in their seats and wait for the speaker to say something that grabs their attention. Every once in a while the speaker rewards them with a joke, a dramatic story, or a startling fact. Then the note taker seizes pen, jots down a few words, and leans back dreamily to await the next fascinating tidbit. By the end of the lecture the note taker has a set of tidbits—and little or no record of the speaker's important ideas.

As these examples illustrate, most inefficient note takers suffer from one or both of two problems: they don't know *what* to listen for, and they don't know *how* to record what they do listen for. The solution to the first problem is to focus on a speaker's main points and evidence. But once you know what to listen for, you still need a sound method of note taking.

Although there are a number of systems, most students find the *key-word outline* best for listening to classroom lectures and formal speeches. As its name suggests, this method briefly notes a speaker's main points and supporting evidence in rough outline form. Suppose a speaker says:

> Elephants have long been hunted for their ivory tusks. In the 1920s thousands of elephants were killed to meet demand in the United States for 60,000 ivory billiard balls every year and hundreds of thousands of piano keys. Today the ivory trade is centered in the Far East—especially Japan and China—where ivory ornaments are highly prized.

key-word outline
An outline that briefly notes a speaker's main points and supporting evidence in rough outline form.

According to *Time* magazine, more than 3,900 tons of ivory were imported into Hong Kong alone during the 1980s. That represents the death of more than 400,000 elephants.

Despite international agreements designed to reduce the ivory trade, poaching continues to take its toll. As recently as 1980, 1.3 million elephants roamed Africa. According to the World Wildlife Federation, today that number has been reduced by at least 50 percent, and in some locations by more than 75 percent. *U.S. News and World Report* states that if the carnage continues, elephants will be threatened with extinction.

Class Activity
Bring two short editorials to class. Read one of the editorials to your students. Have them take notes and try to identify the main points and evidence of the editorial. Check the results in a class discussion and give pointers for listening and taking notes more effectively. Then read the second editorial and give students a chance to apply those pointers. Again, check the results in a class discussion.

A key-word note taker would record something like this:

Elephants long hunted
    1920s—U.S.
    Today—Far East
        Hong Kong: 3,900 tons
        Death of 400,000 elephants

How serious a problem?
    1.3 million elephants in 1980
    Reduced by 50–75 percent today
    U.S. News: could threaten extinction

Notice how brief the notes are. They contain only 35 words (compared with the speaker's 155), yet they accurately summarize the speaker's ideas. Also notice how clear the notes are. By separating main points from subpoints and evidence, the outline format shows the relationships among the speaker's ideas.

Perfecting this—or any other—system of note taking requires practice. But with a little effort you should see results soon. As you become a better note taker, you will become a better listener. There is also a good chance you will become a better student. Common sense and experience suggest that students who take effective notes usually receive higher grades than those who do not.[19]

Summary

Most people are poor listeners. Even when we think we are listening carefully, we usually grasp only half of what we hear, and we retain even less. Improving your listening skills can be helpful in every part of your life, including speechmaking. The best speakers are often the best listeners. Your speech class gives you a perfect chance to work on your listening skills as well as your speaking skills.

The most important cause of poor listening is giving in to physical and mental distractions. Many times we let our thoughts wander rather than concentrating on what is being said. Sometimes, however, we listen *too* hard. We try to remember every word a speaker says, and we lose the main message by concentrating on details. In other situations, we may jump to conclusions and prejudge a speaker without hearing out the message. Finally, we often judge people by their appearance or speaking manner instead of listening to what they say.

You can overcome these poor listening habits by taking several steps. First, take listening seriously and commit yourself to becoming a better listener. Second, work at being an active listener. Give your undivided attention to the speaker in a genuine effort to understand her or his ideas. Third, resist distractions. Make a conscious effort to keep your mind on what the speaker is saying. Fourth, try not to be diverted by appearance or delivery. Set aside preconceived judgments based on a person's looks or manner of speech.

Fifth, suspend judgment until you have heard the speaker's entire message—even if you think you are going to disagree. Sixth, focus your listening by paying attention to main points, to evidence, and to the speaker's techniques. Finally, develop your note-taking skills. When done properly, note taking is an excellent way to improve your concentration and to keep track of a speaker's ideas. It almost forces you to become a more attentive and creative listener.

Key Terms

hearing (56)

listening (56)

appreciative listening (57)

empathic listening (57)

comprehensive listening (57)

critical listening (58)

spare "brain time" (58)

active listening (64)

key-word outline (69)

Review these terms by doing the Chapter 3 crossword puzzle at www.mhhe.com/lucas8.

ONLINE LEARNING CENTER

Review Questions

After reading this chapter, you should be able to answer the following questions:

1. What is the difference between hearing and listening?

2. How is listening connected with critical thinking?

3. Why is it important to develop strong listening skills?

4. What are the four main causes of poor listening?

5. What are seven ways to become a better listener?

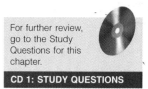

For further review, go to the Study Questions for this chapter.

CD 1: STUDY QUESTIONS

Exercises for Critical Thinking

1. Which of the four causes of poor listening do you consider the most important? Choose a specific case of poor listening in which you were involved. Explain what went wrong.

2. Using the Listening Self-Evaluation form on page 63, undertake a candid evaluation of your major strengths and weaknesses as a listener. Explain what steps you need to take to become a better listener.

3. Watch the lead story this week on "60 Minutes," "20/20," or another news magazine program. Using the key-word method of note taking, record the main ideas of the story.

4. Choose a lecture in one of your other classes. Analyze what the lecturer does most effectively. Identify three things the lecturer could do better to help students keep track of the lecture.

Cross Reference

For discussion of the Exercises for Critical Thinking, see the *Instructor's Manual*, pp. 112–113. For additional exercises, check the *Instructor's Manual*, pp. 114–116, as well as the five volumes of *Selections from the Speech Communication Teacher* that accompany *The Art of Public Speaking*.

Notes

[1]Larry Barker and Kittie Watson, *Listen Up* (New York: St. Martin's Griffin, 2000), p. 5.

[2]Michael P. Nichols, *The Lost Art of Listening* (New York: Guilford, 1995).

[3]Quoted in Ralph G. Nichols and Leonard A. Stevens, *Are You Listening?* (New York: McGraw-Hill, 1957), p. 141.

[4]Beverly Davenport Sypher, Robert N. Bostrom, and Joy Hart Seibert, "Listening, Communication Abilities, and Success at Work," *Journal of Business Communication,* 26 (1989), pp. 293–303.

[5]See the studies cited by Andrew D. Wolvin and Carolyn Gwynn Coakley, "A Survey of the Status of Listening Training in Some Fortune 500 Corporations," *Communication Education,* 40 (1991), p. 153.

[6]Wolvin and Coakley, "Survey of the Status of Listening Training," pp. 152–162.

[7]Carolyn Coakley and Andrew Wolvin, "Listening in the Educational Environment," in Deborah Borisoff and Michael Purdy (eds.), *Listening in Everyday Life: A Personal and Professional Approach,* 2nd ed. (Lanham, MD: University Press of America, 1997), pp. 163–164.

[8]Andrew W. Wolvin and Carolyn Gwynn Coakley, *Listening,* 5th ed. (Dubuque, IA: Brown and Benchmark, 1995), pp. 223–396.

[9]Mortimer J. Adler, *How to Speak, How to Listen* (New York: Macmillan, 1983), pp. 85–86.

[10]For more on this point, see Virginia O'Keefe, *Developing Critical Thinking: The Speaking/Listening Connection* (Portsmouth, NH: Boynton/Cook, 1999).

[11]Florence I. Wolff and Nadine C. Marsnik, *Perceptive Listening,* 2nd ed. (Fort Worth, TX: Harcourt Brace Jovanovich, 1992), p. 66.

[12]Louis Nizer, *My Life in Court* (New York: Doubleday, 1961), pp. 297–298.

[13]Adapted from Lyman K. Steil, Larry L. Barker, and Kittie W. Watson, *Effective Listening* (Reading, MA: Addison-Wesley, 1983).

[14]For an excellent discussion of this and other aspects of effective listening, see Patricia Scileppi Krivanek, *How Then Shall We Live: Values for Interpersonal Communication* (New York: McGraw-Hill, 2000), pp. 56–99.

[15]George H. Putnam, *Abraham Lincoln* (New York: Putnam, 1909), pp. 44–45.

[16]M. Scott Peck, *The Road Less Traveled: A New Psychology of Love, Traditional Values, and Spiritual Growth,* 2nd ed. (New York: Touchstone Books, 1998), p. 127.

[17]Tess Canja, "Breaking Through: A New Age of Health for Women," *Vital Speeches,* 74 (2001), pp. 390–395.

[18]Nichols and Stevens, *Are You Listening?,* pp. 113–114.

[19]For a recent study that confirms the multiple benefits of note taking, see B. Scott Titsworth, "The Effects of Teacher Immediacy, Use of Organizational Lecture Cues, and Students' Notetaking on Cognitive Learning," *Communication Education,* 50 (2001), 283–297.

APPENDIX
Giving Your First Speech

Preparing Your Speech

Developing the Speech

Organizing the Speech

Delivering Your Speech

Speaking Extemporaneously

Rehearsing the Speech

Presenting the Speech

Sample Speeches with Commentary

Y ou may be surprised to learn that one of your first assignments is to give a speech. You say to yourself, "What am I going to do? I have barely started this course, yet I'm supposed to stand up in front of the whole class and give a speech! I've only read a few pages in the textbook, and I don't know much about public speaking. Where do I begin?"

If these are your thoughts, you aren't alone. Most beginning speech students have a similar reaction. Fortunately, giving your first speech sounds a lot harder than it is. The purpose of this appendix is to help you get started on preparing and delivering your speech.

Preparing Your Speech

Usually a brief, simple presentation, the first assignment is often called an ice-breaker speech because it is designed to "break the ice" by getting students up in front of the class as soon as possible. This is an important step because much of the anxiety associated with public speaking comes from a lack of experience giving speeches. Once you have broken the ice by giving a speech, you will feel less anxious and will have taken the first step on the road to developing sound public speaking habits that lead to confidence.

Developing the Speech

There are a number of possible assignments for the first speech. One is a speech of self-introduction that provides insight into the speaker's background, personality, beliefs, or goals. In other cases, students are asked to introduce a classmate, rather than themselves. Some instructors require yet a different kind of speech. No matter which you are assigned, be sure to focus your presentation sharply so it conforms to the assigned time limit. One of the most common mistakes students make on their first speech is trying to cover too much material. You should select a limited number of points and illustrate them clearly.

Speech Assignment
For several approaches to the first speech assignment, see the *Instructor's Manual,* pp. 30–33. Also see the entries under "Speech Assignments—Introductory/ Ice Breaker Speeches" in the five volumes of *Selections from the Speech Communication Teacher* that accompany *The Art of Public Speaking.*

It would be impossible, for example, to tell your audience everything about your life in a two- or three-minute speech. A better approach would be to focus on one or two major events that have helped define who you are—competing in the state track meet, volunteering to tutor disadvantaged children, getting your first job, and the like. This allows you to make a few well-developed points about a clearly defined subject.

On the other hand, avoid the temptation to narrow the focus of your topic too much. Few listeners would be pleased to hear a two- or three-minute discussion of advanced trumpet-playing techniques. Such a speech would be too specialized for most classroom audiences.

Once you have a topic for your speech, be creative in developing it. Think of ways to make your presentation mysterious or suspenseful. Suppose you are telling the audience about your "brush with greatness," in which you met a celebrity, visited a famous place, or participated in a newsworthy event. Rather than identifying the celebrity at the outset, you might save his or her name for the end of your speech. As your story unfolds, tantalize your classmates with clues about your celebrity's gender, physical characteristics, special talents, and the like, but keep the name a secret until the last moment. The idea is to hold your classmates on the edges of their seats as they listen.

In addition to mystery and suspense, audiences are naturally interested in dangerous situations, adventure, and drama. If your task is to introduce a fellow student, find out if she or he has ever been in danger. Suppose your classmate went on a white-water rafting expedition and fell overboard. The story of how this person was rescued would be very dramatic. Or perhaps you spent a year in Africa with the Peace Corps. The details of such an adventure would make excellent material for a speech of self-introduction.

If you think about it, every person has faced risk, done the unusual, or triumphed over hardship. Try to find ways to include such fascinating experiences in your speech.

You can also make your speech interesting by using colorful, descriptive language. One speaker used this technique when introducing a fellow student, named Reva, to the class. The speaker began by saying:

> Drawers pulled open. Clothes scattered all over the floor. A little girl with white blonde curls is digging through her father's chest of drawers. "At last," she exclaims. "I found you." She pulls the expensive European cigars out from the drawer and holds them triumphantly in the sun. Little Reva was not going to let her father ruin his health. Without hesitation, she hoists the cigars out the open window and skips out of the room.

This speaker could have said, "When she was young, our classmate Reva threw her father's cigars out the window because she didn't want him to smoke." Instead, the speaker painted a word picture so her listeners could visualize the chest of drawers, the scattered clothes, the little girl's blonde curls, and the expensive European cigars. Colorful and concrete illustrations like this are always more interesting than dull language and abstract generalizations.

You might wonder whether you should use humor to make your first speech entertaining. Audiences love witty remarks, jokes, and funny situations, but like anything else, humor is only effective when done well. It should flow naturally out of the speech content rather than being contrived. If you are not normally a funny person, you are better off giving a sincere, enthusiastic speech and leaving out the jokes. In no case should you include humor that involves obscenity, embarrasses individuals, or negatively stereotypes groups of people. The best kind of humor gently pokes fun at ourselves or at universal human foibles.

Organizing the Speech

Regardless of your topic, your speech will have three main parts—an introduction, a body, and a conclusion. Your first job in the introduction is to get the attention and interest of the audience. You can do this by posing a question, telling a story, making a startling statement, or opening with a

Teaching Tip
Because the aim of an ice breaker speech is to give students a brief, initial exposure to speaking in front of an audience in a low-risk situation, many instructors do not affix a grade to it. Others, having found that students take the speech more seriously if they know they are being graded, weight it at no more than 5 percent of the total class grade.

View the beginning of Kristin Berg, "A Family Tradition."

CD 1: VIDEO A1.1

quotation. The purpose of all these methods is to create a dramatic, colorful opening that will make your audience want to hear more.

For an excellent example, look at the speech excerpt on CD 1, Video A1.2. The speaker's assignment was to present a narrative about a significant experience in her life. This is how she began:

View the beginning of Gurpreet Paul, "Kiyomi and Me."

CD 1: VIDEO A1.2

> Her name was Kiyomi. She was a mysterious Japanese dancer. Last autumn I got to meet her. How, you ask. Well, actually, she was a character in a play. I met her the day I became her. That day was one of the happiest days of my life. I wanted that part so desperately it was all I could think about. Being Kiyomi was one of the most memorable experiences of my life.

After this introduction, the speaker's classmates were eager to hear more about Kiyomi and her role in the speaker's life.

In addition to gaining attention and interest, the introduction should orient your listeners toward the subject matter of your speech. In the longer speeches you will give later in the term, you will usually need to provide an explicit preview statement that identifies the main points to be discussed in the body of your speech. (For example, "Today I will inform you about the symptoms, causes, and treatment of hepatitis C." Or "This afternoon we will explore the problem of childhood obesity in the United States and look at some solutions to the problem.")

Because your introductory speech is so short, you may not need as detailed a preview statement. But you still need to give your audience a clear sense of the topic and purpose of your speech. Look back for a moment at the introduction about Kiyomi quoted earlier. Notice how it moves from arousing curiosity about the identity of Kiyomi to letting the audience know that the rest of the speech will focus on why "becoming" Kiyomi was one of the most significant experiences in the speaker's life. By the end of the introduction, there is no doubt about the topic of the speech. (Be sure to check with your instructor to see what kind of preview statement he or she prefers for the introductory speech.)

After getting the audience's attention and revealing your topic, you are ready to move into the body of your speech. In some speeches, the body seems to organize itself. If you have been assigned to tell a story about a significant experience in your life, you will relate the events in the order they occurred. The basic structure for such a speech is chronological: "This happened; then this happened; then this happened."

But not all speeches follow such a format. Suppose you have been asked to give a presentation introducing a classmate. You could organize the most important biographical facts about your subject in chronological order, but this might result in a dull, superficial speech: "In 1985 Alicia was born in Cleveland, attended King Elementary School from 1990 to 1997, and graduated from South High School in 2003."

A better way of structuring your remarks might be to discuss three of the most important aspects of Alicia's life, such as hobbies, career goals, and family. This is called the topical method of organization, which subdivides the speech topic into its natural, logical, or conventional parts. Although there are many other ways to organize a speech, your first presentation will probably use either chronological or topical order.

Regardless of the method of organization you use, remember to limit the number of main points in the body of your speech. If you have too many points, your audience will struggle to recognize the most important ideas. In a two-minute speech, you won't have time to develop more than two or three main points.

Once you have selected those points, make sure each one focuses on a single aspect of the topic. For example, if your first point concerns your classmate's hometown, don't introduce irrelevant information about her job or favorite music. Save this material for a separate point, or cut it from the speech altogether.

Try to make your main points stand out by introducing each with a transition statement. In a speech introducing a classmate, you might begin the first main point by saying:

> Erin's family moved a great deal throughout her childhood.

When you reach the second point, you might introduce it like this:

> Moving a lot led to Erin's outgoing nature and confidence in making friends. In fact, she has friends all around the world with whom she corresponds regularly over e-mail.

You have now let your audience know that the first main point is over and that you are starting the second one. The third main point might begin as follows:

> Corresponding with people all over the world is more than just a hobby for Erin, since she is majoring in international relations.

Transition statements such as these will help your audience keep track of your main ideas.

When you finish discussing your final point, you will be ready to move into your conclusion. You need to accomplish two tasks in this part of the speech. First, you should let the audience know you are about to finish your speech. Second, you should reinforce the major theme of the speech.

If possible, try to end on a dramatic, clever, or thought-provoking note. For example, in the speech whose introduction we looked at earlier, the student devoted the body of her speech to explaining how she won the role of Kiyomi and what happened when she performed the role on stage. Then, in her conclusion, she wrapped up by saying:

> I needed this experience to appreciate who I was. I realized that I should be myself and not long to be someone else. So what if I'm not the most graceful or feminine person? So what if I don't possess all the wonderful characteristics of Kiyomi? I am still me—not a character in a play. Yet by playing that character, I learned one of the most important lessons of my life. I learned that by becoming a woman who never was, I became proud of who I am.

The final lines bring the speech to a dramatic close and underscore why the experience of playing Kiyomi was so important to the speaker.

Videotape Supplement
To give students an overview of the speechmaking process before their first presentations, show them either *Be Prepared to Speak* (27 minutes) or *Speaking Effectively to One or One Thousand* (20 minutes), both of which are available as supplements to *The Art of Public Speaking*. Both tapes also provide helpful advice on dealing with stage fright.

View the ending of Gurpreet Paul, "Kiyomi and Me."
CD 1: VIDEO A1.3

Delivering Your Speech

Once you have selected a subject and organized the content into a clear structure, it is time to work on the delivery of your speech. Because this is your first speech of the term, no one expects you to give a perfectly polished presentation. Your aim is to do as well as possible while also laying a foundation you can build upon in later speeches. With this is mind, we'll look briefly at the extemporaneous method of speech delivery, the importance of rehearsing your speech, and some of the major factors to consider when speech day arrives.

Speaking Extemporaneously

Class Activity
On the day of the ice breaker speech, begin class by having your students move so they are all standing a foot or two away from the wall. Have them face the wall and deliver their speeches. All the students should speak at once, and they should speak just as they plan to when addressing the class. The immediate result is a couple minutes of garbled noise, but it does wonders to calm the students' nerves while also giving them a last-minute rehearsal of their speech. Don't tell students about this activity in advance—part of its effectiveness depends on the element of surprise. At first they will doubt whether you are serious, but once they go through the experience, they often ask to be able to do the same thing for later speeches.

You might be inclined, as are many beginning speakers, to write out your speech like an essay and read it word for word to your listeners. The other extreme is to prepare very little for the speech—to wing it by trusting to your wits and the inspiration of the moment. Neither approach is appropriate for your introductory talk. Reading your speech from a manuscript runs the risk of poor eye contact with the audience and a stiff, unenthusiastic delivery. On the other hand, ad-libbing is a recipe for disaster. The outcome is usually an aimless talk that either is embarrassingly short or rambles on far too long.

Most experts recommend speaking extemporaneously, which combines the careful preparation and structure of a manuscript presentation with the spontaneity and enthusiasm of an unrehearsed talk. Your aim in an extemporaneous speech is to plan your major points and supporting material without trying to memorize the precise language you will use on the day of the speech.

The extemporaneous method requires you to know the content of your speech quite well. In fact, when you use the extemporaneous method properly, you become so familiar with the substance of your talk that you need only a few brief notes to remind you of the points you intend to cover. The notes should consist of key words or phrases that jog your memory, rather than of complete sentences and paragraphs. This way, when you stand up in front of the audience, you will tell them what you know about the topic in your own words.

Prepare your notes by writing or printing key terms and phrases on index cards or sheets of paper. Some instructors require students to use index cards because they are small and unobtrusive, don't rustle or flop over, and can be held in one hand, which allows the speaker to gesture more easily. Other teachers recommend sheets of paper because you can get more information on them and because it is easier to print out computer files on paper. If you are unsure what your instructor prefers, be sure to ask well before your speech is due.

Whether you use index cards or sheets of paper, your notes should be large enough to decipher clearly at arm's length. Many experienced speakers prefer to double- or triple-space their notes because this makes it easier to see them at a glance during the speech. Write or print on one side only of the index card or paper, and use the fewest notes you can manage and still present the speech fluently and confidently.

You can see an example of extemporaneous delivery on CD 1, Video A1.4. The speaker, Katherine Hillman, is giving a speech of self-introduction using a personal object—in this case, a shoe—to explain something important about herself. As you view the excerpt from Katherine's speech, notice how her points are well planned, yet she is not tied to a manuscript. She walks away from the lectern, holds up her shoe, and points to things on it that reflect different aspects of her life. All the while, she speaks directly to her classmates and makes strong eye contact with them.

View an excerpt from Katherine Hillman, "A Mile in My Shoes."

CD 1: VIDEO A1.4

At first, it may seem very demanding to deliver a speech extemporaneously. In fact, you already have a great deal of experience using the extemporaneous method in everyday conversation. Do you read from a manuscript when you tell your friends an amusing story or relate the events of a trip or an unusual experience? Of course not. You recall the essential details of your story and tell the tale to different friends, on different occasions, using somewhat different language each time. You feel relaxed and confident with your friends, so you just tell them what is on your mind in a conversational tone. You should try to do the same thing in your speech.

Rehearsing the Speech

When you watch a truly effective extemporaneous speaker, the speech comes out so smoothly that it seems almost effortless. In fact, that smooth delivery is the result of a great deal of practice. As your speech course progresses, you will gain more experience and will become more comfortable delivering your speeches extemporaneously.

The first time you rehearse your introductory speech, however, you will probably struggle. Words may not come easily, and you may forget some things you planned to say. Don't become discouraged. Keep going and complete the speech as well as you can. Concentrate on gaining control of the ideas rather than on trying to learn the speech word for word. Every time you practice, you will get better and better.

For this approach to work, you must rehearse the speech out loud. Looking silently over your notes is not enough. Speaking the words aloud will help you master the content of your talk. Once you have a fairly good grasp of the speech, ask friends or family members to listen and to give constructive feedback. Don't be shy about asking. Most people love to give their opinion about something, and it's crucial that you rehearse with a live audience before presenting the speech in class.

As you practice, time your speech to make sure it is neither too long nor too short. Because of nerves, most people talk faster during their first speech than when they practice it. When you rehearse at home, make certain your speech runs slightly longer than the minimum time limit. That way, if your speaking rate increases when you get in front of your classmates, your speech won't end up being too short.

Don't be surprised if the timing of your speech varies somewhat as you practice. It would be a bad sign if your speech took exactly the same amount of time during each rehearsal, because that would indicate that you were reading it from manuscript or had memorized it verbatim.

Presenting the Speech

When it is your turn to speak, move to the front of the room and face the audience. Assume a relaxed but upright posture. Plant your feet a bit less than shoulder-width apart and allow your arms to hang loosely by your side. Arrange your notes before you start to speak. Then take a moment to look over your audience and to smile. This will help you establish rapport with your classmates from the start.

Once you are into the speech, feel free to use your hands to gesture, but don't worry overly about planning your gestures ahead of time. If you don't normally use your hands expressively during informal conversation, then you shouldn't feel compelled to gesture a lot during your speech. Whatever gestures you do use should flow naturally and spontaneously from your feelings.

Above all, don't let your gestures or bodily actions distract listeners from your message. Do your best to avoid nervous mannerisms such as twisting your hair, wringing your hands, shifting your weight from one foot to the other, rocking back and forth, tapping your fingers on the lectern, or jingling coins in your pockets. No matter how nervous you feel, try to appear calm and relaxed.

During your talk, look at your classmates as often as you can. One of the major reasons for speaking extemporaneously is to maintain eye contact with your audience. In your own experience, you know how much more impressive a speaker is when she or he looks at the audience while speaking.

If you have practiced the extemporaneous method of delivery and prepared your notes properly, you should be able to maintain eye contact with your audience most of the time. Be sure to look to the left and right of the room, as well as the center, and avoid the temptation to speak exclusively to one or two sympathetic individuals. When you are finished speaking, your classmates should have the impression that you established a personal connection with each of them.

Try to use your voice as expressively as you would in normal conversation. Concentrate on projecting to the back of the room. Unless you see your classmates cringing and covering their ears, you will probably not be too loud. Despite your nerves, fight the temptation to race through your speech. If you make a conscious effort to speak up, slow down, and project clearly, you will be on the right track to an effective presentation.

Look, for example, at CD 1, Video A1.5, which presents excerpts from two ice breaker speeches given by students at the University of Wisconsin. Neither student had taken a public speaking class before, yet both rose to the occasion by focusing on the basic elements of delivery we have just discussed. As you watch the video, notice how both—despite their nervousness—convey a sense of poise and confidence, establish strong eye contact with their classmates, and use the extemporaneous method of delivery to communicate personably and expressively. Work on doing the same in your first speech.

Finally, as we saw in Chapter 1, remember that it's normal to be nervous before delivering a speech. You can deal with your nerves by preparing thoroughly, thinking positively, and visualizing yourself giving a successful speech. If you have butterflies in your stomach before delivering your speech, sit quietly in your chair and take several slow, deep breaths.

Teaching Tip
Be sure to have students applaud after each of their classmates' ice breaker speeches. If you have time in class to discuss the speeches after they are presented, be sure to keep the discussion low-key. Because students are especially anxious at the start of the term, take care to avoid negative comments about delivery. Do all you can to create a supportive atmosphere so students will feel comfortable as they work on their future speeches.

View excerpts from Sakhouy Lay, "My Eye on the World," and Bekah Diehl, "The Rare Phobia."

CD 1: VIDEO A1.5

You can help reduce your tension by tightening and relaxing your leg muscles, or by squeezing your hands together and then releasing them. Keep in mind that while you may be anxious about giving your speech, usually your nervousness will not be visible to your audience.

All the topics discussed in this appendix are developed in much more detail in the rest of this book. As the course progresses, you will acquire more knowledge about how to prepare and present a speech, and you will gain experience as a speaker.

For now, keep your introductory assignment in perspective. Remember that neither your audience nor your instructor expects perfection. You are not a professional speaker, and this is the first speech of the class. Do your best on the assignment and have fun with it. Plan what you want to say, organize the material clearly, practice thoroughly, and use the extemporaneous method of delivery. You may be surprised by how much you enjoy giving your first speech.

Sample Speeches with Commentary

The following speeches were presented by students in beginning speech classes at the University of Wisconsin. The first is a speech of self-introduction; the second is a speech introducing a classmate. As you read the speeches, notice how clearly they are organized and how creatively they are developed.

View Bekah Diehl "The Rare Phobia," and Mike Davis II "Steady and True."

CD 2: FULL SPEECH

The Rare Phobia

Commentary	Speech

Bekah Diehl

Beginning with a series of statements about different kinds of phobias helps the speaker gain attention and arouses curiosity about where the speech will go next. The specific details make the introduction much more effective than if the speaker had simply said, "Lots of people suffer from phobias."

Everyone in the world today suffers from some kind of fear. However, about 4 to 5 percent experience a more severe form of fear known as phobias. Some of the most common phobias are claustrophobia, agoraphobia, which is the fear of public spaces, and arachnophobia, the fear of spiders. Then there are the more uncommon phobias—such as peladophobia, the fear of bald people, or geniophobia, the fear of chins. There is even a name for the fear of Friday the 13th—paraskevidekatriaphobia.

The speaker completes her introduction by revealing her particular phobia—the fear of baseballs. As you can see from CD 1: Video A1.5, she presents her ideas with strong eye contact and excellent vocal variety.

According to the latest count, there was a total of 530 named phobias. However, my particular phobia is so rare that it doesn't even have a name. It is simply called the fear of baseballs. That's right, you heard me, the fear of baseballs. I know it sounds stupid, but it's true. I am terrified of baseballs. Even holding one in my hand sends shivers down my spine.

The speaker begins the body of her speech by clarifying the nature of her fear of baseballs.

People don't understand this. They do not understand that this is a real fear. I know it's been said that the only thing to fear is fear itself. But that's not true. I'm not scared of being scared of baseballs. I'm scared of the ball itself—the hard, round object that is usually flying fast through the air.

This paragraph presents the first of two narratives in the body of the speech and illustrates the seriousness of the speaker's aversion to baseballs.

But some people will fight to the death with me about this. For example, just this weekend I was at my friends' apartment and they found out that I have an extreme fear of baseballs. So what do they do? They decide they're going to help cure me of this fear by playing catch with the ball over my head. I get so scared that I have to leave the room and sit on the stairway. And believe me, this is not the first time something like this has happened.

The speaker's second narrative explains how she acquired her fear of baseballs. As in the previous paragraph, she tells her story clearly and engagingly.

You may be wondering how I acquired this phobia. I was about four years old and on a tee-ball team. I was just learning, so my catching skills weren't quite as good as they needed to be. Then, one day at practice, some guy threw a ball at me as hard as he could. He hit me directly in the head and knocked me out cold. Needless to say, I didn't stick with the sport, and ever since I've been scared to death of baseballs.

This paragraph provides an important clarification about the speaker's fear of baseballs and helps lead into her conclusion.

Now it's not like I hate the sport of baseball. I'm a huge Chicago Cubs fan—I can just never attend the games in person.

The speaker begins her conclusion by referring briefly to incidents discussed in the body of her speech. She then wraps everything up by returning to some of the phobias cited in her introduction. The last line is consistent with the lighthearted tone of the speech as a whole.

In conclusion, my unusual fear of baseballs is something real that I have to live with. And while it is inconvenient at times—like when I can't attend the Cubs' games or occasionally have to leave social situations—I take comfort in the fact that at least I'm not afraid of bald people, or public places, or spiders, or even Friday the 13th. So I suppose it could be worse.

Steady and True

Commentary	Speech

Mike Davis II

This paragraph serves as the speaker's introduction. The opening lines get attention by relating to the audience. They also present a creative image—the middle lane divider—that the speaker will return to as a unifying theme throughout the speech. The final sentence identifies the subject of the speech and connects it to the image of the lane divider.

As you hit the road with your best friend on a trip cross country in an old convertible, you see so many different sights that it's easy to overlook the one constant that is always in the same place and is always there. The lane divider is always present—dead center in the middle of the road. Our classmate Beth Michalski fits right in the middle—just like the lane divider.

The speaker begins the body of his speech by presenting information about Beth's parents and siblings. Just as Beth was born in the middle, the speaker says, she usually sticks to the middle of the road when having fun. This continues the theme advanced in the introduction and provides a creative framework for the ideas discussed in this paragraph.

The speaker focuses on Beth's love for volleyball. He relates that love to the thirst one might experience driving down an open road on a hot day. He then compares Beth's experience playing volleyball in high school to the way the lines move faster as one speeds up while driving down the road.

The speaker finishes his discussion of Beth's interest in volleyball by explaining how her "thirst" for the game (mentioned in the previous paragraph) was balanced in college by her "hunger" for academic success.

Continuing the imagery he uses throughout the speech, the speaker talks about the "road" Beth followed in deciding to attend the University of Wisconsin.

The speaker notes Beth's dream of becoming an interior designer in a city such as New York. He then concludes by returning to the imagery of the middle lane divider. All in all, this speech is an excellent example of how one can use creativity to craft an interesting first speech.

Beth was born right between her older sister Katie and her younger brother Max, by her parents Carol and Phil. Perhaps it is not surprising, then, that when it comes to having fun, Beth usually sticks to the middle of the road. Even though she is a shy person, she loves to goof around and have a good time. She loves any water sport, whether it's waterskiing, swimming, or riding a wave runner, but she won't take it to the extreme by bungee jumping or skydiving. On the other hand, you won't catch Beth sitting around all day turning into a couch potato.

In fact, one of Beth's favorite activities is playing competitive volleyball. Her love for this game gives her a thirst comparable to the one you would get if you were on the open road on a hot day. And when you speed up while driving on the road, the lines speed faster too. This same thing happened to Beth while she played varsity volleyball in high school for three years—the competition increased, and so did her level of play.

She loves the game and plays with a fierce passion, but she knows it's not everything in life. She thought long and hard about whether she was going to play here at the university, but her thirst for the game was conquered by her hunger to achieve academic success, and so she decided to focus solely on her schoolwork.

Beth followed a road to college that was already paved and, to her, very familiar. She was born and raised here in Madison, Wisconsin, and she attended Edgewood High School, where she was a superb student. When it came time for college, she chose to stay close to home and attend the University of Wisconsin.

But just because Beth's going to college close to home doesn't mean she will never move in another direction. She aspires to become an interior decorator and designer in a large city such as New York. While there is no way to know whether she will in fact achieve this dream one day, we can all be sure that as Beth travels down the road of her life, she will be steady and constant as that middle lane divider.

Chapter Four

SELECTING A TOPIC AND PURPOSE

s you read through this book, you will find examples of hundreds of speeches that were delivered in classrooms, in the political arena, in community and business situations. Here is a very small sample of the topics they cover:

Undoubtedly you noticed that the list runs from A to Z. This array of topics wasn't planned. It happened naturally in the course of presenting many different kinds of speeches. The list is given here simply to show you that there are literally endless possibilities for speech topics—from A to Z.

Choosing a Topic

The first step in speechmaking is choosing a topic. For speeches outside the classroom this is seldom a problem. Usually the speech topic is determined by the occasion, the audience, and the speaker's qualifications. When Condoleeza Rice lectures on a college campus, she is invited to speak about foreign policy and current events. Carly Fiorina will discuss women and business leadership. Roger Ebert might share his views about the latest in filmmaking. The same is true of ordinary citizens. The doctor is asked to inform high-school athletes and their parents about sport injuries, the head of a neighborhood coalition speaks about zoning regulations, the florist discusses how to grow thriving houseplants.

In a public speaking class the situation is different. Most of your speech assignments will not come with a designated topic. Students generally have great leeway in selecting subjects for their speeches. This would appear to be an advantage, since it allows you to talk about matters of personal interest. Yet there may be no facet of speech preparation that causes more gnashing of teeth than selecting a topic.

Chapter Focus
With this chapter, students begin the process of speech preparation. The chapter opens by exploring several strategies for selecting a speech topic. After discussing the general purpose of a speech, it looks closely at how to determine and phrase the specific purpose. It concludes by explaining how to develop a well-worded central idea. For a full outline of the chapter, see the *Instructor's Manual*, pp. 122–124.

topic
The subject of a speech.

When you look for a speech topic, keep in mind special expertise you may have or sports, hobbies, travel, and other personal experiences that would make for an interesting presentation.

It is a constant source of amazement to teachers that students who regularly chat with their friends about almost any subject under the sun become mentally paralyzed when faced with the task of deciding what to talk about in their speech class. Fortunately, once you get over this initial paralysis, you should have little trouble choosing a good topic.

There are two broad categories of potential topics for your classroom speeches: (1) subjects you know a lot about and (2) subjects you want to know more about. Let's start with the first.

Topics You Know a Lot About

Most people speak best about subjects with which they are most familiar. When thinking about a topic, you draw on your own knowledge and experience. You may think to yourself, "That's impossible. I've never done anything fascinating. My life is too ordinary to interest other people." Everyone knows things or has done things that can be used in a speech.

Think for a moment about unusual experiences you may have had. Think also about special knowledge or expertise you may have acquired. You are bound to come up with something. One student, who grew up in Pakistan, presented a fascinating speech about daily life in that country. Another used her knowledge as a jewelry store salesperson to prepare a speech on how to judge the value of cut diamonds. A third student, who had lived through a tornado, gave a gripping speech about that terrifying experience.

Too dramatic? Nothing in your life is as interesting? Yet another student, who described herself as "just a housewife who is returning to school to finish the education she started 20 years ago," delivered a witty and highly entertaining speech on the adjustments she had to make in coming back to college. This speaker talked about the strange feelings of sitting in class with

Class Activity
Ask students to divide a sheet of paper into two columns: "Things I Know About" and "Things I'd Like to Learn More About." After giving students a few minutes to write potential topics in each column, have them share their ideas with the class. Not only does this activity help students generate subjects for their own speeches, but they are often aided by hearing the results of their classmates' brainstorming.

students young enough to be her children, the difficulty of balancing her academic work against her family commitments, and the satisfaction of completing the education she had begun years earlier.

Here are a few more examples of speech topics based largely on the students' personal knowledge and experience:

Hong Kong: City of Paradox

The Basics of Backpacking

Making a Difference: The Peace Corps

A Tour of Old Jerusalem

Jai Alai: The World's Fastest Sport

Scuba Diving: A New World Under Water

Performing with the Native American Dance Troupe

Diabetes: You Can Live with It

How to Have a Successful Job Interview

Topics You Want to Know More About

On the other hand, you may decide to make your speech a learning experience for yourself as well as for your audience. You may choose a subject about which you already have some knowledge or expertise but not enough to prepare a speech without doing additional research. You may even select a topic that hasn't touched you at all before but that you want to explore. Say, for example, you've always been interested in extrasensory perception but never knew much about it. This would be a perfect opportunity to research a fascinating subject and turn it into a fascinating speech.

Or suppose you run across a subject in one of your other classes that catches your fancy. Why not investigate it further for your speech class? One student used this approach to develop a speech on the use of edible insects as a human food source. After hearing about the topic in a biology lecture, the student checked with his professor for additional readings, which he was able to find in the library. As it turned out, the professor was an internationally known expert on the role of insects as a food source, so the student also arranged an interview with the professor. (See Chapter 6 for information on conducting a research interview.) Using what he learned in his research, the student put together a captivating speech that kept everyone's attention from beginning to end.

Still another possibility—especially for persuasive speeches—is to think of subjects about which you hold strong opinions and beliefs. Imagine you are at dinner with a friend and find yourself arguing that television broadcasters should not report the projected results of presidential elections until polls have closed throughout the country. Why not give a speech in class on the same topic? Or suppose you believe your school should set up a program to help reduce burglaries on campus. Why not try to convince your classmates and get them to petition for such a program?

View an excerpt from Chinaka Steady, "Edible Insects."

CD 1: VIDEO 4.1

Like everyone else, you surely have issues about which you care deeply. They may include national or international concerns such as gun control, protection of the environment, or the threat of terrorism. Or perhaps you are closely involved in a local issue, such as a teachers' strike, the campaign for mayor, or a proposal to increase tuition. Not all such topics must be "political." They can deal with anything from graduation requirements to helping people with physical disabilities, from vegetarianism to preserving a nature sanctuary, from dormitory regulations to building a church recreation center.

Brainstorming for Topics

After all this, you may still be thinking, "I *don't* care about edible insects. I've *never* been to Pakistan. I'm *not* active in politics. WHAT am I going to talk about?" If you are having trouble selecting a topic, there are a number of brainstorming procedures you can follow to get started.

brainstorming
A method of generating ideas for speech topics by free association of words and ideas.

Personal Inventory

First make a quick inventory of your experiences, interests, hobbies, skills, beliefs, and so forth. Jot down anything that comes to mind, no matter how silly or irrelevant it may seem. From this list may come a general subject area out of which you can fashion a specific topic. This method has worked for many students.

Clustering

If the first method doesn't work, try the second. It's a technique called clustering. Take a sheet of paper and divide it into nine columns as follows: People, Places, Things, Events, Processes, Concepts, Natural Phenomena, Problems, and Plans and Policies. Then list in each column the first five or six items that come to mind. The result might look like this:

People	**Places**	**Things**
Colin Powell	Iraq	robots
Hillary Clinton	Mexico City	cell phones
George W. Bush	Grand Canyon	cartoons
my family	San Francisco	dream catchers
Mia Hamm	Alcatraz	Bible
Oscar de la Hoya	my hometown	mosques

Events	**Processes**
September 11, 2001	learning CPR
Passover	cooking Thai food
Chinese New Year	avoiding credit card debt
raves	taking photographs
Cinco de Mayo	studying abroad

Class Activity
Using the method of clustering, lead a class brainstorming session designed to generate 50 potential speech topics in as short a time as possible. Write the topics on the chalkboard and have the class identify those on which they would particularly like to hear speeches.

Concepts	Natural Phenomena
Afrocentrism	earthquakes
medical ethics	hurricanes
conservatism	global warming
free-speech theories	asteroids
Confucianism	lightning

Problems	Plans and Policies
terrorism	homeland security
airline security	protecting civil liberties
racial profiling	ballistic fingerprinting
identity theft	domestic partner benefits
campus crime	school vouchers
illegal business practices	building a new library

Class Activity
To help your students generate speech topics about which they truly care, have them complete the following sentences on a sheet of paper: "I feel really angry when . . . ," "It's unfair that . . . ," "The world would be better off if . . . ."

Very likely, several items on your lists will strike you as potential topics. If not, take the items you find most intriguing and compose sublists for each. Try to free-associate. Write down a word or idea. What does that trigger in your mind? Whatever it is, write that down next, and keep going until you have six or seven ideas on your list. For example, working from the lists printed above, one student composed sublists for cartoons, campus crime, and lightning:

Teaching Tip
Some students are inclined to put off deciding on a subject for their speeches until they find the "perfect" topic. But, of course, there is no such thing. The key to any speech is not the choice of topic per se, but how well the speaker develops the topic. Encourage your students to think carefully about their topics, but also remind them that they must choose a topic expeditiously and get to work as quickly as possible on researching and developing the speech itself.

Cartoons	Campus Crime	Lightning
television	vandalism	thunder
movies	police	noise
Academy Awards	fingerprints	traffic
prizes	hands	air pollution
lotteries	gloves	gasoline
gambling	cold weather	motorcycles

Can you follow her trail of association? In the first column cartoons made her think of television. Television reminded her of movies. Movies suggest the Academy Awards. The Academy Awards are prizes. Prizes reminded her of lotteries. Lotteries are a form of gambling. Suddenly, this student remembered a magazine article she had read on the growing problem of gambling addiction in America. The idea clicked in her mind. After considerable research she developed an excellent speech entitled "Gambling Addiction: Why You Can't Beat the Odds."

That's a far cry from cartoons! If you started out free-associating from cartoons, you would doubtless end up somewhere completely different. This is what clustering is all about.

Reference Search

By clustering, most people are able to come up with a topic rather quickly. But if you are still stymied, don't despair. There is a third technique you can use. Go to the reference room of the library and browse through an encyclopedia, a periodical database, or some other reference work until you stumble across what might be a good speech topic. As an experiment, one student decided to scan the CD-ROM version of *The American Heritage Dictionary,* limiting herself to the letter *b*. Within 10 minutes she had come up with these potential topics:

Bible	bonsai	Baja California	bar mitzvah
backpacking	blackjack	Braille	backgammon
Bill of Rights	bioethics	bicycle	Beatles
ballet	Beethoven	Beijing	beer
beta-carotene	birthstones	botulism	Buddhism

With proper research and development, any one of these could make an excellent speech.

Internet Search

Yet another possibility is to connect to a subject-based search engine, such as Yahoo or the Librarians' Index to the Internet. You will see a screen much like the one in Figure 4.1, which lists the major categories of subjects indexed

Teaching Tip
For two interesting approaches to selecting speech topics, see Hollis F. Glaser, "Focusing the Students on Three Speech Topics," and Loren O. Murfield, "Generating Interest and Community Involvement in Student Speeches," in *Selections from the Speech Communication Teacher, 1996–1999*, pp. 17, 83–84, which accompanies *The Art of Public Speaking.*

Cross-Reference
See Chapter 6, pp. 147–157, for full discussion of how to use Yahoo and other Internet tools in speech research.

Web Site Directory - Sites organized by subject

Business & Economy
B2B, Finance, Shopping, Jobs...

Computers & Internet
Internet, WWW, Software, Games...

News & Media
Newspapers, TV, Radio...

Entertainment
Movies, Humor, Music...

Recreation & Sports
Sports, Travel, Autos, Outdoors...

Health
Diseases, Drugs, Fitness, Medicine...

Government
Elections, Military, Law, Taxes...

Regional
Countries, Regions, US States...

Society & Culture
People, Environment, Religion...

Education
College and University, K-12...

Arts & Humanities
Photography, History, Literature...

Science
Animals, Astronomy, Engineering...

Social Science
Languages, Archaeology, Psychology...

Reference
Phone Numbers, Dictionaries, Quotations...

Buzz Index - **Yahoo! Picks** - **New Additions** - **Full Coverage**

powered by *hp*

Figure 4.1

> - **Yahoo! Health**
>
> ---
>
> **Categories**
>
> - **Alternative Medicine** *(594)*
> - **Children's Health** *(228)* New!
> - **Death and Dying** @
> - **Dentistry** @
> - **Disabilities** @
> - **Diseases and Conditions** *(10214)* New!
> - **Emergency Services** *(585)*
> - **Employment** *(117)*
> - **Environmental Health** *(213)*
> - **Fitness** *(159)*
> - **General Health** *(101)*
> - **Health Care** *(318)*
> - **Hospitals and Medical Centers** *(46)*
> - **Institutes** *(35)*
> - **Medicine** *(5193)* New!
>
> - **Men's Health** *(48)* New!
> - **Mental Health** *(864)* New!
> - **Nursing** *(489)*
> - **Nutrition** *(374)*
> - **Organizations** *(22)*
> - **Pet Health** @
> - **Pharmacy** *(1592)*
> - **Procedures and Therapies** *(600)* New!
> - **Public Health and Safety** *(3814)* New!
> - **Reproductive Health** *(817)*
> - **Traditional Medicine** *(178)* New!
> - **Travel Health and Medicine** *(27)*
> - **Weight Issues** *(160)* New!
> - **Women's Health** *(206)* New!
> - **Workplace** *(71)*

Figure 4.2

Teaching Tip
You can also help students develop speech topics by encouraging them to keep abreast of current issues as they arise in the press. For one approach, see Susan Duffy, "Using News Magazines to Stimulate Topic Choices for Speeches," in *Selections from the Speech Communication Teacher, 1986–1991,* pp. 16–17, which accompanies *The Art of Public Speaking.*

by Yahoo. If you select one of those categories—say, Health—the next screen will show all subcategories indexed under that heading. The result will look something like Figure 4.2, which lists 30 subcategories for Health, any one of which might strike your fancy as a potential speech topic.

One of the advantages of using Yahoo as a brainstorming aid is that you can continue to make your search more and more specific until you find just the right topic. Suppose, for example, that as you look at the subheadings for Health, your attention is grabbed by the first item—Alternative Medicine. If you click on this item, you will get another screen with a detailed list of subheadings for Alternative Medicine. Working from that list, you can link up to other sites that will help you narrow and focus your topic even further. This process is much faster than leafing through reference works in the library, and it can be a great spur to thinking creatively about a topic.

Whatever the means you use for selecting a topic, *start early.* The major reason students have difficulty choosing speech topics is that, like most people, they tend to procrastinate—to put off starting projects for as long as possible. Since choosing a topic is your first step in the process of speech preparation, it is only natural to postpone facing up to it. But if you postpone it for too long, you may dig yourself into a hole from which you cannot escape.

Start thinking about your topic as soon as each assignment is announced. Pay attention to interesting subjects in class and conversation, on the radio and television, in newspapers and magazines. Jot down in your notebook ideas for topics as they occur to you. Having an inventory of possible topics to choose from is much better than having to rack your brain for one at the last minute. If you get an early start on choosing a topic, you will have plenty of time to pick just the right one and prepare a first-rate speech.

Determining the General Purpose

Along with choosing a topic, you need to determine the *general purpose* of your speech. Usually it will fall into one of two overlapping categories—to inform or to persuade.

When your general purpose is to *inform,* you act as a teacher or lecturer. Your goal is to convey information—and to do so clearly, accurately, and interestingly. If you describe how to lift weights, narrate the major events of the latest Middle East crisis, give an account of your trip to Spain, report on your sorority's financial position, or explain how the government's forest management plan works, you are speaking to inform. Your aim is to enhance the knowledge and understanding of your listeners—to give them information they did not have before.

general purpose
The broad goal of a speech.

When your general purpose is to *persuade,* you act as an advocate or a partisan. You go beyond giving information to espousing a cause. You want to *change* or *structure* the attitudes or actions of your audience. The difference between informing and persuading is the difference between explaining and exhorting. If you try to convince your listeners that they should start a regular program of weight lifting, that the United States should modify its policy in the Middle East, that more students should take advantage of the study-abroad program, that your sorority should start a fund-raising drive to balance its budget, or that the federal government should change its methods of forest management to reduce the incidence of forest fires—then you are speaking to persuade. In doing so, you cannot help but give information; but your primary goal is to win over your listeners to your point of view—to get them to believe something or do something as a result of your speech.

Cross-Reference
See Chapter 14 for full discussion of speaking to inform.

In speech classes, the general purpose is usually specified as part of the speech assignment. For speeches outside the classroom, however, you have to make sure of your general purpose yourself. Usually this is easy to do. Are you going to explain, report, or demonstrate something? Then your general purpose is to inform. Are you going to sell, advocate, or defend something? Then your general purpose is to persuade. But no matter what the situation, you must be certain of exactly what you hope to achieve by speaking. Knowing your general purpose is the first step. The next step is determining your specific purpose.

Cross-Reference
See Chapters 15–16 for full discussion of speaking to persuade.

Determining the Specific Purpose

Once you have chosen a topic and a general purpose, you must narrow your choices to determine the *specific purpose* of your speech. The specific purpose should focus on one aspect of a topic. You should be able to state your specific purpose in a single infinitive phrase (to inform my audience

specific purpose
A single infinitive phrase that states precisely what a speaker hopes to accomplish in his or her speech.

about . . . ; to persuade my audience to . . .) that indicates *precisely* what you hope to accomplish with your speech. Perhaps an example will help clarify the process of choosing a specific purpose.

Meg Fugate, a student at the University of Wisconsin, decided to give her first classroom speech on a topic from her personal experience. In her job as a lifeguard during the previous four summers, Meg had dealt with emergencies ranging from drownings to second-degree burns to heart attacks. Knowing that most people will face an emergency at some point in their lives, Meg wanted to share what she had learned with her classmates. This gave her a topic and a general purpose, which she stated this way:

Topic: Emergencies

General Purpose: To inform.

So far, so good. But what aspect of her topic would Meg discuss? The different kinds of emergencies? The emergency situations she had faced? Specific techniques such as water rescue, applying first aid, or preventing a person from going into shock? She had to choose something interesting that she could cover in a six-minute speech. Finally, she settled on explaining the major steps involved in responding to an emergency. She stated her specific purpose this way:

Specific Purpose: To inform my audience of the major steps in responding to an emergency.

This turned out to be an excellent choice, and Meg's speech was among the best in the class.

Notice how clear the specific purpose statement is. Notice also how it relates the topic directly to the audience. That is, it states not what the *speaker* wants to *say*, but what the speaker wants the *audience* to *know* as a result of the speech. This is very important, for it helps keep the audience at the center of your attention as you prepare the speech.

Look what happens when the specific purpose statement does not include the audience.

Specific Purpose: To explain the major steps in responding to an emergency.

Cross-Reference
Keeping one's audience in mind while formulating a specific purpose statement is just as important for a classroom speech as for a speech in any other setting. The nature of the classroom audience is discussed in more detail in Chapter 5, pp. 112–114.

Explain to whom? To a group of medical students? To an introductory Red Cross class? Those would be two different speeches. The medical students already know the basic facts about responding to an emergency. For them, the speaker might provide a more advanced discussion. But the people in the basic Red Cross class will not have anywhere near the knowledge of the medical students. To communicate effectively with them, the speaker will need to prepare a more general speech.

When the audience slips out of the specific purpose, it may slip out of the speaker's consciousness. You may begin to think your task is the general one of preparing "an informative speech," when in fact your task is the specific one of informing a particular group of people. This may seem like

Having trouble choosing a speech topic? Try browsing through the subject categories at the Librarians' Index to the Internet (www.lii.org). You will find a wealth of high-quality materials that can help get your creative juices flowing.

Another valuable website for anyone thinking about speech topics is www.britannica.com, which provides an electronic version of the *Encyclopaedia Britannica,* as well as hundreds of links to other resources.

You can link to these websites at www.mhhe.com/ lucas8.

ONLINE LEARNING CENTER

a small point right now, but as we shall see in the next chapter, it is almost impossible to prepare a good speech without keeping constantly in mind the *people* for whom it is intended.

Tips for Formulating the Specific Purpose Statement

Formulating a specific purpose is the most important early step in developing a successful speech. When writing your purpose statement, try to follow the general principles outlined below.

Write the Purpose Statement as a Full Infinitive Phrase, Not as a Fragment

Ineffective: Calendars.

More Effective: To inform my audience about the four major kinds of calendars used in the world today.

Ineffective: Stem cell research.

More Effective: To persuade my audience that the federal government should increase funding for stem cell research.

The ineffective statements above are adequate as announcements of the speech topic, but they are not thought out fully enough to indicate the specific purpose.

Express Your Purpose as a Statement, Not as a Question

Ineffective: What is Día le los Muertos?

More Effective: To inform my audience about the history of Mexico's Día de los Muertos celebration.

Ineffective: Is the U.S. space program necessary?

More Effective: To persuade my audience that the U.S. space program provides many important benefits to people here on earth.

Class Activity

The third Exercise for Critical Thinking at the end of this chapter is an excellent vehicle for helping students understand the differences between effective and ineffective specific purpose statements. For full discussion of the exercise, see the *Instructor's Manual,* p. 125.

The questions might make adequate titles, but they are not effective as specific purpose statements. They give no indication about what direction the speech will take or what the speaker hopes to accomplish.

Avoid Figurative Language in Your Purpose Statement

Overhead Transparency
For ease of classroom discussion, all the tips for formulating a specific purpose explained on pages 95–98 are included in the binder of full-color overhead transparencies that accompanies *The Art of Public Speaking*.

Ineffective: To inform my audience that yoga is extremely cool.

More Effective: To inform my audience how yoga can improve their health.

Ineffective: To persuade my audience that the campus policy on roller blading really stinks.

More Effective: To persuade my audience that the campus policy on roller blading should be revised.

Although the ineffective statements indicate something of the speaker's viewpoint, they do not state concisely what he or she hopes to achieve. Metaphors, analogies, and the like are effective devices for reinforcing ideas within a speech, but they are too ambiguous for specific purpose statements.

Limit Your Purpose Statement to One Distinct Idea

Ineffective: To persuade my audience to become literacy tutors and to donate time to Habitat for Humanity.

This purpose statement expresses two unrelated ideas, either of which could be the subject of a speech. The easiest remedy is to select one or the other as a focus for your presentation.

More Effective: To persuade my audience to become literacy tutors.

Or:

More Effective: To persuade my audience to donate time to Habitat for Humanity.

Teaching Tip
Determining the specific purpose may be the most important early step in the process of speech preparation. To help your students with this step, have them submit specific purpose statements well before the due dates for their speeches. You can provide feedback to students individually, or you can solicit feedback from the class as a whole.

Does this mean you can never use the word "and" in your specific purpose statement? Not at all. Suppose your specific purpose is "To inform my audience about the causes and effects of epilepsy." In this case, "and" is entirely appropriate because it connects two related parts of a unified topic. What you need to avoid is not simply the word "and," but a specific purpose statement that contains two unrelated ideas, either of which could easily be developed into a speech in its own right.

Make Sure Your Specific Purpose Is Not Too Vague or General

Ineffective: To inform my audience about the Civil War.

More Effective: To inform my audience about the role of African American soldiers in the Civil War.

You can turn to many resources when working on your speeches. Internet sites such as Yahoo can help you brainstorm for topics, as well as provide materials for developing the speech itself.

The ineffective purpose statement above falls into one of the most common traps—it is too broad and ill-defined. It gives no clues about what aspect of the Civil War the speaker will cover. The more effective purpose statement is sharp and concise. It reveals clearly what the speaker plans to discuss.

Here is another example, this time from a persuasive speech:

Ineffective: To persuade my audience that something should be done about medical care.

More Effective: To persuade my audience that the federal government should adopt a system of national health insurance for all people in the United States.

Again, the ineffective purpose statement is vague and indistinct. It gives no indication of the speaker's stance toward the topic. The "something" that "should be done" could include anything from clamping down on abuses by HMOs to reforming Medicare and Medicaid. The more effective purpose statement is crisp and clear. It does not leave us guessing what the speaker hopes to accomplish.

The more precise your specific purpose, the easier it will be to prepare your speech. Consider this topic and specific purpose:

Topic: Hot-air balloons.

Specific Purpose: To inform my audience about hot-air balloons.

With such a hazy purpose, you have no systematic way of limiting your research or of deciding what to include in the speech and what to exclude. The origins of hot-air balloons, how they work, their current popularity—all

Teaching Tip
It is especially important that students avoid broad and ill-defined specific purpose statements. Otherwise, they will have great difficulty focusing their research and deciding what to include in the speech and what to leave out. Remind students that formulating a sharp, tightly focused specific purpose statement will yield many benefits throughout the rest of the speech preparation process.

could be equally relevant to a speech designed "to inform my audience about hot-air balloons."

In contrast, look at this topic and specific purpose:

Topic: Hot-air balloons.

Specific Purpose: To inform my audience about the scientific uses of hot-air balloons.

The Specific Purpose Checklist can help you prepare your speeches.

CD 1: SPEECH CHECKLIST

Now it is easy to decide what is germane and what is not. The origins of hot-air balloons, how they work, their popularity for recreation—all are interesting, but none is essential to the specific purpose of explaining "the scientific uses of hot-air balloons." Thus you need not worry about researching these matters or about explaining them in your speech. You can spend your preparation time efficiently.

Questions to Ask About Your Specific Purpose

Sometimes you will arrive at your specific purpose almost immediately after choosing your topic. At other times you may do quite a bit of research before deciding on a specific purpose. Much will depend on how familiar you are with the topic, as well as on any special demands imposed by the assignment, the audience, or the occasion. But whenever you settle on your specific purpose, ask yourself the following questions about it.

Does My Purpose Meet the Assignment?

Students occasionally stumble over this question. Be sure you understand your assignment, and shape your specific purpose to meet it. If you have questions, check with your instructor.

Can I Accomplish My Purpose in the Time Allotted?

Teaching Tip
Make sure students are well aware of the time limits for their speeches. Decide how strictly you will enforce those limits, and state clearly what consequences students will incur for exceeding the limits. Also remind students that they need to rehearse their speeches fully to make sure they fit within the allotted time.

Most classroom speeches are quite short, ranging from four to ten minutes. That may seem like a lot of time if you have never given a speech before. But you will quickly find what generations of students have discovered, much to their surprise—time flies when you are giving a speech! Most people speak at an average rate of 120 to 150 words a minute. This means that a six-minute speech will consist of roughly 720 to 900 words. That is not long enough to develop a highly complex topic. Here are some specific purpose statements that would defy being handled well in the time normally allocated for classroom speeches:

To inform my audience about the role of technology in human history.

To inform my audience about the rise and fall of ancient Rome.

To persuade my audience to convert to Buddhism.

You are much better off with a limited purpose that you have some reasonable hope of achieving in the short span of four to ten minutes.

Is the Purpose Relevant to My Audience?

The price of retirement homes in Sun City might be an engrossing topic for older citizens who are in the market for such dwellings. And the quality of hot lunches in the elementary schools is of great concern to the students who eat them and the parents who pay for them. But neither subject has much relevance for an audience of college students. No matter how well you construct your speeches, they are likely to fall flat unless you speak about matters of interest to your listeners.

This is not to say you must select only topics that pertain *directly* to the college student's daily experience—the grading system, dormitory conditions, parking spaces on campus, and the like. Most students have wide-ranging backgrounds, interests, ideas, and values. And most of them are intellectually curious. They can get involved in an astonishing variety of subjects. Follow your common sense, and make sure *you* are truly interested in the topic. Also, when speaking on a subject that is not obviously relevant to your listeners, take time in your speech to tie the subject in with their goals, values, interests, and well-being. We'll discuss how to do this in the next chapter.

Is the Purpose Too Trivial for My Audience?

Just as you need to avoid speech topics that are too broad or complicated, so you need to steer clear of topics that are too superficial. How to build a fire without matches might absorb a group of Cub Scouts, but your classmates would probably consider it frivolous. Unfortunately, there is no absolute rule for determining what is trivial to an audience and what is not. Here are some examples of specific purposes that most people would find too trivial for classroom speeches:

Discussion Prompt
Sometimes students disagree about what might be considered trivial for a classroom speech. Have students generate their own examples of trivial topics and discuss those examples with the class.

> To inform my audience about the parts of a backpack.

> To inform my audience how to tie a bow tie.

> To persuade my audience that espresso is better than cappuccino.

Is the Purpose Too Technical for My Audience?

Nothing puts an audience to sleep faster than a dry and technical speech. Beware of topics that are inherently technical and of treating ordinary subjects in a technical fashion. Although you may be perfectly familiar with the principles and vocabulary of quantum physics, physical anthropology, molecular biology, clinical psychology, or constitutional law, most of your classmates probably are not. There are aspects of these and similar subjects that can be treated clearly, with a minimum of jargon. But if you find that you can't fulfill your specific purpose without relying on technical words and concepts, you should reconsider your purpose.

Here are some examples of specific purposes that are overly technical for most classroom speeches:

Discussion Prompt
Ask students if there are ways to develop technical topics into interesting and entertaining speeches. What methods—visual aids, comparisons, vivid language, etc.—can a speaker use to make technical information comprehensible and engaging?

> To inform my audience about the solution to Fermat's Last Theorem.

> To inform my audience about the principles of neutrino physics.

> To inform my audience about the methods of encryption technology.

We shall discuss the details of audience analysis and adaptation in Chapter 5. For the moment, remember to make sure that your specific purpose is appropriate for your listeners. If you have doubts, ask your instructor, or circulate a questionnaire among your classmates (see pages 127–130).

Phrasing the Central Idea

What Is the Central Idea?

central idea

A one-sentence statement that sums up or encapsulates the major ideas of a speech.

The specific purpose of a speech is what you hope to accomplish. The *central idea* is a concise statement of what you *expect to say*. Sometimes it is called the thesis statement, the subject sentence, or the major thought. Whatever the term, the central idea is usually expressed as a simple, declarative sentence that refines and sharpens the specific purpose statement.

Imagine you run into a friend on your way to speech class. She says, "I have to dash to my history lecture, but I hear you're giving a speech today. Can you tell me the gist of it in one sentence?" "Sure," you reply. "America's prison system suffers from three major problems—overcrowding of inmates, lack of effective rehabilitation programs, and high expense to taxpayers."

Your answer is the central idea of your speech. It is more precise than your topic (America's prison system) or your specific purpose statement ("To inform my audience of the three major problems facing America's prison system"). By stating exactly what the three major problems are, the central idea sums up your speech in a single sentence.

residual message

What a speaker wants the audience to remember after it has forgotten everything else in a speech.

Another way to think of the central idea is as your *residual message*—what you want your audience to remember after they have forgotten everything else in the speech. Most of the time the central idea will encapsulate the main points to be developed in the body of the speech. To show how this works, let's take a few of the examples we saw earlier in this chapter and develop them from the topic, general purpose, and specific purpose to the central idea.

We can start with the speech about responding to an emergency situation.

Topic: Emergencies.

General Purpose: To inform.

Specific Purpose: To inform my audience of the major steps in responding to an emergency.

Central Idea: The major steps in responding to an emergency are surveying the scene, contacting an emergency medical service, and starting CPR if needed.

View the introduction from Meg Fugate, "CPR."

CD 1: VIDEO 4.2

Look carefully at this example. It shows how the speaker might start with a broad subject (emergencies) that becomes narrower and narrower as the speaker moves from the general purpose to the specific purpose to the central idea. Notice also how much more the central idea suggests about the content of the speech. From it we can expect the speaker to develop three main points in the speech—each corresponding to one of the major steps in responding to an emergency.

This sharpening of focus as one proceeds to the central idea is crucial. Here is another example:

Topic: Día de los Muertos.

General Purpose: To inform.

Specific Purpose: To inform my audience about the history of Mexico's Día de los Muertos celebration.

Central Idea: Día de los Muertos can be traced to the Aztecs, was moved from summer to fall by Spanish priests, and today is celebrated in a number of ways in different regions of Mexico.

Teaching Tip
Explain that the central idea of a speech is essentially the same as the thesis statement in a written composition. I use the phrase "central idea" so as to distinguish the process of speech preparation from that of writing an essay.

This central idea is especially well worded. We can assume from it that the body of the speech will contain three main points—on the origins of Día de los Muertos among the Aztecs, on how it was changed by the Spanish, and on the ways it is celebrated today.

Much the same is true of the following example:

Topic: Alternative-fuel vehicles.

General Purpose: To persuade.

Specific Purpose: To persuade my audience that the federal government should speed up efforts to develop alternative-fuel vehicles.

Central Idea: Developing alternative-fuel vehicles will help reduce American dependence on foreign oil and will help reduce air pollution.

Class Activity
The fourth Exercise for Critical Thinking at the end of this chapter provides an excellent way to clarify the relationships among the general purpose, specific purpose, central idea, and main points of a speech. For variations on this exercise, see the Additional Exercises for Critical Thinking on pp. 128–132 of the *Instructor's Manual.*

From this central idea we can deduce that the speaker will develop two main points in the speech: (1) alternative-fuel vehicles have the potential to reduce America's need for imported oil, and (2) alternative-fuel vehicles will help reduce the air pollution caused by automobile and truck exhaust.

There is something else important about these examples. Notice in each case how much more the central idea reveals about the content of the speech than does the specific purpose. This is not accidental. Often you can settle on a specific purpose statement early in preparing your speech. The central idea, however, usually emerges later—after you have done your research and have decided on the main points of the speech. The process may work like this:

As an environmental science major, Marcia Esposito had learned that many experts fear the world may face a severe water shortage by the year 2020. She decided this would make a good topic for her informative speech. Tentatively, she adopted the following specific purpose statement: "To inform my audience about the seriousness of the growing international water crisis." Then Marcia started her research.

An article in *Newsweek,* which she located through ProQuest, explained how the population in countries such as China, Egypt, and Mexico is outstripping the available supply of fresh water. According to the article, one-third of the wells in Beijing, China's capital, have gone dry, and the water table in Mexico City is dropping at the rate of 11 feet per year.

Next Marcia found a report on the Worldwatch Institute website about the impact of pollution on the water supply. The report stated that, in many parts of the world, urban and industrial contamination is creating "a water supply too polluted for their people to drink."

Then Marcia hit upon the idea of interviewing one of her environmental science professors. In addition to confirming Marcia's research about the impact of population growth and pollution, the professor mentioned the problems caused by mismanagement of water supplies. Around the world 65 to 70 percent of the water people use is lost to waste, evaporation, and other inefficiencies; the rate in the United States is about 50 percent.

Marcia digested all this information. Now she was ready to formulate her central idea: "Population growth, pollution, and mismanagement are creating a serious shortage of fresh water in many parts of the world."

Guidelines for the Central Idea

What makes a well-worded central idea? Essentially the same things that make a well-worded specific purpose statement. The central idea should (1) be expressed in a full sentence, (2) should not be in the form of a question, (3) should avoid figurative language, and (4) should not be vague or overly general.

Here, for example, are four poorly written central ideas. See if you can identify the problem with each and figure out how each might be phrased more effectively:

Ineffective: Paying college athletes a salary is a good idea.

Ineffective: Problems of fad diets.

Ineffective: How does indoor soccer differ from outdoor soccer?

Ineffective: Mexico's Yucatán Peninsula is an awesome place for a vacation.

The first, of course, is too general. To say that paying college athletes a monthly salary is a "good idea" does not convey the speaker's viewpoint sharply and clearly. What does the speaker mean by a "good idea"? That paying athletes a monthly salary is justified given the millions of dollars generated for universities by sports such as football and basketball? That the salary should be paid to all athletes, or just to those in major revenue-producing sports? That the salary should be $250 a month? If so, the central idea should say as much. A revised central idea for this speech might be:

More Effective: Because college athletes in revenue-producing sports such as football and basketball generate millions of dollars in revenue for their schools, the NCAA should allow such athletes to receive a $250 monthly salary as part of their scholarships.

The second ineffective central idea is also too general, but it suffers further from not being written as a complete sentence. "Problems of fad diets" might work as a topic statement, but it does not reveal enough about the content

Teaching Tip

One of the points this chapter seeks to make is that speech preparation is a systematic process that includes consciously selecting a topic, narrowing the topic to an achievable specific purpose, and developing a central idea that reflects the main points developed in the body of the speech. Encourage students to become increasingly systematic in the choices they make as they work on their speeches throughout the course.

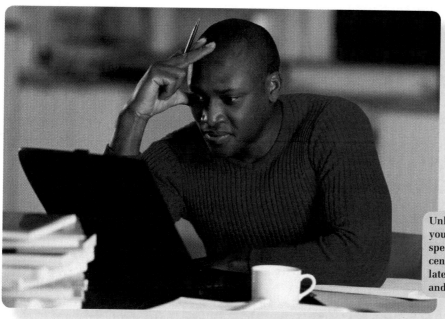

Unlike the specific purpose, which you need to settle on early in the speech preparation process, the central idea usually takes shape later, as a result of your research and analysis of the topic.

of the speech to serve as the central idea. It should be rewritten as a full sentence that identifies the problems of fad diets to be discussed in the speech:

More Effective: Although fad diets produce quick weight loss, they can lead to serious health problems by creating deficiencies in vitamins and minerals and by breaking down muscle tissue as well as fat.

The third poorly written central idea is phrased as a question rather than as a full declarative sentence. Asking "How does indoor soccer differ from outdoor soccer?" might be a good way to catch the interest of your listeners, but it does not encapsulate the main points to be developed in the speech. A more effective central idea would be:

More Effective: Played on a smaller, enclosed field that resembles a hockey rink with artificial turf, indoor soccer involves faster action, more scoring, and different strategies than outdoor soccer.

The final ineffective central idea is flawed by its use of figurative language. To say that the Yucatán Peninsula is an "awesome" place for a vacation does not state the speaker's central idea clearly and concisely. It does not indicate what characteristics of the Yucatán Peninsula the speaker intends to discuss. Moreover, "awesome" could mean quite different things to different people. A better central idea might be:

More Effective: Mexico's Yucatán Peninsula has many attractions for vacationers, including a warm climate, excellent food, and extensive Mayan ruins.

Overhead Transparency
For ease of classroom discussion, all the guidelines for phrasing a central idea are included in the binder of full-color overhead transparencies that accompanies *The Art of Public Speaking*.

The Central Idea Checklist can help you prepare your speeches.

CD 1: SPEECH CHECKLIST

Notice that in all these examples the more effective central idea encapsulates or sums up the main points of the speech in a single sentence. If you are having trouble phrasing your central idea, the reason may be that you do not yet have a firm grasp on the main points of your speech. Do not worry too much about your central idea until after you have developed the body of your speech (see Chapter 8). If, at that point, you still can't come up with a clear, concise central idea, it may be that your speech itself is not very clear or concise. Keep working on the speech until you can compose a central idea that fits the criteria just discussed. The result will be a sharper central idea and a tighter, more coherent speech.

Summary

The first step in speechmaking is choosing a topic. For classroom speeches it is often best to choose a subject you know well or in which you have personal experience, but you can also succeed with a topic you research especially for the speech. If you have trouble picking a topic, you can follow at least four brainstorming procedures. First, make a quick inventory of your hobbies, interests, skills, experiences, beliefs, and so forth. Second, use the technique of clustering and write down on a sheet of paper the first topics that come to mind in several categories. Third, look through a reference work for ideas. Fourth, use a World Wide Web subject directory such as Yahoo! to help you scan possible topics.

After you choose a topic, you need to settle on the general purpose of your speech. Usually the general purpose will be to inform or to persuade. When your general purpose is to inform, you act as a teacher. Your goal is to communicate information clearly, accurately, and interestingly. When your general purpose is to persuade, you act as an advocate. You go beyond giving information to espousing a cause. Your goal is to win listeners over to your point of view.

Once you know your topic and general purpose, you must focus in on a specific purpose that you can express as a single infinitive phrase. The phrase should indicate precisely what your speech seeks to achieve; for example, "To inform my audience of the major kinds of canoe races." The specific purpose statement should (1) be a full infinitive phrase, not a fragment; (2) be phrased as a statement, not a question; (3) avoid figurative language; (4) concentrate on one distinct idea; (5) not be too vague or too general.

In addition, keep several questions in mind as you formulate your specific purpose statement: Does my purpose meet the assignment? Can I accomplish my purpose in the time allotted? Is the purpose relevant to my audience? Is the purpose too trivial or too technical for my audience?

The central idea refines and sharpens your specific purpose. It is a concise statement of what you will say in your speech, and it usually crystallizes in your thinking after you have done your research and have decided on the main points of your speech. An example of a central idea is, "The three major kinds of canoe races are marathon races, white-water races, and flat-water races." As you can see, the central idea usually encapsulates the main points to be developed in the body of your speech.

Key Terms

Review these terms by doing the Chapter 4 crossword puzzle at www.mhhe.com/lucas8.

ONLINE LEARNING CENTER

topic (86)

brainstorming (89)

general purpose (93)

specific purpose (94)

central idea (100)

residual message (100)

Review Questions

After reading this chapter, you should be able to answer the following questions:

1. What four brainstorming methods can you follow if you are having trouble choosing a topic for your speech?

2. What are the two general purposes of most classroom speeches? How do they differ?

3. Why is determining the specific purpose such an important early step in speech preparation? Why is it important to include the audience in the specific purpose statement?

4. What are five tips for formulating your specific purpose?

5. What are five questions to ask about your specific purpose?

6. What is the difference between the specific purpose and the central idea of a speech? What are four guidelines for an effective central idea?

For further review, go to the Study Questions for this chapter.

CD 1: STUDY QUESTIONS

Exercises for Critical Thinking

1. Using one of the four brainstorming methods described in this chapter, come up with three topics you might like to deal with in your next classroom speech. For each topic, devise two possible specific purpose statements suitable for the speech assignment. Make sure the specific purpose statements fit the guidelines discussed in the chapter.

2. Below is a list of nine topics. Choose three, and for each of the three compose two specific purpose statements—one suitable for an informative speech and one suitable for a persuasive speech.

Example

Topic: School buses

Informative: To inform my audience of the dangerous conditions of many school buses in the United States.

Persuasive: To persuade my audience that the federal government should impose stronger safety standards for school buses in the United States.

education	technology	crime
sports	politics	prejudice
science	music	health

Cross-Reference

For discussion of the Exercises for Critical Thinking, see the *Instructor's Manual*, pp. 124–127. For additional exercises, check the *Instructor's Manual*, pp. 128–132, as well as the five volumes of *Selections from the Speech Communication Teacher* that accompany *The Art of Public Speaking*.

3. Here are several specific purpose statements for classroom speeches. Identify the problem with each, and rewrite the statement to correct the problem.

To inform my audience how to make perfect popcorn every time.

To inform my audience about the growth of credit card fraud and the methods of sound financial planning.

What is obsessive compulsive disorder?

To inform my audience why square grooves are superior to U-shaped grooves on golf clubs.

To inform my audience about Thailand.

Donate blood.

To persuade my audience that something has to be done about the problem of antibiotic-resistant bacteria.

4. Below are three sets of main points for speeches. For each set, supply the general purpose, specific purpose, and central idea.

General Purpose:

Specific Purpose:

Central Idea:

Main Points: I. The first step in making pottery is preparing the clay until it is soft and smooth.

    II. The second step in making pottery is shaping the clay to the desired form.

    III. The third step in making pottery is decorating and glazing the shaped clay.

    IV. The fourth step in making pottery is firing the finished product to make it hard and strong.

General Purpose:

Specific Purpose:

Central Idea:

Main Points: I. You should volunteer as a literacy tutor because it helps children.

    II. You should volunteer as a literacy tutor because it strengthens the community.

    III. You should volunteer as a literacy tutor because it is personally rewarding.

General Purpose:

Specific Purpose:

Central Idea:

Main Points: I. As a painter, Leonardo da Vinci produced *The Last Supper,* the *Mona Lisa,* and other masterpieces.

    II. As an inventor, Leonardo da Vinci drew plans for such devices as a parachute and a flying machine.

    III. As an astronomer, Leonardo da Vinci concluded that the earth revolves around the sun.

Applying the POWER of PUBLIC SPEAKING

Your chemistry degree and excellent communication skills have helped you land a job in the office of Public Information in your state's Department of Health. With a particularly dangerous strain of type-A influenza moving through your state, a news briefing has been scheduled to inform residents about the disease. You are selected to present the briefing.

After gathering information from your agency's medical personnel, you plan what you will say in the briefing. You decide that you will (1) report the symptoms of the disease, (2) identify the people—young children, the elderly, and others—who are most at risk to catch the disease, (3) explain preventive measures to avoid getting the disease, and (4) relate how to treat the disease if one does come down with it.

Following the format used in this chapter, state the general purpose, specific purpose, main points, and central idea of your speech.

Cross-Reference

For discussion of this Applying the Power of Public Speaking scenario, see the *Instructor's Manual,* pp. 127–128.

Chapter Five

ANALYZING
THE AUDIENCE

ew speakers in recent memory have faced a tougher situation than Barbara Bush when she delivered the commencement address at Wellesley College on June 1, 1990. Bush was invited to speak after the students' first choice, author Alice Walker, had declined. In protest of Bush's selection, more than one-fourth of the graduating class signed a petition charging that she was not a good role model for career-oriented women and had been chosen simply because she was the wife of the President of the United States.

The petition ignited a month-long national controversy. As educators, politicians, and editorialists debated the students' actions, Bush remained silent. By the day of the speech, interest had grown to the point that her remarks were broadcast live by all the television networks. The public wanted to hear what she would say and to see how the students would react.

Speaking with a blend of grace and humor, Bush acknowledged that the students had preferred Walker, "known for *The Color Purple*," and had instead got her, "known for the color of my hair!" Rather than being defensive or scolding the students, Bush spoke with them personably about her views on the difficult choices facing women in balancing their careers with commitments to friends and family. She capped off the speech by suggesting that someone in the audience might follow in her footsteps and one day preside over the White House as the President's spouse. "I wish *him* well," she added, to thunderous cheering and applause.

Deemed "a triumph" by *The New York Times,* the speech garnered universal praise. Even students who had been critical of Bush beforehand were impressed. "She was wonderful and funny," one of them stated. "She could have addressed more women's issues. But she was sincere and she touched our hearts." NBC News anchor Tom Brokaw called it "one of the best commencement speeches I've ever heard."

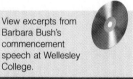

View excerpts from Barbara Bush's commencement speech at Wellesley College.

CD 1: VIDEO 5.1

Audience-Centeredness

audience-centeredness
Keeping the audience foremost in mind at every step of speech preparation and presentation.

Bush's speech points up an important fact: Good public speakers are *audience-centered*. They know the primary purpose of speechmaking is not to browbeat the audience or to blow off steam. Rather, it is to gain a desired response from listeners. No matter what Barbara Bush felt about the petition against her selection as speaker, she had nothing to gain by complaining about it. Nor, under the circumstances, could she ignore it. By respecting the students and their concerns, she was able to establish common ground with her audience and gain a hearing for her ideas.

Being audience-centered does not involve taking any means to an end. You should not compromise your beliefs to get a favorable response from the audience. Nor should you use devious, unethical tactics to achieve your goal. As did Barbara Bush, you can remain true to yourself and speak ethically while adapting your message to the needs of a particular audience.

To be audience-centered, you should keep several questions in mind when you work on your speeches:

To whom am I speaking?

What do I want them to know, believe, or do as a result of my speech?

What is the most effective way of composing and presenting my speech to accomplish that aim?

The answers to these questions will influence every decision you make along the way—selecting a topic, determining a specific purpose, settling on your main points and supporting materials, organizing the message, and, finally, delivering the speech.

Because political candidates deal with many different groups of listeners, it can be instructive to watch how they deal with audience-centeredness. Suppose a person is running for Congress and is giving a series of speeches on the concerns of various constituents. To a meeting of senior citizens she might talk about Social Security benefits; to a group of farmers she might emphasize agricultural price supports; to urban apartment dwellers she might stress methods to counteract street crime. This strategy is perfectly legitimate, provided that all the policies mentioned are part of the candidate's overall program. If the candidate were to concentrate on agricultural price supports before a group of white-collar workers, they might conclude that she is out of touch with their needs and concerns. It only make sense to focus on subjects that are most important to her listeners.

This is not very different from what you do in your daily social contacts. Few people would walk into a party and announce, "What a jerk the governor is!" Or, "You know, those people protesting at the administration building are way over the edge!" If you made either of these statements, you would risk having among your listeners (1) an ardent supporter of the governor, (2) someone who participated in the protest at the administration building, (3) both of the above. The resulting situation could be rather embarrassing.

People usually prefer to open controversial topics with a fairly non-committal position. You might say, "Did you hear what the governor did today?" Or, "What's going on at the administration building?" Then when you have heard and processed your companion's response, you can present your position accordingly. (You don't have to *agree* with a viewpoint different from your own, but neither do you have to hit your listeners over the head with your own opinion.)

Effective public speakers seek to create a bond with their listeners by emphasizing common values, goals, and experiences. Communication scholars call this process *identification*. Barbara Bush created identification with her audience of career-oriented graduates at Wellesley by showing that she understood the difficult choices they would face in balancing the demands of their jobs with their commitments to friends and family. She also indicated that she agreed at least in part with their feminist sensibilities by implying that one day the United States will have a woman president.

When you make a speech, either in class or in some other forum, keep in mind the need to be audience-centered. Think in advance about your listeners' background and interests, about their level of knowledge regarding the speech topic, and about their attitudes regarding your stance on the topic. As you develop the speech, work on explaining your ideas so they will be clear, interesting, and persuasive to the audience.

At this point, you may be nodding your head and saying, "Of course, everyone knows that. It's only common sense." But knowing a precept and putting it into practice are two different matters. The aim of this chapter is

Chapter Focus
This chapter begins by explaining why a public speaker needs to be audience-centered and why students should regard their classmates as a real audience. After discussing the psychology of audiences, it looks at the factors to be considered in demographic and situational audience analysis. It then explains how to get information about an audience and how to adapt to an audience both before and during a speech. For a full outline of the chapter, see the *Instructor's Manual*, pp. 136–140.

identification
A process in which speakers seek to create a bond with the audience by emphasizing common values, goals, and experiences.

to introduce the basic principles of audience analysis and adaption. Chapters 14–16 will deal with those features of audience analysis unique to informative and persuasive speaking.

Your Classmates as an Audience

There is a tendency—among students and teachers alike—to view the classroom as an artificial speaking situation. In a way, it is. Your speech class is a testing ground where you can develop your communication skills before applying them outside the classroom. No elections, no verdicts, no business decisions, no promotions ride on your performance. The most serious measure of success or failure is your grade, and that is determined ultimately by your teacher.

Because of this, it is easy to lose sight of your fellow students as an authentic audience. But each of your classmates is a real person with real ideas, attitudes, and feelings. Your speech class offers an enormous opportunity to inform and persuade other people. As one student wrote on her evaluation form at the end of her speech class, "I thought the speeches would all be phony, but they weren't. Some of them really hit me hard. I've not only learned a lot about speaking—I've learned a lot about other things from listening to the speeches in class."

The best classroom speeches are those that take the classroom audience as seriously as a lawyer, a politician, a minister, or an advertiser takes an audience. Public speaking is not acting. The essence of speechmaking is not to learn a role that can be played over and over without variation, but to adapt one's ideas to particular audiences on particular occasions. If you regard your audience as artificial, you will probably give a speech that sounds artificial.

One key to successful speaking is to consider every audience—inside the classroom and out—as worthy of your best efforts to communicate your knowledge or convictions. At the least you show respect for your listeners. At the most you could make a real difference in their lives. The following story demonstrates the latter:

> Crystal Watkins gave an informative speech on the subject of small claims court, where ordinary people can press lawsuits involving up to $3,000 without lawyers. Part of her speech went like this: "It's two weeks after you have moved into a new apartment. A letter arrives from your old landlord. Expecting to get back your $600 security deposit, you joyfully tear open the envelope. Inside is a form letter explaining why your security deposit is not being refunded. What can you do about it? Nothing, right? Wrong! You can file a claim in small claims court."
>
> Lee Callaway, one of Crystal's classmates, paid close attention. At the end of the previous term, he had run into a situation just like the one Crystal described. Not having money to hire a lawyer, he assumed he would have to forfeit his security deposit. But now, as he listened to Crystal's speech, Lee decided he would try to get his money back in small claims court. He filed suit the next week, and within a month he had his money back—thanks in part to his classmate's speech!

Class Activity
To help your students think of their classmates as a real audience, give the class several different specific purpose statements. For each specific purpose statement, lead a discussion that seeks to answer the question, "What steps should a speaker with this specific purpose statement take to adapt her or his speech to the interests, knowledge, and attitudes of this class?"

Most of your classroom speeches won't have this much immediate impact. Nevertheless, any topic that you handle conscientiously can influence your listeners—can enrich their experience, broaden their knowledge, perhaps change their views about something important.[1]

The Psychology of Audiences

What do you do when you listen to a speech? Sometimes you pay close attention; at other times you let your thoughts wander. People may be compelled to attend a speech, but no one can make them listen unless they want to. It's up to the speaker to make the audience *choose* to pay attention.

Even when people do pay attention, they don't process a speaker's message exactly as the speaker intends. Auditory perception is always selective. Every speech contains two messages—the one sent by the speaker and the one received by the listener. As we saw in Chapter 1, what a speaker says is filtered through a listener's frame of reference—the sum of her or his needs, interests, expectations, knowledge, and experience. As a result, we constantly listen and respond to speeches not as they are, but as we are. Or, to borrow from Paul Simon's classic song "The Boxer," people hear what they want to hear and disregard the rest.

What do people want to hear? Very simply, they usually want to hear about things that are meaningful to them. People are *egocentric*. They pay closest attention to messages that affect their own values, their own beliefs, their own well-being. Listeners typically approach speeches with one question uppermost in mind: "Why is this important to *me?*" As Harry Emerson Fosdick, the great preacher, once said: "There is nothing that people are so interested in as themselves, their own problems, and the way to solve them. That fact is basic. . . . It is the primary starting point of all successful public speaking."[2]

egocentrism
The tendency of people to be concerned above all with their own values, beliefs, and well-being.

What do these psychological principles mean to you as a speaker? First, they mean your listeners will hear and judge what you say on the basis of what they already know and believe. Second, they mean you must relate your message to your listeners—show how it pertains to them, explain why they should care about it as much as you do. Here's an example:

Cheryl Amato had graduated with a degree in public health and was thrilled to be hired by a local hospital to develop a new program on preventing domestic violence. A survey of patients had shown that almost none of the battered women who came into the emergency room had ever told their doctors they were being abused—and that their doctors hadn't asked. It would be Cheryl's job to train physicians in the hospital's managed care network to recognize the warning signs of abuse in their patients and to intervene swiftly.

Drawing on the latest research, Cheryl put together a cutting-edge presentation complete with video clips and PowerPoint slides. After practicing it several times, she asked a couple doctors in the network for their feedback. "You obviously know a lot about the subject," one of them said. "But let's be realistic. Because of managed care, even doctors who are well informed about domestic violence have almost no time to spend with their patients. When are we supposed to talk with them about such a complex issue?"

Good speakers are audience-centered. Whether speaking formally or informally, they work hard to find creative ways to evoke an enthusiastic response from their listeners.

Class Activity
For an activity that helps students understand the multiple frames of reference in an audience and the importance of taking those frames of reference into account when preparing a speech, see Donald C. Smith, "Look Who's Listening: The Importance of Sub-Audiences in Public Speaking," in *Selections from the Speech Communication Teacher, 1994–1996*, p. 10, which accompanies *The Art of Public Speaking*.

Cheryl was taken aback, but she answered quickly: "You're right. So what are some simple, practical things a concerned physician can do?" In the discussion that followed, the doctors came up with a number of suggestions.

The next day, Cheryl reworked her presentation and gave it a new title: "Preventing Domestic Violence: Tips for the Busy Physician." When the first group of doctors came for training the following week, she began: "A survey of patients here in our own hospital showed that most abused women who come to the emergency room have never talked about domestic violence with their doctors. One reason is that doctors today are too busy to spend much time with their patients. Today I'd like to share some tips from doctors like yourselves about how to spot the warning signs of domestic violence, even in a busy practice." In a few moments, Cheryl had everyone's attention and her speech was off to a great start.

As Cheryl's experience shows, you need some grasp of what your listeners know, believe, and care about. As Saul Alinksy, the noted community organizer, advises, "People only understand things in terms of their experience," which means that to communicate with them, "you must get inside their experience."[3]

Of course, you can't actually get inside another person's experience. But you can learn enough about your audience to know what you should do to make your ideas clear and meaningful. How you can do this is our next topic.

Demographic Audience Analysis

One of the ways speakers analyze audiences is by looking at demographic traits such as age; gender; sexual orientation; religion; group membership; racial, ethnic, or cultural background; and the like. This is called *demographic audience analysis*. It consists of two steps: (1) identifying the general demographic features of your audience, and (2) gauging the importance of those features to a particular speaking situation.

While demographic audience analysis can be a useful tool in understanding your audience, like all tools, it can be used improperly. When analyzing demographic information about your audience, it is essential that you avoid stereotyping. Stereotyping involves creating an oversimplified image of a particular group of people, usually by assuming that all members of the group are alike. Examples of stereotyping include the erroneous notions that all women oppose war, that all men are afraid of commitment, that all African Americans are athletic, or that all Asians excel in science. Looking at demographic factors can provide important clues about your audience, but you must use those factors prudently and responsibly.

In addition, as we shall see later in this chapter, you should always combine your demographic audience analysis with situational audience analysis. The importance of any given demographic factor will vary from audience to audience depending on the occasion and the speech topic. If you keep this in mind, demographic analysis can be a valuable starting point in gauging your audience's background, interests, values, and beliefs. Here are a few of the major demographic factors you should consider.

demographic audience analysis
Audience analysis that focuses on demographic factors such as age, gender, religion, sexual orientation, group membership, and racial, ethnic, or cultural background.

stereotyping
Creating an oversimplified image of a particular group of people, usually by assuming that all members of the group are alike.

Age

Are you a member of Generation X? Generation Y? Twenty-something or Thirty-something? A baby boomer or a senior citizen? To some extent these are merely labels. All Gen X'ers do not think alike; all baby boomers do not buy the same products; all senior citizens do not vote for the same political candidates.

Yet as Aristotle noted over 2,000 years ago and as researchers have confirmed many times since, few things affect a person's outlook more than his or her age. Each generation has more or less common values and experiences that set it apart from other generations. No matter how hard they try, for example, many people who grew up during the 1940s will never be fully comfortable with hip-hop, body piercing, and couples living together outside of marriage. On the other hand, to people in their late teens or early twenties, Pearl Harbor, Marilyn Monroe, Vietnam, John Kennedy, Watergate—all are just people and events out of the past. Whatever your age, you are a product of your world.

You can see what this means for your speeches. Suppose you address an audience of older people. If you refer offhandedly to your "roommate"—making it clear that your roommate is someone with whom you are romantically involved—your audience may be disturbed and tune out the rest of your speech. Similarly, if you speak to an audience of young adults and casually mention Joseph McCarthy (an anti-Communist Senator of the 1950s) or the Tet offensive (an important campaign of the Vietnam War), they may not know what you are talking about. Even if younger listeners do recognize the names, they will not have the emotional associations of older people who lived through the 1950s or the war in Vietnam.

Depending on the composition of your speech class, you may face an audience that is mostly in their late teens and early twenties. If so, you can assume a common level of age experience. On the other hand, 45 percent of

Discussion Prompt
If your class contains a wide range of age groups, ask students to identify situations—from public speaking or everyday conversation—in which they have been misunderstood because of a difference in age between themselves and their listeners. In retrospect, what steps would they take to communicate their ideas more effectively? What steps could their listeners have taken to better understand the speaker's message?

college students today are age 25 or older, and many classrooms include students in their thirties, forties, fifties, and beyond. You may then have to tackle two or three generations. This will give you good practice for speeches outside the classroom, where age is usually a major factor in audience analysis.

Gender

Related Reading

For a broader discussion of gender issues in communication, see Julia T. Wood, *Gendered Lives: Communication, Gender, and Culture,* 5th ed. (Belmont, CA: Wadsworth, 2003); and Diana K. Ivy and Phil Backlund, *Exploring GenderSpeak: Personal Effectiveness in Gender Communication,* 2nd ed. (New York: McGraw-Hill, 2000).

As the new sales director for a national computer firm, Alex Kvalo was looking forward to his first meeting with the company's district managers. Everyone arrived on time, and Alex's presentation went extremely well. He decided to end the meeting with a conversation about the importance of the district managers to the company's plans.

"I believe we are going to continue to increase our share of the market," he began, "because of the quality of the people in this room. The district manager is the key to the success of the sales representatives in his district. He sets the tone for everyone else. If he has ambitious goals and is willing to put in long hours, everyone in his unit will follow his example."

When Alex was finished, he received polite applause, but hardly the enthusiastic response he had hoped for. Later, he spoke with one of the senior managers. "Things were going so well until the end," Alex lamented. "Obviously, I said the wrong thing."

"Yes," the district manager replied. "Half of our managers are women. Most have worked their way up from sales representatives, and they're very proud of the role they've played in the company's growth. They don't care a hoot about political correctness, but they were definitely surprised, and distressed, to be referred to as *he.*"

Alex should not have been surprised at the lukewarm response to his speech. Although he did not mean to cause offense, by calling all the district managers "he," Alex disregarded half of his audience and their contributions to the company. The same would have been true if he had referred to all the managers as "she." A speaker who ignores the gender of his or her listeners is almost certain to offend some members of the audience.

Discussion Prompt

Is word choice the only aspect of communication to be conscious of when taking into account gender differences between a speaker and an audience? What about the choice of topic? Are there certain topics that are more suitable for audiences composed primarily of women or primarily of men? If so, what aspects of a speech other than language choice can a speaker adjust to communicate on a topic that may not be intrinsically interesting to an audience on gender grounds?

In speechmaking you must be wary of making assumptions with respect to gender until you have tested those assumptions and found them to be correct. Social distinctions between the sexes have been eroding for some years. Men now cook, keep house, work as receptionists, and volunteer in their children's schools. Women work in construction trades, run corporations, enlist in the armed forces, and serve as college athletic directors. Men and women today share a much broader range of experiences, interests, and aspirations than they once did.

In addition, the "typical" composition of audiences has also changed. At one time local civic groups such as Kiwanis and Rotary clubs were all-male. Today most have sizable contingents of women. Parent associations, which were once composed almost solely of women, now include plenty of interested fathers. Here, as in other areas, the old stereotypes no longer apply.

This is not to say that women and men are alike in all their values and beliefs. When it comes to politics, for instance, American women tend to be more concerned about issues such as education, health care, and social justice, whereas men tend to stress economics and military defense. But keep in mind that these are generalizations. There are lots of women who believe military defense comes first, just as there are plenty of men who give priority to social issues. An astute speaker will be equally attuned to both the differences *and* the similarities between the sexes.

An astute speaker will also take care to avoid using sexist language. Almost any audience you address will contain people—men and women alike—who will take offense at words and phrases that convey gender stereotypes or demean people on the basis of their gender. In Chapter 11, we will look more closely at sexist language and how to avoid it in your speeches. For now, it is enough to know that refraining from sexist language is an important part of being an audience-centered public speaker.[4]

Sexual Orientation

Phillip Ward, president of a major engineering firm, was hosting his annual awards banquet to recognize outstanding employees. After presenting all the plaques and checks, he said, "Now that we have honored these fine people for their career and community accomplishments, I would like to take a moment to recognize the spouses and partners who have supported their exceptional efforts." The room filled with applause.

After the ceremony, Ward made his way around the room shaking hands and chatting with award winners. "I want to congratulate you again on your superior design for the Houston water project," he said to Joanne Fitzpatrick.

"Thank you for the award," Joanne replied. "And I also want to thank you for being sensitive to the fact that many of us are supported by partners as well as by spouses. It really meant a lot to Julie and me to feel recognized and included."

As an experienced speaker and successful businessperson, Philip Ward is well aware of the need in contemporary society to adapt to his audience on the basis of sexual orientation. By mentioning "partners" as well as "spouses," he took an inclusive stance acknowledging the fact that couples can be same-sex or opposite-sex (or married or unmarried). No matter what one's attitude toward gays, lesbians, or heterosexuals, audience-centered speakers are alert to how their messages will be received by people of various sexual orientations.

We saw in Chapter 2 that there is no place in ethical public speaking for name-calling and abusive language, regardless of the group being attacked. Moreover, inflammatory words and phrases that demean gays and lesbians are offensive to most other people as well. A speaker who uses such language—whether in a classroom speech, a business presentation, or a political address—will alienate a significant portion of the audience.

As with Philip Ward, an audience-centered public speaker will also be alert to more subtle uses of language with regard to sexual orientation. The label "homosexual," for example, is considered derogatory by lesbians and gay men. So are references to a gay or lesbian "lifestyle." Such references are also inaccurate because they imply that all gays and lesbians live the same way. Just as there is no single heterosexual lifestyle, there is no single lesbian or gay lifestyle.

When you work on your speeches, keep an eye out for language, examples, and other elements that may unintentionally exclude listeners with same-sex partners. In a speech about financial planning, rather than saying "most of us hope to graduate, find a good job, and get married," you could say "most of us hope to graduate, get a good job, and find a person to share our lives with." In a speech about the soaring cost of housing, you might say "young couples are finding it harder to afford buying a home," rather than referring to "young married couples."

Related Reading

There are a number of Web resources for information on issues related to public speech and sexual orientation. Two of the best are the American Civil Liberty Union's Lesbian and Gay Rights site (www.aclu.org/LesbianGayRights/LesbianGayRightsMain.cfm) and Gay/Lesbian Politics and Law (www.indiana.edu/glbtpol/).

You can link to these websites at www.mhhe.com/lucas8.

THE *INTERNET Connection*

The Internet is rich in resources that can help speakers with demographic audience analysis. A good starting point for accessing those resources is Yahoo: Regional (http://dir.yahoo.com/Regional/Countries), which provides links to countries around the world. For religious information, check the Librarians' Index to the Internet: Religion (www.lii.org/search/file/religion).

You can learn a great deal by seeing how experienced public speakers deal with audience analysis and adaptation. A terrific website for this purpose is Gifts of Speech: Women's Speeches from Around the World (http://gos.sbc.edu), where you will find speeches by more than 200 influential contemporary women.

You may be inclined to dismiss these suggestions as merely another form of political correctness, but just as audiences often include people of varying ages, races, and religions, so too do they contain people of different sexual orientations. Effective public speakers take all these demographic factors into account when preparing their remarks.

Racial, Ethnic, and Cultural Background

As we saw in Chapter 1, the United States has long been a multicultural society. Populated originally by Native Americans and then by immigrants from all over the world, it is today a multiracial, multiethnic country of unmatched diversity. Although there are exceptions, the majority of Americans support this diversity and see it as a positive development in today's globalized world. Attitudes about race and ethnicity are quite different from what they were even a few decades ago.

Understanding those attitudes is crucial for public speakers whether they are addressing a mixed-race audience or one with little apparent racial diversity. Consider, for example, the case of U.S. Senator Trent Lott:

> First elected to Congress in 1972 from the state of Mississippi, Trent Lott rose steadily through the ranks of the Republican Party from one leadership post to another. By the end of 2002, he was poised to become Senate majority leader, one of the most powerful positions in all of American politics.
>
> Then Lott made the following statement during an informal speech at the 100th-birthday party of South Carolina Senator Strom Thurmond: "I want to say this about my state: When Strom Thurmond ran for president, we voted for him. We're proud of it. And if the rest of the country had followed our lead, we wouldn't have had all these problems over all these years, either."
>
> Lott's listeners were shocked, and a number gasped. When Thurmond campaigned for president in 1948, he did so on a platform of racial segregation. Because Lott's words appeared to indicate that he still supported that platform, his comments ignited

Class Activity

For a class activity that encourages students to explore the role of ethnic and gender differences in communication, see Ken Hawkinson, "Two Exercises on Diversity and Gender," in *Selections from the Speech Communication Teacher, 1991–1994,* pp. 24–25, which accompanies *The Art of Public Speaking.*

a political firestorm. Similar words from past speeches by Lott surfaced in the press. African-American leaders condemned Lott, and President George W. Bush stated, "Any suggestion that our segregated past was acceptable or positive is wrong."

Barely two weeks after his original statement, which was criticized by blacks, whites, Democrats, and Republicans alike, Lott was forced to step down from his leadership position.

The fate of Trent Lott illustrates just how important it is for speakers to be sensitive to issues of race, ethnicity, and cultural background. As one political columnist explained, "To win nationally, the leader of the party must pay tribute to the tolerance and open-mindedness of the nation at large." Lott's comments struck most Americans—regardless of race or political party—as inappropriate for a national leader "in a multiracial democracy in the opening years of the 21st century."[5]

In addition to keeping in mind general attitudes about race and ethnicity, public speakers also need to consider how racial, ethnic, and cultural differences among audience members might affect their reactions to a speech. Despite their similarities as Americans, people of European descent, blacks, Latinos, Asians, and others may have different customs and beliefs that bear upon your speech topic. Because we live in an age of globalization, you may also find yourself addressing audiences with listeners from countries other than your own. Here's what happened to one student who forgot to allow for such listeners:

After spending an exciting summer as an intern in a law firm, Lindsey Feldman decided to give her informative speech on how successful women handle themselves in professional situations. Part of her speech dealt with the importance of making a positive first impression.

"One of the things I learned from my internship," she said "is how much depends on that initial handshake. A strong handshake is essential to any woman who wants to be taken seriously in law or business. It conveys confidence, honesty, and friendliness, all at once. You have to reach forward energetically, grasp firmly, and look the person straight in the eye. Most men know how to do this. And so does every successful woman."

Lindsey expected everyone to nod their heads on this line, but she got some quizzical expressions as well. At the end of class, Lindsey spoke with her classmate Daniela, a Chilean student spending a year in the U.S. "I liked most of your speech," Daniela said, "except for the part about shaking hands. In Chile, we greet people with a kiss. To us, a handshake is cold and impersonal." "But in business," objected Lindsey, "you really need to shake hands, especially if you're a woman."

"Maybe here," replied Daniela, "but not at home. My mother is a very successful lawyer in Santiago. For her, a kiss on the cheek works better every time."

What happened to Lindsey, of course, could happen to anyone who is not familiar with South American culture. Even business leaders and heads of state sometimes misstep when speaking to people of different racial, ethnic, and cultural backgrounds. Several years ago, during his first presidential trip to a foreign land, Bill Clinton rose to make a speech during a state dinner in South Korea. He referred several times to South Korean President Kim Young-sam and his wife, "Mrs. Kim." But Korean women keep their birth names. Clinton should have addressed President Kim's wife as "Mrs. Sohn Myong-suk" or as "Mrs. Sohn."[6]

Related Reading

Not only is racial, ethnic, and cultural diversity an important factor in speeches delivered in the United States, but it is also a major concern for speakers who find themselves addressing audiences from other parts of the world. See Patricia L. Kurtz, *The Global Speaker: An English Speaker's Guide to Making Presentations Around the World* (New York: AMACOM, 1995), for a helpful guide to public speaking in an international setting.

Cross-Reference

See Chapter 1, pp. 22–27, for fuller discussion of cultural diversity and its role in contemporary speechmaking.

How can you avoid these kinds of gaffes in your speeches? The first step is to recognize that some of your listeners may indeed have racial, ethnic, or cultural perspectives that will affect their attitudes toward your speech topic. The second step is to try to determine what those perspectives are and how they are likely to affect the audience's response to your message. The third step is to adjust your speech so it will be as clear, suitable, and convincing as possible. No matter who the speaker, no matter what the occasion, adapting to people of diverse racial, ethnic, and cultural backgrounds is a vital aspect of the art of public speaking.

Religion

Related Reading
Diana L. Eck, *A New Religious America* (New York: HarperCollins, 2001). This highly readable study by a prize-winning scholar provides an eye-opening look at the history and current state of religious diversity in the United States. The many specific examples provide excellent material for class discussion.

Russell Middleton, the director of the town's public library, was delighted to be invited to address his local civic association. He needed volunteers to help paint the reading rooms, and he felt sure he could recruit some from the association.

On the evening of his speech, Russell explained the painting project, making special mention of the fact that anyone who volunteered would help the library save money for more books and better programs. "Most of our work will be on Saturdays," he said. "We might also work in the evening, or maybe on a Sunday afternoon. But don't worry. We won't work on Sunday morning because that's when everyone will be at church." He finished by asking volunteers to sign up on a clipboard near the door.

At the end of the evening, Russell was pleased to see plenty of names on his clipboard, but he also found the following note. "Mr. Middleton," it began, "your project seems excellent, and I will be pleased to help. But I think you should remember that there are people in this community who do not go to church or worship on Sunday morning. I am Muslim, and some of the people sitting near me are Jewish. Fortunately, I had a chance to hear about your project before the comment about attending church on Sunday. If I hadn't, I might have concluded that you were not interested in my help. Please give me a call when you are ready to start the painting. Hamid Shakir."

Teaching Tip
Have students prepare an Audience Analysis and Adaptation Worksheet in conjunction with one or more of their speeches. Distribute the worksheets early so students can use them throughout the speech preparation process. You can have students turn in the worksheets at the same time as their initial preparation outline, or you can require that they be turned in on the day of each student's speech. To help ensure that students take the worksheet seriously, many instructors make it a graded assignment. For a sample worksheet, see the *Instructor's Manual*, pp. 148–149.

This story illustrates a factor you must take into account in all your speeches. You cannot assume that your views on religion—whatever they may be—are shared by your listeners. As current events around the world demonstrate, religious views are among the most emotionally charged and passionately defended of all human concerns. Even your small speech class might include a wide range of faiths, as well as atheists and agnostics.

As the United States has become more diverse culturally, it has also become more diverse religiously. The traditional mix of Protestantism, Catholicism, and Judaism has been enriched by growing numbers of Buddhists, Muslims, Hindus, Sikhs, Russian Orthodox, and others. One leading scholar on the subject says the United States is now "the most religiously diverse nation in the world."[7]

You can see this diversity in towns and cities across the land. There are more than twenty Buddhist temples in the greater Seattle area; four Hindu temples in San Diego; a Sikh gurudwara in Omaha; five Muslim mosques in Dallas; a Jain temple in Allentown, Pennsylvania; and Baha'i centers in Topeka, Kansas, and Anchorage, Alaska. Nationwide there are more than 1,800 houses of worship for Muslims, 1,600 for Buddhists, and 600 for Hindus.[8]

There is also great diversity within different faiths. You cannot assume that all Catholics support the official view of their church on such matters as birth control or women in the priesthood, any more than you can stereotype all Baptists as being born-again or all Muslims as favoring a subservient status for women. In matters of religion, the United States is truly a nation of many faiths, many voices, many views.

Whenever you speak on a topic with religions dimensions, then, be sure to consider the religious orientations of your listeners. Doing so can help you avoid potentially embarrassing pitfalls; in some cases, it may make the difference between an unsuccessful speech and a successful one.

Group Membership

"Tell me thy company," says Don Quixote, "and I'll tell thee what thou art." For all our talk about rugged individualism, Americans are very group-oriented. Workers belong to unions, businesspeople to chambers of commerce. Hunters join the National Rifle Association, environmentalists the Sierra Club, feminists the National Organization for Women. Doctors enroll in the American Medical Association, lawyers in the American Bar Association. There are thousands of such voluntary organizations in the United States.

Similar groups abound on campus. Some of your classmates may belong to fraternities or sororities, some to Campus Crusade for Christ, some to the Young Republicans, some to the film society, some to the ski club, and so forth. For speeches in the classroom, as well as for those outside the classroom, the group affiliations of your audience may provide excellent clues about your listeners' interests and attitudes.

Class Activity
The second Exercise for Critical Thinking at the end of this chapter focuses on the role of demographic factors in audience analysis and adaptation. For full discussion of the exercise, see the *Instructor's Manual*, pp. 141–142.

Age; gender; sexual orientation; religion; racial, ethnic, and cultural background; group membership—these are just a few of the variables to consider in demographic audience analysis. Others include occupation, economic position, social standing, education, intelligence, and place of residence. Indeed, *anything* characteristic of a given audience is potentially important to a speaker addressing that audience. For your classroom speeches, you may want to learn about your classmates' academic majors, years in school, extracurricular activities, living arrangements, and job aspirations.

Perhaps the most important thing to keep in mind about demographic audience analysis is that it is not an end in itself. Your aim is not just to list the major traits of your listeners but to find in those traits clues about how your listeners will respond to your speech. Once you have done that, you are ready to move on to the next stage of audience analysis.

Situational Audience Analysis

Situational audience analysis usually builds on the demographic analysis. It identifies traits of the audience unique to the speaking situation at hand. These traits include the size of the audience, attitudes influenced by the physical setting, and the disposition of the audience toward the subject, the speaker, and the occasion.

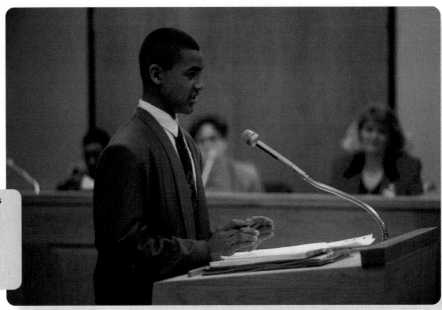

Situational audience analysis is a vital element in public speaking. Whenever you present a speech, be sure to adapt to the size of the audience and the physical setting for the speech.

situational audience analysis

Audience analysis that focuses on situational factors such as the size of the audience, the physical setting for the speech, and the disposition of the audience toward the topic, the speaker, and the occasion.

Size

Outside the classroom, the size of an audience can, with the aid of television and radio, range in the millions. Most speech classes, however, consist of between 15 and 30 people—a small- to medium-sized audience. This is a good size for beginning speakers, most of whom are horrified at the prospect of addressing a huge crowd. As you gain more experience, though, you may welcome the challenge of speaking to larger groups. Some speakers actually prefer a large audience to a small one.

No matter what size group you are addressing, bear in mind one basic principle: The larger the audience, the more formal your presentation must be. Audience size will have the greatest impact on your delivery, but it may also affect your language, choice of appeals, and use of visual aids.

Physical Setting

The receptivity of listeners to your speech frequently will be influenced by factors beyond their control—and sometimes beyond your control. Which of the following would you rather address?

An audience assembled immediately after lunch, crammed into an overheated room with inadequate seating

An audience assembled at 10:00 in the morning, comfortably seated in an airy, well-lighted room

Undoubtedly you chose the second option. Any of the adverse conditions listed in the first could seriously impair your audience's willingness to accept your ideas or even listen to you at all.

When you face any speaking situation, it is important to know in advance if there will be any difficulties with the physical setting. For classroom speeches, of course, you already do know. But speeches outside the classroom can confront you with many unpleasant surprises unless you do your homework beforehand.

When you are invited to speak, don't be shy about asking questions of the person who arranged the speech. If possible, look over the room yourself a few days in advance, or else arrive early on the day of your speech to give the room a quick inspection. If it is too warm or too cold, see about adjusting the thermostat. Check the seating arrangements and the location of the lectern to be sure your audience can see you properly. In short, do everything you can to control the influence of physical setting on your audience.

But, you may wonder, what about circumstances you can't control? Your speech *is* scheduled directly after lunch or dinner. The room *is* too small for the audience expected. The heat *cannot* be regulated. Then you are simply going to have to work harder to adapt to these aspects of your listeners' discomfort. When faced with an audience that is potentially hot, sleepy, and cross, do your best to make the speech as interesting and lively as you can. Above all, don't let *yourself* be influenced by the poor physical setting. If your audience sees that you are energetic, alert, and involved with your topic, chances are they will forget their discomfort and come right along with you.

Teaching Tip
Note that experienced public speakers routinely check out the physical setting for a speech in advance of the final presentation. If possible given the time and circumstances, many speakers rehearse the full speech at least once in the room where it will be presented.

Disposition Toward the Topic

As we saw in Chapter 4, you should keep your audience in mind when choosing a topic. Ideally, you will pick a topic that suits them as well as it suits you. Once you have your topic, however, you must consider in more detail how your listeners will react to it. In particular, you need to assess their interest in the topic, their knowledge about it, and their attitudes toward it.

Interest

Outside the classroom, people do not often expend the time and effort to attend a speech unless they are interested in the topic. But the members of your speech class are a captive audience. Sometimes they will be deeply interested in your topic, particularly if it relates directly to them. Most of the time they will range from fairly interested to mildly curious to downright indifferent.

One of your tasks will be to assess their interest in advance and to adjust your speech accordingly. Most important, if your topic is not likely to generate great interest, you must take special steps to get your classmates involved. Here are two brief examples of how to do this:

View the beginning of Jennifer Conard, "The Ultimate Gift," and Alice Pearson, "Universal Health Care."

CD 1: VIDEO 5.2

Jennifer wanted to persuade her classmates to donate blood on a regular basis. At the beginning of her speech, she said: "Are you at least 17 years old? Do you weigh more than 110 pounds? Do you consider yourself fairly healthy? If you answered yes to all of these questions, you should be donating blood every two months."

Alice's speech was about the need for national health insurance in the United States. She started by saying: "Suppose you come down with a serious but treatable illness. You are too sick to go to class, too sick to work. What do you do? You go to the doctor, right? What if, when you got to the doctor, you were turned away because you couldn't pay and were sent home to suffer alone?"

In the chapters that follow, we'll look closely at all the ways you can develop interest in your topic—by an arresting introduction, provocative supporting materials, vivid language, dynamic delivery, visual aids, and so forth.

Knowledge

There is often a strong correlation between interest in a topic and knowledge about it. People tend to be interested in what they know about. Likewise, they are inclined to learn about subjects that interest them. But there are exceptions. Few students know much about handwriting analysis, yet most would find it an absorbing topic. On the other hand, almost all know a lot about checking books out of the library, but few would find it a fascinating subject for a speech.

Why is it important to gauge your listeners' knowledge about your topic? Quite simply, because it will to a large extent determine what you can say in your speech. If your listeners know little about your topic—whether or not they find it interesting—you will have to talk at a more elementary level. If they are reasonably well informed, you can take a more technical and detailed approach.

Attitude

attitude

A frame of mind in favor of or opposed to a person, policy, belief, institution, etc.

The attitude of your listeners toward your topic can be extremely important in determining how you handle the material. If you know in advance the prevailing attitude among members of your audience, you can adjust your speech to address their concerns or to answer their objections against your point of view. Consider the experiences of the following two students—one who did not account for listener attitude and one who did:

Brad Kaminski spoke about the effects on human health of pesticides and other chemicals found in the environment. On the basis of his research, he believed that the dangers of exposure to pesticide residues in our food have been exaggerated by the popular press. His position was interesting but highly controversial. Unfortunately, rather than citing his sources and acknowledging that his point of view was unusual, Brad presented his material as though it were general knowledge.

The speech was not well received. In fact, the class found Brad's approach so inconsistent with everything they had read about pesticides and food that they couldn't accept it. As one student said after the speech, "You may be right in what you said, but I have trouble believing it. We've all heard so much about the dangers of pesticides—can it all be wrong? I think you would have been more persuasive if you had looked at both sides of the issue rather than just your own."

Had Brad taken the skepticism of his audience into account, he could have established the scientific credibility of his material, and thereby made his arguments more persuasive to his audience.

Compare the approach of Lee Hawkins, who also espoused a controversial viewpoint:

A firm opponent of capital punishment, Lee decided to give his persuasive speech in opposition to the death penalty. After distributing a questionnaire among his classmates, Lee found that three-fourths of them favored capital punishment. They gave two reasons. First, they believed the death penalty was a just punishment for some-one who commits a crime such as murder. Second, they believed capital punishment works as a deterrent to crime.

Although Lee disagreed with those beliefs, he realized he could neither ignore them nor insult his classmates for holding them. He knew he would have to discuss these points logically and with hard evidence if he were to have any chance of per-suading his audience.

View an excerpt from Lee Hawkins, "Capital Punishment."

CD 1: VIDEO 5.3

As it turned out, Lee did convince some members of the class to reconsider their beliefs. He could not have done so without first investigating what those beliefs were and then adapting his message to them.[9]

Disposition Toward the Speaker

Let's return for a moment to Brad's speech about pesticide residues in food. Brad was a sophomore business major with no special scientific or nutritional background. It's not surprising that his classmates took his statements with a large grain of salt. But suppose Brad had been a recog-nized expert on pesticides and the food chain. Then his listeners would have found him much more believable. Why? Because an audience's re-sponse to a message is invariably colored by their perception of the speaker.

The more competent the listeners believe a speaker to be, the more likely they are to accept what the speaker says. Likewise, the more listeners be-lieve that a speaker has their best interests at heart, the more likely they are to respond positively to the speaker's message.

We will come back to this subject in detail when we deal with strate-gies for persuasive speaking in Chapter 16. For now, keep in mind that your listeners will always have *some* set of attitudes toward you as a speaker. Es-timating what those attitudes are and how they will affect your speech is a crucial part of situational audience analysis.

Disposition Toward the Occasion

It was Martin Luther King Day, and the city was holding a public program celebrating King's life and legacy. More than 1,000 people, including hundreds of schoolchildren, were in attendance. All the prominent figures of the city—politicians, clergy, business-people, community leaders—were on the platform. Between songs and other performances, they came to the microphone to talk briefly about the great civil rights leader and what his memory meant to them.

One of the last to speak was James Irvin, the developer of a proposed busi-ness complex that he hoped to locate in one of the city's more impoverished neigh-borhoods. Irvin began his speech by invoking the memory of Dr. King. He then continued: "Some people say I'm out to exploit the poor people of this city and get tax breaks for myself. All I want to do is bring money into the community and make a fair profit on my investment. But to do that I need the support of every one of the people sitting up here with me today, and I want all of you to hold them accountable."

The people on the platform merely looked uncomfortable, but the audience re-acted with boos and hisses.

Class Activity

Barbara Bush's commence-ment address at Wellesley College, which is discussed at the beginning of this chap-ter, provides an excellent ex-ample of a prominent public speaker adapting to the audi-ence, situation, and occasion. Have students analyze the full text of the speech (pp. A4–A7) as a homework assignment and focus class discussion on how Bush adapts her message in light of the controversy that pre-ceded her speech. For fuller discussion of the speech, see the *Instructor's Manual*, pp. 143–144. A videotape of Bush's address is available as part of the instructional sup-plement to *The Art of Public Speaking*.

Adapting to expectations about the occasion is part of being an audience-centered speaker. Here Vinnie Lauwers accepts his award for World Sportsperson of the Year with a Disability.

On other occasions Irvin's comments would not have touched off such an angry response. But the Martin Luther King Day gathering was understood by the organizers—and the audience—to be an occasion for commemoration and reverence. The last thing they expected to hear was a pitch for a business project. What angered the audience was not what Irvin said, but that he exploited the occasion for his own purposes.

No matter what the situation, listeners have fairly definite ideas about the speeches they consider appropriate. They expect to hear political speeches in Congress, sermons in church, after-dinner speeches after dinner, and so forth. Speakers who seriously violate these expectations can almost always count on infuriating the audience.

Perhaps most important, the occasion will dictate how long a speech should be. When you are invited to speak, the chairperson will usually say how much time you have for your talk. If not, be sure to ask. And once you know, pare down your speech so it fits easily within the allotted time. Do not exceed that time under any circumstances, for you are likely to see your audience dwindle as you drone on. (This is one reason why most teachers insist that classroom speeches be kept within the designated time limit. It provides crucial training for speeches you will give outside the classroom.)

There are other audience expectations that apply to your classroom situation. One is that speeches will conform to the assignment. Another is that speakers will observe appropriate standards of taste and decorum. Failure to adhere to these expectations may disturb your classmates and will almost certainly damage your grade.

Getting Information About the Audience

Now that you know *what* to learn about an audience, the next question is, *how* do you learn it? A person running for high political office can rely on hired professional pollsters. If, as is more likely, you are invited sometime to address a particular group—say a meeting of the local Rotary club—the person who invites you can usually provide a good sketch of the audience. Ask your contact with the group where you can find out more about its history and purpose. Best of all, if you know someone who has spoken to the same group, be sure to sound out that person.

What about your classmates as an audience? You can learn a lot about them just by observation and conversation. Still, you probably will need to know more about their backgrounds and opinions in relation to specific speech topics. Some teachers require students to do a formal audience analysis—either through interviews or through written questionnaires—for at least one of their speeches.

Interviewing

The face-to-face interview (see Chapter 6) is highly flexible and allows for in-depth questioning. When properly planned, structured, and conducted, it can be a superb way of learning about individual members of an audience. The great drawback is the cost in time and energy. Interviewing each member of a class before every speech may be the most thorough method of audience analysis, but it is seldom practical. Therefore, most teachers encourage their students to rely on questionnaires.

Questionnaires

Like interviewing, constructing a good questionnaire is an art you cannot be expected to master in a speech class. By following a few basic guidelines, however, you can learn to develop a questionnaire that will be more than adequate for analyzing your classroom audience.

There are three major types of questions to choose from: fixed-alternative questions, scale questions, and open-ended questions.

Fixed-alternative questions, as their name implies, offer a fixed choice between two or more responses. For example:

Do you know what the insanity plea is in the U.S. legal system?

Yes _____

No _____

Not sure _____

Do you know of any legal cases in which the insanity plea was used?

Yes _____

No _____

Not sure _____

Class Activity
The first Exercise for Critical Thinking at the end of this chapter uses magazine advertisements to illustrate the general principles of audience analysis and adaptation. Because most magazine ads are fairly transparent in their audience appeals, they usually work well in promoting class discussion.

fixed-alternative questions
Questions that offer a fixed choice between two or more alternatives.

By limiting the possible responses, such questions produce clear, unambiguous answers. They also tend to yield superficial answers. Other techniques are needed to get beneath the surface.

Scale questions resemble fixed-alternative questions, but they allow more leeway in responding. For example:

How often do you believe the insanity plea is used in U.S. court cases?

Very   Very
seldom ———————|———————|———————|———————|——————— often

Do you agree or disagree with the following? Expert psychologists can determine with a high degree of accuracy whether or not a defendant is criminally insane.

Strongly agree	Mildly agree	Undecided	Mildly disagree	Strongly disagree
———————|———————				

Questions like these are especially useful for getting at the strength of a respondent's attitudes.

Open-ended questions give maximum leeway in responding. For example:

What is your opinion about the insanity plea in U.S. court cases?

Under what circumstances do you think the insanity plea is legitimate in a criminal trial? Please explain.

Although open-ended questions invite more detailed responses than the other two types of questions, they also increase the likelihood of getting answers that do not give the kind of information you need.

Because each type of question has its advantages and disadvantages, many questionnaires contain all three types. Figure 5.1 shows a questionnaire that was distributed before a classroom speech on volunteering for a community, religious, or charitable organization. By using all three types of questions, the speaker did two things—elicited specific information about the audience and probed more deeply into their attitudes toward the speech topic. The results of the questionnaire survey broke down as follows:

1. Less than half of the class had participated as a volunteer. Therefore, the speaker knew she would have to explain clearly what was involved in this kind of work.

2. Five students knew someone close to them who had benefited from volunteer work by a community, religious, or charitable organization; most said they were not sure. Thus the speaker could not depend on a high degree of personal involvement among the audience.

3. All but one of the students who had engaged in volunteer work rated it as "very rewarding" or "somewhat rewarding." Not only would this portion of the audience be inclined to support the speaker's position, but the speaker could point to their attitude as proof that work as a volunteer is a rewarding experience.

4. Nearly 75 percent of the respondents either "strongly agreed" or "mildly agreed" that people have an obligation to help those in less fortunate

scale questions
Questions that require responses at fixed intervals along a scale of answers.

open-ended questions
Questions that allow respondents to answer however they want.

Class Activity
Although speakers outside the classroom seldom employ questionnaires, using them in the classroom is an excellent way for students to engage in systematic audience analysis. As explained in the third Exercise for Critical Thinking at the end of this chapter, have students design and circulate among their classmates an audience-analysis questionnaire like the one described here. For full discussion of this activity, see the *Instructor's Manual*, p. 142.

Figure 5.1 Sample Questionnaire.

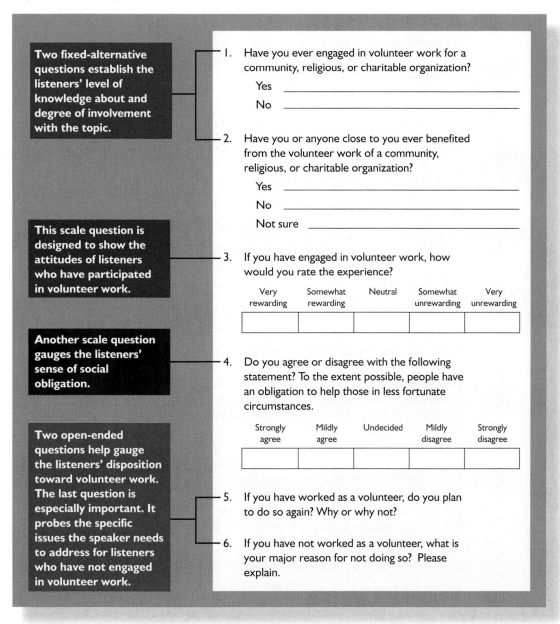

circumstances. No one strongly disagreed. The speaker could therefore depend on an audience favorably inclined to the basic premise underlying
volunteer work.

5. Answers to the fifth question—"If you have worked as a volunteer, do
you plan to do so again? Why or why not?"—were interesting. All the respondents indicated that they planned to engage in volunteer work again,
but most said they were not likely to do so while in college because they
were too busy with other activities.

6. Nearly 90 percent of the students who had not engaged in volunteer work stated that their major reason for not doing so was a lack of time. In combination with the answers to question 5, these responses showed that the speaker would have to deal persuasively with the time issue if she were to be successful in convincing people to volunteer while they were enrolled in school.

This questionnaire worked extremely well. It revealed a great deal about the listeners' knowledge, attitudes, and concerns. You should be able to put together an equally useful questionnaire. In doing so, keep the following principles in mind:

View how the speakers in Videos 5.2 and 5.3 used audience-analysis surveys in their speeches.

CD 1: VIDEO 5.4

1. Plan the questionnaire carefully to elicit precisely the information you need.

2. Use all three types of questions—fixed-alternative, scale, and open-ended.

3. Make sure the questions are clear and unambiguous.

4. Keep the questionnaire relatively brief.

Adapting to the Audience

Once you have completed the audience analysis, you should have a pretty clear picture of your listeners. You should know their relevant demographic characteristics, their interest in and knowledge about the topic, their attitudes toward the topic and the speaker, and their expectations about the occasion. Knowing all this, however, does not guarantee a successful speech. The key is how well you *use* what you know in preparing and presenting the speech.

This point deserves special attention because it poses one of the hardest tasks facing novice speakers. Most people can identify the major character-istics of their audience, but many have trouble *adapting* their ideas to the audience. There are two major stages in the process of audience adaptation—the first occurs before the speech, as part of your preparation and rehearsal; the second occurs during the presentation of the speech itself.

Audience Adaptation Before the Speech

As we have seen, you must keep your audience in mind at every stage of speech preparation. Keeping your audience in mind, however, involves more than simply remembering who your listeners will be. Above all, it means two things: (1) assessing how your audience is likely to respond to what you will say in your speech and (2) adjusting what you say to make it as clear, appropriate, and convincing as possible.

This is not always easy to do. We are all so wrapped up in our own ideas and concerns that we have trouble seeing things from other people's perspective—especially if their perspective is quite different from ours. If, for example, you speak on a subject in which you are expert, you may find it hard to put yourself in the place of someone who knows nothing about it. To step outside your own frame of reference and see things from another person's point of view is a real achievement.

Yet this is what a successful speaker eventually learns to do. You must submerge your own views so completely that you can adopt, temporarily, those of your listeners. When you do this, you will begin to hear your speech through the ears of your audience and to adjust it accordingly.

You must keep your listeners constantly in mind as you prepare your speech. Try to imagine what they will like, what they will dislike, where they will have doubts or questions, whether they will need more details here or fewer there, what will interest them and what will not.

At every point you must *anticipate* how your audience will respond. How will they react to your introduction and conclusion? Will they find your examples clear and convincing? Will your visual aids help them grasp your ideas? How will they respond to your language and manner of delivery? As you answer these questions, consciously identify with your listeners. Put yourself in their place and respond to your speech as they would.

Here is how one student worked out his problems of audience adaptation:

Juan Ruiz, a junior geology major, decided to give an informative speech about how earthquakes occur. From his audience analysis he learned that only two or three of his classmates knew much of anything about geology. To most of them, a tectonic plate would be found on a dinner table rather than below the surface of the earth. Juan realized, then, that he must present his speech at an elementary level and with a minimum of scientific language.

As he prepared the speech, Juan kept asking himself, "How can I make this clear and meaningful to someone who knows nothing about earthquakes or geological principles?" Since he was speaking in the Midwest, he decided to begin by noting that the most severe earthquake in American history took place not in California or Alaska, but at New Madrid, Missouri, in 1811. If such an earthquake happened today, it would be felt from the Rocky Mountains to the Atlantic Ocean and would flatten most of the cities in the Mississippi Valley. That, he figured, should get his classmates' attention.

Throughout the body of the speech, Juan dealt only with the basic mechanics of earthquakes and carefully avoided technical terms such as "asthenosphere," "lithosphere," and "subduction zones." He also prepared visual aids diagramming fault lines so his classmates wouldn't get confused.

To be absolutely safe, Juan asked his roommate—who was not a geology major—to listen to the speech. "Stop me," he said, "anytime I say something you don't understand." Juan's roommate stopped him four times, and at each spot Juan worked out a way to make his point more clearly. Finally, he had a speech that was interesting and perfectly understandable to his audience.

As you work on your speeches, try to keep your listeners constantly in mind. Anticipate how they will respond to your ideas. Be creative in thinking about ways to adapt your message to them. Like Juan, you will give a much better speech.

Audience Adaptation During the Speech

No matter how hard you work ahead of time, things may not go exactly as planned on the day of your speech. For speeches in the classroom you may find that the overhead projector for your visual aids is not available or that another student has the same topic as you. For speeches outside the classroom you might learn that the room for your speech has been changed,

Speech Assignment
For a creative speech assignment that requires students to utilize the principles of audience analysis and adaptation described here, see Sharon D. Downey, "Audience Analysis Exercise," in *Selections from the Speech Communication Teacher, 1986–1991*, pp. 12–13, which accompanies *The Art of Public Speaking*.

Cross-Reference
In Chapter 15, the general principles of audience analysis and adaptation are extended to incorporate the target audience and its role in persuasive speaking.

that the audience will be much larger (or smaller) than you had anticipated, or even that the amount of time available for your speech has been cut in half because a previous speaker has droned on for too long.

If something like this happens to you, don't panic. Find another way to present your visual aids. Modify your introduction to mention the other student's speech on your topic. Adjust your delivery to the changed audience size. And if you find you have less time for your speech than you had planned, don't simply talk twice as fast to get everything in—that would be worse than not talking at all. Instead, condense your speech to its most essential points and present them in the time available. Your listeners will sympathize with your predicament and will appreciate your regard for their time. This will more than compensate for your lost speaking time.

Finally, be sure to keep an eye out during your speech for audience feedback. If your listeners are sitting forward in their chairs, looking at you with interest, and nodding their heads in approval, you can assume things are going well. But suppose you find them frowning or responding with quizzical looks. Then you may need to back up and go over your point again, as in this example:

Michelle Voss, a business major, had worked diligently to make sure her informative speech on how the stock market works was not too technical for her classmates, most of whom were engineering and humanities students. She explained everything from the ground up, prepared two excellent visual aids, and practiced giving the speech to her best friend, an art major and self-confessed "economics imbecile."

On the day of Michelle's speech, everything went well until she got to her second main point, when she noticed that several of her classmates seemed puzzled by the relationship between common stock and preferred stock. Knowing they would be lost for the rest of the speech if they didn't understand that relationship, Michelle paused and said, "I can see some of you are confused by my explanation. Let me try it again from another angle."

As Michelle went through the material a second time, she could see her classmates nodding their heads in understanding. She could now go on with her speech, confident that her audience was ready to go with her.

Adapting to your audience—both before the speech and during it—is one of the most important keys to successful public speaking. Like other aspects of speechmaking, it is sometimes easier said than done. But once you master it, you'll see that it pays dividends in more personal facets of your life—when you adapt to an audience of one.

Summary

Good speakers are audience-centered. They know that the aim of speechmaking is to gain a desired response from listeners. When working on your speeches, keep three questions in mind: To whom am I speaking? What do I want them to know, believe, or do as a result of my speech? What is the most effective way of composing and presenting my speech to accomplish that aim? Your classroom speeches will give you excellent practice in dealing with these questions, provided you always think of your classmates as a *real* audience.

To be an effective speaker, you should know something about the psychology of audiences. Auditory perception is selective. Even when people pay close attention, they don't process a speaker's message exactly as the

Speech Assignment
Because of their lack of speaking experience, most students have great difficulty adjusting to an audience during the course of a speech. For one instructor's approach to teaching this aspect of audience adaptation, see C. Darrell Langley, "The Heckling Speech," in *Selections from the Speech Communication Teacher, 1986–1991*, p. 67, which accompanies *The Art of Public Speaking*.

speaker intended. People hear what they want to hear. People also are egocentric. They typically approach speeches with one question uppermost in mind: "Why is this important to *me?*" Therefore, you need to study your audience and adapt your speech directly to their beliefs and interests.

The first stage in learning about your audience is to undertake a demographic audience analysis. This involves identifying important demographic traits of your audience such as age, gender, sexual orientation, religion, group membership, and racial, ethnic, or cultural background. The second stage in learning about your audience is to conduct a situational audience analysis. This involves identifying traits of the audience unique to the particular speaking situation at hand. These traits include the size of the audience, attitudes influenced by the physical setting, and your listeners' disposition toward the topic, toward you as a speaker, and toward the occasion.

For speeches outside the classroom, you can best get information about the audience by asking the person who invites you to speak. If possible, you should also sound out someone else who has spoken to the same group. For your classroom speeches, you can learn much about your audience by observation and conversation. You also can do a more formal audience analysis by interviewing members of the audience or by circulating a questionnaire.

Once you complete the audience analysis, you must adapt your speech so it will be clear and convincing to your listeners. Keep them in mind constantly as you prepare the speech. Put yourself in their place. Try to hear the speech as they will. Anticipate questions and objections, and try to answer them in advance.

When you deliver your speech, keep an eye out for audience feedback. If you see frowns or puzzled looks on your listeners' faces, you may need to adjust your remarks in response. Like other aspects of audience adaptation, this may be difficult at first, but if you work at it, you should soon see results.

Key Terms

audience-centeredness (110)
identification (111)
egocentrism (113)
demographic audience
    analysis (115)
stereotyping (115)

situational audience analysis (122)
attitude (124)
fixed-alternative questions (127)
scale questions (128)
open-ended questions (128)

Review these terms
by doing the
Chapter 5 crossword
puzzle at
www.mhhe.com/lucas8.

ONLINE LEARNING CENTER

Review Questions

After reading this chapter, you should be able to answer the following questions:

1. Why must a public speaker be audience-centered?

2. What does it mean to say that people are egocentric? What implications does the egocentrism of audiences hold for you as a public speaker?

3. What are the six demographic traits of audiences discussed in this chapter? Why is each important to audience analysis?

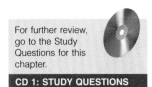

For further review, go to the Study Questions for this chapter.

CD 1: STUDY QUESTIONS

4. What is situational audience analysis? What factors do you need to consider in situational audience analysis?

5. How can you get information about an audience?

6. What are the three kinds of questions used in questionnaires? Why is it a good idea to use all three in audience analysis?

7. What methods can you use to adapt your speech to your audience before the speech? During the speech?

Exercises for Critical Thinking

1. Advertisers are usually very conscious of their audience. Choose an issue of a popular magazine such as *Time, Newsweek, Sports Illustrated, Cosmopolitan,* or the like. From that issue select five advertisements to analyze. Try to determine the audience being appealed to in each advertisement, and analyze the appeals (verbal and visual) used to persuade buyers. How might the appeals differ if the ads were designed to persuade a different audience?

Cross-Reference

For discussion of the Exercises for Critical Thinking, see the *Instructor's Manual,* pp. 140–144. For additional exercises, check the *Instructor's Manual,* pp. 145–149, as well as the five volumes of *Selections from the Speech Communication Teacher* that accompany *The Art of Public Speaking.*

2. Below are three general speech topics and, for each, two hypothetical audiences to which a speech might be delivered. For each topic, write a brief paragraph explaining how you might adjust your specific purpose and message according to the demographic characteristics of the audience.

    a. *Topic:* "Superconductivity"

    Audience #1: 50% physics majors, 30% engineering majors, 20% music majors

    Audience #2: 40% English majors, 40% business majors, 20% physics majors

    b. *Topic:* "Sexual Assault: The Biggest Campus Crime"

    Audience #1: 80% female, 20% male

    Audience #2: 80% male, 20% female

    c. *Topic:* "The 1986 *Challenger* Explosion"

    Audience #1: Day class: 70% age 18 to 22, 30% age 23 and over

    Audience #2: Evening class: 50% age 35 and over, 30% age 23 to 34, 20% age 18 to 22

3. For your next speech, design and circulate among your classmates an audience-analysis questionnaire like that discussed on pages 127–130. Use all three kinds of questions explained in the text: fixed-alternative questions, scale questions, and open-ended questions. After you have tabulated the results of the questionnaire, write an analysis explaining what the questionnaire reveals about your audience and what steps you must take to adapt your speech to the audience.

4. Read Barbara Bush's "Choices and Change" in the appendix of sample speeches following Chapter 18. Focus on how Bush adapts her message to her audience in light of the controversy that preceded her speech. Be prepared to discuss your ideas in class.

Applying the **POWER** *of* PUBLIC SPEAKING

As a university professor, your research, writing, and teaching in the area of gender communication has attracted media attention. It seems that nearly everyone is interested in the differences between the communication styles of men and women. You have been asked to address the managers of a large local manufacturing company on the topic of gender communication in the workplace.

Cross-Reference
For discussion of this Applying the Power of Public Speaking scenario, see the *Instructor's Manual,* pp. 144–145.

To prepare for your speech, you have scheduled a meeting with the company's human resource director who contacted you. Having taken a public speaking class in college, you know how important it is to analyze the audience you will be addressing. List (1) the three most important questions you want to ask the resource director about the demographics of your audience, and (2) the three most important questions you want to ask about the situational traits of your audience. Be specific in your questions, and be prepared, if necessary, to explain your choice of questions.

Notes

[1] Seeing the speech classroom as a real audience is also important because it engages students in a form of rhetorical activity that is vital to participatory democracy. As Rosa Eberly states, "By studying and practicing rhetoric together in classrooms understood as protopublic spaces, students have the potential to understand themselves, invent arguments, make judgments, and engage in conjoint actions" as "citizens who share common interests." See Rosa A. Eberly, "Rhetoric and the Anti-Logos Doughball: Teaching Deliberating Bodies the Practices of Participatory Democracy," *Rhetoric and Public Affairs,* 5 (2002), p. 296.

[2] Quoted in Halford R. Ryan, "Harry Emerson Fosdick," in Bernard K. Duffy and Halford R. Ryan (eds.), *American Orators of the Twentieth Century* (New York: Greenwood Press, 1987), p. 148.

[3] Saul Alinsky, *Rules for Radicals* (New York: Random House, 1971), p. 81.

[4] For a broader discussion of gender issues in communication, see Julia T. Wood, *Gendered Lives: Communication, Gender, and Culture,* 5th ed. (Belmont, CA: Wadsworth, 2003); Diana K. Ivy and Phil Backlund, *Exploring GenderSpeak: Personal Effectiveness in Gender Communication,* 2nd ed. (New York: McGraw-Hill, 2000).

[5] Paul Krugman, "The Other Face," *New York Times,* December 13, 2002, p. 3A; Jon Meacham, "A Man Out of Time," *Newsweek,* December 23, 2002, p. 36.

[6] David Foster, "Cultural Concierges on Alert," *Wisconsin State Journal* (November 19, 1993).

[7] Diana L. Eck, *A New Religious America* (New York: HarperCollins, 2001), p. 4.

[8] Sources for the information in this paragraph include "List of Hindu Temples in U.S.A." (www.geocities.com/kalyan.geo/temple1.html); "Jain Temples in U.S." (www.adherents.com/largecom/templjain_statesUS.html); "Gurudwaras in United States of America" (http://allaboutsikhs.com/gurudwaras/gurud_55.htm); and the Pluralism Project's Directory of Religious Centers (www.pluralism.org/directory/search.php).

[9] There is a substantial body of research to show that speakers are usually more persuasive when they attempt to refute opposing arguments rather than ignoring them. See Daniel J. O'Keefe, *Persuasion: Theory and Research,* 2nd ed. (Thousand Oaks, CA: Sage, 2002), pp. 247–249.

Chapter Six

GATHERING MATERIALS

S uppose you want to create an entertainment system for your home or apartment. You want to select the best components (television, receiver, DVD player, speakers, and so on) you can get for the amount of money you have to spend. How do you go about it?

You can talk to people who have put together entertainment systems and ask them for advice. You can get magazines from the library or search the Internet for information. On the other hand, if you've purchased electronics before, you can rely on your experience and adapt it to your current needs. Since you want your system to be perfect, you gather as much information as you can before you make your purchases.

Gathering material for a speech is like gathering information for any other project. Many resources are available to you if you take advantage of them. How do you get material for your speeches? There are several ways. You can interview people with specialized knowledge on a given topic. You can do research on the Internet or in the library. Sometimes you can use yourself as a resource—whenever you have personal experience or more than average knowledge about a subject. Let's turn first to the resource of your own experience.

Chapter Focus
This chapter explains how to gather materials for a speech by drawing upon one's personal knowledge and experience, by using library resources, by searching the Internet, and by conducting a research interview. It ends with tips for doing research systematically and efficiently. For a full outline of the chapter, see the *Instructor's Manual,* pp. 157–162.

Using Your Own Knowledge and Experience

Everybody is an expert on something, whether it is video games, child care, or backpacking. As we saw in Chapter 4, we often speak best about subjects with which we are familiar. This is why teachers encourage students to capitalize on their own knowledge and experience in developing speech topics.

When you choose a topic from your own experience, you may be tempted to depersonalize it by relying solely on facts and figures from books. Such outside information is almost always necessary. But supplementing it with the personal touch can really bring your speeches to life.

Teaching Tip
Students often ask whether they can use personal stories in their speeches. Reassure them that such stories can lend interest, realism, and vividness to a speech.

One student, afflicted with diabetes, chose to explain how a person can live with the disease on a daily basis. He cited statistics on the incidence of diabetes in the United States, identified symptoms of the disease, and related how it is treated. Along the way he illustrated his points by talking about his personal experiences. Here is part of what he said:

> Being a diabetic presents a challenge one cannot afford to lose. On a personal note, I have tried not to let my diabetes affect my lifestyle. Last year I spent nine months traveling in Central and South America. The trip was very memorable, but I had one particularly frightening experience that quickly makes you realize just how vulnerable a diabetic is. On the fifth day of a two-week excursion down the Amazon River in Brazil, our canoe tipped, dumping everything into the river.
>
> Although I recovered my pack, part of its contents—including my insulin—were swallowed up by the river. Without insulin I could not eat any food, for if I did, my blood sugar level would become too high and I could eventually go into convulsions, slip into a coma, and die. We returned back up the Amazon and traveled three days until we reached the first village and I could radio for more medicine. I was hot and hungry, but alive.

This speech has color and emotion. By drawing on his own experience, the speaker conveyed his point much more meaningfully than he could have in any other way.

Even if your life stories are not that dramatic, you can still put them to work for you. After all, you are the one who was there. You did, saw, felt, heard whatever it is you are speaking about. By thinking over your past experiences—gathering material from yourself—you can find many supporting details for your speeches.

Doing Library Research

Some students regard the library as a place to be entered only in the most desperate circumstances. Then they take a speech class and discover that the library is not so forbidding after all. You will get many of the materials for your speeches from the library. Thus you need to know the basic techniques of doing library research. Of course, you may know them already, in which case you need only review this section of the book.

There are quick, easy, systematic ways to find whatever you need in the library. The first step is to learn your way around. Take the orientation tour offered by your library. While on the tour, you will probably receive a brief handbook or series of leaflets explaining what is in the library and how to find it. Keep this material with your class notes. It takes only a few minutes to read and will be helpful later.

Ultimately, the only way to become adept at library research is to do it—and to do it properly. You have five important resources for finding what you need in the library: librarians, the catalogue, periodical databases, newspapers, and reference works. We'll look at each in turn.[1]

Librarians

Thanks to movies, comic strips, and television commercials, librarians have a bad image. They are typically portrayed as cold, stuffy, bespectacled figures whose main goal in life is to keep people from speaking above a whisper. In fact, most librarians are friendly men and women who can be of enormous help.

Too often students waste their time wandering aimlessly in search of a source because they are afraid to ask for assistance. They don't want to appear stupid or to "bother" anyone. But would you be as sensitive about asking a doctor for help with a medical problem? Librarians are experts in their own field, trained in library use and research methods. If you have a question, don't hesitate to ask a librarian. She or he can help you find your way, locate sources, even track down a specific piece of information.

The Catalogue

The catalogue lists all the books, periodicals, and other resources owned by the library. Although there are many different computer systems for library catalogues, most allow you to search for books by author, title, or subject.

Teaching Tip
Arrange for your students to take a tour of the campus library. Contact the library well in advance to set up the tour. Be sure to explain the research tasks your students will face in preparing their speeches, and indicate any particular features of the library you want the tour to emphasize. If possible, arrange for students to get hands-on experience with the catalogue and with periodical databases. Students usually find the tour so helpful that they often rank it—and the development of their research skills—as one of the most valuable aspects of their speech class.

catalogue
A listing of all the books, periodicals, and other resources owned by a library.

Figure 6.1   Sample Catalogue Entry for a Book.

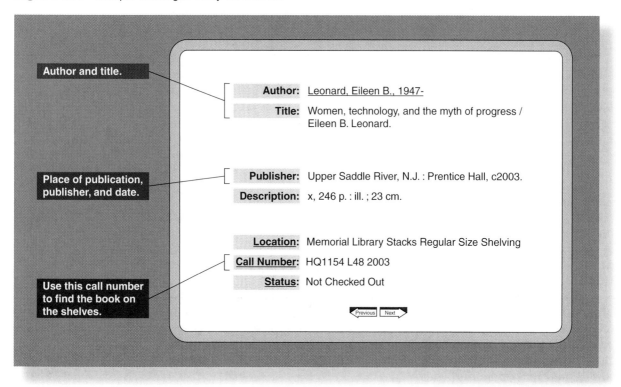

They also are set up for keyword searches, which means you can locate a book by typing in a significant word or phrase, even if that word or phrase is not part of the book's title. The catalogue also tells you whether the book you want is available or is already checked out.

Figure 6.1 shows a sample catalogue entry for a book. As you can see, it gives quite a bit of information. The key to finding the book on the shelves is the *call number*. Once you have the call number, all you have to do is find the right section of the shelves (or stacks, as they are called in some libraries) and retrieve your book.

call number
A number used in libraries to classify books and periodicals and to indicate where they can be found on the shelves.

Periodicals are listed in the catalogue by title. Libraries usually have a special room in which they keep the latest issues of magazines and newspapers. Bound volumes of issues from past years are kept on the book shelves, where they can be located by call number. You may also be able to find the full text of specific articles through the library's periodical databases.

periodical database
A research aid that catalogues articles from a large number of journals or magazines.

Periodical Databases

Periodical databases do for articles in magazines and journals what the catalogue does for books. Just as the catalogue helps you locate specific books from among all the books in the library, a periodical database helps you locate specific magazine or journal articles.

Accessing a periodical database is as easy as using the library's catalogue. Type the subject on which you want information in the database's search box, and citations of articles on your subject will appear on screen. Depending on the database you are using, you may be able to call up the full text of the articles. If the full text is not available, you can use the citations to locate the articles you need on the shelves or in the periodicals section of the library.

Most databases also provide an *abstract* that summarizes the content of each article you access. Keep in mind, however, that an abstract is only a summary of the article, written by someone other than the original author. The purpose of the abstract is to help you decide whether the article will be of use in your speech. You should never cite an article in your speech on the basis of the abstract alone. You should always consult the full article.

Because each database has its own methods of finding materials, you should take time before starting your search to click the "Help," "Tips," or "Search Guide" button on the database's homepage. This will bring up a screen that explains the procedures for conducting searches at different levels of specificity—basic, guided, and advanced. If you don't check this information, you may well miss citations in the database that are important to your speech.

Altogether there are hundreds of databases, covering topics from agriculture to zoology. The exact databases you can use will depend on what is available in your library. Here are a few of the major ones you are most likely to use in preparing your speeches. They are divided into two groups— general databases and special databases. Knowing how to use them will benefit you long after you have finished your speech class.

General Databases

As their name implies, general databases cover a wide range of periodicals and subjects. They usually include popular magazines such as *Time*, *Newsweek*, *Scientific American*, *Ebony*, *Sports Illustrated*, *Ms.*, *Vital Speeches*, *Rolling Stone*, and *Psychology Today*. Some of them also include academic journals and technical publications. Here are four major general databases. Odds are that your library will have at least one of them:

ProQuest Research Library. An excellent database that indexes more than 2,000 general-interest periodicals and academic journals, and provides the full text of articles from nearly 1,000 of them. Dates vary, but many of the full-text articles go back to 1988. Figure 6.2 (page 142) shows a sample screen from ProQuest Research Library with a typical magazine citation and abstract.

Academic Search. An extremely valuable resource that provides the full text of articles from more than 3,000 periodicals, popular and scholarly alike. It also indexes articles from *The New York Times*, *The Wall Street Journal*, and *The Christian Science Monitor*. A special feature translates articles from English to Spanish, French or German.

Reader's Guide Full Text. The electronic counterpart of the printed *Reader's Guide to Periodical Literature,* this database indexes and abstracts articles from more than 240 general-interest publications. Full-text articles are provided for 120 periodicals.

abstract
A summary of a magazine or journal article, written by someone other than the original author.

Teaching Tip
Make sure students understand that they need to locate the full texts of magazine and newspaper articles rather than relying on abstracts of the articles.

Class Activity
As a homework assignment, have students locate three magazine articles on the subject of their next speech using one of the periodical databases discussed on pp. 140–142. Students should prepare a preliminary bibliography entry for each article, locate the text of each article, and prepare a one- to two-sentence summary of each article. Select a few students to report to the class on their findings. Use the reports as a springboard for discussion about how to use periodical databases in researching a speech.

Figure 6.2 Sample Periodical Entry from ProQuest Research Library.

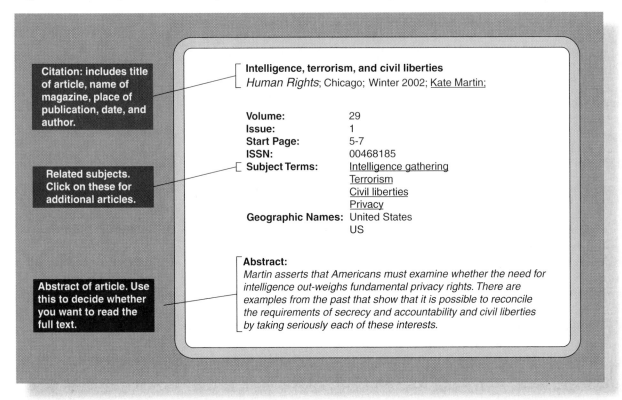

Lexis/Nexis Academic Universe. Composed of roughly 5,000 legal, news, reference, and business sources, this powerful database provides full-text access to a wide range of periodicals and other sources, including television broadcast transcripts and U.S. and international newspapers.

Special Databases

Sometimes you may need more specialized information than you can find in the kinds of publications covered in general periodical databases. If so, check with your librarian, who will direct you to a special database. Examples include:

Business Full Text

Contemporary Women's Issues

ERIC (Education Resources Information Center)

Ethnic Newswatch

General Science Full Text

HAPI Online (Hispanic American Periodicals Index)

Humanities Full Text

Public Affairs Information Service International

Newspapers

Newspapers are invaluable for research on many topics, historical as well as contemporary. If you are looking for information from your local newspaper, your library will probably have current issues in the periodicals room. Back issues may be available on microfilm.

For national and international newspapers, consult one of the following databases:

ProQuest Newspapers. Indexes articles from more than 500 U.S. and international newspapers. Includes full-text articles for most major newspapers back to 1995.

Lexis/Nexis Academic Universe. In addition to magazine articles, Lexis/Nexis furnishes full-text articles from a large number of U.S. and international newspapers, as well as daily updates from news services such as Reuters, United Press International, and the Associated Press. (See Figure 6.3 for a sample screen from Lexis/Nexis.)

Global NewsBank. Provides full-text articles from more than 1,500 international sources, including newspapers.

Teaching Tip
Students sometimes ask how they can acquire transcripts from television news programs. Recent transcripts are often available on a given network's website. Transcripts of many archived programs—including evening news broadcasts—are available through Lexis/Nexis.

Figure 6.3 Sample Newspaper Entry from Lexis/Nexis.

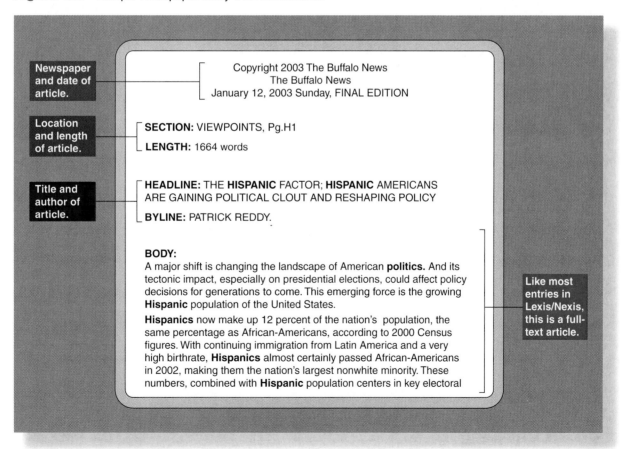

Finally, you should know about *Editorials on File*. Although available only in print form, it contains editorials from hundreds of newspapers across the United States and is an excellent source of informed opinion on current events. Published twice monthly, it reprints nearly 5,000 editorials a year. A cumulative index makes it easy to find what you need.

Reference Works

reference work
A work that synthesizes a large amount of related information for easy access by researchers.

How far is it from Los Angeles to Tokyo? What are the origins of the phrase "raining cats and dogs"? How many people in the United States die in fires each year? Who won the Academy Award for Best Actor in 1993? Which city has the highest murder rate in the U.S.?

These are all questions that could arise in the process of researching a speech. You could try to answer them by rummaging through a dozen books or thumbing through a batch of magazines or newspapers in hopes of finding what you need. The easy, efficient approach, however, would be to consult the library's collection of reference works.

Reference works are usually kept in a separate part of the library called the reference section. The right reference work can save you hours of time by putting at your fingertips a wealth of information that might be difficult to locate through a database or the library catalogue. The major kinds of reference works are encyclopedias, yearbooks, dictionaries, biographical aids, atlases, and gazetteers. Here are the ones you should find most valuable in preparing your speeches.

Encyclopedias

general encyclopedia
A comprehensive reference work that provides information about all branches of human knowledge.

We are all familiar with general encyclopedias such as the *Encyclopaedia Britannica* and the *Encyclopedia Americana*. They seek to provide accurate, objective information about all branches of human knowledge and are an excellent place to begin your research. Both *Britannica* and *Americana* are arranged alphabetically and issue annual supplements to update what is contained in the basic volumes. Many general encyclopedias—including *Britannica*—can also be accessed online.

In addition to general encyclopedias, there are special encyclopedias devoted to particular subjects such as religion, art, law, science, literature, music, education, and the like. They cover their fields in much more depth and detail than do general encyclopedias. Some of the most frequently used special encyclopedias are:

special encyclopedia
A comprehensive reference work devoted to a specific subject such as religion, art, law, science, music, etc.

African American Encyclopedia

Asian American Encyclopedia

Dictionary of Art

Encyclopedia of Philosophy

Encyclopedia of Religion

Grove's Dictionary of Music and Musicians

Latino Encyclopedia

McGraw-Hill Encyclopedia of Science and Technology

Library research is vital for most speeches. Knowing the resources available in your library and how to use them efficiently will make the research process much more productive.

Yearbooks

As the name implies, yearbooks are published annually. They contain an amazing amount of current information that would otherwise be all but impossible to track down. Here are three of the most valuable yearbooks:

> *Statistical Abstract of the United States.* Published since 1878 by the U.S. Bureau of the Census and now available online as well, the *Statistical Abstract* is the standard reference work for numerical information on social, political, and economic aspects of American life. Among the incredible array of facts it contains are the U.S. fertility rate, labor union membership, death rates from various diseases, median family income by state, and so on.

> *World Almanac and Book of Facts.* Unlike the *Statistical Abstract,* the *World Almanac* is not limited to the United States or to numerical data. Among the things you can discover in it are all the Nobel Prize winners since 1901, the most-watched television shows of the previous year, records for professional and collegiate sports, the literacy rate in Afghanistan, and the natural resources of Peru.

> *Facts on File.* Available in both print and online versions, *Facts on File* is a weekly digest of national and foreign news events. It covers politics, sports, medicine, education, religion, crime, economics, and the arts. At the end of the year, all the weekly issues are published together as *Facts on File Yearbook.* This is an excellent place to check quickly on something that happened in a given year.

Dictionaries

There are several excellent dictionaries of the English language, including *Webster's* and the *American Heritage Dictionary,* both of which are available

yearbook
A reference work published annually that contains information about the previous year.

Class Activity
For an excellent activity that requires students to gain familiarity with the library's reference sources and to prepare brief speeches on those sources, see Mark Gellis, "Teaching Research, Teaching Speech," in *Selections from the Communication Teacher, 1999–2002,* pp. 65–67, which accompanies *The Art of Public Speaking.*

electronically as well as in book form. If you are interested more in the history of a word than its present meaning, you should turn first to the *Oxford English Dictionary.* There are also a number of specialized dictionaries that cover a wide range of topics. Some examples are the *Computer Dictionary, Black's Law Dictionary,* the *Dictionary of Feminist Theory,* and the *Morris Dictionary of Word and Phrase Origins.*

Quotation Books

Teaching Tip
Quotation books can be valuable in many ways. When he was a young man, Winston Churchill studied *Bartlett's Familiar Quotations* intently. "The quotations," he said, "when engraved upon the memory give you good thoughts. They also make you anxious to read the authors and look for more."

The best-known collection of quotations is *Bartlett's Familiar Quotations.* With more than 25,000 quotations from historical and contemporary figures, it has long been regarded as an indispensable source for speakers and writers alike. Other excellent quotation books include:

Oxford Dictionary of Quotations

Harper Book of American Quotations

The New Quotable Woman

My Soul Looks Back, 'Less I Forget: A Collection of Quotations by People of Color

Ancient Echoes: Native American Words of Wisdom

Fire in Our Souls: Quotations of Wisdom and Inspiration by Latino Americans

A Treasury of Jewish Quotations

All these works are indexed to help you locate quotations by subject as well as by author.

Biographical Aids

biographical aid
A reference work that provides information about people.

When you need information about people in the news, check the reference section, where you will find books that contain brief life and career facts about contemporary men and women. Here are some of the ones you are likely to find most useful:

International Who's Who

Who's Who in America

Who's Who of American Women

Contemporary Black Biography

Dictionary of Hispanic Biography

Native American Women

Who's Who Among Asian Americans

Class Activity
The fifth Exercise for Critical Thinking at the end of this chapter gives students firsthand experience with a variety of reference works. For full discussion of the exercise, see the *Instructor's Manual,* pp. 163–165. Also see the Additional Exercises for Critical Thinking on pp. 167–172 of the *Instructor's Manual.*

If you need more detailed information than these guides provide, your best bet is *Current Biography.* During the year it offers some 400 articles about newsworthy people all over the world. Each article is three to four pages long, and the fields covered include politics, science, the arts, labor, sports, and business. At the end of the year, the articles are revised and collected alphabetically in a single volume titled *Current Biography Yearbook.* Articles are also available online through the Reader's Guide Full Text database.

Atlases and Gazetteers

Atlases, of course, contain maps. But most modern atlases also include a variety of charts, plates, and tables that furnish information about the geography of states, regions, and countries. The leading all-purpose atlas is the *Rand McNally Cosmopolitan World Atlas,* which includes maps of the world by region, as well as maps of each state of the United States.

Gazetteers, or geographical dictionaries, follow the same alphabetical format as regular dictionaries, but all entries deal with geographical topics. The best-known gazetteer is *Merriam-Webster's Geographical Dictionary.* This fascinating volume lists more than 48,000 places around the world—countries, regions, cities, islands, mountains, rivers—and gives concise facts about each. You should look here to find such things as the height of Mount Everest, the state flower of Florida, and all the places in the world named Athens.

atlas
A book of maps.

gazetteer
A geographical dictionary.

Searching the Internet

The Internet has been called the world's biggest library. Through it you can read electronic versions of the *New York Times,* the *Tokyo Shimbun,* and the *Jerusalem Post.* You can visit the great museums of Europe, browse through the Library of Congress, and get up-to-the-minute bulletins from CNN and Reuters News Service. You can access government agencies and most major corporations. You can read texts of Supreme Court decisions and of the latest bills proposed in Congress. You can check stock market prices, conduct word searches of the Bible, and find statistics on virtually every topic under the sun.

Unlike a library, however, the Internet has no central information desk, no librarians, no catalogue, and no reference section. Nor does it have a person or department in charge of choosing new materials to make sure they are of high quality. You can unearth a great deal of information on the Internet, but you cannot always find the same range and depth of research materials as in a good library. This is why experts advise that you use the Internet to supplement, not to replace, library research.

In this section, we will look at ways you can go beyond surfing the Web and turn it into a powerful research tool for your speeches. We'll begin by looking at search aids and other resources for conducting efficient, focused inquiries. Then we'll look at some specialized research resources that are especially valuable for classroom speeches. Finally, we'll explain how to evaluate the reliability and objectivity of the research materials you find on the Web and how to cite them in your speeches.

Search Aids

Instead of haphazardly surfing the Web, the smart approach is to use a search aid to find exactly what you need. Because there are so many documents

search aid
A program used to find information on the World Wide Web.

on the Web, no search aid can provide a comprehensive catalogue of all of them. Each aid has its strengths and weaknesses, and each has its own procedures for in-depth searches. New search aids keep cropping up, and existing ones continue to be refined. The three major kinds of aids are search engines, metasearch engines, and virtual libraries.

Search Engines

Search engines index Web pages and scan them to find what you want. Because each works a little differently and indexes different pages, the results of any search will vary depending on the engine you use. Taken together, the major search engines cover about 40 percent of the total number of Web pages, and no single search engine covers more than 15 or 20 percent.[2] Depending on the topic of your speech and the information you're looking for, you may find exactly what you need right away. If not, don't despair—it may well show up on another search engine.

Here are some of the major search engines currently in operation:

Google (www.google.com)

Yahoo! (www.yahoo.com)

Fast Search (www.alltheweb.com)

Teoma (www.teoma.com/)

AltaVista (www.altavista.com)

Northern Light (http://northernlight.com)

Of all these search engines, Google is the most widely used by serious researchers. About half of all Web searches in the world are performed by Google. In addition to providing access to more than 3 billion websites, it has specialized search tools devoted to images (Google Image) and news stories (Google News), and it can even translate foreign-language search results. Google is so efficient that its technology is used by other companies such as Yahoo and America Online.[3] While there is no guarantee that you'll find exactly what you need with Google, it's a great place to start your Internet research.

Metasearch Engines

Metasearch engines are the search engines of search engines. They send your request to several search engines at the same time, allowing you to cast a broader net than is possible with a single engine. This can be a great advantage—especially when you are looking for something very obscure. Trying to find it by going through a number of search engines one by one would be extremely time-consuming. By using a metasearch engine, you can scan a dozen or more search engines simultaneously.

It's important to know that metasearch engines vary in the specific search engines they cover, the number of search engines they can access at one time, the length of time they devote to searching each engine, and the number of records they can retrieve from it. If you decide to use a metasearch engine, be sure to check which engines it includes so you will know if there are others you want to access in addition.

There are a large number of metasearch engines. Here are four of the better ones:

Dogpile (www.dogpile.com)

MetaCrawler (www.metacrawler.com)

Ixquick Metasearch (www.ixquick.com)

ProFusion (www.profusion.com)

Virtual Libraries

Search engines help you find what's on the Web, but few evaluate the quality of the sources they retrieve. Faced with the fact that anyone can post anything on the Internet, librarians and other information specialists are working to make it easier to locate reliable, high-quality Web resources. One result of their efforts is the creation of *virtual libraries*—search aids that combine Internet technology with traditional library methods of cataloguing and assessing data to create first-class research collections.[4]

Mostly nonprofit ventures associated with colleges or universities, virtual libraries are much smaller than commercial search engines. What they lack in size, however, they more than make up in quality. You will not retrieve nearly as many sources with a virtual library as with a commercial search engine, but you can be confident that the ones you do get have been screened for accuracy and reliability.

Virtual libraries are also valuable because they can help you locate materials that are overlooked by even the most thorough of search engines. These materials are part of what is called the *invisible Web*—millions of databases and other resources that, because of technological factors, are not indexed by search engines. By accessing this invisible Web, virtual libraries expand the kinds of Internet resources available to you.[5]

As time goes on, we can expect more virtual libraries to be developed. For now, here are seven that you may find helpful as you work on your speeches. All have clear, user-friendly systems that make searching for information easy and efficient.

Librarian's Index to the Internet (www.lii.org)

Internet Public Library (www.ipl.org)

Invisible Web Directory (www.invisible-web.net)

Infomine (http://infomine.ucr.edu)

Social Science Information Gateway (www.sosig.ac.uk)

National Science Digital Library (www.nsdl.org)

Direct Search (www.freepint.com/gary/direct.htm)

Once you have selected a search aid, you will proceed by conducting either a keyword search or a subject search. Both methods are similar to keyword and subject searches in the library, and both are equally effective depending on the topic of your speech and the kind of information you are seeking.

virtual library
A search aid that combines Internet technology with traditional library methods of cataloguing and assessing data.

invisible Web
The multitude of Web databases and other resources that are not indexed by search engines.

Related Reading
For a fascinating look at the invisible Web and its many resources, see Chris Sherman and Gary Price, *The Invisible Web; Uncovering Information Sources Search Engines Can't See* (Medford, NJ: Information Today, 2001).

Keyword Searches

When you undertake a keyword search with a search aid that you have not used before, you should start by clicking the "Help" or "Tips" button on the search aid's homepage. The resulting screen will tell you how to use that particular aid most efficiently. This is especially important if you are using multiple words in your search. You will need a search strategy that will get you to the specific information you need.

Class Activity
You can help your students learn to conduct focused Internet searches by giving them very specific facts to locate on the Web. For one approach, see Michael L. Kent, "Getting the Most from Your Search Engine," in *Selections from the Communication Teacher, 1999–2002,* pp. 68–70, which accompanies *The Art of Public Speaking.* Although Kent focuses on metasearch engines, the activity can easily be adapted for search engines or virtual libraries.

Suppose, for example, that you are using Google to look for information about Ritalin abuse by college students. If you simply enter the word *Ritalin* in the search box, you will get a list of every document catalogued by Google that contains the word *Ritalin* in its index field—about 205,000 in all. Some of these will deal with Ritalin abuse on college campuses, but the vast majority will not. Some will explain the chemical composition of Ritalin; others will deal with Ritalin as a treatment for attention deficit disorder. You will also get links to an underground pharmacy where you can order Ritalin without a prescription, a clothing outlet that sells T-shirts with silk-screen Ritalin designs, and a festival of short plays called *The Ritalin Readings.* Scanning through everything to find what you need would be a daunting task.

How do you limit your search to get more manageable results? If you type *Ritalin abuse* in Google's search box, you will come up with 30,200 citations—far fewer than the original 205,000, but still overwhelming. However, if you type "Ritalin abuse" in quotation marks, you will get only documents that contain the exact phrase "Ritalin abuse"—1,220 in all.

This is much better, but it's still too many to go through one by one. So you narrow your search still further. This time you type the following entry into Google's search box:

"Ritalin abuse" + "college students"

The + sign limits the search to items that contain both sets of keywords, "Ritalin abuse" and "college students." Bingo! This time you get a list of 135 documents, all of which deal with Ritalin abuse by college students.

If you were using a search engine other than Google, you might enter different commands. But the basic principles for doing precise, pinpointed searches are fairly similar from search engine to search engine. If you understand those principles, you will greatly increase your odds of finding exactly what you need for your speeches.

Subject Searches

In addition to searching the Web by keyword, you can explore it by subject. The most popular subject-based search aid is Yahoo. If you access the Yahoo homepage, you will find links to a number of general topic areas, including Business and Economy, Education, Government, Health, News and Media, Science, and Society and Culture. If you click one of these topic areas, you will get a screen with a list of subtopics. If you click one of the subtopics, you will get a screen that divides the subtopic into smaller categories. You will continue moving from screen to screen until you find the websites you want to visit.

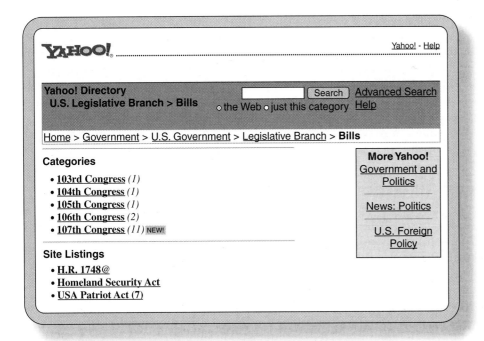

Figure 6.4

Exploring the Web by subject has many advantages. Suppose you need information about a bill currently being debated in the U.S. Congress. You could try to find it with a keyword search, but looking by subject would be much faster. The first step is to access the Yahoo homepage and click "Government." The next screen will give you several options, including "U.S. Government."

If you select "U.S. Government" from this screen and "Legislative Branch" from the next, you will come to a screen that includes "Bills" among its options. By choosing "Bills," you will get a screen similar to that in Figure 6.4. Click "Search Full Text of Bills" and pick the particular bill you want from a subsequent screen. What could be easier?

Bookmarks

Whether you are searching the Web by subject or by keyword, you need to keep track of all the useful-looking resources you uncover. Otherwise, you may never find them again.

As a library book or periodical is identified by its call number, an Internet site is identified by its URL (Uniform Resource Locator), which is often referred to as the site's "address." Once you find an Internet site that looks as if it may be relevant to your speech, you should record its URL in your preliminary bibliography (see page 164 for a sample bibliography entry for an Internet document). If you are doing your research at an on-campus computer center, you can write the site's URL by hand. A better method, however, is to use the computer's copy-and-paste function to transfer the URL to a floppy disk. This way you avoid the possibility of handwriting errors and ensure that the URL is recorded with absolute accuracy.[6]

Teaching Tip
Stress the importance of clicking a search engine's "Help" or "Tips" link for advice on how to conduct fast, focused searches. Most search engines also have guided or advanced options for more in-depth explorations.

URL (Uniform Resource Locator)
The string of letters or numbers that identifies a website's address.

bookmark
A feature in a Web browser that stores links to websites so they can be easily revisited.

If you have your own computer, you can record the URL by using your browser's "Bookmark" or "Favorites" feature. In Microsoft Explorer, for example, you will see the word "Favorites" at the top of the screen. If you click that word, one of your choices in the resulting menu will be "Add to Favorites." By clicking "Add to Favorites," you will automatically store the URL of the website currently on your screen. Not only does this give a record of the URL for your bibliography, but you can revisit that same site whenever you want simply by calling it up from your list of favorites.

Specialized Research Resources

Search aids are extremely helpful, but they are not the only vehicles for finding information on the Web. Because the Web is so vast, you may find it helpful to have a brief list of stable, high-quality websites that you can turn to with confidence in case a search aid doesn't turn up what you're looking for. In compiling the following list, I have concentrated on the kinds of sites that are most likely to be helpful as you work on your speeches.

Given the dynamic nature of the Internet, some sites may change their addresses by the time you read this book. If they do, you will probably find a new address at the old URL. If there is no new address, use a search engine to look for the site by name. (It's possible, of course, that a site will cease to exist, but most of those listed below should be around for some time.)

Related Reading
There are several general guides to the full range of Internet research. Two of the best are Alan M. Schlein, *Find It Online: The Complete Guide to Online Research*, 3rd ed. (Tempe, AZ: Facts on Demand Press, 2001), and Mary McGuire, Linda Stillborne, Melinda McAdams, and Laurel Hyatt, *The Internet Handbook for Writers, Researchers, and Journalists, 2002/2003 Edition* (New York: Guilford, 2002).

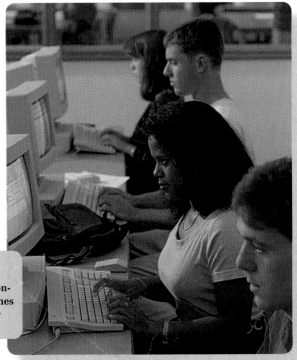

Researching on the Internet has many advantages, especially if you learn how to conduct efficient, focused searches that lead you to high-quality sources of information.

Government Resources

One of the great strengths of the Internet as a research tool is the access it provides to government documents and publications. Whether you are looking for information from a federal bureau in Washington, D.C., or from a state or local agency, chances are you can find it by starting your search at one of these websites:

FirstGov (www.firstgov.gov). The official U.S. gateway to all government information. Provides connections to more than 50 million Web pages from federal, state, local, and tribal governments, as well as from foreign nations around the world. A powerful search engine helps locate information quickly and accurately.

Federal Web Locator (www.infoctr.edu/fwl). One-stop shopping site for federal government information on the Web. Contains links to all major U.S. government websites, including Congress, the White House, the FBI, the Department of Education, the Food and Drug Administration, the Centers for Disease Control and Prevention, and the Environmental Protection Agency.

You can link to the websites identified on this page at www.mhhe.com/lucas8.

ONLINE LEARNING CENTER

State and Local Government on the Net (www.statelocalgov.net/index.cfm). Provides links to all 50 state governments, to Guam, Puerto Rico and other U.S. territories, and to cities and towns throughout the nation. Whether you're looking for the police department in Soldotna, Alaska, or the mayor's office in New York City, this is the website for you.

Reference Resources

The Internet cannot take the place of your library's reference section, with its encyclopedias, yearbooks, biographical aids, and the like. But it does contain a number of sites that can come in handy when you need a reference source. These sites include:

Virtual Reference Collection (http://libraries.mit.edu/research/virtualref.html). Offers links to a wide range of online reference sources, including encyclopedias, yearbooks, dictionaries, atlases, and biographical guides. A great spot as well for finding phone numbers of people and organizations around the world.

Galaxy Quotation (http://galaxy.einet.net/galaxy/Reference/Quotations.html). A comprehensive roster of links to collected quotations on the Web. Includes everything from Shakespeare to an electronic version of *Bartlett's*.

World Factbook (www.odci.gov/cia/publications/factbook/index.html). Published annually by the U.S. Central Intelligence Agency, the *World Factbook* is a rich compendium of information on every country in the world. Topics include people, government, economy, communication, transportation, and transnational issues.

Statistical Abstract (www.census.gov/pub/statab/www). Provides frequently requested tables and other selected data from the annual *Statistical Abstract of the United States*. Despite being less comprehensive than the printed *Statistical Abstract*, it is an excellent site for quantitative information on life in the U.S.

Class Activity
As a homework project, have each student visit one of the websites listed on pp. 152–154. Each student should spend time exploring the site and should bring to class a printout of the homepage for his or her site. Select a few students to report to the class about their sites. Use the reports to stimulate class discussion about the kinds of research resources available on the Web.

News Resources

The Web is a superb place to find information about news and current events. Not only are *Time, Newsweek, U.S. News and World Report,* and many other leading magazines available online, but there is a growing roster of periodicals that exist only in electronic form. In addition, most U.S. newspapers have their own websites—as do the major television news organizations. You can access any given publication or network by looking for it by name with a search engine, or you can go through one of the sites listed below.

Google News (http://news.google.com). Presents information culled from 4,000 news sources worldwide. Coverage is updated throughout the day, and a lightning-fast search engine allows you to find just what you need. The Web's most comprehensive source for up-to-the-minute news coverage.

NewsDirectory.com (www.ecola.com). Offers links to hundreds of magazines, newspapers, and television stations in the U.S. and around the globe. Has an excellent search engine and also provides access to campus papers from American colleges and universities.

Columbia Newsblaster (www.cs.columbia.edu/nlp/newsblaster/). Provides summaries of major daily news articles from a wide range of sources. An extensive archive makes it easy to access past articles from specific dates.

Multicultural Resources

As its name implies, the World Wide Web is a global phenomenon, and it mirrors the internationalism and diversity of our modern age. If you are speaking on a topic with multicultural dimensions, you may find help at one of the following sites:

Yahoo! Regional (www.yahoo.com/Regional/). A great starting point that offers links to scores of countries and regions around the world, as well as to all 50 states of the U.S.

WWW Virtual Library: American Indians (www.hanksville.org/NAresources). Comprehensive, well-organized resource with hundreds of links to sites dealing with Native American history, language, culture, education, health, art, and the like.

Asian American Resources (www.ai.mit.edu/people/irie/aar/). Provides links to scores of websites that feature topics, writings, and organizations of special interest to Asian Americans.

Latino/Hispanic Resources (www-rcf.usc.edu/~cmmr/Latino.html). Maintained by the University of Southern California's Center for Multilingual, Multicultural Research, this outstanding site provides links to a treasure trove of resources devoted to Latino- and Latina-related issues.

African American Web Connection (www.aawc.com). Award-winning website that deals with all aspects of African-American life, including history, business, politics, and religion. Also provides links to organizations such as the National Urban League, the Congressional Black Caucus, and the NAACP.

You can link to the websites identified on this page at www.mhhe.com/lucas8.

ONLINE LEARNING CENTER

Teaching Tip
Decide whether you will allow students to conduct all their speech research on the Internet. To help ensure that students develop their library skills rather than relying solely on the Internet, some instructors require a specified number of library sources for each speech.

Of course, there are thousands of other useful websites. But the ones discussed above, in conjunction with one of the Web's search aids, should help get your research off to a good start.

Evaluating Internet Documents

When you do research in a library, everything you find has been evaluated in one way or another before it gets to you. Books, magazines, and journals have editorial procedures to determine whether a given work should or should not be published. Once a work is published, it has to be approved by the acquisitions staff for inclusion in the library.

The Internet, of course, is a very different story. The most trusted resources on the Web are those derived from printed works—government records, newspaper articles, research reports, and the like. But most Web documents exist only in electronic form. Of these, few have gone through the kind of editorial review that is designed to ensure a basic level of reliability in printed works. The Web is "the largest self-publishing experiment in history."[7] Anyone with a computer and access to the Internet can share his or her opinions with a discussion group, publish an electronic newsletter, or create a personal Web page. Charlatans, extremists, and malcontents circulate their ideas on equal footing with CNN, the Library of Congress, and Nobel Prize winners. Never has the adage been more true than when applied to the Internet: "Don't believe everything you read."[8]

In Chapter 7, we will discuss how to judge the soundness of supporting materials in general. Here we look at three criteria you can use to help distinguish between the jewels and the junk on the Internet.[9]

Related Reading
A growing body of literature, much of it online, is devoted to the criteria and methods of assessing websites and Internet documents. For links to the major sources, see "Selected Internet Sites for Evaluating Internet Resources" (www.lib.vt.edu/research/libinst/evalbiblio.html).

Authorship

Is the author of the Web document you are assessing clearly identified? If so, what are his or her qualifications? Is the author an expert on the topic? Can her or his data and opinions be accepted as objective and unbiased? Just as you should not cite a book or magazine article without identifying the author and his or her credentials, so you should not cite an electronic work in the absence of this information.

In a book or magazine article, information about the author is usually fairly easy to find. Too often, however, it is not made available on the Internet. If you can't find information about the author in the document itself, look for a link to the author's homepage or to another site that may explain the author's credentials. Some Internet documents include the author's e-mail address, which you can use to request further information.

Often you can learn about an author by typing her or his name in the Google search box. If the author is an accepted authority on the subject, there's a good chance Google will turn up information about their credentials, publications, and affiliation. If that doesn't work, trying checking one of the printed biographical aids discussed earlier in this chapter (pages 146–147).

Sponsorship

Many Web documents are published by business, government agencies, public-interest groups, and the like rather than by individual authors. In such cases, you must judge whether the sponsoring organization is impartial enough to cite in your speech. Is the organization objective in its research and fair-minded in its statements? Is it economically unbiased with regard to the issue under discussion? Does it have a history of accuracy and nonpartisanship?

Over the years, some organizations have developed strong reputations for their expertise and objectivity. Many of these are public-interest groups such as Consumers Union, Common Cause, and the American Cancer Society. Others include the National Archives, the Centers for Disease Control, and similar government agencies. Private think tanks such as RAND, the Cato Institute, and the Brookings Institution often have definite political leanings, but are usually well respected for the quality and substance of their research.

sponsoring organization

An organization that, in the absence of a clearly identified author, is responsible for the content of a document on the Internet.

On the other hand, you need to be wary of groups that sound respectable but in fact are not. Don't let a fancy-sounding name trick you into accepting a sponsoring organization's credibility at face value. For example, the World Internet News Distributary Source sounds like a nonpartisan news service. In fact, it has been categorized by Yahoo as a white pride and racialist group, and it refuses to identify the names or credentials of the authors who write under its sponsorship.

One way to way to gauge the credibility of a website is to look at the last three letters of its URL. These letters identify whether the website is maintained by a government agency (gov), an educational institution (edu), a nonprofit group (org), or a commercial organization (com or net).

You can also check the "About" or "Welcome" link on the sponsoring organization's homepage. Often the resulting screen will identify the site's founders, purpose, or philosophy. If the homepage does not contain an "About" or "Welcome" link, this may be a sign that the sponsoring organization is less than forthright and does not meet the necessary standards of objectivity and expertise.

What do you do if you can't verify the credentials of an author or identify a credible sponsoring organization for an Internet document? The answer is easy: Don't use the document in your speech! In this regard, the same standards apply whether you are dealing with a printed work or an electronic one.

Recency

One of the advantages of using the Internet for research is that it often has more recent information than you can find in print sources. But just because a document is on the Internet does not mean its facts and figures are up-to-the-minute.

The best way to determine the recency of an Internet document is to look for a copyright date, publication date, or date of last revision at the top or bottom of the document. If you are using a source located through a virtual library, you can usually be confident of its currency, as well as its objectivity and reliability. Government and academic sites almost always include the date on which the site was last updated.

Once you know the date of the document, you can determine whether it is current enough to use in your speech. This is especially important with regard to statistics, which you should never cite from an undated source, whether in print or on the Internet. If you can't find the date on which a Web document was created or last modified, you should search for another work whose recency you can verify.

Citing Internet Sources

Careful listeners are skeptical. They keep an ear out both for the speaker's information and for the sources of that information. Whether your research is based primarily on the Internet or on print works such as books, newspapers and magazines, you need to identify the sources of the facts, figures, and testimony you cite in your speeches.

One step in identifying your sources is to include them in your speech bibliography. As you prepare your bibliography, don't forget to mention the Internet sources, as well as the print sources, that you used in preparing the speech. When citing Internet sources, include the same information you provide for print works—author, title, date of publication, and the like. You should also include the URL for each Internet document, plus the date on which you accessed the document.

On CD 1, you will find a complete set of sample bibliography citations for various kinds of Internet sources formatted according to American Psychological Association (APA) and Modern Language Association (MLA) guidelines. Check these formats and follow the one your instructor specifies for your class.

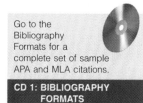

Go to the Bibliography Formats for a complete set of sample APA and MLA citations.

CD 1: BIBLIOGRAPHY FORMATS

In addition to including Internet sources in your speech bibliography, you need to cite them in the speech itself so listeners will know what those sources are. It would take far too much time if you recited orally the full citation as written in your bibliography. On the other hand, you should not simply say, "As I found on the Web," or "As the Internet states."

If you are citing the testimony of a specific person, you should identify her or him and the website on which you found the testimony. If you are citing an organization rather than an individual, you need to provide the name of the organization. Here, for example, are two Internet citations from student speeches. The first is from an informative speech about sign language:

> Some people think that sign language is a primitive substitute for spoken language, but in fact sign language is just as rich and expressive as spoken language. For example, Karen Nakamura states in the online *Deaf Resources Library* that American Sign Language "should not be considered in any way to be a broken, mimed, or gestural form of English." According to Nakamura, ASL is a complex, full, and natural language in its own right, with "its own beautiful grammar."

View these excerpts from Leah Pogoriler, "Sign Language," and Jennifer Conard, "The Ultimate Gift."

CD 1: VIDEO 6.1

The second is from a persuasive speech urging the audience to become blood donors:

> According to the American Red Cross Web pages, where I obtained an enormous amount of information, in the United States alone someone undergoes a blood transfusion once every three seconds, which amounts to 3,000 gallons of blood every hour, day and night.

In both cases, the speaker makes clear exactly where she obtained her information. You should do the same when citing Internet sources in your speeches.

Interviewing

Most people think of interviewing in terms of job interviews or conversations with celebrities. But there is another kind of interview—the research (or investigative) interview. Among journalists it is a time-honored way to collect information. It is also an excellent way to gather materials for speeches.

research interview
An interview conducted to gather information for a speech.

Suppose you are explaining the latest advances in personal computers. Why not contact a local computer dealer as one source of information? Or suppose you are dealing with the problem of binge drinking among college students. Why not get in touch with the dean of students to find out the situation at your school? Once you begin to think about the possibilities, you will discover many people on your campus and in your community who can contribute to your speeches.

When done well, interviewing (like many things) looks deceptively easy. In practice, it is a complex and demanding art. So before you dash off to conduct your interviews à la Larry King or Barbara Walters, you should understand a few basic principles of effective interviewing. They fall into three groups—what to do before the interview, what to do during the interview, and what to do after the interview.

To illustrate, we'll follow the entire interview process for a hypothetical speech about current issues in college athletics.

Before the Interview

Just as the outcome of most speeches is decided by how well the speaker prepares, so the outcome of most interviews is decided by how well the interviewer prepares. Here are five steps you should take ahead of time to help ensure a successful interview.

Define the Purpose of the Interview

You have done Internet and library research about current issues in college athletics and have begun to grasp the major points of view fairly well. At this stage you think it would be helpful to get the perspective of someone involved with the athletic program at your school. You get some information from the newspaper and some more from the athletic department's website. But you still have many questions. You decide the only way to get answers is to interview someone associated with the athletic program. In that decision you have begun to formulate a purpose for the interview.

Decide Whom to Interview

There are several possibilities—players, coaches, administrators. You elect to start at the top—with the athletic director. Isn't that a bit presumptuous? Why not begin with someone a little further down the line—an assistant director or a coach, for instance? You could. But in dealing with administrative organizations, it is usually best to go to the leaders first. They are likely to have a broad understanding of the issues. And if you need more specific information than they have, they can get it for you or put you in touch with the right person.

Arrange the Interview

Because the athletic director is a very busy person, you work out a plan for setting up the interview. Knowing that it's easier to brush someone off over e-mail or the telephone than in person, you go to the athletic office to request the interview. You introduce yourself, identify your exact purpose, and explain why the interview is important. The athletic director agrees, and you set up the interview for three days later.

(You are astonished to get the interview, but you shouldn't be. Nearly everyone likes to be interviewed. If you conduct yourself well, the person you ask is likely to cooperate.)

Decide Whether to Record the Interview

The major advantage of recording an interview is that it gives you an exact record of the interview that you can check later for direct quotes and important facts. Even if you use a recorder, however, you should still take notes by hand in case the recorder malfunctions.

Some interviewees are not comfortable being recorded. If that's the case in your situation, you will need to rely solely on your handwritten notes. Whatever you do, never smuggle a recorder in without the knowledge or consent of the person being interviewed. Not only is it unethical to do so, but the interviewee is bound to find out and you will cause yourself far more trouble than you had hoped to avoid.

Prepare Your Questions

You now face the most important of your preinterview tasks—working out the questions you will ask during the interview. You should devise questions that are sensible, intelligent, and meaningful. Here are some types of questions to *avoid:*

- Questions you can answer without the interview. (How many sports does your school offer? What is the size of its athletic budget?) Queries like these just waste the subject's time and make you look foolish. Research this information yourself before the interview.

- Leading questions. (Opinion polls show that most Americans believe athletics today have little relation to the academic purposes of a college education. You *do* think it's a problem, too, *don't you*?)

- Hostile, loaded questions. (I think it's disgraceful that many schools spend gobs of money on salaries for football and basketball coaches. Don't you think good teachers for all students are more important than coaches for a few athletes? What do you say to *that,* hmmm?)

You need not shy away from tough questions; just phrase them as neutrally as possible and save them until near the end of the interview. That way, if your interviewee becomes irritated or uncooperative, you'll still get most of the information you want.

Speech Assignment
Have students interview someone on campus or in the community who must speak in public as part of her or his job. On the basis of that interview, students should prepare a five-minute speech explaining the role of public speaking in the interviewee's work, the interviewee's approach to public speaking, and how that approach compares with the approach of the student conducting the interview.

When you are finished preparing, you should have a set of direct, specific, reasonable questions, such as the following:

■ Recent studies have shown that most colleges—large and small—lose money on athletics. You were quoted last month as saying that our athletic department faces a potential deficit next year. What plans are there to deal with it?

■ Do you agree with those who say that college sports are too commercialized? If so, what do you think should be done to solve the problem?

■ What is your position on raising eligibility requirements and penalizing schools that do not maintain acceptable graduation rates for athletes?

■ Maintaining gender equity is a major issue in college athletics. How do you think large schools will fund programs for women if there is a reduced emphasis on revenue-producing sports such as football and basketball?

■ In an ideal world, what do you believe should be the role of athletics on a college campus? Do you think we will be closer to that ideal in 10 years than we are today?

Although some experienced journalists conduct interviews with only a few key-word notes on the areas to be covered, you want to be sure not to forget anything during the interview. So you arrange your questions in the order you want to ask them and take the list with you to the interview.

During the Interview

Every interview is unique. Just as a speaker adapts to the audience during a speech, so must an interviewer adapt to the person being interviewed. Because the session will seldom go exactly as you plan, you need to be alert and flexible. Here are several steps you can take to help make the interview proceed smoothly.

Dress Appropriately and Be on Time

The athletic director has a busy schedule and is doing you a favor by agreeing to an interview, so you make every effort to show up on time. Since the interview is a special occasion, you dress appropriately. This is one way of telling the athletic director that you regard the interview as serious business. In return, he or she is likely to take you more seriously.

Repeat the Purpose of the Interview

The athletic director invites you into the office; you exchange a few introductory remarks. Now, before you plunge into your questions, you take a moment to restate the purpose of the interview. This refreshes the athletic director's memory and gives the interview a sharper focus. You are more likely to get clear, helpful answers if your subject knows why you are following a certain line of questioning.

Speech Assignment
As an alternative to the preceding assignment, have students select a period of history or a significant historical event and interview someone—relative, family friend, community figure, etc.—who has firsthand experience with that period or event. After the interview, students should prepare a five-minute informative speech explaining the historical period or event and the interviewee's perspective on it.

Relating Reading
Of all the books explaining how to conduct research interviews, the most helpful remains Ken Metzler's *Creative Interviewing: The Writer's Guide to Gathering Information by Asking Questions*, 3rd ed. (Boston: Allyn and Bacon, 1996).

Interviewing people with expertise on your speech topic can provide valuable information. When conducting an interview, be sure to listen attentively and to take accurate notes.

Set Up the Recorder, If You Are Using One

If your subject has agreed to being recorded, keep one principle in mind: the recorder should be as casual and inconspicuous as possible. Don't thrust the microphone into your subject's face. Don't fiddle endlessly with the machine. You should have practiced in advance to make sure you understand how the recorder works. Set up the recorder, turn it on, and then try to ignore it for the rest of the interview. With luck, your subject will ignore it too.

Keep the Interview on Track

Your goal in the interview is to get answers to the questions you have prepared. Suppose, however, that in answering one of your questions, the athletic director brings up an important point that is not covered anywhere on your list of questions. Rather than ignoring the point, you decide to veer slightly from your prearranged list to pursue the new issue. You pose a couple questions about it, get helpful answers, then keep the interview on track by returning to your list of prepared questions.

This is pretty much how things go throughout the interview. You pursue new leads when they appear, improvise probing follow-up questions when called for, then lead on again in an orderly fashion. When the interview is over, you have answers to all your prepared questions—and a lot more.

Listen Carefully

During the interview, you listen attentively to the athletic director's answers. When you don't understand something, you ask for clarification. If you are not using a recorder and you hear a statement you want to quote directly, you ask the athletic director to repeat it to make sure you get it exactly right.

Teaching Tip
Remind students that they may be able to get research information by conducting a phone interview—especially if they have only a few questions for the person being interviewed. Lengthier interviews, however, should be conducted in person whenever possible.

Chances are the athletic director will have been misquoted more than once in the press, so he or she will be happy to oblige.

Don't Overstay Your Welcome

Try to keep within the stipulated time period for the interview, unless your subject clearly wants to prolong the session. When the interview is over, you thank the athletic director for taking the time to talk with you.

After the Interview

Although the interview is over, the interviewing process is not. You must now review and transcribe your notes.

Review Your Notes As Soon As Possible

Discussion Prompt

What is the best way to thank an interviewee for an interview? Is a simple "thank you" at the end of the interview sufficient? When is a brief note of thanks more appropriate?

When you leave the athletic director's office, the interview is fresh in your mind. You know what the cryptic comments and scrawls in your notes mean. But as time passes, the details will become hazy. Don't let something like this true story happen to you:

Years ago, a prominent woman—writer and diplomat—was being interviewed by a young reporter. Among other things, the reporter asked about hobbies and leisure activities. The woman replied that she enjoyed skeet shooting and raised Siamese cats. The reporter scribbled in her notes "shoots" and "cats"—but didn't bother to put a comma or a dash between the words. The interview was published. And ever since, that prominent woman has been trying to live down the reputation that she "shoots cats."

In reviewing your notes, try to concentrate on two things—discovering the main points that emerged during the interview and pulling out specific information that might be useful in your speech.

The best way to locate the main points is to decide what you would answer if someone asked you to summarize the interview in one minute or less. As you look through your notes, you see three ideas that surface over and over in the athletic director's comments: (1) Maintaining adequate funding for a full slate of men's and women's sports is the major challenge facing athletic departments throughout the country; (2) Division I football and basketball have become highly commercialized, but the revenue they provide is crucial to funding the rest of the athletic program; (3) Tougher academic standards for eligibility and progress toward graduation would benefit athletes and schools alike as long as the standards are fairly determined and consistently applied.

Related Reading

For insight on a wide range of interview situations and how to deal with them, see Charles J. Stewart and William B. Cash, Jr., *Interviewing: Principles and Practices*, 10th ed. (New York: McGraw-Hill, 2003).

As you review the interview, you also seize on several specific items—figures, anecdotes, quotations—that look promising as supporting materials for your speech. If any of them are unclear, call the athletic director to make sure you have the facts right.

Transcribe Your Notes

Once you settle on the most important ideas and information from the interview, you should transcribe that material so it is in the same format as the rest of your research notes (see pages 165–167). By putting all your research notes in a consistent format, you can arrange and rearrange them easily when you start to organize your speech.[10]

Tips for Doing Research

Few people regard doing research as one of life's great joys. There are ways, however, to make it less tedious and more productive. Here are four ways that are guaranteed to help.

Start Early

The biggest mistake students make when faced with a research project is waiting too long to begin. The longer you wait, the more problems you will encounter. You may find that a vital book has been checked out of the library or that you no longer have time to arrange a crucial interview. Starting early also eases the tension of completing an assignment. Instead of sweating under intense time pressure, you can work at your convenience. No matter what kind of research you do, you can be sure of one thing. It will *always* take longer than you expect. So get started early and avoid the pitfalls that come from procrastinating.

Starting early also gives you plenty of time to think about what you find. In researching, you will collect much more material than you will actually use in the speech. Preparing a speech is a little like constructing a jigsaw puzzle. Once you gather the pieces, you have to decide how they fit together. The more time you give yourself, the more likely you are to get the pieces to fit just right.

Make a Preliminary Bibliography

In your research, you will run across the titles of books, magazine articles, Internet documents, and so on that look as if they might contain helpful information about your speech topic. Enter each item you find in your preliminary bibliography.

For books, record the author, title, place of publication, publisher, date of publication, and call number. You may also want to include a brief comment indicating why the book may be valuable for your speech. Figure 6.5 shows a preliminary bibliography entry for a book.

preliminary bibliography
A list compiled early in the research process of works that look as if they might contain helpful information about a speech topic.

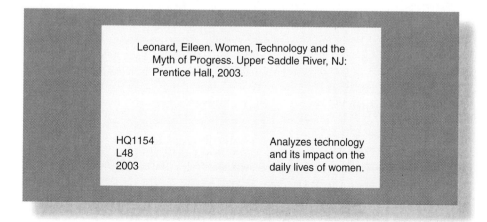

Leonard, Eileen. Women, Technology and the Myth of Progress. Upper Saddle River, NJ: Prentice Hall, 2003.

HQ1154
L48
2003

Analyzes technology and its impact on the daily lives of women.

Figure 6.5
Preliminary Bibliography Entry for a Book.

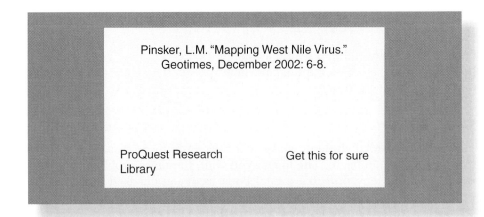

Figure 6.6
Preliminary Bibliography
Entry for a Magazine
Article.

For magazine articles, record the author, title of the article, name of the magazine, date of publication, and page numbers. You should also indicate where you can find the full text of the article—computerized database or call number in the library shelves. As with book entries, you may also want to include a note to yourself about the article. Figure 6.6 shows a preliminary bibliography entry for a magazine article.

For Internet documents, cite the author or sponsoring organization, title of the document, date of Internet publication or of latest update, URL, and the date on which you accessed the document. Figure 6.7 shows a preliminary bibliography entry for an Internet document.

One important point needs to be stressed. You should include in your preliminary bibliography *each* book, article, Internet document, and the like that looks as if it *could be* helpful in preparing your speech. As a result, you may well have 15 or 20 works in your preliminary bibliography. But remember that you have not yet examined those works. Of the 15 or 20 preliminary sources, only 7 or 8 are likely to be of much use in drafting the speech. It is an inevitable fact of research that you must sift through

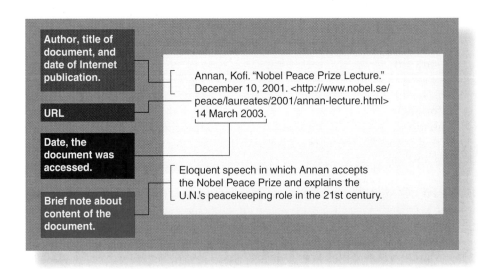

Figure 6.7
Preliminary Bibliography
Entry for an Internet
Document.

many sources to find what you need. If you prepare a skimpy preliminary bibliography, you may well end up with a skimpy speech.

As we mentioned earlier in this chapter, there are two major formats for citing documents in a bibliography. One comes from the Modern Language Association (MLA), the other from the American Psychological Association (APA). If you have questions about either, you can find a full set of sample citations on CD 1 for all manner of sources—including Internet documents, books, magazine articles, interviews, even television programs. Be sure to check with your instructor to see if she or he has a preference for which format you should use in your bibliography.

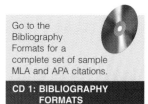

Go to the Bibliography Formats for a complete set of sample MLA and APA citations.

CD 1: BIBLIOGRAPHY FORMATS

Take Notes Efficiently

Asia Marshall started her speech preparation with the best of intentions. She was excited about her topic, "Great Women of Jazz," and she logged on to the Internet to begin researching the same day the assignment was announced. She found several interesting sources and took some notes about them. That evening she checked out a book about Billie Holiday and brought it back to her room. The book was so interesting that she read it straight through. She didn't bother taking notes because she was sure she'd remember it all. The next day she stopped by the reference section of the library to look through the *Encyclopedia of Jazz* and jotted a few notes about it on the back of her speech syllabus.

Then Asia remembered she had a test in another class. Somewhat panicked, she put aside her speech research to study for the test. When she got back to working on the speech, the deadline was only four days away. She dug out the notes she had made, but what did they mean? Most of them were far too brief to be of much help. One said, "Medford—*important!!!*" But who or what was Medford? An author? A musician? Or could it be a place? Asia had thought she'd remember all about the Billie Holiday book, but without notes it was mostly a blur by now. With a sense of doom, she faced up to the fact that she would have to start over—and finish in four days.

Sound familiar? This has happened to almost everyone at least once. But once is enough. There is a better way to take research notes. Here is a method that has worked well for many students:

Take Plenty of Notes

Few things are more aggravating than trying to recall some bit of information you ran across in your research but neglected to record. You might have said to yourself, "That's sort of interesting, but I don't know whether it's important. I'll remember it if I need it." Now, of course, you don't remember it exactly. Worse yet, you don't remember where you read it. So you log back on to the Internet or head back to the library hoping you can relocate the information. Even if you do find it, you have wasted a lot of time.

The moral is clear: If there is even an outside chance that you may need a piece of information, make a note of it. This will take a little extra time in the short run, but in the long run it can save you much grief.

Record Notes in a Consistent Format

You should use the same format for all your research notes, whether they come from Internet sources, library documents, or personal interviews. In each case, record the note, the source of the note, and a heading indicating the subject of the note (see Figure 6.8, page 166).

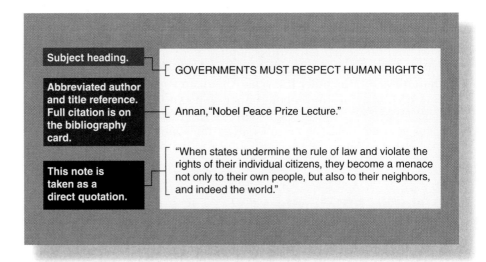

Figure 6.8
Sample Research Note.

The importance of the subject heading cannot be overemphasized. It is the first step to more efficient note taking. By telling you at a glance what each note is about, it will greatly simplify the task of organizing your notes when you start to compose the speech. Once you start using subject headings, you'll see how helpful they can be.

Make a Separate Entry for Each Note

Many students try to record all the information from one source on a single note. This is not an effective procedure because it makes your notes almost impossible to review and organize. A better approach is to make a separate note for *each* quotation or piece of information you record. Although you may end up with several notes from the same document, you will find that this approach allows you to keep better track of your research.

Distinguish Among Direct Quotations, Paraphrases, and Your Own Ideas

As we saw in Chapter 2, it's easy to plagiarize accidentally by not taking careful research notes. As you do research for your speeches, be sure to use quotation marks whenever you copy the exact words of a source. If you paraphrase, rather than quote verbatim, don't forget to include the source when you record the note. By keeping track of quotations and paraphrases, you will be able to separate your own words and ideas from those of other people. This will help you avoid the trap of inadvertent plagiarism when you put your speech together.

Use Index Cards If You Write Notes by Hand

One of the most challenging parts of research is keeping track of all the information you find and being able to organize it quickly when you start to compose your speech. If you take notes on a computer, you can cut and paste quotations, statistics, and the like to get them in the order you want. If you are taking notes by hand, however, you need a method that will let you rearrange your notes as easily as if you were working on a computer.

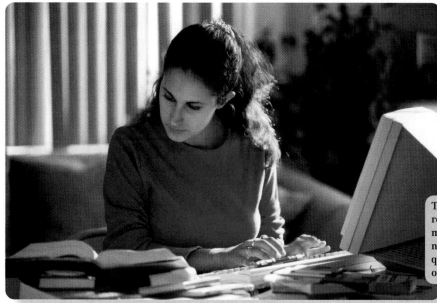

To take research notes efficiently, record them in a consistent format, make a separate entry for each note, and distinguish among direct quotations, paraphrases and your own ideas.

The best solution is to use index cards. Most people prefer the 4 × 6 or 5 × 8 size. They are large enough to hold quite a bit of information, yet they can be sorted easily when you start to organize your speech. If you write your research notes by hand and haven't used index cards before, give them a try. You may be surprised at how much time and frustration they save.

Think About Your Materials as You Research

Students often approach research as a mechanical routine that simply involves gathering the materials to be used in a speech or paper. But when done properly, research can be extremely creative.

If you *think about* what you are finding in your research, you will see your topic just a little bit differently with each note you take. You will find new relationships, develop new questions, explore new angles. You will, in short, begin to write the speech in your head even as you do the research. As you learn more about the topic, you will formulate a central idea, begin to sketch out main points and supporting points, experiment with ways of organizing your thoughts. You may even change your point of view, as did this student:

Francesca Lopez began her speech preparation with this central idea in mind: "Wild animals make more interesting pets than dogs and cats." She went about her research conscientiously, spending many hours online and in the library. In the process, she came upon some disturbing information about the capture of wild animals. She read that young chimpanzees and other apes were literally snatched out of their mothers' arms, and that the mothers were afterward heard to cry almost like humans. Back in her room that night, Francesca couldn't get her mind off the baby chimpanzees.

Teaching Tip
Make sure students understand the minimum number of sources they are required to have for each speech.

The next day Francesca found some more disturbing material. One source told about the extraordinarily high death rate of wild animals during shipment to the United States. Again, that night, Francesca brooded about the young animals dying of fear and cold in the cargo holds of airplanes.

By the time she finished her research, Francesca's central idea was completely different. When she spoke, her central idea was, "The importation of wild animals for use as pets is inhumane."

This is an example of creative research—and of critical thinking. Francesca kept her mind open, read everything she could find about her topic, and thought seriously about what she found. Because of this thoughtful approach, she changed her mind.

Your own speech preparation may not cause you to reverse your position, but it should give you new insights into your topic. If you approach research in this way, you may well find that the time you spend researching is the most productive of all the time you devote to preparing your speech.[11]

Summary

Gathering materials for a speech is like gathering information for any project. Many resources are available if you take advantage of them. When you have personal experience or more-than-average knowledge about a topic, you can use yourself as a resource. Most of the time, however, you will need outside information, which you can get in the library, on the Internet, or by interviewing people with specialized information about your topic.

Finding what you need in the library is largely a matter of knowing how to search for information. The catalogue lists all the books, periodicals, and other resources owned by the library. Databases help you find articles in magazines, journals, and newspapers. The reference section contains a wealth of resources—including encyclopedias, yearbooks, dictionaries, biographical aids, and gazetteers. If you have trouble finding something, don't hesitate to ask a librarian.

When researching on the Web, you should use a search engine, a metasearch engine, or a virtual library to find exactly what you need. Keyword or subject searches can be equally effective depending on the topic of your speech and the kind of information you need. Given the lack of editorial review for most documents on the Web, it is especially important to evaluate the authorship, sponsoring organization, and recency of the research materials you find there. It's also vital to cite Internet sources fully, clearly, and consistently in your bibliography and in the speech itself.

You can also get information by conducting a personal interview with someone on campus or in the community. Before the interview, you should define its purpose, decide whom you are going to interview, and make an appointment with that person. You should also prepare the questions you are going to ask during the interview. Once the interview begins, be sure to keep it on track, to listen attentively, and to take accurate notes. Afterward, review and transcribe your notes as soon as possible, while they are still fresh in your mind.

No matter what sources you draw upon in gathering information, your research will be more effective if you start early and make a preliminary bibliography to keep track of all the books, articles, and Internet documents that look as if they might be helpful. By learning to take research notes effectively, you will save yourself time and energy every step of the way. And if you think about your materials as you research, you may find that gathering materials is the most creative part of your speech preparation.

Key Terms

catalogue (139)
call number (140)
periodical database (140)
abstract (141)
reference work (144)
general encyclopedia (144)
special encyclopedia (144)
yearbook (145)
biographical aid (146)
atlas (147)
gazetteer (147)

search aid (147)
search engine (148)
metasearch engine (148)
virtual library (149)
invisible Web (149)
URL (Uniform Resource Locator) (151)
bookmark (152)
sponsoring organization (156)
research interview (158)
preliminary bibliography (163)

Review these terms by doing the Chapter 6 crossword puzzle at www.mhhe.com/lucas8.

ONLINE LEARNING CENTER

Review Questions

After reading this chapter, you should be able to answer the following questions:

1. Why is it important to draw on your own knowledge and experience in gathering materials for your speeches?

2. What are five important resources for finding what you need in the library?

3. What are the differences among search engines, metasearch engines, and virtual libraries? How can you use each to find information systematically on the Internet?

4. What are three major criteria for evaluating the soundness of research materials that you find on the Web?

5. What are the three stages of interviewing? What should you do as an interviewer in each stage to help ensure a successful interview?

6. Why is it important to start your speech research early?

7. What is a preliminary bibliography? Why is it helpful to you in researching a speech?

8. What five things should you do to take research notes efficiently?

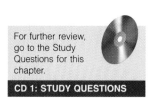

For further review, go to the Study Questions for this chapter.

CD 1: STUDY QUESTIONS

Exercises for Critical Thinking

Cross-Reference

For discussion of the Exercises for Critical Thinking, see the *Instructor's Manual,* pp. 162–165. For additional exercises, check the *Instructor's Manual,* pp. 166–172, as well as the five volumes of *Selections from the Speech Communication Teacher* that accompany *The Art of Public Speaking.*

1. Using one of the general periodical databases discussed on pages 141–142, find three magazine or journal articles on the topic of your next speech. Prepare a preliminary bibliography entry for each article. Read the full text of the articles and assess their value for your speech.

2. Using one of the news databases discussed on pages 143–144, find three newspaper articles on the topic of your next speech. Prepare a preliminary bibliography entry for each article. Read the full text of the articles and assess their value for your speech.

3. Using the procedures for keyword searches explained on page 150, find three Internet documents on the topic of your next speech and prepare a preliminary bibliography entry for each document. Assess all three documents in light of the criteria discussed on pages 155–157 for evaluating Internet documents. Be specific.

4. Plan to conduct an interview for one of your classroom speeches. Be sure to follow the guidelines presented in this chapter for effective interviewing. Afterward, evaluate the interview. Did you prepare for it adequately? Did you get the information you needed? What would you do differently if you could conduct the interview again?

5. This exercise is designed to give you firsthand experience with some of the major reference works discussed on pages 144–147. Your task is to answer each of the following questions. Some of the questions indicate where you will find the answer, and some do not. If necessary, look back through the chapter to see in which reference works you are most likely to find the answers. For each question, record both your answer and where you found it.

   Example

   Question: Who said, "Who knows what women can be when they are finally free to become themselves"?

   Answer: Betty Friedan said, "Who knows what women can be when they are finally free to become themselves." *Bartlett's Familiar Quotations,* 15th edition, page 898.

   a. According to the *Oxford English Dictionary,* what are the origins of "terrorism" as a political term?

   b. What is the opening quotation by Jordan's Queen Rania in the article about her in the 2001 *Current Biography Yearbook*?

   c. How many U.S. towns or cities are named Paris, and in which states are they located?

   d. As explained in the *Encyclopedia of Computer Science,* where and when were the first e-mail messages sent?

   e. What does the *Latino Encyclopedia* identify as the origins of El Día de la Raza?

   f. According to the 2001 *Statistical Abstract of the United States,* what percentage of people 18 to 34 years old had Internet access at home or at work in 2000? What was the percentage for people 55 years old and over?

   g. What were listed in *Facts on File* as the three top-rated prime-time U.S. television programs for the period April 29 to June 2, 2002?

h. As explained in the *Asian American Encyclopedia,* what is the global Hmong population, and how many Hmong clans are there?

i. What is the definition of "fog" in the *McGraw-Hill Encyclopedia of Science and Technology?*

Applying the **POWER** *of* PUBLIC SPEAKING

Your eight-year-old daughter has recently been diagnosed as being allergic to latex, making her one of the growing number of people nationwide with this serious condition. After speaking with other parents in your daughter's school, you discover there are several other children with latex allergies. For the last year an informal group has been meeting to exchange ideas on balancing treatment plans and preventive strategies while maintaining regular family life. Now you have volunteered to do research on whether there is a national support network for people with latex allergies and how you can contact them about setting up your own formal organization.

Find the information you need by conducting a subject search through the Librarians' Index to the Internet.

Cross-Reference
For discussion of this Applying the Power of Public Speaking scenario, see the *Instructor's Manual,* pp. 165–166.

Notes

[1] I would like to thank Abbie Loomis and the reference staff of Memorial Library, University of Wisconsin–Madison, for their assistance with this section of the chapter.

[2] Steve Lawrence and Lee Giles, "Accessibility of Information on the Web," *Nature,* 400 (1999), pp. 107–109. As Randolph Hock explains in *The Extreme Searcher's Guide to Web Search Engines: A Handbook for the Serious Researcher,* 2nd ed. (Medford, NJ: Information Today, 2001), p. 21, some search engine producers have argued that these figures are too low. Beyond dispute, however, is the fact that even the best search engines index only a fraction of the total information available on the Web.

[3] Steven Levy, "The World According to Google," *Newsweek* (December 16, 2002), pp. 46–51.

[4] For information on the development of virtual libraries, see Amy Tracy Wells, Susan Calcari, and Travis Koplow, *The Amazing Internet Challenge: How Leading Projects Use Library Skills to Organize the Web* (Chicago: American Library Association, 1999).

[5] Chris Sherman and Gary Price, *The Invisible Web: Uncovering Information Sources Search Engines Can't See* (Medford, NJ: Information Today, 2001).

[6] Andrew Harnack and Eugene Kleppinger, *Online! A Reference Guide to Using Internet Sources,* 3rd ed. (New York: St. Martin's, 2000), p. 96.

[7] Evan Morris, *The Book Lover's Guide to the Internet* (New York: Fawcett Columbine, 1996), p. 106.

[8] "Call It Cybernoia," *Philadelphia Daily News,* March 1, 1997, p. 11.

[9] These criteria are adapted from Elizabeth Kirk, "Evaluating Information Found on the Internet," June 5, 2002. <www.library.jhu.edu/elp/useit/evaluate/> January 21, 2003.

[10] For more information on the ins and outs of conducting research interviews, see Ken Metzler's excellent *Creative Interviewing: The Writer's Guide to Gathering Information by Asking Questions,* 3rd ed. (Boston: Allyn and Bacon, 1996). Charles J. Stewart and William B. Cash, Jr., *Interviewing: Principles and Practices,* 10th ed. (New York: McGraw-Hill, 2003), provides insight on the full range of interview types and situations.

[11] For a fascinating discussion of the creative dimensions of research, see Howard S. Becker, *Tricks of the Trade: How to Think About Your Research While You're Doing It* (Chicago: University of Chicago Press, 1998).

Chapter Seven

SUPPORTING
YOUR IDEAS

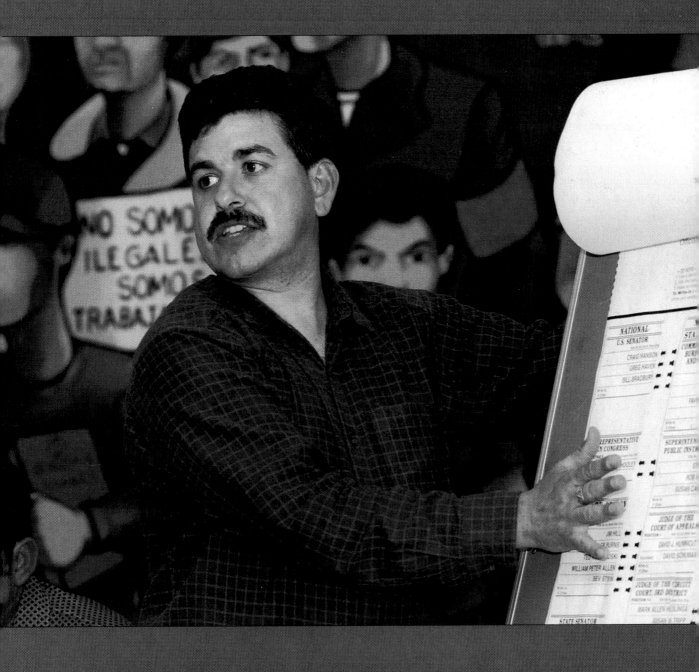

H eather Kolpin decided to give her first classroom speech on the benefits of good nutrition. A dedicated fitness enthusiast, she had recently switched to a high-protein diet. Part of her speech ran like this:

"For years we've been told that meat, eggs, and cheese are bad for us and that we should eat more carbohydrates like cereal, grains, pasta, and rice. But too many carbohydrates can unbalance the body and make you tired and overweight. Do you want more energy? Do you want to concentrate better and get higher grades? Do you want to enjoy real meals and still lose those unsightly pounds? If so, you should eat more protein. I've been on a high-protein diet for six months, and I've never felt better or done better in my classes!"

After the speech, Heather's classmates were interested but skeptical. As one remarked, "I know high-protein diets are popular right now, but Heather's no expert on nutrition. Besides, there are lots of diets around, and they all claim to work wonders. Personally, I'd be more convinced if Heather gave some scientific evidence to back up her opinion."

Good speeches are not composed of hot air and generalizations. They need strong supporting materials to bolster the speaker's point of view. In Heather's case, although there is plenty of evidence on the need to balance protein and carbohydrate consumption, many nutritionists have warned about the dangers of overloading on protein. So Heather's listeners were right to be skeptical. Heather made the mistake of generalizing from her own experience with nothing concrete to support her ideas.

The problem with generalizations is that they do not answer the three questions listeners always mentally ask of a speaker: "What do you mean?" "Why should I believe you?" "So what?" Consider, for example, the following sets of statements:

General	Less General	Specific
Hepatitis C is a serious problem.	A deadly disease, Hepatitis C is spreading rapidly in the United States.	Hepatitis C currently infects 3 to 4 million people in the U.S. and is four times as widespread as AIDS. It kills 10,000 Americans each year, and by 2010 the number of deaths could reach 30,000 annually—twice the toll of AIDS.
There are lots of people in Asia.	More than half the world's population lives in Asia.	If the earth's population were envisioned as a village with exactly 100 persons, the breakdown would be as follows: 57 Asians, 21 Europeans, 14 North and South Americans, and 3 Africans, with the remaining 5 scattered.[1]

Chapter Focus
A public speaker needs strong supporting materials to back up her or his claims. This chapter discusses the three major kinds of supporting materials—examples, statistics, and testimony—and presents guidelines for using them ethically and effectively. A full sample speech with commentary illustrates all three types of supporting materials in action. For a full outline of the chapter, see the *Instructor's Manual*, pp. 176–179.

Discussion Prompt
What makes the statements in the right-hand column more interesting and more convincing than those in the left-hand and center columns?

| The World Cup is very popular. | The World Cup has the largest TV audience of any sporting event on earth. | The 2002 World Cup soccer matches drew a global TV audience of more than 40 billion people. In contrast, the latest Super Bowl had only 135 million viewers worldwide, and the entire 2000 Summer Olympic Games had only 3.2 billion viewers. |

Class Activity
For an excellent activity that introduces students to supporting materials and the importance of thinking critically about them, *see* James Kauffman, "Collecting and Evaluating Evidence," in *Selections from the Speech Communication Teacher 1991–1994*, pp. 18–19, which accompanies *The Art of Public Speaking.*

Which group of statements do you find most interesting? Most convincing? Chances are you will prefer those in the right-hand column. They are sharp and specific, clear and credible—just the sort of thing a speech needs to come alive.

Supporting Materials and Critical Thinking

The skillful use of supporting materials often makes the difference between a poor speech and a good one. It is also closely related to critical thinking. Using supporting materials is not a matter of haphazardly tossing facts and figures into your speech. You must decide which ideas need to be supported given your audience, topic, and specific purpose. You must do research to find materials that will bring your ideas across clearly and creatively. And you must evaluate your supporting materials to make sure they really do back up your ideas.

As you put your speeches together, you will need to make sure your supporting materials are accurate, relevant, and reliable. You will find yourself asking such questions as, "Are my examples representative?" "Am I using statistical measures correctly?" "Am I quoting reputable, qualified sources?" Assessing the supporting materials in your speeches—as well as in the speeches of your classmates—is yet another way in which critical thinking is part of public speaking.

In Chapters 14 and 16, we will look at special uses of supporting materials in informative and persuasive speeches. In this chapter, we focus on the basic kinds of supporting materials—examples, statistics, and testimony—and on general principles for using them effectively and responsibly.

supporting materials
The materials used to support a speaker's ideas. The three major kinds of supporting materials are examples, statistics, and testimony.

Examples

Kelly Reyher stood in the crowded 78th-floor elevator lobby of World Trade Center 2. It was just after 9 a.m. on September 11, 2001. Fifteen minutes earlier a Boeing 767 had flown into the North Tower, touching off a fireball that, across the 140 feet separating the buildings and through the windows on the 103rd floor, still felt to one of Reyher's colleagues, Judy Wein, "like putting your head in an oven."[2]

These lines are from the opening of an article in *Newsweek* magazine about the handful of people who survived the attacks on the World Trade Center despite initially being trapped on the upper floors by wreckage and fire. It illustrates a device well known to magazine writers—and speech-makers: Get the audience involved.

See how skillfully this example accomplishes the goal. It begins by focusing on a particular person (Kelly Reyher). It then sets the scene with details of time, place, even the type of airplane the terrorists piloted into the North Tower. We almost feel ourselves up there with Kelly, braving the heat of the fireball created after the plane smashed into the building. We would not be nearly as involved if the article had merely said, "The attack on the World Trade Center was a horrifying event." The *example* touches something in us that no generalization can.

Research has shown that vivid, concrete examples have strong impact on listeners' beliefs and actions.[3] Without examples, ideas often seem vague, impersonal, and lifeless. With examples, ideas become specific, personal, and lively. This is nowhere better illustrated than in the Bible and the Koran, both of which use all manner of stories, parables, and anecdotes to make abstract principles clear and compelling. There are several kinds of examples you may want to try in your speeches.

example
A specific case used to illustrate or to represent a group of people, ideas, conditions, experiences, or the like.

Brief Examples

brief example
A specific case referred to in passing to illustrate a point.

Brief examples—also called specific instances—may be referred to in passing to illustrate a point. The following excerpt uses a brief example to illustrate the miraculous nature of recent advances in creating artificial limbs for accident victims:

> Changes in technology have made it possible for doctors to work wonders that once seemed impossible. *Roger Charter, for example, lost both his feet when they were crushed in a truck accident. Now he has new feet*—made of a springy plastic alloy that duplicates a normal arch. Not only can Roger walk normally, but he can run and play sports again!

A brief example may also be used to introduce a topic:

> When archaeologists broke the seal on Tutankhamen's tomb in the autumn of 1922, they uncovered an amazing treasure—a storehouse of ancient Egyptian art of priceless beauty that had lain, untouched and unseen, for more than 3,000 years. Archaeology is a profession of endless drudgery, painstaking research, and the occasional—very rare—marvelous find.

Another way to use brief examples is to pile them one upon the other until you create the desired impression. Here is how the technique might be used to reinforce the point that Mexican Americans have made many valuable contributions to U.S. life and culture:

> Many of us are familiar with prominent Chicanos and Chicanas such as comedian George Lopez, singer Selena, baseball player Luiz Gonzalez, and guitarist Carlos Santana. But you may be less familiar with other Americans of Mexican origin who have made important contributions to U.S. society. Nancy Lopez played a crucial role in popularizing

women's professional golf and won 48 tour championships. Dr. Ellen Ochoa is an astronaut who has logged more than 480 hours in space and has invented several optical methods that greatly aid space exploration. Dr. Mario Molina won the 1995 Nobel Prize in Chemistry for his research on the formation and decomposition of the ozone layer.

Extended Examples

Extended examples are often called narratives, illustrations, or anecdotes. They are longer and more detailed than brief examples. By telling a story vividly and dramatically, they pull listeners into the speech. Here is such an example, from a speech by Sun Yan, a student at Fudan University in Shanghai, China. Participating in China's 2001 national English-language speech competition, Sun Yan used an extended example to illustrate the spirit of the Olympic Games:

extended example
A story, narrative, or anecdote developed at some length to illustrate a point.

> In the history of the Olympic Games, there have been many shining stars. Among them was a European girl. With the lapse of time, her name has faded from memory, yet her unbending spirit shall never perish. It was she who highlighted the Olympic Creed.
>
> In the lead though she had been, she stumbled near the terminus and her leg was injured. Competitors passed her from behind in succession until finally only her weak and lonely figure remained on the track. Doctors came and offered to take her away. Yet she refused. With the only strength left in her, she managed to get up and shuffled feebly to the endpoint with drops of blood along her trail.
>
> But cheers broke out. Though she failed in the race, the girl won applause from people all over the world. It was she who elucidated the Olympic creed of participation. It was she who instilled perseverance in our minds.[4]

View this portion of Sun Yan's speech on the Olympic spirit.

CD 1: VIDEO 7.1

This long example captures vividly the courage of the Olympic runner and her personification of the Olympic spirit. The speaker could merely have said, "Olympic athletes often display great fortitude," but the story makes the point far more vividly.

Hypothetical Examples

Whether brief or extended, examples can be either factual or hypothetical. All the examples presented up to now have been factual; the incidents they refer to really happened. Sometimes, however, speakers will use a hypothetical example—one that describes an imaginary situation. Usually such examples are brief stories that relate a general principle.

hypothetical example
An example that describes an imaginary or fictitious situation.

Here is how one student used a hypothetical example to illustrate the need for college students to protect themselves against crime:

> You're tired; you're hungry. You've just spent a long day at College Library and you can't wait to get back to your room. Glancing outside, you remember how quickly it becomes dark. You don't think much of it, though, as you bundle up and head out into the gusty wind. Not until you spy the shadows on the sidewalk or hear the leaves rustling beside you do you wish you weren't alone. You walk quickly, trying to stop your imagination from thinking of murderers and rapists. Only when you are safely inside your room do you relax and try to stop your heart from pounding out of your chest.

Can you remember a time when you felt this way? I would be surprised if you never have. The FBI reported last year that there were three murders, approximately 430 aggravated assaults, 1,400 burglaries, and 80 rapes here in Madison alone. And while these statistics are quite alarming, they don't compare to the numbers of larger metropolitan areas.

View this portion of Rebecca Hanson, "Self-Defense on Campus."

CD 1: VIDEO 7.2

This hypothetical example is particularly effective. The speaker creates a realistic scenario, relates it directly to her listeners, and gets them involved in the speech. In addition, she uses figures from the FBI to show that the scenario could really happen to any of her classmates. Whenever you use a hypothetical example, it is a good idea to follow it with statistics or testimony to show that the example is not far-fetched.

Tips for Using Examples

Use Examples to Clarify Your Ideas

You probably use clarifying examples all the time in everyday conversation. If you were explaining to a friend about different body types, you might say, "Look at Professor Shankar. He's a typical ectomorph—tall, thin, and bony." Examples are an excellent way to clarify unfamiliar or complex ideas. This is why so many teachers use examples in the classroom. Examples put abstract ideas into concrete terms that listeners can easily understand.

This principle works exceptionally well in speeches. Suppose you are talking about suspension bridges. You could give a technical description:

> The suspension bridge has a roadway suspended by vertical cables attached to two or more main cables. The main cables are hung on two towers and have their ends anchored in concrete or bedrock.

If your audience were made up of people familiar with structural systems, they might be able to visualize what a suspension bridge looks like. But for listeners lacking this background, you might want to add a simple example:

> Two well-known suspension bridges are the Golden Gate Bridge in San Francisco and the Brooklyn Bridge in New York.

Because almost everyone has at least seen a picture of the Golden Gate Bridge or the Brooklyn Bridge, using them as examples clarifies your meaning quickly and effectively.

Use Examples to Reinforce Your Ideas

In a speech entitled "Boxing: The Most Dangerous Sport," student Rob Goeckel argued that professional boxing should be banned in the United States. In addition to noting the dozens of deaths caused by boxing, he deplored the irreparable brain damage sustained by many fighters. He explained that a punch thrown by a heavyweight boxer lands with a force of more than 1,000 pounds, and he provided testimony from neurologists about the consequences of receiving repeated blows to the head. To reinforce his point, Rob cited the example of Muhammad Ali, who suffers from a severe case of Parkinson's disease brought on by his years in the ring. His symptoms include impaired hand-eye

Class Activity

As a homework assignment, have each student create an extended hypothetical example suitable for use in his or her next classroom speech. Provide time in class for students to present their examples orally. In addition to getting feedback on the clarity and vividness of their examples, students will gain another brief speaking experience.

View this portion of Rob Goeckel, "Boxing: The Most Dangerous Sport."

CD 1: VIDEO 7.3

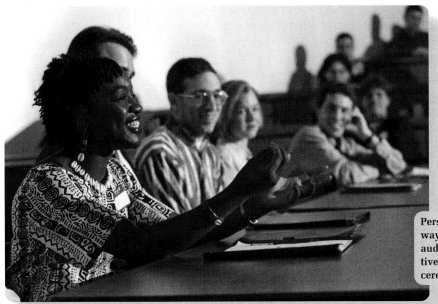

Personal examples are an excellent way to clarify ideas and to build audience interest. To be most effective, they should be delivered sincerely and with strong eye contact.

coordination, slurred speech, reduced muscle strength, and chronic fatigue. Once the heavyweight champion of the world, Ali "has been reduced to a mere shell of a man, a shaking, silent reminder of the brutality of boxing."

This example was especially effective. It put the medical facts about boxing and brain damage in vivid, human terms that everyone could understand. When you use such an example, make sure it is representative—that it does not deal with unusual or exceptional cases. Your listeners are sure to feel betrayed if they suspect you have chosen an atypical example to prove a general point.

Use Examples to Personalize Your Ideas

People are interested in people. As social psychologist Eliot Aronson explains, "Most people are more deeply influenced by one clear, vivid, personal example than by an abundance of statistical data."[5] Whenever you talk to a general audience (such as your speech class), you can include examples that will add human interest to your speech. So far in this section we have seen a number of such examples—Kelly Reyher, who was in the World Trade Center on 9-11; accident victim Roger Charter; and so on. The abstract becomes more meaningful when applied to a person. Which of the following would you be more likely to respond to?

There are many hungry families in our community who could benefit from food donations.

Or:

Let me tell you about Arturo. Arturo is four years old. He has big brown eyes and a mop of black hair and an empty belly. In all his four years on this earth, Arturo has never once enjoyed three square meals in a single day.

Class Activity
Have students find and bring to class a story from a popular magazine such as *Time, Newsweek, Sports Illustrated, Ms., Reader's Digest, Smithsonian,* that contains at least one extended example—preferably on the topic of the students' next speech. Students should be prepared to deliver the example and to explain the role it plays in the story.

Try using examples with human interest in your speeches. You will soon discover why accomplished speakers consider them "the very life of the speech."[6]

Make Your Examples Vivid and Richly Textured

The richly textured example supplies everyday details that bring the example to life. Recall the example on page 177 of the Olympic runner. The speaker provided us with many details about the runner's bravery in the face of adverse conditions. The runner stumbles and injures her leg near the end of the race. She is passed by other competitors until she alone is left on the track. Doctors offer to help, but she refuses their assistance. With drops of blood along her trail, she shuffles to the finish line with all her remaining strength.

How much less compelling the example would have been if the speaker had merely said:

One Olympic runner courageously completed her race despite being injured and exhausted.

Instead, the details let us *see* the runner as she battles through her pain and misfortune to win the applause of people around the globe. She is much more likely to stay in our minds than a "brave runner who completed her race." The more vivid your examples—brief or extended—the more impact they are likely to have on your audience.

Practice Delivery to Enhance Your Extended Examples

An extended example is just like a story or narrative. Its impact will depend as much on delivery as on content. Many students have discovered this the hard way. After spending much time and energy developing a splendid example, they have seen it fall flat on the day of the speech because they did not take the extra step to make it vivid and gripping for listeners.

Look again at the speaker in CD 1, Video 7.1. Notice how she uses her voice to increase the impact of her story about the Olympic runner. Like that speaker, you should think of yourself as a storyteller when you use an extended example. Don't rush through the example as though you were reading the newspaper; use your voice to get listeners involved. Speak faster here to create a sense of action, slower there to build suspense. Raise your voice in some places; lower it in others. Pause occasionally for dramatic effect.

Most important, maintain eye contact with your audience. The easiest way to ruin a fine example is to read it dully from your notes. As you practice the speech, "talk through" your extended examples without relying on your notes. By the day of your speech, you should be able to deliver your extended examples as naturally as if you were telling a story to a group of friends.

Statistics

We live in an age of statistics. Day in and day out we are bombarded with a staggering array of numbers: Garth Brooks has sold over 97 million albums; 12 percent of U.S. children under the age of 18 suffer from some form of psychological illness; Russia produces about 333 million gallons of vodka annually; the adult literacy rate of Brazil is 83 percent; Americans consume more than 4 million pounds of peanut products each day.

What do all these numbers mean? Most of us would be hard-pressed to say. Yet we feel more secure in our knowledge when we can express it numerically. According to Lord Kelvin, the 19th-century physicist, "When you can measure what you are speaking about, and express it in numbers, you know something about it. But when you cannot measure it, when you cannot express it in numbers, your knowledge is . . . meager and unsatisfactory." It is this widely shared belief that makes statistics, when used properly, such an effective way to clarify and support ideas.[7]

Like brief examples, statistics are often cited in passing to clarify or strengthen a speaker's points. The following examples show how three students used statistics in their speeches:

> To show the dangers posed by running red lights: "According to the U.S. Department of Transportation, 200,000 people are injured and more than 800 are killed every year in the U.S. due to motorists who run red lights."

> To illustrate the growing popularity of organic foods: "Consumers Union reports that sales of organic crops now exceed $9 billion a year and are increasing at the rate of 20 percent annually."

> To document the problem of identity theft: "As stated by *Newsweek* magazine, identity theft has become the leading source of consumer fraud in the U.S., with an estimated 500,000 to 700,000 victims each year."

Statistics can also be used in combination—stacked up to show the magnitude or seriousness of an issue. We find a good instance of this technique in a student presentation on the dangers of chewing tobacco. To help demonstrate her point that the use of chewing tobacco is a widespread problem, the speaker cited the following figures:

> According to the American Cancer Society, 1 in every 12 Americans is a regular user of chewing tobacco. The average age of first use is just 10 years old, which means that many children are chewing tobacco when they are in fourth grade. The American Cancer Society also reports that 40 percent of high-school boys have tried chewing tobacco—and, what's worse, 21 percent of kindergartners have tried it. Children are using chewing tobacco before they can even read the warning labels.

This is a well-supported argument. But what if the speaker had merely said:

> Lots of people, including many children, use chewing tobacco.

The second statement is neither as clear nor as convincing as the one containing statistics. The statistics make the speaker's claim credible and specific. Of course, the audience didn't remember all the numbers, but that's all right. The purpose of presenting a series of figures is to create an *overall* impact on listeners. What the audience did recall is that an impressive array of statistics supported the speaker's position.

statistics
Numerical data.

Class Activity
According to the principles of active learning, one of the best ways to master a subject is to teach it. For an excellent activity that utilizes these principles, see Amy R. Slagell, "Speech Coach: An Exercise in Teaching by Learning," in *Selections from the Communication Teacher, 1999–2002*, pp. 11–13, which accompanies *The Art of Public Speaking*.

Understanding Statistics

In his classic book *How to Lie with Statistics,* Darrell Huff exploded the notion that numbers don't lie. Strictly speaking, they don't. But they can be easily manipulated and distorted. For example, which of the following statements is true?

a. Enriched white bread is more nutritious than whole-wheat bread because it contains as much or more protein, calcium, niacin, thiamine, and riboflavin.

b. Whole-wheat bread is more nutritious than white bread because it contains seven times the amount of fiber, plus more iron, phosphorus, and potassium.

As you might expect, *both* statements are true. And you might hear either one of them—depending on who is trying to sell you the bread.

One can play with statistics in all kinds of areas. Which of these statements is true?

a. The cheetah, clocked at 70 miles per hour, is the fastest animal in the world.

b. The pronghorn antelope, clocked at 61 miles per hour, is the fastest animal in the world.

The cheetah, right? Not necessarily. It's true the cheetah can go faster, but only for short sprints. The antelope can maintain its high speed over a much greater distance. So which is faster? It depends on what you're measuring. Put in terms of human races, the cheetah would win the hundred-yard dash, but the antelope would win the marathon.

When you are dealing with money, statistics become even trickier. For instance, consider the following facts:

a. In 1942 President Franklin D. Roosevelt earned a salary of $75,000.

b. In 1972 President Richard Nixon earned a salary of $200,000.

c. In 2002 President George W. Bush earned a salary of $400,000.

Which President was paid the most money? In purely mathematical terms, Bush is the highest earner. But as we all know, a dollar today does not buy as much as it did when Franklin Roosevelt was President. One measure of the inflation rate is the Consumer Price Index, which allows us to gauge the value of the dollar in any given year against its purchasing power in 1972. If we apply the Consumer Price Index to the three Presidents' salaries, we can see how much each earned in 1972 dollars:

a. In 1942 President Franklin D. Roosevelt earned a salary of $192,000.

b. In 1972 Richard Nixon earned a salary of $200,000.

c. In 2002 George W. Bush earned a salary of $92,800.

In other words, although Bush had the highest salary, the value of his $400,000 was less than half the value of Roosevelt's $75,000.

Related Reading
Since the Publication in 1954 of Huff's *How to Lie with Statistics,* there have been many other books of a similar nature. Two excellent recent entries are Joel Best, *Damned Lies and Statistics: Untangling Numbers from the Media, Politicians, and Activists* (Berkeley: University of California Press, 2001), and Gerd Gigerenzer, *Calculated Risks: How to Know When the Numbers Deceive You* (New York: Simon and Schuster, 2002), both of which are highly readable and contain a wealth of examples that can be used for class discussion.

The point is that there is usually more to statistics than meets the eye.[8] When you track down statistics for your speeches, be sure to evaluate them in light of the following questions.

Are the Statistics Representative?

Say that on your way to class you choose ten students at random and ask them whether they favor or oppose government tax credits for students attending private schools. Say also that six approve of such funding and four do not. Would you then be accurate in claiming that 60 percent of the students on your campus favor spending government money for private schools?

Of course not. Ten students is not a big enough sample. But even if it were, other problems would arise. Do the ten students interviewed accurately reflect your school's proportion of freshmen, sophomores, juniors, and seniors? Do they mirror the proportion of male and female students? Are the various majors accurately represented? What about part-time and full-time students? Students of different cultural and religious backgrounds?

In short, make sure your statistics are representative of what they claim to measure.

Are Statistical Measures Used Correctly?

Here are two groups of numbers:

Group A	Group B
7,500	5,400
6,300	5,400
5,000	5,000
4,400	2,300
4,400	1,700

Let us apply to each group three basic statistical measures—the mean, the median and the mode.

The *mean*—popularly called the average—is determined by summing all the items in a group and dividing by the number of items. The mean for group A is 5,520. For group B it is 3,960.

The *median* is the middle figure in a group once the figures are put in order from highest to lowest. The median for both group A and group B is exactly the same—5,000.

The *mode* is the number that occurs most frequently in a group of numbers. The mode for group A is 4,400. For group B it is 5,400.

Notice the results:

	Group A	Group B
Mean	5,520	3,960
Median	5,000	5,000
Mode	4,400	5,400

mean
The average value of a group of numbers.

median
The middle number in a group of numbers arranged from highest to lowest.

mode
The number that occurs most frequently in a group of numbers.

All these measures have the same goal—to indicate what is typical or characteristic of a certain group of numbers. Yet see how different the results are, depending on which measure you use.

The differences among the various measures can be striking. For instance, the *mean* salary of local TV news anchorpersons is $69,800 a year. But most anchors don't earn anywhere near that amount. The mean is inflated by the huge salaries (up to $1 million a year) paid to a few star anchors in media centers such as New York, Los Angeles, and Chicago. In contrast, the *median* salary of local news anchors is $50,000—not a sum to scoff at, but still $19,800 less than the average salary.[9]

How might a speaker use these different measures? The owner of a television station would probably cite the *mean* ($69,800) to show that local news anchors are handsomely compensated for their work. An organization of news anchors might emphasize the *median* ($50,000) to demonstrate that salaries are not nearly as high as the station owner makes them out to be. Both speakers would be telling the truth, but neither would be completely honest unless she or he made clear the meaning of the statistics.

Are the Statistics from a Reliable Source?

Which is the more reliable estimate of the environmental dangers of toxic waste in a landfill—one from the U.S. Environmental Protection Agency or one compiled by the company that owns the landfill? Easy—the estimate by the EPA, which does not have a vested interest in what the figures look like. What about nutritional ratings for fast foods offered by Consumer's Union (a highly respected nonprofit organization) or by Burger King? That's easy too—Consumer's Union, whose claims are not manipulated by advertising executives.

But now things get tougher. What about the competing statistics offered by groups for and against Medicare reform? Or the conflicting numbers tossed out by a school board and the teachers striking against it? In these cases the answer is not so clear, since both sides would present the facts according to their own partisan motives.

As a speaker, you must be aware of possible bias in the use of numbers. Since statistics can be interpreted so many ways and put to so many uses, you should seek figures gathered by objective, nonpartisan sources.

Tips for Using Statistics

Use Statistics to Quantify Your Ideas

The main value of statistics is to give your ideas numerical precision. This can be especially important when you are trying to document the existence of a problem. Examples can bring the problem alive and dramatize it in personal terms. But your listeners may still wonder how many people the problem actually affects. In such a situation, you should turn to statistics. Research has shown that the impact of examples is greatly enhanced when they are combined with statistics that show the examples to be typical.[10]

Suppose you are talking about the need for tougher driver's license requirements for elderly drivers. Part of your speech deals with the growing number of auto accidents caused by drivers age 70 and older. You give an example, you personalize it, you provide many details, as follows:

Speech Assignment
Students will profit from any extra opportunities they have to speak in front of the class. Toward this end, have students prepare and present a one-point speech in which they state their point, support it with three pieces of supporting material, and then summarize the point. The speech should be 1–2 minutes in length and should be accorded the same weight as a homework activity. For full discussion of this assignment, see the first Additional Exercise for Critical Thinking on p. 186 of the *Instructor's Manual*.

Marie Wyman's 87th birthday celebration at the Lobster Trap and Steakhouse in Winslow, Maine, ended with a bang. As Wyman backed out of her parking spot, she lost control of her Buick and plowed right through the restaurant's crowded dining room. Tables and chairs scattered as terrified diners scrambled for cover. Twenty-seven people were injured, and police say it was a miracle that no one was killed.

Confronted with this example, a listener might think, "Yes, that's very unfortunate, but is the accident rate of older drivers really that serious a problem?" Anticipating just such a response, a sharp speaker would include figures to quantify the problem:

According to the National Highway Traffic Safety Administration, almost 5,000 drivers age 70 or older were killed last year, a 33 percent increase over the past 10 years. In fewer than 20 years, there will be more than 30 million drivers over age 70 in the United States, and highway safety experts warn that the number of people killed in crashes involving elderly motorists is likely to exceed the drunk-driving death toll.

Now the audience is much more likely to agree that there may indeed be a need for tougher licensing requirements.

Use Statistics Sparingly

As helpful as statistics can be, nothing puts an audience to sleep faster than a speech cluttered with numbers from beginning to end. Insert statistics only when they are needed, and then make sure they are easy to grasp. Even the most attentive listener would have trouble sorting out this barrage of figures:

According to the *World Factbook,* life expectancy at birth in the United States ranks 18th among 25 industrialized countries. Life expectancy of women in Japan is 84.25 years compared with 80.2 years for American women, and 77.73 years for Japanese men compared with 74.5 years for American men. The United States ranks 23rd among 25 industrialized nations in infant mortality, with a rate almost twice as high as Japan's. Canada ranks 13th. Americans spend more each year on health care than any other nation—$1 trillion dollars, or 13.7 percent of gross domestic product—yet the World Health Organization ranks the U.S. health care system 37th in overall performance among member nations.

Instead of drowning your audience in a sea of statistics, use only those that are most important. For example:

According to the *World Factbook,* people in the United States have one of the lowest life expectancies among industrialized nations. We also have one of the highest rates of infant mortality. Even though we spend more on health care than any other nation, the World Health Organization ranks 36 other nations ahead of us with regard to the overall performance of our health care system.

This second statement makes the same point as the first statement, but now the ideas are not lost in a torrent of numbers.

Identify the Sources of Your Statistics

As we have seen, figures are easy to manipulate. This is why careful listeners keep an ear out for the sources of a speaker's statistics. One student learned this by experience. In a speech titled "Tax Reform: Fact Versus

Fiction," he claimed that the wealthiest 1 percent of U.S. taxpayers pay 34 percent of federal income taxes, even though they account for only 19 percent of all earned income. He also noted that the wealthiest 25 percent of Americans pay 83 percent of federal income taxes. These are startling statistics—especially given concerns that upper-income Americans do not pay their fair share of taxes. But because the student did not say where he got the figures, his classmates were not willing to accept them. They were sure he must be wrong.

As it turned out, the figures were quite reliable. They had come from a study by the Internal Revenue Service reported in the *New York Times*. If the speaker had mentioned the source in his speech, he would have been more successful.[11]

Explain Your Statistics

Statistics don't speak for themselves. They need to be interpreted and related to your listeners. Notice how effectively U.S. Secretary of State Colin Powell did this in a speech to the United Nations General Assembly during a special session on the international AIDS crisis:

> Many speakers have noted the dreadful toll that AIDS is taking. . . . But let me try to make it more relevant.
>
> This hall holds about 2,000 people. By the time the three hours of this session elapse, 2,000 people around the world—just about the same number who are here—will be newly infected with HIV/AIDS. That's one for every person in this room. In some countries the infection rate is so high that one in three of us—the delegate to your right, the delegate to your left, or you, yourself—would be HIV positive.[12]

Explaining what statistics mean is particularly important when you deal with large numbers, since they are hard to visualize. How, for example, can we comprehend the $6.5 trillion U.S. national debt? We could explain that a trillion is a thousand billion and a billion is a thousand million. But that doesn't do much good, since millions and billions are almost as hard to visualize as trillions. Suppose, instead, we translate the huge numbers into terms a listener can relate to. Here is one speaker's solution:

> How much money is a trillion dollars? Think of it this way. If you had $1 million and spent it at the rate of $1,000 a day, you would run out of money in less than three years. If you had $1 billion and spent it at the rate of $1,000 a day, you would not run out of money for almost 3,000 years. And if you had $1 trillion and spent it at the rate of $1,000 a day, you wouldn't run out of money for nearly 3 million years!

Whenever you use statistics in your speeches, think of how you can make them meaningful to your audience. Rather than simply reciting figures about, say, the short-term and long-term consequences of excessive drinking on college campuses, find a way to bring those figures home to your audience. You might say, as did one speaker:

> According to the Office for Substance Abuse Prevention, alcohol is the leading cause of death among young adults. Furthermore, of college students currently enrolled in the United States, more than 240,000 will eventually lose their lives to alcohol. Two hundred forty thousand—that's the current student population of this university six times over.

When used properly, statistics make us feel more secure in our knowledge. A speech that is supported by statistics is usually more persuasive than an undocumented presentation.

Or suppose you're discussing the crime rate in the United States. You could say, "The Foundation for Crime Prevention Education reports that the rate of assault is six times higher than in 1960, and the FBI indicates that every 16 seconds a murder, rape, robbery, or assault takes place." These are alarming statistics, but they are likely to go in one ear and out the other unless you bring them home to your audience. Here's what one student said in her speech:

According to the Foundation for Crime Prevention Education, violence and crime have dramatically increased. An American is six times more likely to be assaulted with a weapon today than in 1960. The FBI reports that someone is either murdered, raped, assaulted, or robbed every 16 seconds. This means that today, at the end of our 50-minute class period, approximately 187 people will have been victims of a violent crime.

Be creative in thinking of ways to relate your statistics to your audience. This is probably the single most important step you can take to make statistics work in your speeches.

View Joveta Dixon, "Responsible Drinking," and Rebecca Hanson, "Self-Defense on Campus."

CD 1: VIDEO 7.4

Round Off Complicated Statistics

Mount Kilimanjaro is 19,341 feet high; the official world land speed record is 622.287 miles per hour; the world's highest waterfall has a total drop of 3,212 feet; the population of Saudi Arabia is 23,513,330 people; the moon is 238,855 miles from earth.

These are intriguing figures, but they are too complicated to be readily understood by listeners. Unless there is an important reason to give exact numbers, you should round off most statistics. You might say that Mount Kilimanjaro is 19,300 feet high; the world land speed record is more than 622 miles per hour; the world's highest waterfall has a drop of some 3,200 feet; the population of Saudi Arabia is more than 23 million; and the moon is 239,000 miles from earth.

Use Visual Aids to Clarify Statistical Trends

Visual aids can save you a lot of time, as well as make your statistics easier to comprehend. Suppose you are discussing the number of major strikes by labor unions in the United States since World War II. You could start by explaining that after the war, during the early 1950s, there were a record number of strikes involving 1,000 or more workers—including the 1950 walkout of 370,000 United Mine Workers that crippled the nation's industries. Then, after the start of Dwight Eisenhower's presidency in 1953, the number of strikes declined fairly steadily until 1964, when they started climbing to a peak of more than 400 in 1968. After a sharp decline in the early 1970s, they jumped again in 1975 to the highest level in two decades. Finally, the number of strikes took a dramatic turn downward during the Reagan years of the 1980s and reached a record low in 2002 under President George W. Bush.

These are interesting statistics, and you could build a good speech around them. But strung together in a few sentences they are hard to digest. Figure 7.1 shows how much more clearly the points can be made with a simple graph. We shall discuss visual aids in detail in Chapter 13. For the moment, keep in mind that they can be helpful in presenting statistical information.

Where to Find Statistics

Statistics can be found in any kind of reputable publication—books, magazines, newspapers, scholarly journals, government documents, business reports, and so forth. A world almanac (there are several established versions) can be a treasure-trove of interesting numbers.

Teaching Tip
Although a visual aid is not needed for every statistic in a speech, each time a speaker uses statistics, he or she should consider whether a visual aid will enhance the clarity and impact of the statistics. Charts and graphs, the most common types of visual aids for presenting statistics, are discussed fully in Chapter 13.

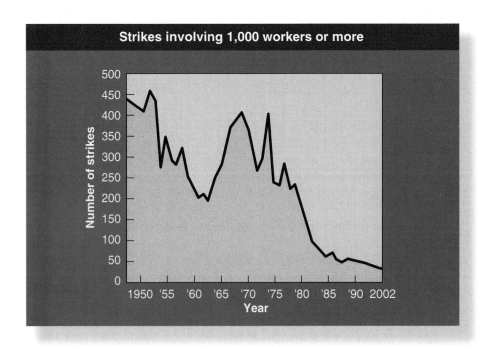

Figure 7.1

There are also some sources devoted solely to statistics. They include the *Statistical Yearbook* (put out by the United Nations) and the *Statistical Abstract of the United States* (published annually since 1878 and also available on CD-ROM). These sources contain statistics on everything from the U.S. economy to world population trends. The *Guinness Book of World Records* offers more esoteric information, such as the weight of the world's largest polished diamond, the internal temperature of the sun, and the number of hours of television the average child watches by the age of 18.

You will find these and other handy sources of statistics in the reference section of your library (see Chapter 6). Besides being easy to use, they can be fascinating to look through. This is why the *Guinness Book of World Records* remains a best-seller year after year.

You can also garner a wealth of statistics from the Internet. Many websites provide numerical data—much of it more current than that found in printed works. As with any kind of information acquired off the Internet, you need to make sure your statistics come from reliable sources such as universities, government agencies, nonpartisan organizations, and the like. One excellent source is the *Statistical Abstract of the United States* website (www.census.gov/statab/www). Another is FedStats, which provides links to more than 70 federal agencies that produce statistics of public interest (www.fedstats.gov). Yet another is the CIA's *World Factbook* site, where you can find figures about every country around the globe (www.cia.gov/cia/publications/factbook/index.html).

Cross-Reference
See Chapter 6, pp. 147–157, for full discussion of how to find statistics and other speech materials on the Internet.

Testimony

Imagine you are talking with a friend about the classes you plan to take next term. You are not sure whether to sign up for Psychology 230 or Accounting 181. Both are requirements; both meet at the same time of day. Your friend says, "I took those classes last year. They're both good, but Professor Hassam was excellent in Psych 230. She's one of the best teachers on campus. If she's teaching the course next term, I'd take it for sure." You check the timetable and find that Professor Hassam is indeed slated for Psychology 230. You sign up for her course.

As this story illustrates, we are often influenced by the *testimony* of other people when making decisions in everyday life. Much the same thing happens in public speaking. Just as you are likely to be swayed by your friend's recommendation about which class to take, so audiences tend to respect the opinions of people who have special knowledge or experience on the topic at hand. By quoting or paraphrasing such people, you can give your ideas greater strength and impact. The two major kinds of testimony are expert testimony and peer testimony.

testimony
Quotations or paraphrases used to support a point.

Expert Testimony

In most speeches you will probably rely on expert testimony—testimony from people who are acknowledged authorities in their fields. Expert testimony is especially helpful for student speakers because students are seldom recognized as experts on their speech topics. Citing the views of people who

expert testimony
Testimony from people who are recognized experts in their fields.

are experts is a good way to lend credibility to your speeches. It shows that you are not just mouthing your own opinions, but that your position is supported by people who are knowledgeable about the topic.[13]

Expert testimony is even more important when a topic is controversial or when the audience is skeptical about a speaker's point of view. The following story explains how one speaker enlisted expert testimony for a speech on reforming the U.S. Social Security system:

> As Julia Wang did her research on how to make Social Security more equitable for younger taxpayers, she became convinced that individual citizens should be allowed to invest a portion of their Social Security funds directly in the stock market. Yet Julia was not an expert on the matter. Nor did she have any firsthand experience with the Social Security system. How could she convince her audience to accept her ideas?
>
> Statistics helped, and so did examples. But on such a controversial topic, that was not enough. So to reinforce her credibility, Julia quoted a wide range of experts who agreed with her—Arizona Senator John McCain; Jeffrey Sachs, a Harvard economics professor; former U.S. Social Security Commissioner Dorcas Hardy; Jose Piñera, founder of the International Center for Pension Reform; former Democratic Senator Daniel Patrick Moynihan, Co-chair of the President's Commission to Strengthen Social Security; and Peter G. Peterson, President of the Concord Coalition. By citing the views of these experts—some of whom might be expected to disagree with her point of view—Julia made her speech much more persuasive.

Peer Testimony

Another type of testimony often used in speeches is peer testimony—opinions of people like ourselves; not prominent figures, but ordinary citizens who have firsthand experience on the topic. This kind of testimony is especially valuable because it gives a more personal viewpoint on issues than can be gained from expert testimony. It conveys the feelings, the knowledge, the insight of people who speak with the voice of genuine experience.

For example, if you were speaking about the barriers faced by people with physical disabilities, you would surely include testimony from doctors and other medical authorities. But in this case, the expert testimony would be limited because it cannot communicate what it really means to have a physical disability. To communicate that, you need statements from people who have physical disabilities—such as the following:

> Itzhak Perlman, the world-renowned violinist whose legs are paralyzed, once said: "When you are in a wheelchair, people don't talk to you. Perhaps they think it is contagious, or perhaps they think crippled legs mean a crippled mind. But whatever the reason, they treat you like a thing."
>
> Paul Longmore, who lost the use of his legs as a child, notes that most people are uncomfortable in the presence of someone who is handicapped. "It's only when they really go out of their way to get to know us," he says, "that they realize we are just as bright, witty, and companionable as they are."

There is no way expert testimony can express these ideas with the same authenticity and emotional impact.

Teaching Tip
Students often think only of books and magazines when looking for expert testimony. Remind them that faculty members are usually more than willing to be interviewed on the subjects of their expertise. For discussion of how to conduct a research interview, see Chapter 6, pp. 156–160.

peer testimony
Testimony from ordinary people with firsthand experience or insight on a topic.

Class Activity
Have students analyze the use of supporting materials in one of the sample speeches in the appendix at the end of the book or in Part V of the *Instructor's Manual*.

Quoting Versus Paraphrasing

The statements from Itzhak Perlman and Paul Longmore are presented as direct quotations. Testimony can also be presented by paraphrasing. Rather than quoting someone verbatim, you present the gist of that person's ideas in your own words—as did one student in her speech about America's potential water crisis:

> Writing in *Audubon* magazine, Dr. Peter Bourne, president of Global Water, a nonpartisan educational group in Washington, D.C., said most Americans do not yet realize the extent and urgency of the water problem. At the present rate, he says, we are headed for a crisis that will change the way we live in every part of the nation.

When should you use a direct quotation as opposed to paraphrasing? The standard rule is that quotations are most effective when they are brief, when they convey your meaning better than you can, and when they are particularly eloquent, witty, or compelling. If you find a quotation that fits these criteria, then recite the quotation word for word.

Paraphrasing is better than direct quotation in two situations: (1) when the wording of a quotation is obscure or cumbersome, as is often the case with government documents; (2) when a quotation is longer than two or three sentences. Audiences often tune out partway through lengthy quotations, which tend to interrupt the flow of a speaker's ideas. Since the rest of the speech is in your own words, you should put longer quotations in your own words as well.

Tips for Using Testimony

Quote or Paraphrase Accurately

Accurate quotation involves three things: making sure you do not misquote someone; making sure you do not violate the meaning of statements you paraphrase; making sure you do not quote out of context. Of these, the last is the most subtle—and the most dangerous. By quoting out of context, you can twist someone's remarks so as to prove almost anything. Take movie advertisements. A critic pans a movie with these words:

> This movie is a colossal bore. From beginning to end it is a disaster. What is meant to be brilliant dialogue is about as fascinating as the stuff you clean out of your kitchen drain.

But when the movie is advertised in the newspapers, what appears in huge letters over the critic's name? "COLOSSAL! FROM BEGINNING TO END—BRILLIANT! FASCINATING!"

This is so flagrant as to be humorous. But quoting out of context can have serious consequences. Consider the following statement by a political candidate:

> Creating a national sales tax would provide needed revenue for programs such as education, health care, and national defense. Several European countries have such a tax, and it could certainly work in the U.S. However, I do not support such a tax here—in fact, I don't support new taxes of any kind.

direct quotation
Testimony that is presented word for word.

paraphrase
To restate or summarize a source's ideas in one's own words.

quoting out of context
Quoting a statement in such a way as to distort its meaning by removing the statement from the words and phrases surrounding it.

Now look what happens when the first part of that statement is quoted out of context by a competing candidate:

Americans already pay too much in taxes. Yet my opponent in this election has stated—and I quote: "Creating a national sales tax would provide needed revenue for programs such as education, health care, and national defense. Several European countries have such a tax, and it could certainly work in the U.S." Well, my opponent may think new taxes are good for Europe, but they're the last thing we need in this country.

By quoting the original statement out of context, the competing candidate has created a false impression of his opponent. Such behavior is highly unethical and has no place in responsible communication of any kind. Be sure, when you quote or paraphrase someone, that you represent their words and ideas with complete accuracy.

Use Testimony from Qualified Sources

We have all become accustomed to the celebrity testimonial in television and magazine advertising. The professional golfer endorses a particular brand of clubs. The movie star praises a certain hair spray or shampoo. The basketball player plugs a type of athletic shoe. So far, so good. These are the tools of the trade for the people who endorse them.

But what happens when a television actor endorses a cell phone company? A tennis player represents a line of cameras? A retired golfer extols the virtues of a brand of motor oil? Do they know more about these products than you or I? Probably not. They have been paid large sums of money to be photographed with the product in hopes that their popularity will rub off on it.

Being a celebrity or an authority in one area does not make someone competent in other areas. Listeners will find your speeches much more credible if you use testimony from sources qualified *on the subject at hand*. As we have seen, this may include either recognized experts or ordinary citizens with special experience on the speech topic.

Use Testimony from Unbiased Sources

In a speech about the controversial sleeping pill Halcion, which has been blamed for causing side effects such as amnesia, anxiety, delusions, and hostility, a student said:

Pharmacologist Robert Shaw, director of project management at the Upjohn Company, the Michigan-based manufacturer of Halcion, maintains that it has no more serious side effects than any other sleeping pill when it is used properly. "The vast majority of studies," Shaw says, "back us up on that point."

As you might expect, the student's classmates were not persuaded. After all, what would you expect someone at Upjohn to say—that its product is unsafe and causes psychiatric disorders? One listener reacted in this way: "For all I know, the statement by Shaw may be true, but he is hardly an unbiased source. I wish you had cited an impartial expert instead."

Do you need supporting materials for your speech? Check out Finding Data on the Internet (www.robertniles.com/data/). Created as a handy resource guide for journalists, this site provides links to facts and figures on dozens of topics of national and international interest.

There are a number of think tanks whose websites provide excellent resources for speech materials. They include the Brookings Institution (www.brook.edu/dybdocroot/), RAND (www.rand.org/), and the Cato Institute (www.cato.org/index.html).

You can link to these websites at www.mhhe.com/lucas8.

ONLINE LEARNING CENTER

Careful listeners are suspicious of opinion from biased or self-interested sources. Be sure to use testimony from credible, competent, objective authorities.

Identify the People You Quote or Paraphrase

The usual way to identify your source is to name the person and sketch her or his qualifications before presenting the testimony. The following excerpt is from a student speech titled "Dying to Be Thin":

> Treatment of anorexia is a lifetime process. According to Dr. Katherine Halmi, director of the eating disorders clinic at New York Hospital, people think that eating disorders are "minor disorders that can be overcome with a little will power and effort, but these are serious, incapacitating illnesses that require professional intervention."

Had the speaker not identified Dr. Halmi, listeners would not have had the foggiest notion who she is or why her opinion should be heeded.

For another example, look at this statement from a speech in favor of beginning foreign language instruction in elementary school:

> John Silber, Chancellor of Boston University and Chairman of the Massachusetts Board of Education, remarks: "It is quite clear that remarkable competence in a language can be achieved in three years—if these years are the ages three, four, and five. There is no question that for the average child to become bilingual, the earlier the better."

After this statement, there is no doubt about Silber's qualifications or why the audience should respect his judgment on the subject of education.

Nor are students the only speakers who need to identify their sources. Whether you are speaking in a classroom or a courtroom, at a business meeting or a technical conference, to a community organization or a religious gathering, you will be much more effective if you make clear to your audience why they should accept the testimony of the people you quote or paraphrase.

Teaching Tip
Remind students that they need to identify the people they quote or paraphrase by stating both the source's full name and her or his qualifications. If the same source is quoted again later in the speech, at that time it is necessary to refer to the source only by name.

View Jennifer Breuer, "Dying to Be Thin" and Renee Varghese, "Multicultural, Multilingual."

CD 1: VIDEO 7.5

As we saw in Chapter 2, identifying the source of testimony is also an important ethical responsibility. If you use another person's words or ideas without giving credit to that person, you will be guilty of plagiarism. This is true whether you paraphrase the original source or quote it verbatim.

Examples, statistics, and testimony are all helpful devices for the speaker. Depending on your topic, you may want to use some of them, all of them, or none of them. Remember, they are tools, and they all serve the same purpose—getting your message across to your listeners.

Sample Speech with Commentary

The following speech illustrates how to work supporting materials into a presentation. As you read, study how the speaker uses a variety of examples, statistics, and quotations to make her ideas clear, credible, and convincing.

Suffer the Children

Commentary	Speech
The speaker begins with an extended example to gain attention and interest. The example is specific and detailed. We are told Matthew Garvey's name and age, where he lived, the kind of work he did, and how he was injured. These are the kinds of details that bring examples to life and help get listeners involved in a speech.	Matthew Garvey was just 13 years old when he was hired by Quality Car Wash in Laurel, Maryland, to towel-dry cars as they came off the line. Not long after he began working, Matthew lost his right leg when it got caught in an industrial machine used to suck the moisture out of the towels. After investigating, the U.S. Department of Labor fined the car wash for illegally hiring a minor and for operating a machine with a broken safety lid.
The speaker moves into testimony suggesting that the opening story is representative of a major problem in the U.S. When you use an extended example, it is usually a good idea to precede or follow the example with statistics or testimony showing that the example is not unusual or exceptional.	This is just one of the more tragic examples of what Jeffrey Newman of the National Child Labor Committee calls the "crisis" of child-labor law abuses in the United States. In researching this speech, I discovered that employers from New York to California are breaking the law by hiring children from ages 7 to 17 who often put in long, hard hours in dangerous conditions. Today I would like to show you the extent of the problem and how it jeopardizes the education and safety of millions of young people.
In her first main point the speaker explores the problem of child-labor law violations in the United States. She begins by summarizing the provisions of the law. Notice how she identifies the website where she acquired the information.	To understand the problem of child-labor law violations, we need to begin by looking at the provisions of the law. As explained on the U.S. Department of Labor website, the Fair Labor Standards Act sets a minimum working age of 14. It limits 14-year-olds and 15-year-olds to three hours of work on school days, prohibits them from working after 7 at night, and allows them a total of 18 work hours per week during the school year. The law also restricts employment of children under 18 in dangerous jobs such as construction, meat-cutting, and mining.

Statistics in this and the next paragraph back up the speaker's point that violations of child-labor laws are widespread in the U.S. Rather than giving the exact number of violations, she rounds them off, making them easier to grasp and recall.

The speaker uses a combination of statistics and testimony to support her point about child-labor abuses in the garment industry. The statement from Thomas Gubiak is an example of expert testimony; the closing quotation from Faviola Flores is an instance of peer testimony.

A series of brief examples supports the speaker's claim about the pervasiveness of child-labor law violations. Because the examples deal with companies throughout the U.S. and in different lines of business, they provide strong evidence to reinforce the speaker's point that violations of the law are widespread.

The speaker begins her second main point— that violations of child-labor laws have serious consequences for the education and physical safety of young workers.

The quotation from Hugh McDaid is a good instance of expert testimony. This quotation, like others in the speech, is short and forceful. There is no reason to use a direct quotation unless it makes the point more clearly and forcefully than you can in your own words.

Here the speaker paraphrases rather than quoting verbatim. Notice that she gives the name of the book she is paraphrasing from

Passed in 1938 and amended several times since, the Fair Labor Standards Act was designed to prevent the exploitation of child labor that took place during the 19th century. Yet today violations of the law are shockingly widespread. According to the Associated Press, 148,000 minors in the U.S. are employed illegally in nonagricultural jobs during an average week, working too many hours or in hazardous conditions. In addition, the National Child Labor Committee reports that more than 110,000 children work illegally on U.S. farms.

Some of the most serious violations occur in garment industry factories known as sweatshops that hire immigrant children at rates well below minimum wage. The Associated Press estimates that as many as 2,600 minors are employed illegally in New York City sweatshops. Thomas Gubiak, head of the city's garment district task force, says "most of the children in these factories are below 18, some as young as 8." Like Faviola Flores, a 15-year-old Mexican girl in a Manhattan sweatshop, they toil long days in unsafe conditions for as little as $3.50 an hour. "I don't like working here," Flores says, "but I have no choice."

Although the exploitation of child labor has been a problem in the garment trade since the 1800s, it can be found in almost every industry that employs minors. In January 2000, Wagner's Meats of New Orleans was fined nearly $150,000 for illegally employing 27 minors in dangerous jobs and for exceeding federal hour limits. In February 2001, Thornton Roofing was fined $34,000 for child-labor violations in connection with the death of a teenage worker in Montgomery, Alabama. In March 2002, the Six Flags amusement parks paid $85,000 in penalties for violating federal child-labor laws.

Like other businesses caught breaking child-labor laws, Wagner's and Six Flags tried to downplay the seriousness of their offenses. But the growing epidemic of child-labor law violations threatens both the education and the physical safety of young workers.

The educational consequences are most damaging to illegal underage employees who work instead of attending school. As Hugh McDaid of New York City's garment task force says, illegal underage workers "sacrifice their education and literally commit themselves to a life of working in a sweatshop. They have no future." But even for children who do attend school, too many hours at work can harm their education. In their book *When Teenagers Work*, psychology professors Ellen Greenberger and Laurence Steinberg note that intensive levels of work among youth tend to produce higher truancy and lower grades.

and identifies its authors. As we saw in Chapter 2, speakers have an ethical obligation to indicate the sources of paraphrases, as well as of quotations.

The examples in this paragraph show specific cases in which teenagers were injured or killed by the violation of child-labor laws. The extended example about Michael Hurcone is especially effective. Filled with specific details that make it interesting and credible, it puts the speaker's point in human terms with which the audience can identify.

In this paragraph the speaker presents testimony and statistics to prove that the examples in the previous paragraph are not atypical. As in other parts of the speech, she is quite specific in identifying the sources of her evidence.

The speaker begins her conclusion by summarizing the two main points she had made in the body of the speech. She then ends with a dramatic quotation. As we shall see in Chapter 9, this is an effective way to pull a speech together and to reinforce its central idea.

According to Greenberger and Steinberg, one study after another has found that working more than a very few hours a week has a negative impact on teenagers' academic performance.

Not only do child workers harm their education, but they often endanger their physical safety as well. Recall the story I told in my introduction about Matthew Garvey, the 13-year-old who lost his leg while working at a car wash. Even more tragic is the case of Michael Hurcone, a 17-year-old Pennsylvania high-school student. While employed at a supermarket, he was working with a bailer—a machine that crushes and binds cardboard boxes and is supposed to be off-limits to minors. Noticing that some material was stuck in the bailer, Michael tried to free up the jam when he got caught in the machine. It crushed his body for 30 minutes before he suffocated.

Nor are these isolated examples. *USA Today* reported on July 12, 2002, that 230,000 teenagers are injured at work each year. According to former U.S. Labor Secretary Alexis Herman, nearly 70 minors are killed on the job annually—most in accidents involving infractions of child-labor laws.

In the light of all this evidence, there can be no doubt that the violation of child-labor laws is a widespread problem with serious consequences. The issue is well summarized by former U.S. Senator Howard Metzenbaum of Ohio, who stated after congressional hearings on the subject, "I shudder to think that children the same age as my own grandchildren are being robbed of an education, their limbs, and indeed, their lives through illegal child labor."

Summary

Good speeches are not composed of hot air and unfounded assertions. They need strong supporting materials to bolster the speaker's point of view. In fact, the skillful use of supporting materials often makes the difference between a good speech and a poor one. The three basic types of supporting materials are examples, statistics, and testimony.

In the course of a speech you may use brief examples—specific instances referred to in passing—and sometimes you may want to give several brief examples in a row to create a stronger impression. Extended examples—often called illustrations, narratives, or anecdotes—are longer and more detailed. Hypothetical examples describe imaginary situations and can be quite effective for relating ideas to the audience. All three kinds of examples help clarify ideas, reinforce ideas, or personalize ideas. To be most effective, though, they should be vivid and richly textured.

Statistics can be extremely helpful in conveying your message as long as you use them sparingly and explain them so that they are meaningful to your audience. Above all, you should understand your statistics and use them fairly. Numbers can easily be manipulated and distorted. Make sure your figures are representative of what they claim to measure, that you use statistical measures correctly, and that you take statistics only from reliable sources.

Testimony is especially helpful for student speakers because students are seldom recognized as experts on their speech topics. Citing the views of people who are experts is a good way to make your ideas more credible. When you include testimony in a speech, you can either quote someone verbatim or paraphrase his or her words. As with statistics, there are guidelines for using testimony. Be sure to quote or paraphrase accurately and to cite qualified, unbiased sources. If the source is not generally known to your audience, be certain to establish his or her credentials.

Key Terms

supporting materials (175)

example (176)

brief example (176)

extended example (177)

hypothetical example (177)

statistics (181)

mean (183)

median (183)

mode (183)

testimony (189)

expert testimony (189)

peer testimony (190)

direct quotation (191)

paraphrase (191)

quoting out of context (191)

Review these terms by doing the Chapter 7 crossword puzzle at www.mhhe.com/lucas8.

ONLINE LEARNING CENTER

Review Questions

After reading this chapter, you should be able to answer the following questions:

1. Why do you need supporting materials in your speeches?

2. What are the three kinds of examples discussed in this chapter? How might you use each kind to support your ideas?

3. What are five tips for using examples in your speeches?

4. Why is it so easy to lie with statistics? What three questions should you ask to judge the reliability of statistics?

5. What are six tips for using statistics in your speeches?

6. What is testimony? Explain the difference between expert testimony and peer testimony.

7. What are four tips for using testimony in your speeches?

For further review, go to the Study Questions for this chapter.

CD: STUDY QUESTIONS

Exercises for Critical Thinking

1. Each of the following statements violates at least one of the criteria for effective supporting materials discussed in the chapter. Identify the flaw (or flaws) in each statement.

   a. In a random survey last month of 470 members of the Sierra Club, 98 percent of those interviewed opposed drilling for oil in the Alaskan wilderness. Clearly, then, the American people oppose such drilling.

   b. In the words of one expert, "Mainstream medical care is not meeting the needs of many Americans. I encourage people to pursue alternative treatments such as acupuncture, chiropractic, and massage therapy."

   c. Statistics compiled by the National Education Association show that the median salary for teachers in our state is $48,835. This shows that teachers average almost $49,000 a year in salary.

   d. According to a survey conducted for Verizon Wireless, most people prefer Verizon's cellular service to that of Cingular, Nextel, or Sprint PCS.

   e. There's no reason insurance companies should charge higher rates for drivers under the age of 25. All my friends drive a lot and almost none of them have been in car accidents.

   f. According to the *New York Times Almanac*, San Francisco has the highest per capita annual income of any U.S. city—$57,414. The lowest per capita annual income belongs to McAllen-Edinburg-Mission, Texas, at $13,344. The average per capita annual income for all U.S. metropolitan areas is $31,332.

   g. As Sean Penn noted in a recent interview, the United States needs to change its foreign policy in the Middle East. Otherwise, Penn said, it will be impossible to bring about lasting peace in the region.

2. Analyze Renee Varghese's "Multicultural, Multilingual," in the appendix of sample speeches following Chapter 18. Identify the main points of the speech and the supporting materials used for each. Evaluate the speaker's use of supporting materials in light of the criteria discussed in this chapter.

Cross-Reference
For discussion of the Exercises for Critical Thinking, see the *Instructor's Manual*, pp. 180–185. For additional exercises, check the *Instructor's Manual*, pp. 186–188, as well as the five volumes of *Selections from the Speech Communication Teacher* that accompany *The Art of Public Speaking*.

Applying the **POWER** *of* PUBLIC SPEAKING

While driving home from Thanksgiving dinner with your family, you are blindsided by a drunk driver. Miraculously, everyone involved is uninjured, but you know the outcome could easily have been different. Shaken by the experience, you have become committed to working for tougher legal and judicial action against drunk driving.

Your state ranks among the lowest in the fight against drunk drivers, but you know a bill will be introduced in the next session of the state senate to change that. To build support for the bill, you will be speaking to several local service organizations. You will tell them about your personal experience and provide testimony in support of the new legislation, but you will also need to support your speech with national and state drunk-driving statistics. Because your accident occurred on Thanksgiving, you also want to know if anyone has compiled figures that correlate drunk-driving accidents with specific holidays throughout the year.

Cross-Reference
For discussion of this Applying the Power of Public Speaking scenario, see the *Instructor's Manual*, pp. 185–186.

As part of your research, you decide to check the website of Mothers Against Drunk Driving (www.madd.org/). What do you find that will help you in your speech? Be specific.

Notes

[1]Tami Longaberger, "Diversity: It's Right, It's Here, Embrace It," *Vital Speeches,* 67 (2000), pp. 89–92.

[2]Jerry Adler, "Five Who Survived," *Newsweek* (September 9, 2002), p. 20.

[3]Daniel J. O'Keefe, *Persuasion: Theory and Research,* 2nd ed. (Thousand Oaks, CA: Sage, 2002), p. 229.

[4]Sun Yan's speech was presented in Beijing during China's 2001 21st Century-Ericsson Cup national English-language public speaking contest. I would like to thank *21st Century* for permission to include video from the speech on the CD that accompanies this edition of *The Art of Public Speaking.*

[5]Eliot Aronson, *The Social Animal,* 8th ed. (New York: W. H. Freeman, 1999), p. 98.

[6]This point was made by James A. Winans in his classic *Speech-Making* (New York: Appleton-Century-Crofts, 1922), p. 141.

[7]Over the years, there has been much debate over whether statistics or examples have more impact on listeners. For a recent study that gives the nod to statistics, see Mike Allen and Raymond W. Preiss, "Comparing the Persuasiveness of Narrative and Statistical Evidence Using Meta-Analysis," *Communication Research Reports,* 14 (1997), pp. 125–131.

[8]For two fascinating recent works on the use and misuse of statistics, see Joel Best, *Damned Lies and Statistics: Untangling Numbers from the Media, Politicians, and Activists* (Berkeley: University of California Press, 2001); Gerd Gigerenzer, *Calculated Risks: How to Know When the Numbers Deceive You* (New York: Simon and Schuster, 2002).

[9]Bob Papper and Michael Gerhard, "2002 Radio and Television Salary Survey," *RTNDA Communicator,* 56 (2002), pp. 20–21.

[10]M. Allen, R. Bruflat, R. Fucilla, M. Kramer, S. McKellips, D. J. Ryan, and M. Spiegelhoff, "Testing the Persuasiveness of Evidence: Combining Narrative and Statistical Forms," *Communication Research Reports,* 17 (2000), pp. 331–336.

[11]For research confirming the importance of citing sources when presenting evidence, see Rodney A. Reynolds and J. Lynn Reynolds, "Evidence," in James Price Dillard and Michael Pfau (eds.), *The Persuasion Handbook: Developments in Theory and Practice* (Thousand Oaks, CA: Sage, 2002), pp. 429–430.

[12]Colin Powell, "U.N. Special Session on HIV/AIDS," *Vital Speeches,* 67 (2001), pp. 578–580.

[13]See O'Keefe, *Persuasion: Theory and Research,* pp. 186–187.

Chapter Eight

ORGANIZING THE BODY OF THE SPEECH

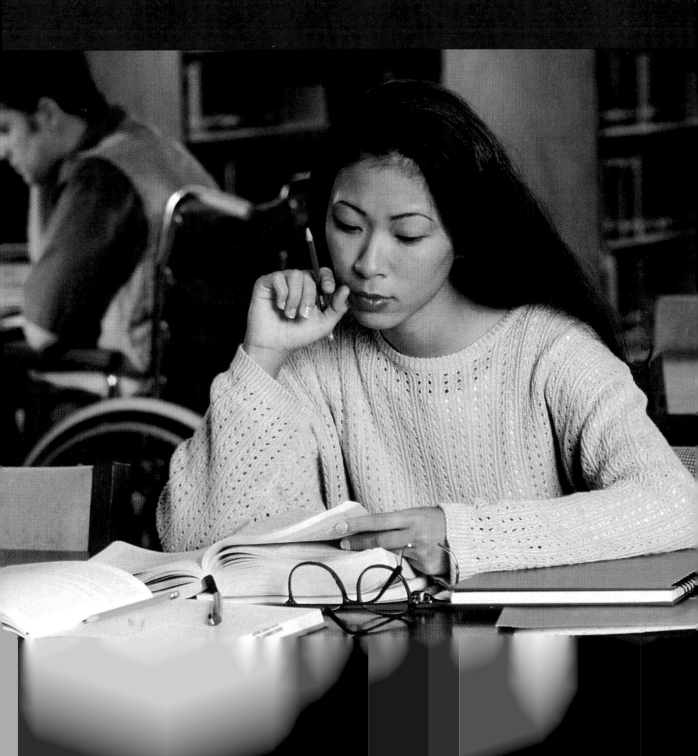

If you thumb through any mail-order catalogue today, you will discover that many of the items for sale are *organizers*—closet organizers, kitchen organizers, office organizers, audio and video equipment organizers. Read enough catalogues, and you must conclude that if something exists, it can be organized.

Why all this quest for organization? Obviously, when the objects you possess are well organized, they serve you better. There's little point in having multiple possessions if you can't find them when you need them. Organization allows you to see what you have and to put your hands immediately on the garment, the tool, the tape, the piece of paper, the CD you want without a frenzied search.

Much the same is true of your speeches. If they are well organized, they will serve you better. Organization allows you—and your listeners—to see what ideas you have and to put mental "hands" on the most important ones.

Organization Is Important

Several years ago a college professor took a well-organized speech and scrambled it by randomly changing the order of its sentences. He then had a speaker deliver the original version to one group of listeners and the scrambled version to another group. After the speeches, he gave a test to see how well each group understood what they had heard. Not surprisingly, the group that heard the original, unscrambled speech scored much higher than the other group.[1]

A few years later, two professors repeated the same experiment at another school. But instead of testing how well the listeners comprehended each speech, they tested to see what effects the speeches had on the listeners' attitudes toward the speakers. They found that people who heard the well-organized speech believed the speaker to be much more competent and trustworthy than did those who heard the scrambled speech.[2]

These are just two of many studies that show the importance of organization in effective speechmaking.[3] They confirm what most of us know from experience. How many times have you listened to someone who rambled aimlessly from one idea to another? You realize how difficult it is to pay attention to the speaker, much less to understand the message. In fact, when students explain what they hope to learn from their speech class, they almost always put "the ability to organize my ideas more effectively" near the top of the list.

This ability is especially vital for speechmaking. Listeners demand coherence. They have little patience with speakers who bounce wildly from idea to idea. Keep in mind that listeners—unlike readers—cannot flip back to a previous page if they have trouble grasping a speaker's ideas. In this respect a speech is much like a movie. Just as a director must be sure viewers can follow the plot of a film from beginning to end, so must a speaker be sure listeners can follow the progression of ideas in a speech from beginning to end. This requires that speeches be organized *strategically*. They should be put together in particular ways to achieve particular results with particular audiences.

Speech organization is important for other reasons as well. As we saw in Chapter 1, it is closely connected to critical thinking. When you work to organize your speeches, you gain practice in the general skill of establishing clear relationships among your ideas. This skill will serve you well throughout your college days and in almost any career you may choose. In addition, there is evidence that using a clear, specific method of speech organization can boost your confidence as a speaker and improve your ability to deliver a message fluently.[4]

The first step in developing a strong sense of speech organization is to gain command of the three basic parts of a speech—introduction, body, and conclusion—and the strategic role of each. In this chapter we deal with the body of the speech. The next chapter will take up the introduction and the conclusion.

There are good reasons for talking first about the body of the speech. The body is the longest and most important part. Also, you will usually prepare the body first. It is much easier to create an effective introduction after you know exactly what you will say in the body.

The process of organizing the body of a speech begins when you determine the main points.

> **strategic organization**
> Putting a speech together in a particular way to achieve a particular result with a particular audience.

Main Points

The main points are the central features of your speech. You should select them carefully, phrase them precisely, and arrange them strategically. Here are the main points of a student speech about the medical uses of hypnosis:

Specific Purpose: To inform my audience about the major uses of hypnosis.

Central Idea: The major uses of hypnosis today are to control pain in medical surgery, to help people stop smoking, and to help students improve their academic performance.

Main Points:
I. Hypnosis is used in surgery as an adjunct to chemical anesthesia.
II. Hypnosis is used to help people stop smoking.
III. Hypnosis is used to help students improve their academic performance.

> **main points**
> The major points developed in the body of a speech. Most speeches contain from two to five main points.

These three main points form the skeleton of the body of the speech. If there are three major *uses* of hypnosis for medical purposes, then logically there can be three *main points* in the speech.

How do you choose your main points? Sometimes they will be evident from your specific purpose statement. Suppose your specific purpose is "To inform my audience about the origins, events, and philosophy of the Special Olympics." Obviously, your speech will have three main points. The first will deal with the origins of the Special Olympics, the second with the events of the Special Olympics, the third with the philosophy of the Special Olympics. Written in outline form, the main points might be:

Specific Purpose: To inform my audience about the origins, events, and philosophy of the Special Olympics.

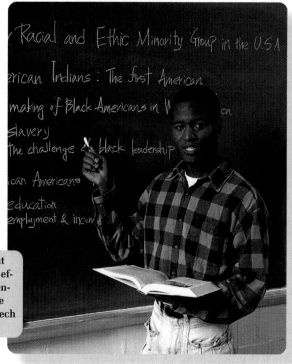

Research studies confirm that clear organization is vital to effective public speaking. Listeners must be able to follow the progression of ideas in a speech from beginning to end.

Central Idea:	The Special Olympics gives people who are mentally or physically challenged a chance to experience athletic competition.

Teaching Tip
Encourage students to notice how the main points flow logically from the specific purpose and the central idea in the examples here and throughout the chapter.

Main Points:	I. The Special Olympics was founded in 1968 to promote fitness for the mentally and physically challenged.
	II. Held locally every year and internationally every four years, the Special Olympics has sports events similar to those in the Olympic Games.
	III. Although medals are awarded, the Special Olympics stresses effort and participation rather than winning.

Even if your main points are not stated expressly in your specific purpose, they may be easy to project from it. Let's say your specific purpose is "To inform my audience of the basic steps in making stained-glass windows." You know each of your main points will correspond to a step in the window-making process. They might look like this in outline form:

Specific Purpose:	To inform my audience of the basic steps in making stained-glass windows.
Central Idea:	There are four steps in making stained-glass windows.

Main Points:	I. The first step is designing the window.
	II. The second step is cutting the glass to fit the design.
	III. The third step is painting the glass.
	IV. The fourth step is assembling the window.

You will not always settle on your main points so easily. Often they will emerge as you research the speech and evaluate your findings. Suppose your specific purpose is "To persuade my audience that our state should not approve proposals for online voting." You know that each main point in the speech will present a *reason* why online voting should not be instituted in your state. But you aren't sure how many main points there will be or what they will be. As you research and study the topic, you decide there are two major reasons to support your view. Each of these reasons will become a main point in your speech. Written in outline form, they might be:

Specific Purpose:	To persuade my audience that our state should not approve proposals for online voting.
Central Idea:	Our state should not approve online voting because it will increase voter fraud and disfranchise people without Internet access.
Main Points:	I. Our state should not approve online voting because it will increase voter fraud.
	II. Our state should not approve online voting because it will disfranchise people without access to the Internet.

Now you have two broad areas around which to organize your ideas.

Number of Main Points

You will not have time in your classroom speeches to develop more than four or five main points, and most speeches will contain only two or three. Regardless of how long a speech might run, if you have too many main points, the audience will have trouble sorting them out. When everything is equally important, nothing is important.

Imagine, for example, that you have a particularly lenient professor who gives everyone in the class an A. Your A won't have much value for you. But if only three students in the class get an A and you are one of them, then you stand out from the crowd. That is what you must aim to do in your speeches—to make a few main points stand out and be remembered.

If, when you list your main points, you find you have too many, you may be able to condense them into categories. Here is a set of main points for a speech about lasers:

| Specific Purpose: | To inform my audience about the uses of lasers. |
| Central Idea: | Lasers harness the power of light for a wide range of uses. |

Discussion Prompt
Ask students to identify speakers they have had trouble listening to because the speakers did not organize their ideas clearly and sharply. In contrast, can students think of speakers whose ideas were well organized and easy to follow? What techniques did the well-organized speakers use to structure and communicate their ideas?

Class Activity
For an activity that helps students work on limiting the number of main points in a speech, see the first Additional Exercise for Critical Thinking in the *Instructor's Manual,* pp. 198–199. To facilitate classroom discussion, this exercise is included in the binder of full-color overhead transparencies that accompanies *The Art of Public Speaking.*

Main Points:
    I. Laser gravity wave detectors allow astronomers to "see" deep into space.
    II. Automobile manufacturers use lasers for many purposes in making cars.
    III. Neurosurgeons use lasers to vaporize brain tumors.
    IV. Lasers help create billions of industrial goods every year.
    V. With lasers, scientists can chart the fastest of chemical reactions.
    VI. The telephone industry sends phone calls underseas to Europe with lasers.
    VII. Eye specialists routinely use lasers to "weld" loose retinas back in place.
    VIII. Lasers allow doctors to make early diagnoses of certain kinds of cancer.

You have eight main points—which is too many. But if you look at the list, you see that the eight points fall into three broad categories: lasers in science, lasers in industry, lasers in medicine. You might, therefore, restate your main points this way:

    I. Lasers have many important uses in science.
    II. Lasers have become indispensable to industry.
    III. Lasers are revolutionizing the practice of medicine.

Strategic Order of Main Points

Once you establish your main points, you need to decide in what order you will present them in your speech. This is extremely important, for it will affect both the clarity and the persuasiveness of your ideas.

The most effective order depends on three things—your topic, your purpose, and your audience. Chapters 14 and 15 will deal with special aspects of organizing informative speeches and persuasive speeches. Here let us look briefly at the five basic patterns of organization used most often by public speakers.

Chronological Order

chronological order
A method of speech organization in which the main points follow a time pattern.

Speeches arranged chronologically follow a time pattern. They may narrate a series of events in the sequence in which they happened. For example:

Specific Purpose: To inform my audience how the Great Wall of China was built.

Central Idea: The Great Wall of China was built in three major stages.

Main Points:
    I. Building of the Great Wall began during the Qin dynasty of 221–206 B.C.
    II. New sections of the Great Wall were added during the Han dynasty of 206 B.C.–220 A.D.
    III. The Great Wall was completed during the Ming dynasty of 1368–1644.

The main points of a speech should be organized to communicate the speaker's message. Chronological order might be highly effective for a speech on how the Great Wall of China was built.

Chronological order is also used in speeches explaining a process or demonstrating how to do something. For example:

Specific Purpose: To inform my audience of the steps in getting a professional tattoo.

Central Idea: There are four main steps in getting a professional tattoo.

Main Points: I. First, the skin is shaved and sterilized in the area to be tattooed.
II. Second, the main lines of the tattoo are traced on the skin with a machine called an outliner.
III. Third, colored pigments are applied inside the outline with a machine called a shader.
IV. Fourth, the tattoo is sterilized and bandaged.

As this outline shows, chronological order is especially useful for informative speeches.

Spatial Order

Speeches arranged in spatial order follow a directional pattern. That is, the main points proceed from top to bottom, left to right, front to back, inside to outside, east to west, or some other route. For example:

spatial order
A method of speech organization in which the main points follow a directional pattern.

Specific Purpose: To inform my audience about the design of the Eiffel Tower.

Central Idea: The Eiffel Tower is divided into three sections.

Main Points:	I. The lowest section of the tower contains the entrance, a gift shop, and a restaurant. II. The middle section of the tower consists of stairs and elevators that lead to the top. III. The top section of the tower includes an observation deck with a spectacular view of Paris.

Or:

Teaching Tip
Stress that the method of organization used in a speech is shaped more by the specific purpose of the speaker than by the general topic of the speech. Indeed, most speech topics can be organized in more than one fashion depending on the specific purpose of the speaker. The second Exercise for Critical Thinking at the end of this chapter provides a good vehicle for exploring this aspect of speech organization. For full discussion of the exercise, see the *Instructor's Manual*, pp. 195–196.

Specific Purpose:	To inform my audience of five major civilizations that existed in different parts of North America centuries before the arrival of Columbus.
Central Idea:	Centuries before the arrival of Columbus there were major civilizations in what is today New York, Florida, New Mexico, the Pacific Northwest, and the Mississippi Valley.
Main Points:	I. In New York, the Onondaga were skilled agriculturalists and fierce warriors. II. In Florida, the Calusa developed one of the most advanced cultures to flourish without agriculture. III. In New Mexico, the people of Chaco Canyon were sophisticated architectural planners and builders. IV. In the Pacific Northwest, the Makah were expert mariners and foresters. V. In the Mississippi Valley, the Cahokia created a complex, prosperous society whose burial mounds are still evident today.

Spatial order, like chronological order, is used most often in informative speeches.

Causal Order

causal order
A method of speech organization in which the main points show a cause-effect relationship.

Speeches arranged in causal order organize main points so as to show a cause-effect relationship. When you put your speech in causal order, you have two main points—one dealing with the causes of an event, the other dealing with its effects. Depending on your topic, you can either devote your first main point to the causes and the second to the effects, or you can deal first with the effects and then with the causes.

Suppose your specific purpose is "To persuade my audience that the widespread use of Ritalin to treat attention deficit hyperactivity disorder (ADHD) is a serious problem." You would begin with the causes for the use of Ritalin and work toward its effects:

Specific Purpose:	To persuade my audience that the widespread use of Ritalin to treat attention deficit hyperactivity disorder (ADHD) is a serious problem.
Central Idea:	Widely prescribed for children who suffer from ADHD, Ritalin has a number of extremely serious side effects.

Main Points:	I. Ritalin is widely prescribed for children who suffer from attention deficit hyperactivity disorder.
	II. Ritalin has been linked with a number of serious side effects, including liver damage, heart disease, depression, stunted growth, and Tourette's syndrome.

When the effects you are discussing have already occurred, you may want to reverse the order and talk first about the effects and then about their causes—as in this speech about the Mayan civilization of Central America:

Specific Purpose:	To inform my audience about the possible causes for the collapse of Mayan civilization.
Central Idea:	The causes for the collapse of Mayan civilization have not yet been fully explained.
Main Points:	I. Mayan civilization flourished for over a thousand years until 900 A.D., when it mysteriously began to disintegrate.
	II. Scholars have advanced three major explanations for the causes of this disintegration.

Because of its versatility, causal order can be used both for persuasive speeches and informative speeches.

Teaching Tip
Be sure to distinguish between a speech organized in causal order and a speech that focuses solely on the causes of an event or a problem. A speech arranged in causal order has two main points—one dealing with the causes of an event, the other with its effects. In contrast, consider a speech with the following central idea: "The three main causes of airplane crashes are pilot error, weather, and mechanical failure." This speech is arranged in topical order, which is discussed on pp. 210–211.

Problem-Solution Order

Speeches arranged in problem-solution order are divided into two main parts. The first shows the existence and seriousness of a problem. The second presents a workable solution to the problem. For example:

problem-solution order
A method of speech organization in which the first main point deals with the existence of a problem and the second main point presents a solution to the problem.

Specific Purpose:	To persuade my audience that legislation is needed to control the abuses of fraudulent charity fund-raisers.
Central Idea:	Fraudulent fund-raising for charities is a serious problem that requires action by government and individuals alike.
Main Points:	I. Fraudulent charity fund-raising has become a widespread national problem.
	II. The problem can be solved by a combination of government initiative and individual awareness.

Or:

Specific Purpose:	To persuade my audience that action must be taken to deal with the environmental hazards created by discarded computers.
Central Idea:	Discarded computers are creating serious environmental hazards that require decisive action by government, consumers, and businesses.

Cross-Reference
See Chapter 15 for fuller discussion of problem-solution order and its use in persuasive speeches.

Main Points: I. Discarded computers have become a major source of lead and radiation pollution in landfills.
II. Solving the problem requires government regulation and personal action by consumers and businesses.

As these examples indicate, problem-solution order is most appropriate for persuasive speeches.

Topical Order

topical order

A method of speech organization in which the main points divide the topic into logical and consistent subtopics.

Speeches that are not in chronological, spatial, causal, or problem-solution order usually fall into topical order. Topical order results when you divide the speech topic into *subtopics,* each of which becomes a main point in the speech. The main points are not part of a chronological, spatial, causal, or problem-solution sequence, but are simply parts of the whole. If this sounds confusing, a few examples should help make it clearer.

Suppose your specific purpose is "To inform my audience of the major kinds of fireworks." This topic does not lend itself to chronological, spatial, causal, or problem-solution order. Rather, you separate the subject—kinds of fireworks—into its constituent parts, so that each main point deals with a single kind of fireworks. Your central idea and main points might look like this:

Specific Purpose: To inform my audience of the major kinds of fireworks.

Central Idea: The major kinds of fireworks are skyrockets, Roman candles, pinwheels, and lances.

Main Points: I. Skyrockets explode high in the air, producing the most dramatic effects of all fireworks.
II. Roman candles shoot out separate groups of sparks and colored flames with a series of booming noises.
III. Pinwheels throw off sparks and flames as they whirl on the end of a stick.
IV. Lances are thin, colorful fireworks used in ground displays.

Discussion Prompt

Of all the methods of organization, topical order is usually the most difficult for students to grasp. You can help them by bringing to class a list of specific purposes for speeches organized in topical order. Ask the class to generate potential main points for a speech on each of the specific purposes. Use the ensuing discussion to clarify the principles of effective topical organization.

To take another example, let's say your specific purpose is "To inform my audience about the athletic achievements of Babe Didrikson." Didrikson, who is considered the greatest American female athlete of all time, competed during the 1930s, 1940s, and 1950s. So you could organize your speech chronologically—by discussing Didrikson's exploits during each decade of her career. On the other hand, you could arrange the speech topically—by dividing Didrikson's accomplishments into categories. Then your central idea and main points might be:

Specific Purpose: To inform my audience about the athletic achievements of Babe Didrikson.

Central Idea: Babe Didrikson was a world-class athlete in track and field, basketball, and golf.

Main Points:
    I. As a track-and-field athlete, Didrikson set two world records in the Olympic Games.
    II. As a basketball player, Didrikson was twice named to the women's All-America team.
    III. As a professional golfer, Didrikson set a record that still stands by winning 17 tournaments in a row.

Teaching Tip
Remind students that although the main points of a speech follow one pattern of organization, the subpoints may follow a different pattern. For example, the main points may be arranged in topical order, while the subpoints developed in one of the main points may be structured chronologically.

Notice that in both of the preceding examples, the main points subdivide the speech topic logically and consistently. In the first example, each main point deals with a single category of fireworks. In the second example, each main point isolates one aspect of Didrikson's achievements as an athlete. But suppose your main points look like this:

I. As a track-and-field athlete, Didrikson set two world records in the Olympic Games.
II. As a basketball player, Didrikson was twice named to the women's All-America team.
III. In the 1940s Didrikson dominated American women's sports.

This would *not* be a good topical order because main point III is inconsistent with the rest of the main points. It deals with a *period* in Didrikson's career, whereas main points I and II deal with *kinds* of athletic events.

All the examples so far refer to informative speeches. But topical order also works for persuasive speeches. Usually the topical subdivisions are the *reasons* why a speaker believes in a certain point of view. Here, for example, are the main points of a speech on why the United States should continue its program of space exploration:

Specific Purpose: To persuade my audience that the United States should continue its program of space exploration.

Central Idea: The United States should continue its program of space exploration because it will open access to vital natural resources, expand scientific knowledge, and further the search for extraterrestrial life.

Overhead Transparency
For ease of classroom discussion, examples of all the patterns of organization discussed on pp. 206–211 are included in the binder of full-color overhead transparencies that accompanies *The Art of Public Speaking.*

Main Points:
    I. Space exploration will open access to vital natural resources that are in limited supply on earth.
    II. Space exploration will produce scientific knowledge that will benefit life on earth.
    III. Space exploration will further the search for extraterrestrial life.

Because it is applicable to almost any subject and to any kind of speech, topical order is used more often than any other method of speech organization.[5]

Tips for Preparing Main Points

Keep Main Points Separate

Each main point in a speech should be clearly independent of the other main points. Take care not to lump together what should be separate main points. Compare these two sets of main points for a speech about the process of producing a Broadway play:

Class Activity
Use the first Exercise for Critical Thinking at the end of this chapter to check how well students understand the methods of organization discussed in the chapter. For full discussion of the exercise, see the *Instructor's Manual,* pp. 194–195.

Ineffective	More Effective
I. The first step is choosing the play.	I. The first step is choosing the play.
II. The second step is selecting the cast.	II. The second step is selecting the cast.
III. The third step is conducting rehearsals and then performing the play.	III. The third step is conducting the rehearsals.
	IV. The fourth step is performing the play.

The problem with the left-hand list is that point III contains two main points. It should be divided, as shown in the right-hand list.

Try to Use the Same Pattern of Wording for Main Points

Consider the following main points for an informative speech about the benefits of exercise.

Teaching Tip
Have students bring to class, early in the speech preparation process, a sheet listing their main points and method of organization. You can discuss the sheets with students individually, or you can divide the class into groups and have group members provide feedback to each other. Regardless of the approach you take, it is important that students start thinking as early as possible about the main points and structure of their speeches.

Ineffective	More Effective
I. Regular exercise increases your endurance.	I. Regular exercise increases your endurance.
II. Your sleeping pattern is improved by regular exercise.	II. Regular exercise improves your sleeping pattern.
III. It is possible to help control your weight by regular exercise.	III. Regular exercise helps control your weight.

The set of main points on the right follows a consistent pattern of wording throughout. Therefore, it is easier to understand and easier to remember than the set on the left.

You will find that it is not always possible to use this kind of parallel wording for your main points. Some speeches just don't lend themselves to such a tidy arrangement. But try to keep the wording parallel when you can, for it is a good way to make your main points stand out from the details surrounding them.

Balance the Amount of Time Devoted to Main Points

Because your main points are so important, you want to be sure they all receive enough emphasis to be clear and convincing. This means allowing sufficient time to develop each main point. Suppose you discover that the proportion of time devoted to your main points is something like this:

I. 85 percent
II. 10 percent
III. 5 percent

A breakdown of this sort indicates one of two things. Either points II and III aren't really *main* points and you have only one main point, or points II and III haven't been given the attention they need. If the latter, you should revise the body of the speech to bring the main points into better balance.

This is not to say that all main points must receive exactly equal emphasis, but only that they should be roughly balanced. For example, either of the following would be fine:

I. 30 percent	I. 20 percent
II. 40 percent	II. 30 percent
III. 30 percent	III. 50 percent

The amount of time spent on each main point depends on the amount and complexity of supporting materials for each point. Supporting materials are, in effect, the "flesh" that fills out the skeleton of your speech.

Supporting Materials

By themselves, main points are only assertions. As we saw in Chapter 7, listeners need supporting materials to accept what a speaker says. When the supporting materials are added, the body of a speech looks like the following in outline form:

I. Hypnosis is used in surgery as an adjunct to chemical anesthesia.
   A. Hypnosis reduces both the physical and psychological aspects of pain.
      1. Hypnosis can double a person's pain threshold.
      2. It also reduces the fear that intensifies physical pain.
   B. Hypnosis is most useful in cases when the patient is known to have problems with general anesthesia.
      1. Quotation from Dr. Harold Wain of Walter Reed Army Hospital.
      2. Story of Linda Kuay.
      3. Statistics from *Psychology Today*.
II. Hypnosis is used to help people stop smoking.
   A. Many therapists utilize hypnosis to help people break their addiction to cigarettes.
      1. The U.S. Department of Health and Human Services considers hypnosis a safe and effective means of stopping smoking.
      2. Success rates are as high as 70 percent.
         a. Story of Alex Hamilton.
         b. Quotation from New York psychiatrist Dr. Herbert Spiegel.
   B. Hypnosis does not work for all smokers.
      1. A person must want to stop smoking for hypnosis to work.
      2. A person must also be responsive to hypnotic suggestion.
III. Hypnosis is used to help students improve their academic performance.
   A. Hypnosis enables people to use their minds more effectively.
      1. The conscious mind uses about 10 percent of a person's mental ability.
      2. Hypnosis allows people to tap more of their mental power.

Class Activity
See Applying the Power of Public Speaking at the end of this chapter for a true-life speaking scenario that students can analyze when working on their skills of speech organization. For discussion of the scenario, see the *Instructor's Manual*, p. 197.

B. Studies show that hypnosis can help people overcome many
   obstacles to academic success.
   1. It improves ability to concentrate.
   2. It increases reading speed.
   3. It reduces test anxiety.

supporting materials
The materials used to support a speaker's ideas. The three major kinds of supporting materials are examples, statistics, and testimony.

In Chapter 7 we discussed the major kinds of supporting materials and how to use them. Here, we need stress only the importance of *organizing* your supporting materials so they are directly relevant to the main points they are supposed to support. Misplaced supporting materials are confusing. Here's an example:

I. There are several reasons why people immigrate to the United
   States.
   A. Over the years, millions of people have immigrated to the United
      States.
   B. Many people immigrate in search of economic opportunity.
   C. Others immigrate to attain political freedom.
   D. Still others immigrate to escape religious persecution.

The main point deals with the reasons immigrants come to the United States, as do supporting points B, C, and D. Supporting point A ("Over the years, millions of people have immigrated to the United States") does not. It is out of place and should not be included with this main point.

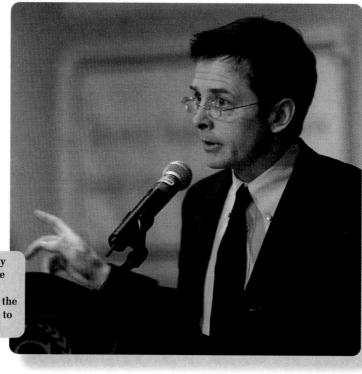

Organizing ideas strategically is important regardless of the speaker or occasion. Here Michael J. Fox speaks about the need for additional research to combat Parkinson's disease.

If you find such a situation in your own speeches, try to reorganize your supporting points under appropriate main points, like this:

I. Over the years, millions of people have immigrated to the United States.
 A. Since the American Revolution, an estimated 60 million people have immigrated to the U.S.
 B. Today there are over 20 million Americans who were born in other countries.
II. There are several reasons why people immigrate to the United States.
 A. Many people immigrate in search of economic opportunity.
 B. Others immigrate to attain political freedom.
 C. Still others immigrate to escape religious persecution.

Cross-Reference
See Chapter 7 for full discussion of supporting materials.

Now you have two supporting points to back up your "millions of people" point and three supporting points to back up your "reasons" point.

Once you have organized your main points and supporting points, you must give attention to the third element in the body of a speech—connectives.

Connectives

Carla Maggio was speaking to her class about the need for students to vote in state and local elections. She had rehearsed the speech several times, had a well-defined central idea, three sharp main points, and strong evidence to support her position. But when Carla delivered the speech, she said "All right" every time she moved from one thought to the next. All told, she said "All right" 10 times in six minutes. After a while, her classmates started counting. By the end of the speech, most had stopped listening. They were too busy waiting for the next "All right." Afterward, Carla said, "I never even thought about saying 'All right.' I guess it just popped out when I didn't know what else to say."

This experience is not unusual. We all have stock phrases that we habitually use to fill the space between thoughts. In casual conversation they are seldom troublesome. But in speechmaking they create a problem—particularly when they call attention to themselves.

What Carla's speech lacked were strong *connectives*—words or phrases that join one thought to another and indicate the relationship between them. Connectives in the body of a speech are like ligaments and tendons in a human body. Without connectives, a speech is disjointed and uncoordinated—much as a person would be without ligaments and tendons to join the bones and hold the organs in place. Four types of speech connectives are transitions, internal previews, internal summaries, and signposts.

connective
A word or phrase that connects the ideas of a speech and indicates the relationship between them.

Transitions

Transitions are words or phrases that indicate when a speaker has just completed one thought and is moving on to another. Technically, the transitions state both the idea the speaker is leaving and the idea she or he is coming up to. In the following examples, the transitional phrases are underlined:

Now that we have a clear understanding of the problem, let me share the solution with you.

transition
A word or phrase that indicates when a speaker has finished one thought and is moving on to another.

I have spoken so far of bravery and patriotism, but it is the sacrifice of the Massachusetts 54th that has etched them into the pages of history.

Now that we've seen how drinking too much is a serious problem for students and their communities, let's look at some causes.

Keeping these points in mind about sign language, let's return to the sentence I started with and see if we can learn the signs for "You are my friend."

Now that we've taken a look at what feng shui is, let's put this ancient art into practice.

Notice how these phrases remind the listener of the thought just completed, as well as reveal the thought about to be developed.

View these transitions from student speeches.

CD 1: VIDEO 8.1

Internal Previews

internal preview
A statement in the body of the speech that lets the audience know what the speaker is going to discuss next.

Internal previews let the audience know what the speaker will take up next, but they are more detailed than transitions. In effect, an internal preview works just like the preview statement in a speech introduction, except that it comes in the body of the speech—usually as the speaker is starting to discuss a main point. For example:

> In discussing how Asian Americans have been stereotyped in the mass media, we'll look first at the origins of the problem and second at its continuing impact today.

After hearing this, the audience knows exactly what to listen for as the speaker develops the "problem" main point.

Internal previews are often combined with transitions. For example:

Teaching Tip
Explain that the preview statement in the introduction is not considered an internal preview. Internal previews occur only within the body of the speech.

> [*Transition*]: Now that we have seen how serious the problem of faulty credit reports is, let's look at some solutions. [*Internal Preview*]: I will focus on three solutions— instituting tighter government regulation of credit bureaus, holding credit bureaus financially responsible for their errors, and giving individuals easier access to their credit reports.

You will seldom need an internal preview for each main point in your speech, but be sure to use one whenever you think it will help listeners keep track of your ideas.

Internal Summaries

internal summary
A statement in the body of the speech that summarizes the speaker's preceding point or points.

Internal summaries are the reverse of internal previews. Rather than letting listeners know what is coming up next, internal summaries remind listeners of what they have just heard. Such summaries are generally used when a speaker finishes a complicated or particularly important main point or set of main points. Rather than moving immediately to the next point, the speaker takes a moment to summarize the preceding point or points. For example:

> In short, palm reading is an ancient art. Developed in China more than five thousand years ago, it was practiced in classical Greece and Rome, flourished during the Middle Ages, survived the Industrial Revolution, and remains popular today in many parts of the world.

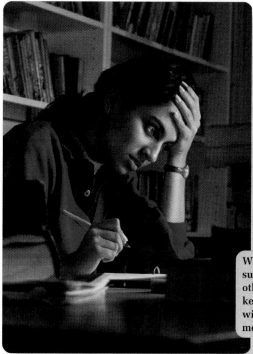

When organizing your speeches, be sure to include transitions and other connectives to help listeners keep track of your ideas. The result will be a crisp presentation that moves clearly from point to point.

I hope I've made clear the benefits of walking as a form of exercise. Unlike running, which often causes as many injuries as it prevents, walking is a gentle but no less effective way to keep in shape. Regular walking at a brisk pace strengthens the heart, increases lung capacity, improves blood circulation, and burns calories—all without the strain on the knees and ankles caused by running.

Such internal summaries are an excellent way to clarify and reinforce ideas. By combining them with transitions, you can also lead your audience smoothly into your next main point:

[*Internal Summary*]: So far we have seen that the normal individual's need for a three-minute burst of stimuli has produced a growing demand for thrill rides and has helped launch a coaster war between amusement parks. Then we looked at the roller coaster's past and present. [*Transition*]: Now I'd like to show you what's in store for us in the future.

[*Internal Summary*]: Let's pause for a moment to summarize what we have found so far. First, we have seen that America's criminal justice system is less effective than it should be in deterring crime. Second, we have seen that prison programs to rehabilitate prisoners have been far from successful. [*Transition*]: We are now ready to explore solutions to these problems.

Signposts

Signposts are very brief statements that indicate exactly where you are in the speech. Frequently they are just numbers. Here is how one student used

signpost
A very brief statement that indicates where a speaker is in the speech or that focuses attention on key ideas.

simple numerical signposts to help her audience keep track of the major causes for the continuing problem of famine in Africa:

The first cause of this problem is inefficient agricultural production.

The second cause is recurrent drought in the affected countries.

The final cause is mismanagement of available food resources by local leaders.

Another way to accomplish the same thing is to introduce your main points with a question, as did one student in his speech titled "Seatbelts: A Habit That Can Save Your Life." His first main point demonstrated the extent to which seatbelts are proven lifesavers. He introduced it this way:

So, first, to what extent will you be protected by wearing a seatbelt?

View these signposts from Andrew Kinney, "Seatbelts: A Habit That Can Save Your Life."

CD 1: VIDEO 8.2

His second main point explained how seatbelts absorb the force of a collision and keep drivers from being thrown around a vehicle's interior. He introduced it like this:

But why is this true? What does a seatbelt do to protect you?

His third main point looked at the reasons people give for not using seatbelts on a consistent basis. He introduced it by saying:

So the evidence is strongly in favor of wearing seatbelts. This brings me to the next question—why don't people wear seatbelts?

Questions are particularly effective as signposts because they invite subliminal answers and thereby get the audience more involved with the speech.

Besides using signposts to indicate where you are in the speech, you can use them to focus attention on key ideas. You can do this with a simple phrase, as in the following example:

Class Activity
Select one of the student speeches at the end of Chapters 14–16 or in the appendix of sample speeches that follows Chapter 18. Assign the speech as a homework assignment and give students three tasks: (1) pick out the main points of the speech; (2) identify its method of organization; (3) locate places where it uses connectives and, in each case, identify the kind of connective used. Also have students identify spots where additional connectives would have enhanced the clarity or coherence of the speech.

The most important thing to remember about abstract art is that it is always based on forms in the natural world.

The underlined words alert the audience to the fact that an especially significant point is coming up. So do phrases such as these:

Be sure to keep this in mind . . .

This is crucial to understanding the rest of the speech . . .

Above all, you need to know . . .

Let me repeat that last statement . . .

Depending on the needs of your speech, you may want to use two, three, or even all four kinds of connectives in combination. You needn't worry too much about what they are called—whether this one is a signpost and that a transition. In fact, many people lump them all together as "transitions." The important thing is to be aware of their functions. Properly applied, connectives can make your speeches much more unified and coherent.

Summary

Clear organization is vital to speechmaking. Listeners demand coherence. They get only one chance to grasp a speaker's ideas, and they have little patience for speakers who ramble aimlessly from one idea to another. A well-organized speech will enhance your credibility and make it easier for the audience to understand your message.

Speeches should be organized strategically. They should be put together in particular ways to achieve particular results with particular audiences. The first step in organizing speeches is to gain command of the three basic parts of a speech—introduction, body, conclusion—and the strategic role of each. In this chapter we have dealt with the body of the speech.

The process of planning the body of a speech begins when you determine the main points. These are the central features of your speech. You should choose them carefully, phrase them precisely, and organize them strategically. Because listeners cannot keep track of a multitude of main points, most speeches should contain no more than two to five main points. Each main point should focus on a single idea, should be worded clearly, and should receive enough emphasis to be clear and convincing.

You can organize main points in various ways. The strategic order will be determined by your topic, your purpose, and your audience. Chronological order means that your speech follows a time pattern. Speeches arranged in spatial order follow a directional pattern. To put your speech in causal order, you organize main points according to their cause-effect relationship. Topical order results when you divide your main topic into subtopics, each of which covers one aspect of the main topic. For problem-solution order you break the body of your speech into two main parts—the first showing a problem, the second giving a solution.

Supporting materials are the backup ideas for your main points. When organizing supporting materials, make sure they are directly relevant to the main points they are supposed to support.

Once you have organized your main points and supporting materials, you are ready to work out the third element in the body of your speech: connectives. Connectives help tie a speech together. They are words or phrases that join one thought to another and indicate the relationship between them. The four major types of speech connectives are transitions, internal previews, internal summaries, and signposts. Using them effectively will make your speeches more unified and coherent.

Key Terms

strategic organization (203)

main points (203)

chronological order (206)

spatial order (207)

causal order (208)

problem-solution order (209)

topical order (210)

supporting materials (214)

connective (215)

transition (215)

internal preview (216)

internal summary (216)

signpost (218)

Review these terms by doing the Chapter 8 crossword puzzle at www.mhhe.com/lucas8.

ONLINE LEARNING CENTER

Review Questions

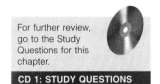

For further review, go to the Study Questions for this chapter.

CD 1: STUDY QUESTIONS

After reading this chapter, you should be able to answer the following questions:

1. Why is it important that speeches be organized clearly and coherently?

2. How many main points will your speeches usually contain? Why is it important to limit the number of main points in your speeches?

3. What are the five basic patterns of organizing main points in a speech? Which are appropriate for informative speeches? Which is used only in persuasive speeches? Which is used most often?

4. What are three tips for preparing your main points?

5. What is the most important thing to remember when organizing supporting materials in the body of your speech?

6. What are the four kinds of speech connectives? What role does each play in a speech?

Exercises for Critical Thinking

Cross-Reference
For discussion of the Exercises for Critical Thinking, see the *Instructor's Manual*, pp. 194–196. For additional exercises, check the *Instructor's Manual*, pp. 198–201, as well as the five volumes of *Selections from the Speech Communication Teacher* that accompany *The Art of Public Speaking*.

1. Identify the organizational method used in each of the following sets of main points.

   I. Cesar Chavez is best known for his efforts to protect the rights of Hispanic farmworkers in California.
   II. Cesar Chavez was also a tireless advocate for Hispanic racial and cultural pride in general.

   I. The game we know as golf originated in Scotland during the 15th century.
   II. Most of golf's rules and traditions developed during the 19th century.
   III. Professional golf tours for men and women emerged during the 20th century.
   IV. Today golf is at a peak of popularity among everyday players and as a spectator sport.

   I. Caused by the bite of infected mosquitos, West Nile virus is spreading throughout the United States.
   II. The effects of West Nile virus include flulike symptoms, convulsions, swelling of the brain, and, in some cases, death.

   I. The outer layer of the skin, the epidermis, is about as thick as a sheet of paper.
   II. The middle later of the skin, the dermis, is 15 to 40 times thicker than the epidermis.
   III. The innermost layer of the skin, the subcutaneous tissue, is by far the thickest layer.

   I. Childhood obesity has reached crisis proportions in the United States.
   II. Solving the problem will require changes in attitudes, eating habits, and exercise.

2. What organizational method (or methods) might you use to arrange main points for speeches with the following specific purpose statements?

   To inform my audience about the major events in the development of the civil rights movement from 1955 to 1970.

   To inform my audience of the causes and effects of the erosion of America's seacoasts.

   To inform my audience about the nonviolent philosophy of Mahatma Gandhi.

   To inform my audience about the geographical regions of the Philippines.

   To persuade my audience that our state legislature should enact tougher laws to deal with the problem of motorists who run red lights.

   To inform my audience about the major kinds of symbols used in traditional Native American art.

3. Turn to the outline of main points and supporting materials for the speech about hypnosis on pages 213–214. Create appropriate transitions, internal previews, internal summaries, and signposts for the speech.

Applying the POWER of PUBLIC SPEAKING

After working for two other firms, you have spent the last several years at a Fortune 500 company that, as part of its operations, is a major manufacturer of lawn care equipment. The company has recently acquired three specialized European businesses that produce similar products. With your engineering degree and experience as part of the fast-growing Product Quality Group, you were the logical candidate to visit the newly acquired companies and evaluate their products for safety, quality, and emissions controls.

You have just returned from a weeklong trip to the three sites in Scotland, France, and Germany. You will deliver your findings and recommendations to the management group for new acquisitions, but you're unsure how best to organize your speech. Your major choices are chronological order, spatial order, and topical order. What might be the main points of your speech in each of these methods of organization? Explain which method you think would be most effective for your presentation.

Cross-Reference
For discussion of this Applying the Power of Public Speaking scenario, see the *Instructor's Manual,* p. 197.

Notes

[1] Ernest C. Thompson, "An Experimental Investigation of the Relative Effectiveness of Organizational Structure in Oral Communication," *Southern Speech Journal,* 26 (1960), pp. 59–69.

[2] Harry Sharp, Jr., and Thomas McClung, "Effects of Organization on the Speaker's Ethos," *Speech Monographs,* 33 (1966), pp. 182–183.

[3] For two recent studies, see B. Scott Titsworth, "The Effects of Teacher Immediacy, Use of Organizational Lecture Cues, and Students' Notetaking on Cognitive Learning," *Communication Education,* 50 (2001), pp. 283–297; Joseph L. Chesebro and James C. McCroskey, "The Relationship of Teacher Clarity and Immediacy with Student State Receiver Apprehension, Affect, and Cognitive Learning," *Communication Education,* 50 (2001), pp. 59–68.

[4] John O. Greene, "Speech Preparation Processes and Verbal Fluency," *Human Communication Research,* 11 (1984), pp. 61–84.

[5] For an interesting study of the role of structure in speeches and other public discourses, see Regina M. Hoffman, "Temporal Organization as a Rhetorical Resource," *Southern Communication Journal,* 57 (1992), pp. 194–204.

Chapter Nine

The Introduction

Get Attention and Interest

Reveal the Topic

Establish Credibility and Goodwill

Preview the Body of the Speech

Sample Introduction with
  Commentary

Tips for Preparing the Introduction

The Conclusion

Signal the End of the Speech

Reinforce the Central Idea

Sample Conclusion with
  Commentary

Tips for Preparing the Conclusion

BEGINNING AND ENDING THE SPEECH

O n the night of October 9, 1986, a conductor stepped up to the podium at Her Majesty's Theater in London, tapped his baton, raised his arms, and signaled the orchestra to play. Moments later the public first heard the dramatic opening chords of the song "The Phantom of the Opera."

Chapter Focus
Effective speeches need appropriate beginnings and endings. This chapter discusses objectives for speech introductions and conclusions and explains methods for achieving those objectives. For a full outline of the chapter, see the *Instructor's Manual*, pp. 204–207.

Like most musical stage plays, *Phantom of the Opera* begins with an overture—an orchestral introduction that captures the audience's attention and gives them a preview of the music they are going to hear. Without such an introduction—if the characters simply walked onstage and began singing or speaking—the beginning of the play would seem too abrupt, and the audience would not be suitably "primed" for the entertainment.

Similarly, nearly all musicals end with a finale, when the whole cast is onstage, elements of the dramatic plot are resolved, portions of the principal songs are recalled, and the music is brought to a dramatic climax. If there were no such conclusion, if the actors merely stopped and walked offstage, the audience would be left unsatisfied.

Just as musical plays need appropriate beginnings and endings, so do speeches. The beginning, or introduction, prepares listeners for what is to come. The conclusion ties up the speech and alerts listeners that the speech is going to end. Ideally, it is a satisfying conclusion.

In this chapter we explore the roles played by an introduction and a conclusion in speechmaking. We also discuss techniques aimed at fulfilling those roles. If you apply these techniques imaginatively, you will take a big step toward elevating your speeches from the ordinary to the splendid.

The Introduction

First impressions are important. A poor beginning may so distract or alienate listeners that the speaker can never fully recover. Moreover, getting off on the right foot is vital to a speaker's self-confidence. What could be more encouraging than watching your listeners' faces begin to register interest, attention, and pleasure? The hardest part of any presentation is the beginning. If you get through the opening stages of your speech without blundering, the rest will go much more smoothly. A good introduction, you will find, is an excellent confidence booster.

In most speech situations, there are four objectives you need to accomplish at the outset:

Teaching Tip
Make sure students understand that an effective introduction should meet all four of these objectives.

- Get the attention and interest of your audience.
- Reveal the topic of your speech.
- Establish your credibility and goodwill.
- Preview the body of the speech.

We'll look at each of these objectives in turn.

Get Attention and Interest

"Unless a speaker can interest his audience at once, his effort will be a failure." So said the great lawyer Clarence Darrow. If your topic is not one of extraordinary interest, your listeners are likely to say to themselves, "So what? Who cares?" No matter how famous the speaker or how vital the topic, the speaker can quickly lose an audience if she or he doesn't use the introduction to get their attention and quicken their interest.

Getting the initial attention of your audience is usually easy to do—even before you utter a single word. After you are introduced and step to the lectern, your audience will normally give you their attention. If they don't, merely wait patiently. Look directly at the audience without saying a word. In a few moments all talking and physical commotion will stop. Your listeners will be attentive. You will be ready to start speaking.

Keeping the attention of your audience once you start talking is more difficult. Here are the methods used most often. Employed individually or in combination, they will help get the audience caught up in your speech.

Relate the Topic to the Audience

People pay attention to things that affect them directly. If you can relate the topic to your listeners, they are much more likely to be interested in it.

Suppose, for example, one of your classmates begins her speech like this:

> Today I am going to talk about collecting postcards—a hobby that is both fascinating and financially rewarding. I would like to explain the basic kinds of collectible postcards, why they are so valuable, and how collectors buy and sell their cards.

This is certainly a clear introduction, but it is not one to get you hooked on the speech. Now what if your classmate were to begin her speech this way—as one student actually did.

> It's Saturday morning, and you are helping clean out your grandmother's attic. After working a while, you stumble upon a trunk, open it, and discover inside hundreds of old postcards. Thinking about getting to the football game on time, you start tossing the cards into the trash can. Congratulations! You have just thrown away a year's tuition.

This time the speaker has used just the right bait. Chances are you will be hooked.

Even when you use other interest-arousing lures, you should *always* relate your topic to the audience. At times this will test your ingenuity, but it pays dividends. Here are two excellent examples. The first is from a speech entitled "Making Campus Accessible for Disabled Students." Notice how the speaker gets her classmates to put themselves in the place of people who are unable to get to class on time because they can't get their wheelchairs or scooters through the snow.

> I'd like to ask you to use your imaginations and think how it would feel if you'd spent an evening studying for an exam, you get up in the morning all set to go to class, you go down, you get to your door, and it won't open. You think, "Oh, I can just use my back door." But you go to your back door, and that won't open either.
>
> It would be pretty frustrating, wouldn't it? That's the kind of frustration handicapped students feel when they can't get to class because of the snow.

Class Activity
Students often have difficulty deciding how to relate their speech topics directly to their classmates. The first Exercise for Critical Thinking at the end of this chapter gives them an opportunity to work on this aspect of creating an introduction. For full discussion of the exercise, see the *Instructor's Manual,* pp. 207–209.

View the beginning of Diane Bright, "Making Campus Accessible for Disabled Students."
CD 1: VIDEO 9.1

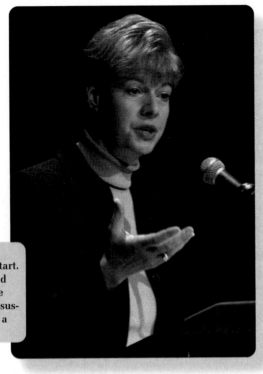

A good introduction will get your speech off to a strong start. To be most effective, it should relate to the audience and be delivered expressively, with sustained eye contact and from a minimum of notes.

The second example is from a student speech about dreams. This is how the speaker began his remarks:

You are being chased by an object of unspeakable horror, yet your legs can only move in slow motion. Each step takes unbearably long, and your frantic struggle to run faster is hopeless. Your pursuer gets closer, and your desperation turns to terror. You know you are not going to escape. You can't breathe, and you gulp for air that isn't there. You are completely helpless—eye to eye with death.

Then you wake up, gasping for air, your heart pounding, your face clammy with sweat. It takes a few minutes for you to reorient yourself to reality, for your heart and breathing to slow down. You reassure yourself that it was "just a dream." Soon you drift back to sleep.

By using vivid language to describe something all his classmates had experienced at some point in their lives, the speaker made sure of an attentive audience.

State the Importance of Your Topic

Presumably, you think your speech is important. Tell your audience why they should think so too. Here is how Susan Paddack, President of the American Medical Association Alliance, used this method to involve her audience in a speech about youth violence to the AMA National Leadership Conference:

Of the many threats to our public health, youth violence is the one that threatens not only each of us an individuals, but also the very fabric of our nation. . . .

I'd like you to imagine some 300 students from our public high schools among us now. Three hundred students would fill about one-third of this room. That's how many students will be attacked or robbed in our country during the 10 minutes I'll be speaking to you. More than 17,000 every day—more than half a million every month. . . . And adolescents in our country suffer the highest rates of murder and suicide among the 26 wealthiest nations.[1]

These are striking statistics. By citing them in the introduction, Paddack emphasized the importance of her topic and captured the attention of her audience.

Clearly this technique is easy to use when discussing social and political issues such as youth violence, endangered species, terrorism, and cloning, but it is appropriate for other topics as well. Here is how one student handled it in a speech about starting a home aquarium:

It is very hard to cuddle a fish. Fish won't roll over or fetch the morning paper. You won't find them curling up on your lap, chasing a ball of string, or rescuing a child from a burning building.

Yet despite these shortcomings, 250 million tropical fish have found their way into 10 million American homes. Tropical fish make up 50 percent of all live animal sales in the United States, and they have earned a spot next to the all-American dog and the cuddly kitten in the hearts of millions of people. Today I would like to explain how you can start a home aquarium and discover the pleasures of owning tropical fish.

The first paragraph—with its clever opening line—grabs the listener's attention. But it is the second paragraph that keeps the attention. Indeed, whenever you discuss a topic whose importance may not be clear to the audience, you should think about ways to demonstrate its significance in the introduction.

Startle the Audience

One surefire way to arouse interest quickly is to startle your listeners with an arresting or intriguing statement. Everyone in the audience paid close attention after this speaker's introduction:

Take a moment and think of the three women closest to you. Who comes to mind? Your mother? Your sister? Your girlfriend? Your wife? Your best friend? Now guess which one will be sexually assaulted during her lifetime. It's not a pleasant thought, but according to the U.S. Department of Justice, one of every three American women will be sexually assaulted sometime during her life.

Notice the gradual buildup to the speaker's arresting statement, "Now guess which one will be sexually assaulted during her lifetime." This statement startles the audience—especially the men—and drives home at a personal level the problem of sexual assault against women. The effect would have been much less if the speaker had said, "Sexual assault against women is a serious problem."

Class Activity
For an excellent activity that uses magazine articles to help students recognize the importance of creative attention getters, see Jean Hibben, "Eliminating the 'My Speech Is About' Introduction," in *Selections from the Speech Communication Teacher: 1991–1994*, p. 37, which accompanies *The Art of Public Speaking*.

Teaching Tip
Stress that speakers should not randomly use startling information just to get their listeners' attention. A startling introduction is effective only when it relates directly to the speech topic.

Sometimes you may want to startle your audience in the very first sentence of your speech. Here is how one student began her speech opposing the use of Native American names for sports teams:

> In tonight's games, the San Antonio Spics are playing the New Jersey Japs, while the Los Angeles Jews will take on the Minnesota Polacks.

Here is a longer example of the same technique, used by a speaker at a professional development seminar on privacy and the Internet:

> Three of you in this room have spent time in jail. Two of you were late on your mortgage payment last month; three more of you didn't make the latest payment on your student loans. Two of the males and three of the females were recently diagnosed with cancer. Five of you are behind in the number of credits needed to maintain your professional certification.
>
> How did I find out all of this? Simply by plugging your first and last names into my computer and searching through specialized sources. I did not enter your addresses, Social Security numbers, driver's license numbers, or any other specific information.

This technique is highly effective and easy to use. Just be sure the startling introduction relates directly to the subject of your speech. The example cited above worked perfectly for a speech on how the Internet is undermining our personal privacy. It would not work for a speech about electronic commerce. If you choose a strong opening simply for its shock value and then go on to talk about something else, your audience will be confused and possibly annoyed.

Arouse the Curiosity of the Audience

People are curious. One way to draw them into your speech is with a series of statements that progressively whet their curiosity about the subject of the speech. For example:

> It is the most common chronic disease in the United States. Controllable but incurable, it is a symptomless disease. You can have it for years and never know until it kills you. Some 40 million Americans have this disease, and 300,000 will die from it before the year is out. Odds are that five of us in this class have it.
>
> What am I talking about? Not cancer. Not AIDS. Not heart disease. I am talking about hypertension—high blood pressure.

For another example, look at this splendid opening from a student speech entitled "The Gift of Life":

> Each of you has a gift. What kind of gift is it? It's not a Christmas gift or a birthday gift. It's not some special talent or skill. It's a gift that could save a life—maybe more than one. If you decide to give it, you lose nothing.
>
> Some people bury their gift. Others burn it. All but one of you who completed my questionnaire would gladly receive the gift, but only 20 percent of you have decided to give it. This gift is the donation of your vital organs when you die.

Not only does this speaker relate the topic directly to his classmates, he gets them further involved by building suspense about the "gift" that each of us has. Notice how much less effective the introduction would have been

Class Activity

Divide the class into small groups. Give each group the same speech topic and have each write an introduction for a speech on that topic using a different method of gaining attention. For example, one group will arouse the curiosity of the audience, another will begin with a quotation, a third will startle the audience, and so forth. Have each group present its introduction to the class and have the class comment on which introductions seem the most effective and why.

if he had simply said, "Today I am going to talk about organ donation." When used appropriately, arousing curiosity is a surefire way to capture and hold your listeners' interest.

Question the Audience

Asking a *rhetorical question* is another way to get your listeners thinking about your speech. Sometimes a single question will do:

How would you respond if a loved one was the victim of terrorism?

What would you think if you went to the doctor because you were ill and she told you to watch *Friends* as part of your treatment?

Do you know how many small businesses are started each year in the United States?

In other circumstances, you may want to pose a series of questions, each of which draws the audience deeper and deeper into the speech. Here is how one speaker used this method:

Have you ever spent a sleepless night studying for an exam? Can you remember rushing to finish a term paper because you waited too long to start writing it? Do you often feel overwhelmed by all the things you have to get done at school? At work? At home?

If so, you may be the victim of poor time management. Fortunately, there are proven strategies you can follow to use your time more effectively and to keep control of your life.

Like beginning with a startling statement, opening with a question works best when the question is meaningful to the audience and firmly related to the content of the speech. It also works most effectively when you pause

Teaching Tip
Note how the examples of rhetorical questions presented here address the audience directly as "you." Make sure students understand the importance of using questions that draw their audience into the speech.

As you research your speeches, keep an eye out for quotations, stories, and other materials that you can use to craft an introduction that will capture the attention of your listeners.

for just a moment after each question. This adds dramatic impact and gives the question time to sink in. The audience, of course, will answer mentally—not out loud.

Begin with a Quotation

Another way to arouse the interest of your audience is to start with an attention-getting quotation. You might choose your quotation from the words of a famous speaker or writer, from Shakespeare or Confucius, from the Bible or Talmud, from a poem or song, even from a television show. One student used the last of these to introduce a speech about the role of women in the United States space program:

> "Space—the final frontier. These are the voyages of the Starship *Enterprise*. Its five-year mission: To explore new worlds. To seek out new life and new civilizations. To boldly go where no man has gone before."
>
> These well-known words, which opened every episode of the original *Star Trek* television series, captured the spirit of adventure that marked American attitudes toward space exploration during the 1960s and 1970s. They also captured the notion that space exploration was essentially a male activity: "To boldly go where no *man* has gone before."
>
> Today, of course, times have changed. Not only are women central characters in all the later *Star Trek* series and movies, but they are playing more and more important roles in the U.S. space program itself. Today I would like to discuss the current status and future prospects of women in the space program.

You need not use a well-known or famous quotation. The following made an effective introduction for a speech about bird-watching:

> "Even to this day I cannot describe what happened without feeling the excitement of the moment. I glimpsed a flash of color in the thicket. I raised my binoculars to my eyes, and then I saw it—a Bachman's Warbler, one of the rarest birds in all of America. For me, this was the equivalent of a coin collector discovering a rare silver dollar, or of a football player scoring a touchdown in the Super Bowl."
>
> This statement was made by my father. He is just one of the millions of people who have discovered the joys and thrills of bird-watching.

A humorous quotation can afford double impact, as in this speech about the need for political reform in the U.S. Congress:

> Mark Twain once said, "It could probably be shown by facts and figures that there is no distinctly American criminal class except Congress."

By opening with Twain's words, the speaker not only got the audience's attention but also foreshadowed a central theme of her speech. Notice, too, that all the quotations used here as examples are relatively short. Opening your speech with a lengthy quotation is a sure way to set your audience yawning.

Tell a Story

We all enjoy stories—especially if they are provocative, amusing, dramatic, or suspenseful. To work well as introductions, they should also be clearly relevant to the main point of the speech. Used in this way, stories are perhaps the most effective way to begin a speech.

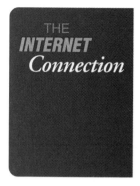

Consider, for example, the story one student, an education major, told to open his speech about the ways American teachers are adapting to the cultural diversity of today's school-age population:

> On a cloudy winter afternoon, Florann Greenberg, a teacher at P.S. 14 in New York City, noticed that her first-grade class was growing fidgety. One girl, dropping all pretense of work, stared at the snow falling outside the schoolroom windows. Annoyed, Greenberg asked her, "Haven't you seen snow before?" The girl whispered, "No." Her classmates began nodding their heads in agreement.
>
> Then it dawned on Greenberg. Of course these children had never seen snow—almost all were immigrants from Colombia and the Dominican Republic. Immediately Greenberg changed her lesson plans. New topics: What is snow? How is it formed? How do you dress in the snow? What games do you play?
>
> This story, reported in *Time* magazine, illustrates the cultural diversity now found in thousands of school classrooms across the United States and how creative teachers are adjusting to that diversity.

Like many good introductions, this one does a double job—it arouses the interest of the audience and gets listeners emotionally involved in the subject of the speech.

You can also use stories based on your personal experience. Here is how one student used such a story in his commencement speech at the University of Richmond. The student had come from Bombay, India, to attend college in the United States. He began by explaining the questions and uncertainties that were running through his mind as he prepared to leave his native land:

View the beginning of Sajjid Zahir Chinoy, "Questions of Culture."

CD 1: VIDEO 9.2

> I can visualize the scene again and again: 11:30 p.m., Saturday night, the 15th of August, 1992, Bombay International Airport, India. I was leaving home for the University of Richmond. And as I said that final goodbye to my parents, my family, and my friends; and as I saw hope, expectation, even a tinge of sadness, in their eyes; and as I stepped aboard the Boeing 747 in front, I knew my life had changed forever.

The effectiveness of any story—especially a personal one—hinges as much on the speaker's delivery as on the content of the story. As you can see from the clip of this speech on CD 1, Video 9.2, the speaker used pauses, eye contact, and changes in his tone of voice to heighten the impact of his words and draw his audience into the speech. See if you can do the same in your speech introductions.

The seven methods discussed above are the ones used most often by student speakers to gain attention and interest. Other methods include referring to the occasion, inviting audience participation, using audio equipment or visual aids, relating to a previous speaker, and beginning with humor. For any given speech, try to choose the method that is most suitable for the topic, the audience, and the occasion.

Reveal the Topic

In the process of gaining attention, be sure to state clearly the topic of your speech. If you do not, your listeners will be confused. And once they are confused, your chances of getting them absorbed in the speech are almost nil. This is a basic point—so basic that it may hardly seem worth mentioning. Yet you would be surprised how many students need to be reminded of it. You may hear speeches in your own class in which the topic is not clear by the end of the introduction. So that you will know what to avoid, here is such an introduction, presented in a public speaking class.

> When Roseanne Taos went to the hospital for knee surgery, her biggest concern was how soon she would be able to go skiing again. Tragically, the answer was never. No, Roseanne didn't die, but an overdose of general anesthesia during surgery left her permanently disabled. She will live the rest of her life under custodial supervision. As this example demonstrates, the use of anesthesia can be the most dangerous part of surgery. Today, I would like to discuss this issue with you.

What is the topic of this speech? The potential dangers of anesthesia? No. The need for periodic recertification of anesthesiologists? No. The limits of modern medicine in general? No. This student was speaking about the ancient Chinese practice of acupuncture as an alternative to anesthesia. But he did not make that clear to his audience. Listening to the introduction, they expected him to talk about the hazards of anesthesia.

This student found a dramatic introduction but ignored the fact that it didn't relate properly to his speech. Certainly the story of Roseanne Taos is an excellent attention getter. But in this case it was wasted. Suppose, instead, the student had begun his speech with a different story:

> The young woman on the operating table at the Institute of Tuberculosis in Beijing, China, is having a diseased lung removed. She has not received any painkilling drugs. Even though she is fully conscious, she experiences no pain and even talks periodically with her surgeons. Her only anesthetic is the array of stainless-steel acupuncture needles in her hands and feet.

This opening would have provided drama and a way to get the listeners' attention, but it also would have related directly to the speech topic.

If you beat around the bush in your introduction, you may lose your listeners. Even if they already know your topic, you should restate it clearly and concisely at some point in the introduction.

Establish Credibility and Goodwill

Besides getting attention and revealing the topic, there is a third objective you may need to accomplish in your introduction—establishing your credibility and goodwill.

Credibility is mostly a matter of being qualified to speak on a given topic—and of being *perceived* as qualified by your listeners. If, for instance, Brad Pitt got up before an audience to speak about nuclear physics, he would have to take drastic steps to establish his credibility on the subject.

Here is how one student established her credibility on the subject of weight lifting without sounding like a braggart:

> What is the fastest-growing sport today among American women? If you answered weight lifting, you are absolutely correct. Once seen as an exclusively male activity, weight lifting has crossed the gender barrier—and with good reason. Regardless of whether you are male or female, weight lifting can give you a sense of strength and power, enhance your self-esteem, and make you look and feel better.
>
> I started lifting weights when I was in high school, and I have kept at it for the past eight years. I have also taught weight lifting in several health clubs, and I am a certified instructor through the Aerobics and Fitness Association of America.
>
> Using some of my experience, I would like to explain the basic kinds of weights and how to use them properly.

Whether or not you lift weights, you will probably be more interested in the speech when you realize the speaker knows what she is talking about.

Your credibility need not be based on firsthand knowledge and experience. It can come from reading, from classes, from interviews, from friends—as in these cases:

> I have been interested in the history of the civil rights movement for several years, and I have read a number of books and articles about it.

> The information I am going to share with you today comes mostly from my biology class and an interview with Reyna Vasquez of the local Audubon Society.

> I've learned a great deal about the problems of early childhood education from my mother, who is a teacher in the San Francisco school system.

Whatever the source of your expertise, be sure to let the audience know.

Establishing your *goodwill* is a slightly different problem. It is often crucial outside the classroom, where speakers have well-established reputations and may be identified with causes that arouse hostility among listeners. In such a situation, the speaker must try to defuse that hostility right at the start of the speech.[2]

Occasionally you may have to do the same thing in your classroom speeches. Suppose you advocate a highly unpopular position. You will need to make a special effort at the outset to ensure that your classmates will at least consider your point of view. This is how one student tried to minimize his classmates' opposition at the start of a speech in favor of building more nuclear power plants to meet America's energy needs during the 21st century.

credibility
The audience's perception of whether a speaker is qualified to speak on a given topic.

Cross-Reference
See Chapter 16 for a detailed discussion of credibility and its role in persuasive speaking.

goodwill
The audience's perception of whether the speaker has the best interests of the audience in mind.

Using the introduction to establish goodwill is often a major concern for speakers who deal with controversial public issues—as in the case of U.N. Secretary General Kofi Annan.

The development of new nuclear power plants in the United States came to a standstill during the 1980s. As *Discover* magazine stated just last month, however, the time has come to look again at the benefits of nuclear power. Unlike fossil fuels, it does not contribute to the greenhouse effect; it does not leave America at the mercy of foreign oil; and, with advances in technology, it is much safer than before.

That is why I am speaking in favor of building more nuclear power plants to meet our future energy needs. I know that most of you oppose nuclear power—I did, too, until I started researching this speech. Today I would like to share with you some of the facts I have found. I know I can't change all your minds. But I do ask you to listen with an open mind and to consider the merit of my arguments.

Class Activity
The second Additional Exercise for Critical Thinking on pp. 211–212 of the *Instructor's Manual* provides flawed introductions for students to analyze and correct. This activity helps students focus on all four major objectives of an introduction.

What reasonable listener could ignore such a sincere, forthright plea?

Preview the Body of the Speech

As we saw in Chapter 3, most people are poor listeners. Even good listeners need all the help they can get in sorting out a speaker's ideas. One way to help your listeners is to tell them in the introduction what they should listen for in the rest of the speech. Here is an excellent example, from a speech by biotechnologist Tony L. White at the Columbia University School of Public Health:

I'm pleased to be here with you, and I'm honored to have been asked to deliver this year's Weiss lecture. . . .

Today I'd like to talk about some of the promises associated with the mapping of the human genome. I'll explain some of the opportunities that have emerged from reaching this milestone, and the impact I think it will have on public health. Finally, I'll call your attention to some of the challenges and issues that accompany this achievement.[3]

After this introduction, there was no doubt about White's topic or the main points he would cover in his lecture.

In some types of persuasive speeches, you may not want to reveal your central idea until later in the speech. But even in such a situation you must be sure your audience is not left guessing about the main points they should listen for as the speech unfolds. Nearly always, you should include some *preview statement* similar to the following:

> In order for you to understand why the mariachis are significant to Hispanic culture, I will be giving you a brief overview of the history of the mariachi, what the word "mariachi" means, their style of dress, and the ways they are used in entertainment today.

> Today I'd like to share some of this information with you by first exposing the presence of insects in our everyday foods. Then we'll consider a history of edible insects, next their nutritional value, and finally we'll see what the possibilities are for making insects a more prevalent part of our diet.

> As you can see, I use a scooter to get around campus, and I have found that this campus is inaccessible due to the uncleared snow. I'd like to share that problem with you and then share my solution.

preview statement
A statement in the introduction of a speech that identifies the main points to be discussed in the body of the speech.

View these preview statements from student speeches.

CD 1: VIDEO 9.3

Preview statements such as these serve another purpose as well. Because they usually come at the very end of the introduction, they provide a smooth lead-in to the body of the speech. They signal that the body of the speech is about to begin.

There is one other aspect you may want to cover in previewing your speech. You can use your introduction to give specialized information—definitions or background—that your listeners will need if they are to understand the rest of the speech. Often you can do this very quickly, as in the following examples:

> "Cryonics" is the science of freezing human organs or body parts in liquid nitrogen to preserve them for later use.

> A "triathlon" is a race made up of three different events completed in succession. The events are usually swimming, biking, and running, though canoeing is sometimes substituted for one of these.

Teaching Tip
Make sure students understand that the preview statement is usually the last component of an introduction and serves as a bridge to the body of the speech.

In other circumstances, you may have to explain an important term in more detail. Here is how one student handled the problem in a speech about the Underground Railroad used by slaves to escape from the South before the Civil War. Although most people have heard the phrase "Underground Railroad," many are not sure exactly what it means. Knowing this, the speaker took time in her introduction to give a precise definition:

> The term "Underground Railroad" was first used about 1830. But in fact, the Underground Railroad was neither underground nor a railroad. It was an informal network that provided runaway slaves food, clothing, directions, and places to hide on their escape routes to the North and to Canada.

Why was it called the Underground Railroad? Because of its secrecy and because many of the people involved used railroad terms as code words. Hiding places, for example, were called "stations," and people who helped the slaves were called "conductors." Over the years, the Underground Railroad helped thousands of slaves make their way from bondage to freedom.

Sample Introduction with Commentary

So far we have seen many excerpts showing how to fulfill the various objectives of an introduction. Now here is a complete introduction from a student speech. The side comments indicate the principles used in developing the introduction.

Canine Companions

Commentary	Introduction
The speaker uses a story to gain attention. This story works particularly well because it is richly detailed and arouses our curiosity about Frances's peculiar behavior.	The doorbell rings. Instantly, Frances jumps up from where she has been sitting, spins around three times, and runs back and forth from the door to the sofa. Next she hops onto the sofa and begins bouncing up and down. Is Frances deranged? No, Frances is a "canine companion," and she has just alerted her deaf owner to the fact that a visitor is at the door.
Now the speaker reveals her topic. She defines what canine companions are and uses statistics to show how many are currently at work. This helps strengthen the audience's interest.	Canine companions are dogs that have been trained to assist people who are hearing-impaired or who have physical disabilities. In addition to answering the door, canine companions perform a wide range of tasks that include locking and unlocking wheelchairs, turning light switches on and off, retrieving books from shelves, even fetching a beer from the refrigerator. According to *Smithsonian* magazine, there are some 3,500 canine companions at work throughout the United States, in addition to the 7,000 "seeing eye" dogs that help guide blind people.
The speaker does an excellent job of establishing her credibility and explaining her personal interest in the topic.	I became interested in canine companions two years ago when my older sister, who was paralyzed in a car accident, received a canine companion named Lucky. Since then I have learned about the subject by watching Lucky, by talking with my sister, and by reading a number of articles and pamphlets.
Here the speaker relates the topic directly to her audience and suggests why they should care about it.	As a result of my sister's accident, I have also gained a greater appreciation of the fact that being physically disabled is the one minority we can all join at any time. Due to an accident or serious illness, any of us could one day be in a situation where we—or someone we love—might require the services of a canine companion. So this afternoon I would like to tell you about canine companions—how they are trained and the many benefits they provide for the people they assist.
By previewing the main points of her speech, the speaker lets her audience know what to listen for. She also provides a good lead-in to the body of the speech.	

Tips for Preparing the Introduction

1. Keep the introduction relatively brief. Under normal circumstances it should not constitute more than about 10 to 20 percent of your speech.

2. Be on the lookout for possible introductory materials as you do your research. File them with your notes, so they will be handy when you are ready for them.

3. Be creative in devising your introduction. Experiment with two or three different openings and choose the one that seems most likely to get the audience interested in your speech. (Don't hesitate to discard a "great" introduction that doesn't quite fit your speech. You'll think of another great one.)

The Speech Introduction Checklist can help you prepare your speeches.

CD 1: SPEECH CHECKLIST

4. Don't worry about the exact wording of your introduction until you have finished preparing the body of the speech. After you have determined your main points, it will be much easier to make final decisions about how to begin the speech.

5. Work out your introduction in detail. Some teachers recommend that you write it out word for word; others prefer that you outline it. Whichever method you use, practice the introduction over and over until you can deliver it smoothly from a minimum of notes and with strong eye contact. This will get your speech off to a good start and give you a big boost of confidence.

The Conclusion

"Great is the art of beginning," said Longfellow, "but greater the art is of ending." Longfellow was thinking of poetry, but his insight is equally applicable to public speaking. Many a speaker has marred an otherwise fine speech by a long-winded, silly, or antagonistic conclusion. Your closing remarks are your last chance to drive home your ideas. Moreover, your final impression will probably linger in your listeners' minds. Thus you need to craft your conclusion with as much care as your introduction.

Teaching Tip
Because students spend so much time working on their introductions, they sometimes neglect their conclusions. Remind them that although the conclusion is usually shorter than the introduction, it still needs careful preparation and rehearsal because of its lasting impression on the audience.

No matter what kind of speech you are giving, the conclusion has two major functions:

- To let the audience know you are ending the speech.

- To reinforce the audience's understanding of, or commitment to, the central idea.

Let us look at each.

Signal the End of the Speech

It may seem obvious that you should let your audience know you are going to stop soon. However, you will almost certainly hear speeches in your class in which the speaker concludes so abruptly that you are taken by surprise. Even in casual conversation you expect some signal that the talk is coming to an end. You are taken aback when the person you are talking with suddenly walks off without warning. The same is true of speechmaking. Too sudden an ending leaves the audience puzzled and unfulfilled.

How do you let an audience know your speech is ending? One way is through what you say. "In conclusion," "One last thought," "In closing," "My purpose has been," "Let me end by saying"—these are all brief cues that you are getting ready to stop.

You can also let your audience know the end is in sight by your manner of delivery. The conclusion is the climax of a speech. A speaker who has carefully built to a peak of interest and involvement will not need to say anything like "in conclusion." By use of the voice—its tone, pacing, intonation, and rhythm—a speaker can build the momentum of a speech so there is no doubt when it is over.

crescendo ending

A conclusion in which the speech builds to a zenith of power and intensity.

One method of doing this has been likened to a musical crescendo. As in a symphony in which one instrument after another joins in until the entire orchestra is playing, the speech builds in force until it reaches a zenith of power and intensity.[4] (This does *not* mean simply getting louder and louder. It is a combination of many things, including vocal pitch, choice of words, dramatic content, gestures, pauses—and possibly loudness.)

A superb example of this method is the memorable conclusion to Martin Luther King's "I've Been to the Mountaintop," the speech he delivered the night before he was assassinated in April 1968. Speaking to an audience of 2,000 people in Memphis, Tennessee, he ended his speech with a stirring declaration that the civil rights movement would succeed despite the many threats on his life:

View the ending of Martin Luther King's "I've Been to the Mountaintop."

CD 1: VIDEO 9.4

> Like anybody, I would like to live a long life. Longevity has its place, but I'm not concerned about that now. I just want to do God's will, and he's allowed me to go up to the mountain, and I've looked over and I've seen the Promised Land. I may not get there with you, but I want you to know tonight that we as a people will get to the Promised Land. So I'm happy tonight. I'm not worried about anything; I'm not fearing any man. Mine eyes have seen the glory of the coming of the Lord.[5]

Another effective method might be compared to the dissolve ending of a concert song that evokes deep emotions: "The song seems to fade away while the light on the singer shrinks gradually to a smaller and smaller circle until it lights only the face, then the eyes. Finally, it is a pinpoint, and disappears with the last note of the song."[6] Here is a speech ending that does much the same thing. It is from General Douglas MacArthur's moving farewell to the cadets at the U.S. Military Academy:

dissolve ending

A conclusion that generates emotional appeal by fading step-by-step to a dramatic final statement.

> In my dreams I hear again the crash of guns, the rattle of musketry, the strange, mournful mutter of the battlefield. But in the evening of my memory always I come back to West Point. Always there echoes and re-echoes: duty, honor, country.
> Today marks my final roll call with you. But I want you to know that when I cross the river, my last conscious thoughts will be of the Corps, and the Corps, and the Corps.
> I bid you farewell.[7]

The final words fade like the spotlight, bringing the speech to an emotional close.

You may think that you couldn't possibly end a speech with that much pathos—and you'd be right. MacArthur was an eloquent speaker discussing a grave issue with extraordinary poignance. This combination rarely occurs. But that doesn't mean you can't use the dissolve ending effectively. One student used it with great effect in a speech about visiting her grandparents' family farm as a young girl. During the body of the speech, the student spoke about the sights and sounds of the farm, the love and laughter she shared there as a child. Then, in conclusion, she evoked the images and sentiments of the farm one last time to create a moving dissolve ending:

> Now, as with so much of our childhood, the farm is no longer the same. Grandpa is gone. The barn has been rebuilt. The softball sits idly on the shelf. Grandma no longer cooks her huge family dinners. Going to the farm is different without these pleasures. But still the memories remain. I can still see the fields. I can still smell the hay. I can still hear the laughter. I can still feel the love.

Both the crescendo and the dissolve endings must be worked out with great care. Practice until you get the words and the timing just right. The benefits will be well worth your time.

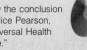

To read these speeches by King and MacArthur, log on to the Top 100 American Speeches of the 20th Century at www.mhhe.com/lucas8.

ONLINE LEARNING CENTER

Reinforce the Central Idea

The second major function of a conclusion is to reinforce the audience's understanding of, or commitment to, the central idea. There are many ways to do this. Here are the ones you are most likely to use.

Teaching Tip
Make sure students understand the importance of strong delivery skills in both the introduction and the conclusion. Also remind them that their nonverbal actions just before they begin to speak and just after they finish can have a powerful impact on the reception of their speech.

Summarize Your Speech

Restating the main points is the easiest way to end a speech. One student used this technique effectively in her persuasive speech about the need for universal health care in the United States:

> In conclusion, we have seen that there are definite problems with the equality and economics of the health care system in the United States which are affecting our citizens and our nation as a whole. I have shown you a viable solution that our entire country would benefit from. Using Canada's system, or one similar to it, would ensure that a much greater percentage of the population receives the health care they need.
>
> Now it is time for our country, considered to be the most advanced in the world, to stop lagging behind other countries in caring for its citizens and begin setting an example of how a country can truly prosper under a universal health care plan.

View the conclusion of Alice Pearson, "Universal Health Care."

CD 1: VIDEO 9.5

The value of a summary is that it explicitly restates the central idea and main points one last time. But as we shall see, there are more imaginative and compelling ways to end a speech. They can be used in combination with a summary or, at times, in place of it.

The conclusion is your last chance to drive home your ideas. Successful speakers such as Bill Moyers craft their endings with great care to leave a strong final impression.

End with a Quotation

A quotation is one of the most common and effective devices to conclude a speech. Here is a fine example, from a speech on the misuse of television advertisements in political campaigns:

> We cannot ignore the evils of television commercials in which candidates for the highest offices are sold to the voters in 30-second spots. These ads cheapen the elective process and degrade our political institutions. In the words of historian Arthur Schlesinger, Jr., "You cannot merchandise candidates like soap and hope to preserve a rational democracy."

The closing quotation is particularly good because its urgency is exactly suited to the speech. When you run across a *brief* quotation that so perfectly captures your central idea, keep it in mind as a possible conclusion.

Make a Dramatic Statement

Rather than using a quotation to give your conclusion force and vitality, you may want to devise your own dramatic statement. Some speeches have become famous because of their powerful closing lines. One is Patrick Henry's legendary "Liberty or Death" oration. It takes its name from the final sentences Henry uttered on March 23, 1775, as he exhorted his audience to resist British tyranny:

> Is life so dear, or peace so sweet, as to be purchased at the price of chains and slavery? Forbid it, Almighty God! I know not what course others may take; but as for me, give me liberty, or give me death.[8]

Although your classroom speeches are not likely to become famous, you can still rivet your listeners—as Henry did—with a dramatic concluding statement. What follows is a particularly striking example, from a speech on suicide prevention. Throughout the speech, the student referred to a friend who had tried to commit suicide the previous year. Then, in the conclusion, she said:

> My friend is back in school, participating in activities she never did before—and enjoying it. I'm happy and proud to say that she's still fighting for her life and even happier that she failed to kill herself. Otherwise, I wouldn't be here today trying to help you. You see, I am my "friend," and I'm more than glad to say, I've made it.

As you can imagine, the audience was stunned. The closing lines brought the speech to a dramatic conclusion.

Here is another example of the same technique—this time from a less unusual situation:

> It is so easy to label the homeless as "bums" and "bag ladies." It is also easy to see them as people who are just looking for a handout—and often we give it to them and walk away. But as we have seen, most homeless people are not simply looking for a handout—they are reaching for a hand. Don't you think we should extend it to them?

This conclusion works because it takes the listener slightly by surprise and creates a lingering impression in the audience. Here the speaker made it even more effective by pausing for just a moment before the last sentence and by using his voice to give the closing words extra emotional force.

Refer to the Introduction

An excellent way to give your speech psychological unity is to conclude by referring to ideas in the introduction. This is an easy technique to use, and it may give your speech an extra touch of class. Here is how one student used the method in her speech about cryonics, the process of freezing people after death in the hope that medical science will be able to revive them in the future:

Introduction: The time is now. Imagine your mother or father has suffered a heart attack. Deprived of its vital blood supply, a part of their heart is dying. Or imagine your grandmother or grandfather lying nearly motionless in their nursing home bed. Advanced age, complicated by pneumonia, is about to end their lives. Or imagine a close friend has just entered the hospital with a massive systemwide infection. AIDS has left their body ravaged by multiple diseases.

For most people, these circumstances would herald the end of life. Today's medicine can no longer help them. But all of you may be able to meet again in the far future. Does this sound like science fiction? Perhaps. But it may one day be possible. How? Through the process of cryonics.

In the body of her speech the student explained the origins of cryonics, the scientific methods used to freeze people, and the problems that must be overcome if they are to be thawed and returned to life in the future. Then, in her conclusion, she returned to the scenarios mentioned in her introduction to tie the whole speech together:

View the beginning and ending of Jayne Richter, "Cryonics."

CD 1: VIDEO 9.6

Conclusion: So think again of your father or mother suffering a heart attack, your grandmother or grandfather dying of pneumonia, or your close friend stricken with AIDS. If they chose to be buried or cremated in traditional fashion, their physical minds and bodies would be destroyed. That is absolutely certain. By contrast, being cryonically frozen offers some small chance that they may be revived in the future. Even if that chance is small, it's more than no chance at all.

Summarizing the speech, ending with a quotation, making a dramatic statement, referring to the introduction—all these techniques can be used separately. But you have probably noticed that speakers often combine two or more in their conclusions. Actually, all four techniques can be fused into one—for example, a dramatic quotation that summarizes the central idea while referring to the introduction.

One other concluding technique is making a direct appeal to your audience for action. This technique applies only to a particular type of persuasive speech, however, and will be discussed in Chapter 15. The four methods covered in this chapter are appropriate for all kinds of speeches and occasions.

Sample Conclusion with Commentary

How do you fit these methods together to make a conclusion? Here is an example, from the speech about canine companions whose introduction we looked at earlier (page 236).

Commentary	Conclusion
The speaker gives an excellent summary of her speech. This is particularly important when you are speaking to inform because it gives you one last chance to make sure the audience remembers your main points.	We have seen, then, that training a canine companion takes a great deal of time and money—up to $10,000 per dog. We have also seen that people who receive the dogs must go through their own training to make sure they and their dog will work as a team. Finally, we have seen the amazing tasks canine companions can perform to help people with physical disabilities enjoy more independent lives.
By referring to her sister, whom she had mentioned in the introduction, the speaker unifies the entire speech. Her closing quotation reinforces the central idea and ends the speech on a strong note.	It has now been two years since my sister received her canine companion. During that time, Lucky has become her hands, her feet, and her best friend. She says of Lucky, "I don't know what I would do without him. He has given my life new meaning."

Tips for Preparing the Conclusion

1. As with the introduction, keep an eye out for possible concluding materials as you research and develop the speech.

2. Conclude with a bang, not a whimper. Be creative in devising a conclusion that hits the hearts and minds of your audience. Work on several possible endings, and select the one that seems likely to have the greatest impact.

3. Don't be long-winded. The conclusion will normally make up no more than about 5 to 10 percent of your speech. Nothing aggravates audiences more than a speaker who says "In conclusion" and then drones on interminably.

4. Don't leave anything in your conclusion to chance. Work it out in detail, and give yourself plenty of time to practice delivering it. Many students like to write out the conclusion word for word to guarantee it is just right. If you do this, make sure you can present it smoothly, confidently, and with feeling—without relying on your notes or sounding wooden. Make your last impression as forceful and as favorable as you can.

The Speech Conclusion Checklist can help you prepare your speeches.

CD 1: SPEECH CHECKLIST

Summary

First impressions are important. So are final impressions. This is why speeches need strong introductions and conclusions.

In most speech situations you need to accomplish four objectives with your introduction—get the attention and interest of the audience, reveal the topic of your speech, establish your credibility and goodwill, and preview the body of the speech. Gaining attention and interest can be done in several ways. You can show the importance of your topic, especially as it relates to your audience. You can startle or question your audience or arouse their curiosity. You can begin with a quotation or a story.

Be sure to state the topic of your speech clearly in your introduction; otherwise, your audience may be confused and wonder where the speech is going. Establishing credibility means that you tell the audience why you are qualified to speak on the topic at hand; establishing goodwill, although less important for classroom speeches than for speeches outside the classroom, may be necessary if your point of view is unpopular. Previewing the body of the speech helps the audience listen effectively and provides a smooth lead-in to the body of the speech.

The conclusion of a speech is particularly important, because the final impression is often what will stick in your listeners' minds. The conclusion has two major objectives—to let the audience know you are ending the speech, and to reinforce their understanding of, or commitment to, your central idea. Too sudden an ending may leave your audience puzzled; it is always a good idea to alert them that you are finishing. You can do this either by your words or by your manner of delivery.

You can use a number of techniques to reinforce your central idea in the conclusion. They include summarizing the speech, ending with a pertinent quotation, making a dramatic statement, and referring to the introduction. Sometimes you may want to combine two or more of these techniques. Be creative in devising a vivid, forceful conclusion.

Key Terms

Review these terms by doing the Chapter 9 crossword puzzle at www.mhhe.com/lucas8.
ONLINE LEARNING CENTER

rhetorical question (229)   preview statement (235)
credibility (233)   crescendo ending (238)
goodwill (233)   dissolve ending (238)

Review Questions

After reading this chapter, you should be able to answer the following questions:

For further review, go to the Study Questions for this chapter.
CD 1: STUDY QUESTIONS

1. What are four objectives of a speech introduction?

2. What are seven methods you can use in the introduction to get the attention and interest of your audience?

3. Why is it important to establish your credibility at the beginning of your speech?

4. What is a preview statement? Why should you nearly always include a preview statement in the introduction of your speech?

5. What are five tips for preparing your introduction?

6. What are the major functions of a speech conclusion?

7. What are two ways you can signal the end of your speech?

8. What are four ways to reinforce the central idea when concluding your speech?

9. What are four tips for preparing your conclusion?

Exercises for Critical Thinking

Cross-Reference
For discussion of the Exercises for Critical Thinking, see the *Instructor's Manual*, pp. 207–209. For additional exercises, check the *Instructor's Manual*, pp. 210–212, as well as the five volumes of *Selections from the Speech Communication Teacher* that accompany *The Art of Public Speaking*.

1. Here are six speech topics. Explain how you might relate each to your classmates in the introduction of a speech.

   Social Security   laughter
   illiteracy   steroids
   soap operas   blood donation

2. Think of a speech topic (preferably one for your next speech in class). Create an introduction for a speech dealing with any aspect of the topic you wish. In your introduction be sure to gain the attention of the audience, to reveal the topic and relate it to the audience, to establish your credibility, and to preview the body of the speech.

3. Using the same topic as in Exercise 2, create a speech conclusion. Be sure to let your audience know the speech is ending, to reinforce the central idea, and to make the conclusion vivid and memorable.

Applying the POWER of PUBLIC SPEAKING

Since leaving college with a degree in education, you have been a classroom teacher, high-school principal, and now assistant superintendent in a large urban school district—the same district in which you, yourself, attended high school. Because of your excellent public speaking skills, you have been chosen to represent the district at a meeting of parents, alumni, and neighborhood residents called to protest the closing of the city's oldest high school. With 1,200 current students and thousands of graduates still in the city, the school has produced many top scholars, as well as championship athletic teams.

Cross-Reference

For discussion of this Applying the Power of Public Speaking scenario, see the *Instructor's Manual*, pp. 209–210.

At the meeting, you will need to explain the decision to close the school and to demolish the 1907 building. Architects, engineers, and city planners agree that renovation of the old structure is impractical and that the city's changing population requires construction of a new school in a new location.

As a graduate of the high school, you understand the feelings of people who want it to remain open. As a member of the school district administration, you understand why it must be closed. You also know that if your speech is to be persuasive, you must use the introduction to establish your credibility and goodwill so the audience will be willing to listen receptively to what you say in the body.

Write a draft of your introduction. In it, be sure to address all four functions of a speech introduction discussed in this chapter.

Notes

[1]Susan Paddack, "Campaigning for Peace: Preventing Youth Violence in America," *Vital Speeches,* 67 (2001), pp. 468–470.

[2]For research on the importance of goodwill to speakers in a variety of situations, see James C. McCroskey and Jason J. Teven, "Goodwill: A Reexamination of the Construct and Its Measurement," *Communication Monographs,* 66 (1999), pp. 90–103.

[3]Tony White, "Smart Medicine Is Coming: Making Intelligent Choices," *Vital Speeches,* 68 (2002), p. 326.

[4]Dorothy Sarnoff, *Speech Can Change Your Life* (Garden City, NY: Doubleday, 1970), p. 189.

[5]Martin Luther King, Jr., "I've Been to the Mountaintop," in Lloyd E. Rohler and Roger Cook (eds.), *Great Speeches for Criticism and Analysis,* 4th ed. (Greenwood, IN: Alistair Press, 2001), p. 363.

[6]Sarnoff, *Speech Can Change Your Life,* p. 190.

[7]Douglas MacArthur, "Farewell to the Cadets," May 12, 1962, in Richard L. Johannesen, R. R. Allen, Wil A. Linkugel, and Ferald J. Bryan (eds.), *Contemporary American Speeches,* 9th ed. (Dubuque, IA: Kendall/Hunt, 2000), p. 284.

[8]Patrick Henry, "Give Me Liberty or Give Me Death," in Owen Collins (ed.), *Speeches That Changed the World,* (Louisville, KY: Westminster John Knox Press, 1998), p. 142.

Chapter Ten

OUTLINING THE SPEECH

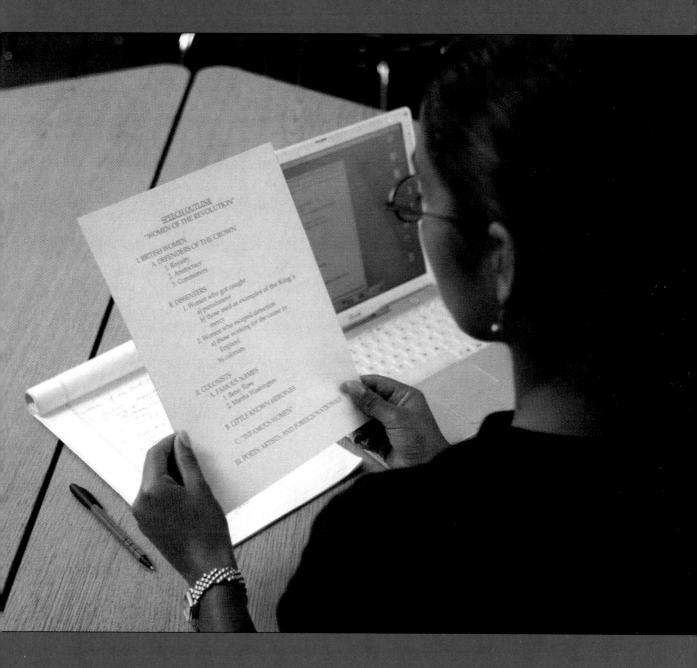

Chapter Focus
Outlining is a crucial step in the process of composing a speech. This chapter presents guidelines for preparation outlines and for speaking outlines. It also includes a complete preparation outline and a complete speaking outline, both with commentary, to help students construct their own outlines. For a complete outline of the chapter, see the *Instructor's Manual*, pp. 214–216.

T hink what might happen if you tried to build a house without a floor plan or an architect's blueprint. You build the kitchen next to the driveway to make it convenient for carrying in groceries. But the dining room turns up at the other end of the house. When you cook and serve a meal, you have to run with the plates to keep the food from getting cold. You put the bathroom at the head of the stairs to make it accessible to visitors. But the door opens in such a way that the unwary guest is catapulted down the steps. You think it's a wonderful idea to have almost no interior walls. After all, the modern living space is supposed to be free and open. But when the first snowfall comes, your (unsupported) roof collapses.

Plans and blueprints are essential to architecture. So, too, are outlines essential to effective speeches. An outline is like a blueprint for your speech. It allows you to see the full scope and content of your speech at a glance. By outlining, you can judge whether each part of the speech is fully developed, whether you have adequate supporting materials for your main points, and whether the main points are properly balanced. An outline helps you make sure that related items are together, that ideas flow from one to another, that the structure of your speech will "stand up"—and not collapse.

Probably you will use two kinds of outlines for your speeches—one very detailed, for the planning stage, and one very brief, for the delivery of the speech.

The Preparation Outline

The preparation outline is just what its name implies—an outline that helps you prepare the speech. Writing a preparation outline means actually putting your speech together. It is the stage at which you decide what you will say in the introduction, how you will organize the main points and supporting materials in the body of the speech, and what you will say in the conclusion.

Guidelines for the Preparation Outline

preparation outline
A detailed outline developed during the process of speech preparation that includes the title, specific purpose, central idea, introduction, main points, subpoints, connectives, conclusion, and bibliography of a speech.

Over the years, a relatively uniform system for preparation outlines has developed. It is explained below and is exemplified in the sample outline on pages 253–255. You should check with your teacher to see exactly what format you are to follow.

State the Specific Purpose of Your Speech

The specific purpose statement should be a separate unit that comes before the text of the outline itself. Including the specific purpose with the outline makes it easier to assess how well you have constructed the speech to accomplish your purpose.

Identify the Central Idea

Some teachers prefer that the central idea be given immediately after the purpose statement. Others prefer that it be given and identified in the text of the outline itself. Check to see which your teacher wants.

Label the Introduction, Body, and Conclusion

If you label the parts of your speech, you will be sure that you indeed *have* an introduction and conclusion and have accomplished the essential objectives of each. Usually the names of the speech parts are placed in the middle of the page or in the far left margin. They are technical labels only and are not included in the system of symbolization used to identify main points and supporting materials.

Use a Consistent Pattern of Symbolization and Indentation

In the most common system of outlining, main points are identified by Roman numerals and are indented equally so as to be aligned down the page. Subpoints (components of the main points) are identified by capital letters and are also indented equally so as to be aligned with each other. Beyond this, there may be sub-subpoints and even sub-sub-subpoints. For example:

I. Main point
  A. Subpoint
  B. Subpoint
    1. Sub-subpoint
    2. Sub-subpoint
      a. Sub-sub-subpoint
      b. Sub-sub-subpoint
II. Main point
  A. Subpoint
    1. Sub-subpoint
    2. Sub-subpoint
  B. Subpoint

The clear *visual framework* of this outline immediately shows the relationships among the ideas of the speech. The most important ideas (main points) are farthest to the left. Less important ideas (subpoints, sub-subpoints, and so on) are progressively farther to the right. This pattern reveals the structure of your entire speech.

Once you have organized the body of your speech (see Chapter 8), you should have identified the main points. You need only flesh out your outline with subpoints and sub-subpoints, as necessary, to support the main points. But suppose, as sometimes happens, you find yourself with a list of statements and are not sure which are main points, which are subpoints, and so forth. Such a list might look like this:

There were 13 people at the Last Supper—Jesus and his 12 disciples.

One of the most common sources of superstition is numbers.

In the United States, 13 is often omitted in the floor numbering of hotels and skyscrapers.

The number 13 has meant bad luck as long as anyone can remember.

Class Activity
For two activities that help students develop an awareness of outlining principles, see Kevin James Brown, " 'Spidergrams': An Aid for Teaching Organization and Outlining," and Virginia B. Mayhew, "Outline the Pictures," both in *Selections from the Speech Communication Teacher 1986–1991*, pp. 53–55, which accompanies *The Art of Public Speaking*.

visual framework
The pattern of symbolization and indentation in a speech outline that shows the relationships among the speaker's ideas.

Teaching Tip
Students are often unsure how long their preparation outlines should be. To give them a sense of what a typical preparation outline looks like, bring in a few samples from previous classes.

Which statement is the main point? The second statement ("One of the most common sources of superstition is numbers"), which is broader in scope than any of the other statements. This would be one of the main ideas of your speech. The fourth statement is the subpoint; it immediately supports the main point. The other two statements are sub-subpoints; they illustrate the subpoint. Rearranged properly, they look like this:

I. One of the most common sources of superstition is numbers.
  A. The number 13 has meant bad luck as long as anyone can remember.
    1. There were 13 people at the Last Supper—Jesus and his 12 disciples.
    2. In the United States, 13 is often omitted in the floor numbering of hotels and skyscrapers.

Above all, remember that all points at the same level should immediately support the point that is just above and one notch to the left in your outline. If this sounds confusing, think of it as a business organization chart:

I. President
  A. Vice president—Operations
    1. Manager—Domestic Operations
      a. Assistant manager—East
      b. Assistant manager—West
    2. Manager—Foreign Operations
      a. Assistant manager—Europe and Asia
      b. Assistant manager—Africa
      c. Assistant manager—Americas
  B. Vice president—Administration
    1. Manager—Finance
    2. Manager—Personnel

As you can see, every person on this chart reports to the person who is above and one notch to the left—except, of course, the president, who is the "main point."

State Main Points and Subpoints in Full Sentences

Below are two sets of main points and subpoints for the same speech on the life of Martin Luther King.

Ineffective	More Effective
I. Montgomery	I. King began his civil rights career in the Montgomery bus boycott of 1955–1956.
II. 1960s	II. King's greatest triumphs came during the early 1960s.
A. Birmingham	A. In 1963 he campaigned against segregation in Birmingham, Alabama.

Overhead Transparency
It is vital that students understand how the proper use of symbolization and indentation in an outline can provide a clear visual framework of the entire speech. This framework can be illustrated with two overhead transparencies—one showing an outline without consistent symbolization and indentation, another showing the same outline with consistent symbolization and indentation. For examples, see the binder of full-color overhead transparencies that accompanies *The Art of Public Speaking*.

Teaching Tip
Students profit enormously from constructive suggestions while they are preparing their speeches. If you require that students turn in their preparation outlines one week before they are scheduled to speak, you can provide feedback about ways to revise the outline and strengthen the speech. Another approach is to pair up students in class and have them read one another's outlines and offer suggestions for improvement.

As blueprints are essential to architecture, so outlines are essential to speechmaking. Developing an outline helps ensure that the structure of your speech is clear and coherent.

B. March	B. Later that year he participated in the famous march on Washington, D.C.
1. 200,000	1. More than 200,000 people took part.
2. "Dream"	2. King gave his "I Have a Dream" speech.
C. Prize	C. In 1964 he received the Nobel Peace Prize.
III. Final years	III. King faced great turmoil during his final years.
A. Criticized	A. He was criticized by more militant blacks for being nonviolent.
B. Vietnam	B. He protested against the war in Vietnam.
C. Assassination	C. He was assassinated in Memphis, Tennessee, on April 4, 1968.

The Preparation Outline Checklist can help you develop your outline.

CD 1: SPEECH CHECKLIST

The sample at left might serve adequately as a speaking outline, but it is virtually useless as a preparation outline. It gives only vague labels rather than distinct ideas. It does not indicate clearly the content of the main points and subpoints. Nor does it reveal whether the speaker has thought out his or her ideas. But there is no concern about any of these matters with the outline on the right.

In sum, a skimpy preparation outline is of little value. Stating your main points and subpoints in full sentences will ensure that you develop your ideas fully.

Label Transitions, Internal Summaries, and Internal Previews

One way to make sure you have strong transitions, internal summaries, and internal previews is to include them in the preparation outline. Usually they are not incorporated into the system of symbolization and indentation, but are labeled separately and inserted in the outline where they will appear in the speech.

Attach a Bibliography

bibliography
A list of all the sources used in preparing a speech.

You should include with the outline a list of the sources you consulted in preparing the speech. The bibliography will show all the books, magazines, newspapers, and Internet sources you consulted, as well as any interviews or field research you conducted.

The two major bibliographic formats are those developed by the Modern Language Association (MLA) and the American Psychological Association (APA). Both are widely used by communication scholars; ask your instructor which he or she prefers. No matter which format you adopt, make sure your statement of sources is clear, accurate, and consistent. For help, check the Bibliography Formats on CD 1, where you will find a complete set of MLA and APA sample citations for a wide range of sources, from books and articles to personal interviews and Internet materials.

Go to the Bibliography Formats for a complete set of sample MLA and APA citations.

CD 1: BIBLIOGRAPHY FORMATS

Give Your Speech a Title, If One Is Desired

In the classroom you probably do not need a title for your speech unless your teacher requires one. In some other situations, however, a speech title is necessary—as when the speech is publicized in advance, when the group inviting you to speak requests a title, or when the speech is going to be published. Whatever the reason, if you do decide to use a title, it should (1) be brief, (2) attract the attention of your audience, and (3) encapsulate the main thrust of your speech.

A good title need not have what Madison Avenue would call "sex appeal"—lots of glitter and pizzazz. By the same token, there is certainly nothing wrong with a catchy title—as long as it is germane to the speech. Here are two groups of titles. Those on the left are straightforward and descriptive. Those on the right are figurative alternatives to the ones on the left.

Teaching Tip
Individual instructors often have their own requirements for titles, connectives, bibliographies, and other elements of a preparation outline. Make sure your students understand exactly what is required of them. It is helpful to prepare a checklist that students can refer to as they develop their outlines.

Group I	**Group II**
Unsafe Drinking Water	Toxins on Tap
Living with Deafness	The Sounds of Silence
The Rage to Diet	The Art of Wishful Shrinking
The United States Mint	The Buck Starts Here
Gambling Addiction	Against All Odds

Which group do you prefer? Neither is perfect. There are advantages and disadvantages to both. Those in the first group clearly reveal the topic of the speech, but they are not as provocative as those in the second group. Those in the second group are sure to arouse interest, but they do not give as clear an idea of what the speeches are about.

There is one other kind of title you should consider—the question. Phrasing your title as a question can be both descriptive and provocative. Using this method, we can construct a third set of titles combining the virtues of groups I and II:

Group III

Is Your Water Safe to Drink?

Can You See What I'm Saying?

Diets: How Effective Are They?

Where Is Making Money a Way of Life?

Do You Really Think You Can Beat the Odds?

The Speech Outliner will guide you through the steps in creating a preparation outline.

CD 1: SPEECH OUTLINER

Sometimes you will choose a title for your speech very early. At other times you may not find one you like until the last minute. Either way, try to be resourceful about creating titles for your speeches. Experiment with several and choose the one that seems most appropriate.

Sample Preparation Outline with Commentary

The following outline for a six-minute informative speech illustrates the guidelines just discussed.[1] The commentary explains the procedures used in organizing the speech and writing the outline. (Check with your teacher to see if she or he wants you to include a title with your outline.)

India: Land of Diversity	
Commentary	*Outline*

Commentary	**Outline**
	Neera Nijhawan
Stating your specific purpose and central idea as separate units before the text of the outline makes it easier to judge how well you have constructed the outline to achieve your purpose and to communicate your central idea.	*Specific Purpose:* To inform my audience about the diversity of India's geography and languages. *Central Idea:* India is a country of great geographical and linguistic diversity.
Labeling the introduction marks it as a distinct section that plays a special role in the speech.	*Introduction*

Opening with a non-English word helps get attention.	I. "Namaste."
	  A. Do you know what I just said?
	  B. I greeted you the way I would in India.
	II. The same word—"Namaste"—is also used when saying goodbye.
	  A. The identical word can have two entirely different meanings.
	  B. This is just one example of the diversity of life in India.

Here the speaker moves from her attention getter to reveal the topic of her speech.	

Now the speaker establishes her credibility and previews the main points to be discussed in the body of the speech.

Including transitions ensures that the speaker has worked out how to connect one idea to the next. Notice that the transition is not included in the system of symbolization and indentation used for the rest of the speech.

Labeling the body marks it as a distinct part of the speech.

Main point I is phrased as a full sentence. As the outline progresses, notice that the main points are arranged in topical order.

The three subpoints are shown by the capital letters A, B, and C, and are written in complete sentences to ensure that the speaker has thought them out fully.

Points below the level of subpoint are indicated by Arabic numerals and lowercase letters. Often they are not written in full sentences. Check to see what your teacher prefers.

When this speech was presented in class, the speaker used a large map as a visual aid throughout main point I so she could point out the regions of India as she discussed them.

The transition shows how the speaker will move from main point I to main point II.

Main point II, like main point I, is phrased as a full sentence.

III. As a first-generation Indian American, I have had firsthand experience with Indian life and culture.
IV. Today I would like to give you a glimpse of India's diversity by looking at its geography and languages.

(*Transition:* Let's start with geography.)

Body

I. India is a land of great geographical diversity.
   A. The northernmost part of India consists of the Himalaya Mountains.
      1. The highest mountain system in the world, the Himalaya separate India from China.
      2. The Indian Himalaya have many mountains more than 20,000 feet high.
   B. The central part of India consists of the Northern Plains.
      1. About 200 miles wide, the Northern Plains stretch across India from the Arabian Sea on the west to the Bay of Bengal on the east.
      2. Within the Northern Plains, there is considerable diversity.
         a. There is fertile farmland.
         b. There are major cities such as Delhi and Calcutta.
         c. There is the great Indian Desert.
   C. The southern part of India consists of the Deccan plateau.
      1. Extending from the edge of the Northern Plains to the southern tip of India, the Deccan plateau is more than 1,200 miles long.
      2. The Deccan plateau includes many geographical features.
         a. It contains farming and grazing land.
         b. It contains tropical forests.
         c. It contains most of India's seacoast.

(*Transition:* Now that you know something about the geographical diversity of India, let's look at its linguistic diversity.)

II. India is a land of great linguistic diversity.
   A. The official language is Hindi.
      1. Hindi is spoken by 40 percent of the people.
      2. The opening word of my speech—"Namaste"—is Hindi.

Notice the pattern of subordination in this section. Subpoint B announces that there are 17 languages besides Hindi recognized in the Indian constitution. Sub-subpoint 1 deals with the distinctiveness of those languages. Because items a and b expand upon the distinctiveness point, they are subordinated to it.

The progressive indentation shows visually the relationships among main points, subpoints, sub-subpoints, etc.

Throughout main point II, the speaker uses well-chosen supporting materials to illustrate India's linguistic diversity in a clear and interesting fashion.

Labeling the conclusion marks it as a distinct part of the speech.

Summarizing the main points is usually standard procedure in an informative speech.

The closing line provides unity by relating back to the introduction.

This is the final bibliography. It lists the sources actually used in writing the speech and is shorter than the preliminary bibliography compiled in the early stages of research. (See Chapter 6 for a discussion of the preliminary bibliography.)

This bibliography follows the Modern Language Association (MLA) format. Check with your instructor to see what format you should use for your bibliography.

B. In addition to Hindi, there are 17 regional languages recognized in the Indian constitution.
  1. These languages are as distinct from each other as English is from French.
    a. Each has its own grammar and pronunciation.
    b. Some have their own alphabet.
  2. Many of these languages have literary traditions that are 2,000 years old.

C. India also has more than 1,000 minor languages and dialects.
  1. These can change entirely from village to village.
  2. This often makes communication very difficult.
D. Most educated Indians also speak English.
  1. The use of English comes from 300 years of British rule.
  2. English is spoken by 2 percent of the population.
  3. It is widely used in colleges and universities.
E. As linguist Kamala Singh has stated, the diversity of India's language is "unrivaled by any other nation."

Conclusion

I. I hope you can see from India's geography and languages why it is such a diverse—and fascinating—country.

II. Thank you and "Namaste."

Bibliography

Books
Arnett, Robert. *India Unveiled.* 3rd ed. Columbus, GA: Atman Press, 2002.
Keay, John. *India: A History.* New York: Grove Press, 2001.

Articles
Dasgupta, Swapan. "What India Thinks: Divided We Stand." *India Today* 26 Aug. 2002: 32–34.
O'Sullivan, John. "Multicultural India Facing Identity Crisis." *Chicago Sun-Times* 5 Mar. 2002: 23.

Internet Sources
"Major Indian Languages." 4 July 2000. 9 May 2003 <http://theory.tifr.res.in/bombay/history/people/language>.
United States. Central Intelligence Agency. "India." *World Factbook 2002.* 1 Jan. 2002. 9 May 2003 <http://www.cia.gov/cia/publications/factbook/geos/in.html>.

The Speaking Outline

Class Activity
The first Exercise for Critical Thinking at the end of this chapter asks students to arrange in proper order a set of randomly organized points from a speech outline. For variations, see Applying the Power of Public Speaking on pages 262–263, as well as the Outlining Exercises on CD 1.

"I was never so excited by public speaking before in my life," wrote one listener in 1820 after listening to Daniel Webster. "Three or four times I thought my temples would burst with the gush of blood. . . . I was beside myself, and am so still."[2]

Such reactions were not unusual among Webster's audiences. He thrilled two generations of Americans with his masterful orations. Incredible as it seems today, he did so while speaking for three, four, even five hours at a time. Equally incredible, he often spoke without using any notes! A reporter once asked how he managed this. "It is my memory," Webster said. "I can prepare a speech, revise and correct it in my memory, then deliver the corrected speech exactly as finished."[3]

Few people have Webster's remarkable powers of memory. Fortunately, it is no longer customary to speak from memory. Today most people speak extemporaneously—which means the speech is thoroughly prepared and carefully practiced in advance, but much of the exact wording is selected while the speech is being delivered (see Chapter 12). Your speeches will probably be of this type. You should know, then, about the *speaking outline*—the most widely recommended form of notes for extemporaneous speeches.

The aim of a speaking outline is to help you remember what you want to say. In some ways it is a condensed version of your preparation outline. It should contain key words or phrases to jog your memory, as well as essential statistics and quotations that you do not want to risk forgetting. But it should also include material *not* in your preparation outline—especially cues to direct and sharpen your delivery.

speaking outline
A brief outline used to jog a speaker's memory during the presentation of a speech.

Most speakers develop their own variations on the speaking outline. As you acquire more experience, you, too, should feel free to experiment. But for now, your best bet is to follow the basic guidelines below and to use the sample speaking outline on pages 259–260 as your model.

Guidelines for the Speaking Outline

Follow the Visual Framework Used in the Preparation Outline

Your speaking outline should use the same visual framework—the same symbols and the same pattern of indentation—as your preparation outline. This will make it much easier to prepare the speaking outline. More important, it will allow you to see instantly where you are in the speech at any given moment while you are speaking. You will find this a great advantage. As you speak, you will look down at your outline periodically to make sure you are covering the right ideas in the right order. It will be of little help if you have to hunt around to find where you are every time you look down.

Compare the following two versions of a partial speaking outline. They are from an informative speech about the history of the U.S. women's rights movement.

Accomplished speakers such as U.S. Senator John McCain often use a brief set of notes, which allows them to maintain eye contact and to communicate directly with the audience.

Ineffective

I. 1840–1860
A. World Anti-Slavery Convention
B. Seneca Falls convention
1. Lucretia Mott
2. Elizabeth Cady Stanton
3. Declaration of Sentiments
II. 1900–1920
A. National American Woman
   Suffrage Association
1. Founding
2. Objectives
B. Nineteenth Amendment
1. Campaign
2. Ratification

More Effective

I. 1840–1860
  A. World Anti-Slavery Convention
  B. Seneca Falls convention
    1. Lucretia Mott
    2. Elizabeth Cady Stanton
    3. Declaration of Sentiments
II. 1900–1920
  A. National American Woman
     Suffrage Association
    1. Founding
    2. Objectives
  B. Nineteenth Amendment
    1. Campaign
    2. Ratification

Class Activity
For an activity that reinforces the importance of speaking from a brief set of notes, see Joan M. Gaulard, "To Read, to Memorize, or to Speak," in *Selections from the Speech Communication Teacher 1986–1991*, pp. 23–24, which accompanies *The Art of Public Speaking.*

The wording of both outlines is exactly the same. But the visual framework of the one on the right makes it easier to take in at a glance and reduces the odds of the speaker losing her or his place.

Make Sure the Outline Is Legible

You would be surprised how many students try to speak from messy, scribbled notes that would be hard to decipher at leisure, much less under the pressures of a speech situation. Your speaking outline is all but worthless unless it is instantly readable at a distance. When you make your outline, use dark ink and large lettering, leave extra space between lines, provide ample margins, and write or type on one side of the paper only.

Some speakers put their notes on index cards. Most find the 3×5 size too cramped and prefer the 4×6 or 5×8 size instead. Other people write their speaking outlines on regular paper. Either practice is fine, as long as your notes are immediately legible to you while you are speaking.

Keep the Outline as Brief as Possible

If your notes are too detailed, you will have difficulty maintaining eye contact with your audience. A detailed outline will tempt you to look at it far too often, as one student discovered:

Angela Granato was speaking about the benefits of Pilates. She had prepared the speech thoroughly and practiced it until it was nearly perfect. But when she delivered the speech in class, she referred constantly to her detailed notes. As a result, her delivery was choppy and strained. After the speech, Angela's classmates remarked on how often she had looked at her notes, and she was amazed. "I didn't even know I was doing it," she said. "Most of the time I wasn't even paying attention to the outline. I knew the speech cold."

Many students have had the same experience. Having lots of notes is a psychological security blanket against the possibility that something will go terribly wrong. The feeling seems to be, "As long as I have plenty of notes, disaster will not strike." In fact, most beginning speakers use far too many notes. Like Angela, they find they don't need all of them to remember the speech. They also discover that too many notes can actually interfere with good communication.

To guard against having too many notes, keep your speaking outline as brief as possible. It should contain key words or phrases to help you remember major points, subpoints, and connectives. If you are citing statistics, you will probably want to include them in your notes. Unless you are good at memorizing quotations, write them out fully as well. Finally, there may be two, three, or four key ideas whose wording is so important that you want to state them in simple complete sentences. The best rule is that your notes should be the *minimum* you need to jog your memory and keep you on track. At first you may find it risky to speak from a brief outline, but you will soon become more comfortable with it.

Give Yourself Cues for Delivering the Speech

A good speaking outline reminds you not only of *what* you want to say but also of *how* you want to say it. As you practice the speech, you will decide that certain ideas and phrases need special emphasis—that they should be spoken more loudly, softly, slowly, or rapidly than other parts of the speech. You will also determine how you want to pace the speech—how you will control its timing, rhythm, and momentum. But no matter how you work these things out ahead of time, no matter how often you practice, it is easy to forget them once you get up in front of an audience.

The solution is to include in your speaking outline *delivery cues*—directions for delivering the speech. One way to do this is by underlining or otherwise highlighting key ideas that you want to be sure to emphasize. Then, when you reach them in the outline, you will be reminded to stress them.

Teaching Tip

Over time every experienced speaker develops her or his own system of speaking notes. In the long run, the key issue is not the exact system used by any given speaker, but whether she or he establishes a strong communicative bond with listeners by speaking fluently, energetically, and with strong eye contact. The same is true with respect to the amount of notes. Some very successful speakers use a lot of notes; others use very few. In speech class, most instructors encourage students to speak from as brief a set of notes as possible so students will get in the habit of talking extemporaneously rather than memorizing their speeches or reading them from manuscript.

delivery cues

Directions in a speaking outline to help a speaker remember how she or he wants to deliver key parts of the speech.

Another way is to jot down on the outline explicit cues such as "pause," "repeat," "slow down," "louder," and so forth. Both techniques are good aids for beginning speakers, but they are also used by most experienced speakers.

Sample Speaking Outline with Commentary

Below is a sample speaking outline for a six-minute informative talk about the geographical and linguistic diversity of India. By comparing it with the preparation outline for the same speech on pages 253–255, you can see how a detailed preparation outline is transformed into a concise speaking outline.

Commentary	Outline

These comments remind the speaker to establish eye contact and not to race through the speech.	*Eye Contact!!*
	 Slow Down
	
	 I. "Namaste."
	     A. Know what I said?
	     B. Greeted as if in India.

The word "pause" reminds the speaker to pause after her opening lines.	— *Pause* —
	
	 II. "Namaste" also used when saying goodbye.
	     A. Two different meanings.
	     B. Example of India's diversity.
	 III. First-generation Indian American.
	 IV. Today—India's diversity in geography and languages.

Including the main ideas of the introduction helps keep the speaker on track at the start of the speech.	(Let's start with geography.)
It's usually a good idea to pause briefly before launching into the first main point. This is another way of signaling that you are moving from the introduction to the body.	— *Pause* —

Most speakers find it helpful to demarcate the body of the speech in the speaking outline as well as in the preparation outline.	*Body*
	
	 I. Great geographical diversity.
	     A. Himalaya Mountains.
	        1. Separate India from China.
	        2. 20,000 feet high.

Notice how the body of the speech follows the same visual format as the preparation outline. This makes the outline easy to read at a glance.	B. Northern Plains.
	        1. 200 miles wide.
	        2. Diversity of Northern Plains.
	           a. Farmland.
	           b. Cities: Delhi and Calcutta.
	           c. Great Indian Desert.

Throughout the outline, key words are used to jog the speaker's memory. Because the final wording of an extemporaneous speech is chosen at the moment of delivery, it will not be exactly the same as that in the preparation outline.

Inserting transitions makes sure the speaker doesn't forget them.

Underlining reminds the speaker to stress key words or ideas.

Quotations are usually written out in full in the speaking outline.

It's usually a good idea to pause before entering the conclusion.

Most speakers label the conclusion in the speaking outline as well as in the preparation outline.

Including the last sentence jogs the speaker's memory and ensures that the speech will end as planned.

C. Deccan plateau.
   1. 1,200 miles long.
   2. Geographical features.
      a. Farming and grazing land.
      b. Tropical forests.
      c. Seacoasts.

(Now you know geographical . . . look at linguistic.)

II. Great linguistic diversity.
   A. Official language is Hindi.
      1. Spoken by 40 percent.
      2. "Namaste" is Hindi.
   B. 17 other major languages in constitution.
      1. Distinct as English and French.
         a. Grammar and pronunciation.
         b. Alphabet.
      2. Literary traditions—2,000 years.
   C. 1,000 minor languages and dialects.
      1. Change from village to village.
      2. Communication very difficult.
   D. Educated also speak English.
      1. 2 percent
      2. Colleges and universities.
   E. Kamala Singh: linguistic diversity "unrivaled by any other nation."

— Pause —

Conclusion

I. Hope you see diversity from geography and languages.
II. Thank you and "Namaste."

Summary

Outlines are essential to effective speeches. By outlining, you make sure that related ideas are together, that your thoughts flow from one to another, and that the structure of your speech is coherent. You will probably use two kinds of outlines for your speeches—the detailed preparation outline and the brief speaking outline.

The preparation outline helps you prepare your speech. In this outline you state your specific purpose and central idea; label the introduction, body, and conclusion; and designate transitions, internal summaries, and internal previews. You should identify main points, subpoints, and sub-subpoints by a consistent pattern of symbolization and indentation. It is usually advisable to state at least main points and subpoints in full sentences. Your teacher may require a bibliography with your preparation outline.

The speaking outline consists of brief notes to help you while you deliver the speech. It should contain key words or phrases to jog your memory, as well as essential statistics and quotations. In making up your speaking outline, follow the same visual framework used in your preparation outline. Keep the speaking outline as brief as possible, and be sure it is legible. You can also give yourself cues for delivering the speech—when to speak more softly or more slowly, when to pause, and so forth.

Key Terms

preparation outline (248)
visual framework (249)
bibliography (252)

speaking outline (256)
delivery cues (258)

Review these terms by doing the Chapter 10 crossword puzzle at www.mhhe.com/lucas8.

ONLINE LEARNING CENTER

Review Questions

After reading this chapter, you should be able to answer the following questions:

1. Why is it important to outline your speeches?

2. What is a preparation outline? What are the eight guidelines discussed in the chapter for writing a preparation outline?

3. What is a speaking outline? What are four guidelines for your speaking outline?

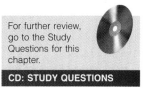

For further review, go to the Study Questions for this chapter.

CD: STUDY QUESTIONS

Exercises for Critical Thinking

1. In the left-hand column on page 262 is a partially blank outline from a speech about sleep deprivation. In the right-hand column, arranged in random order, are the subpoints to fill in the outline. Choose the appropriate subpoint for each blank in the outline.

Cross-Reference

For discussion of the Exercises for Critical Thinking, see the *Instructor's Manual,* pp. 217–222. For additional exercises, check the *Instructor's Manual,* pp. 224–227, as well as the five volumes of *Selections from the Speech Communication Teacher* that accompany *The Art of Public Speaking.*

Outline	**Subpoints**
I. Sleep deprivation is a major cause of traffic accidents and deaths.	Sleep deprivation has been linked to a number of specific disorders.
A.	The *Times* also blames falling asleep at the wheel for 6,500 U.S. traffic deaths each year.
1.	Second, it increases the risk of heart disease.
2.	The statistics linking sleep deprivation to traffic accidents and deaths are alarming.
B.	First, it weakens the immune system.
II. Sleep deprivation also contributes to poor personal health.	Sleep deprivation is second only to alcohol as the leading cause of traffic accidents and deaths.
A.	*Newsweek* reports that "sleep deprivation has become one of the most pervasive health problems facing the U.S."
B.	Third, it contributes to gastrointestinal illness.
1.	The *Los Angeles Times* reports that drowsiness causes 200,000 auto accidents each year.
2.	
3.	

Check your outlining skills by doing the Outline Exercises.

CD 1: OUTLINE EXERCISES

2. Following the format used in the sample preparation outline on pages 253–255, outline "Cryonics," the sample speech at the end of Chapter 14. Be sure to include a specific purpose statement; to identify the central idea; to label the introduction, body, and conclusion; to use a consistent pattern of symbolization and indentation; to state the main points and subpoints in full sentences; and to label transitions and internal summaries.

3. From the preparation outline you constructed in Exercise 2, create a speaking outline that you might use in delivering the speech. Follow the guidelines for a speaking outline discussed in this chapter.

Applying the **POWER** of PUBLIC SPEAKING

Cross-Reference

For discussion of this Applying the Power of Public Speaking scenario, see the *Instructor's Manual,* pp. 222–223.

As the defense attorney in a car theft case, you need to prepare your closing argument to the jury before it begins its deliberations. After reviewing evidence from the trial, you decide to stress the following points to demonstrate the innocence of your client:

a. The stolen car was found abandoned three hours after the theft with the engine still warm; at the time the car was found, your client was at the airport to meet the flight of a friend who was flying into town.

b. Lab analysis of muddy shoe prints on the floor mat of the car indicates that the prints came from a size 13 shoe; your client wears a size 10.

c. Lab analysis shows the presence of cigarette smoke in the car, but your client does not smoke.

d. The only eyewitness to the crime, who was 50 feet from the car, said the thief "looked like" your client; yet the eyewitness admitted that at the time of the theft she was not wearing her corrective lenses, which had been prescribed for improving distance vision.

e. The car was stolen at about 1 P.M.; your client testified that he was in a small town 175 miles away at 11 A.M.

f. In a statement to police, the eyewitness described the thief as blond; your client has red hair.

As you work on the outline of your speech, you see that these points can be organized into three main points, each with two supporting points. Compose an outline that organizes the points in this manner.

Notes

[1]Reprinted with permission of Neera Nijhawan.

[2]Robert T. Oliver, *History of Public Speaking in America* (Boston: Allyn and Bacon, 1965), p. 143.

[3]Oliver, *History of Public Speaking,* p. 145.

Chapter Eleven

USING LANGUAGE

Have you ever played *Pictionary?* The point of the game is to draw words so people watching you can guess them. Some words are easy—"house," "bird," and "television," for instance. Even people without artistic talent can draw these in such a way that observers catch on immediately. But other kinds of words are more challenging. Try drawing "numb," "embarrass," or "dehydrated." The more abstract the word, the more difficult it is to represent visually. How would you draw "improvement" or "appropriate"?

This is why language has evolved. Human beings need to communicate at a level far above what can be shown by pictures. But for language to work there must be a common understanding of what words mean. In effect, we've all made a pact that a certain collection of letters and sounds will mean the same thing to everybody. If you say "book," everybody who speaks English will picture something like what you're holding right now. On the other hand, when you don't use words properly, you "break the pact" and communication breaks down. Suppose you say to a friend, "Abby, you're so pedestrian." You may mean she walks a lot; but Abby is likely to become angry, because you actually called her boring and ordinary.

Chapter Focus

After discussing the importance of language and the differences between denotative and connotative meaning, this chapter explains how to use words accurately, clearly, vividly, and appropriately. It also presents several methods for using inclusive language. For a complete outline of the chapter, see the *Instructor's Manual*, pp. 229–232.

Language Is Important

Good speakers respect language and how it works. How well do you use language? Do you say Kobe Bryant plays basketball *good,* when you mean he plays *well?* Do you say *in the eventuality of* when *if* will do? Do you describe a hurricane as a *terrible disaster,* as if there were such a thing as a *good disaster?* Do you litter your speech with such meaningless words as *you know, like,* and *really?*

If you do these things, you are bound to be less effective as a speaker. And, unfortunately, you are not alone. Much American speech is turning into the linguistic equivalent of junk food. For example:

Related Reading

There are many books on the power of language and the consequences of its misuse. For an entertaining recent work, see William Lutz, *Doublespeak Defined* (New York: HarperCollins, 1999). Lutz provides a wealth of examples that can be used for class discussion.

Sign in an eyeglass shop: "Eyes examined while you wait." (Definitely more comfortable than the alternative.)

A statement from the Federal Aviation Agency, explaining a helicopter crash: "The propeller experienced a case of uncontained blade liberation." (In plain English, "The propeller blade broke off.")

Pittsburgh Steelers football coach Bill Cowher, discussing his quarterback: "Certainly that position is the one that's going to burden the blunt of the responsibilities." (Excuse me?)

A doctor, talking about accident victims: "There were four deaths, only one of which lived more than two months." (Scientific proof of life after death!)

The problem with these statements is not that they violate elitist standards of "good English." People in the United States have always talked casually.

Our language has grown with as much vigor and variety as our population. We have borrowed words from other languages. We have coined new words and dropped old ones.[1] The first edition of *Webster's Collegiate Dictionary,* published in 1898, contained about 70,000 words. The 10th edition, reprinted in 1998, has 215,000 words—and these are just the words deemed necessary for a college education. One expert has estimated that the English language has more than 2 million words, with a thousand new ones being added each year.[2]

There is a big difference, however, between the natural growth of a living language and the misuse of that language. To misuse our language is much more than a matter of mere words. Contrary to popular belief, language does not mirror reality. It does not simply describe the world as it is. Instead, language helps create our sense of reality by giving meaning to events. Language is not neutral. The words we use to label an event determine to a great extent how we respond to it.

Consider the public debate over doctor-assisted suicide. If you see doctor-assisted suicide as "immoral," as a form of "murder," as "a violation of the doctor's duty to save lives," you will likely oppose efforts to allow it in any form. But if you see doctor-assisted suicide as "moral," as a way to provide "death with dignity," as "an acceptable alternative to needless pain and suffering" for the terminally ill, you will likely support efforts to permit it in some circumstances.

What separates these two viewpoints? Not the capabilities of modern medicine; not the conditions of terminally ill patients; not even the act of doctor-assisted suicide itself. All those are the same for both sides. The difference is in the *meaning* given to them by the words that label them. This is why, as one writer has said, a choice of words is also a choice of worlds.[3]

Words are vital to thinking itself. Thought and language are closely linked. We do not get an idea and then come up with words to express it. Rather, we usually think in words. How often have you said, "I know what I want to say, but I just don't know how to say it." In fact, if you truly knew what you wanted to say, you probably would be able to say it. On most occasions when we are looking for "just the right word," what we are really looking for is just the right *idea.*[4]

As a speaker, once you get the right idea, you must decide how best to *communicate* it to listeners. To do this, you need to be especially conscious of what language can do. Unless you use language accurately and clearly, no one will understand your ideas.

Words are the tools of a speaker's craft. They have special uses, just like the tools of any other profession. Have you ever watched a carpenter at work? The job that would take you or me a couple of hours is done by the carpenter in 10 minutes—with the right tools. You can't drive a nail with a screwdriver or turn a screw with a hammer. It is the same with public speaking. You must choose the right words for the job you want to do.

Good speakers are aware of the meanings of words—both their obvious and their subtle meanings. They also know how to use language accurately, clearly, vividly, and appropriately. The balance of this chapter will explore

Discussion Prompt
As the poet Walt Whitman wrote more than a century ago, "the English language is the accretion and growth of every dialect, race, and range of time." Have students discuss the changing nature of language, and see if they can come up with examples of words whose meanings have changed over the years. For an entertaining book on this subject, see John McWhorter, *The Power of Babel: A Natural History of Language* (New York: Henry Holt, 2001).

Class Activity
For a brief exercise that brings home to students the power of language in creating social reality, see Edwin N. Rowley, "More Than Mere Words," in *Selections from the Speech Communication Teacher: 1991–1994,* p. 39, which accompanies *The Art of Public Speaking.*

each of these aspects of language use. We will also give special attention to inclusive language in public speaking.

Meanings of Words

denotative meaning
The literal or dictionary meaning of a word or phrase.

Words have two kinds of meanings—denotative and connotative. *Denotative* meaning is precise, literal, and objective. It simply describes the object, person, place, idea, or event to which the word refers. One way to think of a word's denotative meaning is as its dictionary definition. For example, denotatively, the noun "school" means "a place, institution, or building where instruction is given."

Connotative meaning is more variable, figurative, and subjective. Put simply, the connotative meaning of a word is what the word suggests or implies. For instance, the connotative meaning of the word "school" includes all the feelings, associations, and emotions that the word touches off in different people. For some people, "school" might connote personal growth, childhood friends, and a special teacher. For others, it might connote frustration, discipline, and boring homework assignments.

connotative meaning
The meaning suggested by the associations or emotions triggered by a word or phrase.

Connotative meaning gives words their intensity and emotional power. It arouses in listeners feelings of anger, pity, love, fear, friendship, nostalgia, greed, guilt, and the like. Speakers, like poets, often use connotation to enrich their meaning. For example:

> Terrorists neither listen to reason nor engage in reasoning with others. Their aim is to generate fear—to frighten people into submission. They measure success by the magnitude of the fear they generate through brutal, savage acts of violence. Terrorists are prepared to kill to further whatever cause they claim to be pursuing. And the heinousness of these murders is accentuated by the fact that terrorists murder without passion. They murder with cool deliberation and deliberate planning. They are utterly amoral.

Discussion Prompt
You can illustrate the power of language, as well as the differences between denotative and connotative meaning, by examining the use of language in controversial social issues. For example, ask students to discuss the connotative meanings of the following terms: pro-choice, pro-life, pro-abortion, anti-abortion. Why do anti-abortion advocates prefer to be called "pro-life"? Why do pro-abortion backers prefer the label "pro-choice"?

The underlined words in this passage have powerful connotations that are almost certain to produce a strong emotional revulsion to terrorism.

Here, in contrast, is another version of the same statement—this time using words with a different set of connotations:

> Terrorists do not seek to negotiate with their opponents. They seek victory by using political and psychological pressure, including acts of violence that may endanger the lives of some people. To the terrorist, ultimate objectives are more important than the means used to achieve them.

With the exception of "terrorist," the words in this statement are less likely to evoke an intensely negative response than those in the first statement.

Which statement is preferable? That depends on the audience, the occasion, and the speaker's purpose. Do you want to stir up your listeners' emotions, rally them to some cause? Then select words with more intense connotative meanings. Or are you addressing a controversial issue and trying to seem completely impartial? Then stick with words that touch off less intense reactions. Choosing words skillfully for their denotative and connotative meanings is a crucial part of the speaker's craft.

Using Language Accurately

Using language accurately is as vital to a speaker as using numbers accurately is to an accountant. One student found this out the hard way. In a speech about America's criminal justice system, he referred several times to "criminal *persecution*." What he meant, of course, was "criminal *prosecution*." This one error virtually ruined his speech. As one of his classmates said, "How can I believe what you say about our courts when you don't even know the difference between prosecution and persecution?"

Sometimes inaccuracy results from a misguided attempt to be elegant. This happened to the business manager of a magazine.

Mary Jo Hundt had a special fondness for adding "istic" to the end of a word. Addressing the magazine's editorial staff one day, she said, "We are going to streamline our paperwork to make it more *simplistic*. That's the *modernistic* way to do things. With less paperwork, we'll have more time to devote to the magazine, and that will be *impressionistic* to management."

Mary Jo clearly did not realize that "simplistic" doesn't mean simple or easy but instead refers to *over*simplification on shaky grounds. And "modernistic" refers to a particular style of design, not the general condition of being modern. "Impressionistic,"

Discussion Prompt
Can students think of a time from their experience when using the wrong word created a problem or led to an embarrassing situation?

Words are the tools of the speaker's craft. Good speakers use them accurately and correctly. They also use language that will be clear, vivid, and appropriate for their listeners.

of course, has nothing to do with making an impression on someone; it describes a certain type of art or music. But the editorial staff knew all these things, and they were embarrassed for Mary Jo.

The moral of this story is obvious. Don't use a word unless you are sure of its meaning. If you are not sure, look up the word in a dictionary.

Fortunately, such outright blunders are relatively rare among college students. However, we all commit more subtle errors—especially using one word when another will capture our ideas more precisely. Every word has shades of meaning that distinguish it from every other word. As Mark Twain said, "The difference between the right word and the almost right word is the difference between lightning and the lightning bug."

If you look in a thesaurus, you'll find the following words given as synonyms:

thesaurus
A book of synonyms.

approve	admire
praise	respect

All mean roughly the same thing—to hold a favorable opinion of someone or something. But all these words have different shades of meaning. See if you can fill in the best word to complete each of the sentences below:

1. Everyone in the class decided it was important to _____ each other's right to voice her or his opinion.

2. Often the most encouraging thing you can do for a child is to _____ his or her creative efforts.

3. It is up to the manager to _____ the company's new sales plan.

4. One cannot help but _____ the dedication of Olympic athletes who train for years to capture a gold medal.

The best answers for the four statements are:

1. respect	3. approve
2. praise	4. admire

Each of the words is a little different from the others, and each says something special to listeners.

As you prepare your speeches, ask yourself constantly, "What do I *really* want to say? What do I *really* mean?" Choose words that are precise, exact, accurate. When in doubt, consult a dictionary or thesaurus to make sure you have the best words to express your ideas.

If you have serious aspirations as a speaker, you should work out a systematic plan to improve your vocabulary. Years ago Malcolm X, the famous African-American leader, did this by copying the dictionary, word by word! This method is extreme, and few people would take the time for it. A less arduous plan might be to try using one new word every day—and using the word correctly. The purpose of this is not to learn a lot of big words, but to "learn when certain words should be used, . . . to use the proper word at the proper time."[5]

Related Reading
The experience of Malcolm X illustrates the powerful relationship between language and thought. While in prison, Malcolm realized that the scope of his mind was severely limited by the paucity of his vocabulary, which is why he set about copying the dictionary page by page. The story is vividly recounted in Chapter 11 of *The Autobiography of Malcolm X* (New York: Grove Press, 1965).

Using Language Clearly

Suppose you are standing on a street corner and you see a careless pedestrian about to step into the path of an oncoming car. Do you say, "It would appear from available empirical evidence as if an unsuspecting person is in danger of being struck and injured by an approaching automotive vehicle"? Of course not. You yell, "Look out!"

As many people have discovered, much to their dismay, it is possible to use language accurately without using it clearly. Here is a well-known story that shows how much trouble can be caused by not communicating clearly. A plumber wrote to a government agency to ask whether there was any harm in using hydrochloric acid to clean out drain pipes. The agency replied:

The efficacy of hydrochloric acid is indisputable, but the corrosive effect is incompatible with metallic permanence.

The plumber thanked the agency for approving the use of hydrochloric acid. The agency wrote back, saying:

We cannot assume responsibility for the production of toxic and noxious residue with hydrochloric acid and suggest you use an alternative procedure.

Once more the plumber thanked the agency for its approval. Finally, the agency, alarmed at the prospect of hundreds of ruined drain pipes, called in another scientist. He wrote:

Don't use hydrochloric acid. It eats holes in the pipes!

Remember, people are different. What makes perfect sense to some may be gobbledygook to others. You cannot assume that what is clear to you is clear to your audience. This is particularly true in speechmaking. Listeners, unlike readers, cannot turn to a dictionary or reread an author's words to discover their meaning. A speaker's meaning must be *immediately* comprehensible; it must be so clear that there is virtually no chance of misunderstanding. You can ensure this by using familiar words, by choosing concrete words over abstract words, and by eliminating verbal clutter.

Use Familiar Words

It may seem obvious that familiar words are better than unfamiliar ones. But you would be amazed at how many speakers persist in bombarding listeners with complicated words—usually out of the mistaken belief that such words sound impressive. In truth, filling a speech with long, multisyllabic words only marks the speaker as stuffy and pretentious. Worse, it usually destroys understanding. One of the greatest barriers to clear speech is using big, bloated words where short, sharp ones will do the job better.[6]

Here, for example, are two passages expressing much the same idea. Which is easier to understand?

Class Activity

For a valuable exercise that helps students identify and overcome the ambiguity and imprecision in their language, see Catherine H. Zizik, "Powerspeak: Avoiding Ambiguous Language," in *Selections from the Speech Communication Teacher: 1994–1996*, pp. 44–45, which accompanies *The Art of Public Speaking*.

Class Activity

The second Exercise for Critical Thinking at the end of this chapter asks students to rewrite sentences using clear, familiar words. Divide the class into groups and have each group work on all three sentences. Afterward, ask each group to share its results with the class.

THE INTERNET *Connection*

Looking for just the right word to express your ideas? There's a good chance you will find it at the Merriam-Webster Online Language Center (www.m-w.com). In addition to providing a dictionary and thesaurus, this site contains links to a number of language-related items from Merriam-Webster.

Are you a non-native speaker of English? If so, you will find many helpful resources on the Web. One of the best is Ohio University's Grammar for English Language Learners (www.ohiou.edu/esl/english/grammar/index.html), which provides several dozen language activities, as well as links to sites with additional resources.

> Is this a genuine affirmation that the utterances you anticipate communicating during the time period immediately succeeding the present shall be entirely veracious and devoid of deception, complete in all pertinent minutiae and particularities, and absent of all misleading obfuscation or superfluous and undocumentable specificities, on the authority of your allegiance and fidelity to the supreme deity?

Or,

> Do you swear that the testimony you are about to give shall be the truth, the whole truth, and nothing but the truth, so help you God?

The second passage is the standard oath taken by a witness before testifying in a court of law. It consists of short, simple, familiar words that are easy to comprehend. Its meaning comes across without forcing you to perform complex mental gymnastics. The first passage says essentially the same thing as the second, but is full of stuffy, ostentatious words that make its meaning almost impossible to decipher.

When speaking about technical subjects, you may not be able to avoid unfamiliar words. If this happens, keep the technical terms to a minimum and define clearly those that your audience may not understand. If you work at it, you will almost always be able to translate even the most specialized topic into clear, familiar language.

Here, for instance, are three passages explaining the devastating effects of a pregnant woman's drinking on her unborn child. The first passage is in medical jargon, and it defies comprehension by ordinary listeners:

> Alcohol consumption by the pregnant woman seriously influences the intrauterine milieu and therefore contributes to the morbidity and mortality of children born to these mothers. In regard to the pathophysiology of this syndrome, genetic polymorphism of enzymes for ethanol metabolism may alter fetal susceptibility. There may also be poor microsomal or mitochondrial function or decreased ATP activity.

Teaching Tip
Words that are familiar to native speakers of English may not be familiar to non-native speakers. If you have a fair number of students for whom English is not their primary language, you may profit from the suggestions in Karen Johnson and Paula Golombek, *Public Speaking for Non-Native Speakers: A Handbook for Instructors* (New York: McGraw-Hill, 1996). Written to accompany *The Art of Public Speaking*, this 60-page pamphlet examines the challenges facing ESL students in a public speaking course and provides a wealth of classroom activities and teaching strategies.

Even an educated person without a medical background would have trouble with "pathophysiology" and "polymorphism" and "mitochondrial," much less be able to put them all together.

The second passage represents an attempt to adapt to a nonmedical audience. It is in more familiar language but retains enough obscure words to be difficult:

> The deleterious effects of alcohol on the unborn child are very serious. When a pregnant mother consumes alcohol, the ethanol in the bloodstream easily crosses the placenta from mother to child and invades the amniotic fluid. This can produce a number of abnormal birth syndromes, including central-nervous-system dysfunctions, growth deficiencies, a cluster of facial aberrations, and variable major and minor malformations.

Well-informed listeners could probably figure out "deleterious effects," "central-nervous-system dysfunctions," and "facial aberrations." But these terms don't create a sharp mental image of what the speaker is trying to say. We still need to go one step further away from medical jargon toward ordinary language.

So we come to the third passage, which is utterly clear. It shows what can be done with work, imagination, and a healthy respect for everyday words:

> When the expectant mother drinks, alcohol is absorbed into her bloodstream and distributed throughout her entire body. After a few beers or a couple of martinis, she begins to feel tipsy and decides to sober up. She grabs a cup of coffee, two aspirin, and takes a little nap. After a while she'll be fine.
>
> But while she sleeps, the fetus is surrounded by the same alcoholic content as its mother had. After being drowned in alcohol, the fetus begins to feel the effect. But it can't sober up. It can't grab a cup of coffee. It can't grab a couple of aspirin. For the fetus's liver, the key organ in removing alcohol from the blood, is just not developed. The fetus is literally pickled in alcohol.[7]

This kind of plain talk is what listeners want. You cannot go wrong by following the advice of Winston Churchill to speak in "short, homely words of common usage." If you think big words (or a lot of words) are needed to impress listeners, bear in mind that the Gettysburg Address—considered the finest speech in the English language—contains 271 words, of which 251 have only one or two syllables.

Choose Concrete Words

Concrete words refer to tangible objects—people, places, and things. They differ from abstract words, which refer to general concepts, qualities, or attributes. "Carrot," "pencil," "nose," and "door" are concrete words. "Humility," "science," "progress," and "philosophy" are abstract words.

Of course, few words are completely abstract or concrete. Abstractness and concreteness are relative. "Apple pie" is concrete, but the phrase also has abstract values of patriotism and conventional morals. Usually, the more

Teaching Tip
Using English accurately can pose many challenges for international students and others who are not native speakers of the language. If you have students who are experiencing serious difficulties with English, you may want to refer them to the ESL office or the English for non-native speakers program on your campus. Students with less severe difficulties may profit from books such as *Longman American Idioms Dictionary* (New York: Longman, 2000) and Richard A. Spears, *Common American Phrases in Everyday Contexts*, 2nd ed. (New York: McGraw-Hill, 2002).

concrete words
Words that refer to tangible objects.

abstract words
Words that refer to ideas or concepts.

specific a word, the more concrete it is. Let us say you are talking about golf. Here are several words and phrases you might use:

physical activity — abstract/general

sports

golf

professional golf

Tiger Woods — concrete/specific

Teaching Tip
Be sure to stress the fact that speaking is different from writing in that listeners cannot turn back to a previous page, check a reference work, or pause to meditate upon a speaker's meaning. That meaning must be clear as the words are being uttered. This places great responsibility on the speaker to use language that will be immediately understandable to the audience.

As you move down the list, the words become less abstract and more concrete. You begin with a general concept (physical activity), descend to one type of activity (sports), to a particular sport (golf), to a division of that sport (professional golf), to one specific professional golfer (Tiger Woods).

The more abstract a word, the more ambiguous it will be. Although abstract words are necessary to express certain kinds of ideas, they are much easier to misinterpret than are concrete words. Also, concrete words are much more likely to claim your listeners' attention. Suppose you make a speech about fire ants, which have long plagued the South and are now attacking western states. Here are two ways you could approach the subject—one featuring abstract words, the other concrete words:

Abstract Words

Fire ants have been a problem ever since they arrived in the United States. They have spread across the South and now threaten various parts of the West as well. This is a serious problem because fire ants are highly aggressive. There have even been human casualties from fire ant stings.

Concrete Words

Cross-Reference
See Chapter 14 for discussion of how to use description, comparison, and contrast to avoid abstractions in informative speeches.

Since fire ants came here from South America sometime before World War II, they have spread like a biblical plague across 11 states from Florida to Texas. Now they are invading New Mexico, Arizona, and California. Fire ants attack in swarms and they will climb any foot that is left in the wrong spot for a few seconds. They have even turned up indoors, in clothes hampers, beds, and closets. Fortunately, fewer than 1 percent of people who are stung have to see a doctor, but toddlers who have fallen on fire ant mounds have sometimes died from stings, as have highly allergic adults.[8]

Notice how much more persuasive the second version is. A speech dominated by concrete words will almost always be clearer, more interesting, and easier to recall than one dominated by abstract words.

Eliminate Clutter

Cluttered speech has become a national epidemic. Whatever happened to such simple words as "before," "if," and "now"? When last seen they were being routed by their cluttered counterparts—"prior to," "in the eventuality of," and "at this point in time." By the same token, why can't weather forecasters say, "It's raining," instead of saying, "It appears as if we are currently experiencing precipitation activity"? And why can't politicians say, "We have a crisis," instead of saying, "We are facing a difficult crisis situation that will be troublesome to successfully resolve"?

This type of clutter is deadly to clear, compelling speech. It forces listeners to hack through a tangle of words to discover the meaning. When you make a speech, keep your language lean and lively. Beware of using several words where one or two will do. Avoid flabby phrases. Let your ideas emerge sharply and firmly. Above all, watch out for redundant adjectives and adverbs. Inexperienced speakers (and writers) tend to string together two or three synonymous adjectives, such as "a learned and educated person," or "a hot, steamy, torrid day."

Here is part of a student speech that has been revised to eliminate clutter:

clutter
Discourse that takes many more words than are necessary to express an idea.

Sitting Bull was one of the most important ~~and significant of all~~ Native American leaders.

He was born in ~~the year of~~ 1831 near Grand River, in ~~an area that is now part of the~~ *present-day*

~~state of~~ South Dakota. A fearless ~~and courageous~~ warrior, he ~~ended up being~~ *was* elected

chief of the Hunkpapa Sioux in 1867. In the following years, he also attracted a large

~~and numerous~~ following among the ~~tribes of the~~ Cheyenne and Arapaho. He is best

known ~~to people in this day and age~~ *today* for his ~~instrumental~~ role in ~~helping to lead the~~ *defeating*

~~defeat of~~ General Custer at the Battle of Little Big Horn in 1876. Although eventually

~~required against his will~~ *forced* to live ~~his life~~ on the Standing Rock Reservation in South Dakota,

he never surrendered ~~to anyone~~ his dignity or his ~~personal~~ devotion to the Sioux way

of life.

Notice how much cleaner and easier to follow the revised version is. No longer are the speaker's ideas hidden in a thicket of wasted words.

This kind of pruning is easy once you get the knack of it. The hardest part—and it is often very hard—is recognizing clutter for what it is and then forcing yourself to throw away the unnecessary words. Watch for clutter when you write your speech outlines. Be prepared to revise the outline until your ideas emerge as clearly and crisply as possible. As with revising an essay or a term paper, this will take extra time. But if you keep at it, you will become a much more effective speaker—and writer.

You can also help eliminate clutter by practicing your speeches with a digital recorder. As you play the speech back, keep an ear out not just for flabby phrases but for verbal fillers such as "you know," "like," and "really." Practice delivering the speech again, this time making a special effort to trim it of wasted or distracting words. At first you may feel awkward and unnatural because you are forcing yourself to break old habits. But if

Class Activity
The sixth and seventh Additional Exercises for Critical Thinking on pp. 241–244 of the *Instructor's Manual* give students practice in recognizing and eliminating verbal clutter. For ease of classroom discussion, both exercises are included in the binder of full-color overhead transparencies that accompanies *The Art of Public Speaking*.

Related Reading
Robert Hartwell Fiske and Richard Lederer, *The Dictionary of Concise Writing: 10,000 Alternatives to Wordy Phrases* (Oak Park, IL: Marion Street Press, 2002).

you keep at it, you will gradually develop a new habit of speaking naturally without all that clutter. This will not only make you a better public speaker, but it will help you present ideas more effectively in meetings, conversations, and group discussions.

Using Language Vividly

Just as you can be accurate without being clear, so you can be both accurate and clear without being interesting. Here, for example, is how Martin Luther King *might have* phrased part of his great "I Have a Dream" speech:

> Turning back is something we cannot do. We must continue to work against police brutality, segregated housing, disfranchisement, and alienation. Only when these problems are solved will we be satisfied.

Class Activity
Have students analyze Martin Luther King's "I Have a Dream" as a homework assignment—as directed in the fourth Exercise for Critical Thinking at the end of this chapter. For full discussion of King's speech and of this activity, see the *Instructor's Manual*, pp. 234–237. The text of King's speech is reprinted in the appendix of sample speeches that follows Chapter 18.

Here is what King *actually* said:

> We cannot turn back. There are those who ask the devotees of civil rights, "When will you be satisfied?" We can never be satisfied as long as the Negro is the victim of the unspeakable horrors of police brutality. We can never be satisfied as long as our bodies, heavy with the fatigue of travel, cannot gain lodging in the motels of the highways and the hotels of the cities. . . . We cannot be satisfied as long as a Negro in Mississippi cannot vote and a Negro in New York believes he has nothing for which to vote. No, no, we are not satisfied, and we will not be satisfied until justice rolls down like waters and righteousness like a mighty stream.

Much more stirring, isn't it? If you want to move people with your speeches, use moving language. Dull, dreary words make for dull, dreary speeches. Bring your speeches to life by using vivid, animated language. Although there are several ways to do this, here are two of the most important—imagery and rhythm.

Imagery

One sign of a good novelist is the ability to create word pictures that get you totally involved with a story. These word pictures let you "see" the haunted house, or "feel" the bite of the snow against your face, or "hear" the birds chirping on a warm spring morning, or "smell" the bacon cooking over an open campfire, or "taste" the hot enchiladas at a Mexican restaurant.

imagery
The use of vivid language to create mental images of objects, actions, or ideas.

Speakers can use imagery in much the same way to make their ideas come alive. Three ways to generate imagery are by using concrete words, simile, and metaphor.

Concrete Words

As we saw earlier in this chapter, choosing concrete words over abstract words is one way to enhance the clarity of your speeches. Concrete words

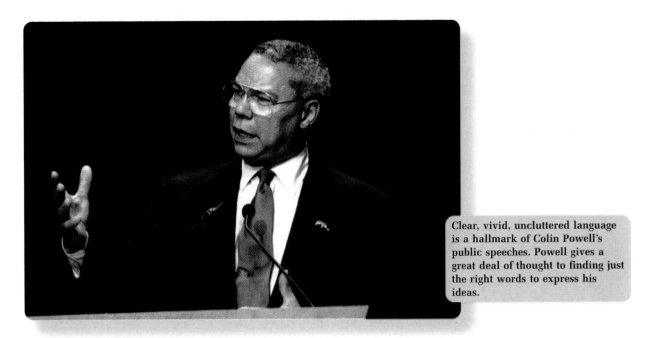

Clear, vivid, uncluttered language is a hallmark of Colin Powell's public speeches. Powell gives a great deal of thought to finding just the right words to express his ideas.

are also the key to effective imagery. Consider the following excerpt from Ronald Reagan's famous address commemorating the 40th anniversary of D-Day. Speaking at the scene of the battle, Reagan dramatically recounted the heroism of the U.S. Rangers who scaled the cliffs at Pointe du Hoc to help free Europe from Hitler's stranglehold:

> We stand on a lonely, windswept point on the northern shore of France. The air is soft, but 40 years ago at this moment, the air was dense with smoke and the cries of men, and the air was filled with the crack of rifle fire and the roar of cannon.
>
> At dawn, on the morning of the 6th of June, 1944, 225 Rangers jumped off the British landing craft and ran to the bottom of these cliffs. . . . The Rangers looked up and saw the enemy soldiers—at the edge of the cliffs shooting down at them with machine guns and throwing grenades. And the American Rangers began to climb. They shot rope ladders over the face of these cliffs and began to pull themselves up.
>
> When one Ranger fell, another would take his place. When one rope was cut, a Ranger would grab another and begin his climb again. They climbed, shot back, and held their footing. Soon, one by one, the Rangers pulled themselves over the top, and in seizing the firm land at the top of these cliffs, they began to seize back the continent of Europe.

View this excerpt from Ronald Reagan's speech at Pointe du Hoc.

CD 1: VIDEO 11.1

For the full text of Reagan's speech, log on to the Top 100 American Speeches of the 20th Century at www.mhhe.com/lucastop100.

ONLINE LEARNING CENTER

Concrete words call up mental impressions of sights, sounds, touch, smell, and taste. In the speech just quoted, we do not merely learn that the U.S. Rangers helped win the battle of D-Day. We visualize the Rangers landing at the foot of the cliffs. We see them fighting their way up the cliffs in the face of enemy grenades and machine guns. We hear the crack of rifle fire and the cries of the soldiers. The concrete words create images of sights and sounds, feelings and emotions that pull us irresistibly into the speech.

Simile

simile
An explicit comparison, introduced with the word "like" or "as," between things that are essentially different yet have something in common.

Another way to create imagery is through the use of simile. Simile is an explicit comparison between things that are essentially different yet have something in common. It always contains the words "like" or "as." Here are some examples from student speeches:

Walking into my grandparents' home when I was a child was like being wrapped in a giant security blanket.

Air pollution is eating away at the monuments in Washington, D.C., like a giant Alka-Seltzer tablet.

These are bright, fresh similes that clarify and vitalize ideas. Some similes, however, have become stale through overuse. Here are a few:

fresh as a daisy	hungry as a bear
fit as a fiddle	busy as a bee
strong as an ox	big as a mountain
stubborn as a mule	happy as a lark
blind as a bat	light as a feather

cliché
A trite or overused expression.

Such *clichés* are fine in everyday conversation, but you should avoid them in speechmaking. Otherwise, you are likely to be "dull as dishwater" and to find your audience "sleeping like a log"!

Metaphor

You can also use metaphor to create imagery in your speeches. Metaphor is an implicit comparison between things that are essentially different yet have something in common. Unlike simile, metaphor does not contain the words "like" or "as." For example:

America's cities are the windows through which the world looks at American society. (Henry Cisneros)

With globalization, the same sea washes all of humankind. We are all in the same boat. There are no safe islands. (Kofi Annan)

metaphor
An implicit comparison, not introduced with the word "like" or "as," between two things that are essentially different yet have something in common.

These are both brief metaphors. Sometimes, however, a speaker will develop a longer metaphor. Here is an excellent example, from a speech delivered in China's 2002 national English-language speech competition. The speaker is Zhang Jiexuan, a student at Fudan University in Shanghai:

Globalization should not be a huge melting pot into which people of uniqueness go only to come out all the same. It should not be a process in which countries gradually lose their identities.

To my understanding, globalization should be a grand orchestra—an orchestra in which every player has his particular position and function; an orchestra where the uniqueness of every member is so cherished that anyone's role is irreplaceable by anyone else; an orchestra based on the joint contribution of every participant, which can and will produce the most beautiful symphony of tomorrow's peace and prosperity.[9]

View this excerpt from Zhang Jiexuan's speech on globalization.

CD 1: VIDEO 11.2

The subject of this metaphor—globalization—is the same as the subject of the metaphor by U.N. Secretary General Kofi Annan quoted earlier in this section. Though different in length, both metaphors convey the speaker's thoughts vividly and memorably. When used effectively, metaphor—like simile—is an excellent way to bring color to a speech, to make abstract ideas concrete, to clarify the unknown, and to express feelings and emotions.[10]

Rhythm

Language has a rhythm created by the choice and arrangement of words. Sometimes the appeal of a statement depends almost entirely on its rhythm—as in this children's verse:

rhythm
The pattern of sound in a speech created by the choice and arrangement of words.

> Pease porridge hot,
>   Pease porridge cold,
> Pease porridge in the pot,
>   Nine days old.

There is little meaning here. The appeal comes from the combination of sounds, which gives the passage an almost musical cadence.[11]

Speakers, like poets, sometimes seek to exploit the rhythm of language. By catching up their listeners in an arresting string of sounds, speakers can enhance the impact of their words—and therefore of their ideas. Winston Churchill was a master at this. Here is a passage from one of his famous speeches during World War II. To emphasize its cadence, the passage has been printed as if it were poetry rather than prose:

> We cannot tell what the course
>   of this fell war will be
> as it spreads remorseless
>   through ever-wider regions.
> We know it will be hard;
>   we expect it will be long.
> We cannot predict or measure
>   its episodes or its tribulations. . . .
> We cannot yet see
>   how deliverance will come,
> or when it will come.
>   But nothing is more certain
> than that every trace of Hitler's footsteps,
>   every stain of his infected and corroding fingers,
> will be sponged and purged
>   and, if need be,
> blasted from the surface of the earth.[12]

View this excerpt from Winston Churchill's speech of June 12, 1941.

CD 1: VIDEO 11.3

The impact of the passage was heightened by Churchill's superb delivery; but even by themselves the words take on an emphatic rhythm that reinforces the message. You can see why one observer said that Churchill "mobilized the English language and sent it into battle."[13]

A speech, however, is not a poem. You should never emphasize sound and rhythm at the expense of meaning. The aim is to think about ways you can use the rhythm and flow of language to enhance your meaning. Although you may never have paid much conscious attention to this subject, you can develop an ear for vocal rhythms by study and practice. What's more, you can easily begin now to use four basic stylistic devices employed by Churchill and other fine speakers to improve the rhythm of their prose.

Parallelism

parallelism
The similar arrangement of a pair or series of related words, phrases, or sentences.

The first device is parallelism—the similar arrangement of a pair or series of related words, phrases, or sentences. For example:

> *Rich and poor, intelligent and ignorant, wise and foolish, virtuous and vicious, man and woman*—it is ever the same, each soul must depend wholly on itself. (Elizabeth Cady Stanton)

> *We defeated* communism. *We defeated* fascism. *We defeated them on the field of* battle, and *we defeated them on the field of* ideas. (Colin Powell)

The effects of parallelism are perhaps best illustrated by seeing what happens when it is absent. For instance, compare this statement:

> I speak as a Republican. I speak as a woman. I speak as a United States Senator. I speak as an American. (Margaret Chase Smith)

with this one:

> I speak as a Republican. I speak as a woman. I speak as a United States Senator. And I am also addressing you as an American.

Class Activity
For an assignment that gives students practice in the use of vivid language, see Susan C. Pendleton, "Using Figurative Language in Persuasive Speeches," in *Selections from the Speech Communication Teacher: 1996–1999*, pp. 64–65, which accompanies *The Art of Public Speaking*.

The first statement is clear, consistent, and compelling. The second is not. By violating the principle of parallel structure, its final sentence ("And I am also addressing you as an American") destroys the progression begun by the preceding three sentences ("I speak as a Republican. I speak as a woman. I speak as a United States Senator"). It thereby turns a strong, lucid, harmonious statement into one that is fuzzy and jarring.

Repetition

repetition
Reiteration of the same word or set of words at the beginning or end of successive clauses or sentences.

The second device you can use to lend rhythm to your speeches is repetition. This means repeating the same word or set of words at the beginning or end of successive clauses or sentences. For example:

> *When you see your* street, *see my* street. *When you see your* house, *see my* house. *When you see your* children, *see my* children. (Whitney Young, Jr.)

> *We will not* tire, *we will not* falter, and *we will not* fail. (George W. Bush)

As you can see, repetition usually results in parallelism. In addition to building a strong cadence, it also unifies a sequence of ideas, emphasizes an idea by stating it more than once, and helps create a strong emotional effect.

Alliteration

The third device you can use to enhance the rhythm of your speeches is alliteration. The most common method of alliteration is repeating the initial consonant sound of close or adjoining words. For example:

> *Peace* is essential for *progress*, but *progress* is no less essential for *peace*. (Liaquat Ali Khan)

> In a nation founded on the promise of human dignity, our colleges, our communities, our country should challenge hatred wherever we find it. (Hillary Rodham Clinton)

By highlighting the sounds of words, alliteration catches the attention of listeners and can make ideas easier to remember. Used sparingly, it is a marvelous way to spruce up your speeches. Used to excess, however, it can be laughable and draw too much attention, so that listeners get more involved in listening for the next alliteration than in absorbing the content of the speech.

Antithesis

Finally, you might try using antithesis—the juxtaposition of contrasting ideas, usually in parallel structure. For example:

> Ask not what your country can do for you; ask what you can do for your country. (John F. Kennedy)

> Your success as a family, our success as a society, depends not on what happens at the White House, but on what happens inside your house. (Barbara Bush)

Antithesis has long been a favorite device of accomplished speakers. Because it nearly always produces a neatly turned phrase, it is a fine way to give your speeches a special touch of class.

You may be thinking that imagery and rhythm are fine for famous people but are too fancy for ordinary speeches like yours. This is not true. Imagery and rhythm are easy to use and can enliven even the most routine of speeches. As an example, take a look at the following excerpt from one student's speech about her grandparents and other survivors of the Holocaust:

> When my grandparents are gone, I will continue to tell their story. I will tell my children about the men and women who were murdered for no cause. . . . And I hope that you, too, will tell stories. For as the Holocaust survivor and writer Elie Wiesel once said, "Not to transmit an experience is to betray it."
>
> To the millions who died in the Holocaust, lie peacefully in your graves, for you have not been forgotten.

alliteration
Repetition of the initial consonant sound of close or adjoining words.

antithesis
The juxtaposition of contrasting ideas, usually in parallel structure.

View the ending of Andrea Besikof, "The Survivors."

CD 1: VIDEO CLIP 11.4

> To the survivors of the Holocaust, rest assured that we have listened to your stories, have learned by your examples, and we, too, are willing to fight for freedom and peace.
>
> May no person around the globe again fall to his or her death murmuring, "How could this happen."

This is vivid, moving language. The imagery is sharp and poignant, the rhythm strong and insistent. Think of how you can do similar things in your own speeches.

Using Language Appropriately

Here is part of a famous oration given by John Hancock in 1774, during the American Revolution. Speaking of the British soldiers who killed five Americans in the Boston Massacre, Hancock exclaimed:

> Ye dark designing knaves, ye murderers, parricides! How dare you tread upon the earth, which has drank in the blood of slaughtered innocents shed by your wicked hands? How dare you breathe that air which wafted to the ear of heaven the groans of those who fell a sacrifice to your accursed ambition? . . . Tell me, ye bloody butchers, ye villains high and low, ye wretches . . . do you not feel the goads and stings of conscious guilt pierce through your savage bosoms?[14]

Speech Assignment
Over the years, I have used a commemorative speech assignment with great success to focus on the devices for enhancing clarity and vividness explained in this chapter. Indeed, students often remark that this is their favorite speech of the entire course. For discussion of the commemorative speech as an address of praise or celebration, see Chapter 17. For sample speeches, see Part V of the *Instructor's Manual*. The commemorative speech assignment is described briefly on p. 35 of the *Manual*.

This is certainly vivid language—and Hancock's audience loved it. But can you imagine speaking the same way today? In addition to being accurate, clear, and vivid, language should be appropriate—to the occasion, to the audience, to the topic, and to the speaker.

Appropriateness to the Occasion

Language that is appropriate for some occasions may not be appropriate for others. "There is a time for dialect, a place for slang, an occasion for literary form. What is correct on the sports page is out of place on the op-ed page; what is with-it on the street may well be without it in the classroom."[15] As a simple example, a coach might address the football team as "you guys" (or worse!), whereas the speaker in a more formal situation would begin with "distinguished guests." Try reversing these two situations, and see how ridiculous it becomes. It's only common sense to adjust your language to different occasions.

Appropriateness to the Audience

Appropriateness also depends on the audience. If you keep this in mind, it will help you greatly when dealing with technical or scientific topics. When addressing an audience of physicians, you might use the word "parotitis" to refer to a viral disease marked by the swelling of the parotid glands. Your audience would know just what you meant. But when talking to a nonmedical audience, such as your classmates, a word like "parotitis" would not be appropriate. The appropriate word in this case would be "mumps."

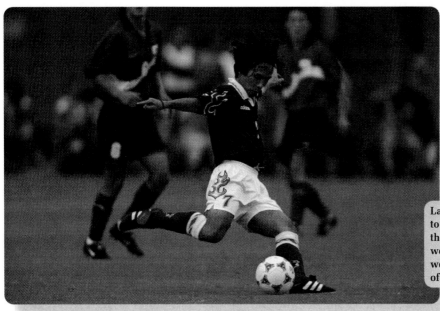

Language needs to be appropriate to a speaker's topic, as well as to the audience. A speech on soccer would use more action-oriented words than a speech about theories of psychology.

You should be especially careful to avoid language that might offend your audience. If you were a stand-up comedian, off-color humor or profanity might be appropriate in a nightclub routine, but most listeners would find it offensive in a formal public speech. Remember, speakers are expected to elevate and polish their language when addressing an audience.

They are also expected to avoid name-calling and other forms of abusive language. As we saw in Chapter 2, such language is ethically suspect because it demeans the basic human worth of the people against whom it is directed. In addition, most listeners take offense at statements that denounce people on the basis of their religious beliefs or ethnic heritage. If you include such statements in your speeches, you will not only violate an important ethical responsibility, but almost surely alienate a good portion of your audience.

Of course, you cannot always be sure of how listeners will respond to what you say. As a general rule, bend over backward to avoid language that may confuse or offend your listeners. When it comes to appropriateness, you will seldom go wrong by erring on the side of caution. (Put simply, "erring on the side of caution" means "when in doubt—don't.")

Appropriateness to the Topic

Language should also be appropriate to the topic. You would not use metaphor, antithesis, and alliteration when explaining how to change a bicycle tire or how to perform routine maintenance on a car. But you might use all three in a speech celebrating the genius of Leonardo da Vinci or

Class Activity

Have the class pay special attention to their classmates' style during the next round of speeches. Afterward, have the class select three or four speeches that were particularly effective in their use of language. What steps did the speakers take to make their ideas clear and lively for the audience?

honoring the crew of the space shuttle *Columbia*. The first two topics call for straightforward description and explanation. The latter two call for special language skills to evoke emotion, admiration, and appreciation.

Appropriateness to the Speaker

No matter what the occasion, audience, or topic, language should also be appropriate to the speaker. Imagine the effect if Dick Cheney tried to adopt the religious imagery and rhythmical cadence of Jesse Jackson. The results would be comical. Every public speaker develops his or her own language style.

"Terrific," you may be thinking. "I have my own style too. I feel more comfortable using abstract words, slang, and technical jargon. That's just me. It's *my* way of speaking." But to say that language should be appropriate to the speaker does not justify ignoring the other needs for appropriateness. There is a difference between one's everyday style and one's *developed* style as a public speaker. Accomplished speakers have developed their speaking styles over many years of trial, error, and practice. They have *worked* at using language effectively.

You can do the same if you become language-conscious. One way to develop this consciousness is to read and listen to the speeches of effective speakers, whether they are current public figures such as Colin Powell and Hillary Clinton or historical figures such as Barbara Jordan and Martin Luther King. Study their techniques for achieving accuracy, clarity, and vividness, and try to adapt those techniques to your own speeches. But do not try to "become" someone else when you speak. Learn from other speakers, blend what you learn into your own language style, and seek to become the best possible you.

Teaching Tip
Mary Fisher's "A Whisper of AIDS" is one of the most eloquent public addresses of recent years. Have students analyze how Fisher uses the resources of language discussed in this chapter to sharpen her message and bring it home to listeners. The text of Fisher's speech is printed in the appendix of sample speeches that follows Chapter 18, and a video of it is available on *Speaking of Diversity: A Videotape Supplement to The Art of Public Speaking*. For full discussion of the speech, see the *Instructor's Manual*, pp. 335–339.

A Note on Inclusive Language

"When a soldier goes to war, he should have the best possible equipment."

"Improving education has always been a high priority for Negro leaders."

"Any discrimination against crippled people is completely unacceptable."

Forty years ago, most people in the United States who heard these statements in a speech would not have given them a second thought. Today the same statements would raise more than a few eyebrows—and perhaps tempers—in almost any audience. Here's why:

Soldiers in the U.S. military include women as well as men. To say, "When a soldier goes to war, he should have the best possible equipment," ignores the existence of female soldiers. It can also be interpreted as meaning that only male soldiers should go to war with the finest possible equipment—hardly a comforting thought to female soldiers or their loved ones!

The word "Negro" has fallen out of common usage and has changed in meaning. While this term was considered acceptable through the 1960s and was used by civil rights leaders such as Martin Luther King, it is now considered offensive. Today the preferred terms are "black" and "African American."

Historically "crippled" was used as a word of ridicule and disparagement. It was replaced some years ago by "handicapped," which has itself been supplanted by "people with disabilities." This last phrase is preferable because it is not judgmental and includes the full range of functional limitations that interfere with a person's ability to see, walk, hear, or learn.

For centuries, the English language has contained countless words and phrases that favor men and convey stereotyped, misleading, or demeaning views of women and minority groups. Today that is changing—not as fast, perhaps, as some people might like, and doubtless too fast for other people—but changing nonetheless. As the United States has become more diverse, our language has evolved to reflect that diversity. Regardless of the situation, audiences today expect public speakers to use inclusive language that is respectful of the different groups that make up American society.

We saw in Chapter 2 that name-calling and other forms of abusive language is ethically suspect because it demeans the dignity of the individuals or groups being attacked and can undermine the right of all groups in a democratic society to be fairly heard. But using inclusive language involves more than avoiding name-calling. Even speakers with the best of intentions can inadvertently use language that stereotypes, demeans, or patronizes people on the basis of gender, race, religion, disabilities, sexual orientation, or other factors.

In addition to its ethical implications, using inclusive language is important as a matter of accuracy. To speak as if all soldiers (or doctors, or lawyers, or firefighters) are men is incorrect—just as it is erroneous to speak as if all secretaries, nurses, or flight attendants are women. Being accurate in such matters is no less important than being accurate in other aspects of your language.

As we saw in Chapter 5, conveying respect for various groups in society is also a vital part of being an audience-centered public speaker. Even if you do not care about inclusive language yourself, you can be sure that almost any audience you address will contain people who do care and who will be upset if you use language that does not reflect a spirit of inclusiveness. This is one reason why governments, businesses, and professional groups invest millions of dollars each year in workshops that help employees and associates understand the importance of respecting diversity and of reflecting that respect in their language.

When editors, linguists, social advocates, and others first proposed inclusive alternatives to traditional words and phrases, some people reacted with shock and indignation. You cannot change the language, they said, without destroying its beauty and purity. But the English language has been changing for centuries—just as it will continue to change in the future. Today a number of principles for inclusive language have become so widespread that no aspiring speaker (or writer) can afford to ignore them. Let's look at several of these principles.

inclusive language
Language that does not stereotype, demean, or patronize people on the basis of gender, race, religion, disability, sexual orientation, or other factors.

Class Activity
For two excellent activities that bring home to students the importance of gender issues in language, see Terilyn Goins Phillips, "Introducing Gender-Biased Language: Much Ado About Something," and Kathryn Sue Young, "Proving the Importance of Inclusive Language in the Basic Course," in *Selections From the Speech Communication Teacher: 1996–1999*, pp. 65–67, which accompanies *The Art of Public Speaking*.

Avoid the Generic "He"

Ineffective: Each time a surgeon walks into the operating room, *he* risks being sued for malpractice.

More Effective: Each time a surgeon walks into the operating room, *she or he* risks being sued for malpractice.

generic "he"
The use of "he" to refer to both women and men.

Often, a more graceful alternative is to pluralize. For example:

More Effective: Whenever surgeons walk into the operating room, *they* risk being sued for malpractice.

Avoid the Use of "Man" When Referring to Both Men and Women

Ineffective: If a large comet struck the Earth, it could destroy all of mankind.

More Effective: If a large comet struck the Earth, it could destroy all human life.

Ineffective: No matter how popular cats have become, the dog is still man's best friend.

More Effective: No matter how popular cats have become, the dog is still a person's best friend.

Avoid Stereotyping Jobs and Social Roles by Gender

Ineffective: Being a small businessman in the current economic climate is not easy.

More Effective: Being a small businessperson in the current economic climate is not easy.

Sometimes you can solve this problem with a simple twist in sentence construction. For example:

More Effective: Owning a small business is not easy in the current economic climate.

Avoid Identifying Personal Traits That Are Unrelated to the Topic

Ineffective: Patrick Spiegel, a stay-at-home father, proposed a bike path plan to the City Council.

More Effective: Patrick Spiegel proposed a bike path plan to the City Council.

Ineffective: Condoleezza Rice, an African-American woman, has had a major impact on U.S. foreign policy.

More Effective: Condoleezza Rice has had a major impact on U.S. foreign policy.

Use Names That Groups Use to Identify Themselves

One of the most fundamental ways of showing respect for others is to refer to them by the names they use to identify themselves and to avoid names they consider offensive.[16]

Related Reading
There are many excellent works on sexist language and its social impact. For two that approach the subject from a communication-oriented perspective, see Diana K. Ivy and Phil Backlund, *Exploring GenderSpeak: Personal Effectiveness in Gender Communication,* 2nd ed. (New York: McGraw-Hill, 2000), and Julia T. Wood, *Gendered Lives: Communication, Gender, and Culture,* 5th ed. (Belmont, CA: Wadsworth, 2003).

Ineffective:	Despite progress in recent years, homosexuals still face many forms of discrimination.
More Effective:	Despite progress in recent years, lesbians and gay men still face many forms of discrimination.
Ineffective:	Michelle Kwan is one of many Orientals who have had a major impact on U.S. life.
More Effective:	Michelle Kwan is one of many Asians who have had a major impact on U.S. life.
Most Effective:	Michelle Kwan is one of many Chinese Americans who have had a major impact on U.S. life.

As this last example suggests, there is currently a trend away from broad words such as "Asian" to more precise terms that do not lump people of distinct nationalities and cultures under one label. Until very recently, "Hispanic" was considered the correct way to designate someone from Latin America, which includes Mexico, Central America, South America, Cuba, and the Carribean Islands. Today, however, many Mexican Americans wish to be called "Chicano" or "Chicana," while people from other Latin American countries frequently prefer the terms "Latino" or "Latina."

The use of specific identifiers is often preferred by other groups as well. For example:

Ineffective:	Indian code talkers were vital to the U.S. armed forces during World War II.
More Effective:	Native American code talkers were vital to the U.S. armed forces during World War II.
Most Effective:	Navajo code talkers were vital to the U.S. armed forces during World War II.

Like many other aspects of American life, questions of inclusive language can sometimes be confusing. Language is alive and constantly evolving, so what is considered inclusive at one point in time may shift down the road. If you do a lot of public speaking (or writing), you should consider purchasing a guidebook such as Rosalie Maggio's *Talking About People: A Guide to Fair and Accurate Language.* Using inclusive and respectful language is not a matter of political correctness, but it is a matter of P.C.—personal courtesy.[17]

Related Reading
Rosalie Maggio, *Talking About People: A Guide to Fair and Accurate Language* (Phoenix, AZ: Oryx Press, 1997) remains the best work on its subject and provides a wealth of examples that can be used for class discussion. Another valuable work for promoting class discussion is Philip H. Herbst, *The Color of Words: An Encyclopaedic Dictionary of Ethnic Bias in the United States* (Yarmouth, ME: Intercultural Press, 1997).

Summary

Of all human creations, language may be the most remarkable. Through language we share experiences, formulate values, exchange ideas, transmit knowledge, and sustain culture. Indeed, language is vital to thinking itself.

Contrary to popular belief, language does not simply mirror reality, but helps create our sense of reality by giving meaning to events.

Good speakers have respect for language and how it works. Words are the tools of a speaker's craft. They have special uses, just like the tools of any other profession. As a speaker, you should be aware of the meanings of words and know how to use language accurately, clearly, vividly, and appropriately.

Words have two kinds of meanings—denotative and connotative. Denotative meaning is precise, literal, and objective. One way to think of a word's denotative meaning is as its dictionary definition. Connotative meaning is more variable, figurative, and subjective. It is whatever the word suggests or implies. Connotative meaning includes all the feelings, associations, and emotions that a word touches off in different people.

Using language accurately is as vital to a speaker as using numbers accurately is to an accountant. Never use a word unless you are sure of its meaning. If you are not sure, look up the word in a dictionary. As you prepare your speeches, ask yourself constantly, "What do I *really* want to say? What do I *really* mean?" Choose words that are precise and accurate.

Using language clearly allows listeners to grasp your meaning immediately. You can ensure this by using words that are known to the average person and require no specialized background; by choosing concrete words in preference to more abstract ones; and by eliminating verbal clutter.

Using language vividly helps bring your speech to life. One way to make your language more vivid is through imagery, or the creation of word pictures. You can develop imagery by using concrete language, simile, and metaphor. Simile is an explicit comparison between things that are essentially different yet have something in common; it always contains the words "like" or "as." Metaphor is an implicit comparison between things that are different yet have something in common; it does not contain the words "like" or "as."

Another way to make your speeches vivid is by exploiting the rhythm of language. Four devices for creating rhythm are parallelism, repetition, alliteration, and antithesis. Parallelism is the similar arrangement of a pair or series of related words, phrases, or sentences. Repetition is the use of the same word or set of words at the beginning or end of successive clauses or sentences. Alliteration is the repetition of the initial consonant sounds of close or adjoining words. Antithesis is the juxtaposition of contrasting ideas, usually in parallel structure.

Using language appropriately means adapting to the particular occasion, audience, and topic at hand. It also means developing your own language style instead of trying to copy someone else's. If your language is appropriate in all respects, your speech is much more likely to succeed.

You will also be more likely to succeed if you use inclusive language in your speeches. Although the subject of inclusive language is complex and controversial, a number of inclusive usages have become so widely accepted that no aspiring speaker can afford to ignore them. They include avoiding the generic "he," dropping the use of "man" when referring to both men and women, refraining from stereotyping jobs and social roles by gender, avoiding identifying personal traits that are unrelated to the topic, and using names that groups use to identify themselves.

Key Terms

Review these terms by doing the Chapter 11 crossword puzzle at www.mhhe.com/lucas8.

ONLINE LEARNING CENTER

denotative meaning (268)

connotative meaning (268)

thesaurus (270)

concrete words (273)

abstract words (273)

clutter (275)

imagery (276)

simile (278)

cliché (278)

metaphor (278)

rhythm (279)

parallelism (280)

repetition (280)

alliteration (281)

antithesis (281)

inclusive language (285)

generic "he" (285)

Review Questions

After reading this chapter, you should be able to answer the following questions:

1. How does language help shape our sense of reality?

2. What is the difference between denotative and connotative meaning? How might you use each to convey your message most effectively?

3. What are the four criteria for using language effectively in your speeches?

4. What are three things you should do to use language clearly in your speeches?

5. What are two ways to bring your speeches to life with vivid, animated language?

6. What does it mean to say you should use language appropriately in your speeches?

7. Why is it important for a public speaker to use inclusive language? What are five usages of inclusive language which have become so widely accepted that no speaker can afford to ignore them?

For further review, go to the Study Questions for this chapter.

CD 1: STUDY QUESTIONS

Exercises for Critical Thinking

1. Arrange each of the sequences below in order, from the most abstract word to the most concrete word.

   a. housing complex, building, dining room, structure, apartment

   b. *Mona Lisa,* art, painting, creative activity, portrait

   c. automobile, vehicle, Ferrari, transportation, sports car

2. Rewrite each of the following sentences using clear, familiar words.

   a. My employment objective is to attain a position of maximum financial reward.

   b. All professors at this school are expected to achieve high standards of excellence in their instructional duties.

   c. In the eventuality of a fire, it is imperative that all persons evacuate the building without undue delay.

Cross-Reference

For discussion of the Exercises for Critical Thinking, see the *Instructor's Manual,* pp. 233–237. For additional exercises, check the *Instructor's Manual,* pp. 238–244, as well as the five volumes of *Selections from the Speech Communication Teacher* that accompany *The Art of Public Speaking.*

3. Each of the statements below uses one or more of the following stylistic devices: metaphor, simile, parallelism, repetition, alliteration, antithesis. Identify the device (or devices) used in each statement.

   a. "We are a people in a quandary about the present. We are a people in search of our future. We are a people in search of a national community." (Barbara Jordan)

   b. "The vice presidency is the sand trap of American politics. It's near the prize, and designed to be limiting." (Howard Fineman)

   c. "We should not demean our democracy with the politics of distraction, denial, and despair." (Al Gore)

   d. "America is not like a blanket—one piece of unbroken cloth, the same color, the same texture, the same size. America is more like a quilt—many patches, many sizes, and woven and held together by a common thread." (Jesse Jackson)

4. Analyze Martin Luther King's "I Have a Dream" in the appendix of sample speeches that follows Chapter 18. Identify the methods King uses to make his language clear, vivid, and appropriate. Look particularly at King's use of familiar words, concrete words, imagery, and rhythm.

Applying the POWER of PUBLIC SPEAKING

Cross-Reference

For discussion of this Applying the Power of Public Speaking scenario, see the *Instructor's Manual,* p. 237.

Since graduating from college, you have developed a successful business that is located near the campus. As part of its plan to involve more alumni and community members in college affairs, the school has asked you to speak with new students during registration week for the fall term. In the opening section of your speech, you want the audience to feel what you felt the first few days you were on campus as a new student. The best strategy, you decide, is to present two or three similes that complete the sentence, "Beginning college is like . . ." Write your similes.

Notes

1. For two highly readable works on the natural evolution of language, see Bill Bryson, *Made in America: An Informal History of the English Language in the United States* (New York: Avon Books, 1996); and John McWhorter, *The Power of Babel: A Natural History of Language* (New York: Henry Holt, 2001).
2. Richard Lederer, *The Miracle of Language,* (New York: Pocket Books, 1991), p. 32.
3. James R. Andrews, *A Choice of Worlds: The Practice and Criticism of Public Discourse* (New York: Harper and Row, 1973).
4. The relationship between thought and language has been explored by many writers. For a recent work, see Steven Pinker, *Words and Rules: The Ingredients of Language* (New York: HarperCollins, 2000).
5. Quoted in Edward P. J. Corbett and Robert J. Connors, *Classical Rhetoric for the Modern Student,* 4th ed. (New York: Oxford University Press, 1999), p. 372.
6. Dorothy Sarnoff, *Speech Can Change Your Life* (New York: Doubleday, 1970), p. 71.
7. Annmarie Mungo, "A Child Is Born," *Winning Orations, 1980* (Mankato, MN: Interstate Oratorical Association, 1980), pp. 49–50.
8. Adapted from Richard Conniff, "You Never Know What the Fire Ant Is Going to Do Next," *Smithsonian,* July 1990, p. 49.

[9]I would like to thank *21st Century* for permission to include video from Zhang Jiexuan's speech on the CD that accompanies this edition of *The Art of Public Speaking.*

[10]For an informative recent study on the functions of metaphor in public address, see Pradeep Sopory and James Price Dillard, "The Persuasive Effects of Metaphor: A Meta-Analysis," *Human Communication Research,* 28 (2002), pp. 382–419.

[11]Thomas R. Arp and Greg Johnson, *Perrine's Sound and Sense: An Introduction to Poetry,* 10th ed. (Boston: Heinle and Heinle, 2000) p. 198.

[12]Winston Churchill, Speech at St. James Palace, London, June 12, 1941, in Lloyd Rohler and Roger Cook (eds.), *Great Speeches for Analysis and Criticism,* 4th ed. (Greenwood, IN: Alistair Press, 2001), p. 94.

[13]Edward Bliss, Jr. (ed.), *In Search of Light: The Broadcasts of Edward R. Murrow, 1938–1961* (New York: Knopf, 1967), p. 276.

[14]John Hancock, Boston Massacre Oration, March 5, 1774, in Ronald F. Reid (ed.), *American Rhetorical Discourse,* 2nd ed. (Prospect Heights, IL: Waveland Press, 1995), pp. 99–108.

[15]William Safire, *On Language* (New York: Times Books, 1980), p. xiv.

[16]Rosalie Maggio, *Talking About People: A Guide to Fair and Accurate Language* (Phoenix, AZ: Oryx Press, 1997), p. 16.

[17]Maggio, *Talking About People,* p. 26.

Chapter Twelve

DELIVERY

Chapter Focus
After defining good delivery and discussing the four major methods of delivery, this chapter explores the vocal and physical factors crucial to public speaking. It then presents a five-step method for practicing extemporaneous speech delivery and concludes by explaining how to handle question-and-answer sessions. For a full outline of the chapter, see the *Instructor's Manual*, pp. 251–257.

nonverbal communication
Communication based on a person's use of voice and body, rather than on the use of words.

I f you were to tape-record one of David Letterman's comedy routines, memorize it word for word, and stand up before your friends to recite it, would you get the same response Letterman does? Not very likely. And why not? Because you would not *deliver* the jokes as Letterman does. Of course, the jokes are basically funny. But David Letterman brings something extra to the jokes—his manner of presentation, his vocal inflections, his perfectly timed pauses, his facial expressions, his gestures. All these are part of an expert delivery. It would take you years of practice—as it took Letterman—to duplicate his results.

No one expects your speech class to transform you into a multimillion-dollar talk show host. Still, this example demonstrates how important delivery can be to any public speaking situation. Even a mediocre speech will be more effective if it is presented well, whereas a wonderfully written speech can be ruined by poor delivery.

This does not mean dazzling delivery will turn a mindless string of nonsense into a triumphant oration. You cannot make a good speech without having something to say. But having something to say is not enough. You must also know *how* to say it.

Speech delivery is a matter of *nonverbal communication.* It is not based on your words, but on how you use your voice and body to convey the message expressed by your words. There is a great deal of research on nonverbal communication in general and on speech delivery in particular. That research shows that the impact of a speaker's words—whether in a formal speech or in daily conversation—is powerfully influenced by the speaker's nonverbal communication.[1] In this chapter, we will explain how you can use your nonverbal communication to deliver your speeches effectively and to increase the impact of your verbal message.

What Is Good Delivery?

Wendell Phillips was a leader in the movement to abolish slavery in the United States during the 1800s. Some people considered him the greatest speaker of his time. The following story suggests one reason why:

> Shortly before the Civil War an Andover student, learning that Phillips was to lecture in Boston, made a 22-mile pilgrimage on foot to hear him. At first the trip seemed hardly worthwhile, for the student discovered that Phillips was not an orator in the grand manner, but spoke in an almost conversational style. He stood on the platform, one hand lightly resting on a table, talked for what seemed to be about 20 minutes, concluded, and sat down. When the student looked at his watch, he found to his astonishment that he had been listening for an hour and a half![2]

Good delivery does not call attention to itself. It conveys the speaker's ideas clearly, interestingly, and without distracting the audience. If you mumble your words, shuffle your feet, gaze out the window, or talk in a monotone, you will not get your message across. Nor will you be effective if you show off, strike a dramatic pose, or shout in ringing tones. Most audiences prefer delivery that combines a certain degree of formality with the best attributes of good conversation—directness, spontaneity, animation, vocal and facial expressiveness, and a lively sense of communication.

When you begin speaking in public, you will probably have many questions about delivery: "Should I be strong and aggressive or low-key?" "Where should I stand?" "How should I gesture?" "How should I handle my notes?" "How fast should I speak?" "When should I pause?" "Where should I look?" "What do I do if I make a mistake?"

There are no hard-and-fast answers to these questions. Speech delivery is an art, not a science. What works for one speaker may fail for another. And what succeeds with today's audience may not with tomorrow's. You cannot become a skilled speaker just by following a set of rules in a textbook. In the long run, there is no substitute for experience. But take heart! A textbook *can* give you basic pointers to get you started in the right direction.

When you plan your first speech (or your second or third), you should concentrate on such basics as speaking intelligibly, avoiding distracting mannerisms, and establishing eye contact with your listeners. Once you get these elements under control and begin to feel fairly comfortable in front of an audience, you can work on polishing your delivery to enhance the impact of your ideas. Eventually, you may find yourself able to control the timing, rhythm, and momentum of a speech as skillfully as a conductor controls an orchestra.

Class Activity
Lead a class discussion in which students develop a set of criteria for effective speech delivery. After the discussion, codify the criteria into an evaluation form that can be used by the class for the remainder of the term. For a full discussion of this activity, see the first Additional Exercise for Critical Thinking on p. 260 of the *Instructor's Manual.*

Methods of Delivery

There are four basic methods of delivering a speech: (1) reading verbatim from a manuscript; (2) reciting a memorized text; (3) speaking impromptu; and (4) speaking extemporaneously. Let us look at each.

Reading from a Manuscript

Certain speeches *must* be delivered word for word, according to a meticulously prepared manuscript. Examples include a Pope's religious proclamation, an engineer's report to a professional meeting, or a President's message to Congress. In such situations, absolute accuracy is essential. Every word of the speech will be analyzed by the press, by colleagues, perhaps by enemies. In the case of the President, a misstated phrase could cause an international incident.

Timing may also be a factor in manuscript speeches. Much of today's political campaigning is done on radio and television. If the candidate buys a one-minute spot and pays a great deal of money for it, that one minute of speech must be just right.

Although it looks easy, delivering a speech from a manuscript requires great skill. Some people do it well. Their words "come alive as if coined on the spot."[3] Others seem to ruin it every time. Instead of sounding vibrant and conversational, they come across as wooden and artificial. They falter over words, pause in the wrong places, read too quickly or too slowly, speak in a monotone, and march through the speech without even glancing at their audience. In short, they come across as *reading to* their listeners, rather than *talking with* them.

manuscript speech
A speech that is written out word for word and read to the audience.

Among current public figures, few are better at avoiding these problems than former Texas governor Ann Richards. Through years of practice, she has learned to sound spontaneous and to communicate heartfelt emotion even though she is delivering the speech word for word. You can see this in the excerpt from her eulogy to Barbara Jordan on CD 1, Video 12.1. Speaking before a packed audience of 1,500 people at Houston's Good Hope Missionary Baptist Church, Richards spoke movingly of Jordan's life and achievements. She communicated as directly with the audience as if she had been speaking informally to a small group of friends.

If you are in a situation where you must speak from a manuscript, do your best to follow Richards's lead. Practice aloud to make sure the speech sounds natural. Work on establishing eye contact with your listeners. Be certain the final manuscript is legible at a glance. Above all, reach out to your audience with the same directness and sincerity that you would if you were speaking extemporaneously.

View an excerpt from Ann Richards's eulogy to Barbara Jordan.

CD 1: VIDEO 12.1

Reciting from Memory

Among the feats of the legendary orators, none leaves us more in awe than their practice of presenting even the longest and most complex speeches entirely from memory. Nowadays it is no longer customary to memorize any but the shortest of speeches—toasts, congratulatory remarks, acceptance speeches, introductions, and the like. If you are giving a speech of this kind and want to memorize it, by all means do so. However, be sure to memorize it so thoroughly that you will be able to concentrate on communicating with the audience, not on trying to remember the words. Speakers who gaze at the ceiling or stare out the window trying to recall what they have memorized are no better off than those who read dully from a manuscript.

Speaking Impromptu

impromptu speech
A speech delivered with little or no immediate preparation.

An impromptu speech is delivered with little or no immediate preparation. Few people choose to speak impromptu, but sometimes it cannot be avoided. In fact, many of the speeches you give in life will be impromptu. You might be called on suddenly to "say a few words" or, in the course of a class discussion, business meeting, or committee report, want to respond to a previous speaker.

When such situations arise, don't panic. No one expects you to deliver a perfect speech on the spur of the moment. If you are in a meeting or discussion, pay close attention to what the other speakers say. Take notes of major points with which you agree or disagree. In the process, you will automatically begin to formulate what you will say when it is your turn to speak.

Whenever you are responding to a previous speaker, try to present your speech in four simple steps: First, state the point you are answering. Second, state the point you wish to make. Third, support your point with appropriate statistics, examples, or testimony. Fourth, summarize your point. This four-step method will help you organize your thoughts quickly and clearly.

If time allows, sketch a quick outline of your remarks on a piece of paper before you rise to speak. Use the same method of jotting down key words and phrases followed in a more formal speaking outline (see Chapter 10). This will help you remember what you want to say and will keep you from rambling.

In many cases, you will be able to speak informally without rising from your chair. But if the situation calls for you to speak from a lectern, walk to it calmly, take a deep breath or two (not a visible gasp), establish eye contact with your audience, and begin speaking. No matter how nervous you are inside, do your best to look calm and assured on the outside.

Once you begin speaking, maintain strong eye contact with the audience. If you are prone to talking rapidly when you are nervous, concentrate on speaking at a slower pace. Help the audience keep track of your ideas with signposts such as "My first point is . . . ; second, we can see that . . . ; in conclusion, I would like to say. . . . " If you have had time to prepare notes, stick to what you have written. By stating your points clearly and concisely, you will come across as organized and confident.

Whether you realize it or not, you have given thousands of impromptu "speeches" in daily conversation—as when you informed a new student how to register for classes, or explained to your boss why you were late for work, or answered questions in a job interview, or tried to persuade your roommate to lend you $20 until next week. There is no reason to fall apart when you are asked to speak impromptu in a more formal situation. If you keep cool, organize your thoughts, and limit yourself to a few remarks, you should do just fine.

As with other kinds of public speaking, the best way to become a better impromptu speaker is to practice. If you are assigned an impromptu speech in class, do your best to follow the guidelines discussed here. You can also practice impromptu speaking on your own. Simply choose a topic on which you are already well informed, and give a one- or two-minute impromptu talk on some aspect of that topic. Any topic will do—no matter how serious or frivolous it may be. Nor do you need an audience—you can speak to an empty room. Better yet, you can speak to a digital recorder or

Speech Assignment
If time permits, give your students an opportunity to practice speaking impromptu. For one approach to the impromptu speech assignment, see the *Instructor's Manual,* pp. 263–265. For additional approaches, check the five volumes of *Selections from the Speech Communication Teacher* that accompany *The Art of Public Speaking.* Whatever approach you adopt, try to ease students' apprehension by maintaining a low-key, supportive atmosphere. You should also give careful thought to the point of the term at which you assign impromptu speeches. If you assign them too early, students may not be comfortable enough with the class to take the psychological risks involved with speaking impromptu.

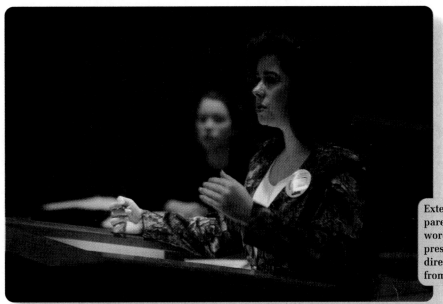

Extemporaneous speeches are prepared ahead of time, but the exact words are chosen at the moment of presentation. This allows for more direct delivery than does reading from a manuscript.

a tape recorder and play the speech back to hear how you sound. The purpose is to gain experience in pulling your ideas together quickly and stating them succinctly. Over the years, many people have found this an effective way to improve their skills of impromptu speaking.

Speaking Extemporaneously

extemporaneous speech

A carefully prepared and rehearsed speech that is presented from a brief set of notes.

In popular usage, "extemporaneous" means the same as "impromptu." But technically the two are different. Unlike an impromptu speech, which is totally off-the-cuff, an extemporaneous speech is carefully prepared and practiced in advance. In presenting the speech, the extemporaneous speaker uses only a set of brief notes or a speaking outline to jog the memory (see Chapter 10). The exact wording is chosen at the moment of delivery.

This is not as hard as it sounds. Once you have your outline (or notes) and know what topics you are going to cover and in what order, you can begin to practice the speech. Every time you run through it, the wording will be slightly different. As you practice the speech over and over, the best way to present each part will emerge and stick in your mind.

The extemporaneous method has several advantages. It gives more precise control over thought and language than does impromptu speaking; it offers greater spontaneity and directness than does speaking from memory or from a full manuscript; and it is adaptable to a wide range of situations. It also encourages the conversational quality audiences look for in speech delivery. "Conversational quality" means that no matter how many times a speech has been rehearsed, it still *sounds* spontaneous to the audience. When you speak extemporaneously—and have prepared properly—you have full control over your ideas, yet you are not tied to a manuscript. You are free to establish strong eye contact, to gesture naturally, and to concentrate on talking *with* the audience rather than declaiming *to* them.

conversational quality

Presenting a speech so it sounds spontaneous no matter how many times it has been rehearsed.

There is no better example of the power of extemporaneous delivery than Elizabeth Dole's renowned speech to the 1996 Republican National Convention in support of her husband's bid for the White House. Speaking to the delegates assembled in San Diego and to a national television audience, Dole broke 150 years of tradition by leaving the lectern and presenting her speech while walking among her listeners on the floor of the auditorium. Speaking extemporaneously, with no notes (and no teleprompter), she was able to break through the physical and psychological barriers that would otherwise have separated her from the audience. As numerous observers commented, it was more like listening to a conversation than to a formal speech.

View excerpts from Elizabeth Dole's speech at the Republican National Convention.

CD 1: VIDEO 12.2

Dole, of course, is one of the most accomplished speakers in the United States. You can't be expected in your speech class to reach the same mastery that she has worked years to achieve. Yet like thousands of previous students, you can become quite adept at speaking extemporaneously by the end of the term and have a solid foundation to build on in the future. As one student commented in looking back on his speech class, "At the start, I never thought I'd be able to give my speeches without a ton of notes, but I'm amazed at how much progress I made. It's still a bit nerve-racking to speak extemporaneously, but I'm confident I can do it, and I know I'll connect better with the audience as a result. This is one of the most valuable things I learned in the entire class."

Most experienced speakers prefer the extemporaneous method, and most teachers emphasize it. Later in this chapter (pages 310–311), we'll look at a step-by-step program for practicing your extemporaneous delivery.

The Speaker's Voice

What kind of voice do you have? Is it rich and resonant like James Earl Jones's? Thin and nasal like Willie Nelson's? Deep and raspy like Al Sharpton's? Soft and alluring like Catherine Zeta Jones's? Loud and irritating like Dick Vitale's?

Whatever the characteristics of your voice, you can be sure it is unique. Because no two people are exactly the same physically, no two people have identical voices. This is why voiceprints are sometimes used in criminal trials as guides to personal identity. The human voice is produced by a complex series of steps that starts with the exhalation of air from the lungs. (Try talking intelligibly while inhaling and see what happens.) As air is exhaled, it passes through the larynx (or voice box), where it is vibrated to generate sound. This sound is then amplified and modified as it resonates through the throat, mouth, and nasal passages. Finally, the resonated sound is shaped into specific vowel and consonant sounds by the movement of the tongue, lips, teeth, and roof of the mouth. The resulting sounds are combined to form words and sentences.

The voice produced by this physical process will greatly affect the success of your speeches. A golden voice is certainly an asset, but you can manage without. Some of the most famous speakers in history had undistinguished voices. Abraham Lincoln had a harsh and penetrating voice; Winston Churchill suffered from a slight lisp and an awkward stammer. Like them, you can overcome natural disadvantages and use your voice to the best effect. If you speak too softly to be heard, constantly stumble over words, spit out your ideas at machine-gun speed, or plod along as if you were reading a grocery list, your speeches will fail. Lincoln and Churchill learned to *control* their voices. You can do the same thing.

The aspects of voice you should work to control are volume, pitch, rate, pauses, variety, pronunciation, articulation, and dialect.

Related Reading
Joni Wilson, *The 3-Dimensional Voice* (San Diego: Blue Loon Press, 2000); Renee Grant-Williams, *Voice Power: Using Your Voice to Captivate, Persuade, and Command Attention* (New York: AMACOM, 2002). Both these books provide excellent, highly practical guides to improving all aspects of the speaking voice.

Volume

At one time a powerful voice was all but essential for an orator. Today, electronic amplification allows even a soft-spoken person to be heard in any setting. But in the classroom you will speak without a microphone. When you do, be sure to adjust your voice to the acoustics of the room, the size of the audience, and the level of background noise. If you speak too loudly, your listeners will think you boorish. If you speak too softly, they will not understand you. Remember that your own voice always sounds louder to you than to a listener. Soon after beginning your speech, glance at the people farthest away from you. If they look puzzled, are leaning forward in their seats, or are otherwise straining to hear, you need to talk louder.

volume
The loudness or softness of the speaker's voice.

Pitch

Pitch is the highness or lowness of the speaker's voice. The faster sound waves vibrate, the higher their pitch; the slower they vibrate, the lower their pitch. Pitch distinguishes the sound produced by the keys at one end of a piano from that produced by the keys at the other end.

In speech, pitch can affect the meaning of words or sounds. Pitch is what makes the difference between the "Aha!" triumphantly exclaimed by Sherlock Holmes upon discovering a seemingly decisive clue and the "Aha" he mutters when he learns the clue is not decisive after all. If you were to read the preceding sentence aloud, your voice would probably go up in pitch on the first "Aha" and down in pitch on the second.

Changes in pitch are known as *inflections.* They give your voice luster, warmth, and vitality. It is the inflection of your voice that reveals whether you are asking a question or making a statement; whether you are being sincere or sarcastic. Your inflections can also make you sound happy or sad, angry or pleased, dynamic or listless, tense or relaxed, interested or bored.

In ordinary conversation we instinctively use inflections to convey meaning and emotion. People who do not are said to speak in a *monotone*— a trait whose only known benefit is to cure insomnia in one's listeners. Few people speak in an absolute monotone, with no variation whatever in pitch, but many fall into repetitive pitch patterns that are just as hypnotic as a monotone. You can guard against this problem by recording your speeches as you practice them. If all your sentences end on the same inflection— either upward or downward—work on varying your pitch patterns to fit the meaning of your words. As with breaking any other habit, this may seem awkward at first, but it is guaranteed to make you a better speaker.

Rate

Rate refers to the speed at which a person speaks. People in the U.S. usually speak at a rate between 125 and 150 words per minute, but there is no uniform rate for effective speechmaking. Daniel Webster spoke at roughly 90 words per minute, Franklin Roosevelt at 110, John Kennedy at 180. Martin Luther King opened his "I Have a Dream" speech at a pace of 92 words per minute and finished it at 145. The best rate of speech depends on several things—the vocal attributes of the speaker, the mood she or he is trying to create, the composition of the audience, and the nature of the occasion.

For example, if you wanted to convey the excitement of the Daytona 500 car race, you would probably speak rather quickly, but a slower rate would be more appropriate to describe the serenity of the Alaskan wilderness. A fast rate helps create feelings of happiness, fear, anger, and surprise, while a slow rate is better for expressing sadness or disgust. A slower tempo is called for when you explain complex information, a faster tempo when the information is already familiar to the audience.

Two obvious faults to avoid are speaking so slowly that your listeners become bored or so quickly that they lose track of your ideas. Novice speakers are particularly prone to racing through their speeches at a frantic rate. Fortunately, once a speaker begins to work on it, this is usually an easy habit to break, as is the less common one of crawling through one's speech at a snail's pace.

The best rate of speech depends partly on the mood a speaker wants to create. To communicate the excitement of kayaking, you would probably speak at a faster-than-normal rate.

The key in both cases is becoming aware of the problem and concentrating on solving it. Use a digital recorder to check how fast you speak. Pay special attention to rate when practicing your speech. Finally, be sure to include reminders about delivery on your speaking outline so you won't forget to make the adjustments when you give your speech in class.

Pauses

Learning how and when to pause is a major challenge for most beginning speakers. Even a moment of silence can seem like an eternity. As you gain more poise and confidence, however, you will discover how useful the pause can be. It can signal the end of a thought unit, give an idea time to sink in, and lend dramatic impact to a statement. "The right word may be effective," said Mark Twain, "but no word was ever as effective as a rightly timed pause."

As Twain knew, the crucial factor is timing. "For one audience," he cautioned, "the pause will be short, for another a little longer, for another a shade longer still." Looking back on his own career as a speaker, he recalled: "When the pause was right the effect was sure; when the pause was wrong . . . the laughter was only mild, never a crash."

Developing a keen sense of timing is partly a matter of common sense, partly a matter of experience. You will not always get your pauses just right at first, but keep trying. Listen to accomplished speakers to see how they use pauses to modulate the rate and rhythm of their messages. Work on pauses when you practice your speeches.

pause
A momentary break in the vocal delivery of a speech.

vocalized pause

A pause that occurs when a speaker fills the silence between words with vocalizations such as "uh," "er," and "um."

When you do pause, make sure you pause at the end of thought units and not in the middle. Otherwise, you may distract listeners from your ideas. Most important, do not fill the silence with "uh," "er," or "um." These *vocalized pauses,* as they are called, are always annoying, and they can be devastating. Not only do they create negative perceptions about a speaker's intelligence, but they often make a speaker appear deceptive.[4]

Vocal Variety

Just as variety is the spice of life, so is it the spice of public speaking. A flat, listless, unchanging voice is just as deadly to speechmaking as a flat, listless, unchanging routine is to daily life.

Try reading this limerick aloud:

I sat next to the Duchess at tea.
It was just as I feared it would be:
    Her rumblings abdominal
    Were simply abominable
And everyone thought it was me!

Now recite this passage from James Joyce's "All Day I Hear the Noise of Waters":

The gray winds, the cold winds are blowing
    Where I go.
I hear the noise of many waters
    Far below.
All day, all night, I hear them flowing
    To and fro.[5]

Class Activity

The first Exercise for Critical Thinking at the end of this chapter uses oral interpretation of poetry to help students develop a lively, expressive speaking voice. For full discussion of the exercise, see the *Instructor's Manual*, pp. 257–258. For an alternative activity, see the fifth Additional Exercise for Critical Thinking on pp. 265–266 of the *Instructor's Manual*, which uses group storytelling as a vehicle for working on speech delivery.

Certainly you did not utter both passages the same way. You instinctively varied the rate, pitch, volume, and pauses to distinguish the light-hearted limerick from the solemn melancholy of Joyce's poem. When giving a speech, you should modulate your voice in just this way to communicate your ideas and feelings.

For an excellent example of vocal variety, look at CD 1, Video 12.3. The speaker is Sajjid Zahir Chinoy, who was born and raised in Bombay, India, before coming to the United States to attend college at the University of Richmond. At the end of his senior year, Chinoy was selected as the student commencement speaker in a campuswide competition. He spoke of the warm reception he received at Richmond and of how cultural differences can be overcome by attempting to understand other people.

At the end of his speech, Chinoy received thunderous applause—partly because of what he said, but also because of how he said it. Addressing the audience of 3,000 people without notes, he spoke extemporaneously with strong eye contact and excellent vocal variety. The speech was so inspiring that the main speaker, Harvard psychiatrist Robert Coles, began his presentation by paying tribute to Chinoy. "I've been to a number of commencements," said Coles, "but I've never heard a speech quite like that!"

How can you develop a lively, expressive voice? Above all, by approaching every speech as Chinoy approached his—as an opportunity to

vocal variety

Changes in a speaker's rate, pitch, and volume that give the voice variety and expressiveness.

View an excerpt from Sajjid Zahir Chinoy, "Questions of Culture."

CD 1: VIDEO 12.3

Do you want to learn more about speech delivery? Perhaps gain additional experience after your speech class is over? You can do both by joining an organization such as Toastmasters International, which has more than 175,000 members and 8,800 clubs in 70 countries around the world. For information about Toastmasters, log on to its website at www.toastmasters.org.

If you are a non-native speaker of English and want to work on your skills of spoken English, you will find a number of excellent resources at the English as a Second Language student website (http://owl.english.purdue.edu/handouts/esl/eslstudent.html).

You can link to these websites at www.mhhe.com/lucas8.

ONLINE LEARNING CENTER

share with your listeners ideas that are important to you. Your sense of conviction and your desire to communicate will help give your voice the same spark it has in spontaneous conversation.

Diagnose your present speaking voice to decide which aspects need improvement. Record your speeches to hear how they sound. Try them out on members of your family, a friend, or a roommate. Check with your teacher for suggestions. Practice the vocal variety exercise at the end of this chapter. Vocal variety is a natural feature of ordinary conversation. There is no reason it should not be as natural a feature of your speeches.

Pronunciation

We all mispronounce words now and again. Here, for example, are six words with which you are probably familiar. Say each one aloud.

genuine	err
arctic	nuclear
theater	February

Very likely you made a mistake on at least one, for they are among the most frequently mispronounced words in the English language. Let's see:

Word	Common Error	Correct Pronunciation
genuine	gen-u-wine	gen-u-win
arctic	ar-tic	arc-tic
theater	thee-ate′-er	thee′-a-ter
err	air	ur
nuclear	nu-cu-lar	nu-cle-ar
February	Feb-u-ary	Feb-ru-ary

Teaching Tip
Pronouncing words correctly in English can be very difficult for students who are not native speakers of the language. If you have such students, you may want to refer them to the ESL program on your campus. An excellent resource for students with less severe difficulties is Ann Cook's *American Accent Training: A Guide to Speaking and Pronouncing American English for Everyone Who Speaks English as a Second Language,* 2nd ed. (Hauppague, NY: Barrons, 2000), which comes with five CDs that provide practice in distinguishing and producing sounds in American English.

Every word leads a triple life: it is read, written, and spoken. Most people recognize and understand many more words in reading than they use in ordinary writing, and about three times as many as occur in spontaneous speech.[6] This is why we occasionally stumble when speaking words that are part of our reading or writing vocabularies. In other cases, we may mispronounce the most commonplace words out of habit.

The problem is that we usually don't *know* when we are mispronouncing a word; otherwise we would say it correctly. If we are lucky, we learn the right pronunciation by hearing someone else say the word properly or by having someone gently correct us in private. If we are unlucky, we mispronounce the word in front of a roomful of people, who may raise their eyebrows, groan, or laugh. Even experienced speakers sometimes fall into this trap. In reporting about a recent presidential election, a local TV news anchor referred several times to the number of votes needed to capture a majority in the e-lec-tor'-e-al college. When he had finished, his coanchor said (on the air!), "And it also takes 270 votes to win a majority in the e-lec'-tor-al college." The first announcer tried to shrug it off, but he was noticeably embarrassed.

All of this argues for practicing your speech in front of as many trusted friends and relatives as you can corner. If you have any doubts about the proper pronunciation of certain words, be sure to check a dictionary.

Articulation

Articulation and pronunciation are not identical. Sloppy articulation is the failure to form particular speech sounds crisply and distinctly. It is one of several causes of mispronunciation; but not all errors in pronunciation stem from poor articulation. You can articulate a word sharply and still mispronounce it. For example, if you say the "s" in "Illinois" or the "p" in "pneumonia," you are making a mistake in pronunciation, regardless of how precisely you articulate the sounds.

Errors in articulation can be caused by a cleft palate, by an overly large tongue, by a misaligned jaw, even by a poorly fitted dental plate or braces on the teeth. Serious problems require the aid of a certified speech therapist. But most of the time poor articulation is caused by laziness—by failing to manipulate the lips, tongue, jaw, and soft palate so as to produce speech sounds clearly and precisely. People in the U.S. seem particularly prone to poor articulation. We habitually chop, slur, and mumble our words, rather than enunciating them plainly.

Among college students, poor articulation is more common than ignorance of correct pronunciation. We know that "let me" is not "lemme," that "going to" is not "gonna," that "did you" is not "didja," yet we persist in articulating these words improperly. Here are some other common errors in articulation you should work to avoid:

Word	Misarticulation
ought to	otta
didn't	dint
for	fur

pronunciation
The accepted standard of sound and rhythm for words in a given language.

articulation
The physical production of particular speech sounds.

Teaching Tip
In most cases it is unrealistic to expect students who are non-native speakers of English to have the same command of articulation and pronunciation as do native speakers. For an excellent discussion of the problems faced by ESL students in a public speaking course and of teaching strategies to address those problems, see Karen Johnson and Paula Golombek, *Public Speaking for Non-Native Speakers: A Handbook for Instructors* (New York: McGraw-Hill, 1996), which is available as a supplement to *The Art of Public Speaking.*

don't know	dunno
have to	hafta
them	em
want to	wanna
will you	wilya

If you have sloppy articulation, work on identifying and eliminating your most common errors. Like other bad habits, careless articulation can be broken only by persistent effort—but the results are well worth it. Not only will your speeches be more intelligible, but employers will be more likely to hire you, to place you in positions of responsibility, and to promote you. As Shakespeare advised, "Mend your speech a little, lest you may mar your fortunes."

Dialect

Most languages have dialects, each with a distinctive accent, grammar, and vocabulary. Dialects are usually based on regional or ethnic speech patterns. The United States has four major regional dialects—Eastern, New England, Southern, and General American. These dialects affect the way people talk in different parts of the country. In Boston people may get "idears" about "dee-ah" friends. In Alabama parents tell their children to stop "squinching" their eyes while watching television and to go clean up their rooms "rat" now. In Utah people praise the "lard" and put the "lord" in the refrigerator.[7]

There are also several well-established ethnic dialects in the United States, including Black English, Jewish English, Hispanic English, and Cajun English. In recent years we have also seen the emergence of newer dialects such as Haitian English and Cuban English. As the United States becomes more diverse culturally, it is also becoming more diverse linguistically.

Over the years linguists have done a great deal of research on dialects. They have concluded that no dialect is inherently better or worse than another. There is no such thing as a right or wrong dialect. Dialects are not linguistic badges of superiority or inferiority. They are usually shaped by our regional or ethnic background, and every dialect is "right" for the community of people who use it.[8]

When is a given dialect appropriate in public speaking? The answer depends above all on the composition of your audience. Heavy use of any dialect—regional or ethnic—can be troublesome for a speaker when the audience does not share that dialect. In such a situation, the dialect may cause listeners to make negative judgments about the speaker's personality, intelligence, and competence. This is why professional speakers have been known to invest large amounts of time (and money) to master the General American dialect used by most television news broadcasters. This dialect has become so widely accepted throughout the United States that it is suitable for almost any audience.

Does this mean you must talk like a television news broadcaster if you want to be successful in your speeches? Not at all. Regional or ethnic dialects do not pose a problem as long as the audience is familiar with them and finds them appropriate to the occasion. When speaking in the North, for

dialect
A variety of a language distinguished by variations of accent, grammar, or vocabulary.

Class Activity
An excellent way to help students work on delivery skills, as well as receive valuable feedback while preparing their speech assignments, is to have them deliver their speeches to each other in small groups the session before they deliver the speeches to the entire class. Each group member should give her or his speech in turn, while the other members listen and prepare critiques for the speaker.

Related Reading
See John McWhorter, *Word on the Street: Debunking the Myth of "Pure" Standard English* (Cambridge, MA: Perseus Publishing, 2001), for a controversial and thought-provoking analysis of dialect in contemporary American society.

example, a southern politician will probably avoid heavy use of regional dialect. But when addressing audiences in the South, the same politician may intentionally include regional dialect as a way of creating common ground with his or her listeners.

Although not strictly speaking a matter of dialect, the proficiency of non-native speakers of English often arises in the speech classroom. Fortunately, teachers and students alike usually go out of their way to be helpful and encouraging to international students and others for whom English is not the primary language. Over the years many non-native speakers of English have found speech class a supportive environment in which to improve their proficiency in spoken English.[9]

The Speaker's Body

Class Activity
Most accomplished speakers reach out to listeners with eye contact, gestures, facial expressions, head nods, and the like. You can illustrate this by showing two video-taped speech excerpts with the sound turned off—one from a highly effective speech, the other from a less effective speech. Ask students to identify the physical actions of both speakers. Then show the excerpts again, this time with the sound turned on. What correlations do students notice between the speakers' actions and their overall effectiveness?

Imagine you are at a party. During the evening you form impressions about the people around you. Jonte seems relaxed and even-tempered, Nicole tense and irritable. Megan seems open and straightforward, Bekah hostile and evasive. Amin seems happy to see you; Seth definitely is not.

How do you reach these conclusions? To a surprising extent, you reach them not on the basis of what people say with words, but because of what they say with their posture, gestures, eyes, and facial expressions. Suppose you are sitting next to Amin, and he says, "This is a great party. I'm really glad to be here with you." However, his body is turned slightly away from you, and he keeps looking at someone across the room. Despite what he says, you know he is *not* glad to be there with you.

Much the same thing happens in speechmaking. Here is the story of one student's first two classroom speeches and the effect created by his physical actions on each occasion:

Sean O'Connor's first speech did not go very well. Even though he had chosen an interesting topic, researched the speech with care, and practiced it faithfully, he did not take into account the importance of using his body effectively. When the time came for him to speak, a stricken look crossed his face. He got up from his chair like a condemned man and plodded to the lectern as though going to the guillotine. His vocal delivery was good enough, but all the while his hands were living a life of their own. They fidgeted with his notes, played with the buttons of his shirt, and drummed on the lectern. Throughout the speech Sean kept his head down, and he looked at his watch repeatedly. Regardless of what his *words* were saying, his *body* was saying, "I don't want to be here!"

Finally it was over. Sean rushed to his seat and collapsed into it, looking enormously relieved. Needless to say, his speech was not a great success.

Fortunately, when Sean's problem was pointed out to him, he worked hard to correct it. His next speech was quite a different story. This time he got up from his chair and strode to the lectern confidently. He kept his hands under control and concentrated on making eye contact with his listeners. This was truly an achievement, because Sean was just as nervous as the first time. However, he found that the more he made himself *look* confident, the more confident he *became*. After the speech his classmates were enthusiastic. "Great speech," they said. "You really seemed to care about the subject, and you brought this caring to the audience."

In fact, the wording of Sean's second speech wasn't much better than that of the first. It was his physical actions that made all the difference. From the time he left his seat until he returned, his body said, "I am confident and in control of the situation. I have something worthwhile to say, and I want you to think so too."

Posture, facial expression, gestures, eye contact—all affect the way listeners respond to a speaker. How we use these and other body motions to communicate is the subject of a fascinating area of study called kinesics. One of its founders, Ray Birdwhistell, estimated that more than 700,000 physical signals can be sent through bodily movement. Studies have shown that these signals have a significant impact on the meaning communicated by speakers. Research has also confirmed what the Greek historian Herodotus observed more than 2,400 years ago: "People trust their ears less than their eyes." When a speaker's body language is inconsistent with his or her words, listeners often believe the body language rather than the words.[10]

Here are the major aspects of physical action that will affect the outcome of your speeches.

kinesics
The study of body motions as a systematic mode of communication.

Personal Appearance

If you were Jennifer Lopez, you could show up to make an Academy Award presentation speech wearing a bizarre creation that left little to the imagination. If you were Albert Einstein, you could show up to address an international science conference wearing wrinkled trousers, a sweater, and tennis shoes. While the members of your audience would certainly comment on your attire, your reputation would not be harmed. In fact, it might be enhanced. You would be one of the few, the very few, who live outside the rules, who are expected to be unusual.

Now imagine what would happen if the president of a corporation showed up to address a stockholders' meeting attired like Jennifer Lopez, or if the President of the United States spoke on national television wearing wrinkled clothes and tennis shoes. Both presidents would soon be looking for work. Barring the occasional eccentric, every speaker is expected by her or his audience to exhibit a personal appearance in keeping with the occasion of the speech.

The President of the United States can be photographed in hiking clothes for a quick weekend interview at Camp David, but that same president will don a conservative suit and tie to address a joint session of Congress. Similarly, a business executive speaking at a winter sales conference in Acapulco would probably wear slacks and a casual shirt or blouse because a business suit, in this atmosphere, would seem too formal. But back home in San Francisco, Chicago, or New York, the same executive will be immaculately dressed in a well-tailored suit.

A number of studies have confirmed that personal appearance plays an important role in speechmaking.[11] Listeners always see you before they hear you. Just as you adapt your language to the audience and the occasion, so should you dress and groom appropriately. Although the force of your speech can sometimes overcome a poor impression created by personal appearance, the odds are against it. Regardless of the speaking situation, you should try to evoke a favorable first impression—an impression that is likely to make listeners more receptive to what you say.

Related Reading
Mark L. Knapp and Judith A. Hall, *Nonverbal Communication in Human Interaction*, 5th ed. (Belmont, CA: Wadsworth, 2002). Co-authored by a communication scholar and a social psychologist, this book provides outstanding coverage of the theory and research on all aspects of nonverbal communication.

Movement

Novice speakers are often unsure about what to do with their body while giving a speech. Some pace nonstop back and forth across the podium, fearing that if they stop, they will forget everything. Others are perpetual-motion machines, constantly shifting their weight from one foot to the other, bobbing their shoulders, fidgeting with their notes, or jingling coins in their pockets. Still others turn into statues, standing rigid and expressionless from beginning to end.

Such quirks usually stem from nervousness. If you are prone to distracting mannerisms, your teacher will identify them so you can work on controlling them in later speeches. With a little concentration, these mannerisms should disappear as you become more comfortable speaking in front of an audience.

Teaching Tip
Stress to students the importance of their physical behavior just before they start to speak and just after they finish. Require students to work on this in all their presentations, including their introductory speeches. It will not take them long to look—and to feel—more poised and confident.

As important as how you act during the speech is what you do just *before* you begin and *after* you finish. As you rise to speak, try to appear calm, poised, and confident, despite the butterflies in your stomach. When you reach the lectern, don't lean on it, and don't rush into your speech. Give yourself time to get set. Arrange your notes just the way you want them. Stand quietly as you wait to make sure the audience is paying attention. Establish eye contact with your listeners. Then—and only then—should you start to talk.

When you reach the end of your speech, maintain eye contact for a few moments after you stop talking. This will give your closing line time to sink in. Unless you are staying at the lectern to answer questions, collect your notes and return to your seat. As you do so, maintain your cool, collected demeanor. Whatever you do, don't start to gather your notes before you have finished talking; and don't cap off your speech with a huge sigh of relief or some remark like, "Whew! Am I glad that's over!"

All this advice is common sense; yet you would be surprised how many people need it. When practicing your speeches, spend a little time rehearsing how you will behave at the beginning and at the end. It is one of the easiest—and one of the most effective—things you can do to improve your image with an audience.

Gestures

Few aspects of delivery seem to cause students more anguish than deciding what to do with their hands. "Should I clasp them behind my back? Let them hang at my sides? Put them in my pockets? Rest them on the lectern? And what about gesturing? When should I do that—and how?" Even people who normally use their hands expressively in everyday conversation seem to regard them as awkward appendages when speaking before an audience.

gestures
Motions of a speaker's hands or arms during a speech.

Over the years, more nonsense has been written about gesturing than about any other aspect of speech delivery. Adroit gestures *can* add to the impact of a speech; but there is nothing to the popular notion that public speakers must have a vast repertoire of graceful gestures. Some accomplished speakers gesture frequently, others hardly at all. The primary rule is this: Whatever gestures you make should not draw attention to themselves and distract from your message. They should *appear* natural and spontaneous, help clarify or reinforce your ideas, and be suited to the audience and occasion.

Good speakers use a lively voice to help bring their ideas to life. They also use gestures, eye contact, and facial expressions to create a strong bond with members of the audience.

At this stage of your speaking career, you have many more important things to concentrate on than how to gesture. Gesturing tends to work itself out as you acquire experience and confidence. In the meantime, make sure your hands do not upstage your ideas. Avoid flailing them about, wringing them together, cracking your knuckles, or toying with your rings. Once you have eliminated these distractions, forget about your hands. Think about communicating with your listeners, and your gestures will probably take care of themselves—just as they do in conversation.

Eye Contact

The eyeball itself expresses no emotion. Yet by manipulating the eyeball and the areas of the face around it—especially the upper eyelids and the eyebrows—we are able to convey an intricate array of nonverbal messages. So revealing are these messages that we think of the eyes as "the windows of the soul." We look to them to help gauge the truthfulness, intelligence, attitudes, and feelings of a speaker.

Like many aspects of communication, eye contact is influenced by cultural background. When engaged in conversation, Arabs, Latin Americans, and Southern Europeans tend to look directly at the person with whom they are talking. People from Asian countries and parts of Africa tend to engage in less eye contact. In Kenya a discussion between a woman and her son-in-law may well be conducted with each person turning her or his back to the other![12]

eye contact
Direct visual contact with the eyes of another person.

Class Activity
For a creative exercise that helps students develop better skills of eye contact, see Thomas J. Roach and Lisa J. Goodnight, "Eye Contact Shooting Gallery," in *Selections from the Speech Communication Teacher, 1996–1999,* p. 23, which accompanies *The Art of Public Speaking.*

When it comes to public speaking, there appears to be fairly wide agreement across cultures on the importance of some degree of eye contact.[13] In most circumstances, one of the quickest ways to establish a communicative bond with your listeners is to look at them personally and pleasantly. Avoiding their gaze is one of the surest ways to lose them. There is a great deal of research to show that speakers in the United States who refuse to establish eye contact are perceived as tentative or ill at ease and may be seen as insincere or dishonest. It is no wonder, then, that teachers urge students to look at the audience 80 to 90 percent of the time they are talking.

You may find this disconcerting at first. But after one or two speeches, you should be able to meet the gaze of your audience fairly comfortably. As you look at your listeners, be alert for their reactions. Can they hear you? Do they understand you? Are they awake? Your eyes will help you answer these questions.

It isn't enough just to look at your listeners; *how* you look at them also counts. A blank stare is almost as bad as no eye contact at all. So is a fierce, hostile glower or a series of frightened, bewildered glances. Also beware of the tendency to gaze intently at one part of the audience while ignoring the rest. In speech class some students look only at the section of the room where the teacher is sitting. Others avoid looking anywhere near the teacher and focus on one or two sympathetic friends. You should try to establish eye contact with your whole audience.

View an excerpt from Kristin Berg, "A Family Tradition."

CD 1: VIDEO 12.4

Look at CD 1, Video 12.4 for an excellent example of eye contact. The speech is by Kristin Berg, a student at the University of Wisconsin. Kristin's assignment was to interview one of her classmates, Reva, and to give a brief talk introducing her to the rest of the class. In her speech, Kristin explained how Reva's parents had worked to help their growing family adapt to a new culture after immigrating to the United States. As you can see from the CD, the impact of Kristin's speech was greatly enhanced by her strong eye contact (as well by her vocal variety and communicative gestures).

When addressing a small audience such as your class, you can usually look briefly, as Kristin did, from one person to another. For a larger group, you will probably scan the audience rather than try to engage the eyes of each person individually. No matter what the size of your audience, you want your eyes to convey confidence, sincerity, and conviction. They should say, "I am pleased to be able to talk with you. I believe deeply in what I am saying, and I want you to believe in it too."

Practicing Delivery

Popular wisdom promises that practice makes perfect. This is true, but only if we practice properly. No matter how long and hard you practice playing the piano, you will never make beautiful music if you don't know the difference between a sharp and a flat. By the same token, you will do little to improve your speech delivery unless you practice the right things in the right ways. Here is a five-step method that has worked well for many students:

1. Go through your preparation outline *aloud* to check how what you have written translates into spoken discourse. Is it too long? Too short? Are the main points clear when you speak them? Are the supporting materials distinct, convincing, interesting? Do the introduction and conclusion come across well? As you answer these questions, revise the speech as needed.

2. Prepare your speaking outline. In doing so, be sure to follow the guidelines discussed in Chapter 10. Use the same visual framework as in the preparation outline. Make sure the speaking outline is easy to read at a glance. Keep the outline as brief as possible. Give yourself cues on the outline for delivering the speech.

3. Practice the speech aloud several times using only the speaking outline. Be sure to "talk through" all examples and to recite in full all quotations and statistics. If your speech includes visual aids, use them as you practice. The first couple of times you will probably forget something or make a mistake, but don't worry about that. Keep going and complete the speech as well as you can. Concentrate on gaining control of the *ideas;* don't try to learn the speech word for word. After a few tries you should be able to get through the speech extemporaneously with surprising ease.

4. Now begin to polish and refine your delivery. Practice the speech in front of a mirror to check for eye contact and distracting mannerisms. Record the speech to gauge volume, pitch, rate, pauses, and vocal variety. Most important, try it out on friends, roommates, family members—anyone who will listen and give you an honest appraisal. Don't be shy about asking. Most people love to give their opinion about something. Since your speech is designed for people rather than for mirrors or recorders, you need to find out ahead of time how it goes over with people.

5. Finally, give your speech a dress rehearsal under conditions as close as possible to those you will face in class. Some students like to try the speech a couple of times in an empty classroom the day before the speech is due. No matter where you hold your last practice session, you should leave it feeling confident and looking forward to speaking in your class.

If this or any practice method is to work, you must start early. Don't wait until the day of your speech, or even the night before, to begin working on delivery. A single practice session—no matter how long—is rarely enough. Allow yourself *at least* a couple of days, preferably more, to gain command of the speech and its presentation. No matter how brilliant your preparation outline, what counts is how the speech comes across when you deliver it. Give yourself plenty of time to make sure it comes across well.

Teaching Tip
If possible, arrange to videotape at least one round of your students' speeches. Try to meet individually with each student to review her or his tape. Stop the tape periodically to comment on the speaker's strong points or to indicate where improvement is needed. If you cannot meet individually with students, have them prepare written self-assessments based on their videotapes. Whichever approach you take, videotaping is extremely valuable because it gives students a chance to see and hear themselves as others see and hear them.

Answering Audience Questions

As superintendent of the city's municipal building, Delia Sedano was responsible for presenting its new security plan to the public. City employees, citizens, and reporters gathered in the auditorium to hear her describe the plan. After outlining the main points she would cover, she assured the audience that she would be happy to answer questions at the end of her presentation.

Delia realized the plan was expensive and potentially controversial, so she was not surprised to see a number of hands go up as soon as she finished speaking. An employee from the coroner's office asked, "Will the new system create long lines to get into the building, like the lines at airport security checks?" Delia had anticipated this question and had an answer ready. After repeating the question so everyone could hear it, she explained that a sufficient number of security guards would be working at peak hours to speed things along.

The next question was more confrontational: "Where will the money come from to pay for all of this?" The journalist who asked the question seemed hostile, but Delia was careful not to adopt a defensive tone. She stated that the money would come from the city's general budget. "I know these are tight times," she added, "but everyone agrees on the importance of safeguarding our employees and members of the public who come into the building."

The third question inquired about the training of security guards. After clarifying the gist of the question, Delia introduced the city's director of security personnel and asked him to provide additional information.

Near the end of the 25 minutes she had allotted, Delia said she would take two more questions. When those were finished, she concluded the session with a brief restatement of how the new system would improve security and peace of mind in the municipal building.

After Delia closed, Art Shafer, a member of the security committee, came forward to congratulate her on a successful briefing. "Your presentation was great," he said, "but the Q&A was especially impressive. It showed the audience that we've looked at this from all angles."

If you have ever watched a press conference or heard a speaker answer questions after a talk, you know the question-and-answer session can make or break a presentation. A speaker who handles questions well, as Delia Sedano did, can enhance her credibility and strengthen the impact of her speech. On the other hand, a speaker who evades questions or shows annoyance will almost certainly create the opposite effect.

The question-and-answer session is a common part of public speaking, whether the occasion is a press conference, business presentation, public hearing, or classroom assignment. Depending on the situation, questioning may take place throughout the presentation, or it may be reserved until after the speaker has completed his or her remarks. In either case, an answer to a question is often the final word an audience hears and is likely to leave a lasting impression.

Preparing for the Question-and-Answer Session

The first step to doing well in a question-and-answer session is to take it as seriously as the speech itself. Even experienced speakers have been known to stumble if they fail to prepare thoroughly for the question-and-answer part of their presentation. The two major steps in preparing are working out answers to possible questions and practicing the delivery of those answers.

Formulate Answers to Possible Questions

Once you know your presentation will include questions from the audience, you should be thinking about possible questions even as you are writing your speech. If you practice your speech in front of friends, family, or coworkers, ask them to jot down any questions they may have. Keep track of all the questions and take the time to formulate answers. Write your answers in full to make sure you have thought them through completely.

Speech Assignment

If time permits, include a brief question-and-answer period with the informative and persuasive speeches. The usual way of doing this is to set aside one or two minutes for questions after each speech. Many teachers assign questioners for each speech. To ensure that students take the question-and-answer session seriously, some instructors include it as part of the speech grade. Others assign it a separate grade equal in weight to a homework assignment.

If you are giving a persuasive speech, be sure to work out answers to objections the audience may have to your proposal. No matter how careful you are to deal with those objections in your speech, you can be sure they will come up at some point in the question-and-answer session.

If you are speaking on a topic with technical aspects, be ready to answer specialized inquiries about them, as well as questions that seek clarification in nontechnical terms. You might even prepare a handout that you can distribute afterward for people who want more information than you can provide in the question-and-answer period.

Practice the Delivery of Your Answers

You would not present a speech to a room full of people without rehearsing. Neither should you go into a question-and-answer session without practicing the delivery of your answers. As many speakers have discovered, writing out answers in the privacy of your home or office and vocalizing them coherently under the pressure of an open forum are two different matters. Since you will be presenting your answers out loud, you should rehearse them out loud.

One possibility is to have a friend or colleague listen to your presentation, ask questions, and critique your answers. This method is used by political candidates and business leaders, whose staff members grill them with questions before debates or press conferences. Another possibility is to record your answers to anticipated questions, play them back, and revise your answers until you get them just right.

As you rehearse, work on making your answers brief and to the point. Many simple questions can be answered in 10 or 15 seconds, and even complex ones should be answered in a minute or two. If you practice answering questions beforehand, you will find it much easier to keep to these time limits.

Of course, no matter how much you work ahead of time, there is no way to predict every question you will receive. Some people will ask questions you had not anticipated, and some of the questions you did anticipate may not get asked at all. But if you go into the question-and-answer period fully prepared, you will find it much easier to adapt to whatever occurs.

Managing the Question-and-Answer Session

If you have ever watched a skillful speaker field questions from the audience, you know there is an art to managing a question-and-answer session. Entire books have been written on this subject, but the following suggestions will help get you started on the right foot.

Clarify the Format

If there is any doubt about when you will entertain questions, take time early in your speech to clarify the format you prefer. You can do this by saying something like, "Feel free to ask questions throughout my speech," or "I'll be happy to answer questions at the end of my talk." Of course, if the ground rules are already clear, there is no need to say anything about them.

Teaching Tip
One way to reinforce the importance of planning for audience questions is to compare the question-and-answer session with a job interview. Just as one should not go to an interview without mapping out answers to questions that the interviewer is likely to ask, so one should not enter a question-and-answer session without working out answers to the most probable questions. For an interesting source of examples with respect to job interviews, see Ron Fry's *101 Great Answers to the Toughest Interview Questions*, 4th ed. (Franklin Lakes, NJ: Career Press, 2000).

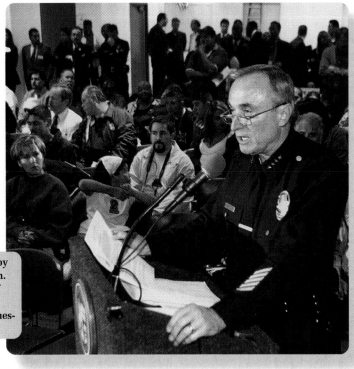

Many speeches are followed by a question-and-answer session. Here Los Angeles police chief William Bratton explains his policies prior to answering questions from the press.

Approach Questions with a Positive Attitude

A positive attitude will help you answer questions graciously and respectfully. Try to view questions from the audience as signs of genuine interest and a desire to learn more about your subject. If someone asks a question about material you feel you have covered or a point that seems clear to you, don't respond by saying, "I discussed that at the beginning of my talk," or "The answer seems obvious." Instead, use moments like these to reiterate or expand upon your ideas. If you insult a questioner by dismissing his or her inquiry, the audience is likely to make negative judgments about your character.

Similarly, a speaker who adopts a sharp or defensive tone while answering questions will alienate many people in the audience. Think of the question-and-answer session as another opportunity to communicate your ideas rather than as a challenge to your competence or personhood.

Even if you are asked a hostile question, keep your cool. Avoid the temptation to answer defensively, sarcastically, or argumentatively. Most people in the audience will respect you for trying to avoid a quarrel.

Listen Carefully

It's hard to answer a question well if you don't listen carefully to it. Give the questioner your full attention. Look directly at her or him rather than glancing around the room, at the floor, or at the ceiling. If an audience member is having a difficult time stating the question, you might even nod in encouragement to help him or her along.

When faced with an unclear or unwieldy question, try to rephrase it by saying something like, "If I understand your question, it seems to me that you are asking . . . " Another option is simply to ask the audience member to repeat the question. Most people will restate it more succinctly and clearly. If you still don't understand, ask the questioner to give an example of what he or she means.

Direct Answers to the Entire Audience

When you are being asked a question, look at the questioner. Direct your answer, however, to the entire audience. Make occasional eye contact with the questioner as you answer, but speak primarily to the audience as a whole. This will help you keep everyone's attention. If you speak just to the questioner, you may well find the rest of your audience drifting off.

When speaking to a large audience, be sure to repeat or paraphrase each question after it is asked. This helps ensure that you understand the question properly. It also involves the entire audience and guarantees that they know the question you are addressing. In addition, repeating or paraphrasing the question gives you a moment to frame an answer before you respond.

Related Reading

Marian K. Woodall, *Thinking on Your Feet: How to Communicate Under Pressure*, 2nd ed. (Lake Oswego, OR: Professional Business Communications, 1996). This book grew out of Woodall's efforts to find ways for students in her technical reporting class to respond competently to questions about their reports.

Be Honest and Straightforward

Some speakers dread question-and-answer sessions because they fear being derailed by a question they can't answer. The world won't end if you can't answer every possible question. If you don't know the answer, say so. Don't apologize, don't evade, and most important, don't try to bluff. Do, however, let the questioner know that you take the question seriously. Offer to check into the answer as soon as possible after the speech. If a more knowledgeable person is at hand, ask if she or he knows the answer.

Stay on Track

It's easy to get diverted or lose control of time in the give-and-take of a lively question-and-answer session. Unless there is a moderator for the session, the speaker is responsible for keeping things on track. Sometimes that means preventing a single questioner from dominating the session. Allow one follow-up question from each person, and don't let yourself be dragged into a personal debate with any questioner. If someone attempts to ask more than two questions, respond graciously yet firmly by saying, "This is an interesting line of questioning, but we need to give other people a chance to ask questions."

Sometimes, a listener will launch into an extended monologue instead of posing a question. When this happens, you can regain control of the situation by saying something like, "Those are very interesting ideas, but do you have a specific question I can answer?" If the person continues, offer to talk individually with him or her after the session.

On some occasions, the length of the question-and-answer session is predetermined by the moderator or by the schedule of the audience. On other occasions, it's up to the speaker to decide how much time to devote to answering questions. Often this requires adapting to the kind and number of questions you are receiving. Make sure you allow enough time to get through issues of major importance, but don't let things drag on after the

Related Reading

For more detail on the elements of speech delivery discussed throughout this chapter, consult Ralph Hillman, *Delivering Dynamic Presentations: Using Your Voice and Body for Impact* (Boston: Allyn and Bacon, 1999).

momentum of the session has started winding down. As the end approaches, offer to respond to another question or two. After answering them, wrap things up by thanking the audience for its time and attention.[14]

Summary

Speech delivery is a matter of nonverbal communication. It is based on how you use your voice and body to convey the message expressed by your words. You can't make a good speech without having something to say, but you also need to know *how* to say it. Rather than calling attention to itself, effective delivery conveys the speaker's ideas clearly, engagingly, and without distracting the audience.

There are four basic methods of delivering a speech: reading verbatim from a manuscript, reciting a memorized text, speaking impromptu, and speaking extemporaneously. The last of these—speaking extemporaneously—is the method you probably will use for classroom speeches and for most speeches outside the classroom. When speaking extemporaneously, you will have a brief set of notes or a speaking outline. You will choose the exact wording of your speech at the moment of delivery.

To use your voice effectively you should work on controlling your volume, pitch, rate, pauses, vocal variety, pronunciation, articulation, and dialect. Volume is the relative loudness of your voice, and pitch is the relative highness or lowness. Rate refers to the speed at which you talk. Pauses, when carefully timed, can add great impact to your speech, but you should avoid vocalized pauses ("er," "um," and the like). Vocal variety refers to changes in volume, pitch, rate, and pauses, and is crucial to making your voice lively and animated. Most of us speak casually in everyday conversation, but for public speaking you should be sure to pronounce words correctly and to articulate them distinctly. You should also avoid heavy use of dialect in situations where the audience does not share the dialect or will find it inappropriate to the occasion.

Posture, personal appearance, facial expression, gestures, and eye contact also affect the way listeners respond to speakers. You can do little to change your face or body, but you can dress and groom appropriately for the situation at hand. You can also learn to control gestures and bodily movements so they enhance your message, rather than distract from it. Making eye contact with listeners is one of the quickest ways to establish a communicative bond with them.

You should practice all these aspects of delivery along with the words of your speech. Start your practice sessions early so you will have plenty of time to gain command of the speech and its presentation.

If your speech includes a question-and-answer session, you will need to prepare for that as well, since it can have a strong impact on the audience's final impression. Anticipate the most likely questions, prepare answers to them, and practice delivering those answers. Once the question-and-answer period is underway, listen carefully to the questions, approach them positively, and respond to them briefly, graciously, and straightforwardly. Direct your answers to the full audience, rather than to the questioner alone, and make sure to end the session in a timely fashion.

Key Terms

nonverbal communication (294)

manuscript speech (295)

impromptu speech (296)

extemporaneous speech (298)

conversational quality (298)

volume (299)

pitch (300)

inflections (300)

monotone (300)

rate (300)

pause (301)

vocalized pause (302)

vocal variety (302)

pronunciation (304)

articulation (304)

dialect (305)

kinesics (307)

gestures (308)

eye contact (309)

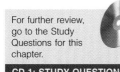

Review these terms by doing the Chapter 12 crossword puzzle at www.mhhe.com/lucas8.

ONLINE LEARNING CENTER

Review Questions

After reading this chapter, you should be able to answer the following questions:

1. What is nonverbal communication? Why is it important to effective public speaking?

2. What are the elements of good speech delivery?

3. What are the eight aspects of voice usage you should concentrate on in your speeches?

For further review, go to the Study Questions for this chapter.

CD 1: STUDY QUESTIONS

4. What are four aspects of bodily action you should concentrate on in your speeches?

5. What are the five steps you should follow when practicing your speech delivery?

6. What steps should you take when preparing for a question-and-answer session? What should you concentrate on when responding to questions during the session?

Exercises for Critical Thinking

1. An excellent way to improve your vocal variety is to read aloud selections from poetry that require emphasis and feeling. Choose one of your favorite poems that falls into this category, or find one by leafing through a poetry anthology. Practice reading the selection aloud. As you read, use your voice to make the poem come alive. Vary your volume, rate, and pitch. Find the appropriate places for pauses. Underline the key words or phrases you think should be stressed. Modulate your tone of voice; use inflections for emphasis and meaning.

   For this to work, you must overcome your fear of sounding affected or "dramatic." Most beginning speakers do better if they exaggerate changes in volume, rate, pitch, and expression. This will make you more

Cross-Reference

For discussion of the Exercises for Critical Thinking, see the *Instructor's Manual*, pp. 257–259. For additional exercises, check the *Instructor's Manual*, pp. 260–267, as well as the five volumes of *Selections from the Speech Communication Teacher* that accompany *The Art of Public Speaking*.

aware of the many ways you can use your voice to express a wide range of moods and meanings. Besides, what sounds overly "dramatic" to you usually does not sound that way to an audience. By adding luster, warmth, and enthusiasm to your voice, you will go a long way toward capturing and keeping the interest of your listeners.

If possible, practice reading the selection into a digital recorder. Listen to the playback. If you are not satisfied with what you hear, practice the selection some more and record it again.

2. Watch a 10-minute segment of a television drama with the sound turned off. What do the characters say with their dress, gestures, facial expressions, and the like? Do the same with a television comedy. How do the nonverbal messages in the two shows differ? Be prepared to report your observations in class.

3. Attend a speech on campus. You may choose either a presentation by a guest speaker from outside the college or a class session by a professor who has a reputation as a good lecturer. Prepare a brief report on the speaker's vocal and nonverbal communication.

In your report, first analyze the speaker's volume, pitch, rate, pauses, vocal variety, pronunciation, and articulation. Then evaluate the speaker's personal appearance, bodily action, gestures, and eye contact. Explain how the speaker's delivery added to or detracted from what the speaker said. Finally, note at least two techniques of delivery used by the speaker that you might want to try in your next speech.

Applying the **POWER** *of* PUBLIC SPEAKING

Cross-Reference

For discussion of this Applying the Power of Public Speaking scenario, see the *Instructor's Manual*, p. 260.

Utilizing your business degree and computer savvy, you have made a success of the online marketing company you started after graduating from college. Now in its third year, the company has prepared a proposal to design the e-commerce site for a major sporting goods retailer. In your 30-minute presentation to the retailer's management team, you will review the homepage designs, site maps, and security protocols.

You notice on the agenda that another 30 minutes has been allotted after your presentation for questions and answers. Knowing from your previous experience with clients how important the Q&A session can be, you want to be sure you are ready for it. What steps will you take to prepare?

Notes

1. For two recent studies, see Carla R. Chamberlin, "Nonverbal Behaviors and Initial Impressions of Trustworthiness in Teacher-Supervisor Relationships," *Communication Education,* 49 (2000), pp. 352–364; Paul L. Witt and Lawrence R. Wheeless, "An Experimental Study of Teachers' Verbal and Nonverbal Immediacy and Students' Affective and Cognitive Learning," *Communication Education,* 50 (2001), pp. 327–342.
2. Irving Bartlett, *Wendell Phillips: Boston Brahmin* (Boston: Beacon Press, 1961), p. 192.
3. A. Craig Baird, *Rhetoric: A Philosophical Inquiry* (New York: Ronald Press, 1965), p. 207.

[4]Daniel J. O'Keefe, *Persuasion: Theory and Research,* 2nd ed. (Thousand Oaks, CA: Sage, 2002), p. 185.

[5]James Joyce, "Chamber Music XXXV," in Harry Levin (ed.), *Collected Poems* (New York: Viking, 1946–1947). Reprinted by permission of Penguin Putnam, Inc.

[6]Dorothy Sarnoff, *Speech Can Change Your Life* (Garden City, NY: Doubleday, 1970), p. 73.

[7]The most authoritative guide to regional dialects in the United States is Frederic G. Cassidy and Joan H. Hall (eds.), *Dictionary of American Regional English,* 4 vols. to date (Cambridge, MA: Harvard University Press, 1985–2002).

[8]For an interesting discussion of this point, see Patrick L. Courts, *Multicultural Literacies: Dialect, Discourse, and Diversity* (New York: Peter Lang, 1997).

[9]For a more detailed guide on vocal communication, consult Jeffrey C. Hahner, Martin A. Sokoloff, and Sandra L. Salisch, *Speaking Clearly: Improving Voice and Diction,* 6th ed. (New York: McGraw-Hill, 2002).

[10]See Mark L. Knapp and Judith A. Hall, *Nonverbal Communication in Human Interaction,* 5th ed. (Belmont, CA: Wadsworth, 2002), pp. 13–16.

[11]O'Keefe, *Persuasion: Theory and Research,* pp. 205–207.

[12]Knapp and Hall, *Nonverbal Communication in Human Interaction,* p. 365.

[13]See, for example, Scott D. Johnson and Ann N. Miller, "A Cross-Cultural Study of Immediacy, Credibility, and Learning in the U.S. and Kenya," *Communication Education,* 51 (2002), pp. 280–292.

[14]For more on managing question-and-answer sessions, consult Natalie H. Rogers, *The New Talk Power: The Mind-Body Way to Speak Without Fear* (Sterling, VA: Capital Books, 2000), pp. 195–210.

Chapter Thirteen

USING VISUAL AIDS

A former lifeguard with training in a number of life-saving techniques, Meg Fugate decided to give her informative speech on the steps one should follow in responding to an emergency situation. Part of her speech was devoted to explaining how to administer cardiopulmonary resuscitation, better known as CPR.

A week before her speech, Meg called the local Red Cross chapter and arranged to borrow a life-size dummy of a human torso on which she could demonstrate CPR. She used the dummy in her practice sessions to make sure she knew exactly what maneuvers she was going to perform and how to coordinate them with her words. By the day of her speech, she was able to move effortlessly between explaining her ideas and performing the procedures of CPR without breaking eye contact or stumbling in her delivery.

By *showing* her classmates how to perform CPR, rather than just telling them about it, Meg made her speech more interesting and communicated her ideas much more effectively. Afterward, one of her classmates commented that the speech was better than the CPR demonstration he had seen at the Red Cross!

View an excerpt from Meg Fugate, "CPR."

CD 1: VIDEO 13.1

As the old saying tells us, one picture is worth a thousand words. People find a speaker's message more interesting, grasp it more easily, and retain it longer when it is presented visually as well as verbally. Can you picture the steps involved in using CPR to save a life? You could if you had watched Meg's speech. Her visual demonstration brought home her ideas more effectively than would have been possible with words alone.

Advantages of Visual Aids

Chapter Focus

Knowing how to use visual aids effectively is crucial to public speaking. After discussing the benefits of employing visual aids in a speech, this chapter looks at the major kinds of visual aids, offers guidelines for preparing effective visual aids, and explains how to integrate visual aids into a speech smoothly and expertly. For a complete outline of the chapter, see the *Instructor's Manual*, pp. 277–280.

Visual aids offer several advantages. The primary advantage is *clarity*. If you are discussing an object, you can make your message clearer by showing the object or some representation of it. If you are citing statistics, showing how something works, or demonstrating a technique, a visual aid will make your information more vivid to your audience. After all, we live in a visual age. Television and movies have conditioned us to expect a visual image. By using visual aids in your speeches, you often will make it easier for listeners to understand exactly what you are trying to communicate.[1]

Another advantage of visual aids is *interest*. The interest generated by visual images is so strong that visual aids are now used routinely in many areas, not just speechmaking. A generation or so ago, most college textbooks were rather dry—page after page of words. Today they are enlivened with photographs, drawings, and other visual aids that clarify the material and make it more interesting. Encyclopedias have blossomed with photographs and maps; even dictionaries contain small drawings to highlight word definitions. You can do the same thing with your speeches.

Still another advantage of visual aids is *retention*. Visual images often stay with us longer than verbal ones. The people who saw Meg Fugate's speech about CPR may not remember everything she said about the details of responding to an emergency, but they will probably remember her demonstration of how to perform CPR. And perhaps they will remember that demonstration if they are ever in a situation where they need to provide CPR for someone who has been in an accident or has suffered a heart attack. We've all heard that words can "go in one ear and out the other." Visual images tend to last.[2]

In fact, when used properly, visual aids can enhance almost *every* aspect of a speech. One study showed that an average speaker who uses visual aids will come across as better prepared, more credible, and more professional than a dynamic speaker who does not use visual aids. According to the same study, visual aids can increase the persuasiveness of a speech by more than 40 percent.[3] Another study found that business speakers who use multimedia in their presentations are significantly more effective than speakers who do not.[4]

There is even research to indicate that visual aids are an excellent way to combat stage fright. They heighten audience interest, shift attention away from the speaker, and give the speaker greater confidence in the speech as a whole.[5]

For all these reasons, you will find visual aids of great value in your speeches. In this chapter we will concentrate primarily on visual aids suitable for classroom speeches. However, the principles outlined here are true for all circumstances. For speeches outside the classroom—in business or community situations, for instance—you should have no difficulty applying the general suggestions given here.

Let us look first at the kinds of visual aids you are likely to use, then at guidelines for preparing visual aids, and finally at guidelines for using visual aids effectively.

Teaching Tip
Stress the fact that the principles discussed in this chapter are applicable to any speech that employs visual aids. Although most students do not have access to the kinds of sophisticated, high-tech visual aids available to business and professional speakers, the guidelines for effective visual aids are the same for classroom speeches as for those presented outside the classroom.

Kinds of Visual Aids

Objects

Tracy Collins is an avid downhill skier. When it came time for her informative speech, she chose as her specific purpose "To inform my audience how to choose the right ski equipment." On the day of her speech, she brought to class a pair of skis, boots, bindings, and ski clothing. It was then easy for her to explain exactly what to look for in each item.

By *showing* her classmates the equipment, Tracy presented her ideas more effectively than she could have by using words alone. She also made her speech more interesting to nonskiers. As one of her classmates said afterward, "I don't ski, but I found your speech fascinating. Using the skis and other equipment as visual aids really helped get me involved. Now I have a little better idea of what my friends who ski are talking about. Without the visual aids I would have been lost."

As in Tracy's speech, bringing the object of your talk to class can be an excellent way to clarify your ideas and give them dramatic impact. If you talk about guitars, why not bring one to class to show your listeners? If you plan to explain the different kinds of golf clubs, what could be better than showing a sample of each kind? Or suppose you want to inform your audience about the Peruvian art of doll making. You could bring several dolls to class and explain to your classmates how they were made.

Teaching Tip
Be sure to inform students of any objects—animals, firearms, illegal substances, etc.—that they are not permitted to use in their speeches.

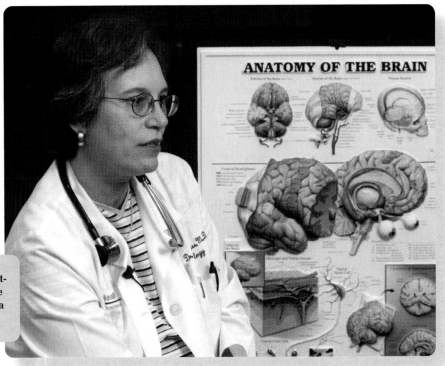

Visual aids make a speaker's message clearer, more interesting, and easier to retain. Here neurologist Anne Weiss uses a visual aid to help explain the effects of West Nile virus.

In certain situations you might use living objects as visual aids. This worked well for a high-school wrestling coach who returned to college to take a night class in public speaking. Not surprisingly, the coach gave one of his speeches about wrestling. On the night of his speech he brought along two of his high-school students, who demonstrated each of the basic holds as the coach discussed them.

Many objects, however, cannot be used effectively in classroom speeches. Some are too big to be hauled into a classroom. Others are too small to be seen clearly by the audience. Still others may not be available to you. If you were speaking about a rare suit of armor in the local museum, you could, theoretically, transport it to class, but it is most unlikely that the museum would let you borrow it. You would have to look for another kind of visual aid.

Models

model

An object, usually built to scale, that represents another object in detail.

If the item you want to discuss is too large, too small, or unavailable, you may be able to work with a model. One option is a life-size model, such as that used by Meg Fugate in the speech on CPR we discussed at the start of this chapter. Another student, an anthropology major, used a full-scale model of a human skull to show how archaeologists use bone fragments to reconstruct the forms of early humans.

You might also be able to use a small-scale model of a large object. One speaker used such a model to help explain the structural factors that contributed to the collapse of the World Trade Center after the attacks of September 11. Another speaker brought to class a scaled-down model of a hang glider to illustrate the equipment and techniques of hang gliding.

A third kind of model is a large-scale representation of a small object. Science teachers use such models to help students visualize molecules and other minuscule structures. A good example of this kind of model came in a speech about extended-wear contact lenses. The speaker wanted to demonstrate the differences in flexibility among hard contact lenses, soft lenses, and extended-wear lenses. Since the lenses themselves were too small for his classmates to see, he used a glass, a paper plate, and a sheet of clear plastic wrap to illustrate the differences among the three kinds of lenses. As you can see from CD 1, Video 13.2, it worked to perfection and allowed the speaker to communicate his ideas more effectively than he could have by words alone.

View the use of visual aids in "Extended-Wear Contact Lenses."

CD 1: VIDEO 13.2

Photographs

In the absence of an object or a model, you may be able to use photographs. Lawyers often employ photographs in trials to show the crime scene; architects to show prospective clients other buildings the firm has designed; drunk-driving activists to demonstrate the tragic results of combining alcohol with driving.

Photographs will not work effectively, however, unless they are large enough for the audience to view without straining. Normal-size photos are not big enough to be seen clearly without being passed around—which only diverts the audience from what you are saying. The same is true of photographs in a book. Even oversize books are too small to be seen clearly by all members of an audience.

How can you get large-scale photos for a speech? One student used art posters to illustrate her points in a speech about the painter Frida Kahlo. Another speaker used enlargements produced by a color copier to show the spectacular markings of various species of saltwater tropical fish. The enlargements were 18 × 24 inches, and the speaker mounted them on white poster board to make them easier to see.

Another option is to take your photographs to a copy service and have them converted to transparencies that can be shown with an overhead projector. The cost is minimal, and the results can be dramatic.

Finally, PowerPoint and other multimedia programs are excellent vehicles for incorporating photographs into a speech. You can use your own photographs or ones you have downloaded from the Web, and you can easily adjust the size and placement of the photos for maximum clarity and impact. (For further explanation, see the appendix on PowerPoint that follows this chapter.)

Speech Assignment
Many teachers assign at least one round of speeches—usually informative—in which students are required to use visual aids. For an explanation of such an assignment, see the Informative Speech, Option B, on p. 33 of the *Instructor's Manual.* If possible, take time after the round of speeches to ask students what they learned about the use of visual aids and what changes they would make in their visual aids if they were to deliver their speeches again.

Drawings

Diagrams, sketches, and other kinds of drawings are superb alternatives to photographs. They are inexpensive to make. Moreover, since they are drawn specifically for one speech, they can be designed to illustrate your points exactly. This more than compensates for what they may lack in realism.

For example, Figure 13.1 (page 326) is a drawing used by a student in a speech about Navajo sandpainting. The student wanted to show his

Figure 13.1

audience what sandpainting looks like and to explain its symbolism and religious significance. As you can imagine, it would have been almost impossible for him to do so without some kind of visual aid.

Figure 13.2 (below) shows a drawing used in a speech about the kinds of problems faced by people who suffer from dyslexia. This aid was particularly effective because it allowed the speaker to translate complex ideas into visual terms the audience could grasp almost immediately.

Figure 13.2

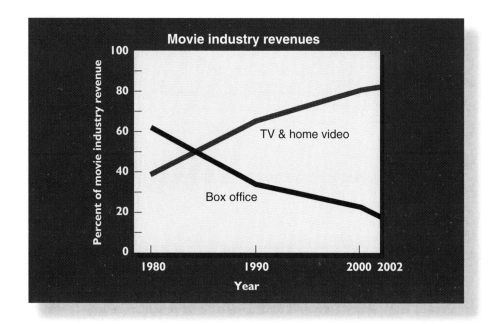

Figure 13.3

Graphs

Graphs are a good way to simplify and clarify statistics. Audiences often have trouble grasping a complex series of numbers. You can ease their difficulty by using graphs to show statistical trends and patterns.

The most common type is the *line graph*. Figure 13.3 (above) shows such a graph, used in a speech about the American movie industry. The speaker explained the graph as follows:

> As you can see from this graph based on figures in *Newsweek* magazine, the video revolution has had a profound impact on the American movie industry. From 1980 to 2002, the percent of movie revenues generated by box office receipts fell dramatically—from 61 percent to 18 percent. At the same time, the percent of movie industry revenues generated by DVD and VHS rentals and sales and by films shown on television more than doubled—from 39 percent in 1981 to 82 percent in 2002.

The *pie graph* is best suited for illustrating simple distribution patterns. You will see such a graph in your newspaper each year to show the division of the national budget. Figure 13.4 (page 328) shows how one speaker used a pie graph to help listeners visualize changes in marital status among working women in the past century. The graph on the left shows the percentages of working women who were single, married, and widowed or divorced in 1900. The graph on the right shows percentages for the same groups in 2000.

These pie graphs helped the speaker make three points: (1) The percentage of working women who are widowed or divorced has remained relatively stable since 1900; (2) the percentage of working women who are single has declined greatly during the past century; (3) the percentage of working women who are married has more than tripled, to the point that they are now far and away the largest group of working women in the United States.

graph
A visual aid used to show statistical trends and patterns.

line graph
A graph that uses one or more lines to show changes in statistics over time or space.

pie graph
A graph that highlights segments of a circle to show simple distribution patterns.

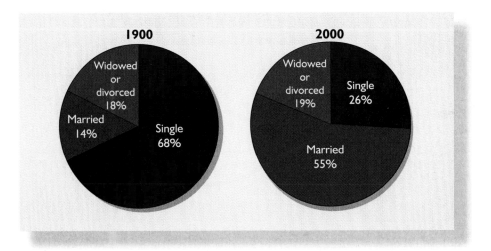

Figure 13.4

Because a pie graph is used to dramatize relationships among the parts of a whole, you should keep the number of different segments in the graph as small as possible. A pie graph should ideally have from two to five segments; under no circumstances should it have more than eight.

The *bar graph* is a particularly good way to show comparisons between two or more items. It also has the advantage of being easy to understand, even by people who have no background in reading graphs. Figure 13.5 (below) is an example of a bar graph from a speech entitled "The Politics of Race in America." It shows visually the relative standing of whites and

bar graph
A graph that uses vertical or horizontal bars to show comparisons among two or more items.

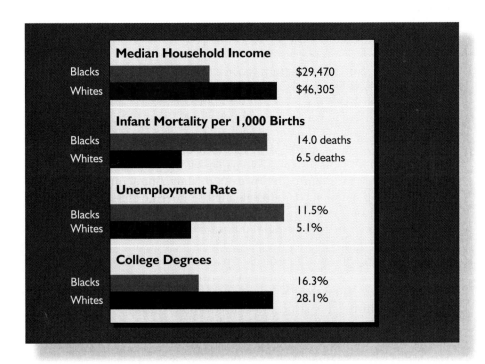

Figure 13.5

Region of Birth	Percent of U.S. Immigrants
Mexico	28 percent
Asia	27 percent
Europe	16 percent
Caribbean	11 percent
Central America	6 percent
South America	6 percent
Africa	2 percent
Other	4 percent

Figure 13.6

blacks with respect to median household income, infant mortality, unemployment, and college education. By using a bar graph, the speaker made her points much more vividly than if she had just cited the numbers orally.[6]

Charts

Charts are particularly useful for summarizing large blocks of information. One student, in a speech titled "The United States: A Nation of Immigrants," used a chart to show the leading regions of the world for U.S. immigrants. (Figure 13.6). These are too many categories to be presented effectively in a pie graph or a bar graph. By listing them on a chart, the speaker made it easier for listeners to keep the information straight.

Charts are also valuable for presenting the steps of a process. One speaker used several charts in a speech about survival techniques in the wilderness, including one outlining the steps in emergency treatment of snakebites. Another speaker used charts effectively to help her listeners keep track of the steps involved in making cappuccino and other specialty coffee drinks.

You can also use charts to present information that your audience may want to write down. In a speech about consumer protection organizations, for example, a speaker might use a chart to let the audience know exactly where to write or phone for consumer services.

The biggest mistake made by beginning speakers when using a chart is to include so much information that the chart is jumbled and hard to read. As we will discuss later, visual aids should be clear, simple, and uncluttered. Lists on a chart should rarely exceed seven or eight items, with generous spacing between items. If you cannot fit everything on a single chart, make a second one.

chart
A visual aid that summarizes a large block of information, usually in list form.

Overhead Transparency
For ease of classroom discussion, examples of drawings, charts, and graphs are included in the binder of full-color overhead transparencies that accompanies *The Art of Public Speaking*.

Video

Video can be extremely effective as a visual aid. If you are talking about the impact caused by even a low-speed automobile accident, what could be more effective than showing slow-motion video of crash tests? Or suppose you are explaining the different kinds of roller coasters found in amusement parks. Your best visual aid would be a video showing those coasters in action. The detail, immediacy, and vividness of video are hard to match.

Despite its advantages, using video in a speech can be complicated. It requires cumbersome equipment, distracts attention from the speaker, and may do more harm than good if used carelessly. If you decide to use video in one of your speeches, you need to follow the lead of Brian Dombkowski, the student who gave the speech on roller coasters mentioned in the previous paragraph. Brian sent away to Arrow Dynamics, Inc., the leading manufacturer of custom roller coasters, for a videotape of their rides. He then went to the audiovisual center on campus and edited several snippets from that tape onto his own tape, which he then showed during his speech.

Knowing that a sloppily edited video is of less value than no video at all, Brian made sure his editing was clean and expert and would not distract from his ideas. He also included the video every time he rehearsed the speech so it would be smoothly integrated with the rest of his presentation. He even made a special trip to campus to practice with the playback equipment in the classroom so he would be able to use it flawlessly on the day of the speech. The result was a memorable presentation that took full advantage of the benefits of video without falling prey to its potential drawbacks.

Transparencies

Earlier in this chapter we mentioned the possibility of converting photographs to transparencies, which can be shown with an overhead projector. You can also use transparencies to present drawings, graphs, and charts. Transparencies are inexpensive, easy to create, and produce a strong visual image. For all these reasons, they are one of the most widely used methods of presenting visual aids.

If you use transparencies, don't try to write or draw on them while you are speaking. Prepare them well in advance and make sure any text is large enough to be seen from the back of the room. A good rule is that all numbers and letters—whether typed or handwritten—should be at least one-quarter inch high (about three times as large as the print on this page).

In addition, check your overhead projector ahead of time to make sure it's working and that you know how to operate it. If possible, arrange to practice with a projector when you rehearse the speech. This will help ensure that your transparencies are well coordinated with the rest of your presentation.

Multimedia Presentations

Multimedia presentations allow you to integrate a variety of visual aids—including charts, graphs, photographs, and video—in the same talk. Presentation software programs include Microsoft PowerPoint, Corel Presentations, and Apple Keynote. Depending on the technological resources at your school, you may be able to give multimedia presentations in your speech class. If so, it will provide training for speeches outside the classroom—especially in business settings, where multimedia presentations are made every day.

In the appendix that follows this chapter, you will find a full discussion of how to use PowerPoint in your speeches. And if you visit *The Art of*

View an excerpt from Brian Dombkowski, "The Thrilling World of Roller Coasters."

CD 1: VIDEO 13.3

transparency
A visual aid drawn, written, or printed on a sheet of clear acetate and shown with an overhead projector.

Teaching Tip
Bring to class samples of well designed and poorly designed transparencies. Show the transparencies on an overhead projector and ask students to point out the strengths and weaknesses of each. This also provides an opportunity for you to demonstrate the techniques of using an overhead projector.

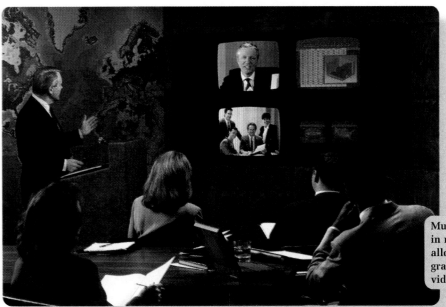

Multimedia presentations are used in many business situations. They allow a speaker to include charts, graphs, slides, photographs, even video and sound in the same talk.

Public Speaking Online Learning Center at www.mhhe.com/lucas8, you will find detailed, how-to guides for the use of PowerPoint 2000 and PowerPoint 2002. Here we will take a brief look at multimedia presentations in general.

Although each multimedia presentation program operates a bit differently, all give you the tools to incorporate a wide range of material into your speech. Suppose you are talking about Mayan architecture and you want to show your audience a photograph of the famous ruins at Chichén Itzá. If the photograph is from the Internet, you can download it directly to your computer for use with your other visual aids. Or suppose you want to create a graph showing the growing number of terrorist incidents in different parts of the world. You can use the presentation software's graph program to generate a professional-looking graph tailored specifically to your needs.

Once you have created all the aids you need for your speech and have them stored on your computer, you can call them up in any order. During the speech, you use a computer to control the presentation of your aids. The computer is usually connected to a television monitor or a large-screen video projector. Some systems have a wireless mouse that lets you move through your presentation with a minimum of fuss.

For all their advantages, multimedia presentations do have some drawbacks—not the least of which is the high cost of the equipment required to show them. It also takes considerable time to learn how to use the software, to design graphs and charts, to edit sound and video clips, and to organize and rehearse a presentation so it is smooth and professional. If you plan to make a multimedia presentation, be sure to give yourself plenty of time to make sure it comes off just right.

With any complex technology, there is always the chance of faulty equipment. Set up your computer, projection unit, and so forth early enough that you can double-check them before the audience arrives. Make sure you know

multimedia presentation

A speech that combines several kinds of visual and/or audio aids in the same talk.

the equipment well enough to handle any basic technical difficulties that may arise. Always carry a backup disk of your presentation just in case you should happen to need it.

Most important, be prepared to give your speech even if all the multimedia equipment were to fall apart. It may not be as dazzling as the speech you had planned, but it will be much better than no speech at all. Your audience will sympathize with your predicament, and they will give you credit for adapting to the situation.

Related Reading
Gene Zelazny, *Say It with Presentations* (New York: McGraw-Hill, 2000); Claudyne Wilder and Jennifer Rotondo, *Point, Click, and Wow: A Quick Guide to Brilliant Laptop Presentations*, rev. ed (San Francisco: Jossey-Bass, 2002). Both of these books focus on business presentations, but the principles they discuss are applicable to multimedia presentations in any setting.

The Speaker

Sometimes you can use your own body as a visual aid—by showing how a conductor directs an orchestra, by demonstrating the skills of modern dance, by doing magic tricks, and so forth. One student gave an informative speech on the art of mime. Throughout the speech she illustrated her points by performing mime routines. In addition to clarifying her ideas, the demonstration kept her classmates deeply engrossed in the speech. Many students have also found that doing some kind of demonstration reduces their nervousness during a speech by providing an outlet for their extra adrenaline.

Doing a demonstration well requires special practice to coordinate your actions with your words and to control the timing of your speech. You can see an excellent example on CD 1, Video 13.4. The subject of the speech is sign language. After providing background about the different kinds of sign language used today, the speaker taught her classmates how to sign the phrase "You are my friend." As you watch, notice how clearly the speaker explains each step along the way and how she gives her classmates time to work on each step before she moves to the next one. Also notice how she communicates directly with the audience and maintains eye contact throughout her demonstration.

View an excerpt from Leah Pogoriler, "Sign Language."

CD 1: VIDEO 13.4

Special care is required if you are demonstrating a process that takes longer to complete than the time allocated for your speech. If you plan to show a long process, you might borrow the techniques of television personalities such as Emeril Lagasse and Martha Stewart. They work through most of the steps in making a perfect enchilada or holiday decoration, but they have a second, finished enchilada or decoration ready to show you at the last minute.

Guidelines for Preparing Visual Aids

Whether you are creating visual aids by hand or designing them on a computer, there are six basic guidelines you should follow to make your aids clear and visually appealing. These guidelines apply whether you are speaking in or out of the classroom, at a business meeting or a political forum, to an audience of 20 or of 200.

Prepare Visual Aids in Advance

No matter what visual aids you plan to use, prepare them well before the day your speech is due. This has two advantages. First, it means you will have the time and resources to devise creative, attractive aids that will truly

Do you want to learn more about PowerPoint presentations, videoconferencing, and other high-tech aspects of public speaking? The website for *Presentations* magazine (www.presentations.com) offers a wealth of helpful tips, as well as updates on the latest technological developments.

Another valuable resource is Presenters University visual aids website (www.presentersuniversity.com/courses/cs_visualaids.cfm). Sponsored by InFocus Corporation, this site provides information about all kinds of visual aids and how to use them effectively.

You can link to these websites at www.mhhe.com/lucas8.

ONLINE LEARNING CENTER

enhance your speech. Audiences respond much more favorably to speakers who have obviously put a great deal of thought and effort into their visual aids.

Second, preparing your visual aids ahead of time means you can use them while practicing your speech. Visual aids are effective only when they are integrated smoothly with the rest of the speech. If you lose your place, drop your aids, or otherwise stumble around when presenting them, you will distract your audience and shatter your concentration. You can avoid such disasters by preparing your visual aids far enough in advance.

Keep Visual Aids Simple

The purpose of a visual aid is to communicate your ideas, not to display your virtuosity as an artist or wizardry with computer graphics. Visual aids should be simple, clear, and to the point. Limit each aid to a manageable amount of information, and beware of the tendency to go overboard when using programs such as PowerPoint. It is possible to create a graphic that displays two charts, a photograph, and 10 lines of text in five different typefaces with 250 colors on the same visual aid. But who would be able to read it? Rather than enhancing your speech, such an aid would detract from it.

The basic rule is to include in your visual aid only what you need to make your point. If you look back at the aids presented earlier in this chapter, you will see that all of them are clear and uncluttered. They contain enough information to communicate the speaker's point, but not so much as to confuse or distract the audience.

Make Sure Visual Aids Are Large Enough

A visual aid is useless if no one can see it. This is one of those points that seems so obvious as to need no comment. But as many speakers have discovered, it is one thing to nod your head in agreement and another to prepare a visual aid properly. Beginning speakers in particular tend to design visual aids that are too small.

Class Activity
When it comes to teaching about visual aids, a picture is truly worth a thousand words. Develop a file of drawings, charts, graphs, and the like from previous classes that you can use to show the traits of effective and ineffective visual aids. Have students identify which aids work well, which do not, and why. For further discussion of this activity, see the first Additional Exercise for Critical Thinking in the *Instructor's Manual*, p. 283.

Figure 13.7

The Checklist for
Preparing Visual
Aids can help you
develop effective
visual aids.

CD 1: SPEECH CHECKLIST

When you design a visual aid, keep in mind the size of the room in which you will be speaking. Make sure the aid is big enough to be seen easily by everyone in the room. If you compose a diagram, chart, or graph by hand, guard against the tendency to write and draw too small. As you prepare the aid, check its visibility by moving to a point as far away from it as your most distant listener will be sitting. If you have trouble making out the words or drawings, your audience will too. By making sure your visual aid is large enough, you will avoid having to introduce it with the comment, "I know some of you can't see this, but . . . "

If you are creating your visual aid by computer, remember that regular-size type (such as that in this book) may be easy to read from two feet away on a computer screen, but it is much too small for a visual aid—even for one that is enlarged with a video unit or an overhead projector. Most experts recommend printing all words and numbers in bold and using 36-point type for titles, 24-point type for subtitles, and 18-point type for other text. Figure 13.7 (above) shows these type sizes in comparison to standard 12-point type.

What about using all capital letters? That might seem a great way to ensure that your print is large enough to be read easily. But research has shown that a long string of words in ALL CAPS is actually harder to read than is normal text. Reserve ALL CAPS for titles or for individual words that require special emphasis.

Use Fonts That Are Easy to Read

font
A complete set of type of
the same design.

Most computer programs come with a large number of fonts, which you can use to vary the style of your visual aids. Although it can be fun to experiment with the fonts, not all are suitable for visual aids. For the most part, you should avoid decorative fonts such as those on the left in Figure 13.8 (page 335). They are hard to read and can easily distract the attention of listeners.

Figure 13.8

In contrast, look at the fonts on the right in Figure 13.8. They are less exciting than those on the left, but they are clear and easy to read. If you use fonts such as these, your visual aids will be audience-friendly.

Use a Limited Number of Fonts

Some variety of fonts in a visual aid is appealing, but too much can be distracting—as in the aid on the left in Figure 13.9 (below), which uses a different font for each line. Most experts recommend using no more than two fonts in a single visual aid—one for the title or major headings, another for subtitles or other text. Standard procedure is to use a block typeface for the title and a rounder typeface for subtitles and text—as in the aid on the right in Figure 13.9.

Ineffective	More Effective
MAJOR CLASSES *of* WINE	**MAJOR CLASSES OF WINE**
appetizer wines	Appetizer Wines
Table Wines	Table Wines
Dessert Wines	Dessert Wines
Sparkling Wines	Sparkling Wines

Figure 13.9

IMPACT ON HEARING	DECIBEL LEVEL	TYPE OF NOISE
Harmful	140	Firecracker
to	130	Jackhammer
hearing	120	Jet engine
Risk	110	Rock concert
hearing	100	Chain saw
loss	90	Motorcycle
Loud	80	Alarm clock
but	70	Busy traffic
safe	60	Air conditioner

Figure 13.10

Use Color Effectively

Color adds clout to a visual aid. When used effectively, it increases recognition by 78 percent and comprehension by 73 percent.[7] The key words, of course, are "when used effectively." Some colors do not work well together. Red and green are a tough combination for anyone to read, and they look the same to people who are color-blind. Many shades of blue and green are too close to each other to be easily differentiated—as are orange and red, and blue and purple.

It is also possible to have too many colors on a visual aid. In most circumstances, charts and graphs should be limited to a few colors that are used consistently and solely for functional reasons. The usual procedure is to use dark print or lettering on a light background—especially if you are using poster board or an overhead transparency. If you are using a video projector as part of a multimedia presentation, you may find that light print on a dark background works better. In either case, make sure there is enough contrast between the background and the text so listeners can see everything clearly.

You can also use color to highlight key points in a visual aid. One student, in a speech about noise pollution, used a chart to summarize the sound levels of everyday noise and to indicate their potential danger for hearing loss (Figure 13.10). Notice, when you look at the chart, how the speaker used color to emphasize the different levels. He put sounds that are definitely harmful to hearing in red, sounds that may cause hearing loss in blue, and sounds that are loud but safe in green. These colors reinforced the speaker's ideas and, at the same time, made his chart easier to read.

Related Reading

For an excellent discussion of fonts, color, and other design elements in visual aids, see Molly W. Joss and Roger C. Parker, *Looking Good in Presentations*, 3rd ed. (Scottsdale, AZ: Coriolis, 2000).

Guidelines for Presenting Visual Aids

In addition to selecting and preparing your visual aids with care, you need to give attention to how you will *present* the aids in your speech. No matter how well designed your visual aids may be, they will be of little value unless you display them properly, discuss them clearly, and integrate them effectively with the rest of your presentation. Here are seven guidelines that will help you get the maximum impact out of your visual aids.

Avoid Using the Chalkboard for Visual Aids

At first thought, using the chalkboard in your classroom to present visual aids seems like a splendid idea. Usually, however, it is not. You have too much to do during a speech to worry about drawing or writing legibly on the board. Many students have marred an otherwise fine speech by turning their backs on the audience to use the chalkboard. Even if your visual aid is put on the chalkboard ahead of time, it will not be as vivid or as neat as one composed on poster board or a transparency.

Display Visual Aids Where Listeners Can See Them

Check the speech room ahead of time to decide exactly where you will display your visual aids. If you are using poster board, make sure it is sturdy enough to be displayed without curling up or falling over. Another choice is foamcore, a thin sheet of styrofoam with graphics-quality paper on both sides.

If you are displaying an object or a model, be sure to place it where it can be seen easily by everyone in the room. Setting it on a table next to the lectern may be fine for listeners seated in front, but the table may be too low for the aid to be visible to people seated farther back. If necessary, hold up the object or model while you are discussing it.

Once you have set the aid in the best location, don't undo all your preparation by standing where you block the audience's view of the aid. Stand to one side of the aid, and point with the arm nearest it. If possible, use a pencil, a ruler, or some other pointer. Using a pointer will allow you to stand farther away from the visual aid, thereby reducing the likelihood that you will obstruct the view of people sitting on the same side of the room as you are standing.

Teaching Tip
Be sure to discuss with students how they will display their visual aids in the classroom. Demonstrate how to set up and display a visual aid, how to explain an aid clearly and concisely, how to maintain eye contact while discussing an aid, and how to move smoothly from one aid to another in the course of a speech.

Avoid Passing Visual Aids Among the Audience

Once visual aids get into the hands of your listeners, you are in trouble. At least three people will be paying more attention to the aid than to you—the person who has just had it, the person who has it now, and the person waiting to get it next. By the time the visual aid moves on, all three may have lost track of what you are saying.

Nor do you solve this problem by preparing a handout for every member of the audience. There is no guarantee they will pay attention to it only when you want them to. In fact, they are likely to spend a good part of the speech looking over the handout at their own pace, rather than listening to you. Although handouts can be valuable, they usually just create competition for beginning speakers.

Every once in a while, of course, you will want listeners to have copies of some material to take home. When such a situation arises, keep the copies until after you've finished talking and can distribute them without creating a distraction. Keeping control of your visual aids is essential to keeping control of your speech.

The Checklist for Presenting Visual Aids can help you use visual aids effectively.

CD 1: SPEECH CHECKLIST

Display Visual Aids Only While Discussing Them

Just as circulating visual aids distracts attention, so does displaying them throughout a speech. Whenever an aid is visible, at least some people will spend their time looking at it rather than listening to you.

If you are using an object or a model, keep it out of sight until you are ready to discuss it. When you finish your discussion, place the object or model back out of sight. The same is true of charts, graphs, or drawings prepared on poster board. If you are using an easel, put a blank sheet of poster board in front of the sheet with the visual aid. When the time comes, remove the blank sheet to show the aid. When you are finished with the aid, remove it from the easel or cover it back up with a blank piece of poster board so it will not divert the attention of your listeners.

Talk to Your Audience, Not to Your Visual Aid

When explaining a visual aid, it is easy to break eye contact with your audience and speak to the aid. Of course, your listeners are looking primarily at the aid, and you will need to glance at it periodically as you talk. But if you keep your eyes fixed on the visual aid, you may lose your audience. By keeping eye contact with your listeners, you will also pick up feedback about how the visual aid and your explanation of it are coming across.

Explain Visual Aids Clearly and Concisely

Visual aids don't explain themselves. Like statistics, they need to be translated and related to the audience. For example, Figure 13.11 (page 339) is an excellent visual aid, but do you know what it represents? You may if you suffer from migraine headaches, since it shows the different regions of pain experienced during a cluster migraine attack. But even then, the full meaning of the drawing may not be clear until it is explained to you. And it certainly will not be clear to a person who knows little about migraines.

A visual aid can be of enormous benefit—but only if the viewer knows what to look for and why. Unfortunately, beginning speakers often rush over their visual aids without explaining them clearly and concisely. Be sure to adapt your visual aids to the audience. Don't just say, "As you can see . . . " and then pass quickly over the aid. Tell listeners what the aid means. Describe its major features. Spell out the meaning of charts and graphs. Interpret statistics and percentages. Remember, a visual aid is only as useful as the explanation that goes with it.

As you can see from CD 1, Video 13.5, the speaker who used the diagram of the migraine headache discussed above did an excellent job of explaining how each color on the drawing corresponds with an area of intense pain suffered during a cluster migraine. Having used the drawing during her practice sessions, she was able to integrate it into the speech smoothly and skillfully—and to maintain eye contact with her listeners throughout her discussion of it. You should strive to do the same when you present visual aids in your speeches.

View an excerpt from Kris Recker, "The Agony of Migraines."

CD 1: VIDEO 13.5

Figure 13.11

Practice with Your Visual Aids

This chapter has mentioned several times the need to practice with visual aids, but the point bears repeating. You do not want to suffer through an experience like the one that follows:

> Several years ago, a young engineer came up with a cutting-edge design for a new machine. He then needed to explain the machine to his supervisors and convince them it was a worthwhile investment. He was told to plan his speech carefully, to prepare slides and other visual aids, and to practice in the conference room, using its complex lectern and projection system.
>
> Unfortunately, although he had done a brilliant job designing the machine, the engineer failed to plan his presentation with similar care. His worst mistake was not practicing with the equipment he now needed to operate. When he dimmed the lights, he couldn't read his text. When the first slide came on, it wasn't his but belonged to a previous speaker. When he reached the first correct slide, the type was too small for anyone past the first row to see.
>
> Unable to turn on the light-arrow indicator to point out the line he was talking about, he walked away from the lectern to point things out directly on the screen. But he left the microphone behind, so people in the back rows could neither see nor hear.
>
> When a slide of his design appeared, he was too close to see the critical parts. Since he couldn't check his text because of the darkness, he lost track of what he was supposed to say. Reaching for a steel-tipped pointer because he couldn't operate the optical one, he managed to punch a hole through the screen.
>
> In desperation, he abandoned his slides, turned up the lights, and raced through the rest of his speech so fast that he was almost unintelligible. Finally, in embarrassment both for himself and the audience, he sat down.[8]

This sounds like a routine from *Saturday Night Live,* but it is a true story. What makes the story especially sad is that it didn't have to happen.

Class Activity
Bring to class a how-to television program (a cooking or gardening show, for instance) or the weather portion of a local newscast. After discussing the kinds of visual aids used in the show, focus attention on how the speaker uses her or his delivery to integrate the aids smoothly with the verbal presentation.

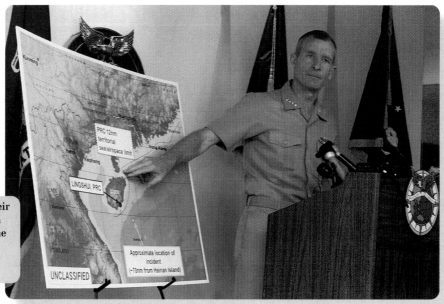

Effective speakers include their visual aids when practicing a speech so they can explain the aids clearly and concisely while maintaining strong eye contact with the audience.

With some effort, thought, and preparation, the engineer could have made a success of his presentation instead of turning it into a fiasco.

You can avoid following in his footsteps if you practice with the visual aids you have chosen. Rehearse with your equipment to be sure you can present your aids with a minimum of fuss. Run through the entire speech several times, practicing how you will show the aids, the gestures you will make, and the timing of each move. In using visual aids, as in other aspects of speechmaking, there is no substitute for preparation.

Summary

There are many kinds of visual aids. Most obvious is the object about which you are speaking, or a model of it. Diagrams, sketches, and other kinds of drawings are valuable because you can design them to illustrate your points exactly. Graphs are an excellent way to illustrate any subject dealing with numbers, while charts are used to summarize large blocks of information. Although video can be useful as a visual aid, it needs to be carefully edited and integrated into the speech. Photographs need to be large enough to be seen clearly by all your listeners. If you have access to the right equipment, you may be able to combine several kinds of visual aids—plus sound—in a multimedia presentation. Finally, you can act as your own visual aid by performing actions that demonstrate processes or ideas.

No matter what kind of visual aid you use, you need to prepare it carefully. You will be most successful if you prepare your aids in advance, keep them simple, make sure they are large enough to be seen clearly, and use color effectively for emphasis and visual appeal. If you are creating visual aids on a computer, use a limited number of fonts and make sure the ones you select will be easy for your audience to read.

In addition to being designed with care, visual aids need to be presented skillfully. Avoid writing or drawing visual aids on the chalkboard. Nor should you pass visual aids among the audience. Instead, display each aid only while you are talking about it, and be sure to display it where everyone can see it without straining. When presenting a visual aid, maintain eye contact with your listeners. Talk to the audience, not to the aid, and explain the aid clearly and concisely. Above all, practice with your visual aids so they fit into your speech smoothly and expertly.

Key Terms

model (324)

graph (327)

line graph (327)

pie graph (327)

bar graph (328)

chart (329)

transparency (330)

multimedia presentation (331)

font (334)

Review these terms by doing the Chapter 13 crossword puzzle at www.mhhe.com/lucas8.

ONLINE LEARNING CENTER

Review Questions

After reading this chapter, you should be able to answer the following questions:

1. What are the major advantages of using visual aids in your speeches?

2. What kinds of visual aids might you use in a speech?

3. What guidelines are given in the chapter for preparing visual aids?

4. What guidelines are given in the chapter for presenting visual aids?

For further review, go to the Study Questions for this chapter.

CD 1: STUDY QUESTIONS

Exercises for Critical Thinking

1. Watch a how-to television program (a cooking or gardening show, for example) or the weather portion of a local newscast. Notice how the speaker uses visual aids to help communicate the message. What kinds of visual aids are used? How do they enhance the clarity, interest, and retainability of the speaker's message? What would the speaker have to do to communicate the message effectively without visual aids?

2. Consider how you might use visual aids to explain each of the following:

    a. How to perform the Heimlich maneuver to help a choking victim.

    b. The proportion of the electorate that votes in major national elections in the United States, France, Germany, England, and Japan, respectively.

    c. Where to write for information about student loans.

    d. The wing patterns of various species of butterflies.

    e. The increase in the amount of money spent by Americans on health care since 1985.

    f. How to change a bicycle tire.

    g. The basic equipment and techniques of rock climbing.

Cross-Reference

For discussion of the Exercises for Critical Thinking, see the *Instructor's Manual*, pp. 281–282. For additional exercises, check the *Instructor's Manual*, p. 283, as well as the five volumes of *Selections from the Speech Communication Teacher* that accompany *The Art of Public Speaking*.

3. Plan to use visual aids in at least one of your classroom speeches. Be creative in devising your aids, and be sure to follow the guidelines discussed in the chapter for using them. After the speech, analyze how effectively you employed your visual aids, what you learned about the use of visual aids from your experience, and what changes you would make in using visual aids if you were to deliver the speech again.

Applying the POWER of PUBLIC SPEAKING

Cross-Reference
For discussion of this Applying the Power of Public Speaking scenario, see the *Instructor's Manual*, p. 282.

As a veterinarian and owner of a small-animal practice, you work closely with your local humane society to help control a growing population of unwanted dogs and cats. You and your staff devote many hours annually in free and reduced-cost medical services to animals adopted from the society. Now you have been asked to speak to the city council in support of legislation proposed by the society for stronger enforcement of animal licensing and leash laws.

In your speech, you plan to include statistics that (1) compare estimates of the city's dog population with the number of licenses issued during the past five years and (2) show the small number of citations given by local law enforcement for unleashed pets during the same period of time. Knowing from your college public speaking class how valuable visual aids can be in presenting statistics, you decide to illustrate one set of statistics with a chart and the other with a graph.

For which set of statistics will a chart be more appropriate? For which set will a graph be more appropriate? Of the three kinds of graphs discussed in this chapter (bar, line, pie), which will work best for your statistics and why?

Notes

[1]Richard E. Mayer and Valerie K. Sims, "For Whom Is a Picture Worth a Thousand Words? Extensions of a Dual-Coding Theory of Multimedia Learning," *Journal of Educational Psychology,* 86 (1994), pp. 389–401.

[2]Michael E. Patterson, Donald F. Danscreau, and Dianna Newbern, "Effects of Communication Aids on Cooperative Teaching," *Journal of Educational Psychology,* 84 (1992), pp. 453–461.

[3]Douglas R. Vogel, Gary W. Dickson, and John A Lehman, *Persuasion and the Role of Visual Presentation Support: The UM/3M Study* (Minneapolis: University of Minnesota School of Management, 1986).

[4]Tad Simons, "Multimedia or Bust," *Presentations* (February 2000), pp. 40–50.

[5]Joe Ayres, "Using Visual Aids to Reduce Speech Anxiety," *Communication Research Reports,* 8 (June–December 1991), pp. 73–79.

[6]For an authoritative look at the art and science of statistical graphics, see Edward R. Tufte, *The Visual Display of Quantitative Information,* 2nd ed. (Cheshire, CT: Graphics Press, 2001).

[7]Claudyne Wilder, *The Presentations Kit: 10 Steps for Selling Your Ideas*, rev. ed (New York: Wiley, 1994), p. 101.

[8]Adapted from Eric A. Walker, "About the 'Death' of an Engineer," *Centre Daily Times,* April 25, 1972.

APPENDIX
Using PowerPoint

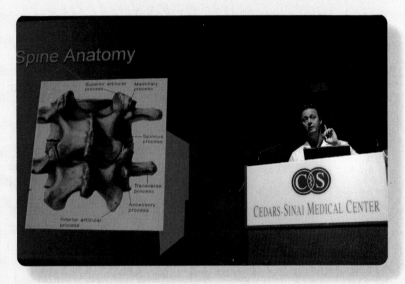

W hat do a business meeting, a courtroom presentation, a military briefing, and a college lecture have in common? In all four situations there is a good chance you will encounter a speaker using PowerPoint to help communicate her or his ideas. A survey of 300 professional speakers showed that 94 percent use PowerPoint during at least part of their talks.[1] Another study revealed that 90 percent of the multimedia presentations in the United States are developed with PowerPoint.[2] Depending on the technology at your school, you may have an opportunity to use PowerPoint in one or more of your classroom speeches.

In Chapter 13, we discussed general principles for effective multimedia presentations. Here we focus specifically on PowerPoint. As with any method of presenting visual or audio aids, PowerPoint has its pluses and minuses. We'll begin by looking at both, as well as at the major factors to consider when planning to use PowerPoint in a speech.

Pluses and Minuses of PowerPoint

When used well, PowerPoint is a great boon to communication. It allows you to employ all the kinds of visual aids discussed in Chapter 13 without having to juggle poster board and overhead transparencies while also trying to operate a CD player, slide projector, and/or video playback unit. Instead, you can use PowerPoint to incorporate text, photographs, charts, graphs, sound, even video into your speech—all with the click of a mouse.

Unfortunately, PowerPoint is not always used well. Too often speakers allow it to dominate their presentations, wowing the audience with their technical proficiency while causing listeners to lose sight of the message in a flurry of spectacular—but haphazard—sounds and images. As technology expert Herb Lovelace states, it sometimes seems that "the fancier the PowerPoint presentation, the less valuable the ideas being presented."[3]

At the other extreme are speakers who throw their presentations together carelessly, assuming that using PowerPoint—no matter how badly—will magically produce a superb speech. Plodding through one poorly designed visual after another with little or no eye contact with an audience seated in a darkened room, these speakers would be better off if they had never heard of PowerPoint.

Another problem is that some speakers use PowerPoint to illustrate every point of their talk, so the speaker is virtually reading the speech to the audience as the words appear on screen. This is no more effective than reading dully from a manuscript, and it seldom produces genuine communication with the audience.

Planning to Use PowerPoint

If you are going to employ PowerPoint effectively, you need a clear idea of exactly why, how, and when you are going to use it in your speech. Rather than falling into the trap of putting everything you say on screen for the audience to read, you need to make choices about which aspects of your speech you will illustrate with visual or audio aids. This requires careful planning.

One of the most surprising aspects of PowerPoint to people who have not used it before is how much time and effort are required to put together a first-rate presentation. Not only are you responsible for all the other activities involved in speechmaking, but you face the additional tasks of deciding where to use PowerPoint in the speech, of gathering images and/or sounds for your presentation, of designing first-rate PowerPoint aids, and of mastering the equipment and PowerPoint commands needed to deliver your speech smoothly and expertly.

The first step is deciding where in the speech you can use PowerPoint to greatest advantage. After you have finished developing the speech, go through it and think about where you might employ PowerPoint to clarify or strengthen your ideas. Rather than using PowerPoint to illustrate every thought, look for spots where it will genuinely enhance your message.

For example, if you're talking about the history of woman's suffrage in the United States, you might include the text of the Nineteenth Amendment, which granted women the vote in 1920; photographs of famous suffrage leaders such as Elizabeth Cady Stanton, Susan B. Anthony, and Carrie Chapman Catt; and a chart with the major events and dates of the suffrage crusade. If you are speaking about West Nile virus, it would make sense to include a diagram showing how the virus is spread, a list of its symptoms, a graph demonstrating the increase in the number of cases in recent years, and a map illustrating the spread of the virus through different regions of the United States.

As you plan your presentation, think about how you can use the tools provided by PowerPoint to go beyond what you might be able to do with traditional visual aids. At the same time, remember that too many visuals— not to mention visuals that are badly designed or poorly explained—can do more harm than good. Be creative and resourceful without allowing PowerPoint to overwhelm your entire speech.

Related Reading

Presentations magazine is an excellent source for keeping track of the latest developments in PowerPoint and other presentation programs. It also provides a wealth of practical advice from experienced speakers about how to develop effective presentations. A month after the publication of each issue, articles are reprinted on the Presentations.com website (www.presentations.com/presentations/index.jsp).

Getting Started in PowerPoint

Once you have decided which aspects of your speech to illustrate with PowerPoint, it's time to start working on your presentation. When you work in PowerPoint, you will be creating *slides* that consist of words, images, and/or sounds that help communicate your ideas to the audience. In the language of PowerPoint, all the slides for a given speech are called a *presentation*. You might think of a PowerPoint slide as equivalent to an individual visual aid, and of a PowerPoint presentation as equivalent to a file folder that holds all the aids for a speech.

slide
A single frame in a PowerPoint presentation.

presentation
A PowerPoint file containing all the slides for a given speech.

Screen Elements

If you have not used PowerPoint before, you should take a moment to familiarize yourself with its screen elements. Figure A.1 (page 346) shows these elements as they appear in PowerPoint 2002. At the top, just below

Figure A.1 PowerPoint 2002 Screen Elements

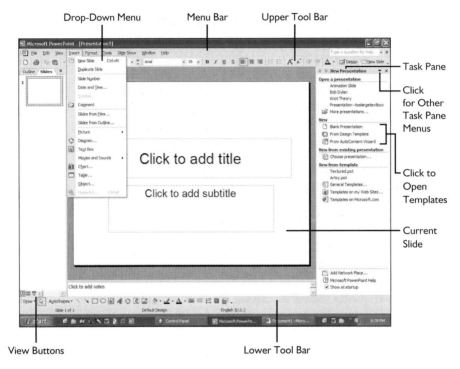

the Microsoft PowerPoint title, is the menu bar, which helps you perform major functions such as opening and closing presentations, choosing fonts, inserting images, and viewing slides. When you click the boxes on the menu bar, drop-down menus appear with more choices. Just below the menu bar is the upper toolbar, which provides shortcuts for such tasks as creating new slides, adding bold or italicized text, undoing your previous action, and saving your work.

Another toolbar stretches across the bottom of the screen. Among the items on this bar are three buttons with icons just above Draw in the lower left-hand corner. These buttons allow you to shift among different views of your presentation. The lower toolbar also includes shortcuts for such functions as adding text boxes, charts, clip art, and color.

The main part of the screen appears in what PowerPoint calls Normal view. This view is divided into three areas. The center area displays your current slide. On the left is a pane that allows you to switch between viewing an outline of all your slides and thumbnails of the slides. On the right is a task pane that provides tools for creating new presentations and for formatting slides.

Templates

PowerPoint gives you three methods for creating a presentation: AutoContent Wizard, Blank Presentation, and Design Templates.

Figure A.2   Design Templates

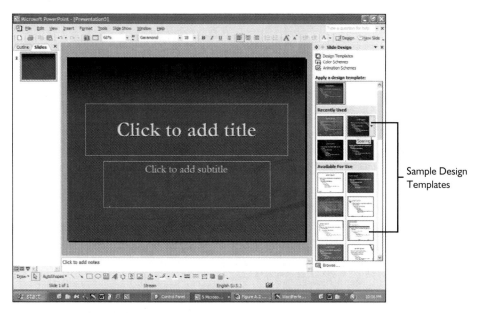

Sample Design
Templates

Designed primarily for business speakers, AutoContent Wizard provides templates with predetermined outlines and sample text for more than 20 kinds of presentations, such as Employee Orientation, Facilitating a Meeting, and Selling a Product or Service. Although helpful in some situations, it is seldom used for speeches outside a business setting.

As its name implies, Blank Presentation does not come with any preset designs. Some experienced speakers prefer the flexibility it provides in designing slides, but it can be daunting for novices.

Most students prefer to start with the Design Template option, which generates a presentation in which all the slides are unified by a prese-lected combination of colors, fonts, and graphics. When you choose De-sign Template, sample templates appear on the right of the screen. By click-ing any template, you can view it in the main part of your screen. (See Figure A.2, above.)

If you use Design Template, be sure to avoid templates with busy back-grounds that may distract from your message. Fortunately, you can easily switch templates partway through a presentation if you decide you don't like your original choice.

Slide Layouts

Both Design Templates and Blank Presentation provide more than two dozen slide layouts for arranging the items on your slides. Thumbnails of these layouts can be viewed in the right pane on your computer screen. (See Figure A.3, page 348.) Click any layout, and it will appear in the mid-dle of your screen.

Figure A.3 Slide Layouts

Once you know your way around the basic elements of PowerPoint, you're ready to begin developing slides for your speech. In the Online Learning Center for your textbook, you will find step-by-step instructions on how to create slides; how to insert text, images, and sounds onto slides; how to format slides for a crisp, professional look; and how to add special features such as animation and transitions to your slides.

If you have not used PowerPoint before, these instructions will provide the information you need to get started on the right track. If you have used PowerPoint before, keep the instructions in mind as a resource you can turn to if you have questions as you work on your slides. You can access the instructions by going to the Online Learning Center at www.mhhe.com/lucas8 and clicking PowerPoint 2000 or PowerPoint 2002, depending on which version is on your computer.

Here we will focus less on technical information than on principles for using PowerPoint effectively in your speeches. As we proceed, we'll illustrate key points with examples from a five-minute informative speech on the Great Wall of China. The full speech is available on CD 1, Video A2.1, and is reprinted at the end of this appendix. You may find it helpful to view the speech now, so you will have it in mind as the discussion unfolds. From time to time, we will also refer you to brief clips from the speech that demonstrate particular points about how you can use PowerPoint to best advantage.

Go to the PowerPoint Tutorials at www.mhhe.com/lucaspowerpoint.

ONLINE LEARNING CENTER

View "The Great Wall of China."

CD 1: VIDEO A2.1

Elements of PowerPoint Slides

The major elements of PowerPoint slides are text, images, and sounds. They can be used individually or in combination, depending on the specific point

Figure A.4
Sample PowerPoint Slide

you wish to communicate. There are also many kinds of images available to you, ranging from video to still images such as photographs, clip art, and graphs. Let's look at each individually.

Text

Most PowerPoint slides contain some kind of text. The text might be no more than a title indicating the subject of the slide, or it might include several lines in the body of the slide. Text can be used by itself, and it can be used in conjunction with photographs, clip art, or other images. For the most part, any text appropriate for a traditional visual aid can be included on a PowerPoint slide.

For example, Figure A.4 shows a slide from the speech on the Great Wall of China. The speaker used this slide in conjunction with his explanation of the first stage of building the Great Wall, during the Qin dynasty. In addition to an image of Qin Shi Huang, the emperor who started construction of the Wall, the slide contains a title plus text identifying Qin Shi Huang and the dates of the Qin dynasty. The slide also includes copyright information for the drawing of Qin Shi Huang.

Photographs

One of the benefits of PowerPoint is the ease with which it allows you to spice up a speech with photographs. If you're speaking on a topic drawn from your personal experience, you can use PowerPoint to display your own photographs. For other topics, you can download photographs from the Web. Here are some of the best online sources for photographs on topics of current and historical interest:

■ *Google Image Search* (www.google.com/imghp?hl=en&ie=UTF-8&oe=UTF-8&q=). The Web's most comprehensive image resource. Allows you to search for photographs on virtually any topic across thousands of websites.

- *Pics4Learning* (http://pics4learning.com). Features thousands of donated images that have no copyright restrictions. Images are divided into categories such as architecture, history, religion, and weather.

- *The Amazing Picture Machine* (www.ncrtec.org/picture.htm). A searchable database especially good for images of astronomy, world leaders, and art.

- *Free Stock Photos* (http://freestockphotos.com/). Provides links to thousands of photographs, historical and contemporary, that can be used without charge for personal purposes.

Clip Art

Clip art includes pictures and symbols that represent common objects, processes, and ideas. Examples of clip art are a drawing of a microscope to stand for science, or a cartoon of an aircraft circling the globe to symbolize travel.

Clip art can be humorous and entertaining, but it can also be distracting and inappropriate. If you employ clip art, avoid using it on every slide and use only one piece of clip art on a given slide. Be certain the images you select convey the same emotional tone as your speech, and make sure all the images are drawn in a consistent style.

There are numerous online sources for clip art. Two of the major ones are:

clip art
Pictures and symbols that represent common objects, processes, and ideas.

- *Microsoft Design Gallery Live* (http://dgl.microsoft.com/?CAG=1). An extensive collection of clip art searchable by category and keyword. Also contains sounds and motions.

- *Barry's Clip Art Server* (www.barrysclipart.com). Contains thousands of pieces of donated clip art that have no copyright restrictions.

Graphs

As we saw in Chapter 13, graphs are excellent for communicating statistical trends and patterns. PowerPoint gives you a number of ways to incorporate graphs into your speeches. One option is to download graphs from the Internet. Websites for government agencies, newspapers, and magazines are all excellent places to look for graphs on current topics. Another option is to use PowerPoint's graph program to create a graph using data you have gathered.

Figure A.5 (page 351) shows what you will see when you enter the graph program. The datasheet is a separate window. As you replace the labels and numbers on the datasheet with your own labels and numbers, the graph will change accordingly. You can also switch to a different kind of graph, such as a pie graph or bar graph. Whichever kind you use, be sure to follow the general principles for effective graphs discussed in Chapter 13.

Sounds

If you're speaking on a topic such as language development, birdcalls, or the jazz violin, you might want to play a sound clip to illustrate your ideas. PowerPoint offers several methods to add sound to your presentation. You

Figure A.5   PowerPoint Graph Program

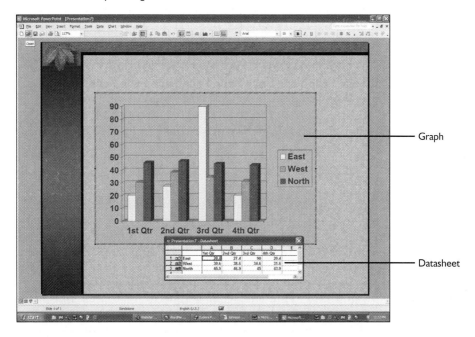

Graph

Datasheet

can play an excerpt from a CD, you can use downloaded sounds from the Web, or you can utilize sounds that you have recorded yourself.

The most important thing to remember with regard to using sounds of any kind is that they should be absolutely essential for communicating your message. You should never add sounds just for the fun of it. Whatever sounds you include should be limited in length so as to illustrate your points without overwhelming them. Remember, the audience has come to listen to you— not to listen to a series of recordings from other people.

Video

PowerPoint offers a number of options for adding video to a speech. For a presentation based on your own experience, you might be able to draw on your personal video collection. These video recordings can be edited and saved on files which are then available for use on PowerPoint slides. Another option is to download nonstreaming video from the Internet, as long as you are careful to observe copyright restrictions (see pages 359–360).

Video, like sound, should be added to a speech only when it is indispensable to communicating your message. It also needs to be skillfully edited and smoothly integrated with the rest of the speech. Be aware that video files take up large amounts of disk space and are often impractical for presentations run from older computers. If you are planning to include video in your speech, be sure to check it ahead of time with the computer you will use on the day of your speech to make sure the video plays at the correct speed and the sound is properly synchronized with the picture.

Related Reading

There are numerous books that provide full-blown guides to the various versions of PowerPoint. Among the best are Faithe Wempen, *Microsoft PowerPoint 2000 Bible* (New York: Hungry Minds, 1999), and Patrice-Ann Rutledge and Tom Mucciolo, *Special Edition Using Microsoft PowerPoint 2002* (Indianapolis, IN: Que 2001).

Formatting Slides

Once you have the text, images, sounds, and/or videos that you want to include on your slides, the next step is to format the slides to communicate your message as effectively as possible. Although PowerPoint provides a number of advanced formatting features, you can start creating sharp, professional-looking slides right away by following a few basic principles for the use of color, fonts, space, and animation. You should also review the guidelines for preparing visual aids discussed in Chapter 13, pages 332–336.

Color

PowerPoint offers a wide selection of colors for your slides, and you may be tempted to try all of them. But to produce effective visual aids, you need to stick to a limited number of colors and use them consistently. Use one color for background, one color for titles, and one color for other text throughout all your slides. Notice, for example, how the Great Wall of China speech uses a red background for all slides, gold for title text, and white for all other text. This consistency unifies the slides and gives the speech a more professional appearance.

When selecting colors, keep in mind that light text against a dark background provides the best contrast for LCD projection. PowerPoint's Color Schemes feature gives you a dozen preset options for different color combinations (see Figure A.6). Clicking any of the options will transfer it to your slides.

Figure A.6   Color Schemes

Serif Fonts	Sans-Serif Fonts
Times New Roman	Arial
Bookman Old Style	Antique Olive
MS Reference Serif	MS Reference Sans Serif
Book Antiqua	Tahoma
Palatino Linotype	Verdana

Figure A.7

Fonts

PowerPoint has dozens of fonts to choose from, but they all fall into one or another of two basic categories—serif or sans-serif. Serif fonts have little tails on each letter, like the type you are reading right now. Sans-serif fonts do not have tails, like the type used for the heading **Fonts** at the start of this section. For examples, see Figure A.7, above.

Serif fonts are easier to read in large patches of text, while sans-serif fonts are better for headings and short bursts of text.[4] Most multimedia experts recommend sans-serif fonts for titles and headings on PowerPoint slides—and there are some who say sans-serif should be used for *all* text in PowerPoint.

The default font for most slides in PowerPoint 2002 is a sans-serif font called Arial. In normal circumstances, there is no reason for you to change from this font. However, if your slides come up with a different font, or if you wish to change the font for some other reason, you can do so fairly easily. When choosing fonts, keep the following guidelines in mind:

- Choose fonts that are clear and easy to read. (For examples, see Chapter 13, pages 334–335.)

- Avoid using ALL CAPS because they are difficult to read.

- Don't use more than two fonts on a single slide—one for the title or major heading and another for subtitles or other text.

- Use the same fonts on all your slides, rather than switching fonts from slide to slide.

- Put titles and major headings in 44- to 36-point type; make subheads and other text 32- to 24-point. The only exception to this rule is copyright credits, which are best in 10-point type.

serif font
A typeface with rounded edges on the letters.

sans-serif font
A typeface with straight edges on the letters.

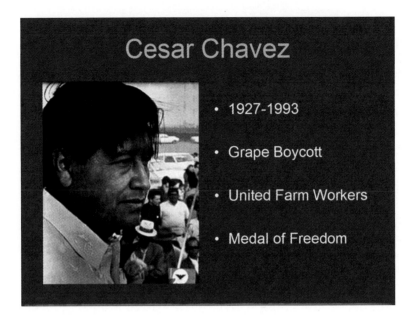

Figure A.8
Effective Visual Balance

Space

One of the biggest mistakes people make when using PowerPoint is putting too much on a single slide. The result is a cluttered, messy slide that detracts from the speaker's message and may well confuse the audience. A general rule for slides that contain only text is to include no more than six lines of type. If you are combining text with images, you may need to limit yourself to fewer lines to keep the text large enough for the audience to read without straining.

Regardless of the elements on your slide, try to achieve a pleasing sense of visual balance when arranging them. Look, for example, at Figure A.8 (above), which shows a slide from a speech about the famous Mexican-American leader Cesar Chavez. Notice how the title is centered at the top of the slide, the photograph fills most of the left side, and the text occupies enough space on the right to compensate for the size of the photograph.

Compare this slide with the one in Figure A.9 on page 355. The second slide contains the same elements as the first, but those elements are not placed effectively. Instead of being centered, the title is located over the photograph, where it takes up two lines rather than one. To compensate, the photograph of Chavez has been reduced in size, so it has less visual impact than the photograph on the first slide. The photograph is also too close to the bottom of the slide, thereby separating it from the title. Finally, the text on the right side is too close to the photograph and is too high on the slide to provide a good sense of visual balance.

If you stick with PowerPoint's default layouts, you should have little trouble creating slides that are visually balanced. Be sure, however, to leave a little extra room at the edges of your slides because what is projected on the viewing screen is sometimes smaller than what you see on your computer.

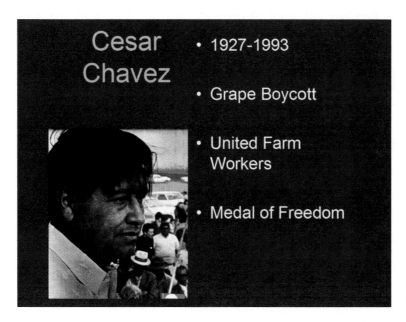

Figure A.9
Ineffective Visual Balance

Animation

When you read the word "animation," you might think of cartoon characters and Walt Disney movies. In PowerPoint, however, animation refers to the way objects enter or exit a slide. Without animation, all the items on a slide appear at the same time when the slide is displayed. With animation, you can control when words, pictures, and even parts of graphs show up on screen. When used properly, it's a terrific way to spruce up your slides.

Recall the speech on the Great Wall of China. For the most part, the speaker avoids special animation effects because they are not necessary to communicate his ideas. However, when explaining the architectural changes made to the Wall during the Ming dynasty, he uses animation to make sure the appropriate text appears on screen just as he begins to discuss each point. By doing so, he focuses the audience's attention and reinforces his ideas at the same time.

When working on your speeches, think about ways you can use animation to help communicate your message. Be wary, however, of animation effects that might distract the attention of listeners. Stick with a limited number of animation effects and use them consistently from slide to slide.

animation
The way objects enter or exit a PowerPoint slide.

View this excerpt from "The Great Wall of China."

CD 1: VIDEO A2.2

Delivering Your Speech with PowerPoint

Once you have created your slides, it's time to work on the delivery of your speech. As with other aspects of PowerPoint, this requires careful planning. Even the most professional-looking slides will do little good if you can't get the computer and projector to work properly, if the slides can't be seen clearly because of poor lighting, or if you forget to display them at the right moment.

Figure A.10 Slide Sorter View

The guidelines presented in Chapter 13 for delivering speeches with other types of visual aids also apply to delivering speeches with Power-Point. Here we will focus on aspects of delivery that are especially important for speakers who employ PowerPoint.

Recheck Your Slides

Before rehearsing your speech, take time to double-check your slides to see if anything is missing, misplaced, or misspelled. You can review all your slides at a glance in Slide Sorter view (see Figure A.10). It's also a good idea to run through your slides in Slide Show view, which displays the slides as they will appear on screen during your speech. Be sure to save any corrections and changes as you go along.

Know Slide Show Commands

When delivering your speech, you should be able to move effortlessly from slide to slide, as well as among animation effects on individual slides. To do so, you have to know the computer commands for these operations. Figure A.11 (page 357) shows some of the most-used commands.

As you can see, there are multiple options for most commands. If you have not used PowerPoint before, practice with the various options and decide which you want to use. Then stick with them throughout your presentation.

As you gain more experience with PowerPoint, its commands will become second nature. However, just in case you forget something during your

Slide Show Commands

Display slides (enter Slide Show view)	Click View on the menu bar at the top of the screen and select Slide Show from the drop-down menu; or click the podium icon on the left of the tool bar at the bottom of the screen.
Show the next slide	Click the mouse; press Enter; press the right arrow button; or press the "N" key.
Show the previous slide	Press Backspace; press the left arrow button; or press the "P" key.
Show a specific slide	Type the number of the slide and press Enter.
End the show	Press Esc.

Check the PowerPoint Tutorials at www.mhhe.com/lucaspowerpoint for additional Slide Show commands.

ONLINE LEARNING CENTER

Figure A.11

speech, you may want to follow the lead of experienced speakers and write the most important commands on a sheet of paper that you can refer to if necessary.

Practice Your Speech with PowerPoint

As we saw in Chapter 13, you should always practice a speech with your visual aids. This is especially important when using PowerPoint. If you don't know the necessary commands, fumble around when operating the equipment, or fail to coordinate your slides with your words, you will quickly lose both your credibility and the attention of listeners.

When you practice your speech using PowerPoint, don't just click the mouse casually or rush quickly over your words. Go through every part of the speech and make sure you know exactly when you want each slide to appear, when you want each to disappear, and what you will say while each is on screen. Mark your speaking notes with cues that will remind you when to display each slide or animation and when to remove it from the screen.

It's usually best to project a slide when you first start discussing the point it illustrates. For a good example, look at the timing of the slides in the speech about the Great Wall of China. The speaker presents each slide at just the right moment and makes sure it is on screen only while he is discussing it. He also times his animation effects to appear just as he is talking about the related point. This kind of precise timing comes from practicing the speech with PowerPoint.

In addition to coordinating your slides with your words, pay attention when you practice to making eye contact with the audience. This is important in any speech, but it is especially challenging when you use PowerPoint because of all the equipment you are operating during the

View an excerpt from "The Great Wall of China."

CD 1: VIDEO A2.3

speech. As you rehearse, work with the mouse and keyboard until you can use both without looking down for more than an instant when advancing your slides.

Also concentrate on presenting the speech without looking back at the screen to see what is being projected on it. You can check what is on screen by glancing at the computer each time you advance a slide. There is nothing wrong with looking at the screen now and again as you explain your slides, but remember to address your remarks to the audience and not to the screen. The Great Wall speech provides a good model in this regard.

Given all the things you have to work on when practicing a speech with PowerPoint, you need to allow more time for rehearsal than with other kinds of speeches. No matter how well designed your slides may be, they won't have much impact if you don't present them effectively. So get an early start and give yourself plenty of time to ensure that your delivery is as impressive as your slides.

Display Slides Only While Discussing Them

As with other types of visual aids, you want your PowerPoint slides to be visible only when you are discussing them. You can achieve this goal by adding blank slides as needed between your other slides. Recall, for example, how the speaker in the Great Wall presentation uses blank slides at various parts of the speech. By doing so, he keeps his listeners focused on what he is saying at the moment, rather than having their attention diverted by the previous slide.

Remember that whenever a visual aid is visible, at least part of the audience will be paying attention to it rather than listening to you. Using blank slides is one way to prevent this from happening when you present aids with PowerPoint. (It's also a good idea to add a blank slide at the end of your presentation, so your last content slide will not continue to be exposed after you have finished discussing it.)

Check the Room and Equipment

In ideal circumstances, you will be able to rehearse at least once in the room in which you will present your speech, with the same computer, mouse, and projector you will use on the day of your speech. If this is not possible, try to stop by the room several days beforehand and work with the equipment. If you can't get to the room before the day of the speech, arrive an hour or so ahead of time to familiarize yourself with the equipment and to make sure it's working properly.

There is wide variation among computers and projectors, as well as among rooms equipped with multimedia connections, so even if you have used PowerPoint on previous occasions, you need to check the setup in the room where you will be speaking. Most experienced speakers arrange ahead of time to have a technician present when they arrive, so she or he can take care of any problems.

Think, too, about the location of your equipment. If you're using a portable projector, you will need a table on which to place it, as well as a table or lectern for your computer, mouse, and speaking notes. Make sure you have a place to stand where you don't block the projector and it doesn't shine directly into your eyes. Depending on the setup in your room, you may need to rearrange some seats—or the location of the projector and screen—so everyone will have a clear view of your slides.

Pay attention to the lighting as well. Check whether the projector is bright enough to overpower the room lights and create a sharp image. If it isn't, see if you can dim the lights near the screen while keeping the rest of the room fully lighted. If you are using a limited number of slides, you may be able to dim the lights just during the time you show the slides. If the light switches are far away from where you will be speaking, arrange for someone to assist you with the lighting and make sure to give him or her clear directions.

This may all seem like a lot of fuss and bother, but anyone who has given speeches with PowerPoint will tell you it's absolutely essential.

Develop a Backup Plan

Despite all your preparation and practice, it's possible that technology will fail you. More than one speaker has arrived with PowerPoint in tow only to discover that the computer is acting up, the projector will not work, or the room's power connections are not compatible with the speaker's computer.

What do you do if this happens to you? You can't just cancel the speech. As the old saying has it, "The show must go on." This is why you always need a backup plan—especially for speeches outside the classroom.

One option is to create overhead transparencies that you can use in place of your PowerPoint slides. Given the fact that overhead projectors are available almost everywhere in the world, professional speakers usually carry a set of transparencies to their speeches just in case they run into a problem with PowerPoint.

Even if you have transparencies as a backup to PowerPoint, you should always be prepared for the possibility that you may have to deliver your speech without either PowerPoint or your transparencies. In such a situation, you can usually adapt by making photocopies of your transparencies and giving your speech with handouts—though there may be circumstances in which even that is impossible. The important thing is to think through the potential complications in advance and have a backup plan ready just in case you need it.

Speech Assignment
For a creative speech assignment that combines collaborative learning with PowerPoint technology, see Nichola D. Gutgold, "Pointing Groups to PowerPoint," in *Selections from the Speech Communication Teacher: 1996–1999*, p. 76, which accompanies *The Art of Public Speaking.*

Copyright and Fair Use

We have mentioned several times the ease with which photographs, clip art, graphs, charts, and videos can be downloaded from the Internet for use with PowerPoint. It's important, when using such materials, to be aware of and to observe copyright laws. These laws are designed to create a financial incentive for writers, artists, musicians, photographers, and the like to produce original work by limiting the reproduction of that work unless the creator is compensated.

fair use

A provision of copyright law that permits students and teachers to use portions of copyrighted materials for educational purposes.

Under copyright law, someone who wishes to use the original work of another person must obtain permission from that person (or whoever owns the material) and often must pay a usage fee. Despite these restrictions, the "fair use" provision of the law permits students and educators to employ portions of copyrighted materials—including images and sounds downloaded from the Web—for educational purposes. Here are basic guidelines for the fair use of electronic materials:[5]

■ You may use portions of copyrighted materials for a multimedia presentation that you create for a specific class. If you include the presentation in an employment portfolio, you may continue to use the copyrighted materials in it.

■ You may *not* post copyrighted materials back to the Web without written permission from the copyright owner. In other words, if you download copyrighted photographs for use in your speech, you need written permission from the owner of the photographs to put your PowerPoint presentation on your personal Web page or any other website.

■ You may use up to three minutes or 10 percent, whichever is less, of a copyrighted film, videotape, or other motion media work without obtaining permission.

■ You may use up to 10 percent but no more than 30 seconds of music and lyrics from an individual musical work without obtaining permission.

■ You may use an entire photograph or illustration without obtaining permission, but you may use no more than 15 images or 10 percent, whichever is less, of a collection of works.

■ You *must* credit your sources and display the copyright symbol—©— when using copyrighted materials in a PowerPoint presentation. For written works, the credit line should include the author, title, and date of publication. For images and sounds, the credit line should include the title of the work (if there is one) and the name of the copyright holder. The usual practice is to type the credit line in 10-point font and to place it immediately under the item for which credit is being given. For an example, see Figure A.4 on page 349.

Keep these guidelines in mind when you search for images and sounds on the Web as well as in books, magazines, and other print sources. Remember to write down credit and copyright information when you download items from the Web; otherwise, you may have to spend extra time searching for it later.

Related Reading
Copyright issues with regard to the Internet continue to evolve as a result of technological changes and developments in case law. For more information on current conditions, check the Copyright and Image Management website (www.utsystem.edu/ogc/intellectualproperty/image.htm#elec) and the Copyright Management Center (www.copyright.iupui.edu/quickguide.htm).

Sample Speech with Commentary

Below is the text of the informative speech on the Great Wall of China that is available for viewing on CD 1, Video A2.1. As you read the text, notice how it fulfills the criteria for effective speeches discussed elsewhere in the book— sharp focus, clear organization, effective connectives, strong supporting materials, and the like. As you view the speech, pay special attention to the quality of the speaker's PowerPoint slides, to the skill with which he integrates the slides into his presentation, and to the way he maintains eye contact with his audience while discussing his slides.

View "The Great Wall of China."

CD 1: VIDEO A2.1

The Great Wall of China

Commentary	Speech
The speaker begins with a quotation to gain attention and interest. He also establishes his credibility by noting that he visited the Great Wall while he was in China.	In China there's a saying, "You won't be considered a great person until you've been to the Great Wall." I visited the wall last year while I was in China. I don't know if it made me a great person, but I do know that the wall is indeed great.
The speaker's first slide is a striking photograph of the Great Wall that shows how it snakes across the tops of the mountains. He then moves to a slide that illustrates the expanse of the wall as it stretches across China. This slide allows people who are not familiar with China's geography to understand where the wall is located. The speaker ends this paragraph by explaining how the Great Wall would stretch from New York City to Berlin, Germany. An animated slide provides visual reinforcement and helps dramatize the extraordinary length of the wall.	As you can see from this photograph, the wall is great in beauty, with its long arms resting on rolling hills and its towers peering across the valleys. The wall stretches across more than half of China, from the sea in the east, past Beijing, to Gansu province in the west. At a total length of 4,000 miles, it is the longest human-made construction in the world. If the Great Wall were transported to the United States and stretched out in a straight line, it would run from New York City completely across the Atlantic Ocean—past Spain, England, and France, all the way to Berlin, Germany.
A clear preview statement specifies the three main points to be covered in the body of the speech. As you watch the speech on CD, notice how the speaker displays a blank slide during this paragraph so as not to distract the audience's attention.	Today I would like to share with you some of the wonders of the Great Wall. I will focus on the three major stages of its construction, moving from the first phase during the Qin Dynasty, to the second phase during the Han Dynasty, and concluding with the third phase during the Ming Dynasty. Let's start more than 2,000 years ago, when the first parts of the wall were built.
The speaker moves into his first main point. As he does so, he projects a slide showing a drawing of Emperor Qin Shi Huang and the dates of the Qin Dynasty. When he finishes this paragraph, he again projects a blank slide so the audience will be focused on his verbal message in the next paragraph.	The beginning of the Great Wall as we know it dates to 221 B.C., when Emperor Qin Shi Huang ordered his top general to lead 300,000 soldiers in rebuilding and connecting separate old walls that had been built by princes of warring states. In just 12 years, Qin had a 3,000-mile wall using primarily wood frames filled with stones and compacted earth.
This paragraph provides interesting details about the building of the wall during the Qin Dynasty. Notice how the speaker identifies	While the wall proved effective in keeping out the tribes who threatened to invade China from the north, it created dissent within China. According to Arthur Waldron's *The Great Wall of China: From History to Myth,* "ditches on the

the source of his quotation about the human cost of the wall's construction.

A signpost at the start of this paragraph alerts the audience that the speaker is moving into his second main point. After showing a slide with the dates of the Han Dynasty and a drawing of Emperor Wu Di, he projects a photograph to demonstrate how different the Han wall was from the Great Wall as it exists today.

As the speaker starts his third main point, he moves immediately from his slide showing the ruins of the Han wall to a slide with a drawing of Emperor Zhu Yuanzhang and the dates of the Ming Dynasty. Because it is parallel in design to the slides used to introduce the first two main points, this slide reinforces the unity and organizational structure of the speech as a whole.

The speaker begins this paragraph by projecting a slide with a photograph that shows the architectural features of the Great Wall. As he discusses each feature, he uses animation to make the appropriate text appear on his slide. This combination of visual and verbal elements, along with the superb timing of the speaker's animation effects, makes this paragraph especially effective and provides an excellent illustration of how to use PowerPoint to maximum advantage.

After signaling that he is moving into his conclusion, the speaker summarizes his main points and ends by reinforcing his central idea. To make sure the audience does not continue to focus on the architectural features of the Great Wall discussed in the previous paragraph, the speaker displays a blank slide that shifts attention back to him during the conclusion.

roadside were filled with corpses of men who had been forced into construction of the Great Wall." Compelled into hard labor and burdened by heavy taxes to finance the project, the people grew unhappy, and a year after Qin's death, the peasants revolted. While the wall stood, the empire collapsed.

The second major period of construction for the Great Wall occurred during the Han Dynasty, which lasted from 206 B.C. to 220 A.D. Emperor Wu Di ordered expansion of the existing wall to protect land won when his armies defeated the northern tribes. Workers added 300 miles to the existing wall. They built wooden frames, which they filled with willow reeds and a mixture of fine gravel and water. As you can see from this picture of ruins of the Han wall, it was very different in construction and appearance from the Great Wall as it exists today.

The third major building period of the Great Wall occurred 1,100 years later during the Ming Dynasty. In 1368, during the first year of the Ming Dynasty, Emperor Zhu Yuanzhang ordered more expansion of the wall. Subsequent Ming emperors strengthened and extended the wall until it reached its current length. Builders of the Ming wall made three important architectural advancements which resulted in the distinctive features of the wall as it exists today.

You can see those features especially well in this photograph. First, rather than using earth and stone, they used kiln-fired bricks to create a stronger wall. Second, they erected more than 3,000 beacon towers to watch the mountain passes for potential invaders. These towers rise from the wall like mighty outposts and are one of the most striking aspects of the wall when you see them in person. Third, the Ming builders made the wall so large that it would be almost impossible to break through. In fact, the wall is so wide that soldiers could ride several horses abreast along the top of the wall.

In conclusion, the Great Wall of China enjoys a rich history. Built over the course of more than 2,500 years during the Qin, Han, and Ming Dynasties, it is a magnificent feat of human engineering. While the wall no longer continues to defend China from invaders, it does continue to play a central role in Chinese culture and international identity. Now that you know a little more about the wall, I hope you have a fuller appreciation of why it's regarded as great, not just in China, but throughout the world.

Key Terms

slide (345)

presentation (345)

clip art (350)

serif font (353)

sans-serif font (353)

animation (355)

fair use (360)

Notes

[1]Joe Downing and Cecile Garmon, "Teaching Students in the Basic Course How to Use Presentation Software," *Communication Education,* 50 (2002), p. 219.

[2]Tad Simons, "Multimedia or Bust," *Presentations* (February 2000), pp. 40–50.

[3]Herbert W. Lovelace, "The Medium Is More Than the Message," *Informationweek.com* (July 16, 2001), p. 74.

[4]Faithe Wempen, *Microsoft PowerPoint 2002 Bible* (New York: Hungry Minds, 1999), pp. 143–144.

[5]Copyright issues are especially complex when it comes to online materials. For more information, check the Copyright and Image Management website (www.utsystem.edu/ogc/intellectualproperty/image.htm#elec) and the Copyright Management Center (www.copyright.iupui/quickguide.htm).

Chapter Fourteen

SPEAKING TO INFORM

Chapter Focus
This chapter introduces students to the task of sharing information accurately, clearly, and engagingly. After exploring four major kinds of speeches to inform, it presents five guidelines for successful informative discourse. It concludes by reprinting a full sample speech with commentary to help students construct their own informative speeches. For a complete outline of the chapter, see the *Instructor's Manual*, pp. 291–294.

ei-Lan Deng is the pharmacy director at a major metropolitan hospital. One morning, after responding to her usual flurry of new e-mail messages, Mei-Lan greeted a pharmaceutical sales rep who had dropped by to discuss a new pain medication the FDA had recently approved for use. She looked through the materials the salesperson brought along, asked numerous questions about how the drug could be used with her hospital's patient population, and took careful notes.

Later that morning, Mei-Lan decided to review the PowerPoint slides for the lunch talk she would be giving in a couple of hours. It was her turn to address a group of pharmacists from area hospitals who met monthly to share ideas. She double-checked the slides on her laptop. They looked terrific, and she knew she could use them again when she spoke to her hospital's administrative council the next week.

The lunch talk went well, and Mei-Lan was back in her office in time for a two o'clock department meeting. She wanted to get her staff members' thoughts on the new pain medication, so she passed around the materials she had received that morning and answered questions based on the notes she had taken.

Back at her desk, Mei-Lan switched on her computer and groaned—20 new messages! What a relief when she realized half were from members of her lunch group, congratulating her on her "fascinating" talk and asking her to e-mail them copies of her "very informative" slides.

Mei-Lan doesn't consider herself a "public speaker," but much of her job involves absorbing and communicating information clearly and effectively. Although Mei-Lan is just a single person, her experience is not unusual. In one survey, graduates from five U.S. colleges were asked to rank the speech skills most important to their jobs. They rated informative speaking number one.[1] In another survey, 62 percent of the respondents said they used informative speaking "almost constantly."[2]

Public speaking to inform occurs in a wide range of everyday situations. What kinds of people make informative speeches? The business manager explaining next year's budget. The architect reviewing plans for a new building. The military officer briefing subordinates. The union leader informing members about details of a new contract. The church worker outlining plans for a fund drive. The teacher in a classroom. There are endless situations in which people need to inform others. Competence in this form of communication will prove valuable to you throughout your life.

One of your first classroom assignments probably will be to deliver an informative speech in which you will act as a lecturer or teacher. You may describe an object, show how something works, report on an event, explain a concept. Your aim will be to convey knowledge and understanding—not to advocate a cause. Your speech will be judged in light of three general criteria:

Is the information communicated accurately?

Is the information communicated clearly?

Is the information made meaningful and interesting to the audience?

informative speech
A speech designed to convey knowledge and understanding.

In this chapter, we will look at four types of informative speeches and the basic principles of informative speaking. Along the way, we will apply various general principles discussed in previous chapters.

Types of Informative Speeches: Analysis and Organization

There are many ways to classify informative speeches. Here we focus on the four kinds of informative speeches you are most likely to give in your speech class: (1) speeches about objects, (2) speeches about processes, (3) speeches about events, and (4) speeches about concepts. These are not hard-and-fast categories, but they provide an effective method of analyzing and organizing informative speeches.

Speeches About Objects

As the word is used here, "objects" include anything that is visible, tangible, and stable in form. Objects may have moving parts or be alive; they may include places, structures, animals, even people. Here are examples of subjects for speeches about objects:

object
Anything that is visible, tangible, and stable in form.

Sitting Bull	subways
Grand Canyon	stock market
the human eye	Elizabeth Cady Stanton
seaweed	digital cameras
comic strips	U.S. Army

You will not have time to tell your classmates everything about any of these subjects. Instead, you will choose a specific purpose that focuses on one aspect of your subject. Working from the topics presented above, the following are examples of good specific purpose statements for informative speeches about objects:

To inform my audience about the social functions of comic strips.

To inform my audience about the geological features of the Grand Canyon.

To inform my audience about the role of Elizabeth Cady Stanton in the U.S. women's rights movement.

To inform my audience what to look for when buying a digital camera.

To inform my audience about the commercial uses of seaweed.

Cross-Reference
See Chapter 4 for full discussion of selecting speech topics and developing specific purpose statements.

Notice how precise these statements are. As we saw in Chapter 4, you should select a specific purpose that is not too broad to achieve in the allotted time. "To inform my audience about cameras" is far too general for a classroom speech. "To inform my audience what to look for when buying a digital camera" is more exact and is a purpose you could reasonably hope to achieve in a brief talk.

If your specific purpose is to explain the history or evolution of your subject, you will put your speech in *chronological* order. For example:

Specific Purpose: To inform my audience about the major achievements of Frederick Douglass.

Central Idea: Although born in slavery, Frederick Douglass became one of the greatest figures in American history.

Main Points:
    I. Douglass spent the first 20 years of his life as a slave in Maryland.
    II. After escaping to the North, Douglass became a leader in the abolitionist movement to end slavery.
    III. During the Civil War, Douglass helped establish black regiments in the Union Army.
    IV. After the war, Douglass was a tireless champion of equal rights for his race.

Teaching Tip
Make sure that students understand the informative speech assignment and that they do not confuse it with speaking to persuade. Although every speech has the potential to persuade depending on how it is interpreted by the audience, there is, in most cases, a sharp difference between a speech designed to convey knowledge and understanding and one designed to change listeners' attitudes, beliefs, or actions. For more on the differences between informative and persuasive speeches, see the Teaching Tip on p. 375.

If your specific purpose is to describe the main features of your subject, you may organize your speech in *spatial* order:

Specific Purpose: To inform my audience about the major land regions in Spain.

Central Idea: There are five major land regions in Spain.

Main Points:
    I. The Northern Mountains extend across northernmost Spain from the Atlantic Ocean to the Coastal Plains.
    II. The Ebro Basin consists of broad plains that extend along the Ebro River in northeastern Spain.
    III. The Coastal Plains stretch along Spain's entire east coast.
    IV. The Guadalquivir Basin is a dry but extremely fertile region in southern Spain.
    V. The Meseta is a huge plateau that covers central Spain.

As often as not, you will find that speeches about objects fall into *topical* order. Here is an example:

Specific Purpose: To inform my audience about the major alternative-fuel cars now being developed.

Central Idea: The major alternative-fuel cars now being developed are powered by electricity, natural gas, methanol, or hydrogen.

Main Points:
    I. One kind of alternative-fuel car is powered by electricity.

II. A second kind of alternative-fuel car is powered by
natural gas.

III. A third kind of alternative-fuel car is powered by
methanol.

IV. A fourth kind of alternative-fuel car is powered by
hydrogen.

No matter which of these organizational methods you use—chronological, spatial, or topical—be sure to follow the guidelines discussed in Chapter 8: (1) limit your speech to between two and five main points; (2) keep main points separate; (3) try to use the same pattern of wording for all main points; (4) balance the amount of time devoted to each main point.

Cross-Reference
See Chapter 8 for full discussion of methods and guidelines for organizing the main points of a speech.

Speeches About Processes

A process is a systematic series of actions that leads to a specific result or product. Speeches about processes explain how something is made, how something is done, or how something works. Here are examples of good specific purpose statements for speeches about processes:

To inform my audience how hurricanes develop.

To inform my audience how to write an effective job resumé.

To inform my audience how to save people from drowning.

To inform my audience how oriental rugs are made.

To inform my audience how to perform Pilates exercises.

process
A systematic series of actions that leads to a specific result or product.

As these examples suggest, there are two kinds of informative speeches about processes. One kind explains a process so that listeners will *understand* it better. Your goal in this kind of speech is to have your audience know the steps of the process and how they relate to one another. If your specific purpose is "To inform my audience how underwater robots work," you will explain the basic tasks and mechanisms of underwater robots. You will not instruct your listeners on how they can *operate* an underwater robot.

A second kind of speech explains a process so listeners will be better able to *perform* the process themselves. Your goal in this kind of speech is to have the audience learn a particular skill. Suppose your specific purpose is "To inform my audience how to take pictures like a professional photographer." You will present the basic techniques of professional photography and show your listeners how they can utilize those techniques. You want the audience to be able to *use* the techniques as a result of your speech.

Both kinds of speeches about processes may require visual aids. At the very least, you should prepare a chart outlining the steps or techniques of your process. In some cases you will need to demonstrate the steps or techniques by performing them in front of your audience. One student did sleight-of-hand magic tricks to show the techniques behind them. Another acted out the basic methods of mime. Yet another executed elementary tai chi maneuvers. In each case, the demonstration not only clarified the speaker's process, but captivated the audience as well. (If you are using visual aids of any kind, be sure to review Chapter 13 before your speech.)

When informing about a process, you will usually arrange your speech in *chronological* order, explaining the process step by step from beginning to end. For example:

Teaching Tip
Many instructors require that students use a visual aid in the informative speech—regardless of whether the speech is about a process, an object, a concept, or an event. Not only does this ensure that all students gain experience using a visual aid in at least one of their speeches, it also increases audience interest, reduces the speaker's nervousness, and encourages extemporaneous delivery. For full discussion of visual aids, see Chapter 13.

Specific Purpose: To inform my audience of the major steps in the classic Japanese tea ceremony.

Central Idea: There are five major steps in the classic Japanese tea ceremony.

Main Points:
I. First, the guests approach the teahouse, taking time on the way to purify their hands.
II. Second, the guests enter the teahouse, admire the hanging scroll and the vase with a flower arrangement, and seat themselves.
III. Third, the tea master prepares a bowl of tea for each guest, following the prescribed ritual.
IV. Fourth, each guest in turn takes exactly three and a half sips of tea.
V. Fifth, the guests admire the tea implements, admire the interior of the teahouse, and depart.

Sometimes, rather than leading your audience through a process step by step, you will focus on the major principles or techniques involved in performing the process. Then you will organize your speech in *topical* order. Each main point will deal with a separate principle or technique. For example:

Specific Purpose: To inform my audience of the common methods used by stage magicians to perform their tricks.

Central Idea: Stage magicians use two common methods to perform their tricks—mechanical devices and sleight of hand.

Main Points:
I. Many magic tricks rely on mechanical devices that may require little skill by the magician.
II. Other magic tricks depend on the magician's skill in fooling people by sleight-of-hand manipulation.

Concise organization is especially important in speeches about processes. You must make sure each step in the process is clear and easy to follow. If your process has more than four or five steps, group the steps into units so as to limit the number of main points. Otherwise, you will have too many main points for listeners to grasp and recall. For example, in a speech explaining how to set up a home aquarium, a student presented the following main points:

I. First you must choose the size of your tank.
II. Then you must determine the shape of your tank.
III. You must also decide how much you can afford to pay for a tank.
IV. Once you have the tank, you need a filter system.
V. A heater is also absolutely necessary.

Informative speeches can be organized in many ways. A speech explaining the major steps in the classic Japanese tea ceremony would most likely be structured chronologically.

VI. You must also get an air pump.
VII. Once this is done, you need to choose gravel for the tank.
VIII. You will also need plants.
IX. Other decorations will round out the effects of your aquarium.
X. Now you are ready to add the fish.
XI. Freshwater fish are the most common.
XII. Saltwater fish are more expensive and require special care.

Not surprisingly, this was too much for the audience to follow. The speaker should have organized the points something like this:

I. The first step in establishing a home aquarium is choosing a tank.
  A. The size of the tank is important.
  B. The shape of the tank is important.
  C. The cost of the tank is important.
II. The second step in establishing a home aquarium is equipping the tank.
  A. You will need a filter system.
  B. You will need a heater.
  C. You will need an air pump.
  D. You will need gravel.
  E. You will need plants.
  F. You may also want other decorations.
III. The third step in establishing a home aquarium is adding the fish.
  A. Freshwater fish are the most common for home aquariums.
  B. Saltwater fish are more expensive and require special care.

Class Activity
It is crucial that students understand the importance of limiting the number of main points in an informative speech about a process. For a helpful activity on this subject, see Applying the Power of Public Speaking at the end of this chapter. For discussion of the activity, see the *Instructor's Manual*, pp. 297–298.

As you can see, the subpoints cover the same territory as that originally covered by the twelve main points. But three main points are much easier to understand and remember than twelve.

Speeches About Events

event
Anything that happens or is regarded as happening.

The *Random House Dictionary* defines an event as "anything that happens or is regarded as happening." By this definition, the following are examples of suitable subjects for informative speeches about events:

Holocaust	mountain climbing
civil rights movement	Paralympics
figure skating	job interviews
Cinco de Mayo	therapeutic massage
attention deficit disorder	Battle of Little Big Horn

As usual, you will need to narrow your focus and pick a specific purpose you can accomplish in a short speech. Here are examples of good specific purpose statements for informative speeches about events:

To inform my audience about the equipment used in mountain climbing.

To inform my audience of the festivities at Mexico's Cinco de Mayo celebration.

To inform my audience about what happened at the Battle of Little Big Horn.

To inform my audience about the techniques of therapeutic massage.

To inform my audience about the experience of working on an archaeological dig.

Speech Assignment
There are many possible approaches to the informative speech assignment, one of which is to have students explain a significant aspect of a culture other than their own. For an explanation of such an assignment, see the *Instructor's Manual,* p. 34. For a more involved approach that combines attention to cultural diversity with small-group discussion and informative speaking, see Kimberly A. Powell, "Increasing Appreciation for Diversity Through the Group Culture Speech," in *Selections from the Speech Communication Teacher, 1994–1996,* pp. 28–29, which accompanies *The Art of Public Speaking.*

As you can see, there are many ways to discuss events. If your specific purpose is to recount the history of an event, you will organize your speech in *chronological* order, relating the incidents one after another in the order they occurred. For example:

Specific Purpose: To inform my audience about the history of the disability rights movement.

Central Idea: The disability rights movement has made major strides during the past 40 years.

Main Points:
    I. The disability rights movement began in Berkeley, California, during the mid-1960s.
    II. The movement achieved its first major victory in 1973 with passage of the federal Rehabilitation Act.
    III. The movement reached another milestone in 1990 when Congress approved the Americans with Disabilities Act.
    IV. Today the movement is spreading to countries beyond the United States.

Do you need quick access to facts about your informative speech topic? Log on to the Internet Public Library's Subject Collection (www.ipl.org/div/subject/), which offers links to a wide range of high-quality resources chosen for their accurate and reliable information.

If you are giving an informative speech on a topic with multicultural dimensions, you may find the following websites useful:

Yahoo Regional   (www.yahoo.com/Regional/)

WWW Virtual Library: American Indians   (www.hanksville.org/NAresources)

Asian American Resources   (www.ai.mit.edu/people/irie/aar/)

Latino/Hispanic Resources   (www-rcf.usc.edu/~cmmr/Latino.html)

African American Web Connection   (www.aawc.com)

You can link to these websites at www.mhhe.com/lucas8.

ONLINE LEARNING CENTER

Instead of recounting the history of an event, you might take a more analytical approach and explain its causes and/or effects. In such a case, you will organize your speech in *causal* order. Let's say your specific purpose is "To inform my audience why so many lives were lost when the 'unsinkable' ocean liner *Titanic* sank." Working from cause to effect, your outline might look like this:

Specific Purpose: To inform my audience why so many lives were lost when the "unsinkable" ocean liner *Titanic* sank.

Central Idea: Inability to remove the passengers and crew from the doomed *Titanic* caused the death of more than two-thirds of those on board.

Main Points:
I. There were two major causes for the great loss of life when the *Titanic* went down.
   A. The *Titanic* carried insufficient lifeboats for the number of people on board.
   B. On the ship *Californian,* which was nearby, the radio operator had shut down the radio and gone to sleep.
II. The effects of these two situations were disastrous.
   A. When all usable lifeboats had been filled, more than 1,500 people remained on board the *Titanic.*
   B. The *Californian,* unaware of the distress signal, steamed on while the *Titanic* went to the bottom.

Speech Assignment
For a different kind of informative speech assignment, have students inform their classmates about a prominent public speaker, either contemporary or historical. Although I have used this assignment most frequently for the final speech of the term, the speech can be reduced in length and complexity so as to be appropriate earlier. For fuller explanation, see the *Instructor's Manual,* p. 37.

There are other ways to deal with an event besides telling what happened or why it happened. Indeed, you can approach an event from almost any angle or combination of angles—features, origins, implications, benefits, future developments, and so forth. In such cases, you will put your speech together in *topical* order. And you should make sure your main points subdivide the subject logically and consistently. For instance:

Specific Purpose: To inform my audience about the four traditional events in women's gymnastics.

Central Idea: The four traditional events in women's gymnastics are floor exercise, vault, balance beam, and uneven parallel bars.

Main Points:
    I. The floor exercise combines dancing, acrobatics, and tumbling.
    II. The vault features explosive strength and dramatic midair maneuvers.
    III. The balance beam requires precise routines and perfect coordination.
    IV. The uneven parallel bars demand great strength, flexibility, and agility.

Speeches About Concepts

concept
A belief, theory, idea, notion, principle, or the like.

Concepts include beliefs, theories, ideas, principles, and the like. They are more abstract than objects, processes, or events. The following are some examples of subjects for speeches about concepts:

Confucianism	film theory
philosophies of education	principles of feminism
original-intent doctrine	Afrocentrism
concepts of science	theories of psychology
religious beliefs	international law

Taking a few of these general subjects, here are some specific purpose statements for speeches about concepts:

To inform my audience about the basic principles of Afrocentrism.

To inform my audience about the doctrine of original intent in constitutional interpretation.

To inform my audience about the different philosophies of family in China and the United States.

To inform my audience about the concept of patriarchy in feminist thought.

To inform my audience about the major principles of film theory.

Speech Assignment
Providing clear explanations of complex ideas is one of the most difficult challenges facing a public speaker. For a valuable exploration of this aspect of informative speaking, see Katherine Rowan, "The Speech to Explain Difficult Ideas," in *Selections from the Speech Communication Teacher 1986–1991*, pp. 69–71, which accompanies *The Art of Public Speaking.*

Speeches about concepts are usually organized in *topical* order. One common approach is to enumerate the main features or aspects of your concept. For example:

Specific Purpose: To inform my audience about the basic principles of Afrocentrism.

Central Idea: The basic principles of Afrocentrism have a theoretical and a practical dimension.

Main Points:
I. The theoretical dimension of Afrocentrism looks at historical and social events from an African rather than a European perspective.
II. The practical dimension of Afrocentrism calls for reforming the school curriculum to fit the needs and cultural experiences of African-American children.

A more complex approach is to define the concept you are dealing with, identify its major elements, and illustrate it with specific examples. An excellent instance of this came in a student speech about Islam:

Specific Purpose: To inform my audience of the basic principles of Islam.

Central Idea: The beliefs of Islam can be traced to the prophet Muhammad, are written in the Koran, and have produced a number of sects.

Main Points:
I. Islam was founded by the prophet Muhammad in the early 600s.
II. The teachings of Islam are written in the Koran, the holy book of Islam.
III. Today Islam is divided into a number of sects, the largest of which are the Sunnis and the Shiites.

Yet another approach is to explain competing schools of thought about the same subject. For example:

Specific Purpose: To inform my audience of the major arguments for and against taxing online commerce.

Central Idea: Supporters and opponents of taxing online commerce both have legitimate economic arguments.

Main Points:
I. Supporters of taxing online commerce maintain that exempting it from taxation gives it an unfair competitive advantage over traditional stores.
II. Opponents of taxing online commerce maintain that subjecting it to taxation could hamper the development of business on the Internet.

As you can see from these examples, speeches about concepts are often more complex than other kinds of informative speeches. Concepts are abstract

Teaching Tip
Students sometimes propose topics for informative speeches about events or concepts that would be more suitable for a persuasive speech on a question of fact. "To inform my audience of the scientific evidence supporting the existence of intelligent extraterrestrial life" is an acceptable specific purpose statement for an informative speech as long as the evidence presented in the speech is truly scientific. In contrast, "To inform my audience about the existence of intelligent extraterrestrial life" is not appropriate for an informative speech. Why? Because there is no consensus in the scientific community about the existence of intelligent extraterrestrial life. Some experts believe in such life; others do not. Because the facts of the matter are so hotly contested, this subject would be better treated as a persuasive speech on a question of fact, with the specific purpose statement "To persuade my audience that there is intelligent extraterrestrial life in the universe." For full discussion of persuasive speeches on questions of fact, see Chapter 15, pp. 400–403.

and can be very hard to explain to someone who is learning about them for the first time. When explaining concepts, pay special attention to avoiding technical language, to defining terms clearly, and to using examples and comparisons to illustrate the concepts and make them understandable to your listeners.

Look, for example, at CD 1, Video 14.1, which presents an excerpt from a student speech about the ancient Chinese art of feng shui. Notice how clearly the student defines feng shui and then explains the concept of chi, which is the most important factor in feng shui. If you give an informative speech about a concept, give special thought to how you can make that concept clear and comprehensible to your listeners.

The lines dividing speeches about objects, processes, events, and concepts are not absolute. Some subjects could fit into more than one category, depending on how you develop the speech. You could treat the Declaration of Independence as an object—by explaining its history and its role in the American Revolution. Or you could deal with the meaning of the Declaration, in which case you would be speaking about a concept—an idea bound up with freedom and democracy.

To take another example, a speech about the destruction of ancient Pompeii by the eruption of Mount Vesuvius would probably deal with its subject as an event, but a speech on what causes volcanoes to erupt would most likely treat its subject as a process. The important step is to decide how you will handle your subject—as an object, a process, an event, or a concept. Once you do that, you can develop the speech accordingly.

One final word about organizing your informative speech: Regardless of which method of organization you use, be sure to give your listeners plenty of help in sorting out facts and ideas during the speech. One way is by using enough transitions, internal previews, internal summaries, and signposts (see Chapter 8). Another way is to follow the old maxim: "Tell 'em what you're going to say; say it; then tell 'em what you've said." In other words, preview the main points of your speech in the introduction, and summarize them in the conclusion. This will make your speech not only easier to understand but also easier to remember.

View an excerpt from Elizabeth Elegant, "Feng Shui."

CD 1: VIDEO 14.1

Overhead Transparency
For ease of classroom discussion, examples of specific purpose statements, central ideas, and main points for all four kinds of informative speeches discussed in this chapter are included in the binder of full-color overhead transparencies that accompanies *The Art of Public Speaking*.

Guidelines for Informative Speaking

All the previous chapters of this book relate to the principles of informative speaking. Choosing a topic and specific purpose, analyzing the audience, gathering materials, choosing supporting details, organizing the speech, using words to communicate meaning, delivering the speech—all of these must be done effectively if your informative speech is to be a success. Here we emphasize five points that will help you avoid the mistakes that plague many informative speakers.

Don't Overestimate What the Audience Knows

In a speech about meteorology, a student said, "If modern methods of weather forecasting had existed in 1900, the Galveston hurricane disaster would never have taken place." Then he was off to other matters, leaving his listeners to puzzle over what the Galveston hurricane was, when it happened, and what kind of destruction it wreaked.

The speaker assumed that the audience already knew these things. But his classmates were not experts on meteorology or on American history. Even those who had heard of the hurricane had only a fuzzy notion of it. Some were not even sure about the location of Galveston. Only the speaker knew that the hurricane, which killed more than 6,000 people when it unexpectedly struck Galveston, Texas, on September 8, 1900, is still the deadliest natural disaster in American history.

As many speakers have discovered, it is easy to overestimate the audience's stock of information. In most informative speeches, your listeners will be only vaguely knowledgeable (at best) about the details of your topic. (Otherwise, there would not be much need for an informative speech!) Therefore, you must lead your listeners step by step, without any shortcuts. You cannot *assume* they will know what you mean. Rather, you must be *sure* to explain everything so thoroughly that they cannot help but understand. As you work on your speech, always consider whether it will be clear to someone who is hearing about the topic for the first time.

Suppose you are talking about the protective tariff. Although many of your classmates might have heard of the protective tariff, you cannot assume they have a firm grasp of it. So you should start by telling them what it is. How will you tell them? Here's one way:

> A protective tariff is a form of customs duty. It is a tax on imported goods, but it differs from other taxes in that its primary purpose is not financial but economic—not to increase a nation's revenue but to protect its domestic industry from foreign competition.

Class Activity
Divide the class into small groups and have them work on the first Exercise for Critical Thinking at the end of this chapter. This exercise gives students practice in developing specific purpose statements for informative speeches and helps them distinguish among informative speeches about objects, concepts, processes, and events. For additional discussion of the exercise, see the *Instructor's Manual*, p. 295.

The principles of informative speaking are applicable to a wide range of situations. Here a traditional Aleut storyteller explains his craft to young Aleut people on the Alaskan coast.

To someone who knows a lot about business and commerce this is perfectly clear. But someone who does not will probably get lost along the way. The tone of the statement is that of a speaker reviewing information already familiar to the audience—not of a speaker introducing new information.

Here, in contrast, is another explanation of protective tariffs:

> What is a protective tariff? Let me explain with an example.
>
> Suppose your business manufactures automobile tires. So does a company in Malaysia. But because of the cost of labor, that company can sell its tires cheaper here than you can. As a result, you are going bankrupt.
>
> So you appeal to the government for help. The government sets up a tariff to protect you from being ruined by the cheap foreign tires. This means that the government puts a tariff—a tax—on every car tire that comes into the U.S. for sale from Malaysia. If the tariff is high enough, the tires from Malaysia will now be more expensive than yours.
>
> Your business has been protected by the tariff. Hence the name, protective tariff.[3]

This statement is clear and simple. Its tone is that of a teacher unraveling a new subject.

Is it too simple? Will your classmates feel as if you are talking down to them? Almost certainly not. Many students hesitate to speak simply because they are afraid they will sound simpleminded. They think they need big words and complicated sentences to sound intelligent. But nothing could be farther from the truth. The test of a good speaker is to communicate even the most complex ideas clearly and simply. Anyone can go to a book and find a learned-sounding definition of a protective tariff like the one above. But to say in plain English what a protective tariff is—that takes hard work and creative thinking.

Also, remember that readers can study a printed passage again and again until they extract its meaning, but listeners don't have that luxury. They must understand what you say in the time it takes you to say it. The more you assume they know about the topic, the greater your chances of being misunderstood.

If you have circulated a questionnaire among your listeners before the speech (see Chapter 5, pages 125–128), you should have a good idea of their knowledge about the topic. If not, you will usually do better to aim for the low end of the knowledge spectrum. Some experts recommend preparing a speech as if the audience had never heard of the subject. That may be a bit extreme, but it is one way to make sure you define every special term, clarify every idea, illustrate every concept, and support every conclusion. You cannot go wrong by following the news reporters' code: "Never *over*estimate the information of your audience; never *under*estimate the intelligence of your audience."

Relate the Subject Directly to the Audience

The British dramatist Oscar Wilde arrived at his club after the disastrous opening-night performance of his new play.

"Oscar, how did your play go?" asked a friend.

"Oh," Wilde quipped, "the play was a great success, but the audience was a failure."

Class Activity

Divide the class into small groups. Have each group select a topic from among the following:

How to tie a shoelace

How to change a car tire

The basic rules of baseball

How to access the Internet

How to program a VCR

The basic rules of checkers

Give each group 15 minutes to work out a 2-minute explanation designed for an audience that knows absolutely nothing about the topic. Each group should select one of its members to present the explanation orally to the class. For further discussion of this activity, see the third Additional Exercise for Critical Thinking on p. 300 of the *Instructor's Manual*.

Speakers have been known to give much the same answer in saving face after a dismal informative speech. "Oh," they say, "the speech was fine, but the audience just wasn't interested." And they are at least partly right—the audience *wasn't* interested. Then was the speech fine? Not by any objective standard. A speech is measured by its impact on a particular audience. There is no such thing as a fine speech that puts people to sleep. It is the speaker's job to get listeners interested—and to keep them interested.

Informative speakers have one big hurdle to overcome. They must recognize that what is fascinating to them may not be fascinating to everybody. A mathematician, for example, might be truly enthralled by a perfect equation, but most people wouldn't want to hear about it. Once you have chosen a topic that could possibly be interesting to your listeners, you should take special steps to relate it to them. You should tie it in with their interests and concerns.

Start in the introduction. Instead of saying,

I want to talk with you about stress.

you could say,

Do you get butterflies in your stomach when you have to give a speech? Can you feel your blood pressure rising when you have an argument with your roommate, spouse, or partner? Are you worried sick about finishing the paper you've been putting off all week? If so, you have experienced the symptoms of stress.

Get your audience involved right at the beginning. Notice how one student did this in her informative speech about Mother Teresa. The speaker's classmates had all heard of Mother Teresa, but the speaker wanted to relate the subject to them on a more personal basis. She began by saying:

Imagine you are a small child lying on the dirt roads of Calcutta, India. You are severely dehydrated because no one you ask will offer you some of their water. You are weak and malnourished because you have not eaten for days. You are hysterically and painfully coughing from your tuberculosis. You have no family, no friends, and, it seems, no future.

As you begin to shut your eyes, gentle but strong arms reach out and pick you up off the dirt road. You regain enough strength to focus your eyes on the face before you. Her face is wrinkled with age and love and is like a ray of light in your dark world.

This is a familiar story for the many poor and needy of India who were touched by Mother Teresa.

Don't stop with the introduction. Whenever you can, put your listeners into the body of the speech. After all, nothing interests people more than themselves. Don't just rattle off statistics and concepts as if you were reciting a shopping list. Find ways to talk about your topic in terms of your listeners. Bring your material home to them. Get it as close to them as possible.

View this excerpt from Mei Chu, "Mother of Love."
CD 1: VIDEO 14.2

Here's an example. Let's say you are explaining how people can discover whether they are "secret southpaws"—that is, people who are naturally left-handed but who have grown up preferring the right hand because they were taught to use it as a child. You have plenty of facts and could recite them like this:

> According to *Science* magazine, half of all people who are naturally left-handed assume they are right-handed because that is the hand they use to eat, to write, and to play sports. But how can it be determined whether one is a natural southpaw? According to Abram Blau, author of *The Master Hand,* there are a number of simple tests. For one thing, most natural left-handers can write spontaneously backward or upside down with the left hand. For another, when left-handers clasp their hands in front of themselves, they usually place the left thumb on top. In contrast, when left-handers grab a broom, they normally place their left hand below the right. Finally, when using the right hand, natural left-handers will draw a circle clockwise, while natural right-handers will draw it counterclockwise. People who give a left-handed response on three or more of these tests may well be secret southpaws.[4]

This is fascinating information, but it is not made fascinating to the audience. Let's try again:

> Just because *you* use *your* right hand to eat, to write, and to play sports, *you* may assume *you* are naturally right-handed. But, says *Science* magazine, half of all people who are naturally left-handed grow up using their right hands. How can *you* tell if *you* are a natural lefty? Dr. Abram Blau, author of *The Master Hand,* gives some tests *you* can try.
>
> First, on a sheet of paper see if *you* can write backward or upside down with *your* left hand. If *you* are left-handed, *you* can probably do this spontaneously, without practice or training.
>
> Second, clasp *your* hands in front of *you;* whichever thumb *you* place on top usually indicates *your* dominant hand.
>
> Third, grab hold of a broomstick. Odds are *you* will place *your* dominant hand on the bottom.
>
> Finally, draw a circle on a piece of paper with *your* right hand. If *you* draw it counterclockwise, *you* are probably a natural right-hander. But if *you* draw it clockwise, *you* are very likely a natural lefty.
>
> If *you* test left-handed on three of these tests, there is a good chance *you* are a secret southpaw.

Look at the frequent use of "you" and "your." The facts are the same, but now they are pointed directly at the audience. This is the kind of thing that gets listeners to sit up and pay attention.

Don't Be Too Technical

What does it mean to say that an informative speech is too technical? It may mean the subject matter is too specialized for the audience. Any subject can be popularized—but only up to a point. The important thing for a speaker to know is what can be explained to an ordinary audience and what cannot.

Say your subject is electronic amplifiers. It's no trick to demonstrate how to operate an amplifier (how to turn it on and off, adjust the volume, set the tone and balance controls). It's also relatively easy to explain what an amplifier

Teaching Tip
Some instructors require that students choose a single topic for both the informative and persuasive speeches. In the informative speech, students provide background information about the topic; in the persuasive speech, they advocate a policy with regard to the same topic. Such an approach eliminates the need for students to spend time selecting two speech topics, and it allows them to research a single topic in more depth than would otherwise be the case.

does (it boosts the sound received from a radio, CD player, or live performance). But to give a full scientific account of how an amplifier works—that is another matter. It cannot be done in any reasonable time unless the audience knows the principles of audio technology. You would be better off not even trying. The material is just too technical to be understood by a general audience.

Even when the subject matter is not technical, the language used to explain it may be. Every activity has its jargon. This is true of golf (bogey, wedge, match play); of chemistry (colloid, glycogen, heavy water); of photography (aperture, f-stop, depth of field); of ballet (arabesque, jeté, pas de deux). If you are talking to a group of specialists, you can use technical words and be understood. But you must do all you can to avoid technical words when informing a general audience such as your speech class.

jargon
The specialized or technical language of a trade, profession, or similar group.

You may find this hard to do at first. Many people are so addicted to the lingo of their subject that they have trouble escaping it. As you give more speeches, though, you will become increasingly adept at expressing your ideas in everyday, nontechnical language.

Here, for instance, are two statements explaining the process of cryonics, which involves freezing people after death in the hope that medical science will be able to restore them to life in the future. The first is heavily laden with specialized language that would have little impact on ordinary listeners:

> Options for cryonic suspension include freezing the subject's head or complete body. In either case, the process entails complex scientific procedures that, for maximum functionality, must be implemented immediately upon the cessation of biological functioning. Measures must be taken to minimize tissue decomposition so as to ensure that the subject can be successfully resuscitated at some undetermined future period.

Overhead Transparency
For ease of classroom discussion, the guidelines for informative speaking discussed on pp. 376–384 are included in the binder of full-color overhead transparencies that accompanies *The Art of Public Speaking*.

The second statement is perfectly understandable. It is from the speech on cyronics reprinted at the end of this chapter, and it shows how technical information can be made clear to the average person:

> Currently, when a person who has signed up to be cryonically suspended dies, a specific procedure, which was outlined in the book *Cryonics: Reaching for Tomorrow*, must be carried out.
>
> First, before death, an individual must decide whether to have his or her entire body frozen or just the head. If the whole body is to be frozen, it must be preserved upon death. Immediately after death—ideally within a matter of minutes—the patient is connected to a heart-lung machine and chemicals such as glucose and heparin are circulated with the oxygenated blood to help minimize the freezing damage. At the same time, the patient's internal temperature is reduced as quickly as possible using cold packs.
>
> If only the head will be frozen, a slightly different procedure must be carried out. The head must be surgically detached from the rest of the body and preserved in a separate container. You may be wondering, "Why would I preserve only my head?" The answer is, with some diseases the body is in a very poor condition. If this is the case and you choose to preserve your head only, you do so with the belief that medical science will be able to create a healthy new body for you in the future.

View this excerpt from Jayne Richter, "Cryonics."

CD 1: VIDEO 14.3

Much clearer, isn't it? The only specialized words in the whole passage are "glucose," "heparin," and "oxygenated blood," and they do not get in the way. The rest of the language is straightforward, the ideas easy to grasp. This is what you should strive for in your informative speeches.

Avoid Abstractions

"My task," said the novelist Joseph Conrad, "is, before all, to make you see." And make the reader see is just what Conrad did. Witness this passage, in which Conrad describes the aftermath of an explosion aboard a ship:

> The first person I saw was Mahon, with eyes like saucers, his mouth open, and the long white hair standing straight on end round his head like a silver halo. He was just about to go down when the sight of the main deck stirring, heaving up, and changing into splinters before his eyes, petrified him on the top step. I stared at him in unbelief, and he stared at me with a queer kind of shocked curiosity. I did not know that I had no hair, no eyebrows, no eyelashes, that my young mustache was burnt off, that my face was black, one cheek laid open, my nose cut, and my chin bleeding.[5]

A speech is not a novel. Still, too many abstractions are tedious—whether in a novel or in a speech. Many informative speeches would be vastly improved by the novelist's bent for color, specificity, and detail.

One way to avoid abstractions is through *description*. When we think of description, we usually think of external events such as the explosion described by Conrad. But description is also used to communicate internal feelings. Here is how one student tried to convey to his audience the sensations he experienced when he first began sky diving:

description
A statement that depicts a person, event, idea, or the like with clarity and vividness.

> As we wait for the plane to climb to the jump altitude of 12,000 feet, my mind races with a frenzied jumble of thoughts: "Okay, this is the moment you've been waiting for. It's going to be great. Am I really going to jump out of an airplane from 12,000 feet? What if something goes wrong? Can I still back out? Come on now, don't worry. It'll be fine."

Even if we have not been sky diving, we have all had the same kinds of emotions on similar occasions. So what happened next?

> Now it is time to jump. My palms are sweating and my heart is pounding so hard I think it may burst. "Get ready," yells the instructor. As I jump into the blue, I wonder, "What am I doing here?"

Yes—and then what?

Class Activity
Have students write one or two paragraphs in which they use description, comparison, and contrast to communicate their internal feelings when speaking in public. Ask students to present their paragraphs aloud.

> The blast of air resistance blows me backward like a leaf at the mercy of an autumn wind. In about 10 seconds my body levels out and accelerates to a speed of 120 miles an hour. The air supports my body like an invisible flying carpet. There is no sound except for the wind rushing around my face. The earth appears soft and green, rivers look like strips of silver, and in every direction the scenery forms a panoramic landscape. Any fears or doubts I had are gone in the exhilaration of free flight. Every nerve in my body is alive with sensation; yet I am overcome by a peaceful feeling and the sense that I am at one with the sky.

As we listen to the speaker, we are almost up there with him, sharing his thoughts, feeling his heart pound, joining his exhilaration as he floats effortlessly through the sky. The vivid description lends reality to the speech and draws us further in.

Whatever the situation, effective informative speakers work on communicating their ideas in clear, nontechnical language that relates the topic to their listeners' knowledge and interests.

Another way to escape abstractions is with *comparisons* that put your subject in concrete, familiar terms. Do you want to convey what would happen if a comet or large asteroid struck the earth? You could say this:

> If a comet or large asteroid struck the earth, the impact would be devastating.

True, but "the impact would be devastating" is vague and abstract. It does not communicate your meaning clearly and concretely. Now suppose you add this:

> To give you an idea how devastating the impact would be, it would be like all the nuclear bombs in the world going off at one spot.

Now you have made the abstract specific and given us a sharp new slant on things.

Like comparison, *contrast* can put an idea into concrete terms. Suppose you want to make the point that a person's chances of winning a state lottery are extremely low. You could say, "The odds, for example, of winning a state lottery are an astronomical 7 million to 1." The word "astronomical" suggests that you consider 7 million to 1 long odds, but long in comparison to what? One speaker offered this contrast:

> The odds of picking the correct six-digit sequence in a typical state lottery are more than 7 million to 1. In contrast, the odds of getting hit by lightning are only 2 million to 1. The chances of being dealt a royal flush in a poker game are 650,000 to 1. The odds of dying in an automobile accident are about 6,000 to 1. In other words, the odds are much stronger that you will get hit by lightning or be killed in a car crash than that you will win the jackpot in a state lottery.

comparison
A statement of the similarities among two or more people, events, ideas, etc.

contrast
A statement of the differences among two or more people, events, ideas, etc.

Now an abstract fact has been put into meaningful perspective. See if you can do something similar in your informative speech.

Personalize Your Ideas

Listeners want to be entertained as they are being enlightened.[6] Nothing takes the edge off an informative speech more than an unbroken string of facts and figures. And nothing enlivens a speech more than personal illustrations. Remember, people are interested in people. They react to stories, not statistics. Whenever possible, you should try to *personalize* your ideas and dramatize them in human terms.

Let's say you are talking about anorexia nervosa, the eating disorder that affects millions of young women in the United States. You would surely note that 1 in every 100 teenage females in the U.S. suffers from anorexia, that the number is rising every year, and that college-age women make up 45 percent of all cases of anorexia. You would also note that the effects of anorexia include extreme weight loss, brittle bones, decreased pulse rate, and brain damage. In addition, you would note that despite drug therapy, hospitalization, and forced feeding, close to 20 percent of the people who are diagnosed with anorexia die from it.

But these are dry facts and figures. If you really want to get your audience involved, you will weave in some examples of people who have suffered from anorexia. One speaker began by telling about her best friend, Julie:

> I was Julie's best friend. I watched her grow from a little girl who was doted on by her parents into a tomboy who carried frogs in her pockets. I watched her become a young woman, fussing with her hair and trying on every outfit in her closet before her first date. I always wanted to be just like her.
>
> But then something went terribly wrong. Julie's shiny hair became dull and brittle. Her eyes lost their sparkle, and she didn't smile that brilliant smile any more. I watched now, as she stepped onto the scale seven times a day, wore baggy clothes to cover her shriveled frame, and kept muttering about losing those last two stubborn pounds. Julie had become anorexic.

During the body of the speech, the speaker mentioned Julie twice more to illustrate different aspects of anorexia. Then, in the conclusion, she brought Julie's story to its tragic end:

> We have seen that anorexia is a serious disease with deep-seated causes and devastating, potentially fatal effects. Julie was one of those who couldn't beat anorexia. She died when she was only 17. We will never go to college together and share a dorm room. She will never fulfill her dream of becoming a nurse. And we will never grow old living beside each other and watching our kids grow up together. Anorexia killed my beautiful, vibrant friend.

It was a powerful ending, and it left the audience stunned. By putting a human face on a familiar topic, the speaker took anorexia out of the realm of statistics and medical jargon and brought it home in personal terms. As one listener said afterward, "Because of your speech, I will never see anorexia in the same way again."

personalize
To present one's ideas in human terms that relate in some fashion to the experience of the audience.

Class Activity
Popular nonfiction writing often provides helpful models of informative discourse on technical topics. Have each student select an article of interest from the medicine, science, or business section of *Time* or *Newsweek*—ideally on the subject of the student's upcoming speech. The student should prepare a brief report (written and/or oral) on the article, explaining how the writer uses the techniques discussed in this chapter to make the subject clear and understandable to ordinary readers.

View these excerpts from Jennifer Breuer, "Dying to Be Thin."

CD 1: VIDEO 14.4

Sample Speech with Commentary

The following classroom speech provides an excellent example of how to apply the guidelines for informative speaking discussed in this chapter. As you study the speech, notice how the speaker takes what could be a highly technical topic and explores it in clear, nontechnical language. Pay attention as well to how crisply the speech is organized, how the speaker uses well-chosen supporting materials to develop her ideas, and how she relates those ideas to her audience at various points throughout the speech.[7]

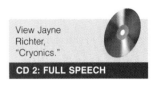

View Jayne Richter, "Cryonics."

CD 2: FULL SPEECH

Cryonics	
Commentary	**Speech**

Jayne Richter

Beginning with a series of brief hypothetical examples is a fine way to capture attention and interest. In this case, the scenarios work particularly well because they relate the topic directly to the audience.

The time is now. Imagine your mother or father has suffered a heart attack. Deprived of its vital blood supply, a part of their heart is dying. Or imagine your grandmother or grandfather lying nearly motionless in their nursing home bed. Advanced age, complicated by pneumonia, is about to end their lives. Or imagine a close friend has just entered the hospital with a massive systemwide infection. AIDS has left their body ravaged by multiple diseases.

The speaker poses two questions that arouse curiosity and get the audience further involved in the speech. Then she reveals her topic.

For most people, these circumstances would herald the end of life. Today's medicine can no longer help them. But all of you may be able to meet again in the far future. Does this sound like science fiction? Perhaps. But it may one day be possible. How? Through the process of cryonics.

The speaker defines cryonics, establishes her credibility, and previews the main points to be discussed in the body of the speech. An explicit preview statement at the end of the introduction is especially important in speaking to inform.

Cryonics is the process of freezing human beings after death in the hope that medical science will be able to revive them in the future. Intrigued by the prospect of being cryonically frozen, I've spent some time researching the subject of cryonics. After reading dozens of newspaper and magazine articles, I would like to give you a brief overview of the history, methods, and future of cryonics. Let's start with the development of cryonics.

Now the speaker moves into her first main point. The information in this paragraph provides historical perspective on the impulse for immortality that underlies the appeal of cryonics.

Although the idea of freezing people is relatively new, the notion of preserving them is old. In the 1770s, for example, Ben Franklin wrote that he wanted to be "immersed in a cask of Madeira wine, 'til that time when he could be recalled to life." It was not to be, but Franklin's dream lived on to be revived in our time as cryonics.

The speaker sketches the development of cryonics in our own time. The details in this paragraph add variety, color, and interest. Imagine, for example, how much less effective the paragraph would have been if the speaker had merely said, "The first case of a person being cryonically frozen occurred in the 1970s." The specific names and dates add depth and texture to the speaker's explanation.

This paragraph completes the speaker's first main point. Because cryonics is so often associated with science fiction, the speaker's classmates were especially intrigued to learn that there are four cryonics institutions in the U.S. and that 80 people have already been cryonically frozen.

The speaker uses questions as signposts to let the audience know she is moving into her second main point.

The explanation in this and the next paragraph provides an excellent model of how to explain technical information in everyday, nontechnical language. Because the speaker is not an expert on cryonics, she is careful to identify the source of her information. You can view this portion of the speech on CD 1, Video 14.3.

Notice how the speaker relates the topic directly to her audience by speaking in terms of "you" and by posing the question that listeners are likely asking mentally.

The speaker completes her discussion of how cryonics works. Notice how she clarifies the meaning of "cryoprotectant" by comparing it

Cryonics has been a staple of science fiction novels, the plot device in movies such as *Austin Powers* and *Sleepers,* and the subject of countless newspaper and magazine articles. Until 1964, however, cryonics remained firmly in the realm of fiction. It was at this time that physics professor Robert Ettinger argued in his book *The Prospect of Immortality* that cryonics was indeed possible. Three years later, on January 12, 1967, 73-year-old James H. Bedford became the first human being to be cryonically frozen.

Ever since Bedford was frozen, cryonics has steadily increased in popularity. Currently there are four cryonic institutions in the United States—two in California and one each in Michigan and Arizona. So far 80 people have been cryonically frozen from around the world, and another estimated 800 people have signed up to be frozen when they die. Their aim is to remain frozen in a state of suspended animation—perhaps for centuries—in the hope that medical science will be able to revive them in the future at a time when cures exist for virtually all of today's diseases and when restoration to full function and health is possible.

So you're probably wondering how will they do it? How does cryonics work?

Currently, when a person who has signed up to be cryonically suspended dies, a specific procedure, which was outlined in the book *Cryonics: Reaching for Tomorrow,* must be carried out. First, before death, an individual must decide whether to have his or her entire body frozen or just the head. If the whole body is to be frozen, it must be preserved upon death. Immediately after death—ideally within a matter of minutes—the patient is connected to a heart-lung machine and chemicals such as glucose and heparin are circulated with the oxygenated blood to help minimize the freezing damage. At the same time, the patient's internal temperature is reduced as quickly as possible using cold packs.

If only the head will be frozen, a slightly different procedure must be carried out. The head must be surgically detached from the rest of the body and preserved in a separate container. You may be wondering, "Why would I preserve only my head?" The answer is, with some diseases the body is in a very poor condition. If this is the case and you choose to preserve your head only, you do so with the belief that medical science will be able to create a healthy new body for you in the future.

Once the head or body is ready for freezing, a liquid called a cryoprotectant, which works as an antifreeze of sorts to help prevent cell damage, is circulated through the body or head.

to an automotive antifreeze. This is a small point, but it illustrates the speaker's efforts throughout the speech to communicate technical terms and concepts in ways her audience can readily understand.

A transition cues the audience that the speaker is moving to her next main point.

Knowing that cost is a common question people have about cryonics, the speaker makes sure to include it in her speech. The quotation at the end of this paragraph adds a bit of wry humor.

A signpost at the beginning of this paragraph gets the speaker into her next subpoint, which deals with the problems involved in rethawing people once they have been cryonically frozen. As in the rest of the speech, the speaker identifies the source of her information and presents that information clearly and forthrightly.

The speaker explains the efforts of scientists to find a way to reduce the damage caused by the freezing process so as to be able to bring frozen patients back to life. This brings her discussion of cryonics fully up to date and completes the body of the speech.

Over a 20-day period, the patient is prepared for long-term storage by cooling the body or head to a temperature of negative 320 degrees Fahrenheit. When this temperature is reached, the patient is stored in a steel cylinder of liquid nitrogen. According to an article in *Omni* magazine, "At this temperature, biological function ceases and the patient will remain unchanged for hundreds of years."

Now that we have explored the development of cryonics and how the freezing process works, you may wonder about questions such as how much it costs and whether the people that are frozen can be rethawed.

According to an article in *Fortune* magazine, the cost of cryonic suspension ranges from $60,000 to $125,000. It can be creatively paid for by making the cryonics institution the beneficiary of your life insurance policy. These costs may be rather steep, but as one cryonics member states, "Facing my own mortality turned out to be much harder than coming up with the cash to pay for life insurance premiums."

But cost is not the only issue. Even if you can afford the cost of being cryonically frozen, scientists have not yet worked out all the details involved in freezing and rethawing. As explained by *New Scientist* magazine, the problem is that the freezing process itself inflicts a crippling amount of cellular damage by dehydrating cells and puncturing their delicate membranes. So far, there are only a few types of human tissue that can be successfully frozen and rethawed, including sperm, embryos, and bone marrow, which contain relatively few cells. It is not yet possible to freeze and rethaw complicated organs such as the heart or liver—not to mention a complete body or brain.

What scientists need is a procedure that will allow them to reduce the damage inflicted by the freezing process. And in fact scientists are currently working on this procedure. Research is being done in the hope of finding better cryoprotectants—or antifreezes—which will reduce the cell damage caused by freezing. According to the book *Cryonics: Reaching for Tomorrow*, scientists are also developing microscopic machines that are capable of repairing cells at the molecular level. These machines might one day make it possible to repair the cell damage caused by the freezing process and thus bring frozen patients back to full life. Until that time, the people that are already frozen will have to remain in their current state of suspended animation in the hope that science will one day work out solutions to the problems involved with freezing and rethawing.

The phrase "In closing" signals that the speaker is moving into her conclusion. She then provides an excellent summary of the main points developed in the body.

In closing, we have seen that cryonics is much more than a plot in a science fiction novel. It has developed from a wholly unrealistic fantasy to the point that 80 people have already been frozen and hundreds more have made the choice to be cryonically frozen when they die. If scientists can ever figure out how to rethaw people successfully, we can be sure that cryonics will become much more popular.

The final paragraph relates the topic to the audience once again and unifies the entire speech by referring to the three hypothetical scenarios mentioned in the introduction. The closing sentence ends the speech on a strong note.

So think again of your father or mother suffering a heart attack, your grandmother or grandfather dying of pneumonia, or your close friend stricken with AIDS. If they chose to be buried or cremated in traditional fashion, their physical minds and bodies would be destroyed. That is absolutely certain. By contrast, being cryonically frozen offers some small chance that they may be revived in the future. Even if that chance is small, it's more than no chance at all.

Summary

Speaking to inform occurs in a wide range of everyday situations. Yet it is a difficult task that requires more skill than you might think. Improving your ability to convey knowledge effectively will be most valuable to you throughout your life.

Informative speeches may be grouped into four categories—speeches about objects, speeches about processes, speeches about events, and speeches about concepts. These categories are not absolute, but they are helpful in analyzing and organizing informative speeches.

Objects, as defined here, include places, structures, animals, even people. Speeches about objects usually are organized in chronological, spatial, or topical order. A process is a series of actions that work together to produce a final result. Speeches about processes explain how something is made, how something is done, or how something works. Clear organization is especially important in speeches about processes because listeners must be able to follow each step in the process. The most common types of organization for speeches about processes are chronological and topical.

An event is anything that happens or is regarded as happening. You can approach an event from almost any angle. You might explain its origins, causes, effects, implications, major features, and so on. Usually speeches about events are arranged in chronological, causal, or topical order. Concepts include beliefs, theories, ideas, and principles. Speeches about concepts are often more complex than other kinds of informative speeches, and they typically follow a topical pattern of organization.

No matter what the subject of your informative speech, be careful not to overestimate what your audience knows about it. In most classroom speeches your listeners will be no more than slightly familiar with your topic. Therefore, you cannot assume they will know what you mean. Explain everything so thoroughly they cannot help but understand. Avoid being too technical. Make sure your ideas and your language are fully comprehensible to someone who has no specialized knowledge about the topic.

Equally important, recognize that what is fascinating to you may not be fascinating to everybody. It is your job to make your informative speech interesting and meaningful to your audience. Find ways to talk about the topic in terms of your listeners. Avoid too many abstractions. Use description, comparison, and contrast to make your audience *see* what you are talking about. Finally, try to personalize your ideas. No matter what your subject, you can almost always find a way to dramatize it in human terms.

Key Terms

informative speech (366)
object (367)
process (369)
event (372)
concept (374)

jargon (381)
description (382)
comparison (383)
contrast (383)
personalize (384)

Review these terms by doing the Chapter 14 crossword puzzle at www.mhhe.com/lucas8.

ONLINE LEARNING CENTER

Review Questions

After reading this chapter, you should be able to answer the following questions:

1. What are the four types of informative speeches discussed in the chapter? Give an example of a good specific purpose statement for each type.

2. Why must informative speakers be careful not to overestimate what the audience knows about the topic? What can you do to make sure your ideas don't pass over the heads of your listeners?

3. What should you do as an informative speaker to relate your topic directly to the audience?

4. What two things should you watch out for in making sure your speech is not overly technical?

5. What are three methods you can use to avoid abstractions in your informative speech?

6. What does it mean to say that informative speakers should personalize their ideas?

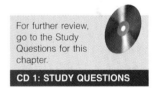

For further review, go to the Study Questions for this chapter.

CD 1: STUDY QUESTIONS

Exercises for Critical Thinking

1. On page 390 is a list of subjects for informative speeches. Your task is twofold: (a) Select four of the topics and prepare a specific purpose statement for an informative speech about each of the four. Make sure that your four specific purpose statements include at least one that deals with its

topic as an object, one that deals with its topic as a process, one that deals with its topic as an event, and one that deals with its topic as a concept. (b) Explain what method of organization you would most likely use in structuring a speech about each of your specific purpose statements.

Cross-Reference
For discussion of the Exercises for Critical Thinking, see the *Instructor's Manual,* pp. 295–296. For additional exercises, check the *Instructor's Manual,* pp. 299–300, as well as the five volumes of *Selections from the Speech Communication Teacher* that accompany *The Art of Public Speaking.*

hobbies	sports
animals	music
science	cultural customs
education	technology
media	health

2. Analyze Jennifer Breuer's "Dying to Be Thin" in the appendix of sample speeches that follows Chapter 18. Identify the specific purpose, central idea, main points, and method of organization. Evaluate the speech in light of the guidelines for informative speaking discussed in this chapter.

Applying the POWER of PUBLIC SPEAKING

As the manager for a local chain of coffeehouses, you have been asked to speak to a gourmet group about how to make genuine Italian cappuccino. As you write down ideas for your speech, you find that you have the following main points:

Cross-Reference
For discussion of this Applying the Power of Public Speaking scenario, see the *Instructor's Manual,* pp. 297–298.

I. First you must make the espresso.
II. Grind the coffee beans so they are fine but not too fine.
III. Place the ground coffee in the filter holder of the espresso machine.
IV. Tamp the coffee once lightly to level the grind in the filter holder.
V. Lock the filter holder onto the brew head of the espresso machine.
VI. Activate the on switch to extract the espresso.
VII. In addition to making the espresso, you must prepare frothed milk for cappuccino.
VIII. Fill a steaming pitcher 1/3 full of very cold milk.
IX. Place the steam vent of the espresso machine just below the surface of the milk in the pitcher.
X. Fully open the steam vent.
XI. Keeping the tip of the steam vent just below the surface of the milk, move the pitcher in a circular motion.
XII. Be careful not to overheat or scald the milk, which will ruin the froth.
XIII. Once you have the desired amount and consistency of froth, turn the steam vent off and remove it from the pitcher.
XIV. Now you are ready to combine the espresso and frothed milk.
XV. The normal proportions for cappuccino are 1/3 espresso to 2/3 frothed milk.
XVI. Some people prefer to pour the espresso into the frothed milk in a cappuccino cup.
XVII. Other people prefer to pour or spoon the frothed milk over the espresso.

Having taken a speech class in college, you know this is too many main points for an audience to keep track of. As you look over your list again, however, you realize that it can easily be reorganized into three main points, each with several subpoints. What are those main points and subpoints?

Notes

[1]John R. Johnson and Nancy Szczupakiewicz, "The Public Speaking Course: Is It Preparing Students with Work-Related Public Speaking Skills?" *Communication Education,* 36 (1987), pp. 131–137.

[2]Andrew D. Wolvin and Diana Corley, "The Technical Speech Communication Course: A View from the Field," *Association for Communication Administration Bulletin,* 49 (1984), pp. 83–91.

[3]Adapted from Rudolf Flesch, *The Art of Readable Writing* (New York: Harper and Row, 1949), p. 82.

[4]Adapted from a speech by Kenda Creasy Dean. Used with permission.

[5]Joseph Conrad, "Youth: A Narrative," in Samuel Hynes (ed.), *Collected Stories of Joseph Conrad* (Hopewell, NJ: Ecco Press, 1991), p. 166.

[6]James Humes, *Roles Speakers Play* (New York: Harper and Row, 1976), p. 25.

[7]Reprinted with permission of Jayne Richter. This speech is also available on the video supplement to *The Art of Public Speaking.*

Chapter Fifteen

2. Identify the kind of reasoning used in each of the following statements. What weaknesses, if any, can you find in the reasoning of each?

   a. According to a study by the American Medical Association, men with bald spots have three times the risk of heart attack as men with a full head of hair. Strange as it may seem, it looks as if baldness is a cause of heart attacks.

   b. Contrary to what the chemical industry argues, limiting pesticide use does not threaten the food supply. Sweden has cut back on pesticides by 50 percent over the last few years with almost no decrease in its harvest. The Campbell Soup Company uses no pesticides at all on tomatoes grown in Mexico, and they reap as much fruit as ever. Many California farmers who practice pesticide-free agriculture have actually experienced increases in their crop yields.

   c. The United States Constitution guarantees all citizens the right to bear arms. Gun control legislation infringes on the right of citizens to bear arms. Therefore, gun control legislation is contrary to the Constitution.

   d. Almost every industrialized nation in the world except for the United States has a national curriculum and national tests to help ensure that schools throughout the country are meeting high standards of education. If such a system can work elsewhere, it can work in the United States as well.

Cross-Reference

For discussion of the Exercises for Critical Thinking, see the *Instructor's Manual,* pp. 330–339. For additional exercises, check the *Instructor's Manual,* pp. 340–347, as well as the five volumes of *Selections from the Speech Communication Teacher* that accompany *The Art of Public Speaking.*

3. Over the years there has been much debate about the role of emotional appeal in public speaking. Do you believe it is ethical for public speakers to use emotional appeals when seeking to persuade an audience? Do you feel there are certain kinds of emotions to which an ethical speaker should not appeal? Why or why not? Be prepared to explain your ideas in class.

4. Analyze Mary Fisher's "A Whisper of AIDS" in the appendix of sample speeches that follows Chapter 18. In your analysis concentrate on how Fisher builds her credibility, employs evidence and reasoning, and generates emotional appeal. In addition, study how she uses the resources of language discussed in Chapter 11 to bring her message home to listeners.

Applying the **POWER** of PUBLIC SPEAKING

As marketing director, you've helped your small company grow from ownership of one health club to nine in as many years. Now one of your less successful competitors is throwing in the towel and has announced plans to sell its seven clubs. Most members of your company's management team want to make an offer to purchase these clubs. However, some members, including yourself, believe the purchase would jeopardize your company's stability by nearly doubling its size overnight.

At a meeting of the management team, you listen as one of the advocates of purchasing the clubs makes his case. Among his points are the following: (1) The company must either purchase the clubs or abandon any thoughts of future growth; (2) If the company can successfully add clubs one at a time, as it has done in the past, then it should be able to add seven

Cross-Reference

For discussion of this Applying the Power of Public Speaking scenario, see the *Instructor's Manual,* pp. 339–340.

at once; and (3) Because a majority of the management team supports the purchase, it must be a good idea.

In your speech, you will point out the fallacy in each of these points. What are those fallacies?

Notes

[1]Roger Dawson Productions, Incorporated, La Habra, California.

[2]For a review of research on the factors of credibility, see Daniel J. O'Keefe, *Persuasion: Theory and Research,* 2nd ed. (Thousand Oaks, CA: Sage, 2002), pp. 182–184.

[3]James C. McCroskey, *An Introduction to Rhetorical Communication,* 8th ed. (Boston: Allyn and Bacon, 2000), pp. 93–103.

[4]Herbert W. Simons, *Persuasion in Society* (Thousand Oaks, CA: Sage, 2001), pp. 79–81.

[5]See O'Keefe, *Persuasion: Theory and Research,* p. 185.

[6]Daniel J. O'Keefe, "How to Handle Opposing Arguments in Persuasive Messages: A Meta-Analytic Review of the Effect of One-Sided and Two-Sided Messages," in James A. Anderson (ed.), *Communication Yearbook 22* (Thousand Oaks, CA: Sage, 1999), pp. 209–249.

[7]John C. Reinard, "The Empirical Study of the Persuasive Effects of Evidence: The Status After Fifty Years of Research," *Human Communication Research,* 15 (1988), pp. 37–38.

[8]Donald Dean Morley and Kim B. Walker, "The Role of Importance, Novelty, and Plausibility in Producing Belief Change," *Communication Monographs,* 54 (1987), pp. 436–442.

[9]Rodney A. Reynolds and J. Lynn Reynolds, "Evidence," in James Price Dillard and Michael Pfau (eds.), *The Persuasion Handbook: Developments in Theory and Practice* (Thousand Oaks, CA: Sage, 2002), pp. 429–430.

[10]O'Keefe, *Persuasion: Theory and Research,* pp. 216–218.

[11]Adapted from James C. Humes, *A Speaker's Treasury of Anecdotes About the Famous* (New York: Harper and Row, 1978), p. 131.

[12]For fuller discussion, see Edward P. J. Corbett and Rosa A. Eberly, *The Elements of Reasoning,* 2nd ed. (New York: Longman, 2000).

[13]In classical systems of logic, reasoning from particular facts to a general conclusion was known as induction. Contemporary logicians, however, have redefined induction as any instance of reasoning in which the conclusion follows from its premises with probability—regardless of whether the reasoning moves from specific instances to a general conclusion or from a general premise to a specific conclusion. In this scheme, reasoning from specific instances is one kind of inductive argument—as are causal reasoning and analogical reasoning. See, for example, S. Morris Engel, *With Good Reason: An Introduction to Informal Fallacies,* 6th ed. (New York: St. Martin's, 2000); Howard Kahane and Nancy Cavender, *Logic and Contemporary Rhetoric: The Use of Reason in Everyday Life,* 9th ed. (Belmont, CA: Wadsworth, 2002).

[14]Lionel Ruby, *The Art of Making Sense* (Philadelphia: Lippincott, 1954), p. 261.

[15]In classical systems of logic, reasoning from a general premise to a specific conclusion was known as deduction. But just as contemporary logicians have redefined induction (see note 13), they have redefined deduction as any instance of reasoning in which the conclusion follows from its premises with certainty. Some deductive arguments move from general premises to a specific conclusion, but others move from specific premises to a general conclusion. Many speech textbooks confuse reasoning from principle, which is one form of deduction, with deductive reasoning in general.

[16]The full text of Anthony's speech is in Karlyn Kohrs Campbell (ed.), *Man Cannot Speak for Her: Key Texts of the Early Feminists* (New York: Praeger, 1989), pp. 289–316.

[17]H. E. Butler (trans.), *The Institutio Oratoria of Quintilian* (Cambridge, MA: Harvard University Press, 1961), Vol. IV, p. 141.

[18]George Campbell, *The Philosophy of Rhetoric,* ed. Lloyd F. Bitzer (Carbondale, IL: Southern Illinois University Press, 1988), p. 77.

[19]For a recent essay that confirms the important role emotion plays in persuasion, see James Price Dillard and Eugenia Peck, "Persuasion and the Structure of Affect: Dual Systems and Discrete Emotions as Complementary Models," *Human Communication Research,* 27 (2001), pp. 38–68.

[20]Research on fear appeals, for example, has demonstrated that messages devoted exclusively to arousing fear in the audience are usually less effective than messages that combine fear appeals with reasonable explanations of how to eliminate or cope with the source of fear. See Paul Mongeau, "Another Look at Fear-Arousing Appeals," in Mike Allen and Ray W. Preiss (eds.), *Persuasion: Advances Through Meta-Analysis* (Cresskill, NJ: Hampton Press, 1997), pp. 87–98.

[21]Reprinted with permission of Rebecca Hanson.

Chapter
Seventeen

Speeches of Introduction

Speeches of Presentation

Speeches of Acceptance

Commemorative
Speeches

After-Dinner Speeches

S pecial occasions are the punctuation marks of day-to-day life, the high points that stand out above ordinary routine. Christenings, weddings, funerals, graduations, award ceremonies, inaugurals, re- tirement dinners—all these are occasions, and they are very spe- cial to the people who take part in them. Nearly always they are occasions for speechmaking. A close friend proposes a toast to the bride and groom; the sales manager presents an award to the sales representative of the year; the president delivers an inaugural address; the basketball coach gives a speech honoring the team's most valuable player; a family member delivers a moving eulogy to the deceased. These speeches help give the occasion its "specialness." They are part of the ceremonial aura that marks the event.

Speeches for special occasions are different from the speeches we have considered so far in this book. They may convey information, but that is not their primary purpose. Neither is their primary purpose to persuade. Rather, they aim to fit the special needs of a special occasion. In this chap- ter we look at the most common special occasions and the kinds of speeches appropriate for each.

Chapter Focus

This chapter explores intro- ductory speeches, presenta- tion speeches, acceptance speeches, commemorative speeches, and after-dinner speeches. A text of each type of speech is included to help students construct their own speeches. For a full outline of the chapter, see the *Instructor's Manual,* pp. 352–355.

Speeches of Introduction

"Distinguished guests, the President of the United States." If you are ever in a situation in which you have to introduce the President, you will need no more than the eight words that begin this paragraph. The President is so well known that any further remarks would be inappropriate and almost foolish.

Most of the time, however, a speech of introduction will be neither this brief nor this ritualized. If you are introducing another speaker, you will need to accomplish three purposes in your introduction:

speech of introduction
A speech that introduces the main speaker to the audience.

Build enthusiasm for the upcoming speaker.

Build enthusiasm for the speaker's topic.

Establish a welcoming climate that will boost the speaker's credibility.

A good speech of introduction can be a delight to hear and can do much to ease the task of the main speaker. Usually you will say something about the speaker and about the topic—in that order. Following are some guide- lines for speeches of introduction.

Be Brief

During World War I, Lord Balfour, Great Britain's foreign secretary, was to be the main speaker at a rally in the United States. But the speaker intro- ducing Lord Balfour gave a 45-minute oration on the causes of the war. Then, almost as an afterthought, he said, "Now Lord Balfour will give his address." Lord Balfour rose and said, "I'm supposed to give my address in the brief time remaining. Here it is: 10 Carleton Gardens, London, England."[1]

Every speaker—and audience—who has ever sat through a long-winded introduction knows how dreary it can be. The purpose of a speech of introduction is to focus attention on the main speaker, not on the person making the introduction. Under normal circumstances, a speech of introduction will be no more than two to three minutes long, and it may be shorter if the speaker is already well known to the audience.

Make Sure Your Remarks Are Completely Accurate

Many an introducer has embarrassed himself or herself, as well as the main speaker, by garbling basic facts about the speaker. Always check with the speaker ahead of time to make sure your introduction is accurate in every respect.

Above all, get the speaker's name right. This may seem obvious, but it needs repeating. Remember that nothing is more important than a person's name. If the speaker's name is at all difficult—especially if it involves a foreign pronunciation—practice saying it well in advance. However, don't practice so much that you frighten yourself about getting it wrong. This was the plight of an announcer whose gaffe is now a classic: "Ladies and gentlemen, the President of the United States—Hoobert Heever!"

Class Activity
Have students attend a speech on campus. Ask them to pay special attention to the speech introducing the main speaker. How well does it fit the guidelines presented in this chapter? For an evaluation form students can use in conjunction with this assignment, see the *Instructor's Manual*, p. 356.

Adapt Your Remarks to the Occasion

In preparing your introduction, you may be constrained by the nature of the occasion. Formal occasions require formal speeches of introduction. If you were presenting a guest speaker at an informal business meeting, you might be much more casual than if you were presenting the same speaker to the same audience at a formal banquet.

Adapt Your Remarks to the Main Speaker

No matter how well it is received by the audience, a speech of introduction that leaves the main speaker feeling uncomfortable has failed in part of its purpose. How can you make a main speaker uncomfortable? One way is to overpraise the person—especially for his or her speaking skills. Never say, "Our speaker will keep you on the edge of your seat from beginning to end!" This is like prefacing a joke with the line, "Here is the funniest joke you've ever heard." You create a set of expectations that are almost impossible to fulfill.

Another way to create discomfort is by revealing embarrassing details of the speaker's personal life or by making remarks that are in poor taste from the speaker's point of view. An introducer may think this line is funny: "Why, I've known Anita Fratello since she was 10 years old and so fat that everybody in the class called her Blimpo!" To the speaker, however, the statement will probably not be a bit funny and may be painful.

Speech Assignment
During the final round of speeches, have each student prepare a one-minute speech of introduction for one of their classmates' speeches. The speech should conform with the guidelines for speeches of introduction presented in this chapter, and it should be delivered in class immediately before the speech it is introducing.

Adapt Your Remarks to the Audience

Just as you adapt other speeches to particular audiences, so you need to adapt a speech of introduction to the audience you are facing. Your aim is to make *this* audience want to hear *this* speaker on *this* subject. If the speaker is not well known to the audience, you will need to establish her or his credibility by recounting some of the speaker's main achievements and explaining why she or he is qualified to speak on the topic at hand. But if the speaker is already personally known to the audience, it would be absurd to act as if the audience had never heard of the person.

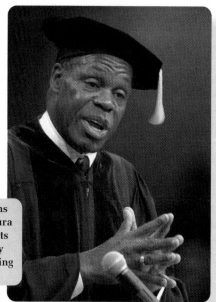

Speeches for special occasions are part of the ceremonial aura that helps make certain events special—as in this address by Danny Glover to the graduating class at Spelman College.

Speech Assignment
As an alternative to the assignment on p. 465, have students present speeches of introduction during each unit of the course. The length and complexity of the introductory speech should vary depending on the kind of speech it is introducing. For an explanation of this assignment, see Shirley Sikes, "Introducing the Speaker," in *Selections from the Speech Communication Teacher, 1991–1994*, pp. 59–60, which accompanies *The Art of Public Speaking*.

Also, you will want to tell each audience what *it* wants to hear—to give the kind of information that is interesting and accessible to the members of that audience. If you were introducing the same speaker to two different groups, some of the information in the speeches of introduction might be the same, but it would be slanted differently. Suppose, for example, the police commissioner of a certain city is going to address two groups—an audience of elementary-school children and the members of the city council. The introduction to the schoolchildren might go something like this:

Children, we have a very important guest with us today. He is the number one policeman in our city, the head of all the other police officers. Besides knowing a lot about crime right here at home, the police commissioner has also spent time working with Interpol—a special group of police officers who deal with crimes around the world. Today he is going to talk about how all of us can work with our neighborhood police officers to prevent crime. Let's give a big round of applause and listen carefully to Police Commissioner Robert Washington.

But the introduction to the city council would be along these lines:

Members of the city council and distinguished guests: It is my privilege to introduce to you today the police commissioner, who will address us on the subject of the community policing program. Most of you know that the commissioner has a distinguished record as head of our police force for more than 10 years. However, you may not know that he also holds a master's degree in criminology and studied abroad for a year with Interpol, the international police force.

The commissioner first introduced the community policing program eight years ago. The idea behind the program is to get police officers out of their cars and into our neighborhoods, where they can talk directly to merchants and residents about the real dynamics of our city. These officers do more than make arrests. They try to find ways to help solve the problems that contribute to crime in the first place. Often that means hooking people up with services offered by other city agencies—schools, hospitals, housing, drug treatment centers.

And the program seems to be working. Crime is down and our citizens report that they feel more secure. Today the commissioner is going to tell us more about this program. Please welcome Police Commissioner Robert Washington.

Try to Create a Sense of Anticipation and Drama

You may have noticed one detail shared by the two speeches introducing the police commissioner: In both cases the speaker's name was saved for last. This is a convention in speeches of introduction. While there may occasionally be a good reason to break the convention, usually you will avoid mentioning the speaker's name until the final moment—even when the audience knows exactly whom you are discussing. By doing this you build a sense of drama, and the speaker's name comes as the climax of your introduction.

Often you will find yourself in the situation of introducing someone who is fairly well known to the audience—a classmate, a colleague at a business meeting, a neighbor in a community group. Then you should try to be creative and cast the speaker in a new light. Try to increase the audience's eagerness to hear the speaker. Talk to the speaker beforehand and see if you can learn some interesting facts that are not generally known—especially facts that relate to the speaker's topic.

Above all, if you expect to be creative and dramatic, be sure to practice your speech of introduction thoroughly. You should be able to deliver it extemporaneously, with sincerity and enthusiasm.

Speech Assignment
Yet another possibility is to have each student give a two-minute speech introducing a famous person to the class. Tell students they should imagine themselves being able to invite any well-known figure, living or dead, to speak to the class on any topic of the student's choice. For a full description of this assignment, see the *Instructor's Manual*, p. 360. You can also use a longer version of this assignment for the final speech of the term. See Charmaine E. Wilson, "Ending the Public Speaking Class on a Positive Note," in *Selections from the Communication Teacher, 1999–2002*, pp. 76–77, which accompanies *The Art of Public Speaking*.

Speeches of Presentation

Speeches of presentation are given when someone is receiving publicly a gift, an award, or some other form of public recognition. Usually such speeches are relatively brief. They may be no more than a mere announcement ("And the winner is . . . ") or be up to four or five minutes in length.

As with other kinds of speeches, speeches of presentation need to be adapted to the audience and to the occasion. The main theme of a speech of presentation is to acknowledge the achievements of the recipient. You need to tell the audience why the recipient is receiving the award. Point out her or his contributions, achievements, and so forth. Do not deal with everything the person has ever done. Focus on achievements related to the award, and discuss these achievements in a way that will make them meaningful to the audience.

Depending on the audience and the occasion, you may also need to discuss two other matters in a speech of presentation. First, if the audience is not familiar with the award and why it is being given, you should explain briefly—or at least allude to—the purpose of the award. Second, if the award was won in a public competition and the audience knows who the losers are, you might take a moment to praise the losers as well.

speech of presentation
A speech that presents someone a gift, an award, or some other form of public recognition.

Below is a sample speech of presentation. It was delivered by President Bill Clinton in presenting the Congressional Gold Medal to former South African President Nelson Mandela at a ceremony in the Rotunda of the United States Capitol in Washington, D.C. Because the Congressional Gold Medal is a special honor bestowed by the U.S. Congress, there are no public competitors for the award. Thus Clinton did not need to say anything about the "losers." His speech focused on Mandela's battle against apartheid and his efforts to promote reconciliation among the people of South Africa.

Presenting the Congressional Gold Medal
Bill Clinton

Speech Assignment
As with speeches of introduction, addresses of presentation and of acceptance
can be used to give students
additional speaking experience. For one approach, see
Randall E. Majors, "Practical
Ceremonial Speaking: Three
Speech Activities," in *Selections from the Speech Communication Teacher, 1986–1991,*
p. 68, which accompanies
The Art of Public Speaking.

To my friend, President Mandela, Americans as one today, across all the lines that divide us, pay tribute to your struggle, to your achievement, and to the inspiration you have given us to do better. Today we offer a man who has received the Nobel Prize the highest honor within the gift of this country. . . .

Those of us who share his vision and lift him up in honor today owe it to him to build a permanent partnership between Americans and Africans—for the education of our children, for the solution of our problems, for the resolution of our differences, for the elevation of what is best about us all. . . .

In forgiving those who imprisoned him, he reminded us of the most fundamental lesson of all—that in the end apartheid was a defeat of the heart, the mind, the spirit. It was not just a structure outside and jail houses within which people were kept; it was a division of the mind and soul against itself. We owe it to Nelson Mandela not simply to give him this award, but to live by the lesson he taught us and to tear down every last vestige of apartheid in our own hearts—everything that divides us, one from another.

For those of us who have been privileged to know this remarkable man, no medal, no award, no fortune, nothing we could give him could possibly compare to the gift he has given to us and to the world. The only gift that is true recompense is to continue his mission and to live by the power of his profound and wonderful example.

Now, as prescribed by the law, it is my privilege to present the Congressional Gold Medal to President Nelson Mandela.

Speeches of Acceptance

The purpose of an acceptance speech is to give thanks for a gift or an award. When giving such a speech, you should thank the people who are bestowing the award, and you should recognize the people who helped you gain it.

acceptance speech
A speech that gives thanks for a gift, an award, or some other form of public recognition.

The acceptance speech that follows is the companion piece to the speech of presentation by Bill Clinton. It was delivered by Nelson Mandela in accepting the Congressional Gold Medal Award, and it exemplifies the major traits of a good acceptance speech—brevity, humility, and graciousness.[2]

Accepting the Congressional Gold Medal

Nelson Mandela

Thank you. President Clinton, Mr. Speaker, distinguished members of the Senate and the House, ladies and gentlemen . . .

It has been my great privilege to serve a people whose bondage to an inhuman system evoked the solidarity of all those who love freedom and justice, a people whose triumph over the divisions of racist doctrine has given new life to humanity's hope for a world without hatred and discrimination. I am conscious that in bestowing the Congressional Gold Medal upon me you are evoking these bonds between our nations and paying tribute to the whole South African nation for its achievements in realizing our shared ideals.

It is in that spirit that I humbly accept the award, aware at the same time of the great honor you do me by using me as the vehicle of a unique distinction conferred by this hallowed institution of American democracy. As one who has dedicated his life to the pursuit of unity, I am moved by the consensus in your nation's regard for the achievements of my people. And I feel a great pride in the fact that with a few citizens of other countries who have received this high honor, the name of an African is now added. . . .

View an excerpt from Nelson Mandela's acceptance speech.

CD 1: VIDEO 17.1

The award with which you honor me today is an expression of the common humanity that binds us, one person to another, nation to nation, and people of the north to people of the south. I receive it with pride as a symbol of partnership for peace, prosperity, and equity as we enter the new millennium. I thank you.

Commemorative Speeches

Commemorative speeches are speeches of praise or celebration. Eulogies, Fourth of July speeches, testimonial addresses, and dedications are examples of commemorative speeches. Your aim in such speeches is to pay tribute to a person, a group of people, an institution, or an idea.

As in an informative speech, you probably will have to give the audience information about your subject. After all, the audience must know *why* your subject is praiseworthy. They will need to know something about the history of the institution or the life of the person being praised. As in other speeches, you may draw on examples, testimony, even statistics to illustrate the achievements of your subject.

Your fundamental purpose in a commemorative speech, however, is not just to inform your listeners but to *inspire* them—to arouse and heighten their appreciation of or admiration for the person, institution, or idea you are praising. If you are paying tribute to a person, for example, you should not compose a biography that simply recounts the details of the person's life. Rather, you should create a speech that goes beyond biography—that penetrates to the *essence* of your subject and generates in your audience a deep sense of respect.

commemorative speech
A speech that pays tribute to a person, a group of people, an institution, or an idea.

When speaking to commemorate, you do not exhort like the advocate or explain like the lecturer. You want to express feelings, to stir sentiments—joy and hope when a new building is dedicated or a new President is inaugurated; anticipation and good wishes at a commencement celebration; lament and consolation at a funeral or memorial service; admiration and respect at a testimonial dinner. In some ways, a commemorative speech is

The primary traits of a good acceptance speech are brevity, humility, and graciousness. Here former President Jimmy Carter accepts the 2002 Nobel Peace Prize in Oslo, Norway.

like an impressionist painting—"a picture with warm colors and texture capturing a mood or a moment."[3]

But while the painter works with brush and colors, the commemorative speaker works with language. Of all the kinds of speeches, perhaps none depends more on the creative and subtle use of language than does the speech to commemorate. Some of the most memorable speeches in history, including Abraham Lincoln's Gettysburg Address, have been commemorative. We remember such speeches—we continue to find them meaningful and inspiring—largely because of their eloquent use of language.

One of the most effective commemorative speakers in our recent history was President Ronald Reagan. After the explosion of the space shuttle *Challenger* in 1986, Reagan delivered a nationally televised eulogy to the astronauts killed in the blast. Below are two versions of Reagan's closing lines. The first is what he *might* have said, stripping the text of its warm emotional content and poignant language:

View the ending of Ronald Reagan's eulogy to the *Challenger* astronauts.

CD 1: VIDEO 17.2

> Like Francis Drake, the great explorer of the oceans, the *Challenger* astronauts gave their lives for a cause to which they were fully dedicated. We are honored by them, and we will not forget them. We will always remember seeing them for the last time this morning as they prepared for their flight.

Here is what Reagan *actually* said:

> There's a coincidence today. On this day 390 years ago, the great explorer Francis Drake died aboard ship off the coast of Panama. In his lifetime the great frontiers were

the oceans, and an historian later said, "He lived by the sea, died on it, was buried in it." Well, today we can say of the *Challenger* crew: Their dedication was, like Drake's, complete.

The crew of the space shuttle *Challenger* honored us by the manner in which they lived their lives. We will never forget them, nor the last time we saw them, this morning, as they prepared for their journey and waved goodbye and "slipped the surly bonds of earth" to "touch the face of God."

The final words—"'slipped the surly bonds of earth' to 'touch the face of God'"—are especially effective. Drawn from a sonnet called "High Flight" that many pilots keep with them, they ennoble the deaths of the astronauts and end the speech on an eloquent, moving, and poetic note.

When speaking to commemorate, you will deal for the most part with intangibles. Your success will depend on your ability to put into language the thoughts and emotions appropriate to the occasion. It is easy—too easy—to fall back on clichés and trite sentiments. Your challenge will be to use language imaginatively in order to invest the occasion with dignity, meaning, and honest emotion.

In doing so, you may want to utilize the special resources of language discussed in Chapter 11 to enhance the imagery and rhythm of your prose. Metaphor, simile, parallelism, repetition, antithesis, alliteration—all are appropriate for commemorative speeches. Some highly acclaimed commemorative speeches—including Martin Luther King's "I Have a Dream" and John Kennedy's inaugural address—are distinguished by their creative use of such devices.

Confronted with the evocative speeches of a Kennedy or a King, you may decide that the speech of commemoration is far beyond your abilities. But other students have delivered excellent commemorative speeches—not immortal, perhaps, but nonetheless dignified and moving. The speech on pages 471–472 was given by Keith Framnes, a student at the University of Wisconsin, in his public speaking class. The assignment was to give a brief speech paying tribute to a person, an institution, or an idea. Keith spoke about the 54th Regiment of the Massachusetts Volunteer Infantry. The first black regiment to fight in the Civil War, the Massachusetts 54th had a distinguished record of bravery and was later immortalized in the movie *Glory*. As you read this speech, notice how effectively Keith uses the resources of language to give his ideas artistic unity and emotional impact.[4]

Speech Assignment
Over the years, I have used a commemorative speech assignment with great success. Students often remark that this is their favorite speech of the course. Because the speech depends so much on the creative use of language, I have students read Chapter 11 in conjunction with this assignment, and I encourage them to employ in their speeches the stylistic devices explained in that chapter. I particularly like the commemorative speech assignment because it takes account of the diversity of student aptitudes and backgrounds. Some students who have difficulty with the more didactic informative and persuasive speeches shine on the commemorative speech, which rewards a different set of skills and sensibilities. For a brief explanation of the commemorative speech assignment, see the *Instructor's Manual*, p. 35.

The Massachusetts 54th

Keith Framnes

Staring at a once beautiful valley now filled with bodies that serve only as a reminder of the morning's gruesome events, a lonely grave digger thinks to himself. Unable to fight in the Civil War because he is black, he can only bury the soldiers that fight and die for his freedom, wondering when he will get his chance to fight.

In the movie *Glory*, this grave digger is played by Morgan Freeman, and he is given his chance to fight as a member of the 54th Regiment of the Massachusetts Volunteer Infantry. The Massachusetts 54th was the first black regiment of the Civil War. Led by Colonel Robert Gould Shaw, the 54th showed remarkable bravery, patriotism, and sacrifice.

Even though the North was opposed to slavery, many Northerners held on to anti-black attitudes. Because of these attitudes, the Massachusetts 54th was given dangerous assignments and equipped with substandard, or even broken, equipment. Wearing shoes no better than wrapped cloth, tattered uniforms that did little or nothing to ward off the cold, and using guns that would misfire every other shot, the 54th still proved to be one of the bravest regiments in the Civil War.

On top of their bravery, the members of the Massachusetts 54th exhibited the highest levels of patriotism. Despite the racism and other struggles they faced, they were proud to wear their uniforms and to carry the Union flag into battle. Their patriotism can best be seen when one observes the number of deserters from this regiment—none. Despite the thousands of desertions suffered by many other regiments on the Northern side, not a single soldier deserted from the Massachusetts 54th.

I have spoken so far of bravery and of patriotism, but it is the sacrifice of the 54th that has etched them into the pages of history. That sacrifice occurred during the assault on Fort Wagner in 1863. This heavily guarded Confederate fort lay on the beaches of South Carolina, nearly unapproachable. A frontal assault was needed to weaken the fort enough to allow for a full-scale attack. It was a suicidal mission, but the 54th volunteered for it.

They were the first regiment to storm Fort Wagner, and so would suffer the highest casualties. Rushing forward, they reached the fort well before any reinforcements that were supposed to back them up. Believing the reinforcements to be close behind, the 54th attacked Fort Wagner and found nothing but the enemy. When the charge was over, more than 250 soldiers from the regiment had been killed, wounded, or captured.

To join an army that didn't believe in you. To fight with an army who didn't like you. To die for an army that didn't respect you. This was the Massachusetts 54th. Today they lay where they died, on the beaches of South Carolina. Colonel Shaw and his men were piled together in a mass grave, which has since been covered by the shifting tides of the Atlantic. A small statue stands in Boston—a reminder of their sacrifice.

Bravery, patriotism, and sacrifice. These are qualities of the Massachusetts 54th. With the help of their efforts, along with all the other black regiments that followed them, slavery did eventually come to an end.

In the movie *Glory,* Morgan Freeman talks of his chance to fight for the freedom of his own people. The 54th grasped this chance, they fought for it, and they eventually died for it. In the words of Union General Truman Seymour, "On every inch of the sands in front of Fort Wagner will be forever traced in undying glory the story of the determination and courage of the Massachusetts 54th."

View Keith Framnes, "The Massachusetts 54th."

CD 2: FULL SPEECH

Video Supplement
"The Massachusetts 54th" is available on the video of student speeches that accompanies this edition of *The Art of Public Speaking.* For full discussion of the speech, see the *Instructor's Manual,* pp. 357–358. Additional samples of student commemorative speeches can be found in Part V of the *Manual.*

After-Dinner Speeches

After-dinner speeches may be harder to define than any other kind of speech. While the custom of saying a few words of tribute or celebration after a meal is as old as civilization itself, after-dinner speeches as a formal type of speech developed in England during the early 1800s. At that time, they were delivered, literally, after dinner. Today, because of the popularity of lunch meetings for various civic and business groups, you are as likely to hear an "after-dinner" speech during the noon hour as during the evening.

Whether given on the world stage or in one's local community, speeches for special occasions should seek to invest the occasion with dignity, meaning, and honest emotion.

After-dinner speeches are best thought of as a kind of speech to entertain. Whether presented after breakfast, lunch, or dinner—in a formal dining room or at an outdoor barbecue—they usually have a lighter tone than a speech to inform or to persuade. This difference in tone will obviously have some impact on your choice of topic. AIDS, child abuse, terrorism, drunk driving, gun violence—all are important, but audiences do not expect to hear about such weighty matters in the relaxed atmosphere of the typical after-dinner speech. For the most part, though, any topic suitable for an informative or persuasive speech can be appropriate for an after-dinner speech, as long as you approach it in a lighthearted manner.

after-dinner speech
A speech to entertain that makes a thoughtful point about its subject in a lighthearted manner.

Suppose your subject is nutrition. If you were giving an informative speech on this topic, your specific purpose might be "To inform my audience of the four basic nutrients in the human diet." If you were presenting a persuasive speech, your specific purpose might be "To persuade my audience that they should reduce their consumption of red meat in favor of more fish, vegetables, and grains." But if you were giving an after-dinner speech on the topic of nutrition, your specific purpose might be "To entertain my audience by showing them the ridiculous extremes some people go to in following special diets."

As this example suggests, after-dinner speeches should not be technical or argumentative. They may contain information that is new to the audience, and they may even have a persuasive impact, but their supporting materials should be chosen primarily for their entertainment value. Audiences for after-dinner speeches are seldom in a mood to follow a close train of reasoning or a complicated set of statistics. They are looking for a good-natured speech that stimulates the imagination by approaching the topic in a novel way, treating it lightly, even whimsically.

As discussed in this chapter, Ronald Reagan's eulogy to the *Challenger* astronauts is one of the most effective commemorative speeches in U.S. history and was judged the eighth best speech of the 20th century. You can read the entire text of Reagan's address, along with the rest of the top 100, at www.mhhe.com/lucastop100.

Presidential inaugural addresses are a major kind of special-occasion speech. You can access these historical documents at either Bartleby's Inaugural Addresses of the Presidents (www.bartleby.com/124/) or the Yale Law School's Avalon Project (www.yale.edu/lawweb/avalon/presiden/inaug/inaug.htm).

Speech Assignment
Toasts are another kind of special-occasion speech that many people will deliver at some point in their lives. For an enjoyable assignment that gives students practice with this kind of speech, see Kathleen W. Williams and Lynn Rinehart, "Here's a Toast," in *Selections from the Speech Communication Teacher, 1996–1999*, pp. 84–85, which accompanies *The Art of Public Speaking*.

This is not to say that after-dinner speeches should be rambling or totally frivolous. Like all other speeches, they require careful preparation and organization. They should have a central theme, and they should strive to make a thoughtful point about that theme—whether it is an aspect of human nature (such as vanity or the desire for immortality), of college life (such as final exams or finding a decent apartment), of work (such as putting up with the boss or dealing with weird customers), of travel (such as poor service by the airlines or dealing with unusual customs abroad), of family life (such as the perils of summer vacations or the experience of being a parent for the first time), or even of current events (such as how we choose presidential candidates or jitters over the stock market).

As you might imagine, humor can be an important part of after-dinner speeches. Some of America's finest after-dinner speakers have been humorists such as Mark Twain and Dave Barry, but you don't need to be a stand-up comic to be a successful after-dinner speaker. The purpose of humor in an after-dinner speech is more to provoke smiles or chuckles than to convulse the audience with a series of one-liners. Nor is humor used merely to make the audience laugh. In the best speeches, humor grows naturally out of the speech materials and helps the speaker make his or her point by providing special insight into the topic.[5]

Tickling an audience's funnybone, however, can be difficult even for accomplished public speakers. If you don't feel confident working for a laugh, don't worry. Humor can contribute to a successful after-dinner speech, but it is not essential. Indeed, the best approach is usually not to work specifically for laughs. If you deal with the topic creatively, select supporting materials that are interesting in their own right, and use the resources of language to create sharp imagery, vivid descriptions, colorful details, and clever phrasing, you should do just fine.

All these traits are represented in the following after-dinner speech. It was given by Julie Daggett, a student at the University of Wisconsin, to her public speaking class.[6]

The Horror of It All

Julie Daggett

They never did find his head or hands. I crouched in the corner, peering through my fingers as he moaned and wailed in an endless search for his missing appendages. I was terrified—but not as terrified as poor Bette Davis. They put her in the nuthouse. I simply turned on the light and ran to the safety of my father's lap. As I perched, shuddering, he said the phrase I was to hear over and over through the coming years, "It's okay, it's only a movie." It did not end for me there, however. The movie *Hush, Hush, Sweet Charlotte* was just the beginning of my love/hate relationship with horror movies.

My scaredy-cat tendencies actually began at a very early age. As a young child, I insisted the hall light be kept on when I went to bed—no measly night-light would do for a hard-core chicken. My parents would come upstairs after the news and tell each other to "turn off the l-i-g-h-t." I could be heard miles away screaming, "NO! I know what that spells!" After *The Ghost and Mr. Chicken* with Don Knotts, my bedtime ritual went something like this—look under the bed, look in the closet, turn off the light, and leap into the sack. As time passed, however, this childish nonsense began to subside. I was growing up.

But then it happened. Theater owners offered up *The Exorcist,* a temptation I could not resist. That delicious, horrible feeling of being terrified was renewed. I was hooked. I stayed pretty sane, though, until I read the book, at which time I discovered I was possessed by the Devil. I had six of the ten symptoms, including headaches, nausea, and loss of sleep. It may not have been Satan himself, but there was definitely a demon lurking somewhere.

Over the next several years, the movie industry fed my passion for terror—and my paranoia. The movie *Halloween* ended any possibility of parking on a deserted road after a date. I was not going to fog up the windows making myself a sitting duck for any escaped mental patient. The *Friday the 13th* series put a stop to any thought of camping overnight in the wilderness, while *Night of the Living Dead* put a dent in my car. I was in such a panic to get out of the dark parking lot after viewing this old classic that I slammed into a pole, causing $300 damage to my trusty Chevy.

My fright-flick fanaticism was taking a toll on my everyday life. I began to notice that guys who took me to these movies didn't often ask me out again—apparently my squirming and screaming in the theater embarrassed them a bit. Some people just don't know how to really get into a movie. I no longer took babysitting jobs because I was afraid to be alone in a strange house. I wouldn't do laundry at night because that meant I had to go down to the basement.

My fears weren't even limited to being alone. One Friday night I was home watching HBO with my Mom. Let me explain that our house is situated in the dead center of a very isolated woods. As a kid I remember thinking it would be an ideal place for escaped convicts to hide out and hold hostages. Anyway, there we were, munching away on junk food, when suddenly the lights went out. Keep in mind that this was a calm summer evening—no rain, no lightning, not even any wind. There was only one explanation—we had a madman in the basement.

In my alarm I turned to the woman who had protected me all my life. My Mom looked at me and said the only thing she could say, "Grab the potato chips." Chips and keys in tow, we bolted for the car. But this was not to be the end of our ordeal—no electricity, no electric garage door opener. I looked at my Mom and said the only thing I could say, "Ram it!" Bravely, Mom kept her head. She crept out of the security of the locked car to manually open the garage door and drive us, in our pajamas, to safety. It was then that I knew I was out of control. It was then that I decided to go cold turkey—no more horror films.

Cross-Reference
For analysis of "The Horror of It All," see the *Instructor's Manual,* pp. 358–359.

Speech Assignment
Although the after-dinner speech is very difficult for most beginning speakers, it can work well with an advanced class or with a class composed mainly of communication majors or honors students. For an explanation of the after-dinner speech assignment, see the *Instructor's Manual,* p. 36.

Related Reading
Paula Wilson Youra and Heidi Koring (eds.), *Pomp & Circumstance: Ceremonial Speaking* (Greenwood, IN: Alistair Press, 2002). This excellent anthology reprints a wide range of commemorative speeches, historical and contemporary alike.

It's been two years now, and I can finally look back at these escapades and laugh. It's been two years now, and I pride myself on the fact that I live alone. The only thing that keeps me awake nights these days is writing speeches. I'm not going to end up in the nuthouse like Bette Davis. But I'm not going to get too overconfident, either. Remember all those unsuspecting kids in *Halloween?* They were just out having a good time when, WHAM—and the rest is history.

Summary

Special occasions include weddings, funerals, dedications, award ceremonies, retirement dinners, and the like. Nearly always they are occasions for speechmaking. In this chapter we have considered speeches of introduction, speeches of presentation, speeches of acceptance, commemorative speeches, and after-dinner speeches.

When you make a speech of introduction, your job is to build enthusiasm for the main speaker and to establish a welcoming climate that will boost his or her credibility and confidence. Keep your remarks brief, make sure they are completely accurate, and adapt them to the audience, the occasion, and the main speaker.

Speeches of presentation are given when someone is receiving publicly a gift or an award. The main theme of such a speech is to acknowledge the achievements of the recipient. The purpose of an acceptance speech is to give thanks for a gift or an award. When delivering such a speech, you should thank the people who are bestowing the award and recognize the contributions of people who helped you gain it. Be brief, humble, and gracious.

Commemorative speeches are speeches of praise or celebration. Your aim in such a speech is to pay tribute to a person, a group of people, an institution, or an idea. When making a commemorative speech you want to inspire your audience—to arouse and heighten their appreciation of and admiration for the subject. Your success will depend largely on how well you put into language the thoughts and feelings appropriate to the occasion.

After-dinner speeches are best thought of as a kind of speech to entertain, and they usually have a lighter tone than informative or persuasive speeches. Neither technical nor argumentative, they seek to stimulate the imagination by approaching the topic in a novel or unexpected way. Although humor can be an important part of after-dinner speeches, it is not essential. If you do use humor, it should grow naturally out of the speech materials and provide insight into the topic.

Key Terms

Review these terms by doing the Chapter 17 crossword puzzle at www.mhhe.com/lucas8.

ONLINE LEARNING CENTER

speech of introduction (464)
speech of presentation (467)
acceptance speech (468)

commemorative speech (469)
after-dinner speech (473)

Review Questions

After reading this chapter, you should be able to answer the following questions:

1. What are the three purposes of a speech of introduction? What guidelines should you follow in preparing such a speech?

2. What is the main theme of a speech of presentation? Depending on the audience and occasion, what two other themes might you include in such a speech?

3. What are the three major traits of a good acceptance speech?

4. What is the fundamental purpose of a commemorative speech? Why does a successful commemorative speech depend so much on the creative and subtle use of language?

5. What is the primary difference between an after-dinner speech and a speech to inform or to persuade? What is the role of humor in after-dinner speaking?

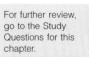
For further review, go to the Study Questions for this chapter.

CD 1: STUDY QUESTIONS

Exercises for Critical Thinking

1. Attend a speech on campus. Pay special attention to the speech introducing the main speaker. How well does it fit the guidelines discussed in this chapter?

2. Observe several speeches of presentation and acceptance—at a campus awards ceremony or on a television program such as the Academy Awards, Grammy Awards, Emmy Awards, or Tony Awards. Which speeches do you find most effective? Least effective? Why?

3. Analyze the commemorative speech by Keith Framnes ("The Massachusetts 54th," pages 471–472). Assess the speech in light of the criteria for commemorative speaking presented in this chapter.

4. Analyze the after-dinner speech by Julie Daggett ("The Horror of It All," pages 475–476). Evaluate the speech in light of the criteria for after-dinner speaking discussed in this chapter.

Cross-Reference
For discussion of the Exercises for Critical Thinking, see the *Instructor's Manual*, pp. 355–359. For additional exercises, check the *Instructor's Manual*, pp. 360–361, as well as the five volumes of *Selections from the Speech Communication Teacher* that accompany *The Art of Public Speaking*.

Notes

[1]James C. Humes, *Roles Speakers Play* (New York: Harper and Row, 1976), p. 8.

[2]For both speeches, see "Remarks by President Clinton and President Nelson Mandela at Presentation of the Congressional Gold Medal to President Nelson Mandela," September 23, 1998. <http://clinton4.nara.gov/WH/New/html/19980923-977.html> January 28, 2003.

[3]Humes, *Roles Speakers Play*, pp. 33–34, 36.

[4]Reprinted with permission of Keith Framnes.

[5]For an interesting recent study with implications for humor in public speaking, see John C. Meyer, "Humor as a Double-Edged Sword: Four Functions of Humor in Communication," *Communication Theory* (2000), pp. 310–331.

[6]Reprinted with permission of Julie Daggett.

Chapter Eighteen

SPEAKING IN SMALL GROUPS

Chapter Focus

This chapter identifies the major traits of a small group, explores the role of leadership in group deliberation, explains the responsibilities of group members, and examines the reflective-thinking method for discussion in problem-solving groups. The chapter concludes by looking at how a group can present its findings in an oral report, a symposium, or a panel discussion. For a full outline of the chapter, see the *Instructor's Manual*, pp. 364–368.

he president of a small company decided to remodel the office space on her management floor. She assigned her youngest vice president, Greg Anapau, to make a plan for remodeling the offices and to carry through the plan.

Greg was very pleased with his plan. He thought he had taken everyone's needs into account, and he had arranged for most of the remodeling to be done over a long weekend so no one's work would be disrupted. On Monday morning, after the remodeling, Greg settled back in his office waiting for congratulations to pour in.

Instead, a crowd of angry people stormed into his office. "There's no telephone jack in my room," said the advertising manager, "and the telephone company says it can't put one in for three weeks. How can I do business without a telephone?"

Right behind him was the administrative assistant. "Do you realize," she said, "how far I have to walk to get to the president's office? It's only 15 feet from my room, but with that new partition, I have to walk halfway around the building!"

Next came the research manager, who said, "What am I supposed to do with my library? All my books are packed up and there's no place to put them."

Angriest of all was another vice president. "For heaven's sake," she said, "why didn't you ask me? The same things happened the *last* time the offices were moved around. I could have told you to watch out for the phone jacks and the research library."

Wearily, Greg went back to his blueprint, making plans to rearrange the offices again.

What went wrong? Greg did not have enough resources on his own to make a successful plan. If a group, instead of a single person, had been assigned to remodel the offices, the problems might have been averted. One person could have taken charge of space needs, another of traffic paths, a third of telephones and other equipment, and so forth. The final plan would have taken *all* factors into account.

Of course, you may have heard the old saying that "a camel is a horse designed by a committee." If you have ever been part of a group that seemed to get nothing done, you may be inclined to say, "Oh, let one person decide and get it over with." The problem in such cases, however, is not that there is a group, but that the group is not functioning properly. A great deal of research shows that if members of a group work well together, they can almost always resolve a problem better than a single person.[1]

This chapter deals with speaking in a particular kind of group—the problem-solving small group.

What Is a Small Group?

dyad
A group of two people.

As its name implies, a small group has a limited number of members. The minimum number is three. (A group of two persons is called a *dyad,* and it operates quite differently from a group of three or more.) There is some difference of opinion about the maximum number of people who constitute a small group. Most experts set the maximum number at seven or eight; some go as high as twelve.[2] The important point is that the group must be small enough to allow free discussion among all members. In small-group communication, all participants are potentially speakers *and* listeners. A manageable number of people permits everyone to shift easily between speaking and listening.

Members of a small group assemble for a specific purpose. They are not just a band of three to twelve people who happen to end up in the same room. Several shoppers milling around the clothing section of a department store are not a small group, even if they speak to one another or comment about high prices and poor service. But if those same shoppers decided to meet together and prepare a formal complaint to the store manager about high prices and poor service, they would then constitute a small group. They would have assembled for a specific purpose.

A *problem-solving small group* is formed to solve a particular problem. Such groups exist in every area of life. Business groups consider ways of increasing sales. Church groups discuss how to raise funds and provide for the needy. Groups of parents work on improving day care facilities. The President's cabinet debates a foreign policy move. A ski club evaluates proposals for the next outing. You will almost surely be a member of many problem-solving small groups during your life.

Although speaking in a small group is not the same as public speaking, it involves many similar skills. Members of a small group influence one another through communication. At times they inform their fellow members. At other times they seek to persuade them. As a participant in a small group, you might influence your colleagues by giving them important information, by encouraging them to speak, by convincing them to change their minds, by leading them into a new channel of communication, even by getting them to end a meeting of the group. All other members of the group have the same opportunity to influence you through effective communication.[3]

small group
A collection of three to twelve people who assemble for a specific purpose.

problem-solving small group
A small group formed to solve a particular problem.

Leadership in Small Groups

We have said that small groups often make better decisions than do individuals. But the word "often" should be stressed here. To make sound decisions, groups need effective leadership.

Kinds of Leadership

Sometimes there is *no specific leader.* In such a situation, members of effective groups tend to have equal influence. When a need for leadership arises, any of the members can—and one probably will—provide the necessary leadership. A typical instance might be a class project, in which you and several classmates are working together. From time to time each of you will help the group move toward its goal by suggesting when and where to meet, by outlining the strengths and weaknesses of a certain viewpoint, by resolving disagreements among other members, and so forth.[4]

In some circumstances a group may have an *implied leader.* For example, if a business meeting includes one vice president and several subordinates, the vice president becomes the implied leader. The same is

leadership
The ability to influence group members so as to help achieve the goals of the group.

implied leader
A group member to whom other members defer because of her or his rank, expertise, or other quality.

true if one member of the group is a specialist in the topic at hand and the others are not. Members will likely defer to the person with the highest rank or greatest expertise, and that person will become the group's implied leader.

emergent leader
A group member who emerges as a leader during the group's deliberations.

Even when a group starts out leaderless, there may be an *emergent leader*. This is a person who, by ability or by force of personality, or just by talking the most, takes a leadership role. The emergence of a leader may or may not be desirable. If the group is stalemated or has dissolved into bickering or making jokes, an emergent leader can put the group back on track. There is a danger, however, that the emergent leader may be not the most effective leader but merely the most assertive personality. Ideally, each member of the group should be prepared to assume a leadership role when necessary.

designated leader
A person who is elected or appointed as leader when the group is formed.

Finally, there may be a *designated leader*—a person elected or appointed as leader when the group is formed. A group that meets for only one session should almost always have a designated leader who takes care of the procedural tasks and serves as spokesperson for the group. Likewise, a formal committee will usually have a designated chairperson. The chair can perform leadership functions or delegate them, but he or she remains in charge of the group.[5]

A group may or may not need a specific leader, but it always needs leader*ship*. When all members of the group are skilled communicators, they can take turns at providing leadership even if the group has a designated or implied leader. As you develop group communication skills, you should be prepared to assume a leadership role whenever necessary.[6]

Functions of Leadership

An effective leader helps the group reach its goals by fulfilling three overlapping sets of needs—procedural needs, task needs, and maintenance needs.

Procedural Needs

procedural needs
Routine "housekeeping" actions necessary for the efficient conduct of business in a small group.

Procedural needs can be thought of as the "housekeeping" requirements of the group. They include:

Deciding when and where the group will meet.

Reserving the room, checking the number of chairs, making sure the heat or air conditioning is turned on.

Setting the agenda of each meeting.

Starting the meeting.

Taking notes during the meeting.

Preparing and distributing any written handouts needed for the meeting.

Summarizing the group's progress at the end of the meeting.

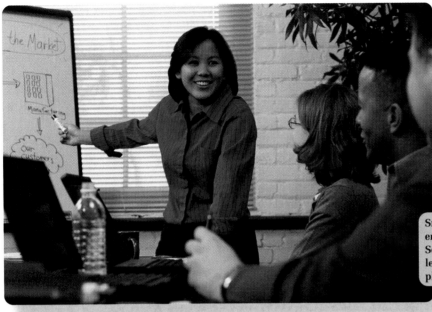

Small groups require effective leadership to accomplish their goals. Some groups have a designated leader, while others have an implied leader or an emergent leader.

If there is a designated leader, she or he can attend to these needs or assign one or more group members to do so. Otherwise, members of the group must devise ways to split the procedural responsibilities.

Task Needs

Task needs go beyond procedural needs and are substantive actions necessary to help the group complete the particular task it is working on. They include:

task needs
Substantive actions necessary to help a small group complete its assigned task.

Analyzing the issues facing the group.

Distributing the workload among the members.

Collecting information.

Soliciting the views of other members.

Keeping the group from going off on a tangent.

Playing devil's advocate for unpopular ideas.

Formulating criteria for judging the most effective solution.

Helping the group reach consensus on its final recommendations.

Most members will help the group satisfy its task needs. Leadership becomes necessary when some task needs are not being fulfilled adequately, as in this example:

A group of students had undertaken to solve the parking problems on their campus. The group had held several meetings, and most of its task needs had been met. Members had done a good job polling students for their opinions, discussing alternative solutions with the administration, and considering the relative merits of each solution. However, one member of the group, Pilar, noticed that two items had not been given enough attention: No one had investigated potential sources of money for new parking facilities, and no one had studied the environmental impact of constructing additional parking spaces. Therefore, Pilar briefly took a leadership role to perform a task need for the group. She pointed out that these two areas had been neglected and recommended that the group explore them further.

The effective leader—whether permanent or temporary—has a realistic notion of the group's task needs and of how to meet them.

Maintenance Needs

maintenance needs
Communicative actions necessary to maintain interpersonal relations in a small group.

Maintenance needs involve interpersonal relations in the group. They include such factors as:

How well members get along with one another.

How willing members are to contribute to the group.

Whether members are supportive of one another.

Whether members feel satisfied with the group's accomplishments.

Whether members feel good about their roles in the group.

If interpersonal problems dominate discussion, the group will have a difficult time working together and reaching a decision. This is one of the more important areas calling for effective leadership. A leader can do much to create and sustain supportive communication in the group. By helping group members handle conflict, by working out differences of opinion, by reducing interpersonal tension, by encouraging participation from all members, by being alert to personal feelings, and by promoting solidarity within the group, a leader can make a tremendous contribution toward helping the group achieve its goals.[7]

Responsibilities in a Small Group

Every member of a small group must assume certain responsibilities, which can be divided into five major categories: (1) commit yourself to the goals of your group; (2) fulfill individual assignments; (3) avoid interpersonal conflicts; (4) encourage full participation; (5) keep the discussion on track. Some of these responsibilities involve leadership roles, but all five are so important that each participant should take them as personal obligations, regardless of the group's leadership. Let us look more closely at each of these responsibilities.

Commit Yourself to the Goals of Your Group

For a group to succeed, members must align their personal goals with the group's goal. This sounds obvious, but it is not always easy. When you are working with other students on a class project, the group goal—and most likely the goal of each member—is to get a good grade, which should ensure a positive attitude toward the group. There is a strong incentive for members to cooperate and commit themselves to completing the task.

Problems arise when one or more members have personal goals that conflict with the group's goal. Here is the kind of situation that can occur:

> Sherri Baines is a member of the committee to buy new equipment for the local newspaper's employee cafeteria. Because the budget is very tight, the committee's goal is to get the best equipment for the lowest price. But unknown to the other members of the group, Sherri's son-in-law is a salesman for a distributor of high-priced kitchen appliances. Privately, Sherri has reasoned that if she can sway the committee toward that company, her son-in-law will get a large commission. Sherri does not mention this fact to the group. Instead, she argues that *quality*—not price—should be the determining factor in the purchase. The group process breaks down because Sherri will not surrender her private goal.

This is an extreme example, but there can be more subtle kinds of private goals, as in the following case:

> Carlos and Rachel are part of a group, and Carlos would like to be on closer terms with Rachel. In order to impress her, he may agree with everything she says, regardless of whether he really shares her views. Consequently, Carlos's expressed views are not his actual views. In short, Carlos has a *hidden agenda* in the group meeting. The group's agenda is to solve the problem, but Carlos's agenda is to get a date with Rachel.

Group members may have all sorts of hidden agendas. One may be experiencing personal problems—lowered grades, a breakup with a friend, trouble at home, or just a bad day. Another may have a commitment to a different group whose goals conflict with those of the present group. A third may want to take charge of the group for reasons of personal power, regardless of the group's task.

Remember that what one member of a group does affects all the other members. You should not try to advance your own interests or boost your own ego at the expense of the group and its goals. Beware of hidden agendas—whether yours or someone else's—and participate with a positive spirit. If a group is to work effectively, all members must commit themselves to the goals of the group and cooperate to achieve them.

Fulfill Individual Assignments

As mentioned earlier, one of the advantages of the group process is that it divides the workload among several people. Work assignments might involve gathering information, making arrangements for a meeting, researching a particular aspect of the group's topic, taking notes at a meeting, and so forth. Unless every member fulfills his or her assignments, the group's entire project may fail—as in the following example:

> Several years ago, one student group decided that as a class project they would bring Easter baskets to the patients in the children's ward of a local hospital. After the

Class Activity
See Janice D. Hamlet, "When Does a Group Become 'A Group'? Solving the Puzzle," in *Selections from the Communication Teacher, 1999–2002,* pp. 52–54, which accompanies *The Art of Public Speaking,* for a creative activity that introduces students to the nature and functions of small-group communication.

hidden agenda
A set of unstated individual goals that may conflict with the goals of the group as a whole.

project had been approved, assignments were given out. Navid would coordinate with the hospital authorities. Corrine would handle fund-raising for the needed supplies. Jesse would supervise the egg-decorating team. Xunhua would be responsible for buying baskets and chocolate bunnies. Justin would arrange for transportation to the hospital.

Everybody completed their assignments except Justin, who was busy writing a term paper. He asked a friend to pick up a bus schedule and assumed everything would be fine. On Easter morning the group assembled at the bus stop, loaded down with baskets for the children. And they waited and waited. After an hour Justin called the bus company, only to discover that the buses did not run on holidays. By the time Justin had made other arrangements to get to the hospital, visiting hours were over, and the group could not get in.

Discussion Prompt

Have students ever been involved in a small group in which one or two members didn't pull their own weight? What was that experience like? What steps can group members take to help ensure that each member fulfills his or her responsibilities?

No matter what other assignments they may have, *all* members of a group have one very critical assignment—listening. If you tune out the person who is speaking, or if you concentrate entirely on what *you* plan to say next, the group is not going to make much progress.

Effective listening is vital to small-group communication. First, it helps you understand what is happening in the group. And unlike a public speaking situation, you can stop the speaker and ask for clarification on any point about which you are confused. Second, listening helps you evaluate the merits of the speaker's position in relation to your own. Third, listening provides support for the speaker and helps establish a positive climate for discussion. In group discussion, as in other kinds of situations, listening is crucial to effective communication.[8]

Avoid Interpersonal Conflicts

Teaching Tip

If you have students participate in a major small-group project out of class, distribute copies of the Group Discussion Participant Evaluation Form printed on p. 382 of the *Instructor's Manual*. Because this form focuses on individual group members, it usually gives a pretty clear picture of who met their responsibilities in the group and who did not. Be sure to let students know that their evaluations will be kept confidential.

If groups were made up of robots, there would be no problem with interpersonal conflicts. But groups are made up of people—people with likes and dislikes and animosities and prejudices and very different personalities. It is vital to the group process that disagreements be kept on a task level, rather than on a personal level.

Suppose you disagree with another member's idea. Disagreement on the personal level could sound like this: "That's the most stupid idea I ever heard of! Do you realize how much money it would cost to do that?" But on the task level, disagreement is aimed at the *idea,* not the person: "Potentially that's a very good solution, but I'm not sure we have enough money to accomplish it."

When disagreements are allowed to become personal, some members may start to see the group as a kind of debating society. Rather than focusing on the task, they may spend their time getting even with other participants, defending themselves, trying to score points, and jumping on people's ideas. Other members—especially those who are shy or soft-spoken—may recoil from the verbal combat and withdraw from active participation in the group's deliberations.

No matter what the group, personal antagonism leaves a bad taste in everyone's mouth and harms the performance of the group. It's essential that someone take a leadership role and bring the discussion back to the relevant

Interested in learning more about leadership? Log on to the Center for Creative Leadership's research site at www.ccl.org/research/projects.htm. The center works with individuals and groups around the world to help organizations of all kinds improve their managerial and leadership skills.

The University of North Texas Center for the Study of Work Teams deals with a wide range of topics relevant to small-group communication. You can access the center's website at www.workteams.unt.edu/.

issues. Let's say your group is considering the practicality of adding a vegetarian section to the dormitory food service. The discussion might go like this:

Miguel: It seems to me a waste of time, money, and space to make a special section for vegetarians. There are plenty of vegetables on the menu now. Anyone who doesn't want to eat the meat doesn't have to.

Liu: You're not getting the point. Vegetarian menus have to be *balanced* with enough vegetable protein. It's not enough to say, "Don't eat the meat." We need a special section where the menus are planned for a nutritious vegetarian diet.

Miguel: Oh, for pity's sake, you food freaks are all alike. You think you've got the true faith and all the rest of us are sinners just because we eat a hamburger now and then.

Liu: If you want to kill innocent animals to eat, that's none of my business. Go ahead, ruin your health, load yourself up with cholesterol. I don't care. But don't stand in the way of people who really care about their bodies.

Leader: Just a minute. Before we go on with this part of the discussion, don't we have some figures on how many students would actually use the vegetarian section? Lisa, I think that was your department. What did you find out?

None of this is to say that members of a group should never disagree. In fact, a serious problem occurs when members get along so well and are so concerned about maintaining the harmony of the group that they will not disagree with one another about anything. Whenever one member makes a suggestion, everybody else thinks it's a wonderful idea. When this happens, the group misses the benefit of having a group in the first place. There is no chance to reach the best decision by exploring an array of perspectives, opinions, and information. A group that is concerned above all with dodging disagreement will not be any more effective than one that dissolves into personal quarreling.

The point, then, is not that groups should avoid conflict but that they should keep it at the task level and not allow it to degenerate into personal

Related Reading

If you have international students in your class, they may have quite different expectations about the conduct of small-group discussion than do students from the United States. For two valuable readings on this subject, see Richard E. Porter and Larry A. Samovar, "Communication in the Multicultural Group," and Myron W. Lustig and Laura L. Cassotta, "Comparing Group Communication Across Cultures: Leadership, Conformity, and Discussion Processes," both in Robert S. Cathcart, Larry A. Samovar, and Linda D. Henman (eds.), *Small Group Communication: Theory and Practice,* 7th ed. (Madison, WI: Brown and Benchmark, 1996), pp. 306–326.

feuding. There is usually little achievement—and even less feeling of satisfaction—when a group is consumed by personal bickering and antagonism.

Encourage Full Participation

If a group is to work effectively, all members must contribute fully and share their ideas with one another. Every member of a group should take responsibility for encouraging other members to participate. You can do this, first of all, by listening attentively. Listening provides support for the speaker. After all, how would you like to speak in a group where everybody else appears bored or distracted?

If there are one or two quiet members in the group, you can draw them into the discussion by asking their opinions and showing your interest in their ideas and information. For instance, you can say something like, "We haven't heard from Jason in a while, and he has some personal experience in this matter. Jason, can you tell the others what you told me about this plan?"

Another way to encourage participation is to help build a supportive environment. When a member speaks, you can say, "That's an interesting idea." Or "I never knew that; can you tell us more about it?" Conversely, try to avoid negative comments that will squelch a speaker before she or he has finished—comments like "Oh, no, that never works" or "What a dumb idea." Supportive comments create goodwill among group members and make everyone feel free to discuss their ideas without ridicule or embarrassment.

If you are shy or afraid your ideas will be taken too critically, you may be unwilling to participate at first. To overcome your diffidence, try to remember that your contribution is necessary to the group. This is why you are there. At the very least, you can help provide a supportive environment for discussion by listening, reacting, and encouraging the free exchange of ideas.

Keep the Discussion on Track

In some groups the discussion proceeds like a stream-of-consciousness exercise. Here is a hypothetical example in which a town planning board is considering installing a new traffic light at a busy intersection:

Sharif: You know, we're going to have trouble getting cars to come to a full stop even if we do put in a traffic light.

Diana: Tell me about it! I came through there yesterday and hit my brakes, and the car just kept going. Maybe I need the brakes adjusted, though.

Mike: Get ready to pay through the nose. I had a brake job on my car last week, and it was nearly twice as much as last time.

Rico: That's nothing. Have you looked at lawnmowers lately? And if you think lawnmowers are high . . .

Jill: Who mows lawns? I had my yard planted with ground cover and put gravel over the rest. It's . . .

Leader: Excuse me, folks, but weren't we talking about the *traffic light?*

In effective small groups, all members participate fully and interact with each other. They also feel that their contributions are respected and valued by the full group.

Every member has a responsibility to keep the discussion on track and to intervene if the group wanders too far afield. There is nothing wrong with a little casual conversation to break the tension or provide a brief respite from work, but it shouldn't be allowed to get out of hand. When working in a problem-solving group, make sure the group's ultimate goal is always in the forefront. Do your best to see that discussion proceeds in an orderly fashion from one point to the next and that the group does not get bogged down in side issues.

On the other hand, you need to guard against the tendency to progress to a solution too quickly, without thoroughly exploring the problem. This concern can be especially serious when members of a group are tired or discouraged. If you feel your group is taking the easy way out and jumping at an easy solution, try to make the other members aware of your concern. By suggesting that they talk about the problem in more detail, you may bring out vital information or ideas. One classroom group learned the perils of making a snap decision:

The group's first job was to decide what they should do for a class project. Near the beginning of their first meeting, someone suggested that they observe an established small group—the city council of their community—to see how the group worked. Everyone thought it was a splendid idea, and the class group wrapped up their session, congratulating themselves on having disposed of the problem so quickly.

But what looked at first like a great idea proved to have some crucial drawbacks. First, it turned out that the city council would not meet again until after the group's class project was due. Second, the city council had 20 people on it—not really an appropriate number to study as a small group. The quick solution turned out to be no solution at all.

Group Assignment
Integrating a unit on group discussion into a public speaking class can pose a special challenge. One approach is to have each group report on a major public speaker or speech campaign. Such an assignment is explained by Joe Ayres and Debbie Ayres Sonandré, "Speech Criticism and Group Presentations," in *Selections from the Speech Communication Teacher, 1996–1999*, p. 102, which accompanies *The Art of Public Speaking.*

Fortunately, there are systematic ways to keep the discussion on track and to avoid hasty group decisions. Research shows that if your group follows a tested method of decision making, it will have a much better chance of reaching a satisfactory decision.[9] We turn, therefore, to the most common decision-making technique for small groups—the reflective-thinking method.

The Reflective-Thinking Method

reflective-thinking method
A five-step method for directing discussion in a problem-solving small group.

The reflective-thinking method is derived from the writings of the American philosopher John Dewey. It offers a logical, step-by-step process for discussion in problem-solving groups. The method consists of five steps: (1) defining the problem; (2) analyzing the problem; (3) establishing criteria for solving the problem; (4) generating potential solutions; (5) selecting the best solution. By following these steps, your group will make its work much easier.

Let's take a closer look at the reflective-thinking method. As we do, we'll illustrate each step by following a single group through the entire process.

Define the Problem

Before a problem-solving group can make progress, it must know exactly what problem it is trying to solve. Defining the problem may seem easy, but it is not always so. In a sense, defining the problem for group discussion is akin to settling on a specific purpose for a speech. Unless it is done properly, everything that follows will suffer.

question of policy
A question about whether a specific course of action should or should not be taken.

The best way to define the problem is to phrase it as a question of policy. We discussed questions of policy in Chapter 15 (see pages 405–410). Here it is enough to note that questions of policy inquire about the necessity and/or practicality of specific courses of action. Questions of policy typically include the word "should." For example:

> What measures should our school take to deal with hazing by athletic teams and other groups on campus?
>
> What steps should the federal government take to protect civil liberties without harming the war on terrorism?
>
> What policy should the United States adopt with respect to the exploitation of child labor in other countries around the world?

Overhead Transparency
For ease of classroom discussion, guidelines for phrasing the question for discussion in a problem-solving small group are available in the binder of full-color overhead transparencies that accompanies *The Art of Public Speaking*.

When phrasing the question for discussion, your group should follow several guidelines. First, make sure the question is as clear and specific as possible. For example:

Ineffective: What should be done about fraudulent charities?

More Effective: What should the federal government do to control the activities of fraudulent charities?

Second, phrase the question to allow for a wide variety of answers. Be especially wary of questions that can be answered with a simple yes or no. For example:

Ineffective: Should the city build a new elementary school?

More Effective: What steps should the city take to deal with increasing enrollment in the elementary schools?

Third, avoid biased or slanted questions. For example:

Ineffective: How can we keep the campus bookstore from ripping off students?

More Effective: What changes, if any, should be made in the pricing policies of the campus bookstore?

Fourth, make sure you pose a single question. For example:

Ineffective: What revisions should the college consider in its admissions requirements and in its graduation requirements?

More Effective: What revisions should the college consider in its admissions requirements?

More Effective: What revisions should the college consider in its graduation requirements?

To clarify this first step of the reflective-thinking method, let's see how our model problem-solving group defined the problem:

> As a class project, the group set out to discuss the problem of sharply rising costs for attending college. Following the reflective-thinking method, they began by defining the problem. After several false starts they phrased the problem this way: "What steps should our school take to reduce student costs for attending college?"

Analyze the Problem

After the problem has been defined, the group begins to analyze it. Too often, groups (like individuals) start mapping out solutions before they have a firm grasp of what is wrong. This is like a doctor prescribing treatment before fully diagnosing the patient's ailment. If your group investigates the problem as thoroughly as possible, you will be in a much better position to devise a workable solution.

In analyzing the problem, pay particular attention to two questions. First, how severe is the problem? Investigate the scope of the problem. Determine how many people it affects. Assess what might happen if the problem is not resolved. Second, what are the causes of the problem? Check into the history of the problem. Learn what factors contributed to it. Ascertain its major causes.

As you might imagine, analyzing the problem requires research. Effective group decisions depend on having the best information available. You

Class Activity

The first Exercise for Critical Thinking at the end of this chapter gives students work in phrasing questions for discussion in a problem-solving small group. For full discussion of this activity, see the *Instructor's Manual,* pp. 368–369.

Discussion Prompt

Have students identify a relatively important decision they have made in the last year or two. Ask them to reconstruct how they reached that decision. Then ask them to imagine remaking the decision following the reflective-thinking method. Have students map out what they would do at each stage of the method. Do they still reach the same decision?

can get this information in the same way you gather materials for a speech. Sometimes you can rely on your own knowledge and experience. More often, you need to get information from other sources—by looking on the Internet, by interviewing someone with expertise on the topic, or by working in the library (see Chapter 6). When meeting with your group, make sure you have done the research assigned to you so you can offer complete and unbiased information.

Let's return now to our sample group and see how it analyzed the problem of rapidly escalating student costs for attending college:

> The group talked first about the severity of the problem. Tuition had risen dramatically, as had outlays for books and incidentals. One member offered statistics to show that the cost of attending college had doubled in the past 10 years. Other members noted that the problem was affecting not only students. Merchants within the college community were being hurt because students had less money to spend on such items as clothes and entertainment.
>
> To determine the causes of the problem, the group researched articles in the library about the rise in student costs for attending college across the nation. They also interviewed an economics professor and the head of the student aid program on campus. After studying the matter thoroughly, the group identified several major causes, including administrative costs, faculty salaries, the price of textbooks, and increased living expenses.

Establish Criteria for Solutions

If you planned to buy a car, how would you proceed? You would probably not just walk into a dealer's showroom and buy whatever appealed to you on the spur of the moment. You would most likely decide ahead of time what kind of car you wanted, what options it should have, and how much money you could afford to spend. That is, you would establish *criteria* to guide you in deciding exactly which car to buy.

You should do much the same thing in group discussion. Once your group has analyzed the problem, you should not jump immediately to proposing solutions. Instead, you should take time to establish criteria—standards—for responsible solutions. You should work out (and write down) exactly what your solutions must achieve and any factors that might limit your choice of solutions. If, for example, a committee is authorized to spend a maximum of $1,000 on a club's annual banquet, one of the criteria for the committee's decision will be that the banquet cost no more than $1,000.

A common failing of problem-solving groups is that they start to discuss solutions before agreeing on criteria for the solutions. When this happens, a group runs into trouble. Some people will propose solutions based on one set of criteria, while others will propose solutions based on different criteria. You can avoid such conflicts by making sure the group sets up criteria before proposing solutions.

To give a better idea of how this stage of the reflective-thinking method works, let's look at the cost-cutting group we have been following:

> After some discussion, the group established these criteria for possible solutions: (1) The solution should significantly reduce students' costs. (2) The solution should come into force at the start of the next school year. (3) The solution should not hurt

Group Project

If you assign students a major group project that requires work outside of class, have them prepare a three- to five-page written report on the deliberations of their group. For a full description of this assignment, see the *Instructor's Manual,* pp. 380–381.

criteria

Standards on which a judgment or decision can be based.

the prestige of the college. (4) The cost of the solution should be minimal and should be paid by the administration. (5) The human resources needed to implement the solution should come from administrative personnel already working on the school's staff. (6) The solution should involve only actions controlled by the college—not matters controlled by outside individuals or agencies.

Generate Potential Solutions

Once your group has the criteria firmly in mind, you are ready to discuss solutions. Your goal at this stage is to come up with the widest possible range of potential solutions—not to judge the solutions. That comes later. At this stage you are only suggesting possibilities. One member of the group should be responsible for writing down all the solutions proposed at this time.

Many groups find the technique of *brainstorming* helpful in this stage. Brainstorming allows a group to generate a variety of solutions without prematurely evaluating them. In Chapter 4 we discussed how brainstorming can work for an individual in choosing a speech topic. Here brainstorming is expanded to the whole group.

brainstorming
A method of generating ideas by free association of words and thoughts.

The best approach is to begin by having each member of the group list all the possible solutions he or she can think of. One member of the group should then consolidate the individual lists into a single master list. The group should discuss the master list to make sure potential solutions have not been overlooked. At this stage, members often "piggyback" new ideas onto ideas on the master list. For example, if one suggestion is "Establish food co-ops," a group member might say, "Yes, and we could establish clothing co-ops, too." One member should be responsible for writing down these new ideas and adding them to the master list. The brainstorming process continues until the group cannot think of any more solutions.

Brainstorming in this fashion has two advantages. First, it encourages creativity. There is a great deal of research to show that beginning with written lists produces more and higher-quality ideas than when a group tries to generate potential solutions by oral discussion.[10] Second, this method of brainstorming encourages equal participation. Having each member create his or her own list of potential solutions makes it less likely that one or two members will dominate the process or that anyone will hold back ideas for fear of being hooted down.

The Reflective Thinking Checklist can help your group keep its discussion on track

CD 1: SPEECH CHECKLIST

Let's see how our cost-cutting group handled this stage:

By brainstorming, the group came up with the following possible solutions: (1) reduce the number of required books for each course; (2) cut some of the "fat" from the administrative staff; (3) make all professors teach more courses; (4) approach landlords about stabilizing rent and utility costs; (5) establish food and clothing co-ops; (6) increase financial aid; (7) decrease the amount of money available for faculty research; (8) boycott businesses around the campus where price markups are highest; (9) increase out-of-state tuition; (10) decrease dormitory expenses; (11) organize fundraising programs with the student government, (12) redirect some money from construction of new buildings to student aid. This was a good yield from a brainstorming session—twelve solid suggestions.

Working in a small group requires many of the skills involved in public speaking. Formal presentations may occur during a group's deliberations or when the group presents its report.

Select the Best Solution

After all potential solutions have been listed, it is time to evaluate them and choose the best solution or solutions. The best way to proceed is to take a particular solution, discuss it with regard to the criteria established earlier in the group's deliberations, then move on to the next solution, and so on. This orderly process ensures that all potential solutions receive equal consideration.

As each potential solution is discussed, the group should make every effort to reach *consensus.* A consensus decision is one that all members accept, even though the decision may not be ideal in the eyes of every member. In other words, consensus may range from full approval of a decision to "Well, I can live with it." Because it usually results in superior decisions as well as in a high degree of unity within the group, consensus is the ideal of group decision making. It comes about when members have been so cooperative that they reach a common decision through reasoning, honest exchange of ideas, and full examination of the issues.[11]

Like most ideals, consensus can be difficult to achieve. If there are different viewpoints, members of the group will often try to find the easiest way to resolve the differences. Sometimes a member will call for a vote, which is very agreeable to those holding a majority opinion (since they will win) but not so pleasant for those in the minority. Resorting to a vote does resolve the immediate conflict, but it may not result in the best solution. Moreover, it weakens unity in the group by fostering factions and perhaps by creating bitterness among the members who lose on the vote. A group should vote only when it has failed in every other attempt to find a solution agreeable to all members.

consensus

A group decision that is acceptable to all members of the group.

What kind of final decision did our model cost-cutting group reach? Let's see:

The cost-cutting group had twelve possible solutions to evaluate. Three were rejected because they violated the group's criterion that an acceptable solution must involve only actions controlled directly by the college. Redirecting building money to student aid could be done only by the state legislature. Approaching landlords about stabilizing rent and boycotting campus businesses were also outside the jurisdiction of college administrators.

Three more solutions were rejected because they were economically impractical. Increasing financial aid would hurt many students because the funds would have to come from student fees. Raising out-of-state tuition would drive away 10 percent of the college's out-of-state students. And decreasing dorm costs would make it impossible to provide minimally acceptable services.

The proposal to reduce funds for faculty research was also rejected since most research money comes from government, corporations, and foundations. Besides, research was recognized as a primary means of maintaining the college's prestige. Finally, the suggestion to reduce administrative "fat" was rejected as too costly because a group would have to be established to audit all administrative duties.

After refining the suggestions, the group finally reached consensus on a solution that included the following provisions: (1) A student should not have to spend more than $100 on required books for any single course. (2) The university should authorize the student government to organize food, book, and clothing co-ops. (3) The student government should conduct five fund-raising projects each academic year. (4) Each professor should teach one more class a year.

Once consensus has been reached on a solution or solutions to the problem, the group is ready to present its findings.

Group Project
Divide the class into groups of four to six persons. Each group will be responsible for a problem-solving project in which it investigates a question of policy and recommends solutions to it. Each group will also be responsible for organizing and conducting a symposium in which the group presents its report to the class. For full explanation of this assignment, see the *Instructor's Manual*, p. 38. For other approaches, check the entries under "Group Discussion" in the five volumes of *Selections from the Speech Communication Teacher* that accompany *The Art of Public Speaking*.

Presenting the Recommendations of the Group

The work of a problem-solving group does not end with the last stage of the reflective-thinking process. Once a group has agreed on its recommendations, it usually needs to present them to somebody. A business group might report to the president of the company or to the board of directors. A special committee of the city council reports to the full council. A presidential commission reports to the President and to the nation at large. A classroom group reports to the instructor and to the rest of the class. The purpose of such reports is to present the group's recommendations clearly and convincingly.

Sometimes a group will prepare a formal written report. Often, however, the written report is supplemented with—or replaced by—an oral report, a symposium, or a panel discussion.

Oral Report

An oral report is much the same in content as a written report. If the group has a designated leader, she or he will probably deliver the report. Otherwise, the group will have to select one person for the job.

oral report

A speech presenting the findings, conclusions, decisions, etc. of a small group.

If you are picked to present your group's report, you should approach it as you would any other speech. Your task is to explain the purpose, procedures, and recommendations of your group. As with any speech, your report should have three main sections. The introduction will state the purpose of the report and preview its main points. The body will spell out the problem addressed by your group, the criteria set for a solution, and the solution being recommended. The conclusion will summarize the main points and, in some cases, urge that the group's recommendations be adopted.

As with any other speech, you should adapt your report to the audience. Use supporting materials to clarify and strengthen your ideas, and consider whether using visual aids will enhance your message. Make sure your language is accurate, clear, vivid, and appropriate. Rehearse the report so you can deliver it fluently and decisively. Afterward, you—and possibly other members of the group—may be called on to answer questions from the audience. (Review the section on answering questions in Chapter 12, pages 311–316.)

Symposium

symposium

A public presentation in which several people present prepared speeches on different aspects of the same topic.

A symposium consists of a moderator and several speakers seated together in front of an audience. If the group presenting the symposium has a designated leader, he or she will typically be the moderator. The moderator's job is to introduce the topic and the speakers. Each speaker in turn delivers a prepared speech on a different aspect of the topic. After the speeches, there may be a question-and-answer session with the audience.

The symposium is often used for group reports in speech classes. One way to organize it is to have each member of the group present a brief talk sketching the group's work and decisions during one stage of the reflective-thinking process. Another way is to have each speaker deal with a major issue relating to the discussion topic. A group dealing with capital punishment, for example, might have one speaker present the group's conclusion on the issue of whether capital punishment is an effective deterrent to crime, another speaker present the group's position on the morality of capital punishment, and so forth.

No matter what kind of symposium your group presents, all the speeches should be carefully planned. They should also be coordinated with one another to make sure the symposium reports on all important aspects of the group's project.

Panel Discussion

panel discussion

A structured conversation on a given topic among several people in front of an audience.

A panel discussion is essentially a conversation in front of an audience. The panel should have a moderator, who introduces the topic and the panelists. Once the discussion is under way, the moderator may interject questions and comments as needed to focus the discussion. The panelists speak briefly, informally, and impromptu. They talk to each other, but loudly enough for the audience to be able to hear. As with a symposium, a panel discussion may be followed by a question-and-answer session with the audience.

Because of its spontaneity, a panel discussion can be exciting for participants and audience alike. But, unfortunately, that spontaneity inhibits systematic presentation of a group's recommendations. Thus the panel discussion is seldom used by problem-solving groups, although it can work well for information-gathering groups.

If you are a participant in a panel discussion, beware of the common fallacy that no serious preparation is required. Although you will speak impromptu, you need to study the topic ahead of time, analyze the major issues, and map out the points you want to be sure to make during the discussion. An effective panel discussion also requires planning by the moderator and panelists to decide what issues will be discussed and in what order. Finally, all panelists must be willing to share talking time. One purpose of a panel is to have all participants voice their ideas, not to have one or two members monopolize the discussion.

Whatever method your group uses to present its findings, you can benefit from the public speaking guidelines given throughout this book. The techniques of effective speech need refinement for different situations, but the principles remain the same whether you are one person addressing an audience, part of a small group of people working to solve a problem, or a participant in a symposium or a panel discussion.

Speech Assignment
For an intriguing option for group presentations, see Ann Neville Miller and Linda Bartlett Hobgood, "Invite an Administrator: Using University Administrators as an Audience for Student Presentations," in *Selections from the Communication Teacher, 1999–2002*, pp. 54–55, which accompanies *The Art of Public Speaking*.

Summary

A small group consists of three to twelve people assembled for a specific purpose. A problem-solving small group, as its name implies, is formed to solve a particular problem. When such a group has effective leadership, it usually makes better decisions than do individuals by themselves. Most groups have a designated leader, an implied leader, or an emergent leader. Some groups have no specific leader, in which case all members of the group must assume leadership responsibilities. An effective leader helps a group reach its goals by fulfilling procedural needs, task needs, and maintenance needs. As you develop your skills in group communication, you should be prepared to assume a leadership role whenever necessary.

Apart from leadership, all members of a group have five basic responsibilities. You should commit yourself to the goals of your group, fulfill your individual assignments, avoid interpersonal conflict within the group, encourage full participation by all members, and help keep the group on track. Meeting these responsibilities is vital if your group is to be successful.

Your group will also be more successful if it follows the reflective-thinking method, which offers a logical, step-by-step process for decision making in problem-solving groups. The method consists of five steps: (1) defining the problem as clearly and specifically as possible; (2) analyzing the problem to determine its severity and causes; (3) establishing criteria to guide the group in evaluating solutions; (4) generating a wide range of potential solutions; (5) selecting the best solution or solutions.

Once your group has agreed on its recommendations, it usually has to present them to somebody. Sometimes this presentation will be in the form of a written report. Often, however, it will be an oral presentation—a report by one member of the group, a symposium, or a panel discussion. Whichever kind of oral presentation your group gives will call for the skills of effective speechmaking explained throughout this book.

Key Terms

Review these terms by doing the Chapter 18 crossword puzzle at www.mhhe.com/lucas8.

dyad (480)
small group (481)
problem-solving small group (481)
leadership (481)
implied leader (481)
emergent leader (482)
designated leader (482)
procedural needs (482)
task needs (483)
maintenance needs (484)

hidden agenda (485)
reflective-thinking method (490)
question of policy (490)
criteria (492)
brainstorming (493)
consensus (494)
oral report (496)
symposium (496)
panel discussion (496)

Review Questions

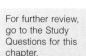

For further review, go to the Study Questions for this chapter.

CD 1: STUDY QUESTIONS

After reading this chapter, you should be able to answer the following questions:

1. What is a small group? What is a problem-solving small group?

2. What are the four kinds of leadership that may occur in a small group? Explain the three kinds of needs fulfilled by leadership in a small group.

3. What are the five major responsibilities of every participant in a small group?

4. What are the stages of the reflective-thinking method? Explain the major tasks of a group at each stage.

5. What are the three methods for presenting orally the recommendations of a problem-solving group?

Exercises for Critical Thinking

1. Identify the flaw (or flaws) in each of the following questions for a problem-solving group discussion. Rewrite each question so it conforms with the criteria discussed in the chapter for effective discussion questions.

   a. Should all students be required to take two years of a foreign language to graduate from college?

   b. What should be done to prevent the utterly ridiculous shortage of computers for students at this school?

c. What should be done about people running red lights?

d. What should our state government do to control taxes and to combat drunk driving?

e. Should the federal government institute a system of standardized national tests for all schoolchildren?

2. If possible, arrange to observe a problem-solving small group in action. You might attend a meeting of your city council, the school board, the zoning commission, a local business, a church committee. To what extent does the discussion measure up to the criteria of effective discussion presented in this chapter? What kind of leadership does the group have, and how well does the leader (or leaders) fulfill the group's procedural needs, task needs, and maintenance needs? How do the other members meet their responsibilities? What aspects of the meeting are handled most effectively? Which are handled least effectively?

3. Identify a relatively important decision you have made in the last year or two. Try to reconstruct how you reached that decision. Now suppose you could remake the decision following the reflective-thinking method. Map out exactly what you would do at each stage of the method. Do you still reach the same decision? If not, do you believe the reflective-thinking method would have led you to a better decision in the first place?

4. Attend a symposium or panel discussion on campus. Prepare a brief analysis of the proceedings. First, study the role of the moderator. How does she or he introduce the topic and participants? What role does the moderator play thereafter? Does she or he help guide and focus the panel discussion? Does she or he summarize and conclude the proceedings at the end?

Second, observe the participants. Are the speeches in the symposium well prepared and presented? Which speaker (or speakers) do you find most effective? Least effective? Why? Do participants in the panel discussion share talking time? Does their discussion appear well planned to cover major aspects of the topic? Which panelist (or panelists) do you find most effective? Least effective? Why?

Cross-Reference

For discussion of the Exercises for Critical Thinking, see the *Instructor's Manual*, pp. 368–370. For additional exercises, check the *Instructor's Manual*, pp. 370–382, as well as the five volumes of *Selections from the Speech Communication Teacher* that accompany *The Art of Public Speaking*.

Notes

[1]Charles Pavitt and Ellen Curtis, *Small Group Discussion: A Theoretical Approach,* 2nd ed. (Scottsdale, AZ: Gorsuch Scarisbrick, 1994), pp. 25–62.

[2]For a summary of research on the question of group size, see Richard L. Moreland, John M. Levine, and Melissa L. Wingert, "Creating the Ideal Group: Composition Effects at Work," in Erich H. Witte and James H. Davis (eds.), *Understanding Group Behavior: Small Group Processes and Interpersonal Relations* (Mahwah, NJ: Lawrence Erlbaum, 1996), II, pp. 12–15.

[3]The importance of communication to effective group discussion is stressed by Charles Pavitt, "Does Communication Matter in Social Influence During Small Group Discussion? Five Positions," *Communication Studies,* 44 (1993), pp. 216–227. For a review of scholarship in this area, see Marshall Scott Poole, "Group Communication Theory," in Lawrence R. Frey, Dennis S. Gouran, and Marshall Scott Poole (eds.), *Handbook of Group Communication Theory and Research* (Thousand Oaks, CA: Sage, 1999), pp. 37–70.

[4]See David Barry, "The Bossless Team," in Robert S. Cathcart, Larry A. Samovar, and Linda D. Henman (eds.), *Small Group Communication: Theory and Practice,* 7th ed. (Madison, WI: Brown and Benchmark, 1996), pp. 411–424.

[5]For an excellent discussion of the responsibilities of designated group leaders, see John K. Brilhart, Gloria J. Galanes, and Katherine Adams, *Effective Group Discussion,* 10th ed. (New York: McGraw-Hill, 2001), pp. 215–245.

[6]J. Kevin Barge, "Leadership as Communication," in Lawrence R. Frey and J. Kevin Barge (eds.), *Managing Group Life: Communicating in Decision-Making Groups* (Boston: Houghton Mifflin, 1997), pp. 202–233.

[7]For research on this aspect of group interaction, consult Joann Keyton, "Relational Communication in Groups," in Frey, Gouran, and Poole, *Handbook of Group Communication Theory and Research,* pp. 192–222.

[8]See Larry L. Barker, Kathy J. Wahlers, and Kittie W. Watson, *Groups in Process: An Introduction to Small Group Communication,* 6th ed. (Boston: Allyn and Bacon, 2001), pp. 83–114.

[9]Charles Pavitt and Kelly K. Johnson, "Scheidel and Crowell Revisited: A Descriptive Study of Group Proposal Sequencing," *Communication Monographs,* 69 (2002), pp. 19–32.

[10]See Carl M. Moore, *Group Techniques for Idea Building,* 2nd ed. (Thousand Oaks, CA: Sage, 1994).

[11]Joann Keyton, *Communicating in Groups: Building Relationships for Effective Decision Making,* 2nd ed. (New York: McGraw-Hill, 2003), pp. 173–175.

APPENDIX

Speeches for Analysis and Discussion

Questions of Culture
Sajjid Zahir Chinoy

Choices and Change
Barbara Bush

I Have a Dream
Martin Luther King, Jr.

Dying to Be Thin
Jennifer Breuer

A Whisper of AIDS
Mary Fisher

The Ultimate Gift
Jennifer Conard

Multicultural, Multilingual
Renee Varghese

Questions of Culture
Sajjid Zahir Chinoy

Seldom does a student commencement address upstage the featured speaker—especially when that speaker is a Pulitzer prize winner from Harvard University. Yet that is exactly what happened when Sajjid Zahir Chinoy spoke to his fellow graduates at the University of Richmond on May 12, 1996.

Born and raised near Bombay, India, Chinoy was selected to speak as the result of a campuswide competition. After describing the jumble of emotions that filled his mind as he came to the United States to attend school, he spoke movingly of the warm reception he received in Richmond and of how cultural differences can be overcome by attempting to understand other people.

Addressing his audience of 3,000 people extemporaneously and without notes, Chinoy received thunderous applause, and his remarks were widely reported in the press. His speech was so inspiring that the main speaker, Harvard psychiatrist Robert Coles, began his address by paying tribute to Chinoy. "I've been to a number of commencements," said Coles, "but I've never heard a speech quite like that."

The text of this speech has been transcribed from a video recording and is reprinted with permission from Sajjid Zahir Chinoy and the University of Richmond. It is also available on the CD-ROM and video supplements to *The Art of Public Speaking*.

1 Distinguished guests, faculty, staff, students, ladies and gentlemen, and, most of all, the Class of 1996:

2 I can visualize the scene again and again: 11:30 P.M., Saturday night, the fifteenth of August, 1992, Bombay International Airport, India. I was leaving home for the University of Richmond. And as I said that final good-bye to my parents, my family, and my friends; and as I saw hope, expectation, even a tinge of sadness, in their eyes; and as I stepped aboard the Boeing 747 in front, I knew my life had changed forever.

3 The next 36 hours on board the aircraft were a time of questions, of concerns, of tremendous uncertainty.

4 Had I made the right choice in leaving home? Had I made the right choice in leaving my parents, my family, my home? Had I made the right choice in leaving my country, my culture, my background? Had I made the right choice in choosing the University of Richmond?

5 And then, of course, there was that one nagging question, that one overriding concern: As one of only three Indian students on a Richmond campus of 3,000, would I ever fit in?

6 My country was different. My culture was different. My experiences were different. My background was different. My language was different. My accent was different. Would I ever fit in?

7 And so here I was, high above the clouds, grappling with questions of culture, of interaction, of ethnicity. What I didn't know was that 30,000 feet below, on the ground, the world was faced with these very same questions—the question of culture, the question of interaction, the question of ethnicity.

8 And so whether my aircraft took off from Bombay, where the Hindus and the Muslims lived together in a most fragile peace; or whether my aircraft was over Africa, where the Hutus and Tutsis of Rwanda and Burundi

had long-standing animosity; or whether my aircraft was over Bosnia, where the Serbs, the Croats, the Muslims, and the Bosnians had broken yet another truce, the question was the same—could different cultures ever come together to reinforce one another?

9 Ladies and gentlemen, after that bumpy aircraft ride, this young Indian student had found his answer. He had been witness to the four most spectacular years of his life at the University of Richmond. The academics were great; the extracurriculars were great; his graduate plans were great.

10 But what left an indelible impact on his mind was none of this. No, instead it was those special moments, those moments of human interaction, those human relationships that can never quite be translated into words:

11 The time this young Indian student spent his first Thanksgiving dinner with his debate team coach. That Thanksgiving evening when I ate my first American turkey and saw my first American football game, not knowing the difference between a tackle and a touchdown. And yet, all of a sudden, just like that, this very different Indian student had become an inherent part of the great American tradition of giving thanks.

12 The time I spent my first Christmas Eve with my journalism professor. That Christmas evening when the relationship wasn't of a faculty member and a student anymore, but of two buddies who fought fiercely over every point in Ping-Pong.

13 The time I had a long and honest talk with an American friend on the eve of a calculus exam. I didn't learn much calculus that night, but what I did learn was that as different as we are—different countries, different cultures, different continents—inherently we are still the same.

14 The time in December 1992 when India was hit by communal riots, when violence and bloodshed were but a few hundred yards from my family and my home, and when my fantastic roommate from my freshman year sat up the entire night, giving me hope, strength, and courage at every step.

15 Yes, four years after that bumpy aircraft ride, I have found the answer to the question of culture.

16 I have found that it has taken just a little understanding, just a little sensitivity, just a little open-mindedness, just a little empathy on the part of this community—this University of Richmond community—to change my life like never before.

17 I have found that it makes no difference what culture you follow, what your background is, what your experiences are, what language you speak, what accent you have. The commonality of the human bond far transcends these superficial differences.

18 And yet look around at the world today. Look around at the very regions that were faced with the same question of culture that I was faced with four years ago.

19 Look at Bosnia, where, between 1992 and 1996, 300,000 people had been slaughtered—Bosnians, Serbs, Croats, Muslims—all because they came from a slightly different heritage or culture or history.

20 Look at Bombay, India. In one maddening week in 1992, 2,000 Indians—Hindus and Muslims—lost their lives fighting with one another. They fought over a mosque; they fought over a structure made of brick and mortar. Two thousand human beings lost their lives.

21 Look at Africa, where, between 1992 and 1996, 1 million Hutus and Tutsis lost their lives. Just comprehend that for a moment. Between the time you were a freshman and a senior, 1 million lost their lives fighting over culture, over history, over background.

22 Yes, just look at the madness. The world has fought hard to highlight its differences. We have forgotten our inherent similarities. All because what was missing was a little understanding. Just a little sensitivity. Just a little open-mindedness. Just a little empathy.

23 Two similar questions of culture in 1992. Two diametrically opposite results in 1996.

24 And so, to the Class of 1996, I say go and distinguish yourselves like never before. Go get the best of jobs, the most rewarding of careers. Go to the best of graduate programs. And make a real difference in your communities.

25 But not for one moment, not for one moment, ever forget the memory of these four years—the memory that just a little understanding, just a little sensitivity, just a little open-mindedness, just a little empathy on your part can mean the difference between complete despair for one young boy in Bosnia and remarkable hope for another young boy at Richmond.

26 Thank you.

Choices and Change
Barbara Bush

Barbara Bush's commencement address at Wellesley College on June 1, 1990, is one of the best known speeches of recent years. Bush was invited to speak by the senior class when their first choice, Alice Walker, author of *The Color Purple,* could not attend. In protest, 150 Wellesley seniors—about one-fourth of the graduating class—signed a petition charging that Bush was not a good role model for career-oriented students at a women's college and had been chosen because of the man she married rather than for her own achievements.

The petition touched off a storm of controversy. Throughout the month before Bush's speech, educators, newspaper columnists, and others debated the petition and the larger issue of women's role in American society. The media spotlight became so intense that Bush's speech was broadcast live by all the major television networks.

In her speech, Bush dealt with one of the most important issues facing modern women—how to balance their careers with their commitments to friends and family. She urged her audience to respect difference, to get involved in social issues, and to cherish human relationships as "the most important investments you will ever make." She capped off the speech by suggesting that someone in the audience might follow in her footsteps as the President's spouse. "I wish *him* well," she added, to thunderous cheering and applause.

Bush's blend of humility and humor won many accolades. NBC News anchor Tom Brokaw called her address "one of the best commencement speeches I've ever heard," while the *New York Times* judged it "a triumph." Many Wellesley students who had been skeptical about Bush's appearance also said they were pleasantly surprised by the speech. "She was wonderful and funny," one of them stated. "I think she could have addressed more women's issues. But she was sincere and she touched our hearts."

The text of this speech is taken from a videotape supplied by Wellesley College, and it includes several impromptu comments and other changes from the version published in the press. The speech is also included in the video supplement to *The Art of Public Speaking.*

1 Thank you very, very much President Keohane, Mrs. Gorbachev, trustees, faculty, parents, and, I should say, Julia Porter, class president, and certainly my new best friend, Christine Bicknell—and of course the Class of 1990. I am really thrilled to be here today and very excited, as I know all of you must be, that Mrs. Gorbachev could join us. These are exciting times— they're exciting in Washington, and I had really looked forward to coming to Wellesley. I thought it was going to be fun; I never dreamt it would be this much fun. So thank you for that.

2 More than 10 years ago when I was invited here to talk about our ex- periences in the People's Republic of China, I was struck by both the natu- ral beauty of your campus and the spirit of this place.

3 Wellesley, you see, is not just a place, but an idea, an experiment in excellence in which diversity is not just tolerated, but is embraced.

4 The essence of this spirit was captured in a moving speech about tolerance given last year by a student body president of one of your sister colleges. She related the story by Robert Fulghum about a young pastor who, finding himself in charge of some very energetic children, hits upon the game called "Giants, Wizards and Dwarfs." "You have to decide now," the pastor instructed the children, "which you are—a giant, a wizard or a dwarf." At that, a small girl tugging at his pants leg asks, "But where do the mermaids stand?"

5 And the pastor tells her there are *no* mermaids. And she says, "Oh yes there are—I am a mermaid."

6 This little girl knew what she was and she was not about to give up on either her identity or the game. She intended to take her place wherever mermaids fit into the scheme of things. Where *do* the mermaids stand—all those who are different, those who do not fit the boxes and the pigeonholes? "Answer that question," wrote Fulghum, "and you can build a school, a nation, or a whole world."

7 As that very wise young woman said, "Diversity, like anything worth having, requires effort." Effort to learn about and respect difference, to be compassionate with one another, to cherish our own identity, and to accept unconditionally the same in others. You should all be very proud that this is the Wellesley spirit.

8 Now I know your first choice today was Alice Walker—guess how I know!—known for *The Color Purple.* Instead you got me—known for the color of my hair! Alice Walker's book has a special resonance here. At Wellesley, each class is known by a special color. For four years the class of '90 has worn the color purple. Today you meet on Severance Green to say goodbye to all of that, to begin a new and a very personal journey to search for your own true colors.

9 In the world that awaits you beyond the shores of Lake Waban, no one can say what your true colors will be. But this I do know: You have a first-class education from a first-class school. And so you need not, probably

cannot, live a "paint-by-numbers" life. Decisions are not irrevocable. Choices do come back. And as you set off from Wellesley, I hope that many of you will consider making three very special choices.

10 The first is to believe in something larger than yourself, to get involved in some of the big ideas of our time. I chose literacy because I honestly believe that if more people could read, write and comprehend, we would be that much closer to solving so many of the problems that plague our nation and our society.

11 Early on I made another choice which I hope you'll make as well. Whether you're talking about education, career, or service, you're talking about life, and life really must have joy. It's supposed to be fun!

12 One of the reasons I made the most important decision of my life, to marry George Bush, is because he made me laugh. It's true, sometimes we've laughed through our tears, but that shared laughter has been one of our strongest bonds. Find the joy in life, because as Ferris Bueller said on his day off: "Life moves pretty fast. You don't stop and look around once in a while, you're gonna miss it!" (I'm not going to tell George you clapped more for Ferris than you clapped for George!)

13 The third choice that must not be missed is to cherish your human connections: your relationships with family and friends. For several years, you've had impressed upon you the importance to your career of dedication and hard work—and of course that's true. But as important as your obligations as a doctor, a lawyer, a business leader will be, you are a human being first, and those human connections—with spouses, with children, with friends—are the most important investments you will ever make.

14 At the end of your life, you will never regret not having passed one more test, not winning one more verdict, or not closing one more deal. You will regret time not spent with a husband, a child, a friend, or a parent.

15 We are in a transitional period right now, fascinating and exhilarating times, learning to adjust to changes and the choices we, men and women, are facing. As an example, I remember what a friend said, on hearing her husband complain to his buddies that he had to babysit. Quickly setting him straight, my friend told her husband that when it's your own kids, it's not called babysitting!

16 Now, maybe we should adjust faster; maybe we should adjust slower. But whatever the era, whatever the times, one thing will never change: fathers and mothers, if you have children, they must come first. You must read to your children, and you must hug your children, and you must love your children. Your success as a family, our success as a society, depends not on what happens in the White House, but on what happens inside your house.

17 For over 50 years, it was said that the winner of Wellesley's annual hoop race would be the first to get married. Now they say the winner will be the first to become a CEO. Both of those stereotypes show too little tolerance for those who want to know where the mermaids stand. So I want to offer a new legend: the winner of the hoop race will be the first to realize her dream—not society's dream, her own personal dream. And who knows? Somewhere out in this audience may even be someone who will one day follow in my footsteps and preside over the White House as the president's spouse. And I wish him well!

18 Well, the controversy ends here. But our conversation is only beginning. And a worthwhile conversation it has been. So as you leave Wellesley today, take with you deep thanks for the courtesy and the honor you have shared with Mrs. Gorbachev and with me. Thank you. God bless you. And may your future be worthy of your dreams.

I Have a Dream
Martin Luther King, Jr.

Martin Luther King's "I Have a Dream" is widely regarded as a masterpiece. It was delivered August 28, 1963, to some 200,000 people who had come to Washington, D.C., to participate in a peaceful demonstration to further the cause of equal rights for African Americans. King spoke from the steps of the Lincoln Memorial, in the "symbolic shadow" of Abraham Lincoln, and the crowd filled the vast area between the Memorial and the Washington Monument. In addition, millions of Americans watched the speech on television or listened to it on the radio.

Like most ceremonial addresses, "I Have a Dream" is relatively short. Although it took King only 16 minutes to deliver the speech, he prepared it more carefully than any other speech in his career to that time. His purpose was to set forth as succinctly and as eloquently as possible the guiding principles of the civil rights movement, and to reinforce the commitment of his listeners to those principles.

One of the most interesting features of this speech is King's use of language to make the abstract principles of liberty and equality clear and compelling. Throughout, King relies on familiar, concrete words that create sharp, vivid images. He uses many more metaphors than do most speakers, but they are appropriate to the occasion and help to dramatize King's ideas. Finally, King makes extensive use of repetition and parallelism to reinforce his message and to enhance the momentum of the speech.

If you have heard a tape recording of "I Have a Dream," you know its impact was heightened by King's delivery. In his rich baritone voice, marked by the fervor of the crusader and modulated by the cadences of the Southern Baptist preacher, King gained the total involvement of his audience. As William Robert Miller says, "The crowd more than listened, it participated, and before King had reached his last phrase, a torrent of applause was already welling up."

The text of this speech was taken from a tape recording and is reprinted with permission of Joan Daves. Copyright 1963 by Martin Luther King, Jr. The speech is also available on the video supplement to *The Art of Public Speaking.*

1 I am happy to join with you today in what will go down in history as the greatest demonstration for freedom in the history of our nation.

2 Five score years ago, a great American, in whose symbolic shadow we stand today, signed the Emancipation Proclamation. This momentous decree came as a great beacon light of hope to millions of Negro slaves, who had been seared in the flames of withering injustice. It came as a joyous daybreak to end the long night of their captivity.

3 But one hundred years later, the Negro still is not free. One hundred years later, the life of the Negro is still sadly crippled by the manacles of segregation and the chains of discrimination. One hundred years later, the Negro lives on a lonely island of poverty in the midst of a vast ocean of

material prosperity. One hundred years later, the Negro is still languished in the corners of American society and finds himself an exile in his own land. And so we've come here today to dramatize a shameful condition.

4 In a sense we've come to our nation's Capitol to cash a check. When the architects of our republic wrote the magnificent words of the Constitution and the Declaration of Independence, they were signing a promissory note to which every American was to fall heir. This note was a promise that all men—yes, black men as well as white men—would be guaranteed the unalienable rights of life, liberty, and the pursuit of happiness.

5 It is obvious today that America has defaulted on this promissory note insofar as her citizens of color are concerned. Instead of honoring this sacred obligation, America has given the Negro people a bad check—a check which has come back marked "insufficient funds."

6 But we refuse to believe that the bank of justice is bankrupt. We refuse to believe that there are insufficient funds in the great vaults of opportunity of this nation. And so we've come to cash this check—a check that will give us upon demand the riches of freedom and the security of justice.

7 We have also come to this hallowed spot to remind America of the fierce urgency of now. This is no time to engage in the luxury of cooling off or to take the tranquilizing drug of gradualism. Now is the time to make real the promises of democracy. Now is the time to rise from the dark and desolate valley of segregation to the sunlit path of racial justice. Now is the time to lift our nation from the quicksands of racial injustice to the solid rock of brotherhood. Now is the time to make justice a reality for all of God's children.

8 It would be fatal for the nation to overlook the urgency of the moment. This sweltering summer of the Negro's legitimate discontent will not pass until there is an invigorating autumn of freedom and equality. Nineteen sixty-three is not an end, but a beginning. Those who hope that the Negro needed to blow off steam and will now be content will have a rude awakening if the nation returns to business as usual. There will be neither rest nor tranquility in America until the Negro is granted his citizenship rights. The whirlwinds of revolt will continue to shake the foundations of our nation until the bright day of justice emerges.

9 But there is something that I must say to my people, who stand on the warm threshold which leads into the palace of justice. In the process of gaining our rightful place, we must not be guilty of wrongful deeds. Let us not seek to satisfy our thirst for freedom by drinking from the cup of bitterness and hatred.

10 We must forever conduct our struggle on the high plane of dignity and discipline. We must not allow our creative protest to degenerate into physical violence. Again and again we must rise to the majestic heights of meeting physical force with soul force.

11 The marvelous new militancy which has engulfed the Negro community must not lead us to a distrust of all white people. For many of our white brothers, as evidenced by their presence here today, have come to realize that their destiny is tied up with our destiny. They have come to realize that their freedom is inextricably bound to our freedom. We cannot walk alone.

12 As we walk, we must make the pledge that we shall always march ahead. We cannot turn back. There are those who are asking the devotees of civil rights, "When will you be satisfied?" We can never be satisfied as long as the Negro is the victim of the unspeakable horrors of police brutality. We can never be satisfied as long as our bodies, heavy with the fatigue of travel, cannot gain lodging in the motels of the highways and the hotels of the cities. We cannot be satisfied as long as the Negro's basic mobility is from a smaller ghetto to a larger one. We can never be satisfied as long as our children are stripped of their selfhood and robbed of their dignity by signs stating "For Whites Only." We cannot be satisfied as long as a Negro in Mississippi cannot vote and a Negro in New York believes he has nothing for which to vote. No, no, we are not satisfied, and we will not be satisfied until justice rolls down like waters, and righteousness like a mighty stream.

13 I am not unmindful that some of you have come here out of great trials and tribulations. Some of you have come fresh from narrow jail cells. Some of you have come from areas where your quest for freedom left you battered by the storms of persecution and staggered by the winds of police brutality. You have been the veterans of creative suffering. Continue to work with the faith that unearned suffering is redemptive.

14 Go back to Mississippi, go back to Alabama, go back to South Carolina, go back to Georgia, go back to Louisiana, go back to the slums and ghettos of our Northern cities, knowing that somehow this situation can and will be changed. Let us not wallow in the valley of despair.

15 I say to you today, my friends, so even though we face the difficulties of today and tomorrow, I still have a dream. It is a dream deeply rooted in the American dream.

16 I have a dream that one day this nation will rise up and live out the true meaning of its creed, "We hold these truths to be self-evident, that all men are created equal."

17 I have a dream that one day on the red hills of Georgia the sons of former slaves and the sons of former slaveowners will be able to sit down together at the table of brotherhood.

18 I have a dream that one day even the state of Mississippi, a state sweltering with the heat of injustice, sweltering with the heat of oppression, will be transformed into an oasis of freedom and justice.

19 I have a dream that my four little children will one day live in a nation where they will not be judged by the color of their skin but by the content of their character. I have a dream today.

20 I have a dream that one day, down in Alabama, with its vicious racists, with its governor having his lips dripping with the words of interposition and nullification, one day right there in Alabama little black boys and black girls will be able to join hands with little white boys and white girls as sisters and brothers. I have a dream today.

21 I have a dream that one day every valley shall be exalted, every hill and mountain shall be made low, the rough places will be made plane and the crooked places will be made straight, and the glory of the Lord shall be revealed, and all flesh shall see it together.

22 This is our hope. This is the faith that I go back to the South with. With this faith we will be able to hew out of the mountain of despair a stone of hope. With this faith we will be able to transform the jangling discords of our

nation into a beautiful symphony of brotherhood. With this faith we will be able to work together, to pray together, to struggle together, to go to jail together, to stand up for freedom together, knowing that we will be free one day.

23 This will be the day—this will be the day when all of God's children will be able to sing with new meaning, "My country 'tis of thee, sweet land of liberty, of thee I sing. Land where my fathers died, land of the pilgrim's pride, from every mountainside, let freedom ring." And if America is to be a great nation, this must become true.

24 So let freedom ring from the prodigious hilltops of New Hampshire. Let freedom ring from the mighty mountains of New York. Let freedom ring from the heightening Alleghenies of Pennsylvania!

25 Let freedom ring from the snowcapped Rockies of Colorado! Let freedom ring from the curvaceous slopes of California!

26 But not only that. Let freedom ring from Stone Mountain of Georgia!

27 Let freedom ring from Lookout Mountain of Tennessee!

28 Let freedom ring from every hill and molehill of Mississippi. From every mountainside, let freedom ring.

29 And when this happens, when we allow freedom ring—when we let it ring from every village and every hamlet, from every state and every city— we will be able to speed up that day when all of God's children, black men and white men, Jews and Gentiles, Protestants and Catholics, will be able to join hands and sing in the words of the old Negro spiritual, "Free at last! Free at last! Thank God almighty, we are free at last!"

Dying to Be Thin
Jennifer Breuer

Despite receiving a great deal of medical attention in recent years, anorexia remains a serious problem in the United States. In fact, reports the *New York Times,* the rate of anorexia is growing by 5 percent a year, and more than 40 percent of all anorexics are young women.

In the following informative speech, Jennifer Breuer, a student at the University of Wisconsin, explores these and other facts about the symptoms, causes, and treatment of anorexia. As you read the speech, notice how Jennifer organizes her ideas and draws upon the experience of her friend Julie to illustrate the devastating consequences of anorexia.

This speech is printed with permission from Jennifer Breuer. It is also available on the CD-ROM and video supplements to *The Art of Public Speaking.*

1 I was Julie's best friend. I watched her grow from a little girl who was doted on by her parents into a tomboy who carried frogs in her pockets. I watched her become a young woman, fussing with her hair and trying on every outfit in her closet before her first date. I always wanted to be just like her.

2 But then something went terribly wrong. Julie's shiny hair became dull and brittle. Her eyes lost their sparkle, and she didn't smile that brilliant smile anymore. I watched now, as she stepped onto the scale seven times a day, wore baggy clothes to cover her shriveled frame, and kept muttering about losing those last two stubborn pounds. Julie had become anorexic.

3 One in every 100 teenage females in America suffers from anorexia, and the *New York Times* says this number is rising by 5 percent every year. Although this disease does strike men, says the *Times,* 90 percent of its victims are women, and 44 percent of those victims are college-age females.

4 From my research and my personal experience with Julie, I have discovered that anorexia is an extremely serious disease that strikes a large number of Americans. Today I will tell you what anorexia is, what causes it, and what methods are used to treat it. Let's start by examining what anorexia is.

5 Anorexia nervosa, one of a number of eating disorders, is a disorder of self-starvation. Simply put, a person who is anorexic refuses to eat normal amounts of food. An article in *Maclean's* states that there are four characteristics of all anorexics: (1) refusal to maintain normal body weight, (2) loss of more than 15 percent of original body weight, (3) a distorted image of one's own body, and (4) an intense fear of becoming fat.

6 The refusal of anorexics to eat has many serious physical consequences. Hair and skin become dry and brittle, and a fine growth of hair may cover the entire body in an attempt to compensate for a lower body temperature. As the anorexia progresses, lack of calcium causes bones to become brittle and break easily. According to an article in *Sports Illustrated,* "The X-rays of a young person who has been anorexic for five to six years and those of a 70-year-old are almost identical." Lack of nutrition can also cause brain damage, blackouts, and a decreased pulse rate. In the most severe cases, anorexia can prove fatal.

7 In Julie's case, she suffered from many of the symptoms of anorexia. I saw her 5′7″ frame drop to 86 pounds. She became weak and pale. Even in the middle of the summer, she was cold all the time. I just wanted to say to her, "Julie, please, can't you see what you're doing to yourself!" But, like most anorexics, she just couldn't see.

8 What causes people like Julie to become anorexic? Scientists have identified three main causes of anorexia. An article in *Newsweek* attributes the rise in cases of anorexia to the pressure in our society to be thin. The media constantly bombards us with images of thin people as ideals. Fat-free products and diet aids have become multimillion-dollar industries. These images and these industries project the idea that being anything but slender is something to be feared and shunned.

9 The second major factor in causing anorexia is the personality of the victim and his or her reaction to the pressures of society. The book *Dying to Please* states that most anorexics fit a basic profile. Many are overachievers or perfectionists. They excel in school and are involved in a variety of extracurricular activities. They seek to please parents, teachers, and friends. Anorexics see being thin as a way to please others. In fact, most will limit their food intake to try to fulfill expectations of perfection from family and friends.

10 A third possible cause of anorexia has only been discovered within the past year. Doctors at the University of Pittsburgh School of Medicine found that when anorexics don't eat, they experience a rise in their level of opiates, natural brain chemicals that produce a sense of happiness. The researchers also found that when anorexics do eat, their bodies produce higher than normal levels of serotonin, a brain chemical that causes a sense

of anxiety. According to the doctors, these chemical changes may make anorexia as physically addictive for the anorexic as alcohol or drugs are for the alcoholic or drug addict.

11 Julie always wanted to be perfect. She was prom queen, a straight-A student, and a member of every team, club, and organization imaginable. But then Julie decided she needed to go on a diet. She started constantly comparing herself to pictures of models in magazines. She was just sure that if she could look like the models, her life would truly be perfect. But losing weight never made Julie's life perfect.

12 What kinds of treatment could have helped Julie and others like her? Treatment of anorexia is a lifetime process. According to Dr. Katherine Halmi, director of the eating disorders clinic at New York Hospital, people think that eating disorders are "minor disorders that can be overcome with a little will power and effort, but these are serious, incapacitating illnesses that require professional intervention."

13 Methods of treatment used to treat anorexia include group therapy, drug therapy, and individual counseling. In severe cases, hospitalization and forced feeding are used to provide nutrition for the anorexic until he or she will eat a sufficient amount. Most anorexics are never cured and must fight the disease daily. Another article in the *New York Times* states that more than 80 percent of anorexics will have several relapses before they are cured. As Angie Melnyk, a 14-year-old who has been anorexic for two years, stated, "If you could cure anorexia in 30 days, it would be a lot less trouble."

14 As I mentioned before, for some anorexics, no treatment is successful. For 18 percent of diagnosed anorexics, the disease proves fatal.

15 We have seen that anorexia is a serious disease with deep-seated causes and devastating, potentially fatal effects. Julie was one of those who couldn't beat anorexia. She died when she was only 17. We will never go to college together and share a dorm room. She will never fulfill her dream of becoming a nurse. And we will never grow old living beside each other and watching our kids grow up together. Anorexia killed my beautiful, vibrant friend.

A Whisper of AIDS

Mary Fisher

Mary Fisher's emergence as an AIDS activist demonstrates how the need for public speaking can touch anyone sometime in her or his life. Only a year before Fisher rose to give the following speech to the Republican National Convention in Houston, Texas, she learned that she had contracted the HIV virus from her ex-husband. Resolving to do all she could to fight the disease, she became an outspoken advocate of the need for public understanding and resources in the battle against AIDS.

After telling her story to the Republican Platform Committee in May 1992, Fisher, a former staff assistant to President Gerald Ford, was invited to address the party's national convention that summer. Feeling, as she said later, like "the only HIV-positive Republican," she was deeply concerned about how her message of compassion and awareness would be received.

It did not take long, however, for Fisher's audience to realize that they were hearing a very special speech. Within a few minutes, the Astrodome turned eerily silent as the delegates stopped their chatting and gave Fisher their undivided attention. Some were moved to tears. Across the United States, millions watched on television, captivated by Fisher's somber words and heartfelt delivery. The *New York Times* deemed the address "exceptional for its deep emotion and sharp message."

One of the most admired public speeches of recent years, Fisher's address has been widely reprinted. The text here is from Fisher's book, *Sleep with the Angels: A Mother Challenges AIDS,* and is presented with permission from Moyer Bell Publishers, Wakefield, Rhode Island. Copyright 1994 by Family AIDS Network, Incorporated.

1 Less than three months ago, at platform hearings in Salt Lake City, I asked the Republican Party to lift the shroud of silence which has been draped over the issue of HIV/AIDS. I have come tonight to bring our silence to an end.

2 I bear a message of challenge, not self-congratulation. I want your attention, not your applause. I would never have asked to be HIV-positive. But I believe that in all things there is a good purpose, and so I stand before you, and before the nation, gladly.

3 The reality of AIDS is brutally clear. Two hundred thousand Americans are dead or dying; a million more are infected. Worldwide, 40 million, or 60 million, or a hundred million infections will be counted in the coming few years. But despite science and research, White House meetings and congressional hearings, despite good intentions and bold initiatives, campaign slogans and hopeful promises—despite it all, it's the epidemic which is winning tonight.

4 In the context of an election year, I ask you—here, in this great hall, or listening in the quiet of your home—to recognize that the AIDS virus is not a political creature. It does not care whether you are Democrat or Republican. It does not ask whether you are black or white, male or female, gay or straight, young or old.

5 Tonight, I represent an AIDS community whose members have been reluctantly drafted from every segment of American society. Though I am white and a mother, I am one with a black infant struggling with tubes in a Philadelphia hospital. Though I am female and contracted this disease in marriage, and enjoy the warm support of my family, I am one with the lonely gay man sheltering a flickering candle from the cold wind of his family's rejection.

6 This is not a distant threat; it is a present danger. The rate of infection is increasing fastest among women and children. Largely unknown a decade ago, AIDS is the third leading killer of young-adult Americans today—but it won't be third for long. Because, unlike other diseases, this one travels. Adolescents don't give each other cancer or heart disease because they believe they are in love. But HIV is different. And we have helped it along—we have killed each other—with our ignorance, our prejudice, and our silence.

7 We may take refuge in our stereotypes, but we cannot hide there long. Because HIV asks only one thing of those it attacks: Are you human? And this is the right question: Are you human? Because people with HIV have not entered some alien state of being. They are human. They have not earned

cruelty and they do not deserve meanness. They don't benefit from being isolated or treated as outcasts. Each of them is exactly what God made: a person. Not evil, deserving of our judgment; not victims, longing for our pity. People. Ready for support and worthy of compassion.

8 My call to you, my Party, is to take a public stand no less compassionate than that of the President and Mrs. Bush. They have embraced me and my family in memorable ways. In the place of judgment, they have shown affection. In difficult moments, they have raised our spirits. In the darkest hours, I have seen them reaching not only to me, but also to my parents, armed with that stunning grief and special grace that comes only to parents who have themselves leaned too long over the bedside of a dying child.

9 With the President's leadership, much good has been done; much of the good has gone unheralded; as the President has insisted, "Much remains to be done."

10 But we do the President's cause no good if we praise the American family but ignore a virus that destroys it. We must be consistent if we are to be believed. We cannot love justice and ignore prejudice, love our children and fear to teach them. Whatever our role, as parent or policy maker, we must act as eloquently as we speak—else we have no integrity.

11 My call to the nation is a plea for awareness. If you believe you are safe, you are in danger. Because I was not hemophiliac, I was not at risk. Because I was not gay, I was not at risk. Because I did not inject drugs, I was not at risk.

12 My father has devoted much of his lifetime to guarding against another holocaust. He is part of the generation who heard Pastor Niemoeller come out of the Nazi death camps to say, "They came after the Jews and I was not a Jew, so I did not protest. They came after the Trade Unionists, and I was not a Trade Unionist, so I did not protest. They came after the Roman Catholics, and I was not a Roman Catholic, so I did not protest. Then they came after me, and there was no one left to protest."

13 The lesson history teaches is this: If you believe you are safe, you are at risk. If you do not see this killer stalking your children, look again. There is no family or community, no race or religion, no place left in America that is safe. Until we genuinely embrace this message, we are a nation at risk.

14 Tonight, HIV marches resolutely towards AIDS in more than a million American homes, littering its pathway with the bodies of the young. Young men. Young women. Young parents. Young children. One of the families is mine. If it is true that HIV inevitably turns to AIDS, then my children will inevitably turn to orphans.

15 My family has been a rock of support. My 84-year-old father, who has pursued the healing of the nations, will not accept the premise that he cannot heal his daughter. My mother has refused to be broken; she still calls at midnight to tell wonderful jokes that make me laugh. Sisters and friends, and my brother Phillip (whose birthday is today)—all have helped carry me over the hardest places. I am blessed, richly and deeply blessed, to have such a family.

16 But not all of you have been so blessed. You are HIV-positive but dare not say it. You have lost loved ones, but you dared not whisper the word AIDS. You weep silently; you grieve alone.

17 I have a message for you: It is not you who should feel shame; it is we. We who tolerate ignorance and practice prejudice, we who have taught you to fear. We must lift our shroud of silence, making it safe for you to reach out for compassion. It is our task to seek safety for our children, not in quiet denial but in effective action.

18 Some day our children will be grown. My son Max, now four, will take the measure of his mother; my son Zachary, now two, will sort through his memories. I may not be here to hear their judgments, but I know already what I hope they are.

19 I want my children to know that their mother was not a victim. She was a messenger. I do not want them to think, as I once did, that courage is the absence of fear; I want them to know that courage is the strength to act wisely when most we are afraid. I want them to have the courage to step forward when called by their nation, or their Party, and give leadership—no matter what the personal cost. I ask no more of you than I ask of myself, or of my children.

20 To the millions of you who are grieving, who are frightened, who have suffered the ravages of AIDS firsthand: Have courage and you will find comfort.

21 To the millions who are strong, I issue this plea: Set aside prejudice and politics to make room for compassion and sound policy.

22 To my children, I make this pledge: I will not give in, Zachary, because I draw my courage from you. Your silly giggle gives me hope. Your gentle prayers give me strength. And you, my child, give me reason to say to America, "You are at risk." And I will not rest, Max, until I have done all I can to make your world safe. I will seek a place where intimacy is not the prelude to suffering.

23 I will not hurry to leave you, my children. But when I go, I pray that you will not suffer shame on my account.

24 To all within sound of my voice, I appeal: Learn with me the lessons of history and of grace, so my children will not be afraid to say the word AIDS when I am gone. Then their children, and yours, may not need to whisper it at all.

25 God bless the children, and God bless us all.

The Ultimate Gift
Jennifer Conard

As the Red Cross states, "Blood is like a parachute. If it's not there when you need it, chances are you'll never need it again." Although Americans take it for granted that they will be able to get a transfusion whenever they need one, blood donations have dipped so low in recent years that a serious, nationwide shortage could result. "When you need surgery, when you need cancer treatment, when a woman gives birth—we all assume the blood will be there," says Dr. Arthur Caplan of the University of Pennsylvania. "You can't make that assumption any more."

In the following speech, Jennifer Conard, a student at the University of Wisconsin, urges her classmates to become regular blood donors. Like many speeches that seek immediate action, this one follows Monroe's motivated sequence. As you read it, study how the speaker develops each step in the motivated sequence. How does she gain the attention of her listeners? Does she present a convincing case that there is a need for blood donors? Is her plan explained in sufficient detail? How does she visualize the benefits of her plan? Does her call for action have strong persuasive appeal?

This speech is presented with permission from Jennifer Conard and is also available on the CD-ROM and video supplements to *The Art of Public Speaking.*

1 Are you at least 17 years old? Do you weigh more than 110 pounds? Do you consider yourself fairly healthy?

2 If you answered yes to all of these questions, you should be donating blood every two months. In my survey of the class, I found that only 50 percent of you have ever donated blood and that only 1 out of 13 of you donate on a regular basis. The lack of participation of eligible donors is a serious problem that requires immediate action. Through extensive research and two years of faithfully donating blood, I have come to realize the magnitude of this problem and just how easy the solution can be.

3 Today I would like to show why blood donors are in such desperate need and encourage you to take action to combat this need. Let's first take a look at the overwhelming need for blood donors.

4 The lack of participation of eligible blood donors poses a threat to the lives of many Americans. According to the American Red Cross Web pages, where I obtained an enormous amount of information, in the United States alone someone undergoes a blood transfusion once every three seconds, which amounts to 3,000 gallons of blood every hour, day and night. People who benefit from donations range from cancer patients to organ transplant patients to surgical patients; even premature infants and trauma victims benefit from donations. The need for blood never takes a vacation and neither should donors.

5 Let me tell you about Brooke, a three-year-old girl with long, curly blond hair and bright blue eyes. Brooke is a victim of cancer and had major surgery to remove a large tumor in her abdomen. She has spent approximately half of her life in the hospital receiving chemotherapy and other treatments for infections that resulted from a decrease in her white blood cell count after each session.

6 According to Texas Children's Hospital, Brooke's treatment will require blood products with a replacement value of 508 units of blood, of which only 250 units have been replaced. She still needs more than 250 units of blood to continue her treatment. If she doesn't receive this blood, she will not live to attend kindergarten, to go to the prom in high school, or to get married—luxuries we all too often take for granted.

7 Cases like Brooke's are becoming all too common these days, with only 1 in 20 eligible Americans donating blood and the donor rate dropping steadily at 2 percent annually. These facts are particularly distressing considering that nearly half of us here will receive blood sometime in our lives.

8 You can now see the magnitude of the problem with the lack of blood donations. Fortunately, it is a problem that can be easily solved. Each and every one of you can be part of the solution. All you have to do to save priceless lives is go to the nearest Red Cross and donate your blood.

9 For those of you who have never donated blood before, the process is so simple and easy. First, you fill out a donor information form that asks you questions about your sexual history and health. You will then receive

a miniphysical. They will take a drop of blood from your finger to measure the percent of red cells in your blood. Then they will take your blood pressure, as well as your temperature and pulse. So not only are you saving lives by donating blood, you are also checking on your own.

10 After your physical, you will be asked from which arm you prefer to donate. Then you will be asked to lie on a donor chair. A staff member will clean your arm and insert a sterile, nonreusable needle, so there is no way to contract AIDS from donating blood. After a pint of your blood has been taken, which usually takes about 10 minutes, you will be asked to rest for 10 to 15 minutes while you enjoy juice and cookies. The process is over, and in eight weeks you can donate again.

11 Many of you may be scared at the thought of the anticipated pain and needles. I admit I was terrified the first time I gave blood, but then I realized I was scared over nothing. The extent of the pain as they insert the needle is equivalent to someone scratching your arm for a brief second, and while the needle is in your arm, you don't feel a thing. And as I stated before, it is impossible to contract AIDS from donating blood.

12 Now that you know how easy and safe the solution is to the lack of blood donations, let's take a look at just how much difference your donations can make. Every unit of blood you donate can help save up to three lives. You see, the blood you donate is divided three ways—into red blood cells, white blood cells, and platelets. Each of these are stored separately and used for different types of treatment. Red blood cells are used to treat anemia. White blood cells are used to fight infections, while platelets are important to control bleeding and are used in patients with leukemia and other forms of cancer.

13 The joy you get from helping three people can be increased many times over. You see, you can donate blood six times in a year. Those six donations could help as many as 18 people. Just think, if you donated for 10 years, you could help save the lives of nearly 180 people. Who knows—one of those lives could be that of a friend, a family member, or even your own, since you can now donate in advance of your own surgery.

14 Now that you know what a difference just one donation can make, I want to encourage you to take action. I urge you to take a stand and become a regular blood donor. Forty-five minutes out of your day is a small price to pay for the lifetime of satisfaction you receive by knowing you may have saved a life. If you have never donated blood before, pull deep inside yourself to find some courage and become a proud wearer of the "I am a first time blood donor" sticker. If you have donated before, think back to the feeling of pride you received from making your donation.

15 Finally, I ask all of you to think of a loved one you hold so dear to your heart. Imagine they need a blood transfusion and there is a shortage of donations that day so they can't receive the treatment they so desperately need—just like Brooke, the three-year-old girl I talked about earlier. Go to the nearest Red Cross in Madison, which is on Sheboygan Avenue, or attend the next blood drive here on campus. These drives are held in various parts of campus, including the dorms. In fact, the next drive will be held in the Ogg Residence Hall in two weeks.

16 Please take this opportunity to save lives and make yourself feel like a million bucks. Give the ultimate gift—the gift of life. Donate blood!

Multilingual, Multicultural
Renee Varghese

Washington Irving described Americans in 1804 as "a strange set of fellows that run about all parts of the world without caring to learn the language beforehand." Irving's words were written 200 years ago, but they are still true today. Foreign language instruction in the United States lags far behind that in most other nations, and few native-born adult Americans can converse in any tongue other than English.

In the following persuasive speech, Renee Varghese, a student at the University of Wisconsin, argues that knowledge of a foreign language has become essential for a nation that depends on a global economy and is becoming increasingly multicultural. Citing research that shows children learn a foreign language best when they are very young, she advocates mandatory foreign language instruction in all elementary schools.

As you read the speech, study how the speaker uses statistics, examples, and testimony to support her ideas. Does she convince you that knowledge of a second language is essential in today's world? Does she present a workable program for starting foreign language instruction earlier in the educational process? How does she demonstrate the practicality of her program? How could she have made the speech more convincing?

This speech is presented with permission from Renee Varghese. It is also available on the CD-ROM and video supplements to *The Art of Public Speaking.*

1 ¿Perdóneme señor; me perdí. Podría decirme cómo ir al Hotel del Sol?

2 A few of you may know I just said, "Excuse me, sir. I'm lost. Could you tell me how to get to the Sun Hotel?" However, some of you may not, even though you had three to four years of Spanish in high school. I have one question for you: Would you be able to get around in a foreign country where the language you studied was spoken?

3 According to a class survey I conducted, all of you said that you studied a foreign language in high school, the majority of you for three to four years. Yet most of you do not have enough knowledge of the language to use it correctly. In addition, 92 percent of you said you thought it would have been more helpful to have started your foreign language study earlier.

4 Today I hope to convince you that knowledge of a foreign language is important and that it would be more beneficial to begin foreign language study earlier in our education. With the world economy globalizing and our country becoming increasingly multilingual, knowledge of a foreign language is now a necessity. Through my own experience and research, I have discovered that starting foreign language instruction in elementary school is most advantageous because our language-acquisition skills are the sharpest at that time. Let's begin with why knowledge of a second language is critical for the world today.

5 The first reason such knowledge is critical is because it is essential for global communication. According to an article in *Current* magazine, Americans both in and out of government proclaim the new global economy the defining reality of our age. With technology growing faster and faster, we have now become closer to our global neighbors than ever before. Governments and businesses will increasingly need workers who can communicate with our global partners in Latin America, Africa, and Europe.

6 According to an article in the *Foreign Language Annals,* "The number of foreign-based industries doing business in the United States has tripled in the last 10 years, while the U.S. has doubled overseas business." A recent issue of *Career World* states that some accountants at Chase Manhattan Bank and National City Bank must have a good grasp of foreign languages because these banks have branched out abroad. One study in the *Journal of Education for Business* showed that among both United States and foreign firms, 51 percent of the responding firms would give hiring preferences to those accounting and business majors skilled in a foreign language.

7 Not only is knowledge of a foreign language necessary for business communication, but the United States itself is a country of mixed cultures, nationalities, and tongues and is growing more multilingual every day.

8 According to Table 57 in the *Statistical Abstract of the United States,* people born in another country make up 9 percent of the American population. An article in the *Population Bulletin* states that 32 million people reported to the last United States Census that they spoke a language other than English at home. This number is larger than the populations of New York, Pennsylvania, and Colorado combined and is six times larger than the number of people that live here in Wisconsin.

9 According to the Census Bureau, more than 17 million people in the U.S. speak Spanish as their primary language. In many parts of the country, knowledge of Spanish has become a vital day-to-day issue. Kathy Lemmons, chairwoman of the foreign language department at Fayetteville High School in Arkansas, says, "When I talk to doctors, they wish they would have taken Spanish; when I talk to lawyers and business people, they say the same thing."

10 But whether Spanish, Japanese, German, Italian, Chinese, or Polish, it is obvious that proficiency in another tongue is needed. To meet this need, I propose a solution that mandates state governments to require foreign language instruction in all elementary schools. The program I advocate is called FLES, the Foreign Languages in Elementary Schools Program. This program is based mostly on the spoken word versus writing and interpretation, and it starts teaching foreign languages as early as the first grade or even kindergarten.

11 It's important to note that much of the foreign language instruction done in this program is very basic. Olwen Bell, a French teacher at an Arkansas elementary school that has implemented the program, states that "There's a lot of role playing, singing, and chanting." Classroom teachers can easily take courses to learn how and what to teach the kids. It's not necessary for teachers to go back to school to get a degree in a foreign language. However, teachers should take instructional courses so they have opportunities for continued professional growth.

12 This program is working in Arkansas and other states. North Carolina, Oklahoma, Montana, and Arizona either have or are planning to institute similar programs. It is time for the rest of the U.S. to follow their lead. This would be a huge change in American education, but it's something that is vital if students are to be prepared for the world they will live in.

13 For years European and Asian countries have begun mandatory English in early grades. Other English-speaking countries such as Australia do extensive foreign language training in the early grades of their schools. Foreign language instruction works in these countries, and it can work in the U.S. as well.

14 In fact, there is abundant evidence that the optimum time to learn a foreign language is before the age of 10 because the brain is most receptive at this time. According to the book *Teaching Foreign Languages to the Very Young,* specific skills such as the ability to distinguish between foreign sounds and to reproduce them are more effective before the age of 10. The same book states that after the age of six the capabilities for pronunciation rapidly begin to deteriorate.

15 John Silber, Chancellor of Boston University and Chairman of the Massachusetts Board of Education, remarks, "It is quite clear that remarkable competence in a language can be achieved in three years—if these years are the ages three, four, and five. There is no question that for the average child trying to become bilingual, the earlier the better."

16 Finally, although some people wonder whether early foreign language instruction gets in the way of learning other subjects, according to the book *Foreign Languages and the Elementary School Child,* experiments done in public schools in Minnesota, Pennsylvania, and New York showed that learning foreign languages had no adverse effects on achievement in subject areas such as math and social studies. In some cases, kids who had foreign language instruction performed better in subjects such as spelling, reading, arithmetic, and language usage.

17 Furthermore, studying a language can help students better understand those outside their own culture and aid them in becoming more tolerant.

18 ¿Cuándo visitamos un país extranjero, estamos suponiendo que alguien habla Inglés? ¿Depende de un diccionario? To put it in English, "When we visit a foreign country, are we to expect that someone will speak English? Depend on a foreign language dictionary?"

19 People from other countries know to expect little from Americans as far as speaking foreign languages is concerned. However, it is time to stop this stereotype.

20 As we have seen, there is strong evidence that knowledge of a second language is vital for interaction both within the United States and on a global scale. We can provide that knowledge by instituting foreign language study in all elementary schools. Evidence shows that this is the best time to begin foreign language acquisition and that instruction in a second language can even help in learning other subjects.

21 With this in mind, hopefully one day when our children are lost somewhere in a foreign country, unlike their parents before them, they will know exactly what to say and do.

Photo Credits

CREDITS

Index

I1